Secondary Influences on Neuropsychological Test Performance

National Academy of Neuropsychology Series on Evidence-Based Practices

SERIES EDITOR

L. Stephen Miller

SERIES CONSULTING EDITORS

Glenn J. Larrabee
Martin L. Rohling

Civil Capacities in Clinical Neuropsychology
Edited by George J. Demakis

Secondary Influences on Neuropsychological Test Performance
Edited by Peter A. Arnett

Secondary Influences on Neuropsychological Test Performance

EDITED BY PETER A. ARNETT

OXFORD
UNIVERSITY PRESS

OXFORD
UNIVERSITY PRESS

Oxford University Press is a department of the University of Oxford.
It furthers the University's objective of excellence in research, scholarship,
and education by publishing worldwide.

Oxford   New York
Auckland   Cape Town   Dar es Salaam   Hong Kong   Karachi
Kuala Lumpur   Madrid   Melbourne   Mexico City   Nairobi
New Delhi   Shanghai   Taipei   Toronto

With offices in
Argentina   Austria   Brazil   Chile   Czech Republic   France   Greece
Guatemala   Hungary   Italy   Japan   Poland   Portugal   Singapore
South Korea   Switzerland   Thailand   Turkey   Ukraine   Vietnam

Oxford is a registered trademark of Oxford University Press in the
UK and in certain other countries

Published in the United States of America by
Oxford University Press
198 Madison Avenue, New York, NY 10016

www.oup.com

Library of Congress Cataloging-in-Publication Data
Secondary influences on neuropsychological test performance / edited by Peter Arnett.
p. cm. — (National academy of neuropsychology series on evidence-based practices)
Includes index.
ISBN 978-0-19-983861-5
1. Neuropsychological tests.   2. Cognition disorders.   3. Cognition disorders—Case
studies.   I. Arnett, Peter (Peter A.)
RC386.6.N48S43 2013
616.8′0475—dc23
2012030195

9 8 7 6 5 4 3 2 1
Printed in the United States of America
on acid-free paper

Contents

Preface to the *National Academy of Neuropsychology Series on Evidence-Based Practices*

The field of clinical neuropsychology has advanced extensively and successfully in the worlds of psychology and neurology by following two major tenets. The first has been the constant focus on exploring and understanding the complex and intricate relationship between observed behavioral function and brain structure (and, of course, changes to that structure). From early observation of the relationship between injury and behavior to today's combination of psychometric testing, cognitive neuroscience, and functional neuroimaging techniques, this focus has served the field extremely well. The second tenet has been the rigorous adherence to careful, replicable scientific principles of questioning and theorizing, data collection, and use of sophisticated statistical analysis in testing, evaluating, and interpreting information about brain–behavior relationships. It is in the spirit of this strong foundation of empirical evidence aimed at improving the quality of informed clinical decision making that the *National Academy of Neuropsychology Neuropsychology Series on Evidenced-Based Practices* developed and came to fruition.

For a significant amount of time, members of the neuropsychology community and in particular the membership of the National Academy of Neuropsychology have voiced a desire for the development and availability of thorough and accurate resources that are directly applicable to the everyday needs and demands of clinical neuropsychology in a meaningful and accessible way but provide the latest knowledge based on the most recent and rigorous scientific evidence within the field. The *National Academy of Neuropsychology Book Series on Evidence-Based Practices* is meant to provide just such a series of resources.

At its formation, it was important to first identify an excellent publisher with a history of publishing significant psychological and scientific volumes who would share this vision and provide significant support for a quality product. After lengthy research and discussions with multiple publishers, the venerable Oxford University Press (OUP), one of the most renowned and respected publishing companies in existence, was selected by the NAN Board of Directors. For their part, OUP has committed to the long-term development and support of the NAN Series and, as can be seen in the pages here, have spared no effort or expense to provide the finest quality venue for the success of the Series.

The Series is designed to be a dynamic and ever-growing set of resources for the science-based clinical neuropsychologist. As such, the volumes are intended to individually focus on specific significant areas of neuropsychological inquiry in depth and together cover the majority of the broad clinical area of neuropsychology. This is a challenging endeavor and one which relies on the foremost experts in the neuropsychological field to provide their insight, knowledge, and interpretation of the empirically supported evidence within each focused topic. It is our hope that the reader recognizes the many established scholars from our field who have taken on the tasks of volume editor and chapter author.

While each volume is intended to provide an exhaustive review of their respective topic, there are a number of constants across the volumes. Importantly, each volume editor and respective chapter authors have committed to constraining themselves to providing only evidence-based information that meets the definition of such information. Second, each volume maintains a broad consistency in format, including an introductory chapter outlining the volume and a final discussion chapter summarizing the current state-of-the-art research and practice within the respective topic area. Each volume provides a comprehensive index, and each chapter provides relevant references for the reader. Third, each volume is designed to provide information that is directly and readily usable, in both content and format, to the clinical neuropsychologist in everyday practice. As such, each volume and chapter within the volume is obliged to provide information in such a way as to make it accessible as a "pull off the shelf" resource. Finally, each volume is designed to work within a pedagogical strategy such that it educates and informs the knowledgeable neuropsychologist, giving a greater understanding of each particular volume focus, and provides meaningful (i.e., read "useful") information geared toward enhancing her or his practice of neuropsychology.

In keeping with the educational focus of the Series, an additional aspect is a collaboration of the Series contributors and the NAN Continuing Education Committee so that each Series Volume is available to be used as a formal continuing education text via the CEU system of NAN.

It is my hope, and the hope of the consulting editors who provide their time, expertise, and guidance in the development of the NAN Series, that this will become an often used and ever-expanding set of efficient and efficacious resources for the clinical neuropsychologist and others working with the plethora of persons with brain disorders and dysfunction.

L. Stephen Miller
Editor-in-Chief
National Academy of Neuropsychology
Book Series on Evidence-Based Practices

Preface to the Second Volume in the *National Academy of Neuropsychology Series on Evidence-Based Practices: Secondary Influences on Neuropsychological Test Performance*

Neuropsychologists take extreme pains to carefully assess the myriad of cognitive performance in their patients and to explicate the causes that result in brain injury or change underlying that performance. This information is essential for the accurate diagnosis and treatment of persons with cognitive dysfunction and is a hallmark of the field. In order to effectively and accurately succeed in this assessment, the challenge of identifying factors thought to influence that performance and yet less directly causal of performance becomes critically important. To have a sense of the appropriate representativeness of the data, the relative impact of these "other" factors, and the interactions of the two, has been the subject of much debate. This challenge has been accepted in this second volume of the *National Academy of Neuropsychology Series on Evidenced-Based Practice, Secondary Influences on Neuropsychological Test Performance*, under the guidance of the Volume Editor, Peter A. Arnett. Dr. Arnett is Professor of Psychology and Director of Training at Penn State University and is a recognized expert in the neuropsychology of multiple sclerosis and in sports concussion. Professor Arnett is also a practicing clinician who deals with these issues within the scope of his own neuropsychology practice. By bringing together a stellar group of experts in factors that are important to consider in not only the interpretation of assessment data but also in relation to specific disorders, Professor Arnett has provided us with a substantive set of treatises that present the current state of evidence about the influence of the most common secondary factors that neuropsychologists deal with in their practice. These factors include the influence of symptom validity, depression, anxiety, pain, and fatigue. Highlights of this volume include the exploration of potential influences often encountered but seldom researched, such as oral motor impairment and diagnosis threat. After providing individual chapters focusing on the current knowledge base of these factors, the volume presents discussion of secondary factors within the context of a number of individual neurological disorders common to the neuropsychologist's patient population. These include traumatic brain injury, multiple sclerosis, the dementias, Parkinson's disease, HIV, and epilepsy. Through these chapters, the reader is provided with reviews of the current state-of the-art research on the impact of secondary factors on these disorders, followed by evidenced-based guidelines for attending to these factors in clinical practice. Further, most of the chapters provide direct clinical examples as a context for their findings and guidelines. Like the first volume in the Series, this volume is aimed primarily at neuropsychologists, but it should also be of use to any professionals who deal with elucidating the tangle of potential causative variables in cognitive-performance measurement.

L. Stephen Miller
Editor-in-Chief
National Academy of Neuropsychology
Book Series on Evidence-Based Practices
July 2012

Contributors

Peter A. Arnett, PhD
Department of Psychology
Penn State University
State College, PA

Michael R. Basso, PhD
University of Tulsa
Tulsa, OK

Amber Baxley, BA
Department of Neurology
University of North Carolina—Chapel
Hill
Chapel Hill, NC

Brian Bell, PhD
Department of Neurology
University of Wisconsin School of
Medicine and Public Health
Madison, WI

Kaitlin Blackstone, BA
San Diego State University/
University of California—San Diego
Joint Doctoral Program in Clinical
Psychology
San Diego, CA

Kyle B. Boone, PhD
Alliant International University
California School of Forensic Studies
Alhambra, CA

Jared M. Bruce, PhD
Psychology Department
University of Missouri
Kansas City, MO

Bruce K. Christensen, PhD, CPsych
Department of Psychiatry and
Behavioural Neuroscience
McMaster University
Hamilton, ON

Patrick Clarke, PhD
Centre for the Advancement of
Research on Emotion
The University of Western Australia
Crawley, WA, Australia
Australian Bushfire Collaborative
Research Centre
East Melbourne, Victoria, Australia

Dennis Combs, PhD
Department of Psychology and
Counseling
University of Texas
Tyler, TX

John DeLuca, PhD
Departments of Physical Medicine and
Rehabilitation, and Neurology and
Science
University of Medicine and
Rehabilitation
New Jersey Medical School
Newark, NJ
Kessler Foundation Research Center
West Orange, NJ

Jake Epker, PhD
Mobile, AL

Eduardo Estevis, MA
University of Tulsa
Tulsa, OK

Bruce Hermann, PhD
Department of Neurology
University of Wisconsin School of
Medicine and Public Health
Madison, WI

Matthew J. King
Ryerson University
Toronto, ON

David Loring, PhD
Department of Neurology
Emory University
Atlanta, GA

Colin MacLeod, PhD
Centre for the Advancement of
Research on Emotion
The University of Western
Australia
Crawley, WA, Australia
Australian Bushfire Collaborative
Research Centre
East Melbourne, Victoria, Australia

Ashley Miller
University of Tulsa
Tulsa, OK

L. Stephen Miller, PhD
Psychology Department
University of Georgia
Athens, GA

David J. Moore, PhD
Department of Psychiatry
HIV Neurobehavioral Research
Program
University of California—San Diego
San Diego, CA

Melissa Ogden, PhD
Mobile, AL

Lindsay P. Prizer, MSW
Department of Neurology
University of North Carolina—Chapel
Hill
Chapel Hill, NC

Antonio N. Puente, MS
Psychology Department
University of Georgia
Athens, GA

Dalin Pulsipher, PhD
Department of Psychology
University of New Mexico
Albuquerque, NM

Amanda R. Rabinowitz, PhD
Department of Psychology
Penn State University
State College, PA

Chad Sanders, MS
Department of Psychology
Washington State University
Pullman, WA

Maureen Schmitter-Edgecombe, PhD
Department of Psychology
Washington State University
Pullman, WA

Michael Seidenberg, PhD
Department of Psychology
Rosalind Franklin University of
Science and Medicine
North Chicago, IL

Lauren B. Strober, PhD
Department of Physical Medicine and
Rehabilitation
University of Medicine and
Rehabilitation
New Jersey Medical School
Newark, NJ
Kessler Foundation Research Center
West Orange, NJ

Julie A. Suhr, PhD
Department of Psychology
Ohio University
Athens, OH

Joanie M. Thelen, BA
Psychology Department
University of Missouri
Kansas City, MO

Alexander I. Tröster, PhD, ABPP
Department of Clinical
Neuropsychology, Muhammad Ali
Parkinson Center, and Barrow Center
for Neuromodulation
Barrow Neurological Institute
Phoenix, AZ

Dede Ukueberuwa, MS
Department of Psychology
Penn State University
State College, PA

Gray A. Vargas, MS
Department of Psychology
Penn State University
State College, PA

Christina Wei, MS
Department of Psychology
Ohio University
Athens, OH

Holly Westervelt, PhD
Department of Psychiatry and Human
Behavior
Alpert Medical School
Brown University
Providence, RI

Steven Paul Woods, Psy. D
Department of Psychiatry
HIV Neurobehavioral Research
Program
University of California—San Diego
San Diego, CA

Elizabeth A. Ziegler, PhD
Department of Veterans Affairs
Spokane VA Medical Center
Spokane, WA Secondary Influences on
Neuropsychological Test Performance

Secondary Influences on Neuropsychological Test Performance

1

Introduction to Secondary Influences on Neuropsychological Test Performance

PETER A. ARNETT

The focus of this book can best be understood by considering two broad influences on cognitive functioning, known as primary and secondary influences. *Primary influences* are the direct result of the extent and location of damage to the brain. For example, someone who suffers from a left-hemisphere stroke and is subsequently unable to produce speech has experienced a primary influence of brain damage on language functioning; the location of the brain affected by the stroke is directly responsible for the onset of the cognitive impairment. *Secondary influences* are the result of something associated with brain injury or disease besides the specific areas of the brain affected. For example, someone experiencing depression from a stroke may have poor memory and attention that is a secondary effect of the depression, not arising from the specific location of damage to the brain caused by the stroke. Also, although a stroke may directly cause depression, the depression may then impact cognitive functioning.

The focus of this book is on secondary factors associated with cognitive functioning. In addition to depression, secondary factors involve influences on cognitive functioning such as anxiety, fatigue, pain, motivation, and primary motor impairments, to name a few. Because the impact of primary influences on cognitive functioning is often salient in neurological disorders and conditions, it can be easy to overlook the possible influence of secondary factors. As this book will demonstrate, research suggests that these also often can account for significant variance in cognitive functioning. An appealing feature of understanding secondary influences is that, if they cause cognitive difficulties, then treatment of these factors may result in improved cognitive performance. Of course, it is probable that secondary factors in some patients do not cause cognitive difficulties but are in fact a *result* of cognitive problems. For example, a patient may become depressed because of cognitive difficulties. It is also likely that the link between some secondary factors and cognitive deficits is mediated by some third variable, such as damage to a particular part of the brain leading to cognitive problems and, say, depression or anxiety. However, even if treatment of these factors does not result in improved cognitive functioning, awareness of secondary factors can provide a more accurate picture of the various contributors and sequelae of cognitive dysfunction in neurological disorders.

An important nuance in considering secondary factors is that they can be caused by the direct biological consequences of the disease or by the limitations and psychosocial stressors caused by the disease. For example, taking multiple sclerosis (MS) as an illustration, it has been established that lesion and brain atrophy measures predict depression. Depression has also been shown to be highly associated with coping strategies, stress, and social support. Regardless of the cause of depression in MS, depression would still be considered a secondary influence because that influence on cognitive functioning is not a *direct* consequence of the disease process. Even in the case of lesion load and brain atrophy causing depression, the latter influence on cognitive functioning is still one step removed from the direct consequence of the disease process on cognitive functioning.

Consideration of secondary factors can provide a more complete and nuanced picture of the contributors to cognitive impairment in neurological and neuropsychiatric conditions. Although significant research literatures have emerged that evaluate the impact of secondary factors, prior to the publication of this volume there has been no one source that provides a comprehensive review of them. Additionally, there is no single source that provides evidence-based guidelines for considering secondary factors more generally and in neurological and neuropsychiatric conditions in particular. The goal of this edited volume is to provide such a source.

The book is divided up into two sections. Part I is devoted to examining secondary influences that cut across disorders, including symptom invalidity, depression, anxiety, fatigue, pain, motor impairments, and diagnosis threat. Each of these influences is considered as an entity in and of itself, outside of the context of particular neurological disorders. There are two chapters on depression. As readers will see, the research on this secondary influence is extensive, with two sets of literature that have evolved in tandem with one another. One literature focuses on the impact of depression on the *level of cognitive functioning*, that is, the extent to which depression influences overall cognitive performance. Basso, Miller, Estevis, and Combs provide a scholarly comprehensive review of this literature that sometimes involves summarizing the results of several meta-analyses. The other literature focuses more on the impact of depression on the *content of cognitive functioning*, that is, the bias that depressed individuals often show in focusing on or remembering or differentially attending to information with a negative affective tone (e.g., affectively negative words or faces). Christiansen and King provide an outstanding comprehensive review of this literature.

In Part II, the focus is on the complexities of assessing secondary influences in the context of specific neurological conditions. The goal of these chapters is to explore how these secondary factors get manifested in several neurological conditions commonly seen by neuropsychologists. Each chapter is written by experts on common neurological disorders who tie the more general research findings to practical suggestions on how to address these issues in the particular disorder. Rather than being limited to discussing one secondary factor, as in the first section of the book, these chapters address all relevant secondary factors for a particular disorder. As readers will come to appreciate, secondary factors do not impact all neurological disorders equally. As such, these chapters provide specific, evidence-based guidelines regarding the most important secondary factors for a particular disorder.

A central goal of Part II is to provide some consistency across the disorders with regard to an empirically supported evaluation of the roles that relevant variables play in these disorders. To achieve this goal, a similar chapter format is used for each disorder. Each chapter provides a brief overview of the characteristics of the disorder as well as the cognitive dysfunction profile typically found. The chapters then address those secondary factors that are most salient. For some disorders there is extensive evidence on a range of secondary factors being important in cognitive function (e.g., MS; see Chapter 10, by Bruce and colleagues), whereas for other disorders (e.g., HIV; see Chapter 11, by Blackstone and colleagues), there is little evidence to support the impact of secondary factors on cognitive functioning. Even in the latter situations, however, the authors consider ways in which secondary factors may affect other aspects of patients' functioning (e.g., quality of life) and provide guidelines for measuring the most important factors.

In addition to being evidence based, an important feature of this book is that most chapters include a case study that illustrates some of the core principles outlined in the chapter. Another central feature of the book is that it is designed to be practical and accessible to clinicians so that the scholarship reviewed can be applied in practice.

In the final chapter in the book I consider things we know at this stage in the field and outline some future directions. As readers will see, much has been learned about secondary influences on cognitive functioning, but there is still much that is unknown.

I hope that when involved in applied work, you will find this book to be a valuable tool in clinical practice. In research, this volume should provide a comprehensive overview of this often overlooked topic in neuropsychology that can be applied to scholarship. I hope you enjoy this book and find it useful in your research and clinical endeavors, as I have.

PART I

Relationship of Affective Disorders, Anxiety Disorders, Fatigue, Motor Impairments, Diagnosis Threat, and Effort to Cognitive Functioning

Symptom Invalidity on Neuropsychological Testing

ELIZABETH A. ZIEGLER AND KYLE B. BOONE

Over the past 25 years, clinical and forensic neuropsychology has witnessed considerable growth in understanding the complexities of feigned and exaggerated cognitive and psychological impairment. Research has shown that negative response bias accounts for more variance in cognitive scores than even a severe traumatic brain injury or other neurological and psychiatric conditions (Green, Rohling, Lees-Haley, & Allen, 2001; Iverson, 2005; Rohling & Demakis, 2010). If examinees do not perform to true capability and noncredible test performance is not detected, neuropsychologists risk interpreting invalid data and potentially contributing to inaccurate diagnoses and treatment recommendations, and/or increasing the chances of an examinee receiving a potentially undeserving compensable or medical claim (e.g., disability payments, lawsuit settlement, stimulant medications).

Recently published practice guidelines and position papers from key neuropsychological organizations (Bush et al., 2005; Heilbronner et al., 2009) have emphasized the importance of including symptom validity tests (SVT) in neuropsychological evaluations. Recent survey data show that over 50% of National Academy of Neuropsychology (NAN) members administer at least one measure of symptom validity in cognitive assessments (Sharland & Gfeller, 2007), and nearly 80% of neuropsychologists conducting neuropsychological evaluations in compensation-seeking contexts reported administration of at least one SVT (Slick, Tan, Strauss, & Hultsch, 2004). The goal of this chapter is to educate the reader on evidence-based guidelines for the assessment of feigned or exaggerated cognitive impairment, with a primary focus on the assessment of noncredible test performance in various contexts (e.g., disability seeking, civil courts, correctional settings, learning disability clinics).

DIAGNOSTIC ALGORITHMS

According to the *Diagnostic and Statistical Manual of Mental Disorders–4th Edition-Text Revision* (*DSM-IV-TR*; American Psychiatric Association [APA], 2000), *malingering* is a conscious process that involves "the intentional production of false or grossly exaggerated physical or psychological symptoms, motivated by external incentives such as avoiding military duty, avoiding work, obtaining financial compensation, evading criminal prosecution, or obtaining drugs." In civil litigation, secondary gain factors typically involve financial settlement, lost wages, and medical expenses. In a correctional setting, evading prison, the death penalty, or both and receiving a lesser sentence are common external incentives. In educational assessment settings, academic accommodations (e.g., increased time for tests or homework) and stimulant medications are often pursued in attention deficit/hyperactivity disorder (ADHD) and learning disability (LD) evaluations. An understanding of the specific external incentives can help guide the assessment and determine what particular SVTs should be incorporated.

Noncredible test performance and symptom reporting can also occur in the absence of secondary gain, and in these contexts, primary gain (i.e., psychological) factors drive the negative response bias and can be conscious (factitious disorder) instead of nonconscious (somatoform disorders). While factitious disorder and malingering both involve intentional exaggeration, the primary difference between the two is the goal of the feigned or exaggerated behavior. In *factitious disorder*, the patient has a primary gain or psychological need to adopt the sick role in order to garner attention from medical professionals, whereas in *malingering*, the individual intentionally exaggerates symptoms for a secondary gain such as disability payments, financial settlement, or evading legal consequences. In factitious disorders and malingering, the goal of symptom exaggeration or embellishment is to deceive others and only occurs in the presence of an audience, whereas in somatoform disorders, the person has deceived himself or herself regarding the presence of illness and as a result adopts the sick role continuously (Boone, 2007a; Boone, 2009).

The *DSM-IV-TR* indicates that the presence of malingering should be considered when there is (1) a medicolegal context of presentation, (2) marked discrepancy between the person's claimed stress of disability and the objective findings, (3) lack of cooperation during the diagnostic evaluation and in complying with the prescribed treatment regimen, and (4) presence of antisocial personality disorder. Other published diagnostic classifications systems specific to malingered cognitive and pain symptoms have appeared more recently (Bianchini, Greve, & Glynn, 2005; Slick, Sherman, & Iverson, 1999). The diagnostic algorithm by Slick et al. (1999) for malingered neurocognitive dysfunction (MND) is commonly employed in forensic neuropsychological settings and is based on four major criteria: (A) presence of a substantial external incentive, (B) evidence from neuropsychological testing, (C) evidence from self-report, and (D) behaviors meeting necessary criteria from groups B or C that are not fully accounted for by psychiatric, neurological, or developmental factors.

Evidence from neuropsychological testing would include significantly below-chance performance on forced-choice SVTs ("definite" MND) or "failure" on other types of SVTs ("probable" MND), and discrepancies between test data and known patterns of brain functioning (e.g., dementia-like performance in a 30-year-old with a remote mild traumatic brain injury), between test data and observed behavior (e.g., patient has dementia level scores but lives independently), between test data and reliable collateral reports (e.g., patient is functioning well on the job and in school but obtains IQ scores within the extremely low range), and between test data and documented background history (e.g., impaired verbal memory scores in the context of claimed traumatic brain injury with no loss of consciousness and normal neurological exams and no concurrent other medical or psychiatric conditions that would account for the findings). Criteria C, evidence from self-report, considers a number of factors such as self-reported history discrepant from documented history; self-reported symptoms discrepant with known patterns of brain functioning, behavioral observations, and information obtained from collateral informants; and evidence of exaggerated or fabricated psychological dysfunction on psychodiagnostic measures such as the Minnesota Multiphasic Personality Inventory–Second Edition-Restructured Form (MMPI-2-RF; Ben-Porath & Tellegen, 2008) or the Personality Assessment Inventory (PAI; Morey, 1991). Subsequently, Boone (2007b, 2011) and Larrabee, Greiffenstein, Greve, and Bianchini (2007) have suggested modifications to the Slick et al. (1999) criteria, including replacing the term "malingering" (which requires documentation of intent) with "noncredible neurocognitive dysfunction"; operationalizing "definite" noncredible performance as failure on at least three independent and validated SVTs rather than limiting the term to significantly below-chance performance on forced-choice paradigms; investigating whether there is redundancy between some B and C criteria; adapting C5 (i.e., evidence of exaggerated or fabricated psychological dysfunction) to refer to personality test scales that identify noncredible cognitive symptom overreport; changing the B2 criterion (i.e., probable response bias) to require failure on at least two SVTs; requiring only one marked discrepancy for B6 (i.e., discrepancy between neurocognitive test data and neurological/psychiatric condition or history); giving C and B criteria equal weight (which would allow for determination of malingering in the absence of test data); and requiring more stringent specifications of the inconsistencies required for criteria B4 (i.e., discrepancy between test data and observed behavior), B5 (i.e., discrepancy between test data and reliable collateral reports), and C1 through C4 (i.e., self-reported discrepancies between documented history, known patterns of brain functioning, behavioral observations, and collateral informants).

Bianchini, Greve, and Glynn (2005) modeled their criteria for malingered pain-related disability (MPRD; definite, probable, and possible) on the Slick et al. algorithm: (A) evidence of significant external incentive, (B) evidence from physical evaluation, (C) evidence from cognitive/perceptual (neuropsychological) testing, (D) evidence from self-report, and (E) behavior meeting necessary criteria from groups B, C, and D are not fully accounted for by psychiatric, neurological, or developmental factors.

METHODS FOR EVALUATING VERACITY OF COGNITIVE PERFORMANCE

Fortunately, numerous symptom validity techniques to assess negative response bias on cognitive testing have been validated and are now available (cf. Boone, 2007a; Larrabee, 2007; Victor, Kulick, & Boone, 2012a, 2012b). The basic rationale underpinning SVTs is that they appear to measure a particular ability (e.g., memory); however, in reality, they are so simple that even persons with significant cognitive impairment perform well on them.

Freestanding SVTs are independent, stand-alone measures that have a single purpose in assessing cognitive symptom validity. Although they add additional time to the test battery, freestanding SVTs are typically the best researched measures. In contrast, *embedded* SVTs are those derived from standard cognitive tests and allow measurement of response bias in "real time" (during actual measurement of the cognitive skill in question).

Freestanding and embedded SVTs can be categorized as either *forced-choice* or *non-forced-choice* measures. In forced-choice tests, which primarily check for veracity of performance on memory tasks, the examinee is exposed to a series of stimuli, usually visual, which are subsequently each paired with a novel stimuli, and the test taker is asked to identify the previously seen item. If examinees perform worse than chance (e.g., ≤ 17 out of 50 trials), this suggests that they knew the correct answer and intentionally chose the incorrect answer. However, relatively few noncredible subjects score significantly below chance (e.g., <10%; Kim et al., 2010), requiring that cutoff scores above chance level be developed that effectively discriminate between credible and noncredible test takers. Several forced-choice tests are available, including the Word Memory Test (Green, 2005), Warrington Recognition Memory Test—Words (Kim et al., 2010), Victoria Symptom Validity Test (Slick, Hopp, Strauss, & Thompson, 1996), and Portland Digit Recognition Test (2003). Dozens of publications support the accuracy of forced-choice SVTs (e.g., Bianchini, Mathias, & Greve, 2001; Millis & Volinsky, 2001; Vickery, Berry, Inman, Harris, & Orey, 2001), and practice surveys of neuropsychological test usage have shown that forced-choice measures are among the most frequently administered SVTs (Sharland, Gfellar, Justice, Ross, & Hughes, 2005).

Non-forced-choice format SVTs allow for a range of responses (tapping speed, circling recognized items in an array, verbal repetition, selection from multiple choice options, etc.) and can evaluate for presence of response bias across a variety of domains, such as processing speed (b Test, Boone, Lu, & Herzberg, 2002a), motor and sensory function (Finger Tapping, Arnold et al., 2005; Finger Agnosia, Trueblood & Schmidt, 1993), attention (Reliable Digit Span, Babikian, Boone, Lu, & Arnold, 2006), visual perceptual/spatial skills (Picture Completion Most Discrepant Index, Solomon et al., 2010), and counting/simple math calculations (Dot Counting Test, Boone, Lu, & Herzberg, 2002b), as well as verbal (Rey Recognition Memory Test, Nitch, Boone, Wen, Arnold, & Alfano, 2006; Rey Auditory Verbal Learning Test Effort Equation, Boone, Lu, & Wen, 2005) and nonverbal (Rey Osterrieth Effort Equation, Lu, Boone, Cozolino, & Mitchell, 2003) memory.

Current recommended practice is to administer SVTs throughout a test battery in order to enhance diagnostic accuracy (Boone, 2009b; Bush et al., 2005; Heilbronner et al., 2009; Lynch, 2004), with a reliance on both forced-choice and non-forced-choice formats from freestanding and embedded indicators.

Heilbronner et al. (2009) suggest that researchers and clinicians develop a working knowledge of common diagnostic statistics such as sensitivity, specificity, and positive and negative predictive values. *Sensitivity* refers to the proportion of persons with the disorder who obtain a positive score on the symptom validity measure, whereas *specificity* refers to the proportion of persons without the disorder who obtain a negative score on the task (i.e., pass the SVT). *Positive predictive value* (PPV) is the proportion of subjects with positive test results who are correctly classified. *Negative predicted value* (NPV) is the proportion of individuals with negative test results who are correctly classified. PPV and NPV, unlike sensitivity and specificity, vary as a function of the prevalence (i.e., base rate) of the disorder.

METHODS FOR EVALUATING CREDIBILITY OF SYMPTOM REPORT

A major component of a neuropsychological evaluation, both in forensic and clinical contexts, is obtaining information from the examinee regarding current complaints. Noncredible subjects can also provide inaccurate symptom reports as well as fail performance-based measures of symptom veracity (i.e., cognitive SVTs). Fortunately, general personality inventories such as the MMPI-2-RF (Ben-Porath & Tellegen, 2008) and Minnesota Multiphasic Personality Inventory–2 (MMPI-2; Butcher, Dahlstrom, Graham, Tellegen, & Kaemmer, 1989) have well-researched validity and other scales sensitive to noncredible symptom cognitive and physical symptom report (Symptom Validity Scale [FBS], FBS-r, Fs, Response Bias Scale [RBS]), in addition to scales for detecting noncredible psychiatric symptom report (F, Fp, Fp-r).

Accurate interpretation of the various personality inventory validity scales requires a solid understanding of their research underpinning. For example, while some claim an excessive false positive rate for the FBS (Butcher, Arbisi, Atlis, & McNulty, 2003), an MMPI-2 validity scale that assesses for noncredible physical, cognitive, and nonpsychotic psychiatric symptom report, studies with appropriate methodology find that recommended cut-offs have very high specificity (for reviews see Greiffenstein, Fox, & Lees-Haley, 2007; Larrabee, 2012).

Several "disorder-specific" inventories are in common use but are problematic in forensic settings. The Beck Anxiety Inventory (BAI; Beck & Steer, 1993) and Beck Depression Inventory–Second Edition (BDI-II; Beck, Steer, & Brown, 1996) lack validity indices to measure the credibility of the examinee's responses. However, even for those measures that purportedly contain overreport scales, research has shown that their ability to detect symptom misrepresentation is poor (e.g., Trauma Symptom Inventory, Detailed Assessment of Post-Traumatic Stress; see review in Boone, in press). It should be kept in mind that in a forensic context, data from these measures are no more valid or compelling than a symptom report gathered from a patient interview.

FORENSIC CONTEXTS

Malingering or noncredible test performance occurs in a number of contexts, diagnoses, and cognitive domains. For example, one study of surveyed board-certified neuropsychologists found that malingering or exaggerated cognitive impairment was estimated to occur in 29% of personal injury litigants, 30% of disability seeking claimants, 19% of criminal evaluations, and 8% of medical cases (Mittenberg, Patton, Canyock, & Condit, 2002). When categorized by diagnostic group, 39% of compensation-seekers claiming mild traumatic brain injury (TBI) were judged to be feigning, as well as 35% of those with fibromyalgia/chronic fatigue, 31% with claimed chronic pain, 27% with neurotoxic exposure, and 22% with electrical injury. Similarly, Larrabee (2003a), in a review of 11 studies of mild TBI litigants, reported on overall 40% base rate of malingering (range = 15 to 64.3%). In fact, Larrabee, Millis, and Meyers (2009) proposed 40% ± 10 as representative of the base rate of malingering in neuropsychological evaluations where there is the presence of secondary gain. The following sections will provide a more detailed review of malingering base rate data within various forensic and clinical contexts, and the types of feigned or exaggerated symptoms (e.g., psychosis, memory) typically found in these varying contexts.

Personal Injury

Neuropsychologists are frequently called upon to render an expert opinion in the civil courts, primarily for personal-injury claims. Civil litigation is initiated when one party (plaintiff) claims injury from another party (defendant), most commonly in the context of motor vehicle accidents. Plaintiffs sue for damages, including cognitive, emotional, and/or physical injury. The plaintiff's goal in civil litigation is typically monetary compensation such as a financial settlement, medical expenses, and lost wages. When neuropsychologists are retained in personal-injury cases, their role is typically to assess for the presence and veracity of claimed damages (e.g., cognitive) with measures that have been well researched and are accepted by the larger scientific community.

The most common type of case seen by neuropsychologists in civil forensic settings is mild TBI (Ruff & Richardson, 1999); therefore, it is important to have a sound understanding of the outcome data in mild TBI in order to render a research-informed decision to the courts. Research consistently shows that individuals who experience a mild TBI return to baseline by weeks to 1–3 months post-injury (Belanger, Curtiss, Demery, Lebowitz, & Vanderploeg, 2005; Belanger & Vanderploeg, 2005; Binder, 1997; Binder, Rohling, & Larrabee, 1997; Dikmen, Machamer, Winn, & Temkin, 1995; Frencham, Fox, & Mayberry, 2005; Iverson, 2005; Levin et al., 1987; McCrea, 2008; McCrea et al., 2009; Millis & Volinsky, 2001; Ruff et al., 1989; Schretlen & Shapiro, 2003). If there are persistent deficits or subjective complaints beyond the 1- to 3-month post-injury mark, they are due to non-TBI factors such as litigation or secondary gain and psychiatric factors (Iverson, 2005, McCrea, 2008; McCrea et al., 2009).

Although the research supports complete resolution of mild TBI-related post-concussive symptoms, neuropsychologists are often asked to evaluate litigants who present with myriad symptoms that persist beyond the 1- to 3-month post-injury mark. When forensic experts review medical records, they frequently encounter the diagnosis of "postconcussion syndrome" (PCS) or "postconcussional disor-der" (PCD), which refers to a constellation of somatic (e.g., headache), cognitive (e.g., memory), and emotional symptoms following a head trauma (Alexander, 1995; Axelrod et al., 1996). Per the *DSM-IV-TR*, the individual with PCD typi-cally displays three or more neurobehavioral symptoms such as fatigue, disor-dered sleep, headache, vertigo, irritability, psychiatric changes (e.g., depression, anxiety), personality change, or apathy following a clinically significant head trauma. To qualify as a syndrome, however, the condition must demonstrate a set of specific symptoms broadly present in persons who have the condition and absent in those who do not have it (see Larrabee, 2012). The fact that there is no PCS symptom specific to mild TBI (Dean, O'Neill, & Sterr, 2012; Mittenberg, DiGiulio, Perrin, & Bass, 1992) largely argues against the validity of this alleged syndrome. In fact, a multitude of studies have shown that chronic pain, anxi-ety, depression, female gender, fatigue, and normal day-to-day stressors account for more variability of PCS-like symptoms and neuropsychological functioning than does remote mild TBI (Dischinger, Ryb, Kufera, & Auman, 2009; Garden & Sullivan, 2010; Iverson, 2005; King, 1996; Landre, Poppe, Davis, Schmaus, & Hobbs, 2006; Meares et al., 2006, 2008, 2011; Sawchyn, Brulot, & Strauss, 2000; Trahan, Ross, & Trahan, 2001). For example, Meares et al. (2011) demonstrated that a pre-injury depressive or anxiety disorder, and acute posttraumatic stress predicted PCS, regardless of presence of actual mild TBI.

Other studies have demonstrated that personal-injury litigants not claiming neurological injury report more neuropsychological symptoms than subjects with a reported history of head trauma or toxic exposure (Dunn, Lees-Haley, Brown, Williams, & English, 1995; Lees-Haley & Brown, 1993). For example, Lees-Haley and Brown (1993) obtained data from personal-injury claimants with no his-tory of brain injury or toxic exposure and no documented neuropsychological impairments, and base rates of cognitive, emotional, and somatic symptoms were quite high (e.g., 88% headaches, 79% fatigue, 78% concentration problems, 77% irritability, 53% memory problems, 34% word finding problems). Furthermore, the prevalence of PCS-like symptoms in the normal population (e.g., headache, irritability) is high (Fox, Lees-Haley, Earnest, & Dolezal-Wood, 1995; Garden & Sullivan, 2010; Gouvier, Uddo-Crane, & Brown, 1988; Iverson & Lange, 2003; McLean, Dikmen, & Temkin, 1993; Wang, Chan, & Deng, 2006).

"Misattribution" of normal, minor cognitive "malfunctions," as well as malin-gering, can play a role in chronic PCS symptom report in mild-TBI litigants. Individuals who sustain an injury often underestimate the extent of premorbid symptoms (i.e., "good old days" bias), which can impact their perceived level of current problems and recovery (Iverson, Lange, Brooks, & Rennison, 2010). Iverson et al. (2010) compared a sample of patients with mild TBI who were deemed temporarily fully disabled and receiving financial compensation through the workers' compensation system to a healthy control group. Results demonstrated that the mild-TBI group retrospectively endorsed fewer pre-injury symptoms as compared to the control group ratings of symptoms, and individuals who failed SVTs reported fewer symptoms pre-injury compared to those patients who passed SVTs. The implications of these findings are that when treating providers fail to understand the nonspecificity of PCS-like symptoms and render a diagnosis of "brain injury" based solely on the presence of such self-reported symptoms, they risk significant harm to the patient via iatrogenesis.

The prototypic case encountered by neuropsychologists in a civil-litigation setting is a claim of mild TBI in the context of a minor motor vehicle accident in which, if the patient presents for evaluation in the emergency department, it is generally for orthopedic or head and neck pain but not brain injury symptoms. Emergency medical personnel notations indicate no or questionable loss of consciousness with Glasgow Coma Scale ratings of 15 and no anterograde amnesia, and if brain imaging is obtained, results are normal. The individual is discharged from the emergency department within hours with no diagnosis of concussion or brain injury. However, weeks to months later, the patient presents to a primary care physician or other provider with vague complaints (e.g., headache, memory loss, dizziness, chronic pain) attributed to the accident, and a diagnosis of concussion/mild TBI is first made at this late date. Unfortunately, it will often be noted that the patient was then "educated" regarding postconcussion symptoms, and in particular, that they may take years to resolve, if ever. Subsequent records refer to the TBI diagnosis, with the patient now reporting that loss of consciousness had been present (often for rather lengthy periods) at the time of injury. Recommendations are made for unnecessary procedures, such as cognitive rehabilitation, speech therapy, vestibular treatment, etc., that arguably do more harm than good by provoking and perpetuating misattribution and somatization tendencies and thereby impeding symptom resolution. To determine the presence of an actual brain injury, clinicians should rely on medical records from the day of injury (e.g., paramedic reports, emergency department notes); that is, a traumatic brain injury is to be diagnosed according to acute injury characteristics at the time of the event (e.g., loss of consciousness, Glasgow Coma Scale score, posttraumatic amnesia length), not on presence of PCS symptoms remote from the injury.

Given the high rates of malingering in compensation seekers, and in mild TBI litigants in particular, as summarized above, it is critical that neurocognitive symptom validity be carefully assessed. As such, it is important to administer SVTs that appear to tap the symptoms the patient is endorsing (e.g., reduced memory, attention, processing speed, etc.) and that cover all cognitive domains. As a group, the SVTs that tend to be the most sensitive to feigning in mild TBI litigants, in descending order, are those that measure credibility of performance in verbal memory (Warrington Recognition Memory Test—Words, RAVLT effort equation, Rey Word Recognition; mean sensitivity = 73%), sensory function (finger agnosia; sensitivity = 66%), visual memory (RO Effort Equation, Digit Symbol Recognition, Rey 15-item plus recognition; mean sensitivity = 61%), processing speed (Warrington—Words time, Dot Counting Test, b Test; mean sensitivity = 57%), and visual perception (Picture Completion; sensitivity = 56%). In contrast, tasks involving attention (Digit Span RDS; sensitivity = 36%) and motor function (finger tapping; sensitivity = 42%) were less effective (Cottingham & Boone, in press). We have published cases illustrating that noncredible mild-TBI litigants may present with noncredible performance solely in verbal memory (Boone, 2009), visual perceptual/memory skills and motor function (Boone, 2009), language skills (Cottingham & Boone, 2010), or processing speed/sensory abilities (Cottingham & Boone, in press); if SVTs are not administered that assess symptom validity in these diverse areas, presence of negative response bias may be missed. Fortunately, there has been an explosion of research on "embedded" SVTs derived from standard neurocognitive tests and which allow for comprehensive assessment and monitoring for the presence of response bias without adding to test battery administration time. The interested reader is referred to Victor, Kulick, and Boone (2012a, 2012b) for a listing and critique of non-memory SVTs, including embedded measures, that have been validated in mild-TBI samples.

In addition to assessment of responses bias on performance-based neurocognitive SVTs, it is critical to measure credibility of cognitive, physical, and psychiatric symptom report. The MMPI-2-RF (Ben-Porath & Tellegen, 2008) has several validity scales that specifically assess for general symptom overreport (F-r), somatic symptom overreport (Fs, FBS-r), and cognitive symptom overreport (RBS, FBS-r). This literature is summarized in Boone (in press) and reveals that sensitivity rates associated with cut-scores set to ≥90% specificity are modest in detecting test takers who fail neurocognitive SVTs (38–48%), indicating that data from self-report validity scales are not interchangeable with performance-based symptom validity information.

Disability-Seeking Claimants

The Social Security Administration (SSA) defines *disability* as "the inability to engage in any substantial gainful activity due to any medically determinable physical or mental impairment" and being unable to perform necessary occupational duties given a medical condition, age, education, and work experience (Social Security Advisory Board, 2003; U.S. Department of Health and Human Services, 1994, revised 2006). Mental-disorder disability is documented through evidence of impairment via self-reported symptoms and findings of the objective medical examination (Conroe, 2009). Claimants that are allegedly impaired from a mental standpoint are referred for a Psychological Consultative Examination (PCE) by the Disability Determination Services (DDS), which is to focus on activities of daily living, ability to maintain close relationships, and emotional stability (U.S. Department of Health and Human Services, 1994, revised 2006). If the claimant is found to have objective evidence of physical or mental impairment, they may be awarded Social Security Disability Insurance (SSDI) or Supplemental Security Income (SSI). These incentives provide secondary gain during the PCE, and, as such, the assessment of noncredible psychological and cognitive functioning becomes an important factor.

The prevalence of malingering in disability evaluations is generally estimated to be between 30% and 60%. The Mittenberg et al. (2002) survey of neuropsychologists documented an estimated 30% base rate of malingering in private disability seeking claimants. However, prevalence rates based on actual performance of disability claimants on symptom validity measures have generally been higher. Miller, Boyd, Cohn, Wilson, and McFarland (2006) reported a 52% failure rate in DDS claimants on the Computerized Assessment of Response Bias (CARB; Conder, Allen, & Cox, 1992) and Word Memory Test (WMT; Green & Flaro, 2003), while Chafetz, Abrahams, and Kohlmaier (2006) found that 56% of DDS claimants failed the Test of Memory Malingering (TOMM; Tombaugh, 1996) and 61% scored below cutoffs for the Medical Symptom Validity Test (MSVT; Green, 2004). On the DDS Malingering Rating Scale, a measure specifically developed and validated in this population, 52–59% of adults obtained failing scores (Chafetz, Abrahams, & Kohlmaier, 2007), although in a follow-up study that eliminated truly impaired individuals, data were consistent with a 41.8% SVT failure rate (Chafetz, 2010).

Disability claimants often have low IQ or present with bona fide neurological impairment. Chafetz et al. (2007) reported that 76.3% of their adult sample had a history of special education and 85.5% had completed less than 12 years of education. As such, the impact of low IQ on SVT performance is of particular concern in this population. Dean, Victor, Boone, and Arnold (2008) found a higher rate of SVT failures in credible patients with low IQ. In their study, participants with the lowest IQ (50–59) failed approximately 60% of the SVTs administered, while patients with an IQ of 60 to 69 failed 44%, and individuals with an IQ of 70 to 79 exhibited a 17% failure rate. All patients with IQ <70 failed at least one neurocognitive SVT. Hurley and Deal (2006) observed that 41% of individuals with IQs from 50 to 78 failed the recommended cutoff scores on the TOMM and 89% fell below the established cutoff on the Rey 15-Item Test. However, a recent study of low-IQ individuals suggested that motivation explained SVT failure, rather than low IQ (Chafetz, Prentkowski, & Rao, 2011). In this study, claimants for Social Security Disability compensation (mean FSIQ = 62.5) failed the MSVT at high rates, compared to claimants from a vocational rehabilitation program who were seeking to work (mean FSIQ = 68.3) and parents seeking reunification with their children (mean FSIQ = 71.7). Despite comparable mean IQs, 45% of the DDS claimants met Slick et al. (1999) criteria for at least probable malingering, whereas only a small percentage of vocational rehabilitation subjects, and none of the parents seeking reinstatement of parental role, failed SVTs. Interestingly, the few vocational rehabilitation subjects who failed symptom validity testing were also seeking disability benefits. The discrepancy between Chafetz et al.'s (2011) and Dean et al.'s (2008) findings may be related to differences between samples; the Dean et al. (2008) subjects were drawn from a population referred for neuropsychological testing and had comorbid diagnoses in addition to low IQ, and the Hurley and Deal (2006) subjects were residing in residential facilities, whereas the Chafetz et al. (2011) sample generally did not have concurrent neurological or severe psychiatric conditions and were relatively functional in independent activities of daily living (ADLs) (e.g., were obtaining job training and petitioning to resume parenting). These findings suggest that individuals with low IQ scores are heterogeneous in regard to functionality in ADLs and performance on SVTs, necessitating future research on identification of appropriate SVTs for discrete subgroups.

Further complicating the situation, measurement of response bias in government-sponsored disability programs has been compromised because of constraints placed on psychological practice. Specifically, the SSA actually discourages formal testing of negative response bias (Social Security Administration, 2008, pp. 1–2). Furthermore, there is apparently no payment to psychologists for administration of SVTs, with determinations regarding disability status derived from behavioral observations, mental status examination results, Wechsler scales, and other evidence gathered by examiners in the DDS office (Chafetz et al., 2007). Consequently, clinicians must rely on embedded SVTs. To this end, the DDS Rating Scale (Chafetz et al., 2007), developed in low-functioning claimants, shows promise; it incorporates 11 validity variables including measures of overlearned information (e.g., simple arithmetic tasks, personal information such as age and birthday), as well as Wechsler items such as RDS, the number of low average scale scores, the number of errors on the Coding subtest, and the number of subtests in which items are missed before the start point.

Military and Veteran Disability

The evaluation of noncredible cognitive performance and psychological symptom reports within military and veteran samples is crucial given the financial incentives associated with disability evaluations, unemployability benefits, and pensions (Armistead-Jehle, 2010; Cooper, Nelson, Armistead-Jehle, & Bowles, 2011; Freeman, Powell, & Kimbrell, 2008; Nelson et al., 2010; Whitney, Shepard, Williams, Davis, & Adams, 2009). Veterans can receive a service-connection (SC) disability rating (0% to 100%) for alleged conditions or injuries (e.g., posttraumatic stress disorder [PTSD], diabetes, tinnitus, TBI) incurred during military service and receive monthly disability payments if they are found to be at least 10% disabled. Veterans often apply for multiple conditions or injuries, which can result in high total SC ratings and disability payments, although even a single condition can be compensable up to 100%. Depending on SC ratings, veterans may also qualify for Individual Unemployability benefits, which pay a "total disability" rate even if the disabling conditions are not 100% service connected. The Veterans Benefits Administration (VBA) also offers pensions to wartime veterans who have limited or no income, and who are age 65 or older, or if under 65, are permanently and totally disabled. They can also receive a large lump sum payment for a traumatic injury (up to $100,000) from the Traumatic Service Members' Group Life Insurance (TSGLI), with potential payment exceeding $100,000 for multiple events (Traumatic Insurance Protection, 2007). Furthermore, veterans can apply for Social Security Disability in addition to their VBA disability benefits, which can lead to substantial monthly payments that often exceed what would be made in a general workforce labor position. These multiple incentives actually deter some veterans from returning to work, even if they are physically and mentally capable of competitive employment. For example, if a veteran collects $5000/month in combined disability payments, and would only make $2000 to $3000/month in the general workforce, there is significant incentive to maintain disability status.

Given all of these factors, the issue of secondary gain within the veteran population is substantial and must be carefully considered in neuropsychological assessments in this context. Reported base rates of malingered cognitive symptoms have been highly variable and appear to vary depending on the evaluation context (Armistead-Jehle, 2010; Nelson et al., 2010; Whitney et al., 2009). For example, Nelson et al. (2010) noted failed SVT performance in 8% of veteran mild-TBI research subjects, whereas 67% of veteran disability claimants failed SVTs in the context of compensation and pension examinations. Clinical samples of Operation Enduring Freedom/Operation Iraqi Freedom (OEF/OIF) veterans have demonstrated SVT failure rates between 17% and 58% (Armistead-Jehle, 2010; Belanger, Kretzmer, Yoash-Gantz, Pickett, & Tupler, 2009; Whitney et al., 2009). Because of these concerns, the Military TBI Task Force (McCrea et al., 2008) suggests consideration of symptom validity or response bias measures in evaluations of veterans in the context of alleged mild TBI.

High prevalence rates have also been reported for feigned psychiatric symptoms, including PTSD, in veteran samples. In Vietnam-era veterans, Freeman, Powell, and Kimbrell (2008) reported a 53% rate of symptom exaggeration on the Structured Interview of Reported Symptoms (SIRS; Rogers, Bagby, & Dickens, 1992), and Frueh et al. (2005) noted that in those claiming combat-related PTSD, military records did not corroborate reports of combat exposure in almost 40% of cases. Thus claims of PTSD and other psychiatric symptoms must be carefully verified with appropriate measures of psychological symptom validity, such as the MMPI-2-RF, Structured Interview of Reported Symptoms, 2nd edition (SIRS-2; Rogers, Sewell, & Gillard, 2010), and Miller Forensic Assessment of Symptoms Test (M-FAST, Miller, 2001).

Criminal Forensic

Forensic neuropsychology is becoming increasingly popular in the criminal arena, with typical referral questions including competence to stand trial, criminal responsibility, and competence to be executed. Forensic psychologists and psychiatrists have typically dominated this arena, although as questions related to brain–behavior relationships have come to the forefront in legal proceedings, neuropsychological data have become increasingly relied upon. For example, a defendant may allege that a brain injury precludes his or her ability to assist counsel and thus claim incompetence to stand trial. A neuropsychologist may then be retained to conduct a neuropsychological evaluation of the defendant to provide information regarding competence.

In the pivotal case of *Dusky v. United States* (1960), the U.S. Supreme Court determined that a defendant accused of a criminal offense must be mentally fit to stand trial. The Supreme Court ruled that "the test must be whether the defendant has sufficient present ability to consult with his attorney with a reasonable degree of rational understanding and a rational as well as factual understanding of the proceedings against him." In other words, the defendant must possess the understanding of the charges against him or her and have the ability to assist counsel in his or her own defense, which includes knowledge and understanding of all participants who take part in the legal proceedings such as the roles of the judge, jury, defense attorney, and prosecutor. Neuropsychological evaluations are particularly suited to provide objective information regarding cognitive competency.

Whereas competence to stand trial focuses on the defendant's current state of mind, the central role of the forensic evaluator in criminal responsibility evaluations is to provide data and analysis concerning the defendant's functioning, mental status, and capacities at the time of the alleged offense (Packer, 2009), and conclusions must be consistent with the legal definition of criminal responsibility in the court's jurisdiction. Jurisdictions differ not only in the legal standard for insanity but also in the terms used for the threshold question about mental condition, such as whether the defendant had a "mental illness," "mental disease," "mental defect," or "mental retardation" at the time of the alleged offense.

In *Atkins v. Virginia* (2002), the U.S. Supreme Court ruled that executions of mentally retarded criminals are "cruel and unusual punishments" prohibited by the Eighth Amendment. Defendants in capital cases thus require objective evaluations of their intellectual functioning to assist the court on determining competence to be executed.

Given the incentives in criminal evaluations (e.g., avoiding execution, lesser criminal charges, placement in state psychiatric facility rather than prison setting), the assessment of malingering becomes a key consideration. The Mittenberg et al. (2002) survey results revealed that neuropsychologists estimated that malingering or exaggerated cognitive impairment occurred in 19–23% of criminal evaluations. In contrast, higher prevalence rates have been found in studies reporting SVT performance. Ardolf, Denney, and Houston (2007) observed that 89.5% of their sample failed a single cognitive SVT, 70.5% failed two, and 53.3% failed three or more indicators; based on the Slick et al. criteria (1999), the combined rate of probable and definite MND was 54.3%.

In addition to neurocognitive SVTs, symptom validity techniques specific to the criminal forensic setting are now available to the clinician; for example, the Inventory of Legal Knowledge (ILK; Otto, Musick, & Sherrod, 2010) is a recently published measure of feigned incompetence to stand trial. Frederick and Denney (1998) reported that 25% of individuals claiming amnesia for the crime scored significantly below chance on standard forced-choice recognition tests, and Denney (1996) has described how the forced-choice SVT paradigm can be adapted and customized to evaluate veracity of claimed amnesia for a crime.

As discussed by Victor and Boone (2007), many forensic clinicians assume that standard neurocognitive SVTs are robust to low intelligence and that failure on such tasks identifies symptom fabrication. As described earlier, Dean et al. (2008) observed a higher rate of SVT failures in credible patients with low IQ, although other authors, such as Chafetz, Prentkowski, and Rao (2011), have not found an impact of low intelligence on SVT performance (for reviews, see Dean et al., 2008; Victor & Boone, 2007). Clearly more information is needed regarding the moderating impact of IQ on SVT performance; in the interim, the clinician must employ SVTs cautiously when evaluating for feigned versus actual mental retardation.

Significantly below-chance performance on forced-choice symptom validity measures would appear to provide definitive evidence of feigning in individuals of very low intelligence; however, sensitivity rates are poor at these levels, necessitating the use of additional SVTs. Victor and Boone (2007) observed that the highest specificity rates in credible low-IQ individuals were found for the Rey Complex Figure Test/RAVLT discriminant function (Sherman, Boone, Lu, & Razano, 2002) and the Warrington Recognition Memory Test—Words, while Marshall and Happe (2007) reported that 89% of their credible low IQ sample passed the forced-choice portion of the CVLT-II. They also note that the WMT and Digit Memory Test (DMT; Guilmette, Hart, Giuliano, & Leininger, 1994) may be helpful in assessing credibility of performance in mentally retarded populations, but additional data are needed to validate their use. Victor and Boone (2007) caution that it may be naïve to assume that most SVTs developed for use in a population of normal intelligence can be successfully applied to individuals of low intelligence, and they suggested that new SVTs specific for use in individuals with low intelligence may be required. In this vein, the DDS Malingering Rating Scale (Chafetz et al., 2007), discussed earlier, which was specifically developed for low-functioning individuals in a disability-seeking setting, may hold promise in the differential between actual and feigned low intelligence in a criminal forensic settings.

Many prominent criminal cases have involved claims that defendants had dementia and thus were not competent to stand trial, but on evaluation, these individuals were determined to be malingering (e.g., Vincent the Chin Gigante, head of the Genovese crime family; and Ku Klux Klan member Bobby Frank Cherry, convicted of a bombing in Alabama that killed four African American school girls). Boone, Lu, Back, et al. (2002) observed that inmates determined by staff to be malingering at a prison mental hospital faked more blatantly on the Dot Counting Test than individuals determined to be noncredible in the context of civil litigation or disability-seeking. The former subjects appeared to be feigning a dementia presentation, as well as severe psychiatric symptoms, in their quest to remain housed in the more desirable hospital setting. Thus, clinicians evaluating in the correctional context will frequently be required to evaluate whether a defendant has actual or feigned dementia.

However, as with individuals with low intelligence, individuals with actual dementia fail cognitive SVTs a high rate despite performing to true capability; for example, in patients with MMSE scores of >20, 36% of SVTs were failed, but with MMSE scores of 15–20 only 53% of SVTs were passed, and in patients with

MMSE <15, only 17% of SVTs were passed (Dean, Victor, Boone, Philpott,, & Hess, 2009). Dean and colleagues showed that the neurocognitive SVTs most impervious to actual dementia were time scores on Forward Digit Span, finger tapping, and Rey Word Recognition. In an attempt to develop techniques better able to discriminate between actual and feigned dementia, Green (2004; see also Howe & Loring, 2009) identified a genuine memory profile; however, while specificity is high, questions have been raised regarding sensitivity of this technique (Axelrod & Schutte, 2010; Chafetz, 2011). Similarly, some SVTs, such as the Dot Counting Test, have cutoffs that maintain adequate specificity (≥90%) for patients with mild (MMSE >20) and moderate (MMSE = 10–20) dementia; however, use of these adjusted cut-scores results in sacrifice to sensitivity (Boone, Lu, & Herzberg, 2002a). Currently, determination of feigned dementia must rely on the following: (1) the few symptom validity techniques that have adequate specificity in dementia, (2) observations of marked inconsistency between neurocognitive scores and evidence of normal function in ADLs and spontaneous behaviors (e.g., scores at chance levels on memory testing but the patient is able to provide a complete and coherent personal history as well as a listing of daily life activities), and (3) marked discrepancies across test performances and behaviors (e.g., patient cannot rapidly count dots when requested, but is noted to spontaneously accurately and rapidly count on a unrelated test that was not introduced as a counting task).

As in most forensic evaluations, the evaluator of criminal defendants must consider assessment of noncredible performance in both psychiatric (e.g., feigned psychosis) and cognitive domains (e.g., feigned memory/amnesia). Some measures exist to detect feigned psychosis in the criminal arena, such as the MMPI-2/MMPI-2-RF, SIRS, and M-FAST.

Testing of Athletes and Sports-Related Mild Traumatic Brain Injury

Current practice standards recommend that athletes undergo testing preseason, and then serially if or when they sustain a TBI (Barth et al., 1989; Echemendia & Cantu, 2003; Echemendia & Julian, 2001; Erlanger, Kutner, Barth, & Barnes, 1999). Comparison of post-injury data with baseline testing informs return-to-play decisions; that is, low scores after concussion relative to baseline are suggestive of continuing brain dysfunction and would argue for continued convalescence. Thus, in this situation the injured individual is motivated to underperform *before* injury, in contrast to civil litigation and veteran contexts, in which test takers are incentivized to underperform post-injury. Athletes have, in fact, admitted that they have intentionally underperformed on pre-season and baseline testing:

> They have these new [brain] tests we have to take. Before the season, you have to look at 20 pictures and turn the paper over and then try to draw those 20 pictures. And they do it with words, too. Twenty words, you flip it over, and try to write those 20 words. Then, after a concussion, you take the same test and if you do worse than you did on the first test, you can't play. So I just try to do badly on the first test. (Peyton Manning, Indianapolis Colts quarterback, 2011)

Deliberate underperformance on baseline cognitive testing is a major concern because, as outlined by Bailey et al. (2006), if athletes are returned to play while experiencing the acute effects of a mild TBI, they are at increased risk of further injury (Gerberich, Priest, Boen, Straub, & Maxwell, 1983; Guskiewicz, Weaver, Padua, & Garrett, 2000).

One novel method for identifying deliberate underperformance on baseline evaluation is a finding of post-injury scores substantially higher than baseline performance. For example, if an athlete obtains scores at the 16th percentile on a cognitive measure at baseline, yet obtains a score at the 84th percentile 1 week after mild TBI, this is a likely indicator of invalid baseline data. Bailey, Echemendia, and Arnett (2006) adopted this approach in examining archival data on collegiate athletes from the Penn State Concussion Program. The sample was divided into those with baseline "suspect motivation" (i.e., scored ≥1 standard deviations below the mean on baseline testing for a specific measure) or "high motivation" (i.e., scored ≥1 standard deviations above the mean of all athletes on the baseline testing for a specific measure). The authors hypothesized greater post-injury improvement in scores in the former group, and results in fact confirmed larger gains in the "suspect motivation" group for Trail Making Test A & B, Digit Span, and Stroop-Color Word tests.

The findings of Bailey et al. (2006) clearly demonstrate the need for follow-up studies and incorporation of formal SVTs during the baseline assessment. However, athletes may intuit that substantially impaired underperformance on baseline testing is incompatible with ability to perform on the field, which may limit the utility of many symptom validity measures. Bailey et al. (2006) commented that SVTs such as the TOMM or WMT might not be adequately sensitive to the milder symptom feigning likely adopted at baseline by some athletes. As such, SVTs and cutoffs that are specific to this population may need to be developed.

ADHD and Learning Disabilities

Feigning or exaggeration of symptoms of attention deficit/hyperactivity disorder (ADHD) and learning disability (LD) during educational assessments has only recently received attention. Adults with ADHD/LD may exaggerate or feign cognitive impairment and symptoms in order to receive academic accommodations, such as extra time on examinations and homework assignments, as mandated under the Americans with Disabilities Act (U.S. Department of Justice, 2004), or obtain stimulant medications. Several investigators have found base rates of malingering of 12% to 47.6% in academic evaluations (Harrison, Rosenblum, & Currie, 2010; Suhr, Hammers, Dobbins-Buckland, Zimak, & Hughes, 2008; Sullivan, May, & Galbally, 2007).

Mapou (2009) has outlined a research-informed approach to ADHD/LD evaluations that includes a thorough history (with a particular focus on early development, problems in education); record review (individualized educational programs [IEPs], grades, standardized test scores, prior evaluations); behavioral rating scales; semistructured interview focused on specific symptoms; and neuropsychological assessment including IQ and academic achievement measures, objective personality measures, and symptom validity testing.

Lee Booksh, Pella, Singh, and Drew Gouvier (2010) documented that ADHD simulators were able to successfully feign ADHD symptoms on a retrospective self-report measure and performed similarly to a clinical ADHD comparison sample on cognitive measures (e.g., WAIS-III subtests). Similarly, Tucha, Sontag, Walitza, and Lange (2009), Harrison, Edwards, and Parker (2007), Young and Gross (2011), Jachinowicz and Geiselman (2004), and Sollman, Ranseen, and Berry (2010) also found that ADHD simulators were able to successfully feign ADHD on self-report rating measures. These findings have spurred research into validation of neurocognitive SVTs in the detection of feigned ADHD.

Continuous performance tests (CPTs) have received wide acceptance in detecting attentional problems in ADHD. A meta-analysis of CPT measures demonstrated that ADHD samples displayed twice as many missed targets and false hits as non-ADHD groups (Losier, McGrath, & Klein, 1996). Given that CPT measures are commonly employed in ADHD and LD evaluations, research has examined use of these measures to identify feigned performances. Studies have shown that malingerers score worse than individuals diagnosed with ADHD (Leark, Dixon, Hoffman, & Huynh, 2002; Lee Booksh et al., 2010; Quinn, 2003; Suhr, Sullivan, & Rodriguez, 2011) and that performance on the Conners' CPT was more related to motivation than ADHD condition (Sollman et al., 2010). Lack of internal consistency in CPT scores may be useful in identifying malingering (Sattler, 1998). Quinn (2003) hypothesized that excessive between-item variance and reaction-time variance on CPTs may be particularly sensitive to malingering. In a study with ADHD undergraduate college students, simulators, and controls, malingerers significantly differed from the other groups on 81% of the Integrated Visual and Auditory CPT subscales (Quinn, 2003), and their approach included feigning general attention (61%) and ignoring visual (43%) and auditory (17%) stimuli. Furthermore, most malingerers produced commission errors (57%) and deliberate omission errors (35%), used a random response strategy (9%), "double clicked the mouse" to demonstrate symptoms of hyperactivity (30%), and exhibited generalized "fidgety behaviors" (13%). On the Test of Variable Attention (TOVA), ADHD college student simulators made significantly more commission and omission errors than when completing the task in an "honest" condition; specifically, when feigning, students demonstrated nearly four times the number of missed targets (Leark et al., 2002). Of interest, cutoff scores applied to the TOVA have also been found to discriminate noncredible from credible litigants (96% mild TBI; Henry, 2005).

Several recent studies have examined the use of neurocognitive SVTs in identification of feigned ADHD. Suhr, Sullivan, and Rodriguez (2011) analyzed archival data on the Conners' CPT on college students referred for concerns about ADHD, finding that those who failed the WMT were more "impaired" on the CPT. In a prior study, Suhr and colleagues (2008) observed that those individuals failing the WMT were indistinguishable from subjects passing the WMT and diagnosed with ADHD on current ADHD symptom report or retrospective childhood symptom report, which demonstrated the vulnerability of self-reported ADHD symptoms to noncredible presentation. In regard to cognitive test performance, the malingerers performed worse on neuropsychological tests, particularly on memory and executive measures. Similarly, Sullivan et al. (2007) reported that, in a clinical sample of adults referred for either ADHD or LD assessment, failure on the WMT was related to poorer performance on intelligence and memory measures (Sullivan et al., 2007) and negatively correlated with self-report symptom inventory scores.

Sollman and colleagues (2010) reported that cognitive SVTs (i.e., TOMM, Digit Memory Test, Letter Memory Test, and Nonverbal Medical Symptom Validity Test) demonstrated high specificity in actual ADHD (93% to 100%, with the exception of TOMM Trial 1 = 83%) and generally moderate sensitivity in ADHD simulators (43% to 52%, with the exception of 87% for TOMM trial 1). Presence of ≥2 versus 1 SVT failure resulted in only modest declines in sensitivity (50% versus 63%) but increased specificity (83% to 93%), whereas 3 failures was associated with 100% specificity at 47% sensitivity. A recent cross-validation study (Jasinski et al., 2011) showed that the TOMM, Letter Memory Test, Digit Memory Test, Nonverbal Medical Symptom Validity Test, and the b Test were reasonably successful at discriminating feigned and genuine ADHD; failure on ≥2 of the SVTs detected almost half of the simulators (47.5%) and resulted in no false positive identifications. In a large "real-world" sample of adults undergoing evaluation for ADHD (n = 268), the WMT, TOVA omission errors and reaction time variability, and the b Test, as well as the infrequency scale from the Clinical Assessment of Attention Deficit-Adult, achieved relatively good sensitivity (47% to 64%) at cutoffs associated with at least 90% specificity (Marshall et al., 2010). Harrison, Rosenblum, and Currie (2010) reported that WAIS-III Digit Span ACSS and RDS cutoff scores of <8 were associated with 100% specificity and 53% sensitivity in small samples of actual ADHD students and those meeting Slick et al. (1999) criteria for malingered neurocognitive dysfunction. In an earlier study (Harrison et al., 2007), college students asked to feign ADHD underperformed on reading and processing-speed indices relative to students with actual ADHD, indicating that strategies for feigning were not confined to attentional symptoms.

Interestingly, some psychodiagnostic tests appear to show some promise in detection of feigned ADHD. Young and Gross (2011) found that the MMPI-2 F-p scale best identified ADHD simulators (60% sensitivity at 94% specificity with cutoff of ≥5), followed by F, Fb, RBS, HHI, and FBS. In contrast, Sollman and colleagues (2010), in the simulation study described above, observed that the M-FAST cutoff ≥6 was associated with 100% specificity but only 10% sensitivity.

In identification of feigned LDs, some recent studies have examined use of standard neurocognitive SVTs, as well as dedicated measures designed to assess for feigned reading disability per se. Osmon, Plambeck, Klein, and Mano (2006) compared effectiveness of a reading disability SVT (Word Reading Test [WRT]) with the WMT in normal effort, reading simulator, and processing-speed simulator groups. WMT sensitivity was moderate (65%, at 96% specificity). On the WRT accuracy score, all groups significantly differed from each other, with nonsimulators performing best, speed simulators performing intermediately, and reading simulators performing worst. In contrast, for the WRT speed score, controls and reading simulators performed comparably, and the speed simulators scored significantly lower than the two other groups. A cutoff of ≥ 4 errors was associated with 90% sensitivity for reading simulators and 74% sensitivity for speed simulators at 100% specificity. The authors concluded that the WRT error score was more effective than the WMT in detecting feigned LD. Subsequently, Harrison and colleagues (2008, 2010) developed and validated an additional SVT specific for feigned reading disability (Dyslexia Assessment of Simulation or Honesty [DASH]), and a "feigning index" containing DASH scores as well as data from the Woodcock Johnson Psychoeducational Battery-III. The two measures identified between 83% and 86% of reading disability simulators, with no false positive identifications.

Examination of standard reading tests as embedded symptom validity measures has shown some promise (Lindstrom, Coleman, Thomassin, Southall, & Lindstrom, 2011), particularly for the Comprehensive Test of Phonological Processing; with cutoffs set to maintain specificity of >90%, sensitivity in simulators was 80% to 88% for the Rapid Naming Errors and Rapid Naming subtests, respectively, whereas cutoffs for the Woodcock Johnson-III Reading Fluency only identified approximately 50% of simulators. Standard neurocognitive tests requiring reading also may have utility in detecting noncredible claims of reading impairment. Lu, Boone, Jimenez, and Razani (2004) investigated the use of the Stroop test in a case report of six individuals in compensation-seeking or correctional settings who alleged complete inability to read. These individuals claimed they could not read "red," "green," or "blue" on the word-reading card of the Comalli Stroop Test; however, on the interference trial they were observed to make errors of reading, thereby providing evidence of malingering (i.e., they were observed performing a task they claimed they could not do). These findings suggest that the Stroop interference task may be the instrument of choice with individuals alleging a complete inability to read.

Some neurocognitive SVTs involve basic math skills, reading, and letter identification, skills that might be expected to be compromised in actual learning disability. However, validation studies of the Dot Counting Test (Boone, Lu, & Herzberg, 2002a), b Test (Boone, Lu & Herzberg, 2002b), Rey 15-Item Test plus recognition trial (Boone, Salazar, Lu, Warner-Chacon, & Razani, 2002), and Rey Word Recognition Test (Nitch et al., 2006) have shown low rates of failure on college students receiving services for documented learning disability. Further, in the Harrison et al. (2010) study described earlier, a WAIS-III Digit Span ACSS cutoff of ≤ 5 was associated with 91% specificity in learning-disabled college students (but sensitivity was only 7% in students meeting Slick et al. [1999] criteria for malingering), while an RDS cutoff of ≤ 6 limited false positives to 5% (33% sensitivity). However, learning-disabled students in college may not be representative of the larger learning-disabled population. For example, preliminary data suggest that credible individuals with low math ability (e.g., WAIS-III Arithmetic ACSS ≤ 5) are at increased risk of failure on the Dot Counting Test and Digit Span symptom validity indicators (Ziegler, Boone, Victor, & Zeller, 2008a, 2008b).

In summary, available literature indicates that various free-standing neurocognitive SVTs, as well as embedded symptom validity indicators and data from personality inventories, are effective in identifying feigned symptoms of ADHD and LD. In addition, domain-specific SVTs have been developed that appear to show particular promise in detection of feigned symptoms in these areas. However, many of the studies have relied on simulators rather than known groups study designs, and replication of findings in "real-world" samples is necessary. Also, most studies have been conducted in college samples, and these may represent the mild end of the LD spectrum and thus are potentially problematic when attempting to document SVT specificity rates. In conducting assessments regarding actual versus feigned ADHD and LD, clinicians should select SVTs that do not involve the claimed deficits (e.g., verbal recognition memory tasks requiring reading of words in those individuals claiming reading disability).

EVIDENCE-BASED GUIDELINES FOR THE ASSESSMENT OF NONCREDIBLE TEST PERFORMANCE

Evaluation context should be considered when constructing the neuropsychological assessment battery (e.g., civil litigation, criminal, learning disability clinic), because this will influence how the subject may opt to feign or exaggerate impairment. For example, criminal defendants are more likely to feign dementia and psychosis in the context of evaluation of competence to stand trial, whereas in civil litigation, simulated memory complaints and exaggerated depression and anxiety are more common. Additional recommendations and considerations regarding assessment of symptom validity factors include the following:

- Examinees should not be warned about the presence of SVTs in the battery; but should be encouraged to provide maximum effort during the exam (Boone, 2007). Informing examinees of SVT administration does not deter them from feigning but rather makes them more sophisticated in their approach (Youngjohn, Lees-Haley, & Binder, 1999).
- The examiner should administer several independent neurocognitive SVTs throughout a test battery (Boone, 2009b; Bush et al., 2005; Heilbronner et al., 2009; Lynch, 2004) with a reliance on both forced-choice and non-forced-choice formats from freestanding and embedded indicators. Test takers vary in strategies for feigning and may elect to feign on some tasks and not others; in other words, they typically "pick and choose" during the exam which tasks on which to underperform. If symptom validity is not repeatedly sampled, noncredible performances may not be detected (Boone, 2009b).
- SVTs should be selected that are not highly intercorrelated; highly correlated SVTs provide redundant rather than converging evidence of symptom invalidity.
- Because SVT cutoffs are selected to protect credible patients at the expense of failing to detect some noncredible subjects (i.e., ≥90% specificity), failed

SVT performances are more informative than passing performances, and passed SVTs do not "cancel out" failed SVTs. Failure on three SVTs, regardless of the number of passed SVTs, is associated with essentially 100% specificity (excluding subjects with dementia and extremely low IQ scores; Larrabee, 2003b; Meyers & Volbrecht, 2003; Victor et al., 2009) and is thus virtually 100% predictive of noncredible performance.

- Interpretation of SVT data should consider whether the test taker is in a group at high risk for failure despite performance to true capability (e.g., low intelligence, dementia, etc.), and SVTs should be selected that are most appropriate for the claimed condition.
- The examiner should keep current with available literature on SVTs, as new research on cutoffs and interpretation strategies may supersede that contained in test manuals.
- Individuals who demonstrate invalid test performance on cognitive-based assessments still may obtain scores on some standard neurocognitive tasks in the low-average and higher ranges, and when this occurs, these performances may be interpreted as representing minimum ability level.
- In evaluating validity of self-reported complaints (e.g., cognitive, psychological, somatic), it is best to use psychometric instruments with built-in validity indicators that measure a range of response styles (e.g., MMPI-2-RF).
- Validity of cognitive and psychiatric data should be assessed and interpreted separately. An individual may produce invalid test data on cognitive-based SVTs, but this does not necessarily indicate that psychodiagnostic data are also invalid.
- Substantial inconsistencies between test data and "real-world" functionality, and between self-report and historical records, should be considered in documentation of symptom invalidity (Heilbronner et al., 2009).
- The examiner should keep abreast of the neuropsychological literature of various medical and psychiatric conditions. When performance on a claimed condition (e.g., mild TBI) is largely discrepant from what is demonstrated in the research, credibility of symptom report and test data should be carefully considered.

References

Accident Neurosis. (1961). *British Medical Journal, 1*, 992–998.

Alexander, M. P. (1995). Mild traumatic brain injury: Pathophysiology, natural history, and clinical management. *Neurology, 45*(7), 1253–1260.

American Congress of Rehabilitation Medicine. (1993). Definition of mild traumatic brain injury. *Journal of Head Trauma Rehabilitation, 8*(3), 86–87.

American Psychiatric Association. (2000). *Diagnostic and statistical manual of mental disorders* (4th ed., text rev.). Washington, DC: Author.

Ardolf, B., Denney, R., & Houston, C. (2007). Base rates of negative response bias and malingered neurocognitive dysfunction among criminal defendants referred for neuropsychological evaluation. *The Clinical Neuropsychologist, 21*(6), 899–916.

Armistead-Jehle, P. (2010). Symptom validity test performance in U.S. veterans referred for evaluation of mild TBI. *Applied Neuropsychology, 17*(1), 52–59.

Arnold, G., Boone, K. B., Lu, P., Dean, A., Wen, J., Nitch, S., & McPherson, S. (2005). Sensitivity and specificity of finger tapping test scores for the detection of suspect effort. *The Clinical Neuropsychologist, 19*(1), 105–120.

Atkins v. Virginia, 153 L. Ed. 2d 335 (2002).

Axelrod, B. N., & Schutte, C. (2010). Analysis of the dementia profile on The Medical Symptom Validity Test. *The Clinical Neuropsychologist, 24*(5), 873–881.

Axelrod, B. N., Fox, D. D., Lees-Haley, P. R., Earnest, K., Dolezal-Wood, S., & Goldman, R. S. (1996). Latent structure of the Postconcussion Syndrome Questionnaire. *Psychological Assessment, 8*(4), 422–427.

Babikian, T., Boone, K., Lu, P., & Arnold, G. (2006). Sensitivity and specificity of various digit span scores in the detection of suspect effort. *The Clinical Neuropsychologist, 20*(1), 145–159.

Bailey, C. M., Echemendia, R. J., & Arnett, P. A. (2006). The impact of motivation on neuropsychological performance in sports-related mild traumatic brain injury. *Journal of the International Neuropsychological Society, 12*(4), 475–484.

Bailey, C. M., Samples, H. L., Broshek, D. K., Freeman, J. R., & Barth, J. T. (2010). The relationship between psychological distress and baseline sports-related concussion testing. *Clinical Journal of Sport Medicine, 20*(4), 272–277.

Barth, J. T., Alves, W., Ryan, T., Macciocchi, S., Rimel, R., & Jane, J. J. (1989). Mild head injury in sports: Neuropsychological sequelae and recovery of function. In H. Levin, J. Eisenberg, & A. Benton (Eds.), *Mild head injury* (pp. 257–275). New York: Oxford University Press.

Beaber, R. J., Marston, A., Michelli, J., & Millis, M. J. (1985). A brief test for measuring malingering in schizophrenic individuals. *American Journal of Psychiatry, 142*(12), 1478–1481.

Beck, A. T., & Steer, R. A. (1993). *Beck Anxiety Inventory.* San Antonio, TX: The Psychological Corporation.

Beck, A. T., Steer, R. A., & Brown, G. K. (1996). *Beck Depression Inventory—2nd edition.* San Antonio, TX: The Psychological Corporation.

Belanger, H. G., Curtiss, G., Demery, J. A., Lebowitz, B. K., & Vanderploeg, R. D. (2005). Factors moderating neuropsychological outcomes following mild traumatic brain injury: A meta-analysis. *Journal of the International Neuropsychological Society, 11*(03), 215–227.

Belanger, H. G., Kretzmer, T., Yoash-Gantz, R., Pickett, T., & Tupler, L. A. (2009). Cognitive sequelae of blast-related versus other mechanisms of brain trauma. *Journal of the International Neuropsychological Society, 15*(1), 1–8.

Belanger, H. G., & Vanderploeg, R. D. (2005). The neuropsychological impact of sports-related concussion: A meta-analysis. *Journal of the International Neuropsychological Society, 11*(4), 345–357.

Ben-Porath, Y. S., & Tellegen, A. (2008). *Minnesota Multiphasic Personality Inventory-2 Restructured Form: Manual for administration, scoring and interpretation.* Minneapolis, MN: University of Minnesota Press.

Berry, D. T., Adams, J. J., Clark, C. D., Thacker, S. R., Burger, T. L., Wetter, M. W., & Baer, R. (1996). Detection of a cry for help on the MMPI-2: An analog investigation. *Journal of Personality Assessment, 67*(1), 26–36.

Bianchini, K. J., Greve, K. W., & Glynn, G. (2005). On the diagnosis of malingered pain-related disability: Lessons from cognitive malingering research. *The Spine Journal, 5*(4), 404–417.

Bianchini, K. J., Mathias, C. W., & Greve, K. W. (2001). Symptom validity testing: A critical review. *The Clinical Neuropsychologist, 15*(1), 19–45.

Binder, L. M. (1993). Assessment of malingering after mild head trauma with the Portland Digit Recognition Test. *Journal of Clinical and Experimental Neuropsychology, 15*(2), 170–182.

Binder, L. M. (1997). A review of mild head trauma. part II: Clinical implications. *Journal of Clinical and Experimental Neuropsychology, 19*(3), 432–457.

Binder, L. M., Rohling, M. L., & Larrabee, G. J. (1997). A review of mild head trauma. part I: Meta-analytic review of neuropsychological studies. *Journal of Clinical and Experimental Neuropsychology, 19*(3), 421–431.

Binder, R. L., Trimble, M. R., & McNiel, D. E. (1991). The course of psychological symptoms after resolution of lawsuits. *American Journal of Psychiatry, 148*(8), 1073–1075.

Boone, K. B. (2007a). *Assessment of feigned cognitive impairment: A neuropsychological perspective*. New York: Guilford Press.

Boone, K. B. (2007b). A reconsideration of the Slick et al. (1999) criteria for malingered neurocognitive dysfunction. In K. B. Boone (Ed.), *Assessment of feigned cognitive impairment: A neuropsychological perspective* (pp. 29–49). New York: Guilford Press.

Boone, K. B. (2009a). Fixed belief in cognitive dysfunction despite normal neuropsychological scores: Neurocognitive hypochondriasis? *The Clinical Neuropsychologist, 23*(6), 1016–1036.

Boone, K. B. (2009b). The need for continuous and comprehensive sampling of effort/response bias during neuropsychological examinations. *The Clinical Neuropsychologist, 23*(4), 729–741.

Boone, K. B., Lu, P., Back, C., King, C., Lee, A., Philpott, L., et al. (2002). Sensitivity and specificity of the Rey Dot Counting Test in patients with suspect effort and various clinical samples. *Archives of Clinical Neuropsychology, 17*(7), 625–642.

Boone, K. B., Lu, P., & Herzberg, D. S. (2002a). *The Dot Counting Test manual*. Los Angeles: Western Psychological Services.

Boone, K. B., Lu, P., & Herzberg, D. S. (2002b). *The b Test manual*. Los Angeles: Western Psychological Services.

Boone, K. B., Lu, P., & Wen, J. (2005). Comparison of various RAVLT scores in the detection of noncredible memory performance. *Archives of Clinical Neuropsychology, 20*(3), 301–319.

Boone, K. B., Salazar, X., Lu, P., Warner-Chacon, K., & Razani, J. (2002). The Rey 15-Item Recognition Trial: A technique to enhance sensitivity of the Rey 15-Item Memorization Test. *Journal of Clinical and Experimental Neuropsychology, 24*(5), 561–573.

Bush, S. S., Ruff, R. M., Troster, A. I., Barth, J. T., Koffler, S. P., Pliskin, N. H., et al. (2005). NAN position paper: Symptom validity assessment: Practice issues and medical necessity. *Archives of Clinical Neuropsychology, 20*(4), 419–426.

Butcher, J. N., Arbisi, P. A., Atlis, M. M., & McNulty, J. L. (2003). The construct validity of the Lees-Haley Fake Bad Scale: Does this scale measure somatic malingering and feigned emotional distress? *Archives of Clinical Neuropsychology, 18*(5), 473–485.

Butcher, J. N., Dahlstrom, W. G., Graham, J. R., Tellegen, A., & Kaemmer, B. (1989). *Minnesota Multiphasic Personality Inventory–second edition (MMPI-2)*. Minneapolis, MN: University of Minnesota Press.

Chafetz, M. D. (2010). Symptom validity issues in the psychological consultative examination for Social Security disability. *The Clinical Neuropsychologist, 24*(6), 1045–1063.

Chafetz, M. D. (2011). Reducing the probability of false positives in malingering detection of Social Security disability claimants. *The Clinical Neuropsychologist, 25*(7), 1239–1252.

Chafetz, M. D., Abrahams, J., & Kohlmaier, J. (2006). *Malingering on the Social Security disability consultative exam: A new rating scale*. Philadelphia, PA: American Academy of Clinical Neuropsychology (AACN) Scientific Program.

Chafetz, M. D., Abrahams, J. P., & Kohlmaier, J. (2007). Malingering on the Social Security disability consultative exam: A new rating scale. *Archives of Clinical Neuropsychology, 22*(1), 1–14.

Chafetz, M. D., Prentkowski, E., & Rao, A. (2011). To work or not to work: Motivation (not low IQ) determines symptom validity test findings. *Archives of Clinical Neuropsychology, 26*(4), 306–313.

Cohen, J. (1988). *Statistical power analysis for the behavioral sciences* (2nd ed.). Hillsdale, NJ: Lawrence Erlbaum Associates.

Conder, R., Allen, L., & Cox, D. (1992). *Computerized assessment of Response Bias Test manual*. Durham, NC: Cognisyst.

Conroe, H. G. (2009). Social Security adjudication: Regional consultant. In J. E. Morgan & J. J. Sweet (Eds.), *Neuropsychology of malingering casebook* (pp. 488–493). New York: Psychology Press.

Conti, R. P. (2004). Malingered ADHD In adolescents diagnosed with conduct disorder: A brief note. *Psychological Reports, 94*(3), 987–988.

Cooper, D. B., Nelson, L., Armistead-Jehle, P., & Bowles, A. O. (2011). Utility of the Mild Brain Injury Atypical Symptoms Scale as a screening measure for symptom over-reporting in Operation Enduring Freedom/Operation Iraqi Freedom service members with post-concussive complaints. *Archives of Clinical Neuropsychology, 26*(8), 718–727.

Cottingham, M. E., & Boone, K. B. (2010). Non-credible language deficits following mild traumatic brain injury. *The Clinical Neuropsychologist, 24*(6), 1006–1025.

Dean, A. C., Victor, T. L., Boone, K. B., & Arnold, G. (2008). The relationship of IQ to effort test performance. *The Clinical Neuropsychologist, 22*(4), 705–722.

Dean, A. C., Victor, T. L., Boone, K. B., Philpott, L. M., & Hess, R. A. (2009). Dementia and effort test performance. *The Clinical Neuropsychologist, 23*(1), 133–152.

Dean, P. J., O'Neill, D., & Sterr, A. (2012). Post-concussion syndrome: Prevalence after mild traumatic brain injury in comparison with a sample without head injury. *Brain Injury, 26*(1), 14–26.

Dikmen, S. S., Machamer, J. E., Winn, H. R., & Temkin, N. R. (1995). Neuropsychological outcome at 1-year post head injury. *Neuropsychology, 9*(1), 80–90.

Dischinger, P. C., Ryb, G. E., Kufera, J. A., & Auman, K. M. (2009). Early predictors of postconcussive syndrome in a population of trauma patients with mild traumatic brain injury. *Journal of Trauma: Injury, Infection, and Critical Care, 66*(2), 289–297.

Dunn, J. T., Lees-Haley, P. R., Brown, R. S., Williams, C. W., & English, L. T. (1995). Neurotoxic complaint base rates of personal injury claimants: Implications for neuropsychological assessment. *Journal of Clinical Psychology, 51*(4), 577–584.

Dusky v. United States, 362 U.S. 402 (1960).

Echemendia, R. J., & Cantu, R. C. (2003). Return to play following sports-related mild traumatic brain injury: The role for neuropsychology. *Applied Neuropsychology, 10*(1), 48–55.

Echemendia, R. J., & Julian, L. J. (2001). Mild traumatic brain injury in sports: Neuropsychology's contribution to a developing field. *Neuropsychology Review, 11*(2), 69–88.

Erlanger, D. M., Kutner, K. C., Barth, J. T., & Barnes, R. (1999). Neuropsychology of sports-related head injury: Dementia pugilistica to post concussion syndrome. *The Clinical Neuropsychologist, 13*(2), 193–209.

Flaro, L., Green, P., & Robertson, E. (2007). Word Memory Test failure 23 times higher in mild brain injury than in parents seeking custody: The power of external incentives. *Brain Injury, 21*(4), 373–383.

Forbes, G. B. (1998). Clinical utility of the Test of Variables of Attention (TOVA) in the diagnosis of attention-deficit/hyperactivity disorder. *Journal of Clinical Psychology, 54*(4), 461–476.

Fox, D., Lees-Haley, P., Earnest, K., & Dolezal-Wood, S. (1995). Base rates of post-concussive symptoms in health maintenance organization patients and controls. *Neuropsychology, 9*(4), 606–611.

Frazier, T., Frazier, A., Busch, R., Kerwood, M., & Demaree, H. (2008). Detection of simulated ADHD and reading disorder using symptom validity measures. *Archives of Clinical Neuropsychology, 23*(5), 501–509.

Frederick, R. I. (2003). A review of Rey's strategies for detecting malingered neuropsychological impairment. *Journal of Forensic Neuropsychology. Special issue: Detection of response bias in forensic neuropsychology: Part I, 2,* 1–25.

Frederick, R. I., & Denney, R. L. (1998). Minding Your "ps and qs" when using forced-choice recognition tests. *The Clinical Neuropsychologist, 12*(2), 193–205.

Freeman, T., Powell, M., & Kimbrell, T. (2008). Measuring symptom exaggeration in veterans with chronic posttraumatic stress disorder. *Psychiatry Research, 158*(3), 374–380.

Frencham, K. A., Fox, A. M., & Maybery, M. T. (2005). Neuropsychological studies of mild traumatic brain injury: A meta-analytic review of research since 1995. *Journal of Clinical and Experimental Neuropsychology, 27*(3), 334–351.

Garden, N., & Sullivan, K. A. (2010). An examination of the base rates of post-concussion symptoms: The influence of demographics and depression. *Applied Neuropsychology, 17*(1), 1–7.

Gennarelli, T. A., Thibault, L. E., Adams, J. H., Graham, D. I., Thompson, C. J., & Marcincin, R. P. (1982). Diffuse axonal injury and traumatic coma in the primate. *Annals of Neurology, 12*(6), 564–574.

Gerberich, S. G., Priest, J. D., Boen, J. R., Straub, C. P., & Maxwell, R. E. (1983). Concussion incidences and severity in secondary school varsity football players. *American Journal of Public Health, 73*(12), 1370–1375.

Gervais, R. O., Ben-Porath, Y. S., Wygant, D. B., & Green, P. (2007). Development and validation of a Response Bias Scale (RBS) for the MMPI-2. *Assessment, 14*(2), 196–208.

Gervais, R. O., Ben-Porath, Y. S., Wygant, D. B., & Green, P. (2008). Differential sensitivity of the Response Bias Scale (RBS) and MMPI-2 validity scales to memory complaints. *The Clinical Neuropsychologist, 22*(6), 1061–1079.

Gouvier, W., Uddo-Crane, M., & Brown, L. (1988). Base rates of post-concussional symptoms. *Archives of Clinical Neuropsychology, 3*(3), 273–278.

Green, P. (2004). *Green's Medical Symptom Validity Test.* Edmonton, Alberta, Canada: Green's Publishing.

Green, P. (2005). *Green's Word Memory Test for Microsoft Windows: User's manual.* Edmonton, Alberta, Canada: Green's Publishing.

Green, P., & Flaro, L. (2003). Word Memory Test performance in children. *Child Neuropsychology, 9*(3), 189–207.

Green, P., Iverson, G. L., & Allen, L. M. (1999). Detecting malingering in head injury litigation with the Word Memory Test. *Brain Injury, 13*(10), 813–819.

Green, P., Lees-Haley, P. R., & Allen, L. M. (2002). The Word Memory Test and validity of neuropsychological test scores. *Journal of Forensic Neuropsychology, 2,* 97–124.

Green, P., Rohling, M. L., Lees-Haley, P. R., & Allen, L. M. (2001). Effort has a greater effect on test scores than severe brain injury in compensation claimants. *Brain Injury, 15*(12), 1045–1060.

Greiffenstein, M. F., Fox, D., & Lees-Haley, P. R. (2007). The MMPI-2 Fake Bad Scale in detection of noncredible brain injury claims. In K. Boone (Ed.), *Assessment of feigned cognitive impairment: A neuropsychological perspective* (pp. 210–235). New York: Guilford Publications.

Greve, K. W., Binder, L. M., & Bianchini, K. J. (2009). Rates of below-chance performance in forced-choice symptom validity tests. *The Clinical Neuropsychologist, 23*(3), 534–544.

Gronwall, D., & Wrightson, P. (1975). Cumulative effect of concussion. *The Lancet, 306*(7943), 995–997.

Grote, C. L., Kooker, E. K., Garron, D. C., Nyenhuis, D. L., Smith, C. A., & Mattingly, M. L. (2000). Performance of compensation seeking and non-compensation seeking samples on the Victoria Symptom Validity Test: Cross-validation and extension of a standardization study. *Journal of Clinical and Experimental Neuropsychology (Neuropsychology, Development and Cognition: Section A), 22*(6), 709–719.

Guilmette, T. J., Hart, K. J., Giuliano, A. J., & Leininger, B. E. (1994). Detecting simulated memory impairment: Comparison of the Rey Fifteen-Item Test and the Hiscock Forced-Choice Procedure. *The Clinical Neuropsychologist, 8*(3), 283–294.

Guskiewicz, K. M., Weaver, N. L., Padua, D. A., & Garrett, W. E. (2000). Epidemiology of concussion in collegiate and high school football players. *American Journal of Sports Medicine, 28*(5), 643–650.

Harrison, A. G., Edwards, M. J., & Parker, K. C. (2007). Identifying students faking ADHD: Preliminary findings and strategies for detection. *Archives of Clinical Neuropsychology, 22,* 577–588.

Harrison, A. G., Edwards, M. J., & Parker, K. H. (2008). Identifying students feigning dyslexia: Preliminary findings and strategies for detection. *Dyslexia, 14*(3), 228–246.

Harrison, A. G., Rosenblum, Y., & Currie, S. (2010). Examining unusual digit span performance in a population of postsecondary students assessed for academic difficulties. *Assessment, 17*(3), 283–293.

Heilbronner, R. L., Sweet, J. J., Morgan, J. E., Larrabee, G. J., Millis, S. R., & Conference Participants. (2009). American Academy of Clinical Neuropsychology consensus conference statement on the neuropsychological assessment of effort, response bias, and malingering. *The Clinical Neuropsychologist, 23*(7), 1093–1129.

Henry, G. K. (2005). Probable malingering and performance on the test of variables of attention. *The Clinical Neuropsychologist, 19*(1), 121–129.

Hom, J., & Denney, R. L. (2002). *Detection of response bias in forensic neuropsychology.* Binghamton, NY: Haworth Medical Press.

Howe, L. L., & Loring, D. W. (2009). Classification accuracy and predictive ability of the Medical Symptom Validity Test's Dementia Profile and General Memory Impairment Profile. *The Clinical Neuropsychologist, 23*(2), 329–342.

Hurley, K. E., & Deal, W. P. (2006). Assessment instruments measuring malingering used with individuals who have mental retardation: Potential problems and issues. *Mental Retardation, 44*(2), 112–119.

Iverson, G. L. (2005). Outcome from mild traumatic brain injury. *Current Opinion in Psychiatry, 18*(3), 301–317.

Iverson, G. L., & Binder, L. M. (2000). Detecting exaggeration and malingering in neuropsychological assessment. *Journal of Head Trauma Rehabilitation, 15*(2), 829–858.

Iverson, G. L., & Franzen, M. D. (1998). Detecting malingered memory deficits with the Recognition Memory Test. *Brain Injury, 12*(4), 275–282.

Iverson, G. L., & Lange, R. T. (2003). Examination of "postconcussion-like" symptoms in a healthy sample. *Applied Neuropsychology, 10*(3), 137–144.

Iverson, G. L., & McCracken, L. M. (1997). Postconcussive symptoms in persons with chronic pain. *Brain Injury, 11*(11), 783–790.

Iverson, G. L., Lange, R. T., Brooks, B. L., & Rennison, V. L. (2010). "Good old days" bias following mild traumatic brain injury. *The Clinical Neuropsychologist, 24*(1), 17–37.

Jachinowicz, G., & Geiselman, R. E. (2004). Comparison of ease of falsification of attention deficit hyperactivity disorder diagnosis using standard behavioral rating scales. *Cognitive Science Online, 2*, 6–20.

Jones, A., & Ingram, M. V. (2011). A comparison of selected MMPI-2 and MMPI-2-RF validity scales in assessing effort on cognitive tests in a military sample. *The Clinical Neuropsychologist, 25*(7), 1207–1227.

Killgore, W. D., & DellaPietra, L. (2000). Using the WMS-III to detect malingering: Empirical validation of the Rarely Missed Index (RMI). *Journal of Clinical and Experimental Neuropsychology, 22*(6), 761–771.

Kim, M. S., Boone, K. B., Victor, T. L., Marion, S. D., Amano, S., Cottingham, M. E., et al. (2010). The Warrington Recognition Memory Test for words as a measure of response bias: Total score and response time cutoffs developed on "real world" credible and noncredible subjects. *Archives of Clinical Neuropsychology, 25*(1), 60–70.

King, N. S. (1996). Emotional, neuropsychological, and organic factors: Their use in the prediction of persisting postconcussion symptoms after moderate and mild head injuries. *Journal of Neurology, Neurosurgery & Psychiatry, 61*(1), 75–81.

Landre, N., Poppe, C. J., Davis, N., Schmaus, B., & Hobbs, S. E. (2006). Cognitive functioning and postconcussive symptoms in trauma patients with and without mild TBI. *Archives of Clinical Neuropsychology, 21*(4), 255–273.

Larrabee, G. J. (2003a). Detection of malingering using atypical performance patterns on standard neuropsychological tests. *The Clinical Neuropsychologist (Neuropsychology, Development and Cognition: Section D), 17*(3), 410–425.

Larrabee, G. J. (2003b). Exaggerated pain report in litigants with malingered neurocognitive dysfunction. *The Clinical Neuropsychologist, 17*(3), 395–401.

Larrabee, G. J. (2007). *Assessment of malingered neuropsychological deficits.* New York: Oxford University Press.

Larrabee, G. J. (2012). *Forensic neuropsychology: A scientific approach* (2nd ed.). New York: Oxford University Press.

Larrabee, G. J., Greiffenstein, M. F., Greve, K. W., & Bianchini, K. J. (2007). Refining diagnostic criteria for malingering. In G. J. Larrabee (Ed.), *Assessment of malingered neuropsychological deficits* (pp. 334–371). New York: Oxford University Press.

Larrabee, G. J., Millis, S. R., & Meyers, J. E. (2009). 40 plus or minus 10, a new magical number: Reply to Russell. *The Clinical Neuropsychologist, 23*(5), 841–849.

Leark, R. A., Dixon, D., Hoffman, T., & Huynh, D. (2002). Fake bad test response bias effects on the test of variables of attention. *Archives of Clinical Neuropsychology, 17*(4), 335–342.

Leark, R. A., Greenberg, L. K., Kindschi, C. L., Dupuy, T. R., & Hughes, S. J. (2007). *Test of Variables of Attention: Professional manual.* Los Alamitos: The TOVA Company.

Lee Booksh, R., Pella, R. D., Singh, A. N., & Drew Gouvier, W. (2010). Ability of college students to simulate ADHD on objective measures of attention. *Journal of Attention Disorders, 13*(4), 325–338.

Lees-Haley, P. R., & Brown, R. S. (1993). Neuropsychological complaint base rates of 170 personal injury claimants. *Archives of Clinical Neuropsychology, 8*(3), 203–209.

Levin, H. S., Mattis, S., Ruff, R. M., Eisenberg, H. M., Marshall, L. F., Tabaddor, K., et al. (1987). Neurobehavioral outcome following minor head injury: A three-center study. *Journal of Neurosurgery, 66*(2), 234–243.

Lezak, M. D. (1983). *Neuropsychological assessment* (2nd ed.). New York: Oxford University Press.

Lezak, M. D. (1995). *Neuropsychological assessment* (3rd ed.). New York: Oxford University Press.

Lindstrom, W., Coleman, C., Thomassin, K., Southall, C. M., & Lindstrom, J. H. (2011). Simulated dyslexia in postsecondary students: Description and detection using embedded validity indicators. *The Clinical Neuropsychologist, 25*(2), 302–322.

Loring, D. W., Larrabee, G. J., Lee, G. P., & Meador, K. J. (2007). Victoria Symptom Validity Test performance in a heterogeneous clinical sample. *The Clinical Neuropsychologist, 21*(3), 522–531.

Losier, B. J., McGrath, P. J., & Klein, R. M. (1996). Error patterns on the continuous performance test in non-medicated and medicated samples of children with and without ADHD: A meta-analytic review. *Journal of Child Psychology and Psychiatry, 37*(8), 971–987.

Lu, P. H., Boone, K. B., Cozolino, L., & Mitchell, C. (2003). Effectiveness of the Rey-Osterrieth Complex Figure Test and the Meyers and Meyers Recognition Trial in the detection of suspect effort. *The Clinical Neuropsychologist, 17*(3), 426–440.

Lu, P. H., Boone, K. B., Jimenez, N., & Razani, J. (2004). Failure to inhibit the reading response on the Stroop Test: A pathognomonic indicator of suspect effort. *Journal of Clinical and Experimental Neuropsychology, 26*(2), 180–189.

Lynch, W. J. (2004). Determination of effort level, exaggeration, and malingering in neurocognitive assessment. *Journal of Head Trauma Rehabilitation, 19*(3), 277–283.

Main, C. J. (1983). The Modified Somatic Perception Questionnaire (MSPQ). *Journal of Psychosomatic Research, 27*(6), 503–514.

Mapou, R. L. (2009). *Adult learning disabilities and ADHD: Research-informed assessment.* Oxford, UK: Oxford University Press.

Marshall, P., & Happe, M. (2007). The performance of individuals with mental retardation on cognitive tests assessing effort and motivation. *The Clinical Neuropsychologist, 21*(5), 826–840.

Marshall, P., Schroeder, R., O'Brien, J., Fischer, R., Ries, A., Blesi, B., & Barker, J. (2010). Effectiveness of symptom validity measures in identifying cognitive and behavioral symptom exaggeration in adult attention deficit hyperactivity disorder. *The Clinical Neuropsychologist, 24*(7), 1204–1237.

McCrea, M. (2008). *Mild traumatic brain injury and postconcussion syndrome: The new evidence base for diagnosis and treatment.* Oxford, UK: Oxford University Press.

McCrea, M., Iverson, G. L., McAllister, T. W., Hammeke, T. A., Powell, M. R., Barr, W. B., & Kelly, J. P. (2009). An integrated review of recovery after mild traumatic brain injury (MTBI): Implications for clinical management. *The Clinical Neuropsychologist, 23*(8), 1368–1390.

McCrea, M., Pliskin, N., Barth, J., Cox, D., Fink, J., French, L., et al. (2008). Official position of the military TBI task force on the role of neuropsychology and rehabilitation psychology in the evaluation, management, and research of military veterans with traumatic brain injury. *The Clinical Neuropsychologist, 22*(1), 10–26.

McLean, A., Dikmen, S. S., & Temkin, N. R. (1993). Psychosocial recovery after head injury. *Archives of Physical Medicine and Rehabilitation, 74*(10), 1041–1046.

Meares, S., Shores, E. A., Batchelor, J., Baguley, I. J., Chapman, J., Gurka, J., & Marosszeky, J. E. (2006). The relationship of psychological and cognitive factors and opioids in the development of the postconcussion syndrome in general trauma patients with mild traumatic brain injury. *Journal of the International Neuropsychological Society, 12*(06).

Meares, S., Shores, E. A., Taylor, A. J., Batchelor, J., Bryant, R. A., Baguley, I. J., et al. (2008). Mild traumatic brain Injury does not predict acute postconcussion syndrome. *Journal of Neurology, Neurosurgery, & Psychiatry, 79* (3), 300–306.

Meares, S., Shores, E. A., Taylor, A. J., Batchelor, J., Bryant, R. A., Baguley, I. J., et al. (2011). The prospective course of postconcussion syndrome: The role of mild traumatic brain injury. *Neuropsychology, 25*(4), 454–465.

Mild Traumatic Brain Injury Committee of the Head Injury Interdisciplinary Special Interest Group of the American Congress of Rehabilitation Medicine. (1993). Definition of mild traumatic brain injury. *Journal of Head Trauma Rehabilitation, 8*(3): 86–87.

Miller, H. A. (2001). *M-FAST: Miller Forensic Assessment of Symptoms Test: Professional manual*. Odessa, FL: Psychological Assessment Resources.

Miller, L. S., Boyd, M. C., Cohn, A., Wilson, J. S., & McFarland, M. (2006). *Prevalence of sub-optimal effort in disability applicants*. Poster session, Boston, MA: International Neuropsychological Society.

Millis, S. R., & Volinsky, C. T. (2001). Assessment of response bias in mild head injury: Beyond malingering tests. *Journal of Clinical and Experimental Neuropsychology, 23*(6), 809–828.

Mittenberg, W., DiGiulio, D. V., Perrin, S., & Bass, A. E. (1992). Symptoms following mild head injury: Expectation as aetiology. *Journal of Neurology, Neurosurgery & Psychiatry, 55*(3), 200–204.

Mittenberg, W., Patton, C., Canyock, E. M., & Condit, D. C. (2002). Base rates of malingering and symptom exaggeration. *Journal of Clinical and Experimental Neuropsychology, 24*, 1094–1102.

Morey, L. C. (1991). *Personality Assessment Inventory professional manual*. Odessa, FL: Psychological Assessment Resources.

Moser, R. S., Schatz, P., Neidzwski, K., & Ott, S. D. (2011). Group versus individual administration affects baseline neurocognitive test performance. *The American Journal of Sports Medicine, 39*(11), 2325–2330.

Nelson, N. W., Hoelzle, J. B., McGuire, K. A., Ferrier-Auerbach, A. G., Charlesworth, M. J., & Sponheim, S. R. (2010). Evaluation context impacts neuropsychological performance of OEF/OIF veterans with reported combat-related concussion. *Archives of Clinical Neuropsychology, 25*(8), 713–723.

Nitch, S., Boone, K. B., Wen, J., Arnold, G., & Alfano, K. (2006). The utility of the Rey Word Recognition Test in the detection of suspect effort. *The Clinical Neuropsychologist, 20*(4), 873–887.

Osmon, D. C., Plambeck, E., Klein, L., & Mano, Q. (2006). The Word Reading Test of effort in adult learning disability: A simulation study. *The Clinical Neuropsychologist, 20*(2), 315–324.

Otto, R. K., Musick, J. E., & Sherrod, C. B. (2010). *Inventory of Legal Knowledge: Professional manual*. Lutz, FL: Psychological Assessment Resources.

Packer, I. K. (2009). *Evaluation of criminal responsibility*. New York: Oxford University Press.

Post, R. D., & Gasparikova-Krasnec, M. (1979). MMPI validity scales and behavioral disturbance in psychiatric inpatients. *Journal of Personality Assessment, 43*(2), 155–159.

Quinn, C. (2003). Detection of malingering in assessment of adult ADHD. *Archives of Clinical Neuropsychology, 18*(4), 379–395.

Richman, J., Green, P., Gervais, R., Flaro, L., Merten, T., Brockhaus, R., & Ranks, D. (2006). Objective tests of symptom exaggeration in independent medical examinations. *Journal of Occupational and Environmental Medicine, 48*(3), 303–311.

Rogers, R. (1997). Introduction. In R. Rogers (Ed.) *Handbook of diagnostic and structured interviewing* (pp. 1–19). New York: Guilford Press.

Rogers, R., Bagby, R. M., & Dickens, S. E. (1992). *Structured Interview of Reported Symptoms (SIRS) and professional manual*. Odessa, FL: Psychological Assessment Resources.

Rogers, R., Sewell, K. W., & Gillard, N. D. (2010). *Structured Interview of Reported Symptoms, 2nd edition (SIRS-2): Professional manual*. Odessa, FL: Psychological Assessment Resources.

Rogers, R., Sewell, K. W., & Ustad, K. L. (1995). Feigning among chronic outpatients on the MMPI-2: A systematic examination of fake-bad Indicators. *Assessment, 2*, 81–89.

Rohling, M. L., & Demakis, G. J. (2010). Bowden, Shores, & Mathias (2006): Failure to replicate or just failure to notice. Does effort still account for more variance in neuropsychological test scores than TBI severity? *The Clinical Neuropsychologist, 24*(1), 119–136.

Rosenfeld, B., Sands, S. A., & Van Gorp, W. G. (2000). Have we forgotten the base rate problem? Methodological Issues in the detection of distortion. *Archives of Clinical Neuropsychology, 15*(4), 349–359.

Ruff, R. M., Levin, H. S., Mattis, S., High, W. M., Marshall, L. F., Eisenberg, H. M., et al. (1989). Recovery of memory after mild head injury: A three-center study. In H. S. Levin, H. M., Eisenberg, & A.L. Benton (Eds.), *Mild head injury* (pp. 176–188). New York: Oxford University Press.

Ruff, R. M., & Richardson, A. M. (1999). Mild traumatic brain injury. In J. J. Sweet (Ed.), *Forensic neuropsychology: Fundamentals and practice. Studies on neuropsychology, development, and cognition* (pp. 315–338). Bristol, PA: Swets & Zeitlinger.

Sandford, J. A., & Turner, A. (1995). *Intermediate visual and auditory Continuous Performance Test interpretation manual*. Richmond, VA: Braintrain.

Sattler, J. M. (1998). *Clinical and forensic interviewing of children and families: Guidelines for the mental health, education, pediatric, and child maltreatment fields*. San Diego: Sattler.

Sawchyn, J. M., Brulot, M. M., & Strauss, E. (2000). Note on the use of the Postconcussion Syndrome Checklist. *Archives of Clinical Neuropsychology, 15*(1), 1–8.

Schretlen, D. J., & Shapiro, A. M. (2003). A quantitative review of the effects of traumatic brain injury on cognitive functioning. *International Review of Psychiatry, 15*(4), 341–349.

Sharland, M. J., & Gfeller, J. D. (2007). A survey of neuropsychologists' beliefs and practices with respect to the assessment of effort. *Archives of Clinical Neuropsychology, 22*(2), 213–223.

Sharland, M. J., Gfeller, J. D., Justice, L., Ross, M., & Hughes, H. (2005). A survey of neuropsychologists' beliefs and practices with respect to the assessment of effort. *Archives of Clinical Neuropsychology, 20*(7), 8.

Sherman, D. S., Boone, K. B., Lu, P., & Razano, J. (2002). Re-examination of a Rey Auditory Verbal Learning Test/Rey Complex Figure Discriminant Function to detect suspect effort. *The Clinical Neuropsychologist, 16*(3), 242–250.

Simon, M. J. (2007). Performance of mentally retarded forensic patients on the test of memory malingering. *Journal of Clinical Psychology, 63*(4), 339–344.

Slick, D. J., Hopp, G., Strauss, E. H., & Thompson, G. B. (1996). *The Victoria Symptom Validity Test.* Lutz, FL: Psychological Assessment Resources.

Slick, D. J., Sherman, E. M., & Iverson, G. L. (1999). Diagnostic criteria for malingered neurocognitive dysfunction: Proposed standards for clinical practice and research. *The Clinical Neuropsychologist, 13*(4), 545–561.

Slick, D. J., Tan, J. E., Strauss, E. H., & Hultsch, D. F. (2004). Detecting malingering: A survey of experts' practices. *Archives of Clinical Neuropsychology, 19*(4), 465–473.

Social Security Administration (2008). *Do tests of malingering have any value for SSA evaluations?* Policy Clarification: 1-22-2008.

Social Security Advisory Board (2003). *The Social Security definition of disability.* Washington, DC: Social Security Advisory Board.

Sollman, M. J., Ranseen, J. D., & Berry, D. T. (2010). Detection of feigned ADHD in college students. *Psychological Assessment, 22*(2), 325–335.

Solomon, R., Boone, K. B., Miora, D., Skidmore, S., Cottingham, M., Victor, T., et al. (2010). Use of the WAIS-III picture completion subtest as an embedded measure of response bias. *The Clinical Neuropsychologist, 24*(7), 1243–1256.

Suhr, J., Hammers, D., Dobbins-Buckland, K., Zimak, E., & Hughes, C. (2008). The relationship of malingering test failure to self-reported symptoms and neuropsychological findings in adults referred for ADHD evaluation. *Archives of Clinical Neuropsychology, 23*(5), 521–530.

Suhr, J., Sullivan, B. K., & Rodriguez, J. L. (2011). The relationship of noncredible performance to continuous performance test scores in adults referred for attention-deficit/hyperactivity disorder evaluation. *Archives of Clinical Neuropsychology, 26*(1), 1–7.

Sullivan, B. K., May, K., & Galbally, L. (2007). Symptom exaggeration by college adults in attention-deficit hyperactivity disorder and learning disorder assessments. *Applied Neuropsychology, 14*(3), 189–207.

Tombaugh, T. N. (1996). *TOMM. The Test of Memory Malingering.* North Tonawanda, NY: Multi-Health Systems.

Trahan, D. E., Ross, C. E., & Trahan, S. L. (2001). Relationships among postconcussional-type symptoms, depression, and anxiety in neurologically normal young adults and victims of mild brain injury. *Archives of Clinical Neuropsychology, 16*(5), 435–445.

Trueblood, W., & Schmidt, M. (1993). Malingering and other validity considerations in the neuropsychological evaluation of mild head injury. *Journal of Clinical and Experimental Neuropsychology, 15*(4), 578–590.

Tucha, L., Sontag, T. A., Walitza, S., & Lange, K. W. (2009). Detection of malingered attention deficit hyperactivity disorder. *ADHD Attention Deficit and Hyperactivity Disorders, 1*(1), 47–53.

U.S. Department of Health and Human Services, Social Security Administration (1994, revised 2006). *Disability evaluation under Social Security* (SSA Publication no. 64–039).

U.S. Department of Justice. (2004). *A guide to disability rights laws.* Washington DC: Civil Rights Division Disability Rights.

Vickery, C. D., Berry, D. T., Inman, T. H., Harris, M. J., & Orey, S. A. (2001). Detection of inadequate effort on neuropsychological testing: A meta-analytic review of selected procedures. *Archives of Clinical Neuropsychology, 16*(1), 45–73.

Victor, T. L., & Boone, K. B. (2007). Identification of feigned mental retardation. In K.B. Boone (Ed.), *Assessment of feigned cognitive impairment: A neuropsychological perspective* (pp. 310–345). New York: Guilford Press.

Victor, T. L., Kulick, A. D., & Boone, K. B. (2012a). Assessing noncredible attention, processing speed, language and visuospatial/perceptual function in mild TBI cases. In D. A. Carone & S. S. Bush (Eds.), *Mild traumatic brain injury symptom validity assessment and malingering.* New York: Springer Publishing Company.

Victor, T. L., Kulick, A. D., & Boone, K. B. (2012b). Assessing noncredible sensory-motor function, executive function, and test batteries in mild TBI cases. In D. A. Carone & S. S. Bush (Eds.), *Mild traumatic brain injury symptom validity assessment and malingering.* New York: Springer Publishing Company.

Wang, Y., Chan, R., & Deng, Y. Y. (2006). Examination of postconcussion-like symptoms in healthy university students: Relationships to subjective and objective neuropsychological function performance. *Archives of Clinical Neuropsychology, 21*(4), 339–347.

Warrington, E. K. (1984). *Recognition Memory Test.* Windsor, UK: NFER-Nelson.

Whitney, K. A., Shepard, P. H., Williams, A. L., Davis, J. J., & Adams, K. M. (2009). The Medical Symptom Validity Test in the evaluation of Operation Iraqi Freedom/ Operation Enduring Freedom soldiers: A preliminary study. *Archives of Clinical Neuropsychology, 24*(2), 145–152.

Whitney, K., Davis, J., Shepard, P., & Herman, S. (2008). Utility of the Response Bias Scale (RBS) and other MMPI-2 validity scales in predicting TOMM performance. *Archives of Clinical Neuropsychology, 23*(7–8), 777–786.

Widows, M. R., & Smith, G. P. (2005). *SIMS: Structured Inventory of Malingered Symptomatology: Professional manual.* Lutz, FL: Psychological Assessment Resources.

Wygant, D. B., Sellbom, M., Benporath, Y. S., Stafford, K. P., Freeman, D. B., & Heilbronner, R. L. (2007). The relation between symptom validity testing and MMPI-2 scores as a function of forensic evaluation context. *Archives of Clinical Neuropsychology, 22*(4), 489–499.

Young, J. C., & Gross, A. M. (2011). Detection of response bias and noncredible performance in adult attention-deficit/hyperactivity disorder. *Archives of Clinical Neuropsychology, 26*(3), 165–175.

Ziegler, E. A., Boone, K. B., Victor, T. L. & Zeller, M. (2008a). The specificity of Digit Span effort indicators in patients with poor math abilities. *The Clinical Neuropsychologist, 22,* 435.

Ziegler, E. A., Boone, K. B., Victor, T. L. & Zeller, M. (2008b). The specificity of the Dot Counting Test in patients with poor math abilities. *The Clinical Neuropsychologist, 22,* 435.

Neuropsychological Deficits in Major Depressive Disorder: Correlates and Conundrums

MICHAEL R. BASSO, ASHLEY MILLER,
EDUARDO ESTEVIS, AND DENNIS COMBS

It is well recognized that major depressive disorder (MDD) corresponds with significant morbidity. In particular, depressed individuals manifest diminished functional, vocational, and medical outcomes, and illness coincides with a variety of physiological and cerebral anomalies. These problems occur during acute depressive episodes and in periods of remission, implying that MDD is a chronic syndrome marked by considerable morbidity.

Despite long-standing indications of pervasive abnormalities, the impact of MDD on neuropsychological function received little scientific attention until the 1980s. Since that time, a large body of research has accumulated, and these data indicate that MDD results in significant neuropsychological impairment. Yet, only some depressed people manifest such deficits, and investigators have begun to identify characteristics that moderate risk of neurocognitive impairment. Toward this end, the purpose of this chapter is to review these depressive features. In doing so, we will focus on primary unipolar depression. We will ignore research concerning secondary depression (i.e., depression consequent to primary neurological disease) because it is a different pathological and diagnostic entity and covered in other chapters in this book.

Background

MDD ranks among the most prevalent mental illnesses. Although estimates vary, most investigators agree that 15% of the population will meet diagnostic criteria for MDD during their lifetime (Hasin, Goodwin, Stinson, & Grant, 2005; Kessler et al., 2005), and 7% of the population will become depressed during any one year (Kessler & Merikangas, 2004). Although the median age of onset is 32 years, interquartile ages range from 19 to 44 years, and risk of sustaining a first depressive episode decreases after age 40 (Hasin et al., 2005). Nonetheless, 11% of elderly patients, especially those in skilled nursing facilities, meet criteria for MDD (Kessler, McGonagle, Swartz, Blazer, & Nelson, 1993). Caucasians tend to have higher rates of MDD than those for other ethnic groups (Williams et al., 2007), and women are nearly twice as likely as men to become depressed.

Etiology of the illness is uncertain. Owing to exaggerated prevalence among first-degree relatives of afflicted individuals, genetic influences are likely. Other putative vulnerabilities include temperament and developmental insults, as individuals with high neuroticism or histories of brain trauma are at elevated risk for developing MDD (Kendler, Thornton, & Gardner, 2001). Initial onset of depression seems to correspond with psychosocial stressors (e.g., death of a spouse, divorce, etc.), and these stressors seem to interact with vulnerabilities to yield onset of a MDD episode. In particular, some researchers assert that MDD occurs consequent to an exaggerated immune-mediated stress response resulting in neuronal dysfunction (e.g., Maes, 2011). Hypotheses that MDD is due to a single neurotransmitter deficiency are disputed, and the illness seems to reflect multiple discrete but integrated pathways, including serotonin, norepinephrine, and dopamine (Mayberg, 2003; Trivedi, Hollander, Nutt, & Blier, 2008).

Pathology

With the advent of neuroimaging methods, it became apparent that considerable structural and functional abnormalities exist in people with MDD. Reduced cerebral volumes have been observed in orbital and dorsal lateral frontal cortex, anterior cingulate, hippocampus, amygdala, cerebellum, and basal ganglia structures (Beyer & Krishnan, 2002; Drevets, Price, & Furey, 2008; Mayberg, 2003). Indeed, recent meta-analyses imply that these reduced tissue volumes are a reliable finding across investigations (Arnone, McIntosh, Ebmeier, Munafo, & Anderson, 2012; Bora, Fornito, Pantelis, & Yücel, 2012; Cole, Costafreda, McGuffin, & Fu, 2011; Kempton et al., 2011; Sacher et al., 2012). Areas of reduced volume are present during an initial depressive episode (Cole et al., 2011) and correspond with diminished glial cell counts and density as well as reduced neuronal density (Drevets et al., 2008; Harrison, 2002). In turn, these structural anomalies coincide with functional abnormalities. Although inconsistencies exist, MDD corresponds with hypometabolism in prefrontal cortex, medial frontal structures, and the basal ganglia and with hypermetabolism in anterior subgenual cingulate cortex (Drevets, 2000; Sacher et al., 2012). These abnormal structural and functional changes appear to persist despite remission of symptoms (Drevets, 2000; Rogers, Bradshaw, Pantelis, & Phillips, 1998; Sheline, 2000). Notably, some aspects of abnormal activation correspond with depressive severity and cognitive impairment in people with MDD (Drevets, 2000; Marvel & Paradiso, 2004; Mayberg, 2003). Some investigators assert that these abnormalities reveal dysfunction in multiple neural systems. As depression occurs, frontal-limbic networks become dysregulated, and modulation of frontal and subcortical limbic activation fails. As depression remits, frontal lobe activation increases, and ventral limbic and paralimbic activation diminishes (Mayberg, 2003). Ultimately, these abnormal patterns of cerebral function may underlie neuropsychological impairment in MDD.

Symptoms

MDD is defined by episodes of clinical depression. These episodes are characterized by an interval of at least 2 weeks during which depressed mood, or anhedonia, and four of the following symptoms occur (most of the day, nearly every day): insomnia or hypersomnia, excessive or insufficient appetite, fatigue, inattention, psychomotor retardation or agitation, excessive guilt, or suicidal ideation. Untreated depression tends to be durable, and the median length of a depressive episode is 6 months (Eaton et al., 2008; Hasin et al., 2005). Approximately 40% of depressed individuals will recover in 5 weeks, and 90% will recover within 1 year (Kessler & Wang, 2010). By middle age, patients tend to report an average of five discrete episodes (Hasin et al., 2005), and 80% will sustain a recurrent episode over time (Kessler et al., 2003). Indeed, 26% of patients are likely to sustain a recurrence within 1 year of episode recovery. Ten years after an initial episode, the median number of recurrent episodes was 7. Time to recurrence seems to decrease with subsequent episodes. For example, a second episode occurs about 150 weeks after an initial episode, but a fifth episode will occur approximately 55 weeks after a fourth episode (Solomon et al., 2000).

In some individuals, depression is unrelenting. More than 65% of patients will fail to have a complete remission of symptoms (Trivedi et al., 2006). In a longitudinal study, Eaton et al. (2008) found that 15% reported chronic symptoms over 23 years. Other studies report that 20–35% of patients will manifest chronic symptoms over shorter intervals (Kessler et al., 2005). Chronicity tends to correspond with symptom severity, and about 66% will manifest severe to moderate depression. Notably, severity of depression appears to be a salient predictor of impaired ability to manage activities of daily living (Kessler et al., 2005).

Summary

MDD manifests with recurrent episodes, and a considerable proportion of the patient population will experience relentless symptoms of depression or an incomplete remission. As time passes, recurrence becomes more frequent, and most episodes are marked by considerable severity. In turn, severity of MDD tends to correspond with worsening functional impairment.

NEUROPSYCHOLOGICAL DEFICITS IN MDD

Some of the earliest studies of neuropsychological function in MDD were conducted in the late 1970s. By the mid-1990s, a sufficient number of publications emerged, permitting investigators to conduct meta-analyses. *Meta-analysis* is a quantitative method of summarizing research findings across multiple publications. It indicates whether findings occur reliably across studies, and it can be used to estimate the magnitude of independent variables on dependent variables. Currently, there are at least 10 meta-analyses concerning neuropsychological function in people with MDD. Because meta-analyses provide a composite estimate of effects across studies, these investigations likely provide a more reliable overview of neuropsychological deficits in people with MDD than reviewing a series of individual studies.

Among the first of these meta-analyses, Burt, Zembar, and Niederehe (1995) focused on memory impairment in people with MDD. Summarizing 122 studies, mostly involving middle-aged inpatients with depression, they found moderate to large effect sizes for differences between patients and normal individuals on measures of recall and recognition memory. Overall, depressed patients performed approximately .5 standard deviations below the mean of control subjects. Notably, depressed patients learned and remembered as poorly as schizophrenics, but not as poorly as patients with Alzheimer's disease. Nonetheless, several variables moderated the impact of depression on memory. In particular, inpatients performed worse than outpatients, and outpatients generally performed normally. Compared to age-respective control groups, patients younger than age 60 showed greater memory impairment than those older than 60. Those who were treated with antidepressant medication performed better than those without treatment, and recall was worse for visual than verbal material.

Expanding on the review by Burt et al. (1995), Christensen, Griffiths, MacKinnon, and Jacomb (1997) conducted a meta-analysis that examined other domains of neuropsychological function besides memory. Summarizing the findings of 154 papers, Christensen et al. found that depressed patients performed worse than controls on measures of executive function, memory, working memory, and speed of information processing, and the average overall effect size was moderately large. Notably, however, these effect sizes were mitigated by age. Relative to their respective control groups, depressed individuals who were 60 and older displayed more impairment than younger patients, and this occurred despite equivalent depressive severity. Hospitalized patients with MDD performed far worse than outpatients. Likewise, mild depression coincided with smaller effect sizes than severe depression. Patients whose depression was precipitated by a psychosocial stressor (exogenous depression) performed comparably to those with no identified stressor (endogenous depression). Neuropsychological test difficulty failed to moderate differences between depressed and nondepressed individuals, and recognition memory and recall memory were equally impaired. Depressed individuals had less impairment than those with Alzheimer's disease. Christensen and colleagues further concluded that insufficient effort or poor motivation fails to account for neuropsychological deficits in MDD. Moreover, MDD is not associated with global impairment, as is Alzheimer's disease.

Although elderly patients comprised some of Christensen et al's (1997) meta-analysis, the researchers did not exclusively examine such individuals. Kindermann and Brown (1997) conducted a meta-analysis concerning memory function in elderly depressed patients. They excluded studies that included patients whose depression was due to comorbid medical illness. They combined data from 40 studies, and the average weighted effect size of MDD was in the moderate range at .6. Kindermann and Brown also evaluated several possible moderator variables. Studies that combined unipolar and bipolar depressed patients found worse memory impairment than those involving unipolar patients exclusively. Medication had no impact on memory function. Depression was associated with worse delayed than immediate recall, worse recognition than free recall, and worse figural than verbal memory.

In another investigation concerning elderly depressed patients, Herrmann, Goodwin, and Ebmeier (2007) conducted a meta-analysis of 10 studies. The authors specifically compared patients whose MDD began prior to age 50 with those who became symptomatic after that age. Patients with early- and late-onset depression performed worse than control groups on measures of executive function, psychomotor speed, and memory. Furthermore, on measures of executive function and speed of information processing, patients with late-onset depression performed worse than those who became symptomatic during young adulthood. Presumably, those with late-life onset of MDD became symptomatic secondary to underlying neurological disease (e.g., cerebrovascular disease), leading to them having greater impairment. Regardless, these data suggest that cognitive impairment is present in elderly patients with MDD, but those who sustain a first episode during senescence manifest worse dysfunction than those with a longer history of MDD.

Similar to Christensen et al. (1997), Veiel (1997) conducted a broad meta-analysis involving 13 studies and addressed domains of cognition in addition to memory. In contrast to Christensen et al., Veiel excluded elderly patients. Studies included within Veiel's meta-analysis generally employed inconsistent test batteries. Consequently, many of this investigation's composite effect sizes were based on only three studies. Despite the small number of studies, reliability statistics for the effect sizes were judged satisfactory. Overall, the meta-analysis identified no meaningful effect of depression on measures of attention and working memory. However, depression achieved moderate effects upon recall and retention of verbal and visual information. Moreover, the meta-analysis revealed large effects of depression on executive function. Across the neuropsychological domains, 11% to 50% of patients with MDD performed at the 2nd percentile of control subjects. Collapsing across neuropsychological domains, 40% of patients were judged impaired by this standard, implying that many, but not all, patients with MDD manifest considerable cognitive deficit.

Zakzanis, Leach, and Kaplan (1998) conducted a meta-analysis of 22 studies published since 1980. Collapsing across neuropsychological domains, the median effect size was in the moderate range at .52, and the greatest effects were observed on measures of memory, mental flexibility, speed of information processing, and working memory. To determine whether certain neuropsychological domains were more likely to be impaired than others, Zakzanis and colleagues also computed the sensitivity of various measures to detect cognitive impairment. Although some measures of executive function and new learning had relatively high sensitivities, the authors concluded that few measures reliably discriminated between patients and controls. Indeed, the median sensitivity across domains was .62. This suggests that some domains are more likely to be impaired than others. In addition, because only some of the patients displayed impairment, neuropsychological deficits are not a universal characteristic of MDD.

Relevant to this implication, approximately 25% of patients with MDD will display psychotic symptoms (primarily delusions of guilt), and such individuals experience greater morbidity and worse outcomes than those without psychotic features. In a meta-analysis of five studies, Fleming, Blasey, and Schatzberg (2004) compared depressed individuals with and without psychotic features across a broad range of neuropsychological domains. Limiting its generalizability, three of the studies in the meta-analysis focused on elderly patients. Additionally, the authors did not compare depressed patients with nondepressed control groups. These limitations notwithstanding, the largest effect sizes between the psychotic and nonpsychotic depressed patients appeared on measures of psychomotor speed, executive function, and memory. Moderate effect sizes were observed on measures of working memory and visual-spatial reasoning. Thus, psychotic features connote greater neurocognitive morbidity, and they serve to moderate which depressed patients manifest deficits. Yet, these conclusions are based on only five studies, and most of the patients were elderly. Consequently, their reliability is at least somewhat limited, and some of the elderly patients may have been impaired secondary to latent neurological disease rather than primary mood disorder.

In another effort to examine the effect of patient characteristics, McDermott and Ebmeier (2009) examined whether depressive severity predicted cognitive impairment. In their meta-analysis of 14 studies, the authors showed that increasing severity correlated with worsening executive function, psychomotor speed, and verbal memory. Other domains of neurocognitive function failed to correlate with depressive severity. To some extent, these findings parallel those of Christensen et al. (1997), whose meta-analysis revealed that depressive severity predicted worse impairment. Yet they extend those data by showing that only some domains correspond with depressive severity. Moreover, the magnitude of effects was modest, and depressive severity accounted for approximately 10% of the variance in neuropsychological function. Thus, factors other than overall symptom severity predict cognitive impairment in people with MDD.

McClintock, Husain, Greer, and Munro Cullum (2010) conducted a qualitative review of the literature concerning depressive severity and neuropsychological function. They concluded that depressive severity is inconsistently associated with neuropsychological dysfunction, and insufficient data exist to support firm conclusions. Perhaps explaining their contradictory conclusions, McClintock et al. cited approximately half of the studies cited by McDermott and Ebmeier (2009), and McDermott and Ebmeier cited only some of the papers cited by McClintock et al. The entire universe of available papers was not included in both reviews. Thus, there is modest evidence that depressive severity corresponds with neuropsychological impairment, but further research is warranted.

Although each of the meta-analyses discussed earlier demonstrate that some depressed patients display significant neuropsychological impairment, they provide no indication concerning the durability of cognitive deficits. Douglas and Porter (2009) conducted a meta-analysis of 30 studies that evaluated neuropsychological function across time. The range of follow-up varied from 1 week to 2 years. Most of the studies re-evaluated patients after depressive symptoms had subsided or remitted entirely. As symptoms remitted, verbal memory improved. There was no clear relationship between changes in depressed mood and visual memory. Regarding executive function, working memory, and psychomotor speed, patients continued to demonstrate poor performance despite symptom reduction. In some instances, executive function deficits remained 2 years after the initial examination. Additionally, there was little relationship between changes in depressive symptoms and executive function, working memory, or psychomotor speed. Residual deficits were not due to medication, but older age corresponded with worse neurocognitive outcomes. Notably, verbal and figural fluency improved as depressive symptoms remitted. These aspects of executive function were the sole measures that differentiated patients who responded to treatment from those who retained residual symptoms. Overall, these data imply that some form of residual brain dysfunction remains despite symptom remission. Given the high likelihood of relapse in MDD, perhaps these continued neurocognitive deficits suggest underlying cerebral vulnerability to subsequent depressive episodes.

Most of the meta-analyses reviewed concluded that MDD yields potent deficits on measures of executive function. Among the most sensitive measures of executive function are those that assess verbal fluency. Henry and Crawford (2005) conducted a meta-analysis of verbal fluency deficits in people with major depression. They included 42 studies published from 1982 until 2002. They found moderate differences between depressed and nondepressed individuals on measures of verbal fluency, but the effect size was larger for semantic fluency than phonemic fluency. Therefore, some measures of executive function are more sensitive to depression-related deficits than others.

Summary

Several converging findings emerge from these meta-analyses. MDD corresponds with neuropsychological dysfunction, but this finding is mitigated by several issues. Severity of cognitive deficits varied from mild to severe across studies. For example, Burt et al. (1995) and Christensen et al. (1997) found that depressed patients performed only .5 to .6 standard deviations below nondepressed control subjects, suggesting that MDD corresponds with only mild neuropsychological impairment. In contrast, Veiel (1997) reported that 40% of patients performed 2 standard deviations below normal, implying a more compelling pattern of impairment. Reasons for discrepant rates of impairment are uncertain. Burt et al. focused on memory impairment, whereas Veiel addressed a wider-range of neuropsychological function. Christensen et al. largely examined elderly patients, whereas Veiel's review concerned patients of diverse ages. Regardless, neuropsychological

Table 3.1 COGNITIVE DOMAINS IN MDD

Cognitive Domains Often Impaired in MDD	Cognitive Domains Infrequently Impaired in MDD	Cognitive Domains Sometimes Impaired in MDD
Mental flexibility	Intelligence	Concept formation
Semantic fluency	Receptive language	Phonemic fluency
Working memory	Object naming	Psychomotor speed
Speed of information processing	Visual-spatial perception	
New learning		

dysfunction occurs in MDD, but the prevalence of such impairment remains uncertain. Apart from Veiel (1997), most of the available studies neglect to provide prevalence estimates. Such estimates should be reported in future research.

As summarized in Table 3.1, these meta-analyses indicate that impairment is neither uniform across neuropsychological domains nor global. Rather, deficits appear specific to certain domains. Although executive function, speed of information processing, and new learning tend to be diminished across each of the meta-analyses, deficits do not occur consistently across all measures within these domains. For example, executive function is not uniformly affected. On measures of verbal fluency, phonemic fluency is less vulnerable to MDD than semantic fluency (Henry & Crawford, 2005). Although measures of concept formation may be robust to MDD, depressed patients often perform poorly on measures of mental flexibility (Veiel, 1997; Zakzanis et al., 1998). The status of working memory and new learning is likewise unclear. Some studies reported impaired working memory, whereas others did not. Some investigations implied that visual memory is more impaired than verbal memory (Burt et al., 1995), whereas other studies suggested no difference (Christensen et al., 1997). In contrast to these inconsistencies, the consensus of the meta-analyses implies that intellect, language, and visual-spatial perception are resilient to MDD. The cause of these deficits is uncertain, but it is interesting to note that the deficits involving executive function, memory, and working memory concur with findings of frontal and temporal lobe abnormalities in studies involving neuroimaging methods.

Patient characteristics seem to mitigate neurocognitive morbidity. Those who are elderly, psychotic, more severely depressed, or admitted to a hospital appear most likely to manifest impairment. In contrast, medication status, inadequate effort, or endogenous onset of symptoms does not seem to explain cognitive dysfunction. Additionally, deficits involving executive function, visual memory, working memory, and speed of information processing are durable, and they remain despite decreases in depressive symptoms (Douglas & Porter, 2009). Thus medication may have no clear benefit on neuropsychological function.

Possibly, neurocognitive deficits precede onset of MDD and reveal underlying cerebral vulnerability to depressive episodes. Alternatively, depressive episodes may damage the brain, especially in the frontal–temporal lobes. This damage becomes permanent and may make the patient increasingly more vulnerable to subsequent depressive episodes. Determining the validity of either explanation clearly deserves close scrutiny in subsequent research. Regardless, the presence of residual deficits in some patients with MDD should lead clinicians to monitor neurocognitive function, even after acute symptoms have improved or completely resolved.

Of course, these conclusions are tempered by several considerations. The meta-analyses are based on studies of varying quality and patient composition. For example, some of the meta-analyses were based on a relatively small number of research papers. Consequently, some of the meta-analyses may have yielded results of limited generalizability. Furthermore, the meta-analyses leave several questions unanswered. For example, apart from age, inpatient status, and presence of psychotic features, what other characteristics mitigate neuropsychological dysfunction in MDD? Some studies imply that recurrence of depression or presence of melancholic features exacerbate the severity of neurocognitive impairment (Austin et al., 1999; Basso & Bornstein, 1999). Delineating characteristics that moderate or mediate neuropsychological dysfunction in MDD would help clinicians to identify patients who are likely to display diminished mental status.

MODERATING FACTORS

A number of patient characteristics have been suggested that may moderate neuropsychological dysfunction in MDD. Some have been addressed in the previously reviewed meta-analyses (e.g., psychotic features, age of onset), and conclusions ensuing from those investigations can be made with at least marginal confidence. Other factors have not been addressed within meta-analyses, but a relatively compelling body of research has emerged concerning these variables.

Melancholia

The *Diagnostic and Statistical Manual of Mental Disorders* (4th ed., text rev.; DSM-IV-TR; American Psychiatric Association, 2000) recognizes a melancholic subtype of depression. According to the *DSM-IV-TR*, melancholia is characterized by anhedonia, weight loss, insomnia with early-morning awakening, guilt, and psychomotor agitation or retardation. Parker and Hadzi-Pavlovic (1996) assert that psychomotor retardation is the key defining element of melancholia, and they hypothesize that frontal-striatal dysfunction is the neural substrate of melancholic features. Related to this proposition, Buyukdura, McClintock, and Croarkin (2010) recently reviewed the literature concerning psychomotor retardation in MDD and found that although psychomotor retardation is not specific to melancholic depression, depressed patients with psychomotor retardation display decreased activation in the dorsal-lateral prefrontal cortex, angular gyrus, and anterior cingulate. Psychomotor retardation also predicts poor treatment response in people with MDD.

Inasmuch as frontal-striatal dysfunction is the neural substrate of melancholia, depressed patients with melancholic features may show worse executive function and working memory and slowed speed of information processing compared with those without melancholic features. To investigate this, Austin et al. (1999) studied 28 control subjects and 77 depressed patients, most of whom were inpatients. Patients with MDD performed worse than the control group on measures of memory, working memory, and mental flexibility, but they performed normally on the Wisconsin Card Sorting Test. However, when the depressed patients were dichotomized according to presence of melancholic features, a different pattern of deficits emerged. The melancholic patients performed worse than the control group on measures of memory, working memory, and executive function, including the Wisconsin Card Sorting Test. The nonmelancholic depressed patients performed normally on the neurocognitive battery.

These findings imply that melancholic features predict neuropsychological dysfunction in depressed people, more so than the presence of simple depression alone. Austin et al. (1999) reanalyzed their data, controlling for severity of depressive symptoms. Melancholic features typically emerge only in severely depressed patients, and the authors anticipated that melancholia would be confounded with depressive severity. Their assumption was supported; after covarying the effects of depressive severity, melancholic features failed to account for variance on the neuropsychological battery. This may be an artifact of the measures employed. The authors used the Hamilton Depression Rating Scale to assess depressive severity, and nearly a third of the items comprising that scale pertain to melancholic features. In partialling variance due to symptom severity, variance associated with melancholic features may have been removed because of multicollinearity, rendering effects of melancholic features nonsignificant.

In subsequent research, Michopoulos et al. (2008) administered a neuropsychological battery to 40 depressed patients and a control group of 20 nondepressed individuals. Patients were categorized by presence of melancholic features, resulting in half being melancholic and half having no significant melancholic features. The two depressed groups were equally depressed on the Hamilton Depression Rating Scale. Similar to Austin et al. (1999), Michopoulos and colleagues found that the patients with melancholic features performed worse than the control group across the battery, but the nonmelancholic patients were indistinguishable from the control group. Furthermore, the patients with melancholic features performed worse than the nonmelancholic patients on measures of executive function pertaining to mental flexibility. Likewise, Rogers et al. (2004) administered a brief battery of tests, including the Stroop task, to 8 healthy control subjects and 15 depressed patients, 7 of whom demonstrated melancholic features. The patients with melancholic features performed worse than the control group across all measures, and they performed worse than the nonmelancholic patients only on the Stroop task. The patients without melancholic features were equal to the control group across the entire battery. Moreover, in a study comparing melancholic and nonmelancholic inpatient depressives to a control group, Pier, Hulstijn, and Sabbe (2004) showed that the melancholic patients displayed impaired motor and cognitive slowing compared to the control group and nonmelancholic patients. As in the studies by Michopoulos et al. (2008) and Rogers et al. (2004), the nonmelancholic patients were equal to the control group. The observed deficits were not attributable to medication or demographic confounds; none of the patients were taking medication, and the patients were matched to the control group according to age, education, and sex.

Collectively, these data imply that melancholic features contribute to neuropsychological impairment, and melancholic features appear to be a potent risk factor for neuropsychological impairment in people with MDD. The neuropsychological anomalies are not accounted for by severity of overall depressive symptoms or other patient characteristics, because relative deficits emerge despite controlling for these variables. Moreover, the most salient area of deficit that distinguishes depressed patients with and without melancholic features are those that involve mental flexibility, set-shifting, and speed of information processing. Such measures are typically associated with frontal lobe substrates, thereby supporting assertions that melancholia implies frontal-striatal dysfunction (Austin et al., 1999; Buyukdura et al., 2010). Yet, these conclusions are based on a small number of studies, and some of the studies (e.g., Rogers et al., 2004) were based on very small samples. As a result, their reliability and generalizability is uncertain, and the data merit follow-up investigation.

Unipolar versus Bipolar Mood Disorder

Significant neuropsychological dysfunction occurs in people diagnosed with bipolar disorder, including those who are depressed (Basso, Lowery, Neel, Purdie, & Bornstein, 2002). Surprisingly, few studies have compared neuropsychological function among individuals diagnosed with bipolar or unipolar depression. In one of the first investigations concerning this issue, Borkowska and Rybakowski (2001) administered a lengthy battery to inpatient depressives. Fifteen were diagnosed with bipolar depression, and 30 were diagnosed with unipolar depression. The groups were equivalent with respect to demographic and clinical characteristics (e.g., duration of illness, treatment status, etc.). Although the groups showed equivalent intellect and speed of information processing, the bipolar depressive patients performed worse than the unipolar group on measures of nonverbal intellect, mental flexibility, selective attention, phonemic fluency, and set-shifting ability.

Extending these findings to outpatients, Maalouf et al. (2010) reported a study of 14 depressed bipolar patients, 20 depressed unipolar patients, and 28 control subjects. The patients were equivalent with respect to age, education, and clinical features, and they were administered a brief computerized battery of neuropsychological tests. Compared to the control group, the bipolar and unipolar depressives performed worse on a measure of complex planning. In contrast to the findings of Borkowska and Rybakowski (2001), the bipolar depressives were otherwise indistinguishable from the unipolar depressives. Perhaps the absence of salient differences between the bipolar and unipolar depressives is attributable to Maalouf et al. (2010) including only outpatients; Borkowska and Rybakowski studied inpatients.

Bipolar II is a less malignant form of the disorder than bipolar I. In bipolar II, patients have never experienced a manic episode; they have sustained at least one hypomanic episode, whereas bipolar I patients have sustained at least one manic episode. One study compared unipolar depressed people to depressed patients diagnosed with bipolar type II disorder: Taylor Tavares et al. (2007) administered measures of executive function, memory, and working memory to 17 depressed patients diagnosed with bipolar II disorder and 22 patients with MDD. These outpatients had taken no medication for 3 weeks prior to neuropsychological assessment, and they were compared to a group of 25 healthy control subjects. The two patient groups were equally depressed. The groups failed to differ on most of the measures, but the MDD group performed worse than the control group on one measure of executive function and on a measure of visual working memory. The bipolar II group performed as well as the control group. Thus bipolar II does not appear to contribute to worse neuropsychological function than that of MDD, whereas MDD appears to correspond with abnormal performance.

Overall, the majority of investigations fail to demonstrate significant neuropsychological differences between unipolar and bipolar depressive individuals. For example, several studies compared depressed inpatients with bipolar or unipolar mood disorder (Gruber, Rathgeber, Brünig, & Gauggel, 2007; Mojtabai et al., 2000; Sweeney, Kmiec, & Kupfer, 2000), and others have studied depressed outpatients (Bearden et al., 2006; Godard, Groundin, Baruch, and Lafleur,, 2011; Hermens, Redoblado Hodge, Scott, & Hickie, 2010; Taylor Tavares et al. 2007). Across each of these studies, sample sizes varied from 10 to nearly 60, with most including groups numbering less than 20. With one exception (Taylor Tavares et al., 2007), depressed patients, both bipolar and unipolar, performed worse than control groups on measures of executive function, working memory, and memory, and there was no difference between the bipolar or unipolar patients. Rather, the two patient groups were equally dysfunctional.

To what can the inconsistent findings be attributed? Borkowska and Rybakowski (2001) were the only investigators to find that bipolar depressive individuals performed worse than unipolar patients. Possibly, their study included outliers. With a sample of only 15 bipolar depressives, one or two highly influential outliers could have skewed the distribution of scores, leading to spurious conclusions. Alternatively, the studies finding no differences between unipolar and bipolar depressive patients may have possessed insufficient power; effect sizes were generally not reported in these investigations. Regardless, the consensus of findings implies that bipolar and unipolar depression yields equivalent neurocognitive impairment. Relatively few studies with robust statistical power exist. Thus, this area of research is unsettled and awaits further investigation.

Comorbid Disorders

MDD shares a high rate of comorbidity with anxiety disorders. Kessler and colleagues (2003) estimated that nearly 60% of patients with primary major depression present with at least one comorbid anxiety disorder, and 40% of patients with a primary diagnosis of anxiety disorder meet criteria for major depression (Rodriguez, Bruce, Pagano, & Keller, 2004). Similar to MDD, anxiety disorders appear to coincide with structural and functional brain abnormalities. For example, disorders such as post-traumatic stress disorder, generalized anxiety disorder, panic disorder, and specific phobias are associated with a variety of structural (e.g., Bremner et al., 2003; De Bellis et al., 2000, 2002; Gurvits et al., 1996; Massana et al., 2003; Rauch, Foa, Furr, & Filip, 2004; Vythilingam et al., 2000; Wurthmann et al., 1997) and functional abnormalities (e.g., Charney, 2003; Dewar & Stravynski, 2001; Pissiota et al., 2003; Tankard et al., 2003). Furthermore, deficits involving executive function, attention, working memory, and memory have been reported in people with posttraumatic stress disorder (Danckwerts & Leathem, 2003; Vasterling, Brailey, Constans, & Sutker, 1998; Vasterling, Rogers, & Kaplan, 2000), panic disorder (Asmundson, Stein, Larsen, & Walker, 1994; Lautenbacher, Spernal, & Krieg, 2002; Ludewig, Paulus, Ludewig, & Vollenweider, 2003), and phobia (Asmundson et al., 1994; Cohen et al., 1996). Although the conclusions from this research are tentative because of inconsistencies between studies, such data imply that presence of anxiety disorders increases the risk of cerebral and neuropsychological abnormalities.

A number of studies have addressed consequences of comorbid anxiety disorder on several domains of function. For instance, compared to those with MDD or anxiety alone, patients with comorbid MDD and anxiety have more severe psychopathology, earlier symptom onset, poorer outcomes, greater disability, and worse functional impairment (Andrade, Eaton, & Chilcoat, 1994; Crown et al., 2002; Grunhaus, Pande, Brown, Greden, 1994). Such exacerbated morbidity may correspond with worse neuropsychological function; few studies have addressed this issue.

To this end, Basso et al. (2007) administered a battery of neuropsychological tests to 52 inpatients with MDD and 38 normal-control subjects. Thirty of the inpatients had solitary diagnoses of MDD, and 22 were diagnosed with MDD and a comorbid anxiety disorder. Apart from number of comorbid disorders, the two patient groups were comparable with respect to demographic and clinical characteristics. Both patient groups displayed worse memory performance than the control group, but only the patients with comorbid anxiety disorder performed abnormally on measures of executive function, working memory, and psychomotor speed. The depressed patients without comorbid anxiety were indistinguishable from the control group on those measures. To provide an estimate of overall impairment, Basso and colleagues summed the number of scores accumulated across the battery that fell below the 5th percentile of test norms. The depressed patients with comorbid anxiety had more impaired scores than the control group and patients without an anxiety disorder. Specifically, those with anxiety displayed impaired scores on 50% of the battery, compared to the nonanxious patients (30%) and the control group (12%).

Lyche, Jonassen, Stiles, Ulleberg, and Landro (2010, 2011) have published three papers concerning the same sample of 61 depressed outpatients and 92 control subjects. Twenty-four patients had comorbid anxiety disorders and 37 did not.

Generally, the two patient groups performed worse than the healthy comparison group, especially on measures of executive function, working memory, memory, and speed of information processing. The patients with comorbid anxiety disorders performed worse than the patients without anxiety on a measure of sustained working memory. In no other instance did anxiety exacerbate the severity of neuropsychological impairment. Moreover, the patients generally performed within .5 standard deviations of the control group. Such performance is generally classified as normal. These outpatients demonstrated relatively mild depression and anxiety, and they showed modest performance decrements.

In another study of outpatients, Kaplan et al. (2006) administered many of the same measures employed by Lyche et al. (2010). Eleven patients were diagnosed with MDD and panic disorder, and 11 were diagnosed with panic disorder alone; none were taking medication. These 22 patients were compared to a group of 22 healthy individuals. The patients with panic disorder performed as well as the control group. The patients with comorbid MDD and panic disorder performed abnormally on indices reflecting speed of information processing and visual working memory, and their performances were at least 1 standard deviation below the control group mean. This study did not include a comparison group of patients diagnosed with MDD only. Consequently, the results do not indicate whether MDD with comorbid anxiety exacerbates cognitive dysfunction compared to that of people with MDD alone. Rather, these data show that MDD with comorbid panic disorder exacerbates cognitive impairment in people with panic disorder alone.

Kizilbash, Vanderploeg, and Curtiss (2002) examined the relationship between Minnesota Multiphasic Personality Inventory (MMPI) and California Verbal Learning Test (CVLT) performance among participants in the Vietnam Experience Study. It is uncertain whether any of the 3999 participants had formal diagnoses of depression or anxiety disorders. Participants were not patients, and structured diagnostic interview data were not reported. They were classified as having high or low depression (all with low anxiety), high or low anxiety (all with low depression), and high depression–high anxiety or low depression–low anxiety based on the D and Pt scale scores from the MMPI. There were no significant differences on the CVLT due to anxiety level alone. Those with high depression had slightly lower immediate recall than those with low depression. Those with high depression–high anxiety had lower immediate and delayed recall compared with those with low depression–low anxiety. These data imply that the presence of comorbid anxiety symptoms exacerbated the memory dysfunction among those reporting depressive symptoms. Yet, this study has multiple limitations. There is no clear indication of whether any of the individuals met criteria for MDD or anxiety disorder. There is no direct contrast of individuals with depression and no anxiety with those with depression and anxiety. Rather, Kizilbash et al. analyzed their data using separate one-way analyses of variance. The authors conducted no statistical test of the contrast between depressed individuals with and without anxiety. Hence, these data fail to clarify the potential exacerbating effect of comorbid anxiety in depressed individuals.

Overall, these nascent findings imply that comorbid anxiety disorders exacerbate neuropsychological deficits in people with MDD. At least two investigations (Basso et al., 2007; Lyche et al., 2010) show that comorbid anxiety disorders result in worse executive function, working memory, and speed of information processing than that with MDD alone. Additionally, one study vaguely suggests that anxiety worsens memory performance in people with depression (Kizilbash et al., 2002). This relationship appears to be mitigated by hospitalization status. For instance, the inpatients studied by Basso et al. (2007) had greater dysfunction associated with anxiety than did the outpatients examined by Lyche et al. (2010). These conclusions notwithstanding, many questions remain unanswered. For example, is greater neurocognitive morbidity associated with some anxiety disorders more than others? Basso et al. and Lyche et al. included samples of patients with various anxiety disorders, and no disorder predominated. Additionally, do the detrimental effects of comorbid anxiety disorders generalize across other domains of dysfunction besides executive function, working memory, and speed of information processing? The range of assessment in the existing studies is somewhat limited, thus constraining possible generalizations.

Summary

As summarized in Table 3.2, melancholic features and presence of comorbid anxiety disorders contribute to exacerbated neuropsychological dysfunction in people with MDD. In contrast, history of a prior manic or hypomanic episode does not contribute to increasing neurocognitive morbidity in depressed people. These conclusions should be considered preliminary because they are based on a small number of studies. Indeed, each of these studies varies in sample size, quality of neuropsychological assessment, and patient sample composition. Thus their generalizability is uncertain. Additionally, other patient characteristics may also moderate the effect of MDD on neuropsychological function. This is an area that invites scientific attention. Through future research, clinicians will be better able to determine which patients are most vulnerable to cognitive impairment.

Table 3.2. CLINICAL FACTORS THAT MAY MODERATE NEUROCOGNITIVE DYSFUNCTION IN MDD

Factors That Exacerbate Impairment	Factors with No Compelling Effects on Impairment
Inpatient status	Presence of bipolar depression
Onset in senescence	Medication status
Presence of psychotic features	
Depressive severity	
Melancholia	
Comorbid anxiety disorders	

IMPLICATIONS OF NEUROPSYCHOLOGICAL IMPAIRMENT

Apart from indicating underlying cerebral dysfunction, neuropsychological impairment may be expected to correspond with other domains of function. In particular, a growing literature reveals that cognitive impairment in MDD predicts treatment response and functional outcomes.

Prediction of Treatment Response

To assess treatment response, Dunkin et al. (2000) administered a broad neuropsychological battery to 14 patients with MDD. The patients were enrolled in a 9-week, placebo-controlled, clinical trial involving fluoxetine. The Hamilton Depression Rating Scale served as the outcome measure. Eight of the patients responded to treatment, and six did not. The authors conducted multiple group contrasts and found that baseline performance on the Wisconsin Card Sorting Test and Stroop Test differed between the responders and nonresponders. Although this suggests that executive function, perhaps reflecting frontal lobe dysfunction, can distinguish patients who will and will not respond to medication, doubts still exist. Multiple contrasts were performed, and these two measures were the only ones to emerge as significantly different between groups. With only 14 patients and the number of contrasts exceeding the number of patients, it is questionable whether these results are reliable.

Such doubts notwithstanding, subsequent studies have found similar outcomes. For example, Taylor et al. (2006) administered a brief battery of neuropsychological measures to 37 patients diagnosed with MDD. The patients participated in a 12-week, open-label clinical trial of fluoxetine. At the end of the study, a blinded rater completed an overall clinical-impairment rating and the Hamilton Depression Rating Scale to quantify treatment response. Twenty-five patients were classified as responders, and 12 were designated nonresponders. Baseline scores on the neuropsychological battery were contrasted between the groups. The treatment-responders had better performance on measures of verbal fluency, visual working memory, and speed of information processing. Yet, there were no differences between the groups on the Wisconsin Card Sorting Test or measures of intellect.

Rather than compare baseline neuropsychological performance of responders and nonresponders, Kampf-Sherf et al. (2004) used logistic regression to predict treatment outcomes. They enrolled 55 patients in an open-label study of various serotonin reuptake inhibitors that occurred over 6 weeks of treatment. Outcomes were measured by the Hamilton Depression Rating Scale. The authors found that verbal fluency, working memory, abstract verbal reasoning, and visual memory predicted treatment outcomes, with better baseline performance corresponding with response to treatment. Visual-spatial perception, motor speed, and measures of auditory attention and verbal memory failed to predict treatment response. Gorlyn et al. (2008) reported similar relationships between treatment outcomes and verbal fluency, working memory, and speed of information.

Other investigators have conducted studies involving elderly patients with late-onset depression. Although varying in rigor and sample sizes, similar patterns of results have emerged. Measures of executive function, working memory, and speed of information processing predict treatment response (e.g., Alexopoulos et al., 2005; Marcos et al., 2005), even better than a quantitative index of white matter hyperintensities (Sneed et al., 2007).

Overall, these findings suggest that measures of executive function, working memory, and speed of information processing are predictors of treatment response in MDD. Because such results have emerged across multiple investigations, they possess some degree of consistency and generalizability. Yet, most of these studies can be criticized for similar problems. They typically involve small sample sizes, large numbers of statistical tests, and questionable outcome measures. For instance, criterion for treatment response is often characterized by a reduction of 50% on the Hamilton Depression Rating Scale. Such a reduction may reflect alleviated symptoms or regression to the mean, but it may not indicate a meaningful remission of symptoms. Indeed, in most of the aforementioned investigations, outcome values on the Hamilton Depression Rating Scale often remained elevated, implying that patients displayed residual symptoms. Thus, at best, the data suggest that neuropsychological abilities, especially executive function, working memory, and speed of information processing, correlate with symptom reductions.

Additionally, none of the reviewed studies examined distinct domains of adaptive function as outcome variables. Rather, they only evaluated whether treatment decreased depressive symptoms. People with MDD are prone to having poor functional outcomes, and they do not function well domestically, socially, or vocationally. None of the investigations discussed here examined whether such functional outcomes improved in response to treatment. This is a relevant point, because an emerging literature shows that neuropsychological deficits predict poor functional outcomes in MDD.

Functional Outcomes

The association between depression and activities of daily living (ADLs) is well documented, especially for older adults. Twenty percent of patients are permanently disabled (Andrews, Henderson, & Hall, 2001), and disability rates increase with each additional depressive episode (Beckett et al., 1996). Notably, cognitive dysfunction predicts diminished outcomes. For example, McCall and Dunn (2003) administered the Mini-Mental Status Exam and the Rey Auditory Verbal Learning Test and Rey-Osterrieth Complex Figure to 77 inpatients diagnosed with depression. Although depressive symptoms predicted self-reported ability to manage hygiene and self-care activities, the Mini-Mental Status Exam predicted self-reported ability to manage daily domestic chores (e.g., grocery shopping, paying bills, etc.). In other elderly samples involving mixed samples of depressed and demented patients, executive function and psychomotor speed also predicted ability to manage domestic chores and financial decision-making, more so than depressive severity (Kiosses, Alexopoulos, & Murphy, 2000; Kiosses, Klimstra, Murphy, &Alexopoulos, 2001; Mackin & Areán, 2009). Likewise, in middle-aged samples, psychomotor speed predicts ADLs more than depressive severity (Naismith, Longley, Scott, & Hickie, 2007).

Baune et al. (2010) administered the Repeated Battery for the Assessment of Neuropsychological Status (RBANS) to 26 currently depressed outpatients and 44 outpatients whose depression had remitted. Patients varied from young adult to elderly, with an average age in the mid-40s. Compared to a control group, the depressed patients had worse neuropsychological function. Notably, the unemployed patients had worse scores on the RBANS than those who continued working. Curiously, neuropsychological status did not predict ADLs. In a similar study, Jaeger, Berns, Uzelac, and Davis-Conway (2006) administered an extensive neuropsychological battery to young-adult inpatients with MDD, and patients rated their ability to manage ADLs. After controlling for depressive severity, visual memory, visual reasoning, and psychomotor speed predicted functional outcomes 6 months after discharge from the hospital.

Ability to make decisions regarding medical treatment is a complex ADL. Ghormley, Basso, Candlis, and Combs (2011) administered measures of executive function, memory, and working memory to a group of 31 inpatient depressives and 16 control subjects. They also administered a standardized measure of capacity to provide informed consent concerning medical treatment. Patients displaying impaired neuropsychological function were more likely to show impaired understanding of medical treatment disclosures than the control group. With semantic cueing, however, the impaired patients displayed normal understanding of treatment choices. Regression analyses revealed that memory dysfunction predicted poor understanding of the medical-treatment options. Paralleling these findings, Grisso and Appelbaum (Appelbaum, Grisso, Frank, O'Donnell, & Kupfer, 1999; Grisso & Appelbaum, 1995) conducted similar studies involving mildly depressed outpatients, and found that impaired reasoning corresponded with incompetent decision-making. Thus, cognitive impairment makes depressed patients vulnerable to incompetent choices regarding medical treatment. However, these data were based on a limited neuropsychological battery, and other cognitive domains may have contributed to poor decision-making. Additionally, only understanding of medical options was evaluated, and Ghormley and colleagues neglected to examine patients' ability to evaluate or weigh the consequences of their treatment choices, typically construed as necessary elements of competent decision-making. Other aspects of neurocognitive function may contribute to such domains of medical decision-making.

Collectively, these data suggest that neuropsychological function, especially psychomotor speed, predicts ability to manage ADLs in people with MDD. It is curious, however, that the number of studies concerning this matter is so limited. The literature on this issue in schizophrenia and bipolar disorder is relatively robust, and numerous studies show that neuropsychological dysfunction predicts diminished ADLs, social functioning, and work performance (e.g., Bowie et al., 2010). Furthermore, the research involving depression, neuropsychological function, and ADLs has largely focused on elderly patients rather than young adults, thereby limiting their generalizability. Functional outcomes have primarily been assessed with self-report measures rather than actual behavioral demonstrations. Self-reports in depressed individuals may be biased and may not accurately reflect their genuine ability to manage daily affairs. These issues should be corrected in subsequent research.

Suicidality is an important element of functional outcomes in MDD. Keilp et al. (2001) classified a sample of 50 depressed patients according to history and lethality of suicide attempts. They administered an extensive neuropsychological battery to the patients and to a healthy control group. The patients who had previously made a highly lethal suicide attempt displayed worse performance than that of all other participants on measures of executive function, and they performed worse than the control group on measures of intelligence, memory, and working memory. Furthermore, using a discriminant function analysis, Keilp and colleagues demonstrated that executive function discriminated the patients with highly lethal suicide from other patients, implying that poor problem-solving, reasoning, flexibility, and self-control contribute to dangerous suicidal behaviors. Likewise, in separate samples of young-adult inpatients and elderly outpatients, measures of executive function emerged as salient predictors of suicidality among patients with MDD (Dombrovski et al., 2008; Westheide et al., 2008). Thus, these findings seem reliable and imply that executive dysfunction in MDD is an important morbidity and mortality risk factor. Yet, these studies only addressed prior suicide attempts, and it remains uncertain whether executive dysfunction predicts future attempts.

Summary

Neuropsychological deficits in MDD have potentially important implications. They appear to predict whether patients will benefit from certain treatments. They also correspond with how well patients manage daily affairs and make important decisions regarding medical treatment. Furthermore, cognitive impairment, especially executive dysfunction, correlates with suicidal behaviors.

CASE STUDY

Mrs. X is a 44-year-old divorced, Caucasian female with 12 years of education. She was admitted to the hospital after having deliberately overdosed on antidepressant medication. This is her third psychiatric admission during the past 10 years, each having occurred after a suicide attempt or significant suicidal ideation. She stated that she had always been depressed, but first sought treatment while separated from her first husband at age 23. Since that time, her symptoms have waxed and waned, and she believes that she has never been symptom free. Symptoms worsened after her second divorce at age 35. At that time, she was dismissed from her job as a medical transcriptionist, for excessive absenteeism. Subsequently, she began receiving disability benefits for depression and returned to live with her mother. Recently, her mother announced her intention to move to a distant city to live with Mrs. X's sibling. Mrs. X became increasingly despondent anticipating the loss of her mother's immediate support. Additionally, she anticipated being obligated to leave her mother's home, and she did not appreciate how she might afford to live independently on her disability support. Hence, she attempted suicide.

After becoming medically stable, Mrs. X was transferred to the psychiatry unit and began to receive milieu therapy. She complained of forgetfulness, inattention, and distractibility that interfered with her ability to benefit from treatment and manage daily affairs. A neuropsychological consultation was ordered. She had taken an SSRI the morning of the examination.

A screening battery was administered comprised of the Vocabulary, Block Design, Digit Span, and Letter Number Sequencing subtests from the WAIS-IV; Trail Making Tests A and B; the Verbal Fluency and Figural Fluency subtests from the D-KEFS; California Verbal Learning Test-2; Logical Memory from the WMS-IV; Reading subtest from the WRAT-4; Judgment of Line Orientation Test; Grooved Pegboard Test; the MMPI-2; and the Mini International Neuropsychiatric Interview. Furthermore, to assess performance effort, the Word Memory Test was administered.

Her Vocabulary and Block Design results were average for her age. Semantic fluency was mildly below normal, but phonemic fluency was low-average. Figural fluency was low-average. The Trail Making Test A score was borderline normal, and Test B score was mildly to moderately below normal for age and education. Immediate recall of List A from the CVLT-2 was low-average, but delayed recall was mildly below normal. Recognition memory was mildly below normal. Logical Memory immediate recall was low-average for age, and delayed recall was borderline normal. Her recognition memory was low-average. Reading skill was average for her age and at a high-school level. The Judgment of Line Orientation Test result was low-average, and Grooved Pegboard Test performance was mildly slowed bilaterally. The MMPI-2 was valid and revealed moderate to severe distress characterized by depression, pessimism, hopelessness, anxiety, and worry. During the diagnostic interview, Mrs. X. presented with major depressive disorder, recurrent episode, severe; and panic disorder with agoraphobia.

Accommodations in treatment were recommended and principally attempted to enhance Mrs. X's ability to attend to and remember information delivered in therapy sessions. Additionally, owing to apparent weaknesses involving mental flexibility and ideational fluency, her ability to comprehend material discussed in treatment may be diminished. Delivery of therapeutic information was simplified.

CONCLUSIONS

This review demonstrates that neuropsychological dysfunction occurs commonly in people with MDD. Executive function, memory, working memory, and speed of information processing are the domains most commonly affected, and the severity of dysfunction generally ranges from mild to moderate. These deficits correspond with structural and functional neuroimaging data that show frontal and temporal lobe anomalies in MDD. A variety of patient factors modify the likelihood of dysfunction. Compelling evidence implies that inpatient status, depressive severity, older age, and presence of psychotic or melancholic features contribute to cognitive impairment. There are modest indications that comorbid anxiety disorders exacerbate MDD-related deficits. There is little evidence that depressed patients with bipolar disorder display worse impairment than that of those with unipolar depression.

The presence of neuropsychological deficits in MDD emerges as a salient correlate of functional outcomes. Cognitive dysfunction seems to predict poor response to treatment, decreased ability to manage daily affairs, incapacity to make medical decisions, and history of prior suicide attempts. Thus, neurocognitive dysfunction in MDD is relatively common, and it coincides with potent morbidity and possible mortality.

These conclusions should alert clinicians who treat patients with MDD. Some of their patients are apt to have significant problems in excess of generic depressive symptoms. Patients should be screened for these neurocognitive impairments, and treatment plans should take these deficits into consideration. For example, it seems likely that those patients with significant cognitive impairment will be prone to sustain residual symptoms, and they will require aggressive and coordinated treatment to address this issue. Owing to neuropsychological weaknesses, depressed patients may struggle to incorporate or benefit from psychological treatments, especially those that emphasize abstract concepts pertaining to cognitive-behavioral therapy. Accommodations in therapy may be required for these patients to benefit from treatment. Such patients may benefit from interventions such as occupational or vocational rehabilitation to enhance their ability to fulfill domestic and work-related demands. Additionally, it may be prudent to closely monitor those patients with executive dysfunction for suicidal ideation or behaviors.

For researchers, the literature has not fully delineated the range of patient characteristics that correspond with neuropsychological dysfunction. In addressing this issue, patients who are at increased risk of neurocognitive vulnerability may be identified and appropriately treated. Because neuropsychological dysfunction seems to remain after other symptoms of depression remit, it also seems worthwhile to develop cognitive-rehabilitation methods. In doing so, patient morbidity may be diminished, and functional outcomes may be enhanced. By focusing future efforts in these directions, our understanding of factors that contribute to neuropsychological dysfunction may be refined, and morbidity and mortality associated with MDD may be diminished.

References

Alexopoulos, G. S., Kiosses, D. N., Heo, M., Murphy, C. F., Shanmugham, B., & Gunning-Dixon, F. (2005). Executive dysfunction and the course of geriatric depression. *Biological Psychiatry, 58*, 204–210.

American Psychiatric Association. (2000). *The diagnostic and statistical manual of mental disorders* (4th ed., text rev.). Arlington, VA: Author.

Andrade, L., Eaton, W. W., & Chilcoat, H. (1994). Lifetime comorbidity of panic attacks and major depression in a population-based study. Symptom profiles. *British Journal of Psychiatry, 165*(3), 363–369.

Andrews, G., Henderson, S., & Hall, W. (2001). Prevalence, comorbidity, disability, and service- utilization: Overview of Australian National Mental Health Survey. *British Journal of Psychiatry, 178*, 145–153.

Appelbaum, P. S., Grisso, T., Frank, E., O'Donnell, S., & Kupfer, D. J. (1999). Competence of depressed patients for consent to research. *American Journal of Psychiatry, 156*, 1380–1384.

Arnone, D., McIntosh, A. M., Ebmeier, K. P., Munafo, M. R., & Anderson, I. M. (2012). Magnetic resonance imaging studies in unipolar depression: Systematic review and meta-regression analyses. *European Neuropsychopharmacology, 22*, 1–16.

Asmundson, G. J., Stein, M. B., Larsen, D. K., & Walker, J. R. (1994). Neurocognitive function in panic disorder and social phobia patients. *Anxiety, 1*, 201–207.

Austin, M. P., Mitchell, P., Wilhelm, K., Parker, G., Hickie, I., Brodaty, H., et al. (1999). Cognitive function in depression: a distinct pattern of frontal impairment in melancholia? *Psychological Medicine, 29*(1), 73–85.

Basso, M. R., & Bornstein, R. A. (1999). Relative memory deficits in recurrent versus first-episode major depression on a word-list learning task. *Neuropsychology, 13*, 557–563.

Basso, M. R., Lowery, N., Ghormley, C., Combs, D., Purdie, R., Neel, J., & Bornstein, R. (2007). Comorbid anxiety corresponds with neuropsychological dysfunction in unipolar depression. *Cognitive Neuropsychiatry, 12*(5), 437–456.

Basso, M. R., Lowery, N., Neel, J., Purdie, R., & Bornstein, R. A. (2002). Neuropsychological impairment among manic, depressed, and mixed-episode inpatients with bipolar disorder. *Neuropsychology, 16*, 84–91.

Baune, B. T., Miller, R., McAfoose, J., Johnson, M., Quirk, F., & Mitchell, D. (2010). The role of cognitive impairment in general functioning in major depression. *Psychiatry Research, 176*, 183–189.

Bearden, C. E., Glahn, D. C., Monkul, E. S., Barrett, J., Najit, P., Villarreal, V., & Soares, J. C. (2006). Patterns of memory impairment in bipolar disorder and unipolar major depression. *Psychiatry Research, 142*, 139–50.

Beckett, L. A., Brock, D. B., Lemke, J. H., et al. (1996). Analysis of change in self-reported physical function among older persons in four population studies. *American Journal of Epidemiology, 143*, 766–778. 357–362.

Beyer, J. L., & Krishnan, K. R. R. (2002). Volumetric brain imaging findings in mood disorders. *Bipolar Disorders, 4*, 89–104.

Bora, E., Fornito, A., Pantelis, C., & Yücel, M. (2012). Gray matter abnormalities in major depressive disorder: A meta-analysis of voxel based morphometry studies. *Journal of Affective Disorders, 138*, 9–18.

Borkowska, A., & Rybakowski, J. K. (2001). Neuropsychological frontal lobe tests indicate that bipolar depressed patients are more impaired than unipolar. *Bipolar Disorders, 3*, 88–94.

Bowie, C. R., Depp, C., McGrath, J. A., Wolyniec, P., Mausback B. T., Thornquist, M. H., et al. (2010). Prediction of real-world functional disability in chronic mental disorders: a comparison of schizophrenia and bipolar disorder. *American Journal of Psychiatry, 167*(9), 1116–24.

Bremner, J. D., Vythilingam, M., Ng, C. K., Vermetten, E., Nazeer, A., Oren, D. A., Berman, R. M., & Charney, D. S. (2003). Regional brain metabolic correlates of alpha-methylparatyrosine-induced depressive symptoms: implications for the neural circuitry of depression. *The Journal of the American Medical Association, 289*(23), 3125–3134.

Burt, D. B., Zembar, M. J., & Niederehe, G. (1995). Depression and memory impairment: A meta-analysis of the association, its pattern, and specificity. *Psychological Bulletin, 117,* 285–305.

Buyukdura, J. S., McClintock, S. M., & Croarkin, P. E. (2010). Psychomotor retardation in depression: Biological underpinnings, measurement, and treatment. *Progress in Neuro-Psychopharmacology & Biological Psychiatry, 35,* 395–409.

Charney, D. S. (2003). Neuroanatomical circuits modulating fear and anxiety behaviors. *Acta Psychiatrica Scandinavica, 417,* 38–50.

Christensen, H., Griffiths, K., MacKinnon, A., & Jacomb, P. (1997). A quantitative review of cognitive deficits in depression and Alzheimer-type dementia. *Journal of the International Neuropsychological Society, 3,* 631–51.

Cohen, L. J., Hollander, E., DeCaria, C. M., Stein, D. J., Simeon, D., Liebowitz, M. R., et al. (1996). Specificity of neuropsychological impairment in obsessive-compulsive disorder: A comparison with social phobic and normal control subjects. *Journal of Neuropsychiatry and Clinical Neuroscience, 8,* 82–85.

Cole, J., Costafreda, S. G., McGuffin, P., & Fu, C. H. Y. (2011). Hippocampal atrophy in first episode depression: A meta-analysis of magnetic resonance imaging studies. *Journal of Affective Disorders, 134,* 483–487.

Crown, W. H., Diéras, V., Kaufmann, M., von Minckwitz, G., Kaye, S., Marty, M., Piccart, M., et al. (2002). The impact of treatment-resistant depression on health care utilization and costs. *Journal of Clinical Psychiatry, 63*(11), 963–971.

Danckwerts, A., & Leathem, J. (2003). Questioning the link between PTSD and cognitive dysfunction. *Neuropsychology Review, 13*(4), 221–235.

De Bellis, M. D., Casey, B. J., Dahl, R. E., Birmaher, B., Williamson, D. E., Thomas, K. M., et al. (2000). A pilot study of amygdala volumes in pediatric generalized anxiety disorder. *Biological Psychiatry, 48,* 51–57.

De Bellis, M. D., Keshavan, M. S., Shifflett, H., Iyengar, S., Dahl, R. E., Axelson, D. A., et al. (2002). Superior temporal gyrus volumes in pediatric generalized anxiety disorder. *Biological Psychiatry, 51,* 553–562.

Dewar, K. M., & Stravynski, A. (2001). The quest for biological correlates of social phobia: An interim assessment. *Acta Psychiatria Scandanavica, 103*(4), 244–251.

Dombrovski, A. Y., Butters, M. A., Reynolds, C. F., Houck, P. R., Clark, L., Mazumdar, S., & Szanto, K. (2008). Cognitive performance in suicidal depressed elderly: Preliminary report. *American Journal of Geriatric Psychiatry, 16*(2), 109–115.

Douglas, K. M., & Porter, R. J. (2009). Longitudinal assessment of neuropsychological function in major depression. *Australian and New Zealand Journal of Psychiatry 2009, 43,* 1105–1117.

Drevets, W. C. (2000). Neuroimaging studies of mood disorders. *Biological Psychiatry, 48,* 813–829.

Drevets, W. C., Price, J. L., & Furey, M. L. (2008). Brain structural and functional abnormalities in mood disorders: Implications for neurocircuitry models of depression. *Brain Structure and Function, 213,* 93–118.

Dunkin, J. J., Leuchter, A. F., Cook, I. A., Kasl-Godley, J. E., Abrams, M., & Rosenberg-Thompson, S. (2000). Executive dysfunction predicts nonresponse to fluoxetine in major depression. *Journal of Affective Disorders, 60,* 13–23.

Eaton, W. W., Shao, H., Nestandt, G., Lee, H. B., Bienvenu, O. J., & Zandi, P. (2008). Population-based study of first onset and chronicity in major depressive disorder. *Archives of General Psychiatry, 65*(5), 513–520.

Fleming, S. K., Blasey, C., & Schatzberg, A. F. (2004). Neuropsychological correlates of psychotic features in major depressive disorders: A review and meta-analysis. *Journal of Psychiatric Research, 38*, 27–35.

Ghormley, C., Basso, M., Candlis, P., & Combs, D. (2011). Neuropsychological impairment corresponds with poor understanding of informed consent disclosures in persons diagnosed with major depression. *Psychiatry Research, 187*, 106–112.

Godard, J., Groundin, S., Baruch, P., & Lafleur, M. F. (2011). Psychosocial and neurocognitive profiles in depressed patients depressive disorder and bipolar disorder. *Psychiatry Research, 190*, 244–252.

Gorlyn, M., Kelip, J. G., Grunebaum, M. F., Taylor, B. P., Oquendo, M. A., Bruder, G. E., Stewart, J. W., et al. (2008). Neuropsychological characteristics as predictors of SSRI treatment response in depressed subjects. *Journal of Neural Transmission, 115*, 1213–1219.

Grisso, T., & Appelbaum, P. S. (1995). The MacArthur Treatment Competence Study: III. Abilities of patients to consent to psychiatric and medical treatments. *Law and Human Behavior, 19*, 149–174.

Gruber, S., Rathgeber, K., Bräunig, P., & Gauggel, S. (2007). Stability and course of neuropsychological deficits in manic and depressed bipolar patients compared to patients with major depression. *Journal of Affective Disorders, 104*, 61–71.

Grunhaus, L., Pande, A. C., Brown, M. B., & Greden, J. F. (1994). Clinical characteristics of patients with concurrent major depressive disorder and panic disorder. *American Journal of Psychiatry, 151*(4), 541–6.

Gurvits, T. V., Shenton, M. E., Hokama, H., Ohta, H., Lasko, N. B., Gilbertson, M. W., & Pitman, R. K. (1996). Magnetic resonance imaging study of hippocampal volume in chronic combat-related post traumatic stress disorder. *Biological Psychiatry, 40*(11), 1091–1099.

Harrison, P. J. (2002). The neuropathology of primary mood disorder. *Brain, 125*, 1428–1449.

Hasin, D. S., Goodwin, R. D., Stinson, F. S., & Grant, B. F. (2005). Epidemiology of major depressive disorder: Results from the National Epidemiologic Survey on Alcoholism and Related Conditions. *Archives of General Psychiatry, 62*, 1097–1106.

Henry, J. D., & Crawford, J. R. (2005). A meta-analytic review of verbal fluency deficits in depression. *Journal of Clinical and Experimental Neuropsychology, 27*, 78–101.

Hermens, D. F., Redoblado Hodge, M. A., Scott, E. M., & Hickie, I. B. (2010). Impaired verbal memory in young adults with unipolar and bipolar depression. *Early Intervention in Psychiatry, 3*, 227–233.

Herrmann, L. L., Goodwin, G. M., & Ebmeier, K. P. (2007). The cognitive neuropsychology of depression in the elderly. *Psychological Medicine, 37*, 1693–1702.

Jaeger, J., Berns, S., Uzelac, S., & Davis-Conway, S. (2006). Neurocognitive deficits and disability in major depressive disorder. *Psychiatry Research, 145*, 39–48.

Kampf-Sherf, O., Zlotogorski, Z., Gilboa, A., Speedie, L., Lereya, J., Rosca, P., & Shavit, Y. (2004). Neuropsychological functioning in major depression and responsiveness to selective serotonin reuptake inhibitors antidepressants. *Journal of Affective Disorders, 82*, 453–459.

Kaplan, J. S., Erickson, K., Luckenbaugh, D. A., Weiland-Fiedler, P., Geraci, M., Sahakian, B. J., Charney, D., et al. (2006). Differential performance on tasks of affective processing and decision-making in patients with panic disorder and panic disorder with comorbid major depressive disorder. *Journal of Affective Disorders, 95,* 165–171.

Keilp, J. G., Sackeim, H. A., Brodsky, B. S., Oquendo, M. A., Malone, K. M., & Mann, J. J. (2001). Neuropsychological dysfunction in depressed suicide attempters. *American Journal of Psychiatry, 158*(5), 735–741.

Kempton, M. J., Salvador, Z., Munafò, M. R., Geddes, J. R., Simmons, A., Frangou, S., & Williams, S. C. R. (2011). Structural neuroimaging studies in major depressive disorder: Meta-analysis and comparison with bipolar disorder. *Archives of General Psychiatry, 68*(7), 675–690.

Kendler, K. S., Thornton, L. M., & Gardner, C. O. (2001). Genetic risk, number of previous depressive episodes, and stressful life events in predicting onset of major depression. *American Journal of Psychiatry, 158,* 582–586.

Kessler, R. C., Berglund, P., Demler, O., Jin, R., Koretz, D. Merikangas, K. R., et al. (2003). The epidemiology of major depressive disorder: Results from the National Comorbidity Survey Replication (NCS-R). *Journal of the American Medical Association, 289,* 3095–3105.

Kessler, R. C., Berglund, P., Demler, O., Jin, R., Merikangas, K. R., & Walters, E. E. (2005). Lifetime prevalence and age-of-onset distributions of DSM-IV disorders in the National Comorbidity Survey Replication. *Archives of General Psychiatry, 62*(6), 593–602.

Kessler, R. C., McGonagle, K. A., Swartz, M., Blazer, D. G., & Nelson, C. B. (1993) Sex and depression in the National Comorbidity Survey. I: Lifetime prevalence, chronicity, and recurrence. *Journal of Affective Disorders, 29*(2–3), 85–96.

Kessler, R. C., & Merikangas, K. R. (2004). The National Comorbidity Survey Replication (NCS-R): Background and aims. *International Journal of Methods in Psychiatric Research, 13*(2), 60–68.

Kessler, R. C., & Wang, P. S. (2010). Epidemiology of depression. In I. H. Gotlib & C. L. Hammen (Eds.), *Handbook of depression* (2nd ed., pp. 5–22). New York: Guilford Press.

Kindermann, S. S., & Brown, G. G. (1997). Depression and memory in the elderly: A meta-analysis. *Journal of Clinical and Experimental Neuropsychology, 19,* 625–642.

Kiosses, D. N., Alexopoulos, G. S., & Murphy C. (2000). Symptoms of striatofrontal dysfunction contribute to disability in geriatric depression. *International Journal of Geriatric Psychiatry, 15*(11), 992–999.

Kiosses, D. N., Klimstra, S., Murphy, C., & Alexopoulos, G. S. (2001). Executive dysfunction and disability in elderly patients with major depression. *American Journal of Geriatric Psychiatry, 9*(3) 269–274.

Kizilbash, A. H., Vanderploeg, R. D., & Curtiss, G. (2002). The effects of depression and anxiety on memory performance. *Archives of Clinical Neuropsychology, 17,* 57–67.

Lautenbacher, S., Spernal, J., & Krieg, J. C. (2002). Divided and selective attention in panic disorder: A comparative study of patients with panic disorder, major depression, and healthy controls. *European Archives of Psychiatry and Clinical Neuroscience, 252*(5), 210–213.

Ludewig, S., Paulus, M. P., Ludewig, K., & Vollenweider, F. X. (2003). Decision-making strategies by panic disorder subjects are more sensitive to errors. *Journal of Affective Disorders, 76,* 183–189.

Lyche, P., Jonassen, R., Stiles, T. C., Ulleberg, P., & Landro, N. I. (2010). Cognitive control functions in unipolar major depression with and without comorbid anxiety disorder. *Frontiers in Psychiatry, 1*(149), 1–9.

Lyche, P., Jonassen, R., Stiles, T. C., Ulleberg, P., & Landro, N. I. (2011). Cognitive control functions in unipolar major depression with and without comorbid anxiety disorder. *The Clinical Neuropsychologist, 25*(3), 359–375.

Maalouf, F. T., Klein, C., Clark, L., Sahakian, B. J., LaBarbara, E. J., Versace, A., et al. (2010). Impaired sustained attention and executive dysfunction: Bipolar disorder versus depression-specific markers of affective disorders. *Neuropsychologia, 48*, 1862–1868.

Mackin, R. S., & Areán, P. A. (2009). Impaired financial capacity in late-life depression is associated with cognitive performance on measures of executive function and attention. *Journal of International Neuropsychological Society, 15*, 793–798.

Maes, M. (2011). Depression is an inflammatory disease, but cell-mediated immune activation is the key component of depression. *Progress in Neuro-Psychopharmacology & Biological Psychiatry, 35*, 664–675.

Marcos, T., Portella, M. J., Navarro, V., Gasta, C., Rami, L., Lázaro, L., & Salamero, M. (2005). Neuropsychological prediction of recovery in late-onset major depression. *International Journal of Geriatric Psychiatry, 20*, 790–795.

Marvel, C. L., & Paradiso, S. (2004). Cognitive and neurological impairment in mood disorders. *Psychiatric Clinics of North America, 27*, 19–36.

Massana, G., Serra-Grabulosa, J. M., Salgado-Pineda, P., Gasto, C., Junque, C., Massana, J., et al. (2003). Amygdalar atrophy in panic disorder patients detected by volumetric magnetic resonance imaging. *NeuroImage, 19*, 80–90.

Mayberg, H. S. (2003). Modulating dysfunctional limbic-cortical circuits in depression: Towards development of brain-based algorithms for diagnosis and optimized treatment. *British Medical Bulletin, 65*, 193–207.

McCall, W. V., & Dunn, A. G. (2003). Cognitive deficits are associated with functional impairment in severely depressed patients. *Psychiatry Research, 121*, 179–184.

McClintock, S. M., Husain, M. M., Greer, T. L., & Munro Cullum, C. (2010). Association between severity and neurocognitive function in major depressive disorder: A review and synthesis. *Neuropsychology, 24*, 9–34.

McDermott, L. M., & Ebmeier, K. P. (2009). A meta-analysis of depression severity and cognitive function. *Journal of Affective Disorders, 119*, 1–8.

Michopoulos, I., Zervas, I. M., Pantelis, C., Tsaltas, E., Papakosta, V., Boufidou, F., et al. (2008). Neuropsychological and hypothalamic-pituitary-axis function in female patients with melancholic and non-melancholic depression. *European Archives of Clinical Neuroscience, 258*, 217–225.

Mojtabai, R., Bromet, E. J., Harvey, P. D. Carlson, G. A., Craig, T. J., & Fennig, S. (2000). Neuropsychological differences between first-admission schizophrenia and psychotic affective disorders. *American Journal of Psychiatry, 157*, 1453–1460.

Naismith, S. L., Longley, W. A., Scott, E. M., & Hickie, I. B. (2007). Disability in major depression related to self-rated and objectively-measured cognitive deficits: A preliminary study. *BMC Psychiatry, 7*, 32.

Parker, G., & Hadzi-Pavlovic, D. (1996). *Melancholia: A disorder of movement and mood: A phenomenological and neurobiological review.* New York: Cambridge University Press.

Pier, M. P. B. I., Hulstijn, W., & Sabbe, B. G. C. (2004). Differential patterns of psychomotor functioning in unmedicated melancholic and nonmelancholic depressed patients. *Journal of Psychiatric Research, 38*, 425–435.

Pissiota, A., Frans, O., Michelgard, A., Appel, L, Langström, B., Flaten, M. A., & Fredrikson, M. (2003). Amygdala and anterior cingulated cortex activation during affective startle modulation: A PET study of fear. *European Journal of Neuroscience, 18*(5), 1325–1331.

Rauch, S. A., Foa, E. B., Furr, J. M., & Filip, J. C. (2004). Imagery vividness and perceived anxious arousal in prolonged exposure treatment for PTSD. *Journal of Traumatic Stress, 17*(6), 461–465.

Rodriguez, B. F., Bruce, S. E., Pagano, M. E., & Keller, M. B. (2004). Relationships among psychosocial functioning, diagnostic comorbidity, and the recurrence of generalized anxiety disorder, panic disorder, and major depression. *Journal of Anxiety Disorders, 19*(7), 752–766.

Rogers, M. A., Bradshaw, J. L., Pantelis, C., & Phillips, J. G. (1998). Frontostriatal deficits in unipolar major depression. *Brain Research Bulletin, 47*, 297–310.

Rogers, R. D., Ramnani, N., Mackay, C., Wilson, J. L., Jezzard, P., Carter, C. S., & Smith, S. M. (2004). Distinct proportions of anterior cingulate cortex and medial prefrontal cortex are activated by reward processing in separable phases of decision-making cognition. *Biological Psychiatry, 55*, 594–602.

Sacher, J., Neumann, J., Fünfstück, T., Soliman, A., Villringer, A., & Schroeter, M. L. (2012). Mapping the depressed brain: A meta-analysis of structural and functional alterations in major depressive disorder. *Journal of Affective Disorders, 140*, 142–148.

Sheline, Y. I. (2000). 3D MRI studies of neuroanatomic changes in unipolar major depression: The role of stress and medical comorbidity. *Biological Psychiatry, 48*, 791–800.

Sneed, J. R., Roose, S. P., Kelip, J. G., Krishnan, K. R. R., Alexopoulos, G. S., & Sackeim, H. A. (2007). Response inhibition predicts poor antidepressant treatment response in very old depressed patients. *American Journal of Geriatric Psychiatry, 15*(7), 553–563.

Solomon, D. A., Keller, M. B., Leon, A. C., Mueller, T. I., Lavori, P. W., Shea, M. T., et al. (2000). Multiple recurrences of major depressive disorder. *American Journal of Psychiatry, 157*(2), 229–233.

Sweeney, J. A., Kmiec, J. A., & Kupfer, D. J. (2000). Neuropsychologic impairments in bipolar and unipolar mood disorders on the CANTAB neurocognitive battery. *Biological Psychiatry, 48*, 674–685.

Tankard, C. F., Waldstein, S. R., Siegel, E. L., Holder, L. E., Lefkowitz, D., Anstett, F., et al. (2003). Cerebral blood flow and anxiety in older men: An analysis of resting anterior asymmetry and prefrontal regions. *Brain and Cognition, 52*, 70–78.

Taylor, B. P., Bruder, G. E., Stewart, J. W., McGrath, P. J., Halperin, J., Ehrlichman, H., & Quitkin, F. M. (2006). Psychomotor slowing as a predictor of fluoxetine nonresponse in depressed outpatients. *American Journal of Psychiatry, 163*, 73–78.

Taylor Travares, J. V., Clark, L., Cannon, D. M., Erickson, K., Drevets, W. C., & Sahakian, B. J. (2007). Distinct profiles of neurocognitive function in unmedicated unipolar depression and bipolar II depression. *Biological Psychiatry, 62*, 917–924.

Trivedi, M. H., Hollander, E., Nutt, D., & Blier, P. (2008). Clinical evidence and potential neurobiological underpinnings of unresolved symptoms of depression. *Journal of Clinical Psychiatry, 69*, 246–258.

Trivedi, M. H., Rush, A. J., Wisniewski, S. R., Nierenberg, A. A., Warden, D., Ritz, L., et al. (2006). Evaluation of outcomes with citalopram for depression using measurement-based are in STAR*D: Implications for clinical practice. *American Journal of Psychiatry, 163*(1), 28–40.

Vasterling, J. J., Brailey, K., Constans, J. I., & Sutker, P. B. (1998). Attention and memory dysfunction in posttraumatic stress disorder. *Neuropsychology, 12*, 125–133.

Vasterling, J. J., Rogers, C., & Kaplan, E. (2000). Qualitative block design analysis in post-traumatic stress disorder. *Assessment, 7*, 217–226.

Veiel, H. O. F. (1997). A preliminary profile of neuropsychological deficits associated with major depression. *Journal of Clinical and Experimental Neuropsychology, 19*, 587–603.

Vythilingam, M. Anderson, E. R., Goddard, A., Woods, S. W., Staib, L. H., Charney, D. S., & Bremner, J. D. (2000). Temporal lobe volume in panic disorder—a quantitative magnetic resonance imaging study. *Psychiatry Research, 99*(2) 75–82.

Westheide, J., Quednow, B. B., Kuhn, K., Hoppe, C., Cooper-Mahkorn, D., Hawellek, B., et al. (2008). Executive performance of depressed suicide attempters: The role of suicidal ideation. *European Archives of Psychiatry and Clinical Neuroscience, 258*, 414–421.

Williams, D. R., González, H. M., Neighbors, H., Nesse, R., Abelson, J. M., Sweetman, J., & Jackson, J. S. (2007). Prevalence and distribution of major depressive disorder in African Americans, Caribbean blacks, and non-Hispanic whites: Results from the National Survey of American Life. *Archives of General Psychiatry, 64*(3), 305–315.

Wurthmann, C., Bogerts, B., Gregor, J., Baumann, B., Effenberger, O., & Dohring, W. (1997). Frontal CSF enlargement in panic disorder: A qualitative CT-scan study. *Psychiatry Research, 76*, 83–87.

Zakzanis, K. K., Leach, L., & Kaplan, E. (1998). On the nature and pattern of neurocognitive function in major depressive disorder. *Neuropsychiatry, Neuropsychology, & Behavioral Neurology, 11*, 111–119.

4

The Allure of Emotion: How Affective Stimuli Impact Cognitive Processing Among Patients with Mood Disorders

BRUCE K. CHRISTENSEN AND MATTHEW J. KING

In their most basic form, emotions are adaptive psychological and physiological states, arising from the interplay between internal and external stimuli, to which a value judgment can be assigned (Dolan, 2002). Emotions are adaptive because they signal to the individual experiencing them that something in the environment is of particular importance. Consequently, emotional material frequently gains quicker and easier access to our cognitive systems for processing. For example, fearful stimuli are recognized quicker than neutral stimuli (e.g., Ohman, Flykt, & Esteves 2001); positive memories are recalled in more detail than neutral memories (D'Argembeau, Comblain & Van der Linden, 2003), and appetitive objects obligate our attention more forcefully than neutral objects (e.g., Bradley et al., 2003). These tendencies are robust and often automatic. From an evolutionary perspective, they have undoubtedly served to aid survival. However, they can also confer distinct disadvantages when task goals require a cognitive agent to overcome the influence of emotion in favor of hard-nosed, analytical processing. The negative impacts of emotional stimuli are especially prominent in the domains of attention, memory, and decision making (for a review see Dolan, 2002).

It is the influence of emotional material on cognitive processing that is the central topic of this chapter. We begin by briefly outlining the conceptual and experimental evidence that casts emotional information (rather than nonemotional information) as a priority within our cognitive system. This initial section of the chapter explicitly considers these effects among healthy research participants. Following that, we discuss the consequences to the cognitive system when the individual has a mood disorder, such as major depressive disorder (MDD) or bipolar disorder (BD). Of particular importance, we will address how depression affects the *content* of cognitive functioning (i.e., preferential processing of affectively laden content), not the level of cognitive functioning (i.e., how well an individual does on a task relative to a criterion). Chapter 3 in this book, by Basso and colleagues, addresses the latter topic in detail. We will conclude with a brief case study and potential considerations for clinicians working toward a better our understanding of how emotion influences cognition among their clients.

THE INFLUENCE OF EMOTION ON ATTENTION, MEMORY, AND DECISION MAKING

Attention

At face value, one can readily conceive that emotional stimuli affect attention. From an evolutionary perspective, the ability to readily detect harmful or danger-ous stimuli provides increased chances of survival. Moreover, it stands to reason that systems dedicated to processing dangerous stimuli work quickly and robustly. In a recently published study using a classical visual search paradigm, Notebaert, Crombez, Van Damme, De Houwer, and Theeuwes (2011) showed that threaten-ing stimuli do not capture but *prioritize* attention. The distinction here is subtle: capturing attention implies an effortless or unconscious control of attention, whereas prioritizing attention implies a conscious interplay between the valence of stimuli as well as the perceptual features, which manifest in a more effortful form of guidance (Frischen, Eastwood, & Smilek, 2008). Using the slopes of reac-tion times as indicators of bias, Notebaert et al. (2011) showed that on congruent trials (i.e., when the feared stimulus is in the same location as the target), partici-pants were faster to detect the target than on incongruent trials and baseline (no feared stimulus) trials. If the feared stimulus was being preattentively processed, the slopes should have been equivalent for both congruent and incongruent tri-als. These data support the idea that emotion serves to prioritize or guide atten-tion toward threatening stimuli rather than capture it entirely. Participants in this study consisted of individuals with high and low trait anxiety, as measured by the State Trait Anxiety Inventory. However, no differences were observed between the two groups, suggesting that the effect is present in healthy individuals free of anxiety or other psychopathology.

Another study by Reeck and Egner (2011) supports the notion that emotions prioritize attention. This study used a face-word Stroop paradigm to study the impact of both gender and emotional expression on attention. Healthy partic-ipants made either gender or emotion judgments in the context of competing information. The typical Stroop results were replicated where congruent trials were labeled faster than incongruent trials. Importantly, however, a three-way interaction emerged which showed that gender labels did not affect performance on the emotional judgments, but emotional labels affected performance on the gender judgments. These data show that affective stimuli are able to influence attention, even when they are irrelevant to the task at hand.

Research has also demonstrated that the influence of emotion on attention occurs automatically or even preattentively. For example, recent event-related potential (ERP) studies suggest that the "time signature" of awareness for emo-tional stimuli is much earlier than the perceptual and categorical encoding of the stimuli per se. Eimer and Holmes (2002) showed this using face stimuli, while Ortigue et al. (2004) obtained similar results using emotional words. Further support for the automaticity of emotion awareness or detection comes from affective priming studies, where stimuli presented at an unconscious level (i.e., at durations that preclude conscious processing of the stimuli) are capable of influencing emotional judgments. Using a backward-masking technique and functional magnetic resonance imaging (fMRI), Morris, Ohman, and Dolan (1998) found amygdala activity resulting from emotional stimuli presented at unconscious levels (i.e., without awareness on the part of participants).

Most important to the automaticity argument is the observation that emotional stimuli can be encoded without the use of attentional resources (Taylor & Fragopanagos, 2005). One conventional method to assess this is with the visual search paradigm, where, according to Triesman and Gelade (1980), any targets that are processed preattentively will "pop out" of a visual display, regardless of how many distractor elements are present. By contrast, elements that require serial allocation of attention result in longer search times, directly proportional to the number of elements in the display. Ohman et al. (2001) conducted a study in which participants searched for fear-relevant and fear-irrelevant pictures. Participants' search time for fear-relevant stimuli (snakes and spiders) did not increase as more fear-irrelevant elements were added; instead, fear-relevant stimuli were found quickly regardless of how many elements were in the array. In a similar line of research, healthy participants more readily detected emotional faces displaying negative emotions (fear, anger) than faces displaying positive emotions (Globisch, Hamm, Esteves, & Ohman, 1999; Wells and Matthews, 1994).

Although the evidence for automatic processing of emotional stimuli is compelling and widely accepted, it has not gone unchallenged. Some have criticized previous studies because the competing stimuli were not sufficiently attention-grabbing (Pessoa, McKenna, Gutierrez, & Ungerleider, 2002). These authors charted the fMRI BOLD signal in the amygdala when attention was voluntarily directed toward emotional pictures compared to when the same stimuli were presented as distracters and attention was directed toward another task. Pessoa et al. (2002) argued that if emotional stimuli are processed preattentively, a processing advantage should still exist for emotional stimuli even when the distractor demands a large amount of attentional resource. Instead, they found that amygdala activation was only present in the condition where participants were focused solely on the emotional stimuli; when the distractor task was the primary goal, no amygdala activation was observed. Furthermore, the distractor task did not evoke different responses, suggesting that attention is required for amygdala activation. Here, the authors found that negative stimuli evoked stronger activation in the *visual cortex* than did neutral stimuli. Pessoa and colleagues suggested that the increased activation of the visual cortex in response to emotional stimuli represents emotional modulation—just as attended items are processed more than nonattended items, emotional items are attended more than neutral items. This may imply a top-down influence of emotion on visual attention (Pessoa & Ungerleider, 2004).

Others have also pointed out that the automatic processing of emotional stimuli is not *necessarily* mediated by the amygdala. There is another neural system, although indirect and consciously controlled, that may underlie the privileged attentional processing of emotional material. This system is centered on frontal cortical areas. While the amygdala uses direct connections to associative and sensory cortices to modulate responses, the frontal lobes must modulate responses through the use of cognitive processes, such as prioritizing certain stimuli over others (Taylor & Fragopanagos, 2005). Of particular importance to this network is the dorsolateral prefrontal cortex (DLPFC), which is largely responsible for sustaining task-relevant goals in working memory (Barch et al., 1997). In turn, attention can then be directed toward the task-relevant (e.g., emotional) stimuli while ignoring task-irrelevant (e.g., nonemotional) stimuli. As the frontal lobes are highly interconnected, it is possible that other frontal areas may provide additional influence over the DLPFC during the attainment of behavioral goals (Taylor & Fragopanagos, 2005). For example, the ventromedial prefrontal cortex (VMPFC) shares direct connections with the amygdala (Nolte, 1998) and DLPFC; it is, therefore, possible that emotional stimuli registered by the amygdala are processed through the VMPFC to the DLPFC, allowing these systems to exact a modulatory effect on goal-directed cognition. In this way, there are possibly two pathways by which attention and emotion interact. The first pathway is through the amygdala, which may be considered a bottom-up, automatic, and direct pathway. The second pathway is indirect and requires some top-down cognitive intervention; this system consists of inputs to the DLPFC via the VMPFC from the amygdala.

Memory

Of all the neuropsychological domains known to be influenced by emotion, memory is probably the most studied and well documented (Dolan, 2002; Hamann, 2001). Not only is memory enhanced through general cognitive factors such as rehearsal and elaboration, but there also exist special neural and hormonal mechanisms that are engaged when one remembers (or intends to remember) emotional stimuli (Hamann, 2001). Memory is best conceptualized as a system of several dissociable, but related, components rather than as a unitary construct (Christensen, Carney, & Segal, 2005; Tulving, 1985). One of the most common divisions of memory is between implicit and explicit memory. *Implicit memory* is the recollection or performance of unconscious information and is relatively resistance to neuronal insult (e.g., Milner, 2005). It is assessed with paradigms such as priming and procedural skill learning tasks. A crucial characteristic of implicit memory is that it can occur without awareness. *Explicit memory*, by contrast, requires the conscious recollection of information or events (e.g., recollection of a word list, or an autobiographical experience) and is commonly affected by neuronal damage, including most forms of psychopathology (e.g., Williams et al., 2007). Much evidence suggests that these two types of memory are mediated by different, but overlapping, neural networks. Where implicit memory is largely independent of medial temporal lobe (MTL) function and is reliant on the amygdala, explicit memory is crucially reliant on MTL integrity (e.g., Milner, 2005; Scoville & Milner, 1957). More specifically, explicit memory relies on the dentate gyrus, cornu ammonis 1, 2, and 3 (CA1–3), subiculum, and the entorhinal cortex. For the purposes of this chapter, we will focus on explicit memory, as the majority of data on impairments in implicit memory implicate acquired amygdala damage. Further, the population of interest for this chapter, patients with mood disorders, typically exhibit intact implicit memory against robust impairments in explicit memory (Bazin, Perruchet, De Bonis, & Feline, 1994; Zakzanis, Leach, & Kaplan, 1998).

The influence of emotion on memory has been observed in a wide variety of explicit memory tasks, including recall for list-learning (e.g., Kensinger, Addis, & Atapattu, 2011), directed-forgetting, (Zwissler, Koessler, Engler, Schedlowski and Kissler, 2011), and recall for autobiographical memory tasks (e.g., Bluck, 2003; Conway, 2003). Generally speaking, emotion is known to enhance memory at most stages of mnemonic operation, including encoding, retention/consolidation, and retrieval (Hamann, 2001). These effects are evident at both biological and behavioral levels and include instances when participants first process to-be-remembered material. In an early study, Cahill et al. (1996) showed that participants exhibited more amygdala activity while encoding negative films than that used for neutral films; 3 weeks later, the participants with the highest amygdala activity recalled more of the negative films than did the participants with lower amygdala activity. This finding was not observed for the neutral films. The amygdala can also exert its influence at encoding on positive material; for example, increased bilateral amygdala activity is associated with enhanced recognition of positive and negative stimuli 1 month after initial exposure (Hamann, Ely, Grafton, & Kilts, 1999). At a behavioral level, Cahill and McGaugh (1995) showed participants a narrated emotional and nonemotional slideshow. Importantly, the slideshows used the exact same slides in the same sequence: the key manipulation was the emotional content of narration. The group presented with the emotional story remembered significantly more detail about the story and recalled more individual slides. Using the same paradigm with lesion patients, Hamann, Cahill, McGaugh, and Squire (1997) found that amnesiac patients with varying lesion locations exhibited generally poor recall of verbal material but nonetheless exhibited enhanced recall for the emotional story. Other studies have found the reverse when the amygdala region is damaged (bilaterally) but the hippocampal region is intact—that is, impaired memory for emotional events but spared recall for verbal material (Adolphs, Cahill, Schul, & Babinsky, 1997). This is not to say, however, that patients with amygdala damage cannot remember emotional information; in fact, it has been shown that these patients can remember emotional words high on the valence dimension but low on the arousal dimension better than neutral words (Phelps, LaBar, & Spencer, 1997). Furthermore, they better remember the content of emotional sentences than neutral sentences (Phelps et al., 1998).

The role of emotion in the consolidation of information is less clear. One study using a contextual memory paradigm has recently shed some light on this issue

(Lewis, Cairney, Manning, & Critchley, 2011). In this experiment, participants were presented with neutral images that were superimposed on either neutral or negative backgrounds and were asked to report the initial context in which the image was presented. The manipulation of interest was whether a consolidaton period, consisting of sleep, would have differential effects from an equally long consolidation period of wakefulness. Given that sleep is generally understood to improve memory consolidation, the authors looked to determine whether emotional information was especially well preserved or enhanced after a period of sleep. The authors replicated the finding that participants who sleep after doing a task outperform participants who have a period of equally long wakefulness; however, they did not find any evidence that emotion was especially preserved. This study differed from other studies investigating the role of emotion in consolidation by looking at contextual memory. Other studies have shown that sleep usually enhances memory for negative objects (Nishida, Pearsall, Buckner, & Walker, 2009). Another study has shown that sleep can influence the underlying neurobiology used to retrieve an emotional memory (Payne & Kensinger, 2011). In this study, participants were presented with a negative or neutral image on a neutral background. Importantly, one group of participants was given the task in the morning and had to stay up for 12 hours before being tested, whereas the other group was given the task at night, had a 12-hour period of normal sleep, and was tested in the morning. The group that slept before being tested performed better for negatively valenced objects. Using fMRI, this study was also able to show that the group that slept recruited a more specific set of neural regions, including the amygdala and VMPFC, whereas the non-sleep group recruited a more widespread network for the same material, which included lateral PFC and parietal corticies (Payne & Kensinger, 2011). This latter study shows that emotion impacts memory at both the consolidation and retrieval stages. Although the direct evidence is mixed for the role of emotion in the consolidation process, indirect evidence suggests that emotional memories are more often relived, talked about, and bonded over with more intensity and frequency (Walker, Skowronski, Gibbons, Vogl, & Ritchie, 2009) than mundane memories. According to Nadel and Moscovitch's (1997) multiple trace theory, memories that are more rehearsed become "stronger." As such, one might predict that this is one avenue by which emotion exerts its influence on the consolidation process.

The retrieval of emotional memories has proven more complicated to study empirically. Perhaps the most notable problem arises from the longstanding difficulty separating the effects at encoding from those at retrieval. One attempt to better isolate retrieval function is to employ tasks that involve specific postencoding instructions that bear upon the memorial process. For example, in directed-forgetting studies, participants are presented with a list of words and then instructed to either remember or forget that list before they are given another list (Bjork, LaBerge, & LeGrand, 1968). At recall, participants are asked to recall as many words as possible from both lists, regardless of the original instruction. The general finding from nonemotional directed-forgetting tasks is that the "forget" list is recalled worse than the "remember" list. More recently, Minnema and

Knowlton (2008) showed that emotion can change this finding. They found that when participants were given a list of negative words followed by the "forget" instruction and then given another negative list, the recall of words from the first list was significantly increased, whereas the recall of words from the second list, which is normally better remembered, was decreased. This was not the case when the first list was followed by a neutral list.

In a more direct effort to assess the role of emotion in retrieval, Smith, Stephan, Rugg, and Dolan (2006) had participants undergo an fMRI while performing a contextual memory task. In this task, participants had to make emotional and nonemotional discriminations. For the emotional discriminations, participants had to judge whether a neutral object was paired with an emotional or neutral scene, whereas the nonemotional discrimination required participants to remember whether or not people were in the scenes. Importantly, in both conditions the stimuli were the same and only the instructions at the time of recall differed. Overall, there was greater amygdala, hippocampus, and medial PFC activation in the emotional discrimination task, which suggests that when made explicit, emotions exert a larger influence on the retrieval of information (Smith et al., 2006).

Autobiographical memory, which relies on all memory-processing stages, is the ability to recollect unique individual experiences that are temporally and spatially specific. Although there are currently a wide range of autobiographical memory testing paradigms, the most commonly used is the autobiographical memory test developed by Robinson in 1976 and used famously by Williams and Broadbent in 1986. In this modified Crovitz cue-word paradigm, participants are shown a word that is emotionally laden (positive, negative, or neutral) and asked to recollect an event, specific in time and in place, that manifests the given word. There are two types of responses obtained from this test: specific and overgeneral memories. Specific memories are characterized by being spatially and temporally specific (e.g., "my first day in Spain was exciting"). Overgeneral memories, by contrast, are characterized by either repeated instances (e.g., "every time I walk the dog we pass a park") or summaries of long periods of time (e.g., "during university I drank lots of coffee"), termed *categoric* and *extended*, respectively. This paradigm has shown repeatedly that memories in response to emotional words are more specific than memories in response to neutral words, at least in healthy research participants (e.g., D'Argembeau, Comblain, & Van der Linden, 2003; Nandrino et al., 2002; Williams & Broadbent, 1986).

In real life, memory and emotion are intrinsically intertwined. Not surprisingly, laboratory studies of healthy subjects, such as the studies reviewed above, reliably demonstrate that emotion enhances recall of information when it is instantiated as the target of our memorial efforts. Moreover, the enhanced recall of emotional information is often reflected in the detail or specificity of one's memories. However, when the emotional quality of a stimulus countermands the explicit goal of our memory systems, it can deter recall in the form of distraction or disproportionate salience in ways that unnecessarily obligate memory resources. As we will see later, this system is even more strongly obligated among individuals with mood disorders.

Decision Making

Psychologists have devoted comparatively little effort to studying the impact of emotion on decision making (Mitchell, 2011). Behavioral economists, however, have recently underscored the importance of emotions in everyday decisions. In 2003, Sanfey, Rilling, Aronson, Nystrom, and Cohen had participants perform the ultimatum game while undergoing an fMRI scan. In this game, participants must agree to split a sum of money, which can be done either fairly (each person gets the same amount of money) or unfairly; importantly, only one player can propose what the split should be, while the other player can only choose to accept or reject the offer. A model of purely logical decision-making would suggest that regardless of the split proposed by Player 1, Player 2 should accept the offer, as it will be a net increase in the amount of money they have. However, this is not observed in experiments (e.g., Guth, Schmittberger, & Schwarze, 1982). Instead, people tend to reject offers that are seen as unfair. In the experiment by Sanfey et al. (2003), participants were either paired with a person or with a computer. Participants were less likely to accept an unfair offer from another person, suggesting a greater sense of fairness when other humans are involved. The imaging data showed that unfair offers activated the anterior insula, DLPFC, and the anterior cingulate cortex (ACC) more than fair offers. Interestingly, this effect was more robust when participants were dealing with human partners than with computers (Sanfey et al., 2003). Furthermore, the magnitude of activity of the anterior insula was directly proportional to the degree of unfairness, where greater activation was observed for the increasingly unfair proposals. Given the role of the insula in negative emotional states, these results suggest a strong role for emotions in decision making. A more recent study showed that this effect is amenable to experimental manipulation. Knoch, Pascual-Leone, Meyer, Treyer, and Fehr (2006) had participants play the ultimatum game while being administered transcranial magnetic stimulation (TMS) over either the left or right DLPFC. The authors found that when unfair proposals were made during right DLPFC stimulation, participants were significantly *more* likely to accept the offer than with either left DLPFC or sham stimulation (Knoch et al., 2006). Critically, the participants still recognized the offers as unfair, but they were still more willing to accept the offer. Similar results were obtained by van't Wout, Kahn, Sanfey, and Aleman (2005). These data implicated the DLPFC as having a central role in emotional decision-making.

Further evidence for the role of the PFC in decision making comes from lesion studies; specifically, patients with damage to the VMPFC displayed impaired personal and social decision-making, despite otherwise intact cognitive functioning (Bechara, 2004). In terms of experimentally measuring decision making, gambling tasks, such as the Iowa Gambling Task, are commonly used. Briefly, participants are allowed to choose cards from one of two decks: one deck that has large gains followed by many small losses, which over time accumulate to a loss in points, and another deck with small gains and fewer losses, which over time yields gains. Most healthy participants, as well as participants with brain injuries to areas other than the VMPFC, end up choosing more cards from the second deck. By contrast, patients with VMPFC damage tend to choose the deck with sharper costs and rewards but that ends up in net losses (Bechara, 2004). Results such as these imply that if decision making in a relatively controlled environment is impaired, as indicated by poorer choices, then real-life decisions are likely to be impaired as well. Given this, how does emotion play a role in decision-making processes? The orbitofrontal cortex (OFC) plays a key role in decision making; however, it is not the only neural structure responsible for it. Other cortical and subcortical regions, including the amygdala and somatosensory/insular cortices, as well as the indirect routes, including the spinal cord, vagus nerve, and endocrine system, also influence decision making. These latter three structures are a crucial part of the somatic marker hypothesis, which states that decision making is a process influenced by marker signals that arise from bioregulatory processes, including those that express themselves in emotions and feelings (Bechara, 2004). Bechara and colleagues (1998) have shown that patients with primary polyneuropathies affecting autonomic fibers exhibit mild impairments on gambling tasks.

In addition to these structures, other neural regions with overlapping roles in emotion (regulation) and decision making include the OFC, ventrolateral prefrontal cortex (VLPFC), medial prefrontal cortex (MPFC), and the DLPFC. The OFC and the VMPFC play key roles in the integration of emotional content coming from the limbic system (Krawczyk, 2002) and, as such, are involved in processing the reward value of environmental stimuli. Furthermore, these areas specialize in modulating behavior in response to stimuli that no longer provide rewards, as in reversal learning. Finally, the role of the DLPFC in working memory is well established, and by extension, its integration of information from several sources (emotional or not) (Goldman-Rakic, 1992).

Summary

Emotion plays a key role in a variety of cognitive processes, as illustrated above. This happens, in part, because of the adaptive nature of emotions. In particular, emotion can guide attention to pertinent stimuli, shape memories, and influence decisions. In healthy individuals, this interplay of cognition and emotion serves to optimize human behavior by allowing emotions to sway, temper, and modulate cognitive processes. What happens, however, when the cognitive system and underlying neural networks that serve to treat emotion with some priority are dysfunctional, as in the case of mood disorders? The remainder of this chapter will explore this in relation to each of the major cognitive processes discussed above. To date, most research has focused on attention and memory, while decision making has only recently been investigated.

EMOTIONAL INFLUENCE ON ATTENTION, MEMORY, AND DECISION MAKING IN MOOD DISORDERS

Major depressive disorder (MDD) affects multiple domains of cognition (e.g., Merriam, Thase, Haas, Keshavan, & Sweeney, 1999; Paelecke-Habermann, Pohl, &

Leplow, 2005; for a meta-analysis see Zakzanis, Leach, & Kaplan, 1998). However, the cognitive theory of depression proposed by Beck (1976) suggests that there is a *style* of thinking associated with depression that leads to a certain type of impairment. Specifically, Beck (1976) posits that the thinking of individuals with MDD is characterized by a triad of negative thoughts—about the self, the world, and the future. Related to this, individuals with depression will process information in schema-congruent ways, focusing on negative aspects of situations rather than on positive ones. Most notably, according to Beck, are schemas related to loss, separation, failure, worthlessness, and rejection. Importantly, these deficits are hypothesized to remain even after affective episodes. Research has proven Beck correct in many respects, with an abundance of evidence for negative thinking in depression regardless of mood state (e.g., Mathews & MacLeod, 2005). Beck's cognitive theory of depression makes a crucial prediction with regard to the impact of emotional information on the cognition of affected individuals: although there is a general impairment in cognitive functioning associated with depression, is there a greater deficit in the processing of emotional relative to neutral stimuli? The following sections will review research addressing this question.

Importantly, the processing of affective information in depression activates either different neural circuitry from that in healthy controls (HCs) or varying degrees of the same neural circuitry. Researchers consider both of these activation patterns to be abnormal. For example, in one study looking at the processing of positive and negative pictures, Wagner, Muller, Sommer, Klein, and Hajak (2004) found that, compared to HCs, patients with depression exhibited enhanced hippocampal activity in response to positive pictures as well as enhanced activity in the amygdala, PFC, and OFC in response to negative pictures. Patients with MDD have also been reported to exhibit enhanced amygdala activity in response to emotional faces (e.g., Sheline et al., 2001). Similarly, when judging the valence of emotional words (and the degree to which they are self-relevant), patients with MDD recruited the amygdala to a larger degree than did HCs and for a longer period of time when judging negative, self-relevant words. These activation patterns often result in behavioral responses indicating an affective bias toward negative stimuli, such as enhanced memory for negative pictures (Hamilton & Gotlib, 2008).

Emotion and Attention in Mood Disorders

There is a relatively large literature focusing on the differences and similarities between mood disorders and anxiety disorders with respect to biased attentional processing. Here, we will focus on depression, but briefly highlight the ongoing debate. Two schools of thought emerge. One proposes that anxiety is characterized by automatic processing toward enhancing the detection of threat cues (Williams, Watts, MacLeod, & Matthews, 1988; Williams et al., 1997), which leads to biases in the early stages of processing (attention), whereas depression is influenced by mood-congruent biases, especially in the strategic elaboration of information, causing biases specific to memory. Data exist to support this claim, including the occasional finding that patients with MDD do not exhibit any attentional bias (MacLeod, Mathews, & Tata, 1986; Mogg, Bradley, Williams, & Mathews, 1993). Critically, the studies reporting no attentional bias in depression use exposure times of less than 1 second. The other school of thought comes from Bradley, Mogg, and Lee (1997), who suggest that there is indeed an attentional bias in major depression, but it may not be an initial orienting bias, as in the case with anxiety. Instead, Bradley and colleagues (1997) propose that MDD is characterized by a difficulty disengaging from negatively valenced material once it has grabbed a person's attention. Studies showing an attentional bias for stimuli presented for at least 1 second in MDD support this hypothesis (e.g., Gotlib & Cane, 1987).

In mood-disordered patients' self-report of their own cognitive abilities, a dissociation emerges: they report difficulties concentrating; yet despite this, they are able to easily focus on (or have trouble disengaging from) negative thoughts, especially if they are self-focused (Burt, Zembar & Niederehe, 1995; Matthews & MacLeod, 2005). Empirical work in the behavioral realm indicates that individuals with MDD exhibit processing bias toward negative stimuli and away from positive stimuli in a variety of experimental tasks, including visual Dot-Probe, dichotic listening, affective go/no-go, and emotional Stroop tasks (Gotlib, McLachlan, & Katz, 1988; McCabe & Gotlib, 1993; Williams & Nulty, 1986). Given that these same individuals focus on the negative aspects of events, even if minor, in real-life situations, this is perhaps not surprising (Gotlib & McCabe, 1992). This attentional bias to negative stimuli is also observed at the neurophysiological level (e.g., Siegle, Steinhauer, Thase, Stenger, & Carter, 2002; Surguladze et al., 2005), where patients with MDD exhibit exaggerated amygdala activity in response to explicitly presented sad faces compared to that in HCs.

In a recent meta-analysis, Peckham, McHugh, and Otto (2010) found that processing biases in the domain of attention for individuals with MDD were most strongly captured by the dot probe task. In this task, participants are asked to respond as quickly as possible to a small dot that replaces one of two simultaneously presented emotional words or faces (usually negative vs. neutral or neutral vs. positive). The variable of interest is how much time it takes participants to identify the location of the dot. Experiments show that participants with MDD attend rapidly to the negatively valenced stimuli and slowly to the positively valenced stimuli, at least if the stimulus is presented long enough to enter awareness (Mathews, Ridgeway, & Williamson, 1996; Peckham et al., 2010). In another study, participants with MDD located the dot presented behind sad faces faster than when it was behind positive or neutral faces; this quick detection was faster than for persons with generalized anxiety disorder and for HCs (Gotlib, Kasch, et al., 2004). Importantly, this finding was only true for depression-relevant stimuli (sad faces) and not just negative facial stimuli in general (angry or fearful), and patients with an anxiety disorder did not show this bias toward sad faces. Another study by Gotlib, Krasnoperova, Yue, and Joormann (2004) found that patients with MDD had a greater bias toward sad faces on the dot-probe task than did HCs or patients with generalized social phobia. Again, patients with MDD did not show this pattern toward angry faces.

Other studies using the dot probe paradigm have shown that participants with MDD, instead of exhibiting attention toward negative stimuli, have simply lost the typical positive attentional bias that is usually observed in HCs (Mogg et al., 1991; Gotlib et al., 1988). Some studies have failed to find an attentional processing bias in patients with MDD (e.g., Mathews et al., 1996), but this may be due to methodological differences, such as using words rather than pictorial stimuli. Importantly, as Glaser and Glaser (1989) have shown, faces have preferential access over words to affective storage. As such, studies using words to determine affective attentional biases may not be using the optimal stimuli.

Dichotic listening tasks have participants listen to two separate streams of conversation, one to each ear, while having to repeat one stream and ignoring the other. In an affective dichotic listening task, one stream is affectively valenced while the other is not. This allows researchers to determine approximately how much attention is being paid to the irrelevant emotional stimuli. McCabe and Gotlib (1993) found that patients with MDD exhibited slower response times to an intermittent light when the unattended ear was presented with negatively valenced content, an observation not found in the comparison group. When this same group of depressed patients were remitted from their symptoms, this attentional bias was no longer present, suggesting that it may be a product of current mood state, or depression severity.

The affective go/no-go task involves both the facilitation of responses to emotional stimuli and/or the suppression of responses to irrelevant emotional stimuli. For example, participants may be encouraged to press a button in response to negative words while at the same time discouraged from pressing a button in response to positive words. At some point, this criterion may change. The variable of interest is the reaction time to press the button. As shown by Murphy et al. (1999), participants with MDD were slower when responding to positive, but not negative, words. This study suggests a bias away from positive emotions, not a bias towards negative emotions (see also Williams & Nulty, 1986). In the same study, participants with bipolar disorder (BD) were faster than controls when responding to positive words, a result suggesting a bias toward positive emotions in stages of mania. In another study, Erickson et al. (2005) found that HCs have a bias toward positive words, whereas unmedicated patients with MDD responded faster to sad words, which suggests a bias toward negative words. Using an fMRI version of the go/no-go task, Elliott et al. (2002) found that patients with MDD and HCs showed opposite responses: patients had increased ventral ACC activity to sad targets and decreased activity to happy targets. The pattern of results from the affective go/no-go task are unclear at present and more research is required.

Finally, the emotional Stroop task has been used somewhat extensively to study attentional biases in psychopathology, including generalized anxiety disorder, posttraumatic stress disorder, obsessive-compulsive disorder, specific phobia, and MDD (Williams, Mathews, & MacLeod, 1996). The emotional Stroop task works by the same principle as the classic Stroop task, with the main difference being that participants must name the color of emotional words, in comparison to neutral words (Gotlib & McCann, 1984). In one of the first studies to use this method, Gotlib and McCann (1984) found that patients with MDD were slower to name depression-related words than they were to name neutral- or mania-related words; HCs did not differ in their response latency across any word class. This suggests that patients with MDD are allocating some attentional resources to reading the irrelevant stimuli. More recently, it has been shown that patients with MDD exhibit slightly altered ERP profiles during this task (McNeely, Lau, Christensen, & Alain, 2008). Specifically, these authors found that, although no group differences emerged with respect to accuracy or response times, patients with MDD had larger N450 values over parietal regions for valenced (positive and negative) words than for neutral words. Importantly, the relation between N450 and clinical symptom measures was significant, where patients with higher levels of depression showed larger N450 measures. This may reflect the fact that, as depressive symptoms worsen, patients with MDD have an increasingly difficult time inhibiting word valence.

In agreement with Beck's (1976) notion of mood state specificity, these Stroop interference effects have been reported to disappear after successful treatment when depressive symptoms are no longer present (Williams et al., 1996). In a longitudinal study, Gotlib and Cane (1987) found that reaction times to negative words normalized in patients with clinical depression after successful treatment. Further evidence for this depression severity/mood state–specific notion comes from Gilboa and Gotlib (1997), who found no difference on the emotional Stroop task in previously dysphoric and never-dysphoric individuals. Finally, the emotional Stroop task appears to have some clinical relevance: Segal and Gemar (1997) found that participants who responded to cognitive-behavioral therapy (CBT) showed less pre-therapy interference for negative material, whereas participants who did not respond to treatment showed the typical longer latencies to negative words.

On a neurophysiological level, it has also been shown that patients with MDD exhibit increased amygdala activity in response to sad faces (e.g., Surguladze et al., 2005). In a recent study, Victor, Furey, Fromm, Ohman, and Drevets (2010) used a backward masking paradigm and found that currently unmedicated depressed participants, as well as unmedicated remitted participants, exhibited this same bias for stimuli presented below the level of conscious awareness. Both groups displayed greater amygdala activity when looking at sad faces (although they were unaware that faces were presented) in comparison to HCs. Further, the group that was initially depressed underwent a treatment intervention of sertraline, and upon completion of the 8-week intervention, their bias scores (amygdala activity) became more like those of HCs. Although inconsistent with other treatment studies, these data are interesting in that they suggest a specific effect of treatment in the removal of a processing bias and not the mere remission of depressive symptoms. This finding of an unconscious bias toward sad faces is at odds with some behavioral experiments that show no bias in the early stages of attentional processing in MDD; however, it is in agreement with the studies mentioned above discussing the automatic processing of emotional stimuli (e.g., Eimer & Holmes, 2002).

Emotion clearly plays an important role in the domain of attention in individuals with mood disorders. The empirical literature suggests that this occurs in several experimental paradigms at different stages of attention (early versus late) as well as at the neurophysiological level: patients with mood disorders exhibit increased neural activity at important emotional centers (amygdala) even below the level of awareness. These latter findings hint at altered neural circuitry primed to respond to negative (sad) emotions. Fortunately, as mentioned earlier, treatment appears to ameliorate this response, perhaps suggesting a degree of plasticity in the underlying substrate. With the exception of the study by Victor et al. (2010), most data point toward the idea that the affective bias in attention may be moderated by mood state or depression severity and is not an enduring trait of mood disorders.

Emotion and Memory in Mood Disorders

As noted above, the emotional enhancement of memory has been thoroughly documented in healthy populations (see Labar & Cabeza, 2006 for a review). In individuals with mood disorders, this system is intact; however, it is biased toward the processing of *negative* material specifically. For example, in a meta-analysis, Matt, Vazquez, and Cambell (1992) showed that patients with MDD recalled 10% more negative than positive stimuli, whereas healthy comparison subjects remembered 8% more positive than negative stimuli. This effect was most notable in free recall tasks. This meta-analysis illustrates the core difference in mnemonic processing between HCs and individuals with mood disorder: a positive bias exists for HCs, whereas a negative bias exists for individual with mood disorders. This is an important issue as previous meta-analyses (e.g., Burt et al., 1995) suggest that memory deficits are the result of psychopathology in general and not mood disorders specifically. However, the data reviewed here suggest that this general effect is importantly moderated by valence, such that memory among MDD patients is disproportionately guided to negative material. This section will largely focus on MDD, but relevant (or existing) data on BD will also be included where possible.

Individuals with MDD are more likely to recall negative information than are controls (e.g., Matt et al., 1992). This may be due to an increased elaboration processing during the encoding of negative stimuli, as shown by Deveney and Deldin (2004). In this study, participants were shown positive, negative, and neutral faces and asked to "hold them in mind." Using electroencephalography (EEG), these authors showed that when patients with MDD were shown negative faces, they did not exhibit the same pattern as that in HCs, which involved a decrease in the amplitude of the slow-wave component of the EEG. Instead, participants with MDD processed positive, negative, and neutral faces in the same way. Similarly, decreased elaboration of positive stimuli has been shown in MDD (Shestyuk, Deldin, Brand, & Deveney, 2005). Gotlib, Krasnoperova, et al. (2004b) showed that when participants rated whether affectively valenced adjectives were self-relevant, depressed individuals chose more negative words than did HCs. In addition, during free recall, patients with MDD recalled a higher proportion of negative words than did HCs and individuals with generalized social phobia. Using the same self-relevance task, Timbremont, Braet, Bosmans, and Van Vlierberghe (2008) failed to replicate Gotlib, Krasnoperova, et al.'s (2004) results, perhaps because they were primarily studying adolescents. Although patients with MDD can be taught to intentionally forget negative material, there is a tradeoff involved, whereby the intentional forgetting of negative material also reduces memory performance for previously learned cue words (Joormann, Hertel, Brozovich & Gotlib, 2005). In addition to recalling more negative material than HCs, patients with MDD also appear to be more prone to developing false memories for negative material than HCs (Joormann, Teachman & Gotlib, 2009).

At the neurophysiological level, it has been shown that patients with MDD encode negative stimuli differently than HCs (Hamilton & Gotlib, 2008). Specifically, patients with MDD exhibit an increase in activity in the right amygdala upon the successful encoding of negative, but not positive or neutral, stimuli. In this study, patients with MDD also recalled disproportionately more negative than positive material on the behavioral recognition test, whereas HCs recognized more positive material.

One of the most widely studied areas of memory in MDD is autobiographical memory (for a review, see King et al., 2010). The typical variable of interest in the autobiographical memory literature is the memory *specificity*, which is measured on a scale between specific and overgeneral. *Specific memories* are memories indicative of a one-time, spatially and temporally unique event, whereas an *overgeneral memory* is either a repeated instance or the summary of a longer period of time. These two forms of overgeneral memory are referred to as *categoric* and *extended*, respectively. The literature widely assumes that specific memories are indicative of normal memory function, whereas overgeneral memories are indicative of abnormal memory functioning or dysfunction.

In patients with depression, the effect of positive and negative cue words is conflicting, as many studies show that patients are more overgeneral to positive words, whereas roughly the same number show that patients are more overgeneral to negative words (King et al., 2010). This relation between emotion and autobiographical memory in patients with MDD is complicated by a variety of clinical and demographic factors such as depression severity, age of illness onset, medication status, and mood state at testing. Although the moderating influence of emotion on autobiographical memory recall is not yet well understood, there is no question that patients with MDD submit memories that are overgeneral relative to HCs. In a meta-analysis of studies using the cue word paradigm to assess autobiographical memory, van Vreeswijk and de Wilde (2004) concluded that patients with MDD were indeed more overgeneral than healthy comparison subjects. One other study looking at truly episodic memories (as assessed by the remember/know paradigm) found that patients with MDD exhibited a bias toward negative memories whereas HCs exhibited a bias toward positive memories (Lemogne et al., 2006). Further, it was found that patients with MDD were impaired for positive memories across three criteria for episodic autobiographical memories: they lacked specificity, the memories did not utilize autonoetic consciousness (mental time travel), and the memories were recalled from a third-person perspective.

Similar results have been obtained in BD, although only a few studies exist to date (Mansell & Lam, 2004; Mowlds et al., 2010; Scott et al., 2000; Tzemou & Birchwood, 2007). Two of these studies reported that patients with BD, while euthymic, were more overgeneral to both positive and negative cues relative to matched controls (Scott et al., 2000; Tzemou & Birchwood, 2007). In the Mowlds et al. (2010) study, there was no comparison group, but remitted patients were more overgeneral to positive and negative cues relative to neutral cues. Finally, Mansell and Lam (2004) reported overgenerality only for negative events in remitted patients with BD. No comparison group was used in this study. Interestingly, patients with BD reported recollecting negative events more than positive events on a daily basis, which suggests a bias toward negative thinking.

The preferential recall of negative material is in line with Beck's (1976) cognitive theory of depression. Experimental evidence exists to show that, on average, patients with MDD recall more negative material than do nondepressed controls. It is difficult to separate out whether this enhanced recall of negative material is a memory phenomenon or the result of the enhanced attention toward negative stimuli, as discussed earlier. At any rate, the bulk of empirical work shows that emotion has a different effect on the memory of individuals with MDD than that on those without a mood disorder.

Emotion and Decision Making in Mood Disorders

Neuropsychological studies have shown that individuals with MDD are impaired on measures of executive functioning, including measures of fluency, cognitive flexibility, and dysexecutive syndrome (Paelecke-Habermann et al., 2005). Decision making is considered to fall under the umbrella of executive functioning, as it draws largely on processes like working memory and cognitive control, which in turn, have been associated with emotion regulation (e.g., Miyake & Shah, 1999). In mood disorders, working-memory deficits have been reported in delayed, but not immediate, recall tasks (Ilsley, Moffoot, & O'Carroll, 1995). Using an affective 2-back task, which required participants to judge whether a facial expression matched the same expression presented two faces earlier, Levens and Gotlib (2010) showed that patients with MDD were slower to disengage from negative stimuli, whereas HCs were slower to disengage from positive stimuli. This suggests that each group may have a respective bias in updating the content of working memory. In line with Ilsley et al. (1995), there were no impairments in the 0-back condition, which suggests that immediate processing on working memory tasks is spared in MDD. This inability to disengage from negatively valenced emotional material has been shown with other experimental paradigms as well, such as the Sternberg task (Joormann & Gotlib, 2008). In this task, participants were presented with two rows of three words (affectively valenced) that appeared for 7.8 seconds. This was followed by a blank screen and then a cue screen indicating which row of words was to be recalled, as indicated by the color in which the words were written. This experiment showed that when the cue screen displayed irrelevant negative material (the list *not* to be recalled), participants with MDD were slower to respond than HCs, an effect not observed for positive words. Yet another study found similar results; patients with MDD were less able to suppress negative material than HCs (Joormann, Nee, Berman, Jonides, & Gotlib, 2010). Hence, it appears that individuals with MDD have difficulty disengaging from negative material from working memory. This has important clinical implications: If individuals with MDD are unable to remove the negative information in working memory (i.e., rumination), it can lead to the maintenance of depressive symptoms (Nolen-Hoeksema, Morrow, & Fredrickson, 1993).

Related to decision making is cognitive control, or being able to select task-relevant information. Lau et al. (2007) found that on a measure of cognitive inhibition, a prose-distraction task, patients with MDD were less able to ignore irrelevant negative material than HCs or nondepressed anxious controls. Importantly, in this study, patients with MDD had no affective bias in a motor task, a finding suggesting that the bias is specific to cognition. On classic decision-making tasks such as the Iowa Gambling Task (IGT), studies have shown that males with MDD make less optimal decisions than matched controls and females with MDD (e.g., Han et al., 2012). Another study compared individuals with panic disorder to a group with comorbid panic disorder and major depressive disorder and found that the latter group exhibited greater impairments on a task similar to the IGT, the Cambridge Gambling Task (Kaplan et al., 2006). With regard to BD, impaired decision making has also been observed in the absence of an affective processing bias (Rubinsztein, Michael, Underwood, Tempest, & Sahakian, 2006).

Summary

Evidence clearly indicates that the emotional valence of stimuli affects cognitive processing in the domains of attention, memory, and decision making in healthy individuals and in individuals with mood disorders (see Table 4.1). Important quantitative differences exist between these groups: Individuals with mood disorders exhibit a tendency to orient more strongly toward more negative material on a variety of experimental tasks (e.g., visual dot probe and emotional Stroop tasks) and have greater difficulty disengaging from negative material (Joormann & Gotlib, 2008). These individuals also remember a disproportionate amount of negative material on memory tasks (e.g., Matt et al., 1992) and tend to report overgeneral memories (see King et al., 2010, for a review). Preliminary evidence also suggests that emotion can influence decision-making processes in complex tasks (e.g., gambling tasks) as well as simple tasks (emotion recognition). In addition to the well-documented quantitative difference manifested by patients with mood disorders, there exists some evidence of qualitative differences as well. For example, the affective bias among MDD patients relative to HCs on memory tasks involves distinct valences; that is, both are biased but in the opposite direction, with MDD patients remembering more negative material and HCs remembering more positive material. Similarly, some functional brain imaging studies have

Table 4.1. EFFECT SIZES FOR EMPIRICAL TESTS OF ATTENTION, MEMORY, AND EXECUTIVE FUNCTIONS IN MAJOR DEPRESSION

Cognitive Domain of Bias[1]	Number of Studies[2]	Range of Effect Size[3]
Attention		
Emotional Stroop	****	.17 (*d*)–.98 (*g*)
Dot-probe	****	.52 (*d*)
Affective dichotic listening	*	N/A
Affective go/no-go	**	.42 (*d*)
Memory		
Autobiographical memory	****	.53 (*d*) –.58 (*d*)
Affective list-learning	****	.19 (*d*)
Executive function		
Gambling task(s)	*	.23 (*d*)
Prose distraction	*	.57 (*d*)
Affective *n*-back	*	.31 (*d*)

[1] Comparisons indicate healthy controls versus individuals with major depressive disorder.
[2] Number of studies: *1–5; **6–10; *** >11; ****meta-analysis.
[3] Where available, meta-analyses using Cohen's *d* or Hedge's *g* are reported (Epp, Dobson, Dozois, & Frewen, 2012; Matt et al., 1992; Peckham et al., 2010; van Vreeswijk & de Wilde, 2004). Otherwise, effect sizes were calculated on the basis of published means and standard deviations.

reported distinctly different activation patterns underlying affective biases among patients with MDD compared to patterns in HCs.

CLINICAL RELEVANCE

Given the experimental nature of the tasks presented above, they provide limited help to the clinician attempting to test patients for mood disorder–specific profiles. Currently, there are no commercially available or psychometrically tested instruments that directly assess the degree of affective bias among individual patients. This behooves researchers and clinicians to undertake the appropriate psychometric studies in order to validate and norm some of the more sensitive tasks (e.g., visual dot-probe task, emotional Stroop task, autobiographical memory test) for use with clinical populations. These tests would all be easily incorporated into a neuropsychological battery without adding undue administration time or patient burden. Given the impact of emotional content on the cognitive processing ability of patients with mood disorders, such measures promise to have demonstrable clinical utility.

Having said this, clinicians can use the experimental evidence reviewed here to help guide their assessments of patients with mood disorders, especially with the aid of common sense and clinical discretion. We will now illustrate some of these approaches through a case study of middle-aged woman referred to our service for a neuropsychological evaluation.

CASE STUDY

G.K. was a 49-year-old, Caucasian female referred by her psychotherapist for a neuropsychological evaluation. At the time of the referral she was in the middle of a 20-week, standardized course of therapy using interpersonal psychotherapy to treat MDD. Her therapist had noted vacillating progress and queried whether underlying cognitive deficits might be responsible for her variable response to treatment.

G.K.'s first depressive episode was in her early 20s, while a student in college. At that time she sought counseling at the university student center but did not receive psychiatric treatment or medication. Her symptoms abated and, while she had to reduce her course load for one semester, she was able to continue at college and complete her studies over the normal time course. Following her undergraduate studies, she enrolled in a master's program in journalism, where she did well and achieved high grades. She began working in radio broadcasting as a news writer in her mid-20s. She remained in this line of work, reporting some advancement into editorial and managerial positions, but having to step out of these positions secondary to stress and interpersonal conflicts with colleagues. At the time of the assessment she was working as a writer for a local, classical radio station. During the evaluation, G.K. indicated that her work stress was particularly high as the radio station was undergoing a format change (from classical to jazz) and several layoffs were anticipated. She was unmarried and had no children. She was not currently in a romantic relationship but had been involved in a long-term partnership through her late 30s and early 40s with a bank executive. She began to experience depressive symptoms again in her late 30s after her mother tragically died in a boating accident. She reported three distinct depressive episodes since this time, each lasting between 12 and 18 months. At the time of the evaluation she was prescribed a single SSRI.

G.K. presented as a slight, well-groomed, attractive woman. She was noticeably shy and made little eye contact, at least in the early phases of the assessment. She was articulate and spoke intelligently across an array of topics. She reported being an avid consumer of fiction and classical music. Her principle social contacts outside of work were her sister and book club. She complained of sad mood, anhedonia, low appetite, anxiety, rumination, low self-esteem, sexual disinterest, and occasional low back pain. She was particularly consumed by work stress and interpersonal interactions with a selection of co-workers, including the manager to whom she reported. G.K. was also very concerned about what she perceived to be declining cognitive function. In particular, she noticed substantive problems in her driving and reported several near-miss accidents, missed stop signs, and missed turns. Although a keen reader, she was finding it difficult to concentrate on reading and noticed her mind continually wandering to ruminative topics such as work, relationships, and her depression. She also explained that she was increasingly forgetful and embarrassingly forgot scheduled appointments, people's names, and objects in her home (e.g., reading glasses, car keys). She was also experiencing difficulties meeting deadlines at work and felt that she had become increasingly inefficient with her time.

The results from her evaluation showed general intellectual ability in the very superior range. Roughly consistent with this level of functioning were her language, crystallized knowledge, and problem-solving abilities. Relative minor impairments were noted in visual-spatial processing, executive functioning, and motor speed. More substantive relative deficits (normatively in the mildly impaired range) were revealed on tasks of complex attention, working memory, cognitive control, and memory (both in the verbal and visual-spatial domains). Psychopathology testing suggested moderately elevated depressive symptoms (primarily of an affective and cognitive nature), stress, and anxiety.

Several aspects of G.K.'s presentation and challenges were significantly impacted by affective biases toward negative information. As a starting point, we conceptualized affective bias as either an aid or hindrance, moderated expressly by task demands. That is, if targets of cognitive processing are emotionally valenced, performance is likely to be augmented, whereas if irrelevant stimuli (i.e., distracters, foils) are emotionally valenced, performance is likely to be attenuated. Within this context we set out to explore in detail the behavioral characteristics of G.K.'s reported driving impairment with the assistance of a certified driving coach. Driving simulation and a road test suggested that her driving skills were intact. Through more in-depth interviewing, however, it came to light that while driving, G.K. routinely listened to audio books or radio theater. In particular, she favored fiction in which characters were highly developed, psychologically complex, and dealing with formidable life challenges. Her justification for listening to fiction in the car was sound; in light of her difficulty reading written prose, it was an efficient way for her to keep up her book club activity. We hypothesized, however, that such emotionally laden material would be especially distracting for G.K., and we worked with her to develop a plan to continue using the excellent strategy of listening to audio books but at a time during the day when her attention could be exclusively directed to the story. We also posited that, under the right conditions, listening to emotionally laden fiction was beneficial from a cognitive standpoint. In particular, in most situations the task at hand lacked adequate salience to compete with G.K.'s internal ruminations for cognitive resources—internal negative thoughts were the distracters. By enhancing the emotional content of the target task (i.e., listening to engaging, affective prose), salience was bolstered such that cognitive resource was more easily captured by the target task at the expense of processing irrelevant distraction. Moreover, we emphasized to G.K. that keeping up on her book club activities was important to maintaining social contact, which would continue to mitigate her depression. G.K. was able to quickly implement this recommendation and reported a significant impact on her self-evaluated driving abilities.

A very similar hypothesis was proffered to explain some of her difficulties at work. A more careful behavioral analysis of her occupational performance uncovered several instances of distraction and loss of intention and awareness when engaged in tasks. It also became apparent that many of these distractions were caused by excessive monitoring of the whereabouts and physical proximity of objectionable colleagues. We engaged G.K. to generate strategies for reducing *this type of affectively charged distraction. She implemented several techniques, including regularly closing her office door, listening to music over headphones, and working from home one day per week. She reported that these modifications aided her concentration and that she was meeting deadlines with more ease. Moreover, our clinical sense was that bringing the impact of her monitoring behavior to her awareness also contributed positively to its management.*

The potential problem with affective bias in the case of G.K. was partially illuminated during the initial interview, before the actual neuropsychological assessment. This gave us an opportunity to review the test materials and steer our assessment away from instruments that might include inherently emotional material—for example, HVLT Form 2, BNT, WMS-III Logical Memory, and RBANS Stories. Given the literature reviewed in this chapter, it is recommended that, when assessing patients with mood disorders, clinicians take stock of the materials intended for administration and eliminate, where possible, emotionally provocative stimuli.

Although any form of intervention based on the studies reviewed here is precluded, it is recommended that clinicians provide some form of psychoeducation regarding affective bias to their clients with mood disorders. Specifically, it might be helpful to inform clients with mood disorders that when confronted with emotional material they will experience a natural tendency to be pulled toward negative material. Creating an awareness of these processes in these clients may be enough to buffer them against the affective biases observed in the domains of attention, memory, and decision making. Moreover, normalizing the process as a natural and adaptive one (i.e., a process experienced by all individuals and one that has helped humans survive) may help clients to understand and accept the full implications of such biases.

References

Adolphs, R., Cahill, L., Schul, R., & Babinsky, R. (1997). Impaired declarative memory for emotional material following bilateral amygdala damage in humans. *Learning and Memory, 4*, 291–300.

Barch, D. M., Braver, T. S., Nystrom, L. E., Forman, S. D., Noll, D. C., & Cohen, J. D. (1997). Dissociating working memory from task difficulty in human prefrontal cortex. *Neuropsychologia, 35*(10), 1373–1380.

Bazin, N., Perruchet, P., De Bonis, M., & Feline, A. (1994). The dissociation of explicit and implicit memory in depressed patients. *Psychological Medicine, 24*, 239–245.

Bechara, A. (2004). The role of emotion in decision-making: Evidence from neurological patients with orbitofrontal damage. *Brain and Cognition, 55*, 30–40.

Bechara, A., Tranel, D., Wilson, J., Heberlein, A. S., Ross, M., & Damasio, A. R. (1998). Impaired decision-making in peripheral neuropathy. *Society for Neuroscience Abstracts, 24*, 1176.

Bjork, R. A., LaBerge, D., & LeGrand, R. (1968). The modification of short-term memory through instructions to forget. *Psychonomic Science, 10*, 55–56.

Bradley, B. P., Mogg, K., & Lee, S. C. (1997). Attentional biases for negative information in induced and naturally occurring dysphoria. *Behaviour Research and Therapy, 35*, 911–927.

Bradley, M. M., Sabatinelli, D., Lang, P. J., Fitzsimmons, J. R. King, W., & Desai, P. (2003). Activation of the visual cortex in motivated attention. *Behavioral Neuroscience, 117*(2), 369–380.

Burt, D. B., Zembar, M. J. & Niederehe, G. (1995). Depression and memory impairment: A meta-analysis of the association, its pattern, and specificity. *Psychological Bulletin, 117*, 285–305.

Cahill, L., Haier, R. J., Fallon, J., Alkire, M. T., Tang, C., Keator, D., Wu, J., & McGaugh, J. L. (1996). Amygdala activity at encoding correlated with long-term, free recall of emotional information. *Proceedings of the National Academy of Science of the U.S.A. 93*, 8016–8021.

Cahill, L., & McGaugh, J.L. (1995). A novel demonstration of enhanced memory associated with emotional arousal. *Consciousness & Cognition 4*, 410–421.

Christensen, B. K., Carney, C. & Segal, Z. V. (2005). Cognitive processing models of Depression. In D. J. Stein, D. J. Kupfer, & A. F. Schatzber (Eds.), *Textbook of mood disorders* (pp. 131–144). Washington, DC: American Psychiatric Publishing.

Deveney, C.M., Deldin, P.J. (2004). Memory of faces: A slow wave ERP study of major depression. *Emotion, 4*, 295–304.

Dolan, R. J. (2002). Emotion, cognition and behavior. *Science, 298*, 1191–1194.

Eastwood, J. D., Smilek, D., & Merikle, P. M. (2001). Differential attentional guidance by unattended faces expressing positive and negative emotion. *Perception & Psychophysics, 63*, 1004–1013.

Eimer, M., & Holmes, A. (2002). An ERP study on the time course of emotional face processing. *Neuroreport, 13*, 427–431.

Epp, A. M., Dobson, K. S., Dozois, D. J. A., & Frewen, P. A. (2012). A systematic meta-analysis of the Stroop task in depression. *Clinical Psychology Review, 32*, 316–328.

Erickson, K., Drevets, W. C., Clark, L., Cannon, D. M., Bain, E. E., Zarate, Jr., C. A., et al. (2005). Mood-congruent bias in affective go/no-go performance of unmedicated patients with major depressive disorder. *American Journal of Psychiatry, 162*, 2171–2173.

Frischen, A., Eastwood, J. D., & Smilek, D. (2008). Visual search for faces with emotional expressions. *Psychological Bulletin, 134*, 662–676.

Gilboa, E., & Gotlib, I. H. (1997). Cognitive biases and affect persistence in previously dysphoric and never-dysphoric individuals. *Cognition & Emotion, 11*, 517–538.

Glaser, W. R., & Glaser, M. O. (1989). Context effects in Stroop-like word and picture processing. *Journal of Experimental Psychology: General, 118*, 13–42.

Globisch, J., Hamm, A. O., Esteves, F., & Ohman, A. (1999). Fear appears fast: Temporal course of startle potential in animal fearful subjects. *Psychophysiology, 36*, 66–75.

Goldman-Rakic, P.S. (1992). Working memory and the mind. *Scientific American, 267*, 111–117.

Gotlib, I. H., & Cane, D. B. (1987). Construct accessibility and clinical depression: A longitudinal investigation. *Journal of Abnormal Psychology, 96*, 199–204.

Gotlib, I. H., Kasch, K. L., Traill, S., Joorman, J., Arnow, B. A., & Johnson, S. L. (2004). Coherence and specificity of information processing biases in depression and social phobia. *Journal of Abnormal Psychology, 113*, 3, 386–398.

Gotlib, I. H., Krasnoperova, E., Yue, D. L., & Joormann, J. (2004). Attentional biases for negative interpersonal stimuli in clinical depression. *Journal of Abnormal Psychology, 113*, 127–135.

Gotlib, I. H., & McCabe, S. B. (1992). An information-processing approach to the study of cognitive functioning in depression. In E. F. Walker, B. A. Cornblatt, & R. H. Dworkin (Eds.), *Progress in experimental personality and psychopathology research* (Vol. 15, pp. 131–161). New York: Springer.

Gotlib, I. H. & McCann, C. D. (1984). Construct accessibility and depression: An examination of cognitive and affective factors. *Journal of Personality and Social Psychology, 47,* 427–439.

Gotlib, I. H., McLachlan, A. L., & Katz, A. N. (1988). Biases in visual attention in depressed and nondepressed individuals. *Cognition & Emotion, 2,* 185–200.

Guth, W., Schmittberger, R., & Schwarze, B. (1982). An experimental analysis of ultimatum bargaining. *Journal of Economic Behavior and Organization 3*(4), 367–388.

Hamann, S. B., Cahill, L., McGaugh, J. L., & Squire, L. R. (1997). Intact enhancement of declarative memory for emotional material in amnesia. *Learning and Memory, 4,* 301–309.

Hamann, S. B., Ely, T. D., Grafton, S. T., & Kilts, C. D. (1999). Amygdala activity related to enhanced memory for pleasant and aversive stimuli. *Nature Neuroscience, 2,* 289–293.

Hamilton, J. P., & Gotlib, I. H. (2008). Neural substrates of increased memory sensitivity for negative stimuli in major depression. *Biological Psychiatry, 63,* 1155–1162.

Han, G., Klimes-Dougan, B., Jepsen, S., Ballard, K., Nelson, M., Houri, A., et al. (2012). Selective neurocognitive impairments in adolescents with major depressive disorder. *Journal of Adolescence, 35,* 11–20.

Ilsley, J. E., Moffoot, A. P. & O'Carroll, R. E. (1995). An analysis of memory dysfunction in major depression. *Journal of Affective Disorders, 9, 35*(1–2), 1–9.

Joormann, J., Hertel, P. T., Brozovich, F., & Gotlib, I. H. (2005). Remembering the good, forgetting the bad: Intentional forgetting of emotional material in depression. *Journal of Abnormal Psychology, 114* (4), 640–648.

Joormann, J., Nee, D. E., Berman, M. G., Jonides, J., & Gotlib, I. H. (2010). Interference resolution in major depression. *Cognitive, Affective, and Behavioral Neuroscience, 10*(1), 21–33.

Joormann, J., Teachman, B. A. & Gotlib, I. H. (2009). Sadder and less accurate? False memory for negative material in depression. *Journal of Abnormal Psychology, 118* (2) 412–417.

Kaplan, J. S., Erickson, K., Luckenbaugh, D. A., Weiland-Fiedler, P., Geraci, M., Sahakian, B.J., et al. (2006). Differential performance on tasks of affective processing and decision-making in patients with panic disorder and panic disorder with comorbid major depressive disorder. *Journal of Affective Disorders, 95*(1–3), 165–171.

Kensinger, E. A., Addis, D. R. & Atapattu, R. K. (2011). Amygdala activity at encoding corresponds with memory vividness and with memory for select episodic details. *Neuropsychologia, 49* (4), 663–673.

Knoch, D., Pascual-Leone, A., Meyer, K., Treyer, V., & Fehr, E. (2006). Diminishing reciprocal fairness by disrupting the right prefrontal cortex. *Science, 314,* 829–832.

Levens, S. M. & Gotlib, I. H. (2010). Updating positive and negative stimuli in working memory in depression. *Journal of Experimental Psychology General, 139*(4), 654–664.

Lewis, P. A., Cairney, S., Manning, L., & Critchley, H. D. (2011). The impact of overnight consolidation upon memory for emotional and neutral encoding contexts. *Neuropsychologia, 49,* 2619–2629.

MacLeod, C., Mathews, A., & Tata, P. (1986). Attentional bias in emotional disorders. *Journal of Abnormal Psychology, 95,* 15–20.

Mathews, A. & MacLeod, C. (2005). Cognitive vulnerability to emotional disorders. *Annual Review of Clinical Psychology, 1*, 167–195.

Mathews, A., Ridgeway, V., & Williamson, D. A. (1996). Evidence of attention to threatening stimuli in depression. *Behavior Research & Therapy, 34*, 695–705.

Matt, G. E., Vazquez, C., & Cambell, W. K. (1992). Mood-congruent recall of affectively toned stimuli: A meta-analytic review. *Clinical Psychology Review, 12*, 227–255.

McCabe, S. B., & Gotlib, I. H. (1993). Attentional processes in clinically depressed subjects: A longitudinal investigation. *Cognitive Therapy and Research, 17*, 359–377.

McNeely, H. E., Lau, M. A., Christensen, B. K., & Alain, C. (2008). Neurophysiological evidence of cognitive inhibition anomalies in persons with major depressive disorder. *Clinical Neurophysiology, 119*, 1578–1589.

Milner, B. (2005). The medial temporal-lobe amnesic syndrome. *Psychiatric Clinics of North America 28(3)*, 599–611, 609.

Mitchell, D. G. (2011). The nexus between decision making and emotion regulation: A review of the convergent neurocognitive substrates. *Behavioural Brain Research, 217*, 215–231.

Miyake, A., & Shah, P. (1999). *Models of working memory: Mechanisms of active maintenance and executive control.* New York: Cambridge University Press.

Mogg, K., Bradley, B. P., Williams, R., & Mathews, A. (1993). Subliminal processing of emotional information in anxiety and depression. *Journal of Abnormal Psychology, 102*, 304–311.

Mogg, K., Mathews, A., May, J., Grove, M., Eysenck, M., & Weinman, J. (1991). Assessment of cognitive bias in anxiety and depression using a colour perception task. *Cognition & Emotion, 5*, 221–238.

Morris, J. S., Ohman, A., & Dolan, R. J. (1998). Conscious and unconscious emotional learning in the human amygdala. *Nature, 393*, 467–470.

Murphy, F. C., Sahakian, B. J., Rubinsztein, J. S., Michael, A., Rogers, R. D., Robbins, T. W. & Paykel, E. S. (1999). Emotional bias and inhibitory control processes in mania and depression. *Psychological Medicine, 29*, 1307–1321.

Nadel, L., & Moscovitch, M. (1997). Memory consolidation, retrograde amnesia and the hippocampal complex. *Current Opinion in Neurobiology, 7(2)*, 217–227.

Nishida, M., Pearsall, J., Buckner, R. L., & Walker, M. P. (2009). REM sleep, prefrontal theta, and the consolidation of human emotional memory. *Cerebral Cortex, 19*, 1158–1166.

Nolen-Hoeksema, S., Morrow, J., & Fredrickson, B. L. (1993). Response styles and the duration of episodes of depressed mood. *Journal of Abnormal Psychology, 102*, 20–28.

Notebaert, L., Crombez, G., Van Damme, S., De Houwer, J., & Theeuwes, J. (2011). Signals of threat do not capture but prioritize attention: A condition approach. *Emotion, 11* (1), 81–89.

Ohman, A., Flykt, A., & Esteves, F. (2001). Emotion drives attention: Detecting the snake in the grass. *Journal of Experimental Psychology: General, 130, 3*, 466–478.

Ortigue, S., Michel, C. M., Murray, M. M., Mohr, C., Carbonnel, S., & Landis, T. (2004). Electrical neuroimaging reveals early generator modulation to emotional words. *Neuroimage, 21*, 1242–1251.

Paelecke-Habermann, Y., Pohl, J., & Leplow, B. (2005). Attention and executive functions in remitted major depression patients. *Journal of Affective Disorders, 89* (1–3), 125–135.

Payne, J. D., & Kensinger, E. A. (2011). Sleep leads to changes in the emotional memory trace: Evidence from fMRI. *Journal of Cognitive Neuroscience, 23*, 1285–1297.

Peckham, A. D., McHugh, R. K., & Otto., M. W. (2010). A meta-analysis of the magnitude of biased attention in depression. *Depression and Anxiety, 27*, 1135–1142.

Pessoa, L., McKenna, M., Gutierrez, E., & Ungerleider, L. G. (2002). Neural processing of emotional faces requires attention. *Proceedings of the National Academy of Science of the U.S.A., 99* (17), 11458–11463.

Pessoa, L., & Ungerleider, L. G. (2004). Neuroimaging studies of attention and the processing of emotion-laden stimuli. *Progress in Brain Research, 144*, 171–182.

Phelps, E. A., Labar, K. S., Anderson, A. K., O'Connor, K. J., Fulbright, R. K., & Spencer, D. D. (1998). Specifying the contributions of the human amygdala to emotional memory: A case study. *Neurocase 4*, 527–540.

Phelps, E. A., LaBar, K. S., & Spencer, D. D. (1997). Memory for emotional words following unilateral temporal lobectomy. *Brain and Cognition, 35*, 85–109.

Reeck, C., & Egner, T. (2011). Affective privilege: Asymmetric interference by emotional distracters. *Frontiers in Psychology, 2*, 1–7.

Rubinsztein, J. S., Michael, A., Underwood, B. R., Tempest, M., & Sahakian, B. J. (2006). Impaired cognition and decision-making in bipolar depression but no "affective bias" evident. *Psychological Medicine. 36*(5), 629–639.

Russell, J. A. (1980) A circumplex model of affect. *Journal of Personality and Social Psychology, 39*, 1161–1178.

Sanfey, A. G., Rilling, J. K., Aronson, J. A., Nystrom, L. E., & Cohen, J. D. (2003). The neural basis of economic decision-making in the ultimatum game. *Science, 300*, 1755–1758.

Schooler, J. W., & Eich, E. (2000). Memory for emotional events. In E. Tulving & F. I. M. Craik (Eds.), *The Oxford handbook of memory* (pp. 379–392). Oxford, UK: Oxford University Press.

Scoville, W. B., & Milner, B. (1957). Loss of recent memory after bilateral hippocampal lesions. *Journal of Neurology, Neurosurgery & Psychiatry, 20*, 11–21.

Sheline, Y. I., Barch, D. M., Donnelly, J. M., Ollinger, J. M., Snyder, A. Z., & Mintun, M. A. (2001). Increased amygdala response to masked emotional faces in depressed subjects resolves with antidepressant treatment: an fMRI study. *Biological Psychiatry, 50*, 651–658.

Shestyuk, A. Y., Deldin, P. J., Brand, J. E., & Deveney, C. M. (2005). Reduced sustained brain activity during processing of positive emotional stimuli in major depression. *Biological Psychiatry, 57*, 1089–1096.

Segal, Z. V., & Gemar, M. (1997). Changes in cognitive organization for negative self-referent material following cognitive behaviour therapy for depression: A primed Stroop study. *Cognition & Emotion, 11*, 501–516.

Siegle, G. J., Steinhauer, S. R., Thase, M. E., Stenger, V. A., & Carter, C. S. (2002). Can't shake that feeling: Event-related fMRI assessment of sustained amygdala activity in response to emotional information in depressed individuals. *Biological Psychiatry, 51*(9), 693–707.

Smith, A. P., Stephan, K. E., Rugg, M. D., & Dolan, R. J. (2006). Task and content modulate amygdala-hippocampal connectivity in emotional retrieval. *Neuron, 49*, 631–638.

Surguladze, S., Brammer, M. J., Keedwell, P., Giampietro, V., Young, A. W., Travis, M.J., et al. (2005). A differential pattern of neural response toward sad versus happy facial expressions in major depressive disorder. *Biological Psychiatry, 57*(3), 201–209.

Svoboda, E., McKinnon, M. C., & Levine, B. (2006). The functional neuroanatomy of autobiographical memory: A meta-analysis. *Neuropsychologia, 44*, 2189–2208.

Taylor, J. G., & Fragopanagos N. F. (2005). The interaction of attention and emotion. *Neural Networks, 18*, 353–369.

Timbremont, B., Braet, C., Bosmans, G., & Van Vlierberghe, L. (2008). Cognitive biases in depressed and non-depressed referred youth. *Clinical Psychology & Psychotherapy, 5* (5), 329–339.

Tulving, E. (1985). How many memory systems are there? *American Psychologist, 40,* 385–398.

Van't Wout, M., Kahn, R. S., Sanfey, A. G., & Aleman, A. (2005). Repetitive transcranial magnetic stimulation over the right dorsolateral prefrontal cortex affects strategic decision-making. *NeuroReport, 16*(16), 1849–1852.

Victor, T. A., Furey, M. L., Fromm, S. J, Ohman, A., & Drevets, W. C. (2010). Relationship between amygdala responses to masked faces and mood state and treatment in major depressive disorder. *Archives of General Psychiatry, 67,* 11, 1128–1138.

Wagner, V., Muller, J. L., Sommer, M., Klein, H. E., & Hajak, G. (2004). Changes in the emotional processing in depressive patients: A study with functional magneto resonance tomography under the employment of pictures with affective contents. *Psychiatrische Praxis 31*(Suppl 1), S70–S72.

Walker, W. R., Skowronski, J. J., Gibbons, J. A., Vogl, R. J., & Ritchie, T. D. (2009). Why people rehearse their memories: Frequency of use and relations to the intensity of emotions associated with autobiographical memories. *Memory, 17* (7), 760–773.

Williams, J. M. G., Mathews, A., & MacLeod, C. (1996). The emotional Stroop task and psychopathology. *Psychological Bulletin, 120,* 3–24.

Williams, J. M. G., & Nulty, D. D. (1986). Construct accessibility, depression and the emotional Stroop task: Transient mood or stable structure? *Personality and Individual Differences, 7,* 485–491.

Williams, J. M., Watts, F. N., MacLeod, C., & Mathews, A. (1988). *Cognitive psychology and emotional disorder.* Chichester, UK: Wiley.

Zwissler, B., Koessler, S., Engler, H., Schedlowski, M., & Kissler, J. (2011). Acute psychosocial stress does not disrupt item-method directed forgetting, emotional stimulus content does. *Neurobiology, Learning and Memory, 95*(3), 346–354.

5

The Impact of Anxiety on Cognitive Task Performance

PATRICK CLARKE AND COLIN MACLEOD

It has long been recognized that anxiety can compromise performance on a wide variety of cognitive tasks designed to assess the efficiency and effectiveness of information processing (cf. Eysenck, 1992). Most clinicians who carry out neuropsychological assessment will be sensitive to the possibility that elevated anxiety has the potential to elicit performance deficits despite intact underlying cognitive capabilities. Indeed, within this realm of cognitive assessment, anxiety is likely to be not only one of the greatest non-neurological influences on test performance but also one of the most common. Clients who undergo assessment to determine whether they are suffering cognitive impairments as a result of neurological dysfunction can reasonably be expected to feel apprehensive about these possibilities. Such concerns, when combined with the usual apprehensions associated with testing procedures delivered in unfamiliar environment, often will contribute to increased anxiety. Therefore, the need to dissociate the cognitive characteristics of elevated anxiety from those that instead reflect neuropsychological dysfunction is of major importance. The cognitive characteristics of anxiety are fairly distinctive and do not involve a global deficit observed across all types of processing tasks. They also are marked by particular patterns of processing selectivity that can even enhance cognitive task performance under certain conditions. A good appreciation of the cognitive "signature" of elevated anxiety can assist in determining whether unusual patterns of cognitive performance are likely to reflect inflated levels of anxiety, rather than neuropathology. In this review, we endeavor to familiarize the reader with the ways in which anxiety is known to have an impact on performance across a range of cognitive tasks, describing the profile of these anxiety-related effects and also considering some influential theoretical accounts that have been put forward to explain them.

GENERAL COGNITIVE PERFORMANCE IN ANXIETY: WHEN AND WHY DOES ANXIETY HELP OR HINDER PERFORMANCE ON COGNITIVE TASKS?

Increased anxiety is a common experience of individuals undergoing cognitive assessment (Cassady, 2004), and there is a wealth of evidence to show that elevated anxiety exerts a direct impact on how well cognitive assessment tasks generally are performed (O'Toole & Pedersen, 2011; Skaali et al., 2011). The results of numerous studies have clearly demonstrated that such performance can be expected to suffer when the elevation of anxiety is intense, though it is equally evident that mild elevations of anxiety can serve to improve cognitive performance (cf. Eysenck, 1982). Furthermore, a critical factor in determining whether a given anxiety elevation is more likely to hinder or assist cognitive task performance is the difficulty of the assessment task. Research comparing the impact of anxiety on a range of different assessment tasks has revealed that, while substantially inflated anxiety is likely to compromise performance on difficult cognitive tasks, it may not impair, and indeed might well facilitate, performance on easy cognitive tasks (Pessoa, 2009). Both the magnitude of the anxiety elevation and the difficulty of the cognitive task interactively determine the likelihood of performance impairment, as the intensity of the anxiety elevation required to negatively impact performance is lower for more difficult tasks and higher for easier tasks (Eysenck, Derakshan, Santos, & Calvo, 2007).

Models designed to account for the impact of anxiety on cognitive performance have sought to explain why the prospect of an anxiety-linked performance deficit depends on both the intensity of the anxiety and task difficulty. One of the earliest such models was put forward by Easterbrook (1959). According to this theory, increasing anxiety progressively constrains the breadth of attentional focus, thereby reducing the breadth of informational cues an individual will process when performing any given task. Importantly, Easterbrook argued that as increasing anxiety serves to narrow attentional focus, this initially will progressively reduce the processing of peripheral task-irrelevant cues, without reducing the processing of more central task-relevant cues. Therefore, slight elevations of anxiety may lead to improved task performance by suppressing the processing of distracting and irrelevant information. However, as anxiety increases further, this progressive narrowing of attention will come to compromise the processing of more task-relevant informational cues as well, ultimately resulting in impaired performance when anxiety becomes intense. According to Easterbrook, the breadth of task-relevant informational cues needed to sustain good performance is relatively small for easy tasks and large for hard tasks. Hence, on easy tasks the narrowing of attention associated with increasing anxiety will continue to improve performance until attentional focus is very narrow, as optimal performance will occur when only the few task-relevant informational cues are being processed. However, on hard tasks, less narrowing of attention will result in participants failing to process some of the more extensive range of required informational cues, and so performance decrements will be evident with smaller elevations of anxiety.

Taking a rather different theoretical approach, Spence and Spence (1966) proposed that anxiety serves as a nonspecific motivational drive, which increases the tendency of participants to favor responses that have the greatest "habit strength." Habit strength reflects the degree to which these responses have led to successful performance in the past. According to these theorists, easy tasks are those in which the correct response is likely to have the greatest habit strength, and so on such tasks anxiety will serve to increase the motivational drive to perform what is likely to be the correct response. Difficult tasks, in contrast, are those in which the correct response has a relatively low habit strength, whereas erroneous candidate responses have higher habit strengths. Suppressing competing responses with high habit strength is thus necessary to enable good task performance. By increasing the motivational drive to produce responses with high habit strengths, heightened anxiety will increase the probability that the wrong response will be produced on these harder tasks, resulting in the commonly observed decrement in performance.

While these accounts provide elegant conceptualizations of anxiety-mediated enhancement and impairment of performance on easy and difficult cognitive tasks, their value is compromised by difficulties associated with operationalizing some of their key constructs. For example, Easterbrook's (1959) account is handicapped by the lack of any clear way for researchers to define and quantify relevant and irrelevant informational cues, thus task difficulty continues to be defined in practice by circular reference to the degree to which it elicits improved or impaired performance. Similarly, Spence and Spence's (1966) account is limited by the absence of any obvious way to directly determine the numbers and relative habit strengths of all available responses in any task environment. Despite their limitations, these early accounts have been highly influential in shaping more contemporary explanations of how anxiety influences cognitive task performance.

An important step toward these contemporary conceptions was provided by the early work of M. W. Eysenck, which subsequently has undergone progressive refinement (Eysenck, 1979, 1982, 1988; Eysenck & Calvo, 1992; Eysenck, et al., 2007). Eysenck's account shares with Easterbrook the idea that variations in available processing capacity underpin the observed effects of anxiety on cognitive task performance. Specifically, Eysenck proposes that, as anxiety increases, there often will be a reduction in the degree to which the working-memory system is likely to be deployed to sustain good performance on the types of cognitive tasks commonly delivered in standard psychological assessment. However, he contends that this results from the fact that anxious individuals preferentially employ their working-memory resources to instead process information that, although largely irrelevant to the assessment task they have been given, is highly relevant to their anxiety-related concerns. Like Spence and Spence, Eysenck's account also holds that general motivation or "effort" will also increase with anxiety. Hence the precise impact of elevated anxiety on cognitive task performance will be determined by the combined influence of the reduction in task-relevant processing and this increased motivation. For mild elevations of anxiety, and on simple tasks, the reduction in task-relevant processing may not greatly affect capacity and so will be more than offset by the concurrent increased effort, resulting in enhanced task performance. However, for intense anxiety, and on difficult tasks, this increased motivation will be insufficient to compensate for the detrimental consequences of the associated reductions in task-relevant processing, leading to the impairment of task performance.

A key feature of Eysenck's account, which distinguishes it from previous models but which is a feature of most contemporary cognitive accounts of anxiety, is that it attributes anxiety-related deficits on conventional cognitive assessment tasks to anxiety-linked biases in the way cognitive resources are selectively assigned to alternative processing options. When anxiety impairs performance on a given cognitive assessment task, these anxious participants are preferentially employing their cognitive resources to engage in other types of information processing, which may be irrelevant to the task given them by the experimenter but likely more relevant to their anxious concerns. The implication is that anxious individuals do not necessarily have reduced cognitive capacity but allocate this cognitive capacity in a biased manner, directing it selectively to process information relevant to their anxiety-related concerns. Indeed, according to Eysenck and to others who have built on this theoretical foundation (Mogg & Bradley, 1998; Williams, Watts, MacLeod, & Mathews, 1997), the distinctive cognitive content commonly associated with elevated anxiety is considered to represent the direct consequence of this pattern of selective information processing.

COGNITIVE CONTENT IN ANXIETY: THE PREDOMINANCE OF THREAT-RELATED THINKING

Consistent with the notion that anxious individuals selectively deploy their cognitive resources to preferentially engage in anxiety-relevant processing, a considerable literature demonstrates that people with heightened dispositional anxiety report cognitive content that tends to be anxiety-relevant in nature. Typically, such content involves cognitions concerning a heighted expectation of danger. Early work of this type involving interviews with clinically anxious populations revealed that patients with anxiety experience cognitions concerning the heightened expectation of physical harm or psychosocial trauma, such as embarrassment or ridicule (Beck, Laude, & Bohnert, 1974; Hibbert, 1984). More recent research employing structured questionnaire instruments has corroborated such findings and has shown that inflated rates of cognitions concerning personal danger are particularly evident among those patients who are most disposed to frequently experience anxious mood states (e.g., Kendall & Treadwell, 2007; Niles, Lebeau, Liao, Glenn, & Craske, 2012).

These elevated levels of threat-related cognitive content are not restricted to clinical samples but have been observed in many nonclinical samples reporting elevated levels of anxiety, including children (Broeren, Muris, Bouwmeester, van der Heijden, & Abee, 2011), undergraduate students (Frewen, Evans, Maraj, Dozois, & Partridge, 2008), and people undergoing medical procedures (Loebner et al., 2012). Furthermore, studies in which participants keep detailed diaries of their anxiety levels and their thoughts indicate that the variation in anxiety-relevant cognitive content is predicted by day-to-day variations in level of anxious mood (Hong, 2010; Sewitch & Kirsch, 1984). The observation that stressors known to elicit anxious mood, such as a medical procedures, can serve to induce this selective focus on anxiety-relevant cognitive content is consistent with the idea that elevated anxiety can trigger such cognitive selectivity. But there is also evidence that such negative cognitive content can have a direct impact on anxious mood. Hirsch, Mathews, Clark, Williams, and Morrison (2006) had individuals with low levels of public-speaking fear imagine speech scenarios in which they performed positively or negatively before giving a talk. This manipulation of thought content served to significantly influence the level of anxiety experienced by participants. Thus, heightened levels of anxiety are reliably associated with an increased tendency to devote cognitive resources to sustain patterns of thinking that are anxiety relevant. Such selective cognition may facilitate performance on cognitive tasks that require the processing of anxiety-relevant information while impairing performance on tasks that instead require the processing of anxiety-irrelevant information. We now turn to consider the evidence that anxiety is indeed characterized by such patterns of relative facilitation and impairment, depending on whether the information that must be processed is related or unrelated to anxiety-relevant concerns.

COGNITIVE BIAS IN ANXIETY: INFORMATION-PROCESSING MECHANISMS THAT UNDERPIN COGNITVE THREAT CONTENT

There are a number of basic information-processing mechanisms that could potentially operate selectively in anxious individuals to produce the observed patterns of biased cognitive content described above. Recognition of these alternatives, and appraisal of the experimental findings relevant to the evaluation of each possibility, has given rise to a rich range of theoretical models. It is beyond the scope of this chapter to fully describe these models, hence we refer the reader to Hofmann, Ellard, and Siegle (2012) and to Cisler and Koster (2010) for recent informative overviews. In this chapter we will focus on reviewing the empirical evidence relevant to the main types of anxiety-linked processing selectivity that have been predicted by such accounts and that have been experimentally investigated in sufficient depth to permit considered evaluation. Several candidate cognitive operations have been the focus of theoretical accounts that attribute anxiety-linked cognitive content to selective processing biases in lower-level operations. Many investigators have been motivated by the possibility that anxious individuals' memory may operate in a biased manner, such that threatening information from the past may be disproportionately accessible (cf. Mitte, 2008). Another possibility receiving experimental scrutiny is that anxious individuals may resolve ambiguous aspects of their current experience in a disproportionately threatening manner through the operation of an anxiety-linked interpretive bias (cf. Blanchette & Richards, 2010). A third possibility, which has been the focus of extensive experimental study, is that anxious individuals may attend disproportionately to the more threatening elements of their immediate environment, consequently constructing internal representations that give extra weight to such threatening elements (cf. Cisler & Koster, 2010).

In the following sections we consider the evidence for these putative forms of anxiety-linked cognitive bias, focusing on work that has examined the patterns of selectivity that operate when anxious participants process information that differs in terms of its potential threat value. We will evaluate, in turn, research that has sought to investigate such selectivity in memorial processing, interpretive processing, and attentional processing. In each case, we highlight (1) the major types of cognitive-experimental tasks deployed to assess anxiety-linked biases in that particular cognitive operation, (2) how the findings from these tasks have informed understanding of anxiety-linked selective information processing, and (3) the key issues that remain to be addressed in each domain.

Anxiety and Biased Memory

The relative accessibility of different past experiences not only influences the way in which present situations are construed but also exerts a powerful impact on the predictions people make about the relative likelihood of experiencing similar events in the future (Engelhard, de Jong, van den Hout, & van Overveld, 2009). Hence, a biased capacity to remember past emotional events could readily contribute to distorted expectancies concerning the future. People generally display enhanced recall of emotional material compared to that of nonemotional material (Zimmerman & Kelley, 2010). This appears to reflect the fact that the emotionally positive or negative events are highly distinctive, which contributes to their improved recollection, relative to more neutral memories (Talmi, Luk, McGarry, & Moscovitch, 2007). If anxious individuals are characterized by a memory bias that favors the recollection of emotionally threatening memories relative to emotionally positive memories, then this may explain why they are preoccupied with thoughts concerning the prospect of future dangers. This general idea has been featured in numerous cognitive theories of anxiety dysfunction (Baumeister, Vohs, DeWall, & Zhang, 2007; Beck & Clark, 1997).

One means of experimentally assessing whether such emotional memory biases are evident in anxious individuals is to ask anxious and nonanxious people to voluntarily recall past events related to either positive or negative cue words. Studies examining such cued recall for positive and negative past events have consistently revealed that clinically anxious individuals and high-trait anxious members of the general population can more readily retrieve anxiety-provoking events from autobiographical memory than is the case for less anxious individuals (e.g., Burke & Mathews, 1992; Witheridge, Cabral, & Rector, 2010). This suggests that anxious individuals have a disproportionate capacity to readily recall negative events from their past experience.

However, it would be wrong to infer from this that the memory retrieval process consequently must be biased in anxious individuals. An equally plausible reason for these effects could be that anxious individuals have genuinely experienced a greater number of past negative events. If so, then the unbiased retrieval of information from autobiographical memory would recover negative events more readily in anxious participants, simply because they have more such events to recover. There is evidence to support the idea that anxious individuals may commonly have experienced an above-average number of negative events in the past, as a history of negative life events is known to be a contributing factor to elevated anxiety vulnerability (Spinhoven et al., 2010). Consequently, to determine whether anxiety is truly characterized by the biased retrieval of emotionally threatening information, it is necessary to assess ability to recall emotionally toned information that has been presented in a controlled and equivalent manner to both highly and less anxious participants. In many studies this has been done by assessing later recall of threatening and neutral stimulus words encountered at an earlier stage of an experimental session. In general, neither clinically anxious participants nor individuals with elevated trait anxiety scores show preferential recall for threatening word stimuli in such studies, compared to low-trait anxious control participants (e.g., Mathews & MacLeod, 1985; Mogg & Mathews, 1990; Mogg, Mathews, & Weinman, 1989). More recent reviews evaluating extensive research of this type have concluded that anxious individuals generally do not preferentially recall experimentally presented threatening information. For example, in one meta-analysis, Coles and Heimberg (2002) reported that only one of nine such studies, carried out on participants with generalized anxiety disorder, found evidence of such a recall bias favoring threatening information.

Despite the predominant absence of evidence for a negative recall bias in participants who report elevated levels of general anxiety, there have been occasional reports of such a memory bias in individuals whose anxiety involves panic disorder. Cloitre, Shear, Cancienne, and Zeitlin (1994) presented individuals diagnosed with panic disorder and nonanxious controls with threatening (panic-related), positive, or neutral word pairs. Participants were initially asked to rate the similarity of each word pair. This was followed by a cued-recall task in which participants were shown one member of each word pair and required to recall the other. Compared to control participants, patients with panic disorder recalled a disproportionate number of the threatening panic-related words. Other studies have obtained similar evidence that individuals who suffer panic disorder may show a memory bias for fear-relevant material (e.g., Becker, Rinck, & Margraf, 1994; Nunn, Stevenson, & Whalan, 1984). However, the effect is not a consistent one. Using a cued-recognition task, Beck, Stanley, Averill, Baldwin, and Deagle (1992) failed to find evidence that patients with panic disorder showed superior memory for threatening panic-relevant words; this was also the case in a study by Ehlers, Margraf, Davies, and Roth (1988). Similarly, Rapee (1994) found no evidence to suggest the presence of a recall bias favoring threatening words among panic disorder patients. Thus, even in the case of panic disorder there is no reliable memory bias for anxiety-relevant information, and in general there is little evidence that heightened anxiety generally is characterized by a recall advantage for threatening information.

Drawing the theoretical distinction between elaborative and integrative processing (Graf & Mandler, 1984), Williams, Watts, MacLeod, and Mathews (1988) argued
that anxiety may not increase the elaborative processing of threatening information,
which influences explicit memory, but may rather increase the integrative processing of such information, which instead influences implicit memory. This led to the
prediction that anxious individuals would display an implicit memory advantage
for threat-relevant information, despite showing no enhanced explicit memory for
this type of information. In the first test of this hypothesis, Mathews, Mogg, May, &
Eysenck (1989) presented emotionally threatening words in an initial encoding task
to patients with generalized anxiety disorder and to nonanxious controls. Following
this, participants were provided three-letter word stems that could be completed to
produce either previously encoded words or new, unseen words. Participants were
told to complete the word stems to yield words that they had encountered earlier,
providing a test of explicit memory, or they were told to complete the stems with
the first words that came to mind, in which case implicit memory was revealed
by the tendency to complete stems to yield previously seen words. Consistent with
Williams et al.'s theory, anxious individuals did not differ significantly in terms
of explicit memory for anxiety-related words; however, these individuals did display disproportionately improved implicit memory for such words. MacLeod and
McLaughlin (1995) subsequently corroborated these findings in a conceptual replication of this study. The measure of implicit memory in this later study was provided by a perceptual accuracy task, which indexed implicit memory by assessing
ability to perceptually identify briefly presented threat and neutral stimulus words
that had either been previously seen or not. A number of studies have since reported
evidence of an implicit memory advantage for threatening information in populations with more specific anxiety disorders. For example, Cloitre et al. (1994) found
an implicit memory advantage for anxiety-related threat words among individuals
with panic disorder, using a similar methodology to that employed by Mathews et
al. (1989). Similarly, Amir, Bower, Briks, and Freshman (2003) have reported finding an implicit memory bias of this type, but no evidence of any explicit memory
bias, in a sample of individuals with social anxiety disorder.

However, there also have been a good number of well-designed studies that
have failed to find evidence of an anxiety-related implicit memory bias. Using the
same word-stem memory test as that used by Mathews et al. (1989), Mathews,
Mogg, Kentish, and Eysenck (1995) failed to obtain evidence that individuals with
generalized anxiety show an implicit memory advantage for threatening material. Likewise, Becker, Rinck, and Margraf (1994) found no evidence of such an
implicit memory bias in panic-disorder patients using this word-stem completion
task. Nugent and Mineka (1994) found no difference in relative implicit memory
for anxiety-relevant and neutral information between high- and low-trait anxious
students. Other studies have similarly found no association between explicit or
implicit memory bias and measures of trait anxiety (McCabe, 1999; Oldenburg,
Lundh, & Kivisto, 2002).

Hence, despite the occasional evidence produced from time to time by individual studies suggesting that anxiety may bias either explicit or implicit memory

in ways that favor threatening information, the overall pattern of findings leads to the conclusion that anxiety is not reliably characterized by enhanced memory for anxiety-congruent information. Indeed, this is the conclusion drawn by Mitte (2008) on the basis of a recent large-scale meta-analysis considering the results of 165 studies: the author found that their combined findings did not support an association between anxiety and enhanced memory for threat-related information. While Mitte suggests that future research in this field might usefully differentiate between recollection and familiarity elements of memory performance, to determine whether certain precise facets of memory may reveal an anxiety-linked advantage for threatening information, it seems likely that such effects will be subtle and unlikely to compromise the assessment of memorial functioning on conventional neuropsychological tasks.

Anxiety and Biased Judgment and Interpretation

In contrast to findings in the field of memory performance, the effects of anxiety on measures of judgment and interpretation appear to be quite robust. Anxious individuals tend to form judgments that give extra weight to threatening information, overestimating both the likelihood of future negative events and the cost associated with these (McNally & Foa, 1987; Nelson, Lickel, Sy, Dixon, & Deacon, 2010). Examples of such biased judgments among individuals with anxiety pathology are readily available from the clinical literature. Socially anxious individuals commonly anticipate that intolerable ridicule and embarrassment will result from social interactions; individuals with panic disorder often interpret a racing heart as signaling the imminent onset of cardiac arrest; and people with generalized anxiety consistently overestimate the risk of personal injury or harm befalling them (cf. Barlow, 2002). This judgment bias is not limited to clinically anxious populations but also is more broadly associated with elevated anxiety. When an imminent stressor serves to elevate anxiety, both highly and less anxious individuals experience a concomitant increase in the subjectively perceived risk of experiencing a negative event relating to the stressor, although high-trait anxious individuals also have a tendency to generalize this stress-induced bias by inflating the subjective risk of negative events unrelated to this current stressor (Butler & Mathews, 1987). Hence, when state anxiety is elevated by an impending danger, low-trait anxious individuals perceive increased risk to be associated with this particular danger, while high-trait anxious individuals perceive increased risk everywhere.

Researchers have sought to illuminate the basis of anxiety-related bias in judgment and expectancy by systematically investigating whether anxiety influences the types of interpretations that people impose on ambiguous information. Experimentally assessing the biased interpretation of ambiguity commonly involves two distinct stages: first participants are presented with inherently ambiguous information, then a variety of techniques are used to infer whether they resolved this initial ambiguity in a threatening or benign way. Often the ambiguous information employed in such studies consists of sentences that permit both negative and benign interpretations, such as "When meeting her date, Lisa said, 'You're certainly not what I expected.'" Following exposure to a set of sentences that included some ambiguous items of this type, Constans, Penn, Ihen, and Hope (1999) gave anxious and nonanxious participants a recognition memory task in which they were required to rate how closely a number of new statements agreed with the meaning of statements encountered earlier. In this recognition test, either negative or non-negative interpretations of previously exposed ambiguous sentences were included (e.g., "Lisa was impressed with her date when they met" versus "Lisa was disappointed with her date when they met"). Constans et al. found that, compared to the less anxious participants, the patterns of recognition performance shown by the highly anxious participants suggested that they had imposed more negative resolutions on the initially presented ambiguous information.

Other researchers have investigated anxiety-linked interpretive bias using ambiguous words instead of ambiguous sentences. In the simplest approach, participants are required to write down orally presented words that are ambiguous homophones that could have either a threatening or a neutral interpretation (e.g., pain/pane, die/dye). These words are embedded within longer lists of unambiguous filler words to reduce their salience. The spellings employed by participants are used to index whether they imposed the threatening or neutral interpretation on ambiguous auditory information. Using this and similar methodologies, it has been demonstrated that anxious individuals are significantly more likely than nonanxious individuals to produce threatening, instead of neutral, interpretations of the homophone, a finding again suggesting that anxiety is characterized by an interpretive bias favoring threatening resolutions of ambiguity (Gifford, Reynolds, Bell, & Wilson, 2008; Mogg et al., 1994).

While results derived from the homophone-spelling and ambiguous-sentence recall tasks are consistent with the possibility that anxious individuals resolve ambiguous information in a threatening manner, these techniques share a common limitation. Specifically, individuals may sometimes access both negative and benign meanings of the ambiguity, and the observed effects may reflect anxious individuals' heightened tendency under these circumstances to choose the response options associated with the more negative interpretation. A number of experimental tasks have been developed to overcome the potential influence of such a response bias, and the effects obtained using these task variants continue to support the operation of an anxiety-linked interpretive bias. One such task variant employs homographs not in a spelling task but as primes in a semantic priming task. Amir, Beard, and Przeworski (2005) presented highly and less anxious participants with a task requiring them to perform lexical decisions on target letter strings that were preceded by prime words. In critical trials, these prime words were homographs that permitted both a threat-related and a neutral interpretation (e.g., "bitter"). The ambiguous primes were followed by target words related to either their threat meaning (e.g., "resentful") or their neutral meaning (e.g., "flavor"). It was reasoned that the tendency to impose threat resolutions on the ambiguous prime words would result in the selectively facilitated processing of target words related to the threat meanings of these primes, rather than target words related to their neutral meanings, resulting in shorter response times to identify threat than that used for neutral associates. Consistent with an anxiety-linked interpretive bias, it was found that anxious individuals, relative to nonanxious controls, were consistently faster to perform the lexical decision on target words related to the more threatening meanings of the ambiguous primes. Thus anxiety was associated with an increased tendency to resolve prime ambiguity to yield threat meanings. Other studies have produced similar findings using this paradigm (Hazlett-Stevens & Borkovec, 2004).

While the results of numerous studies suggest that anxiety is associated with an interpretive bias that favors threatening resolutions of ambiguous information, the mechanisms underlying this anxiety-linked bias are not yet fully understood. For example, it may be that this bias reflects the impact of elevated anxiety on increasing the speed with which negative meanings of ambiguous information are activated, or elevated anxiety may make it more difficult to inhibit negative meanings of ambiguity. Both activation and inhibition are intimately involved in resolution of ambiguity, and anxiety may operate via either or both cognitive mechanisms. It also is unknown whether anxiety-linked interpretive bias operates automatically or whether the tendency for anxious individuals to impose threatening interpretations on ambiguity can be influenced by intention and so is amenable to conscious control. This latter issue is likely to be of particular relevance in the clinical setting, where the modification of this anxiety-linked interpretive bias might reasonably be expected to yield therapeutic benefits (Hallion & Ruscio, 2012). Nevertheless, the evidence clearly indicates that, under normal assessment conditions, anxiety is likely to influence the resolution of ambiguity in ways that yield more threatening interpretations, when such interpretations are available.

Anxiety and Biased Attention

Many theorists contend that the threatening cognitive content observed among anxious individuals may reflect a heightened tendency to selectively attend to threatening information in their environment (cf. Cisler & Koster, 2010). This is consistent with Eysenck's (1982; Eysenck et al., 2007) suggestion that anxiety-linked performance decrements on conventional cognitive assessment tasks may reflect not an impairment in processing capabilities but a change in processing priorities, whereby anxious individuals preferentially direct their attentional resources to task-irrelevant but anxiety-relevant information. If this is the case, then it raises the interesting prospect that anxious individuals may in fact show enhanced performance under task conditions that render such selective information processing advantageous. Indeed, much experimental research designed to investigate whether anxious individuals do selectively attend to emotionally threatening information contrives task conditions in which an attentional bias toward threatening information is likely to either enhance or impede task performance.

One method of examining anxiety-linked attentional processing has been through the use of interference paradigms. Typically these require participants to complete a central task in the presence of distracter information. By examining the degree to which threatening and nonthreatening distracter information impairs central task performance, it is possible to infer the extent to which such distracters recruit selective attention. The most widely used interference task employed for this purpose has been a modified variant of the Stroop (1938) color-naming task. The original variant of the Stroop task requires participants to rapidly name the text color of words while ignoring their meaning. Using this task, Stroop revealed that participants could not completely avoid processing word meanings as demonstrated by increased response latencies when the word itself was a color name incongruent with the text color (e.g., naming the text color of the word "red" printed in green). In the emotional variant of the Stroop task, threat words (e.g., "embarrassed," "mutilated") and non-threat words (e.g., "table," "picture") are presented in colored text, and participants must name the color while attempting to ignore word content. The assumption is that a reduced ability to ignore word content will disrupt color-naming performance, and so if anxious individuals have difficulty ignoring the content of the threat words they should display disproportionately long color-naming latencies for such stimuli. Numerous studies employing this task have consistently concluded that, relative to nonanxious individuals, anxious participants selectively attend to the content of more emotionally threatening words, as evidenced by their longer latencies to name the color of such words (cf. Bar-Haim, Lamy, Pergamin, Bakermans-Kranenburg, & van Ijzendoorn, 2007). This effect has been observed in patients suffering from anxiety pathology (El Khoury-Malhame et al., 2011; Wiener, Perloe, Whitton, & Pincus, 2012) as well as in high-trait anxious individuals (Fox, 1993; Krug & Carter, 2010) and in participants experiencing higher levels of current anxious mood due to an impending stressor (Dresler, Meriau, Heekeren, & van der Meer, 2009; Rutherford, MacLeod, & Campbell, 2004).

In the emotional Stroop task, an attentional bias toward threatening information would give rise to impaired task performance when threatening words are present. However, many investigators have noted that such impaired performance by anxious participants in the presence of threatening distracter stimuli need not mean that they selectively attend toward the threatening material. Rather, it has been pointed out that anxiety may be characterized by a greater tendency to "freeze" in the presence of threat, which would disproportionately slow responding on trials in which threat was shown without this reflecting an attentional bias toward such threat (Mogg, Holmes, Garner, & Bradley, 2008). Concerns of this type have led to the development of attentional bias-assessment tasks in which the tendency to selectively attend to threatening information would result in the relative enhancement of performance, rather than impairment of performance, under key experimental conditions. One such assessment approach is the widely used attentional probe task (cf. Cisler & Koster, 2010), which involves the brief, simultaneous presentation of two stimuli—one threat-related (e.g., the word "fear" or a threatening image such as a frowning face) and one threat-unrelated (e.g., the word "book" or a nonthreatening image such as a smiling face). Following the disappearance of this stimulus pair, participants are asked to discern the identity of a small probe that appears where either the threatening or the nonthreatening stimulus was just shown. The assumption is that the probes will be discriminated more rapidly when they are presented in the area of the screen that participants are already attending to. Hence, if anxious individuals do selectively attend toward threatening information, they should show relatively facilitated probe discrimination performance when the probes appear in the vicinity of the threatening members, in contrast to the nonthreatening members, of these stimulus pairs. Using this task, it has been shown that individuals more prone to dispositional anxiety consistently have shorter latencies in detecting probes that appear in the location of threatening stimuli, suggesting an attentional bias favoring threat, whereas nonanxious controls often demonstrate a relative slowing in discriminating probes presented in the location of threat, compared with the time required with nonthreatening stimuli. This effect has been demonstrated in highly anxious members of the general population (Arndt & Fujiwara, 2012) and among individuals with anxiety pathology, including social anxiety disorder (LeMoult & Joormann, 2012), obsessive-compulsive disorder (Cohen, Lachenmeyer, & Springer, 2003), posttraumatic stress disorder (Fani et al., 2012), health anxiety (Jasper & Witthoeft, 2011), and generalized anxiety disorder (Mogg & Bradley, 2005).

Another approach that often has been adopted to demonstrate anxiety-linked attentional bias involves emotional variants of visual search tasks. In these tasks, participants are required to identify a particular type of target stimuli when these are embedded in arrays of background stimuli. Typically, they must search for threatening targets (e.g., threat-related words or angry faces) within arrays of nonthreatening background stimuli (e.g., neutral words or faces) or must search for nonthreatening targets within arrays of threatening background stimuli. Anxious participants show disproportionately good performance on such tasks when searching for threatening targets, consistent with the hypothesis that threat-related information selectively captures their attention (e.g., Hadwin et al., 2003; Miltner, Krieschel, Hecht, Trippe, & Weiss, 2004; Rinck, Reinecke, Ellwart, Heuer, & Becker, 2005). Hence, elevated anxiety results in impaired task performance under those conditions in which an attentional preference for threatening information would be detrimental but enhances task performance under conditions in which such an attentional preference for threatening information would be beneficial.

Much contemporary research has been devoted to establishing the nature of the cognitive mechanisms that give rise to this anxiety-linked attentional bias (Bar-Haim et al., 2007). It would appear that this attentional bias operates quite automatically, as is evidenced by the fact that it continues to be observed even when the opportunity for intentional control of attention is restricted. For example, in some variants of the emotional Stroop task and attentional probe tasks outlined above, the emotional stimuli are exposed too briefly to permit their conscious identification, and yet anxious individuals continue to display patterns of performance that suggest the disproportionate assignment of attention toward the more threatening stimuli (MacLeod & Rutherford, 1992; Mogg & Bradley, 2002). It is not yet clear whether this anxiety-linked attentional bias reflects a heightened tendency to engage attention with threatening information or a difficulty in disengaging attention from threatening stimuli once it has become the focus of attention. Early attempts to differentiate these two facets of attentional selectivity led some investigators to argue in favor of the latter position (e.g., Koster, Crombez, Verschuere, Van Damme, & Wiersema, 2006). However, subsequent work has cast doubt on the veracity of this conclusion, by highlighting the methodological limitations of the techniques employed to distinguish the patterns of selective attentional engagement and disengagement that characterize anxiety (Clarke, MacLeod, & Guastella, in press; Mogg et al., 2008).

While it may take further research to determine the precise mechanisms that underpin anxiety-linked attentional bias, it is clear that attentional bias toward threatening information is particularly evident on materials that closely relate to these anxious individuals' specific domains of concern. Thus, for example, attentional-probe, visual-search, and emotional Stroop tasks have demonstrated that anxious individuals with spider phobia attend specifically to spider-related stimuli (Rinck et al., 2005); those who suffer from social anxiety exhibit biased attentional processing of socially threatening stimuli, such as threatening faces (Mogg & Bradley, 2002); and those with obsessive-compulsive disorder show an attentional preference for threatening material relevant to their domain of concern, such as contamination-related stimuli (Tata, Leibowitz, Prunty, Cameron, & Pickering, 1996). Of specific relevance to the types of anxiety-linked attentional biases likely to influence performance on neurocognitive assessment tasks are those that characterize elevated test anxiety. Participants who report high levels of test anxiety commonly exhibit attentional vigilance for information related to the more negative connotations of assessment when exposed to conditions involving performance evaluation (Putwain, Langdale, Woods, & Nicholson, 2011). This may positively affect performance on tasks that assess the processing of assessment-related stimuli, such as words like "failure." However, on many conventional assessment tasks, which require the processing of only neutral stimulus materials, this increased tendency of attention to be captured by signals relating to potential failure may be more likely to impair overall performance.

PRACTICAL CONSIDERATIONS WHEN ASESSING NEUROCOGNITIVE FUNCTIONING IN ANXIOUS CLIENTS

There are numerous points during and following neurocognitive assessment at which anxiety-linked information-processing biases of the types outlined above could influence outcomes. Cognitive assessment will commonly involve tasks that examine memory, comprehension, and attention, and evidence presented here indicates that at least some of these operations can be biased by the influence of anxiety. In this section we will discuss ways in which these anxiety-linked effects could potentially influence performance on cognitive assessment procedures carried out in a clinical context and will consider what clinicians should perhaps bear in mind when delivering such assessment to anxious clients.

Even the initial assessment of a client's clinical history will be open to the influence of anxiety-linked cognitive bias. As we have reviewed earlier, the experimental evidence provides no compelling basis to anticipate that anxiety will directly influence selective memory retrieval during such assessment. It is not unlikely that dispositionally anxious individuals may report having experienced more negative life events, but this reflects the genuinely elevated probability that they do indeed have such a history (Spinhoven et al., 2010), rather than the operation of an anxiety-linked retrieval bias. However, when past events or experiences can be subjectively construed in alternative ways, as often is the case, then assessors should be mindful that anxiety can be expected to influence how these events and experiences are interpreted and use caution in their assessment. For example, when individuals experience anxiety over the possibility that they may be suffering from neurological dysfunction, it is not unlikely that their consequently heightened tendency to resolve ambiguity in threatening ways could readily contribute to benign instances of cognitive errors being misconstrued as signs of cognitive impairment and being reported as such to the assessing clinician. Hence, an individual who is anxious about the possibility of having developed a degenerative memory condition may interpret benign instances of everyday forgetfulness as evidence for declining memory abilities and report a history indicative of memory dysfunction. Particularly given that emotional memories tend to be better recalled (Zimmerman & Kelley, 2010), such instances of negative interpretation could result in patterns of reporting that wrongly suggest evidence of neuropathology. Indeed, research has demonstrated that higher anxiety and negative affect more generally are associated with the tendency to subjectively report more episodes of forgetting in the absence of any objective cognitive impairment (Dux et al., 2008). Hence it is especially important when dealing with anxious clients to ensure that self-report is supplemented by corroborating information from other sources less susceptible to the potential impact of anxiety-linked interpretive bias, such as independent caregivers.

Memory tasks often feature in neuropsychological test batteries. As long as such memory tasks employ unambiguous stimuli unlikely to invite alternative interpretive options, then even if such material is emotional toned, there is no compelling evidence to suggest that anxiety will systematically bias which stimuli are better retrieved. Rather, the evidence suggests that unambiguous material of any emotional valence (positive, negative, or neutral) is unlikely to selectively enhance or impede recall for anxious individuals. In contrast, there is a possibility that memory would be enhanced or impaired if information encountered during the testing procedure can be interpreted in a positive or negative way. In such instances, there is a greater prospect that anxiety could influence interpretation in ways that would affect the recall of such information. For example, if ambiguous material in a memory test is interpreted negatively because of the operation of anxiety-linked interpretive bias, then it may become more distinctly memorable due to its increased emotionality. The resulting enhanced retrieval of such information could, in principle, obscure underlying deficits in memory performance. To limit the potential influence of such anxiety-linked bias on memory task performance, one would ideally use unemotional and unambiguous material in these tests.

It is important to bear in mind, however, that even when the task-relevant information presented in neurocognitive tests is unambiguous, emotionally neutral, and unrelated to anxious concerns, there is always task-irrelevant information available for processing, which anxious participants may find emotional and of relevance to their concerns. Thus, for example, across most assessment procedures participants are likely to make some errors, and anxiety may influence how clients appraise the significance and implications of their errors. If anxious individuals construe such failures more negatively or infer that they will be judged poorly because of these mistakes, the selective investment of processing resources in sustaining rumination about these task-irrelevant but anxiety-relevant concerns could reasonably be expected to impair performance on the primary assessment task. Hence anxious participants may display a performance decrement due to the cognitive costs associated with task-irrelevant rumination, without this reflecting a genuine deficit in neurocognitive functioning.

Tasks assessing attention and executive control commonly require participants to maintain attentional focus on a central task (e.g., the Stroop test; Dodrill, 1978) or to maintain different pieces of information within current cognitive operations (e.g., Trail Making Test; Reitan, 1971) while suppressing the processing of task-irrelevant information. Clearly, anxiety would likely either enhance or impair performance on such tasks, depending on whether the focal information requiring their attention, or the irrelevant information that must be ignored, is anxiety-relevant in content. Furthermore, the range of information that they find relevant to their anxious concerns need not be universally considered threatening but will depend on the specific concerns of individual participants. As reviewed earlier, attentional bias is evident for information related to anxious individuals' idiosyncratic concerns (e.g., Putwain et al., 2011; Tata et al., 1996). Just as the word "exam" is likely to be relevant to the concerns of an anxious student studying for a major test, so it could reasonably be expected that words such as "forget" or "memory" may be relevant to the concerns of anxious clients who fear that they may be suffering from a neuropsychological impairment.

Even when materials used in tasks assessing attentional/executive control are emotionally neutral in content, performance may be impaired when internally generated emotional content competes for the attention of anxious participants. Such individuals are disproportionately inclined to both generate negative ideation and have their attention captured by such ideation, resulting in the commonly documented phenomenon of intrusive worry (Borkovec, 1994). Some of the performance deficits attributable to anxiety will reflect the tendency for attention to be shifted from task-relevant information toward this task-irrelevant, self-generated cognitive stream of negatively toned cognition. To determine whether observed cognitive impairments may be attributable to the disrupting influence of anxiety-related worry, it may be prudent to directly assess worry when carrying out such cognitive assessment, for example, by using the recently validated Past Day version of the Penn State Worry Questionnaire (Joos et al., 2012). If cognitive deficits are observed in the absence of elevated worry, then this would mitigate against the possibility that such deficits reflect impaired performance as a consequence of distraction from self-generated negative cognition of this type.

Few neurocognitive tasks are designed to directly assess the interpretation of ambiguous information, unlike many of the tests employed by our more psychodynamically oriented forebears (e.g., the Rorschach Task and the Thematic Apperception Task). Although some of these tests do assess high-level comprehension (e.g., word association, similarities), typically the stimulus materials themselves are unambiguous, reducing the potential impact of anxiety-linked interpretive bias on test performance. Nevertheless, many incidental aspects of the assessment process, including some types of information that may come from the examiner, have the potential to introduce ambiguity and so may be differentially interpreted as a function of anxiety in ways that could influence performance. For example, informal nonspecific feedback given by the assessor to encourage continued effort, including comments such as "you're doing okay" or "just do your best" may lend themselves to differential interpretation, such that anxious participants could be overly inclined to construe these comments as discouraging. The potential impact of such an anxiety-linked interpretive bias could be reduced by providing feedback during task performance in a highly structured and formal manner, though it may be better to follow the advice of Lezak (1995) and simply provide no feedback during testing. Even when assessors intend to provide no feedback, their nonverbal signals could be sufficiently ambiguous to be interpreted negatively by anxious clients. Options to minimize the influence of anxiety-linked biases in the interpretation of such nonverbal cues may be as simple as arranging seating such that clients will less exposed to the assessor's facial expressions. However, the increasing availability of automated variants of assessment tasks, such as computer-delivered tests (cf. Kane & Reeves, 1997), will also serve to reduce the degree to which anxiety-linked interpretive bias can affect task performance by influencing how clients construe potentially ambiguous aspects of their interactions with an assessor.

Of course, ultimately the outcomes of neurocognitive assessment must be communicated to clients. This critical component of the assessment process should give the client insight into their particular problem and should convey recommendations concerning how to compensate for any forms of observed cognitive impairment (Lezak, 1995). Here, too, it is important for the clinician to recognize that client anxiety can be expected to distort their interpretation of the information they are given. The potential for misinterpretation is especially great given that it can reasonably be expected that most clients will be highly apprehensive at this point. Hence their interpretations are likely to favor threatening resolutions of any ambiguity they encounter in the information given. To minimize such ambiguity and reduce the prospect that elevated anxiety could compromise the value of this crucial final step of the assessment process, clinicians should avoid the use of jargon when communicating their findings and recommendations and should ensure that written summary feedback in lay terms is provided for reference. Ideally, a family member, friend or caregiver would receive this information together with the client and thus be in a position to clarify aspects of the feedback that an overly anxious client may subsequently misconstrue.

CLOSING COMMENTS

Laboratory-based research investigating the association between cognition and emotion has resulted in a good understanding of the patterns of processing selectivity that characterize heightened anxiety. In this chapter we have sought to review the evidence for anxiety-linked biases in attentional, interpretive, and memory functioning and to illustrate how these biases can be assessed. Table 5.1 summarizes these assessment procedures and indicates the degree of support for each form of cognitive bias by listing the approximate number of studies providing evidence of each anxiety-linked effect. While this summary table should be used in conjunction with the critical review provided within the preceding sections, it clearly demonstrates that anxiety is characterized by reliable patterns of selective information processing, generally operating to favor negative information.

Nevertheless, very little research has yet directly examined the ways in which such anxiety-linked cognitive biases affect performance on the types of

Table 5.1 MEASURES USED TO ASSESS SECONDARY FACTORS INVOLVING ANXIETY-LINKED COGNITIVE BIAS

Type of Cognitive Bias	Assessment Procedure	Number of Studies Showing Significant Association with Anxiety
Memory bias	Free recall of negative and non-native stimuli	*
	Recognition/cued recall	*
	Implicit memory	*
Interpretive bias	Self-reported interpretation of scenarios	****
	Homophone spelling	***
	Ambiguous scenario—recognition memory	**
	Ambiguous scenario/stimulus priming	**
	Classification of facial expressions	**
	Word-sentence association	*
Attentional bias	Emotional Stroop task	*****
	Attentional probe task	****
	Visual search task	**
	Emotional spatial cueing task	**

*1–5 studies.
**6–10 studies.
***11–20 studies.
****21–49 studies.
*****50+ studies.

neuropsychological testing commonly delivered in clinical settings. The time is right for a concerted effort to remedy this situation by directly investigating the contributions made by anxious client's biases in attention, interpretation, and memory to their performance on neurocognitive assessment tasks. Work of this type can be expected to constructively bridge theoretical and applied facets of prior cognition and emotion research and should be driven by the objective of developing assessment tasks that can sensitively distinguish the presence of neuropsychological impairment from the patterns of performance that instead are indicative of elevated anxiety. We hope that this review and our reflections concerning how anxiety might be expected to bear on the performance of clients undergoing neurocognitive assessment may make a useful contribution to this important future endeavor.

ACKNOWLEDGMENT

Preparation of this chapter was partially supported by Australian Research Council grant DP0879589.

References

Amir, N., Beard, C., & Przeworski, A. (2005). Resolving ambiguity: The effect of experience on interpretation of ambiguous events in generalized social phobia. *Journal of Abnormal Psychology, 114*, 402–408.

Amir, N., Bower, E., Briks, J., & Freshman, M. (2003). Implicit memory for negative and positive social information in individuals with and without social anxiety. *Cognition and Emotion, 17*, 567–583.

Arndt, J. E., & Fujiwara, E. (2012). Attentional bias towards angry faces in trait-reappraisal. *Personality and Individual Differences, 52*, 61–66.

Bar-Haim, Y., Lamy, D., Pergamin, L., Bakermans-Kranenburg, M. J., & van Ijzendoorn, M. H. (2007). Threat-related attentional bias in anxious and nonanxious individuals: A meta-analytic study. *Psychological Bulletin, 133*, 1–24.

Barlow, D. H. (2002). *Anxiety and its disorders: The nature and treatment of anxiety and panic* (2nd ed.). New York: Guilford Press.

Baumeister, R. F., Vohs, K. D., DeWall, C. N., & Zhang, L. (2007). How emotion shapes behavior: Feedback, anticipation, and reflection, rather than direct causation. *Personality and Social Psychology Review, 11*, 167–203.

Beck, A. T., & Clark, D. A. (1997). An information processing model of anxiety: Automatic and strategic processes. *Behaviour Research and Therapy, 35*, 49–58.

Beck, A. T., Laude, R., & Bohnert, M. (1974). Ideational components of anxiety neurosis. *Archives of General Psychiatry, 31*, 319–325.

Beck, J., Stanley, M. A., Averill, P. M., Baldwin, L. E., & Deagle, E. A. (1992). Attention and memory for threat in panic disorder. *Behaviour Research and Therapy, 30*, 619–629.

Becker, E. S., Rinck, M., & Margraf, J. (1994). Memory bias in panic disorder. *Journal of Abnormal Psychology, 103*, 396–399.

Blanchette, I., & Richards, A. (2010). The influence of affect on higher level cognition: A review of research on interpretation, judgement, decision making and reasoning. *Cognition & Emotion, 24*, 561–595.

Borkovec, T. (1994). The nature, functions and origins of worry. In G. Davey & F. Tallis (Eds.), *Worrying: Perspectives on theory, assessment and treatment*. Chichester, England: Wiley.

Broeren, S., Muris, P., Bouwmeester, S., van der Heijden, K. B., & Abee, A. (2011). The role of repetitive negative thoughts in the vulnerability for emotional problems in non-clinical children. *Journal of Child and Family Studies, 20*, 135–148.

Burke, M., & Mathews, A. (1992). Autobiographical memory and clinical anxiety. *Cognition and Emotion, 6*, 23–35.

Butler, G., & Mathews, A. (1987). Anticipatory anxiety and risk perception. *Cognitive Therapy and Research, 11*, 551–565.

Cassady, J. C. (2004). The influence of cognitive test anxiety across the learning–testing cycle. *Learning and Instruction, 14*, 569–592.

Cisler, J. M., & Koster, E. H. (2010). Mechanisms of attentional biases towards threat in anxiety disorders: An integrative review. *Clinical Psychology Review, 30*, 203–216.

Clarke, P. J. F., MacLeod, C., & Guastella, A. J. (in press). Assessing the role of spatial engagement and disengagement of attention in anxiety-linked attentional bias: A critique of current paradigms and suggestions for future research directions. *Anxiety, Stress and Coping*.

Cloitre, M., Shear, M., Cancienne, J., & Zeitlin, S. B. (1994). Implicit and explicit memory for catastrophic associations to bodily sensation words in panic disorder. *Cognitive Therapy and Research, 18*, 225–240.

Cohen, Y., Lachenmeyer, J. R., & Springer, C. (2003). Anxiety and selective attention in obsessive-compulsive disorder. *Behaviour Research and Therapy, 41*, 1311–1323.

Coles, M. E., & Heimberg, R. G. (2002). Memory biases in the anxiety disorders: Current status. *Clinical Psychology Review, 22*, 587–627.

Constans, J. I., Penn, D. L., Ihen, G. H., & Hope, D. A. (1999). Interpretive biases for ambiguous stimuli in social anxiety. *Behaviour Research and Therapy, 37*, 643–651.

Dodrill, C. B. (1978). A neuropsychological battery for epilepsy. *Epilepsia, 19*, 611–623.

Dresler, T., Meriau, K., Heekeren, H. R., & van der Meer, E. (2009). Emotional Stroop task: Effect of word arousal and subject anxiety on emotional interference. *Psychological Research-Psychologische Forschung, 73*, 364–371.

Dux, M. C., Woodard, J. L., Calamari, J. E., Messina, M., Arora, S., Chik, H., et al. (2008). The moderating role of negative affect on objective verbal memory performance and subjective memory complaints in healthy older adults. *Journal of the International Neuropsychological Society, 14*, 327–336.

Easterbrook, J. (1959). The effect of emotion on cue utilization and the organization of behavior. *Psychological Review, 66*, 183–201.

Ehlers, A., Margraf, J., Davies, S., & Roth, W. T. (1988). Selective processing of threat cues in subjects with panic attacks. *Cognition & Emotion, 2*, 201–219.

El Khoury-Malhame, M., Lanteaume, L., Beetz, E. M., Roques, J., Reynaud, E., Samuelian, J. C., et al. (2011). Attentional bias in post-traumatic stress disorder diminishes after symptom amelioration. *Behaviour Research and Therapy, 49*, 796–801.

Engelhard, I. M., de Jong, P. J., van den Hout, M. A., & van Overveld, M. (2009). Expectancy bias and the persistence of posttraumatic stress. *Behaviour Research and Therapy, 47*, 887–892.

Eysenck, M. W. (1979). Anxiety, learning, and memory: A reconceptualization. *Journal of Research in Personality, 13*, 363–385.

Eysenck, M. W. (1982). *Attentional and arousal: Cognition and performance*. Berlin: Springer.

Eysenck, M. W. (1988). Anxiety and attention. *Anxiety Research, 1*, 9–15.

Eysenck, M. W. (1992). *Anxiety: The cognitive perspective*. Hove, England: Erlbaum.

Eysenck, M. W., & Calvo, M. G. (1992). Anxiety and performance: The processing efficiency theory. *Cognition & Emotion, 6*, 409–434.

Eysenck, M. W., Derakshan, N., Santos, R., & Calvo, M. G. (2007). Anxiety and cognitive performance: Attentional control theory. *Emotion, 7*, 336–353.

Fani, N., Tone, E. B., Phifer, J., Norrholm, S. D., Bradley, B., Ressler, K. J., et al. (2012). Attention bias toward threat is associated with exaggerated fear expression and impaired extinction in PTSD. *Psychological Medicine, 42*, 533–543.

Fox, E. (1993). Attentional bias in anxiety: Selective or not? *Behaviour Research and Therapy, 31*, 487–493.

Frewen, P. A., Evans, E. M., Maraj, N., Dozois, D. J., & Partridge, K. (2008). Letting go: Mindfulness and negative automatic thinking. *Cognitive Therapy and Research, 32*, 758–774.

Gifford, S., Reynolds, S., Bell, S., & Wilson, C. (2008). Threat interpretation bias in anxious children and their mothers. *Cognition & Emotion, 22*, 497–508.

Graf, P., & Mandler, G. (1984). Activation makes words more accessible, but not necessarily more retrievable. *Journal of Verbal Learning and Verbal Behavior, 23*, 553–568.

Hadwin, J. A., Donnelly, N., French, C. C., Richards, A., Watts, A., & Daley, D. (2003). The influence of children's self-report trait anxiety and depression on visual search for emotional faces. *Journal of Child Psychology & Psychiatry & Allied Disciplines, 44*, 432–444.

Hallion, L. S., & Ruscio, A. M. (2011). A meta-analysis of the effect of cognitive bias modification on anxiety and depression. *Psychological Bulletin, 137*, 940–958..

Hazlett-Stevens, H., & Borkovec, T. D. (2004). Interpretive cues and ambiguity in generalized anxiety disorder. *Behaviour Research and Therapy, 42*, 881–892.

Hibbert, G. A. (1984). Ideational components of anxiety: Their origin and content. *British Journal of Psychiatry, 144*, 618–624.

Hirsch, C. R., Mathews, A., Clark, D. M., Williams, R., & Morrison, J. A. (2006). The causal role of negative imagery in social anxiety: A test in confident public speakers. *Journal of Behavior Therapy and Experimental Psychiatry, 37*, 159–170.

Hofmann, S. G., Ellard, K. K., & Siegle, G. J. (2012). Neurobiological correlates of cognitions in fear and anxiety: A cognitive-neurobiological information-processing model. *Cognition & Emotion, 26*, 282–299.

Hong, R. Y. (2010). Neuroticism, anxiety sensitivity thoughts, and anxiety symptomatology: Insights from an experience-sampling approach. *Cognitive Therapy and Research, 34*, 254–262.

Jasper, F., & Witthoeft, M. (2011). Health anxiety and attentional bias: The time course of vigilance and avoidance in light of pictorial illness information. *Journal of Anxiety Disorders, 25*, 1131–1138.

Joos, E., Vansteenwegen, D., Brunfaut, E., Bastiaens, T., Demyttenaere, K., Pieters, G., et al. (2012). The Penn State Worry Questionnaire-Past Day: Development and validation of a measure assessing daily levels of worry. *Journal of Psychopathology and Behavioral Assessment, 34*, 35–47.

Kane, R. L., & Reeves, D. L. (1997). Computerized test batteries. In A. M. Horton, D. Wedding, & J. Webster (Eds.), *The neuropsychology handbook*. New York: Springer.

Kendall, P. C., & Treadwell, K. R. (2007). The role of self-statements as a mediator in treatment for youth with anxiety disorders. *Journal of Consulting and Clinical Psychology, 75*, 380–389.

Koster, E. H., Crombez, G., Verschuere, B., Van Damme, S., & Wiersema, J. R. (2006). Components of attentional bias to threat in high trait anxiety: Facilitated engagement, impaired disengagement, and attentional avoidance. *Behaviour Research and Therapy, 44,* 1757–1771.

Krug, M. K., & Carter, C. S. (2010). Adding fear to conflict: A general purpose cognitive control network is modulated by trait anxiety. *Cognitive Affective & Behavioral Neuroscience, 10,* 357–371.

LeMoult, J., & Joormann, J. (2012). Attention and memory biases in social anxiety disorder: The role of comorbid depression. *Cognitive Therapy and Research, 36,* 47–57.

Lezak, M. D. (1995). *Neuropsychological assessment* (3rd ed.). Oxford: Oxford University Press.

Loebner, M., Luppa, M., Matschinger, H., Konnopka, A., Meisel, H. J., Guenther, L., et al. (2012). The course of depression and anxiety in patients undergoing disc surgery: A longitudinal observational study. *Journal of Psychosomatic Research, 72,* 185–194.

MacLeod, C., & McLaughlin, K. (1995). Implicit and explicit memory bias in anxiety: A conceptual replication. *Behaviour Research and Therapy, 33,* 1–14.

MacLeod, C., & Rutherford, E. M. (1992). Anxiety and the selective processing of emotional information: Mediating roles of awareness, trait and state variables, and personal relevance of stimulus materials. *Behaviour Research & Therapy, 30,* 479–491.

Mathews, A., & MacLeod, C. (1985). Selective processing of threat cues in anxiety states. *Behaviour Research & Therapy, 23,* 563–569.

Mathews, A., Mogg, K., Kentish, J., & Eysenck, M. (1995). Effect of psychological treatment on cognitive bias in generalized anxiety disorder. *Behaviour Research & Therapy, 33,* 293–303.

Mathews, A., Mogg, K., May, J., & Eysenck, M. (1989). Implicit and explicit memory bias in anxiety. *Journal of Abnormal Psychology, 98,* 236–240.

McCabe, R. E. (1999). Implicit and explicit memory for threat words in high- and low-anxiety-sensitive participants. *Cognitive Therapy and Research, 23,* 21–38.

McNally, R. J., & Foa, E. B. (1987). Cognition and agoraphobia: Bias in the interpretation of threat. *Cognitive Therapy and Research, 11,* 567–581.

Miltner, W. H., Krieschel, S., Hecht, H., Trippe, R., & Weiss, T. (2004). Eye movements and behavioral responses to threatening and nonthreatening stimuli during visual search in phobic and nonphobic subjects. *Emotion, 4,* 323–339.

Mitte, K. (2008). Memory bias for threatening information in anxiety and anxiety disorders: A meta-analytic review. *Psychological Bulletin, 134,* 886–911.

Mogg, K., & Bradley, B. P. (1998). A cognitive-motivational analysis of anxiety. *Behaviour Research and Therapy, 36,* 809–848.

Mogg, K., & Bradley, B. P. (2002). Selective orienting of attention to masked threat faces in social anxiety. *Behaviour Research and Therapy, 40,* 1403–1414.

Mogg, K., & Bradley, B. P. (2005). Attentional bias in generalized anxiety disorder versus depressive disorder. *Cognitive Therapy and Research, 29,* 29–45.

Mogg, K., Bradley, B. P., Miller, T., Potts, H., Glenwright, J., & Kentish, J. (1994). Interpretation of homophones related to threat: Anxiety or response bias effects? *Cognitive Therapy and Research, 18,* 461–477.

Mogg, K., Holmes, A., Garner, M., & Bradley, B. P. (2008). Effects of threat cues on attentional shifting, disengagement and response slowing in anxious individuals. *Behaviour Research and Therapy, 46,* 656–667.

Mogg, K., & Mathews, A. (1990). Is there a self-referent mood-congruent recall bias in anxiety? *Behaviour Research and Therapy, 28,* 91–92.

Mogg, K., Mathews, A., & Weinman, J. (1989). Selective processing of threat cues in anxiety states: A replication. *Behaviour Research and Therapy, 27*, 317–323.

Nelson, E. A., Lickel, J. J., Sy, J. T., Dixon, L. J., & Deacon, B. J. (2010). Probability and cost biases in social phobia: Nature, specificity, and relationship to treatment outcome. *Journal of Cognitive Psychotherapy, 24*, 213–228.

Niles, A. N., Lebeau, R. T., Liao, B., Glenn, D. E., & Craske, M. G. (2012). Dimensional indicators of generalized anxiety disorder severity for DSM-V. *Journal of Anxiety Disorders, 26*, 279–286.

Nugent, K., & Mineka, S. (1994). The effect of high and low trait anxiety on implicit and explicit memory tasks. *Cognition and Emotion, 8*, 147–163.

Nunn, J. D., Stevenson, R. J., & Whalan, G. (1984). Selective memory effects in agoraphobic patients. *British Journal of Clinical Psychology, 23*, 195–201.

O'Toole, M. S., & Pedersen, A. D. (2011). A systematic review of neuropsychological performance in social anxiety disorder. *Nordic Journal of Psychiatry, 65*, 147–161.

Oldenburg, C., Lundh, L.-G., & Kivisto, P. (2002). Explicit and implicit memory, trait anxiety, and repressive coping style. *Personality and Individual Differences, 32*, 107–119.

Pessoa, L. (2009). How do emotion and motivation direct executive control? *Trends in Cognitive Sciences, 13*, 160–166.

Putwain, D. W., Langdale, H. C., Woods, K. A., & Nicholson, L. J. (2011). Developing and piloting a Dot-Probe measure of attentional bias for test anxiety. *Learning and Individual Differences, 21*, 478–482.

Rapee, R. M. (1994). Failure to replicate a memory bias in panic disorder. *Journal of Anxiety Disorders, 8*, 291–300.

Reitan, R. M. (1971). Trail Making Test results for normal and brain-damaged children. *Perceptual and Motor Skills, 33*, 575–581.

Rinck, M., Reinecke, A., Ellwart, T., Heuer, K., & Becker, E. S. (2005). Speeded detection and increased distraction in fear of spiders: Evidence from eye movements. *Journal of Abnormal Psychology, 114*, 235–248.

Rutherford, E. M., MacLeod, C., & Campbell, L. W. (2004). Negative selectivity effects and emotional selectivity effects in anxiety: Differential attentional correlates of state and trait variables. *Cognition & Emotion, 18*, 711–720.

Sewitch, T., & Kirsch, I. (1984). The cognitive content of anxiety: Naturalistic evidence for the predominance of threat-related thoughts. *Cognitive Therapy and Research, 8*, 49–58.

Skaali, T., Fossa, S. D., Andersson, S., Langberg, C. W., Lehne, G., & Dahl, A. A. (2011). Is psychological distress in men recently diagnosed with testicular cancer associated with their neuropsychological test performance? *Psycho-Oncology, 20*, 369–377.

Spence, J. T., & Spence, K. W. (1966). The motivational components of manifest anxiety: Drive and drive stimuli. In C. D. Spielberger (Ed.), *Anxiety and behaviour.* London: Academic Press.

Spinhoven, P., Elzinga, B. M., Hovens, J. G., Roelofs, K., Zitman, F. G., van Oppen, P., et al. (2010). The specificity of childhood adversities and negative life events across the life span to anxiety and depressive disorders. *Journal of Affective Disorders, 126*, 103–112.

Stroop, J. (1938). Factors affecting speed in serial verbal reactions. *Psychological Monographs, 50*, 38–48.

Talmi, D., Luk, B. T., McGarry, L. M., & Moscovitch, M. (2007). The contribution of relatedness and distinctiveness to emotionally-enhanced memory. *Journal of Memory and Language, 56*, 555–574.

Tata, P. R., Leibowitz, J. A., Prunty, M. J., Cameron, M., & Pickering, A. D. (1996). Attentional bias in obsessional compulsive disorder. *Behaviour Research and Therapy, 34,* 53–60.

Wiener, C., Perloe, A., Whitton, S., & Pincus, D. (2012). Attentional bias in adolescents with panic disorder: Changes over an 8-day intensive treatment program. *Behavioural and Cognitive Psychotherapy, 40,* 193–204.

Williams, J. M. G., Watts, F. N., MacLeod, C., & Mathews, A. (1988). *Cognitive psychology and emotional disorders.* Chichester, UK: Wiley.

Williams, J. M. G., Watts, F. N., MacLeod, C., & Mathews, A. (1997). *Cognitive psychology and emotional disorders* (2nd ed.). Chichester, UK: Wiley.

Witheridge, K. S., Cabral, C. M., & Rector, N. A. (2010). Examining autobiographical memory content in patients with depression and anxiety disorders. *Cognitive Behaviour Therapy, 39,* 302–310.

Zimmerman, C. A., & Kelley, C. M. (2010). "I'll remember this!" Effects of emotionality on memory predictions versus memory performance. *Journal of Memory and Language, 62,* 240–253.

6

Fatigue: Its Influence on Cognition and Assessment

LAUREN B. STROBER, AND JOHN DELUCA

Fatigue is one of the most common symptom observed following numerous medical, neurological, and psychological conditions. It is also commonly experienced in everyday life, typically as a result of an illness, a stressful life event, excessive muscular expenditure, or sustained performance. Yet, despite its high prevalence, fatigue is a nonspecific, poorly described, and inadequately understood symptom observed by both laypeople and medical professionals. Physiologically, fatigue can be defined as reduced force production, loss of exercise capacity, increased sense of effort or over perception of force, or decreased power (Davis & Walsh, 2010). However, it is the subjective nature of fatigue which has eluded comprehension, scientific inquiry, and medical understanding. Subjectively, fatigued individuals use the following terms to describe their experience: *tired, exhausted, lacking in energy, drowsy, feelings of weakness, wiped out, uninterested, sleepy,* or *feeling as if everything is an effort,* yet these terms are clearly not synonymous and can be representative of a host of factors. Additionally, while an acute sense of fatigue is common in the general population, chronic fatigue, which is frequent among many disorders, is a much more disabling and distressing symptom. It is this subjective sense of chronic fatigue that is frequently encountered in clinical practice and will serve as the primary focus of this chapter.

Despite being a hallmark of many psychological, medical, and neurological conditions commonly seen by neuropsychologists, fatigue remains a nebulous construct that is poorly understood, defined, assessed, and treated. In general, our understanding of fatigue has advanced little over the past 100 years despite innumerable efforts (DeLuca, 2005b). This lack of progress may have been foreseen by Muscio in 1921, when he recommended that we abandon the study of fatigue all together, having been convinced of the inability to ever measure fatigue adequately (Muscio, 1921). In fact, in Muscio's 1921 article, "Is a Fatigue Test Possible," he stated:

> The conditions of experimentation with the purpose of finding a fatigue test are two:
>
> (a) That we know what we mean by fatigue;
> (b) That we have some method other than the use of a suggested fatigue test by which we can know that different degrees of fatigue are present at certain different times.
>
> That the first of these conditions is necessary is self-evident: it is obviously absurd to set about finding a test of an undefined entity. (p. 31)

Nearly a century later, those attempting to study fatigue have found themselves still grappling with the same challenges and making strikingly similar statements following such pursuits:

> Before a concept can be measured, it must be defined, and before a definition can be agreed, there must exist an instrument for assessing phenomenology. There is unfortunately no "gold standard" for fatigue, nor is there ever likely to be. (Dittner, Wessely, & Brown, 2004, p. 166)

Despite learning relatively little over the past century or so and lacking a definitive definition of fatigue, the issue of fatigue and its influence on cognition remains; it is the primary focus of this chapter. We begin discussing the importance of assessing fatigue and the hurdles in doing so, particularly when using self-report. Next, we offer a brief review of what we know about fatigue—its prevalence and impact on various disorders, its conceptualization and models, and our current understanding of how fatigue may influence cognition, so-called cognitive fatigue. A review of neuroimaging findings of fatigue is also provided, followed by a brief synopsis regarding the use of self-report fatigue instruments and their utility among disorders commonly seen by neuropsychologists. Case examples pertaining to the influence of fatigue on neuropsychological test performance are then provided. Finally, we make a few suggestions as to where the field may need to go in hopes of ever fully appreciating fatigue.

SELF-REPORTED FATIGUE AND COGNITION: CONSIDERATIONS FOR THE CLINICIAN

The subjective feeling of cognitive or mental fatigue experienced in the clinical setting is presumed to influence cognitive performance. Lezak (1995) recommends that individuals be afforded frequent rest periods during an evaluation, that more difficult tests be administered early on in the session, and that shortening or even discontinuing a session be done when patients report or exhibit significant fatigue. She also goes on to say, "In arranging [a] test time, the patient's daily schedule must be considered if the effects of fatigue are to be kept minimal. When necessary, the examiner may insist that the patient take a nap before being tested." This purported detrimental effect of fatigue on neuropsychological performance is taught in training programs. Practitioners are trained to routinely inquire about their patients' level of fatigue throughout an evaluation. Additionally, mention of the patient's level of arousal and fatigue is customary on neuropsychological reports and is taken into account in the final interpretation of test findings. However, what do we really know about the information we are obtaining when we ask about a patients' fatigue? Are we possibly asking about a patient's motivation to continue (which may have nothing to do with fatigue), or if they feel tired (which presumably affects performance)? What we will emphasize in this chapter is that fatigue is a complex construct, and that simple self-report assessments may yield less than we think.

Fatigue is not a unitary construct but, rather, multidimensional, rendering accurate assessment by practitioners a difficult challenge. Back in 1904, Mosso described fatigue as having four components: (1) behavior (i.e., he believed that it was associated with performance decrement); (2) a feeling state (subjective state); (3) a mechanism or intervening variable; and (4) context (e.g., environment, attitudes, culture). His research on fatigue demonstrated that all components need to be taken into consideration when fully appreciating the experience of fatigue and its effects. However, most research as well as clinical assessment has focused primarily on only one of these components—the feeling state, that is, the patient's self-report. As we will see, a patient's feeling of fatigue is an amalgam of a host of factors, rendering a simple self-report score difficult to comprehend. Therefore, before discussing fatigue and its influence on cognition, we will first address the question of what self-reported fatigue tells us about the patient.

Briefly, the findings to date are as follows: (1) self-reported fatigue correlates poorly with objective markers of fatigue; (2) self-reported fatigue has shown an inconsistent association with cognitive performance; and (3) self-reported fatigue is consistently correlated with a host of other factors and outcomes. These factors are important to our patients and our assessments, but they may blur our assessment of fatigue and, consequently, its influence on cognition. Hence, while fatigue may affect cognition, it cannot simply be assumed unless the numerous other components reflected in one's self-report are also considered or ruled out.

CORRELATES OF SELF-REPORTED FATIGUE: WHAT DOES IT TELL US?

Self-reported fatigue correlates poorly with objective markers of fatigue

For over 100 years, numerous studies have shown that subjective, self-reported fatigue does not consistently correlate with objective markers of fatigue. For instance, Paul, Beatty, Schneider, Blanco, and Hames (1998) demonstrated that while individuals with multiple sclerosis (MS) reported greater physical and cognitive fatigue following a cognitive test battery, their objective performance on both physical and cognitive measures (e.g., grip strength, neuropsychological tests) were unchanged from baseline. Reports of subjective fatigue have also failed to show a correlation with muscular endurance in individuals with brain injury (Walker, Cardenas, Guthrie, McLean, & Brooke, 1991). This lack of a relationship between self-report and behavior is perhaps the most consistent research finding regarding fatigue over the last 100 years or so.

Self-reported fatigue is inconsistently related to cognitive performance

Under fatiguing conditions, performance sometimes declines, sometimes remains unchanged, or sometimes even increases as time on task increases. Nonetheless, cognitive fatigue remains an issue of critical importance in the psychological laboratory, the school, the workplace, and the clinic. (Ackerman, 2011, p. 3)

The notion that self-reported fatigue inevitably leads to performance decrements is simplistic and wrong. It stems from research on muscle fatigue where a clear performance decrement is observed with continual repetitive movement. However, its generalization to cognition has not been established. This was exemplified in Davis' (1946) "Cambridge Cockpit" study in which pilots underwent a simulated exercise on instrument training, revealing three contrasting patterns. One group showed no difference in performance over the experiment; one group "withdrew" in the face of a fatiguing condition and subsequently lowered their standards of performance; and one group "overreacted" to the situation and increased their effort and arousal during the task (Davis, 1946). Similar results have been reported numerous times over the years (see Ackerman & Kanfer, 2009). Reasons for the inconsistent relationship between self-reported fatigue and cognition include, but are not limited to, (1) human differences in motivation, personality, or affect, as exemplified in the Davis (1946) study; (2) the use of varying self-report fatigue measures that assess the impact of fatigue on day-to-day functioning as opposed to momentary influences; (3) the use of cognitive tests that may not be most sensitive to fatigue; and (4) the use of varying procedures in which participants are purported to be "fatigued." Regardless of the exact reason, the relationship between self-reported fatigue and cognition is inconsistent, at best.

This lack of a relationship between self-reported fatigue and cognition has also been shown numerous times in clinical samples. For instance, in MS, self-reported, subjective fatigue has been shown to have no relationship to declines in working memory (Johnson, Lange, DeLuca, Korn, & Natelson, 1997), short-term memory (Johnson, DeLuca, Diamond, & Natelson, 1998), executive function or complex attention (Krupp & Elkins, 2000; Rao, Leo, Bernardin, & Unverzagt, 1991), vigilance (Paul et al., 1998), verbal fluency (Rao et al., 1991), or verbal memory (Krupp & Elkins, 2000; Paul et al., 1998; Schwartz, Coulthard-Morris, & Zeng, 1996). More recently, Morrow, Weinstock-Guttman, Munschauer, Hojnacki, and Benedict (2009) examined the relationship between self-reported fatigue and cognitive performance during one of the most widely used neuropsychological test batteries in MS. They concluded that reports of fatigue were unrelated to performance on any of these measures. Among individuals with traumatic brain injury (TBI) it has also been noted that self-reported fatigue and cognitive performance are fairly independent of one another (Azouvi et al., 2004; Borgaro, Baker, Wethe, Prigatano, & Kwasnica, 2005; Brouwer & van Wolffelaar, 1985).

A novel approach taken to examine the role of self-reported fatigue and performance on cognitive tasks was taken by Parmenter, Denney, and Lynch (2003). These investigators reasoned that if fatigue affected cognitive performance, then individuals should perform worse when actually experiencing fatigue. They asked individuals with MS to identify their "highest" and "lowest" times of fatigue and subsequently tested cognitive performance during both time periods, one week apart. While patients consistently reported greater fatigue during their "high" fatigue session, there were no significant effects of fatigue found on any of the cognitive measures (Parmenter et al., 2003). Nonetheless, despite the abundant evidence suggesting there is a poor correlation between self-reported fatigue and cognitive performance, some studies have found a relationship between self-reported fatigue and performance. For instance, Bruce, Bruce, and Arnett (2010) found a significant association between self-reported fatigue and response-time variability over the course of a sustained attention task. Similarly, Ziino & Ponsford (2006a) showed that decrements in performance and greater reaction times of dual-tasked working memory tasks were associated with greater reports of fatigue. Close examination of these and other studies suggests that this positive relationship is nonspecific and may be associated with a particular pattern or model of performance, which will be discussed later.

There is an association between self-reported fatigue and other factors.

In contrast to its inconsistent relationship with cognitive variables, fatigue demonstrates its strongest and most consistent correlation with depression and the presence of other psychological disorders (e.g., anxiety, somatization). In fact, fatigue experienced concomitantly with psychiatric symptoms is particularly debilitating (Cathebras, Robbins, Kirmayer, & Hayton, 1992) and significantly affects daily functional activity. However, despite the strong relationship between fatigue and psychopathology, the presence of one does *not* necessarily prove the presence of the other. There are numerous studies that find patients with significant fatigue without psychopathology.

Reports of pain, sleepiness, and sleep disturbance are also common among those with self-reported fatigue. However, again, the fact that patients may report such complaints does not imply that these complaints are associated with fatigue. For example, while often used interchangeably, there are now numerous studies showing that sleepiness and fatigue arise from different neurological mechanisms (Duntley, 2005). Nonetheless, clinicians and researchers continuously and wrongly attribute the vast literature on the detrimental effects of sleep deprivation on cognition to fatigue. For example, excessive sleepiness is restored with sleep. In persons with medically diagnosed fatigue, complaints of fatigue are not alleviated following rest or sleep. Yet, despite our current knowledge that sleepiness and fatigue represent related but distinct entities, many, if not most, self-reported instruments continue to include questions about sleepiness or feeling "tired."

Fatigue is also thought to have an association with poor self-efficacy and use of inadequate coping strategies, all of which may or may not be related to subjective reports of changes or declines in cognition. Lastly, there are a host of other factors that contribute to the feelings of fatigue, which are reflected in patients' self-report. These include medication effects, illness (e.g., flu), deconditioning, hormonal changes, and stress. Taken together, what then does a patient's self-reported feelings of fatigue tell us? Clearly, simplistic, unidimensional interpretations based on self-report measures no longer have a place in the neuropsychological evaluation. While self-reported fatigue may be associated with significant everyday functional consequences, such as reduced quality of life, increased disability, and potentially significant medical consequences (as discussed within), the attribution of self-reported fatigue to psychopathology is overly simplistic and potentially detrimental to the patient.

CURRENT UNDERSTANDING OF FATIGUE: WHAT WE KNOW

Prevalence

> Fatigue is so common as to be almost normal. (Wessely, Hotopf, & Sharpe, 1998, p. 27)

Acute fatigue, which is typically brought on by a single cause, has a rapid onset and is of short duration; it is common in approximately 10% to 33% of the population (Jason, Evans, Brown, & Porter, 2010). Such fatigue is typically alleviated by rest or lifestyle change, has minimal impact on daily functioning, and is protective in nature. Chronic fatigue by contrast, as discussed above, has a major effect on individuals' functioning and quality of life, has no known function or purpose, may result from numerous etiologies, and is typical in many clinical populations. Chronic fatigue is also described as abnormal, excessive, or unusual and to have no relation to an identifiable trigger such as activity or exertion. It is also not readily ameliorated by rest or other interventions. Such chronic fatigue has been hypothesized to be associated with a variety of mechanisms, including impaired nerve conduction or immune system, neuroendocrine or neurotransmitter dysregulation, proinflammatory cytokines affecting neural metabolism, the hypothalamic–pituitary–adrenal axis, and involvement of several brain regions, including the basal ganglia, thalamus, and frontal regions. Chronic fatigue is also associated with many psychological, medical, and neurological disorders (DeLuca, 2005b).

Further complicating matters, fatigue can be both a symptom and a syndrome. Among psychological disorders, fatigue is considered a symptom of diagnostic criteria for major depressive disorder, dysthymia, and generalized anxiety disorder (American Psychiatric Association, 2000). Fatigue is also an extremely prevalent symptom in various medical conditions, such as cardiovascular disease, cancer, human immunodeficiency virus/acquired immune deficiency syndrome

(HIV/AIDS), infectious disorders, autoimmune disease, inflammatory disease, and thyroid disorder, among others (see Table 6.1). For instance, approximately 69% to 82% of individuals with cardiac disease complain of fatigue (Bartels, 2009) and upwards of 90% of cancer patients report experiencing fatigue at some point during their disease course, describing it as their most distressing symptom (Cheville, 2009). In addition, fatigue is the defining feature of a medical illness, chronic fatigue syndrome (CFS), and a hallmark of illnesses such as fibromyalgia and rheumatoid arthritis, with 76% to 81% and 80% to 93% of individuals complaining of fatigue, respectively (Pan & Bressler, 2009).

Neurological disorders, including MS, stroke, TBI, and Parkinson's disease (PD), are also accompanied by a high rate of patient-reported fatigue. MS-related fatigue is seen in as many as 96% of patients and is commonly described as the most frequent and disabling symptom (Shah, 2009). Rates of post-stroke fatigue range from 23% to 75%, with rates varying by time after stroke (Choi-Kwon & Kim, 2011). Fatigue following a TBI has been reported to range from 50% to 80% (Levine & Greenwald, 2009), and it is the third most common symptom of

Table 6.1 Medical and Neurological Disorders in Which Fatigue Is Common

Medical Conditions
Chronic fatigue syndrome
Fibromyalgia
Cardiovascular disease
Cancer
HIV/AIDS
Thyroid disorder
Infectious diseases (e.g., Lyme disease)
Autoimmune disorders (e.g., lupus)
Inflammatory conditions (e.g., rheumatoid arthritis)
Metabolic conditions (e.g., hypercalcemia)
Anemia
Diabetes
Kidney and liver disease (e.g., end-stage renal disease, hepatitis C)
Chronic obstructive pulmonary disease
Obstructive sleep apnea
Sarcoidosis

Neurological Conditions
Multiple sclerosis
Stroke
Traumatic brain injury
Parkinson's disease
Spinal cord injury
Motor neuron disease
Myasthenia gravis
Neuromuscular disorders (e.g., myotonic dystrophy)

postconcussion syndrome (PCS), with rates as high as 47% the first month following a concussion and up to 37% three months following (LaChapelle & Finlayson, 1998). Among individuals diagnosed with PD, approximately 40% to 65% complain of fatigue and, like MS, describe it as their most disabling symptom (Hagell et al., 2006).

While clinicians often view the symptom of fatigue as indicative of psychopathology (a remnant of "psychopathological thinking" that dominated European psychiatry at the turn of the 20th century; see Shorter [2005]), it is at least equally likely following many medical and neurological conditions and has been shown to have significant medical predictive value. For instance, post-stroke fatigue has been associated with worse outcomes on a variety of metrics and has been shown to be an independent predictor of death one year post-stroke (Stulemeijer, Fasotti, & Bleijenberg, 2005) and with reduced long-term survival (Mead et al., 2011). Post-stroke fatigue has also been shown to be associated with increased risk of "suicidality" (Tang, Lu, Mok, Ungvari, & Wong, 2011) and found to be independently associated with pre-stroke depression, white matter changes, diabetes mellitus, pain, and sleeping disturbances (Naess, Lunde, Brogger, & Waje-Andreassen, 2012). It is also now well established that depressive symptomatology, such as fatigue, predicts the development of coronary heart disease, risk of future cardiac events, and even survival following myocardial infarction. These relationships remain even after controlling for the traditional risk factors (e.g., elevated cholesterol, hypertension, smoking, age). However, while specific symptoms of depression such as hopelessness, depressed affect, and irritability are all predictive of future cardiac problems, when adjusted for fatigue, these factors all lose their predictive power. Thus fatigue has been acknowledged as an independent predictor of risk of myocardial infarction, even after controlling for cholesterol level, age, smoking, and hypertension (Siegel & Schneiderman, 2005). In contrast, there are conditions in which even chronic fatigue is normal (e.g., pregnancy).

In sum, fatigue represents a substantial problem among many psychological, medical, and neurological conditions. Its impact is pervasive, affecting not only one's level of functioning and quality of life but also one's health.

CONCEPTUALIZATION AND MODELS OF FATIGUE

While still an elusive construct, several characterizations of fatigue exist that guide much of our present understanding and its investigation. For one, as stated above, fatigue has been classified as either acute or chronic (Piper, 1989). However, even this distinction has not proved easy. For instance, some define chronic fatigue as lasting at least six months (Fukuda et al., 1994), while others define it as lasting at least six weeks (Multiple Sclerosis Council, 1998). Others classify fatigue as either primary or secondary (DeLuca, 2005b). *Primary fatigue* in MS, for example, is purported to be related to centrally mediated processes of the disease, such as demyelination and axonal loss in the central nervous system or immunological factors. *Secondary fatigue,* by contrast, is linked to the host of factors that may accompany MS (e.g., depression, sleep disturbance, reduced activity, deconditioning, and medication side effects) and is presumed to be more readily treatable and often reversible.

Models differentiating central from peripheral fatigue have also been developed. *Peripheral fatigue* is the "failure in neuromuscular transmission, sarcolemmal excitation, or excitation-contraction coupling" that results in one's failure to sustain force or power (Torres-Harding & Jason, 2005). Peripheral fatigue arises from the muscle and is more associated with peripheral nervous system diseases, such as myasthenia gravis. *Central fatigue*, by contrast, has been described as the failure to initiate or sustain attentional tasks and physical activities requiring self-motivation and involves the central nervous system (Chaudhuri & Behan, 2000). Chaudhuri & Behan (2000) further propose a neural model of central fatigue that implicates the striatal–thalamic–frontal systems as being responsible for fatigue, with the basal ganglia as the primary neural structure (see below).

Finally, there are several theoretical conceptualizations with regard to the underlying mechanisms of fatigue. Aaronson et al. (1999) conceptualize fatigue as "the awareness of a decreased capacity for physical and/or mental activity due to an imbalance in the availability, utilization, and/or restoration of resources needed to perform activity." According to this model, fatigue results when the system is "out of balance"—in other words, when there are insufficient resources because either the demand is too great or because the mechanisms of utilization and restoration are impaired. Others propose that fatigue, particularly that among those with neurological insult, is more related to coping. More specifically, it has been suggested that the fatigue experienced by individuals with TBI is due to the additional effort needed to compensate for their injury when meeting the demands of everyday life (van Zomeren, Brouwer, & Deelman, 1984). Both of these definitions refer to fatigue as being a result of limited resources needed to fulfill the demands placed on an individual and are primarily cognitive in nature.

Cognitive Fatigue

While chronic fatigue is multifaceted, cognitive fatigue and its definition and impact are also complex. A common assumption is that cognitive fatigue does not influence performance on simple, automated tasks, but it may affect performance on more complex tasks (Holding, 1983). Moreover, some contend that cognitive fatigue affects control processes responsible for the *organization* of actions but not *individual* actions (Bartlett, 1943) and that fatigue results in "inaccurate timing of actions, less efficient inhibition of irrelevant information, decreased responsiveness to changes in stimulus information, and reduced anticipation" (Lorist & Faber, 2011). This speaks to the idea that "mental fatigue is mainly characterized by deterioration of executive control... the ability to regulate perceptual and motor processes in order to respond in an adaptive way to novel or changing task demands" (van der Linden, Frese, & Meijman, 2003). This suggestion that fatigue will be most evident on executive "frontal" tasks is also consistent with Chaudhuri and Behan's model of central fatigue implicating the frontal basal ganglia circuitry as the main mechanism of fatigue. Thus, the literature has seen an abundance of studies aimed at examining the effect of mental fatigue on complex attentional and executive tasks, as these functions are thought to be most susceptible. For instance, Ziino and Ponsford (2006b) demonstrated that while mood mediated the relationship between fatigue and cognitive performance on more simple tasks, a direct relationship between self-reported fatigue and cognition existed on more cognitively demanding tasks. This is consistent with reports that self-reported fatigue resulted in impairment on tasks requiring greater executive demands in MS, while mood was related to performance on less demanding tasks (Holtzer & Foley, 2009). Similarly, in a clinical pharmacological treatment study of fatigue in MS, Cohen and Fisher (1989) demonstrated a significant improvement in self-reported fatigue following treatment but found minimal effect on cognitive functioning across the trial, the exception being improved performance on one divided attention task. Taken together, these findings suggest that the relationship between cognition and self-report fatigue may be dependent on the nature of the task as well as the contribution of other factors such as mood, which again, may explain some of the inconsistencies found in the literature.

But, the question remains—can we measure cognitive fatigue and does subjective fatigue correlate with objective cognitive performance? To address this question, investigators have typically adopted three approaches when examining the influence of fatigue on cognitive performance: (1) examine one's performance over a prolonged period of time to measure any decrease in performance; (2) measure performance over an acute period of time, but during a task that requires sustained mental effort; (3) evaluate one's performance after a challenging mental task or physical exertion. We briefly describe examples of these approaches in turn (DeLuca, 2005a).

Fatigue over a prolonged period of time. This model suggests fatigue develops over the course of an extended period of time, such as after a day of work, and this fatigue affects cognitive performance. Johnson et al. (1997) administered a 3-hour neuropsychological test battery to induce fatigue in individuals with MS, depression, chronic fatigue syndrome, and healthy controls. Patients reported their fatigue four times throughout the evaluation and were immediately administered a challenging working-memory and processing-speed task, the Paced Auditory Serial Addition Task (PASAT). Despite reports of increased subjective fatigue, all groups demonstrated an overall improvement in performance on the task, which suggests that while subjectively they were more fatigued, they were still capable of maintaining, if not improving, their level of performance. These and other findings (e.g., Jennekens-Schinkel, Sanders, Lanser, & Van der Velde, 1988; Paul et al., 1998) suggest that prolonged effort may result in an increase in subjective fatigue, but this does not necessarily result in subsequent deficits in cognitive performance. A similar approach resulting in differing findings was taken by Claros-Salinas et al. (2010), who examined MS and stroke patients at three distinct time periods (morning, noon, and afternoon) on two consecutive days. They found that objective markers of cognitive fatigue (e.g., reaction time) were associated with diurnal difference in cognitive performance; however, subjective reports did not correlate with cognitive performance, despite increases in self-reported fatigue being evident for the MS and stroke patients. These authors concluded that objective measures of cognitive performance are more suitable than subjective reports when assessing fatigue-related differences in cognitive functioning (Claros-Salinas et al., 2010). Taken together, while subjective fatigue seems to increase over a prolonged period of time, there appears to be little to no evidence supporting the model that the increase in subjective fatigue is associated with impaired cognitive performance.

Fatigue during sustained and demanding cognitive activity. Another way in which cognitive fatigue has been conceptualized is similar to how muscle fatigue has been examined, that is, during sustained mental effort. Numerous studies of motor or muscle fatigue have demonstrated deteriorating performance with sustained or repetitive motor activity. Thus, many have conceptualized cognitive fatigue in a similar manner. Schwid et al. (2003) examined performance on the PASAT in a sample of individuals with MS and controls to determine whether performance declined *within* the administration of the PASAT (e.g., from the first third to the last third of the task). Individuals with MS, but not controls, demonstrated a decline in performance. This decrement in objective performance was associated with some but not all measures of subjective fatigue (Schwid et al., 2003). Similar declines in objective performance have been shown by several investigators (Bryant, Chiaravalloti, & DeLuca, 2004; Krupp & Elkins, 2000; Kujala, Portin, Revonsuo, & Ruutiainen, 1995); individuals with MS exhibited greater reaction times or made more errors during sustained cognitive activity, but such changes did not always correlate with subjective fatigue. More recently, Bruce et al. (2010) also demonstrated that individuals with MS showed greater response variability than that of healthy controls during a sustained-attention task. This variability correlated with self-reported cognitive fatigue (Bruce et al., 2010). However, it should be noted that the expectation of performance declines based on the muscle fatigue model are not always observed, as some studies have shown improved performance with repetitive cognitive challenge (e.g., Genova, Hillary, Wylie, Rypma, & DeLuca, 2009). Taken together, performance decrements during sustained cognitive effort seems to hold the most promise in objectively documenting cognitive fatigue, although such performance does not appear to reliably correlate with subjective ratings of fatigue.

Evaluation of fatigue following a physically or mentally demanding task. Clinically, fatigued patients often report significantly increased fatigue following either physical or mental exertion. The notion is that physical or mental effort should result in a "buildup" of fatigue, which then has a carryover effect on subsequent activity. Unfortunately, the literature on this is mixed. Krupp and Elkins (2000) administered a "continuous effortful cognitive task" and then repeated a neuropsychological battery that was initially administered several hours earlier. They found a decline in performance on verbal-memory and perceptual planning tasks in an MS group following the cognitively effortful task, although performance did not correlate with subjective fatigue reports. In contrast, healthy controls showed an improvement. The major problem with this study was that the entire test session required 4 hours of testing, and thus the decline in performance may not have been due to a previously mental exertion but to a function of the prolonged battery (i.e., the first model discussed above). Importantly, a study similar to the Krupp and Elkins study found no effect of complex processing on subsequent performance (Ziino & Ponsford, 2006b). Studies looking at cognitive decline following physical exertion in fatiguing populations have shown both support for the model (Blackwood, MacHale, Power, Goodwin, & Lawrie, 1998; LaManca et al., 1998) as well as no influence on cognitive fatigue post-exertion (Claypoole et al., 2001).

Overall, this section illustrates that we frequently refer to cognitive fatigue both clinically and in research; however, our understanding of this construct is rudimentary and unclear. Future research is needed to gain a better understanding of the various factors that influence the self-expression of cognitive fatigue across these situations, as well as which markers are the most accurate assessment of the fatigue experienced.

Neuroimaging of Fatigue

A number of theories have been proposed to explain the underlying etiology and pathophysiology of fatigue. Despite the various models and theories explored, our understanding of the neural mechanisms responsible for fatigue remains elusive.

"Central fatigue," as mentioned earlier, is purported to be the failure to initiate or sustain attentional tasks and physical activities requiring self-motivation. Using this definition, Chaudhuri and Behan (2000) have proposed that the non-motor structures of the basal ganglia serve as the primary neural structure for central fatigue along with its strong connections with the prefrontal cortex and the thalamus. The evidence for basal ganglia involvement in central fatigue is the most compelling model evident to date.

While several structural imaging studies have failed to show any relationship between structural indices and self-reported fatigue (Leavitt & DeLuca, 2010), recent studies have been more promising. These studies have focused on white matter lesions and gray matter alterations in prefrontal regions and the basal ganglia. For example, in MS, fatigue has been associated with left frontal regional lesion load and loss of gray mater volume in frontal regions (Sepulcre et al., 2009). Fatigue severity has been associated with thalamic structural alterations shown by increased T1-relaxation time (Niepel et al., 2006). Using diffusion tensor imaging (DTI), Pardini, Bonzano, Mancardi, and Roccatagliata (2010) showed that self-reported fatigue was associated with decreased white matter integrity in frontostriatal, frontofrontal, and frontolimbic pathways in persons with MS. In persons with TBI, impaired self-reported fatigue has been found to be associated with volume loss in the ventromedial prefrontal cortex (Pardini, Krueger, Raymont, & Grafman, 2010).

Functional imaging studies have also provided support for the critical role of the basal ganglia and frontal regions in fatigue. Using fluorodeoxyglucose positron emission tomography (FDG-PET), Roelcke et al. (1997) showed that self-reported fatigue was related to hypometabolism in the lateral and medial prefrontal cortex, the prefrontal and premotor cortex, and the putamen of persons with MS. Filippi et al. (2002) showed significant correlations between self-reported fatigue scores and prefrontal and thalamic functional magnetic resonance imaging (fMRI) activation in fatigued MS patients, suggesting alterations in frontostriatal functional architecture.

Central or cognitive fatigue was examined by two recent studies using fMRI, designed to specifically test the Chaudhuri and Behan model with fMRI (DeLuca, Genova, Hillary, & Wylie, 2008; Kohl, Wylie, Genova, Hillary, & DeLuca, 2009). DeLuca and colleagues (2008) objectively measured cognitive fatigue in MS patients and healthy controls by administering four trials of a sustained attention task (modified Symbol Digit Modalities Task) during fMRI acquisition, with the idea of "inducing" cognitive fatigue. They found that cognitive fatigue in MS subjects was associated with increased activation in the orbitofrontal cortex, superior parietal cortex, and the basal ganglia (specifically the caudate), areas consistent with the fatigue areas set forth by Chaudhuri and Behan, while healthy controls showed decreased activation in these same regions. Similar findings were observed in a second study by this group using the same procedure but in persons with TBI. That is, relative to healthy controls, the TBI group exhibited greater neural activation in the basal ganglia, middle frontal gyrus, superior parietal cortex, and anterior cingulate (Kohl et al., 2009). Both of these studies also reported involvement of parietal regions, areas not currently associated with the Chaudhuri and Behan model. These and other recent studies that found support for parietal involvement in self-reported fatigue (Morgan et al., 2007) suggest that Chaudhuri and Behan's model may need to be updated to include parietal structures.

Taken together, recent neuroimaging studies support the model that objective and subjective measures of fatigue are associated with striatal–frontal–thalamic structures and suggest a promising direction for future studies examining the relationship between subjective fatigue, behavioral findings, and cerebral activity.

ASSESSMENT OF SUBJECTIVE FATIGUE

Despite the lack of a relationship between subjective and objective measures of fatigue, fatigue is so common following medical, neurological, and psychiatric illness that it cannot be ignored. Despite the long known multidimensional nature of fatigue, clinical definitions of fatigue have focused primarily on subjective self-reported assessments. Once again, it must be emphasized that one cannot determine the nature of fatigue from self-report because of the numerous variables that make up this subjective sense. Nonetheless, self-report remains the "gold standard" and more often than not, when fatigue is a concern, practitioners will assess fatigue through use of a self-report questionnaire or as part of a clinical interview. As such, a brief review of available questionnaires is discussed next.

Existing instruments for self-reported fatigue have been described as being either unidimensional or multidimensional. Unidimensional questionnaires typically focus on the severity of fatigue, whereas multidimensional questionnaires attempt to measure severity as well as the nature of one's fatigue, such as temporal aspects, distress from fatigue, impact of fatigue on daily living, recognized cor-relates of fatigue, and key biological parameters (Aaronson et al., 1999). Fatigue measures can also be divided into generic and disease specific (see Table 6.2). Thus, practitioners and researchers should base their choice of measure on what it is they are actually interested in measuring. For brevity in this review, we excluded measures that include fatigue as a component of a broader health or quality-of-life outcome and less commonly used measures.

Assessment of the clinical and research utility, scale usability, and psychomet-ric properties of 22 commonly used measures resulted in the "endorsement" of six measures (Whitehead, 2009). These included the Fatigue Severity Scale (FSS), the Fatigue Impact Scale (FIS), the Brief Fatigue Inventory (BFI), the Fatigue Symptom Inventory (FSI), the Multidimensional Assessment of Fatigue (MAF), and the Multidimensional Fatigue Symptom Inventory (MFSI). An earlier com-prehensive review of similar measures suggested the FIS, FSI, FSS, and MFSI had reasonably to good psychometric properties and the ability to differentiate patients from non-patients, with the latter two also having good test–retest reli-ability and the FSS being sensitive to change over time and after treatment. The BFI and MAF were also found to be psychometrically sound, but there existed little information as to their test–retest reliability or sensitivity to change (Dittner et al., 2004). However, one must be cautioned against claims that instruments can differentiate components of fatigue such as cognitive fatigue from physical fatigue. For instance, while the Multidimensional Fatigue Inventory (MFI) claims to make such a differential assessment, the following items are included in the instrument: "I have been forgetful"; "I have been less alert"; "I have difficulty pay-ing attention for long periods of time"; "I have trouble concentrating"; or "My thinking has been slowed down." These may all be acknowledged by persons with legitimate cognitive problems yet have no fatigue!

Many existing subjective fatigue scales have been evaluated for use in specific populations commonly seen by neuropsychologists, including patients with MS, PD, stroke, TBI, or epilepsy. It should be noted that these studies have inherent flaws, including but not limited to small sample sizes and a lack of a gold standard of fatigue from which to compare. Dittner, Wessely, and Brown (2004) argue that a disease-specific fatigue measure should be designed to (1) distinguish between cases and non-cases, (2) be capable of distinguishing fatigue severity within that population, and (3) be sensitive to change following treatment or intervention. Few instruments have proven to fulfill these requirements. Nonetheless, the fol-lowing is provided as a "current state-of-affairs" review of present self-report fatigue measures for use in the respective condition.

Multiple Sclerosis

The FSS and FIS were found to adequately assess the *impact* of fatigue, be sen-sitive to intervention, and be capable of differentiating MS from other medi-cal samples. However, these instruments were not adequate at differentiating fatigued from nonfatigued patients or assessing the severity of fatigue, a major

Table 6.2 COMMONLY USED SELF-REPORT FATIGUE MEASURES

	Measure	Purported to Measure
Generic	*Unidimensional*	
	Fatigue Severity Scale (FSS)	Impact on physical and social functioning
	Visual Analog Scale (VAS)	Severity
	Brief Fatigue Inventory (BFI)	Impact on functioning, mood, work, relationships, and enjoyment of life
	Fatigue Assessment Scale (FAS)	Physical and mental fatigue
	Unidimensional Fatigue Impact Scale (U-FIS)	Impact of fatigue
	Multidimensional	
	Fatigue Impact Scale (FIS)	Impact on physical, cognitive, and psychosocial functioning
	Fatigue Impact Scale for Daily Use (D-FIS)	
	Modified Fatigue Impact Scale (MFIS)	
	Fatigue Assessment Inventory (FAI)	Severity, situational specificity of fatigue, consequences of fatigue, and response to rest or sleep
	Multidimensional Fatigue Inventory (MFI)	General fatigue, physical fatigue, mental fatigue, reduced motivation, reduced activity
	Multidimensional Assessment of Fatigue (MAF)	Degree of fatigue, severity, distress, impact on daily living, and timing
	Multidimensional Fatigue Symptom Inventory (MFSI)	General fatigue, emotional fatigue, physical fatigue, mental fatigue, and vigor
	Piper Fatigue Scale	
Disease Specific		
MS	Modified Fatigue Impact Scale	Impact on physical, cognitive, and psychosocial functioning
PD	Parkinson Fatigue Scale (PFS)	Presence and impact of fatigue
	Fatigue Severity Inventory (FSI)	Severity, situational specificity of fatigue, consequences of fatigue, and response to rest or sleep
TBI	Barrow Neurological Institute (BNI) Fatigue Scale	
HIV	HIV-Related Fatigue Scale or Barroso Fatigue Scale (BFS)	
Cancer	The Functional Assessment of Cancer Treatment-Fatigue Scale (FACT-F)	Impact of fatigue
	Fatigue Symptom Inventory (FSI)	Severity, duration, and impact on quality of life
	Schwartz Cancer Fatigue Scale (SCFS)	

flaw in its clinical utility (Dittner et al., 2004). Mathiowetz (2003) examined the test–retest reliability and convergent validity of the FIS and found the instrument to have adequate convergent validity and test–retest reliability with regard to the cognitive and social fatigue subscales, but the test–retest reliability of the physical subscale was less than adequate (Mathiowetz, 2003). Mathiowetz also reported low correlations between the FIS and FSS ($r = .44$) and cautioned that despite many investigations using these measures interchangeably, they may not be measuring the same construct, another very important thing to keep in mind when choosing a subjective fatigue scale. A comparison of the FSS, MS-Specific FSS (MFSS), Visual Analog Scale (VAS), and MFIS found the FSS and MFIS to be superior at identifying patients who reported fatigue as one of their three most disabling symptoms, occurring nearly daily and interfering with their day-to-day activities. A cutoff of 4.6 on the FSS and 38 on the MFIS, respectively, were most indicative of fatigue (Flachenecker et al., 2002). Most recently, Elbers et al.'s (2012) review of the literature on fatigue measures in MS, PD, and stroke resulted in recommending use of the Fatigue Scale for Motor and Cognitive Functions (FSMC) and the Unidimensional Fatigue Impact Scale (U-FIS) among patients with MS.

Parkinson's Disease

The Parkinson's Fatigue Scale (PFS) was developed specifically for use in PD. Its development adopted a qualitative approach and the measure was derived from patient focus groups. The resultant 16-item measure was found to have good internal consistency, split-half reliability, and adequate concurrent validity with a single-item question regarding one's fatigue. While the measure was not examined with regard to its ability to differentiate PD from healthy controls, Receiver Operating Characteristic (ROC) analyses suggested that the PFS has clinical utility in differentiating those with PD who complained of fatigue from those who did not, as well as between those who viewed their fatigue as problematic. A comparison of the FSS and PFS found both to be capable of differentiating PD patients from controls and to have good reliability. However, the FSS question "Exercise brings on my fatigue" proved to be a poor example and should be used with caution among patients with PD. In contrast to those with MS, individuals with PD actually reported that exercise ameliorates their fatigue (Grace, Mendelsohn, & Friedman, 2007). Hagell et al. (2006) examined the Functional Assessment of Chronic Illness Therapy–Fatigue (FACIT-F) and FSS for use in PD and found that both were capable of distinguishing fatigued from nonfatigued patients, had excellent internal consistency, had minimal floor and ceiling effects, and had an absence of differential item functioning. While not examined with the FSS, the test–retest reliability of the FACIT-F was considered to be adequate (Hagell et al., 2006). Finally, the D-FIS accurately distinguished those experiencing fatigue from those who were not, and it proved to have adequate internal consistency and convergent validity in a sample of individuals with PD (Martinez-Martin et al., 2006). Elbers et al.'s (2012) review also recommended the FACIT-F and FSS for use in PD. A commissioned task force of the Movement Disorders Society distinguished between those commonly used measures that are *recommended* for use and those *suggested* for screening and assessing severity in PD (see Table 6.3) (Friedman et al., 2010).

Stroke

When comparing the Fatigue Assessment Scale (FAS) to the general subscale of the MFI, the fatigue subscale of the Profile of Mood States (POMS), and Short-Form 36 (SF-36) vitality component for use in stroke, the FAS was found to have the best test–retest reliability but the worst internal consistency. The remaining measures were found to have adequate values of both indices (Mead et al., 2007). Given this, Elbers et al. (2012) suggested that the POMS fatigue subscale may be most applicable for use in the stroke population.

Brain Injury

In a fairly large sample, the Barroso Fatigue Scale (BFS) was administered to both healthy and TBI samples (Dijkers & Bushnik, 2008). Despite excellent internal consistency and minimal ceiling and floor effects overall between the BFS, FSS, Fatigue Assessment Instrument (FAI), and MAF, factor analysis of the BFS failed to demonstrate an acceptable solution, and the investigators asserted that the BFS was not appropriate for use among a TBI sample. The Barrow Neurological Institute (BNI) Fatigue Scale was developed specifically for individuals who have sustained a TBI, particularly for use in acute inpatient rehabilitation. The BNI Fatigue Scale focuses more on the difficulty of fatigue (e.g., staying alert, maintaining energy). Given the limited scope of the items, principal components factor analysis resulted in one factor, accounting for 65% of the variance. The measure also had excellent internal consistency, but the ability to differentiate patients from controls, its test–retest reliability, and its ability to assess severity were

Table 6.3 Self-Report Fatigue Measures Recommended for Use in Parkinson's Disease by the Movement Disorders Society Task Force

Measure	Screening	Severity
Fatigue Severity Scale	Recommended	Recommended
Functional Assessment of Chronic Illness Therapy–Fatigue	Recommended	Suggested
Fatigue Assessment Inventory	Suggested	Suggested
Multidimensional Fatigue Inventory	Suggested	Recommended
Parkinson Fatigue Scale	Recommended	Suggested
Fatigue Impact Scale for Daily Use		Suggested

Table derived from Friedman et al. (2010).

not assessed; thus further investigation of its clinical utility remains warranted (Borgaro, Gierok, Caples, & Kwasnica, 2004).

Epilepsy

The FSS, FSI, and FAI were examined for use in epilepsy by Hernandez-Ronquillo, Moien-Afshari, Knox, Britz, and Tellez-Zenteno (2011). All measures were found to have high intraobserver reliability and were capable of differentiating people with epilepsy (PWE) from healthy controls, with PWE reporting higher scores across all measures (Hernandez-Ronquillo et al., 2011).

CASE EXAMPLES

The following case examples are provided to illustrate the influence self-reported fatigue has on neuropsychological test performance.

Case 1

Mr. X was seen for a neuropsychological evaluation, given his report of increased stress at work, chronic headaches, and increased mental fatigue when attempting to maintain a consistent level of previous performance at work and at home. History was also significant for a TBI approximately 14 years prior. At the onset of the evaluation, Mr. X described his fatigue as being a "2" to "3" on a scale of "1" to "10" with "10" being the highest. Toward the end of the evaluation, he reported an increase in his fatigue, rating himself a "6." However, test performance across the evaluation did not show a decline or detriment in performance. In fact, on measures presumed to be most susceptible to fatigue, such as those assessing working memory, he performed in the superior to very superior range. Similarly, he placed in the high-average range on measures of information-processing speed, attention/working memory, cognitive flexibility, set shifting, sequencing, and inhibition (the latter being at a time when he reported greater fatigue). In contrast, Mr. X demonstrated only mild deficits on measures assessing confrontation naming and speeded visual perception and scanning. All other measures were in the average to high-average range, consistent with overall level of intellectual functioning. Overall, these findings suggested that there was little to no effect of self-reported fatigue during the neuropsychological evaluation, despite significant reports of mental fatigue and reported impairment in day-to-day functioning. Additionally, assessment of mood and personality was suggestive of increased fluctuations in mood and preoccupation with physical functioning worthy of further attention. When this patient was seen for feedback and presented with the findings, he and the neuropsychologist focused less on what he perceived to be a cognitive complaint and more on the need to treat any existing depression and to employ better strategies at handling stress, which is likely what contributed to his self-reported fatigue. The patient was very amenable to this interpretation and relieved to know that there was no indication of a significant cognitive impairment.

Case 2

This next case example illustrates two points: (1) the interchangeable use of sleepiness and fatigue, and (2) the apparent lack of a relationship between sleepiness/fatigue and cognitive performance during an isolated neuropsychological assessment.

Mr. Y had sustained a right-sided stroke approximately 1 year prior. Since then, he had been unemployed. However, before his injury, he had worked evenings without problems. At the present time, he reported difficulty obtaining adequate sleep in the evenings. He was suspected of having some residual effects of a shift-work sleep disorder. During the neuropsychological evaluation, it was evident that Mr. Y's sleep propensity was high and he would, on occasion, appear to instantly fall asleep. Despite being offered many breaks and the option to continue testing at a later date, he insisted on continuing with the testing. The examiner decided to continue administering the test, as she had also recognized that despite her encouragement to have him "wake up," he was performing at nearly ceiling level. In fact, on one specific task in which she did "wake him up" in between item administration, he performed in the superior range. Overall, this patient of estimated average intelligence actually performed in the average range or higher on all measures, despite the observation that he was obviously sleepy during the evaluation. When Mr. Y returned for feedback, he was encouraged to undergo a sleep study and consider psychological treatment to address his sleep hygiene. Mr. Y was informed that despite his intact cognitive abilities observed during the evaluation, his lack of sleep was likely to be having significant physical and cognitive consequences in his day-to-day functioning. He and his wife agreed with these conclusions and recommendations.

As can be seen in each of these cases, a simple conclusion of fatigue would have been overly simplistic, and practices taught in graduate school to decrease fatigue (e.g., breaks, etc.) would have had little to no impact on performance. In reality, there were particular factors accounting for the stated fatigue or sleepiness reported during the patients' neuropsychological evaluation—depression in Case 1 and a potential sleep disorder in Case 2. There is little doubt that in both cases the patients' self-reported feelings of fatigue were affecting their day-to-day functioning, quality of life, and, likely, their health. However, on objective measures of their cognitive functioning during a neuropsychological evaluation, the association between their momentary self-reported fatigue or sleepiness and their cognitive performance likely had little to no effect on what was truly being experienced in everyday life.

FUTURE DIRECTIONS

Fatigue is a complex construct, unduly simplified by the stubborn reliance on self-report alone. In the end, self-reported fatigue yields little information, as it consists of many variables that are often subjective and unreliable. A main purpose of this chapter was to expose these variables and educate clinicians to avoid simple and outdated constructs, identify several misconceptions, and become more sophisticated in the assessment and interpretation of fatigue.

There are at least two primary misconceptions regarding fatigue (or cognitive fatigue) that need to be highlighted. The first is that there is an association between subjective and objective measures of fatigue. Over 100 years of research, the most common finding is that no such consistent relationship has been observed. It is time to assimilate this fact and to end the quest to find correlations between subjective and objective fatigue. A more useful approach may be to reconceptualize fatigue as affected by two sets of factors—those that initiate fatigue (e.g., systemic disease), causing primary fatigue, and those that perpetuate or exacerbate fatigue (e.g., depression, sleep disturbance, pain, medication effects, deconditioning), causing secondary fatigue. While both primary and secondary factors contribute to the feeling of fatigue, it is likely that the secondary factors are those that complicate the understanding of self-report. Thus, the assessment of fatigue needs to become more multidimensional, taking into account the various components when formulating clinical opinions regarding its impact on behavior.

The second misconception is that fatigue results in performance decrements. This belief is deeply ingrained in our thinking and resistant to extinction, or at least modification, even in light of dozens if not hundreds of studies challenging this strict interpretation. Such misconceptions have clearly thwarted research efforts to develop objective measures of cognitive fatigue. Nevertheless, the behavioral literature is beginning to yield a hint of understanding of how cognitive fatigue affects behavior. The most promising evidence supports a model of cognitive fatigue in which one observes impaired performance during sustained (i.e., maintaining cognitive vigilance) instead of prolonged yet nonsustained mental effort (i.e., the course of a long day). Other avenues exist as well, such as looking at performance variability. Through this investigation we may continue to chip away at older models and begin to establish new scientific approaches to assessing and measuring the impact of cognitive fatigue on objective neuropsychological performance.

Our understanding of cerebral mechanisms underlying cognitive fatigue has shown considerable growth and promise over the last decade, although clearly more work is required. Data from neuroimaging studies suggest that cognitive fatigue may be a failure of the non-motor function of a network comprising the basal ganglia and its connections with thalamic and frontal-lobe structures. Such studies may provide the mechanisms associated with primary fatigue and perhaps be able to yield relationships between brain activity and subjective feelings of fatigue. Such data may ultimately lead to more valid assessment of self-reported fatigue.

Because fatigue is one of the most common symptoms observed in neurological and psychiatric populations and it significantly affects everyday-life activities, the need for its assessment and our understanding of it remains crucial and should not change. It is its interpretation that requires modification.

References

Aaronson, L. S., Teel, C. S., Cassmeyer, V., Neuberger, G. B., Pallikkathayil, L., Pierce, J. et al. (1999). Defining and measuring fatigue. *Image Journal of Nursing Scholarship, 31,* 45–50.

Ackerman, P. L. (2011). Introduction. In P. L. Ackerman (Ed.), *Cognitive fatigue: Multidisciplinary perspectives on current research and future applications* (pp. 3–7). Washington, DC: American Psychological Association.

Ackerman, P. L., & Kanfer, R. (2009). Test length and cognitive fatigue: An empirical examination of effects on performance and test-taker reactions. *Journal of Experimental Psychology:Applied, 15,* 163–181.

American Psychiatric Association (2000). *Diagnostic and statistical manual of mental disorders* (4th ed., text rev.) Washington, DC: Author.

Azouvi, P., Couillet, J., Leclercq, M., Martin, Y., Asloun, S., & Rousseaux, M. (2004). Divided attention and mental effort after severe traumatic brain injury. *Neuropsychologia, 42,* 1260–1268.

Bartels, M. N. (2009). Fatigue in cardiopulmonary disease. *Physical Medicine & Rehabilitation Clinics of North America, 20,* 389–404.

Bartlett, F. C. (1943). Fatigue following highly skilled work. *Proceedings of the Royal Society B, 131,* 247–257.

Blackwood, S. K., MacHale, S. M., Power, M. J., Goodwin, G. M., & Lawrie, S. M. (1998). Effects of exercise on cognitive and motor function in chronic fatigue syndrome and depression. *Journal of Neurology, Neurosurgery, & Psychiatry, 65,* 541–546.

Borgaro, S. R., Baker, J., Wethe, J. V., Prigatano, G. P., & Kwasnica, C. (2005). Subjective reports of fatigue during early recovery from traumatic brain injury. *Journal of Head Trauma and Rehabilitation, 20,* 416–425.

Borgaro, S. R., Gierok, S., Caples, H., & Kwasnica, C. (2004). Fatigue after brain injury: Initial reliability study of the BNI Fatigue Scale. *Brain Injury, 18,* 685–690.

Brouwer, W. H., & van Wolffelaar, P. C. (1985). Sustained attention and sustained effort after closed head injury: Detection and 0.10 Hz heart rate variability in a low event rate vigilance task. *Cortex, 21,* 111–119.

Bruce, J. M., Bruce, A. S., & Arnett, P. A. (2010). Response variability is associated with self-reported cognitive fatigue in multiple sclerosis. *Neuropsychology, 24,* 77–83.

Bryant, D., Chiaravalloti, N. D., & DeLuca, J. (2004). Objective measurement of cognitive fatigue in multiple sclerosis. *Rehabilitation Psychology, 49,* 114–122.

Cathebras, P. J., Robbins, J. M., Kirmayer, L. J., & Hayton, B. C. (1992). Fatigue in primary care: Prevalence, psychiatric comorbidity, illness behavior, and outcome. *Journal of General Internal Medicine, 7,* 276–286.

Chaudhuri, A., & Behan, P. O. (2000). Fatigue and basal ganglia. *Journal of the Neurological Sciences, 179,* 34–42.

Cheville, A. L. (2009). Cancer-related fatigue. *Physical Medicine & Rehabilitation Clinics of North America, 20,* 405–416.

Choi-Kwon, S., & Kim, J. S. (2011). Poststroke fatigue: An emerging, critical issue in stroke medicine. *International Journal of Stroke, 6,* 328–336.

Claros-Salinas, D., Bratzke, D., Greitemann, G., Nickisch, N., Ochs, L., & Schroter, H. (2010). Fatigue-related diurnal variations of cognitive performance in multiple sclerosis and stroke patients. *Journal of the Neurological Sciences, 295,* 75–81.

Claypoole, K., Mahurin, R., Fischer, M. E., Goldberg, J., Schmaling, K. B., Schoene, R. B., et al. (2001). Cognitive compromise following exercise in monozygotic twins discordant for chronic fatigue syndrome: Fact or artifact? *Applied Neuropsychology, 8,* 31–40.

Davis, D. R. (1946). The disorganization of behavior in fatigue. *Journal of Neurology, Neurosurgery, & Psychiatry, 9*, 23–29.

Davis, M. P., & Walsh, D. (2010). Mechanisms of fatigue. *Journal of Supportive Oncology, 8*, 164–174.

DeLuca, J. (2005a). Fatigue, cognition, and mental effort. In J. DeLuca (Ed.), *Fatigue as a window to the brain* (pp. 37–58). Cambridge, MA: MIT Press.

DeLuca, J. (2005b). Fatigue: Its definition, its study, and its future. In J. DeLuca (Ed.), *Fatigue as a window to the brain* (pp. 319–325). Cambridge, MA: MIT Press.

DeLuca, J., Genova, H. M., Hillary, F. G., & Wylie, G. (2008). Neural correlates of cognitive fatigue in multiple sclerosis using functional MRI. *Journal of the Neurological Sciences, 270*, 28–39.

Dijkers, M. P., & Bushnik, T. (2008). Assessing fatigue after traumatic brain injury: An evaluation of the HIV-Related Fatigue Scale [corrected]. *Journal of Head Trauma & Rehabilitation, 23*, 3–16.

Dittner, A. J., Wessely, S. C., & Brown, R. G. (2004). The assessment of fatigue. A practical guide for clinicians and researchers. *Journal of Psychosomatic Research, 56*, 157–170.

Duntley, S. P. (2005). Fatigue and sleep. In J. DeLuca (Ed.), *Fatigue as a window to the brain* (pp. 209–228). Cambridge, MA: MIT Press.

Elbers, R. G., Rietberg, M. B., van Wegen, E. E., Verhoef, J., Kramer, S. F., Terwee, C. B., et al. (2012). Self-report fatigue questionnaires in multiple sclerosis, Parkinson's disease and stroke: A systematic review of measurement properties. *Quality of Life Research, 21*, 925–944.

Filippi, M., Rocca, M. A., Colombo, B., Falini, A., Codella, M., Scotti, G., et al. (2002). Functional magnetic resonance imaging correlates of fatigue in multiple sclerosis. *Neuroimage, 15*, 559–567.

Flachenecker, P., Kumpfel, T., Kallmann, B., Gottschalk, M., Grauer, O., Rieckmann, P., et al. (2002). Fatigue in multiple sclerosis: A comparison of different rating scales and correlation to clinical parameters. *Multiple Sclerosis, 8*, 523–526.

Friedman, J. H., Alves, G., Hagell, P., Marinus, J., Marsh, L., Martinez Martin, P., et al. (2010). Fatigue rating scales critique and recommendations by the Movement Disorders Society Task Force on rating scales for Parkinson's disease. *Movement Disorders, 25*, 805–822.

Fukuda, K., Straus, S. E., Hickie, I., Sharpe, M. C., Dobbins, J. G., & Komaroff, A. (1994). The chronic fatigue syndrome: A comprehensive approach to its definition and study. International Chronic Fatigue Syndrome Study Group. *Annals of Internal Medicine, 121*, 953–959.

Genova, H. M., Hillary, F. G., Wylie, G., Rypma, B., & DeLuca, J. (2009). Examination of processing speed deficits in multiple sclerosis using functional magnetic resonance imaging. *Journal of the International Neuropsychological Society, 15*, 383–393.

Grace, J., Mendelsohn, A., & Friedman, J. H. (2007). A comparison of fatigue measures in Parkinson's disease. *Parkinsonism & Related Disorders, 13*, 443–445.

Hagell, P., Hoglund, A., Reimer, J., Eriksson, B., Knutsson, I., Widner, H., et al. (2006). Measuring fatigue in Parkinson's disease: A psychometric study of two brief generic fatigue questionnaires. *Journal of Pain and Symptom Management, 32*, 420–432.

Hernandez-Ronquillo, L., Moien-Afshari, F., Knox, K., Britz, J., & Tellez-Zenteno, J. F. (2011). How to measure fatigue in epilepsy? The validation of three scales for clinical use. *Epilepsy Research, 95*, 119–129.

Holding, D. (1983). Fatigue. In R. Hockey (Ed.), *Stress and fatigue in human performance* (pp. 145–164). Durham: John Wiley & Sons.

Jason, L. A., Evans, M., Brown, M., & Porter, N. (2010). What is fatigue? Pathological and nonpathological fatigue. *Physical Medicine & Rehabilitation, 2*, 327–331.

Jennekens-Schinkel, A., Sanders, E. A., Lanser, J. B., & Van, der Velde, E. A. (1988). Reaction time in ambulant multiple sclerosis patients. Part I. Influence of prolonged cognitive effort. *Journal of the Neurological Sciences, 85*, 173–186.

Johnson, S. K., DeLuca, J., Diamond, B. J., & Natelson, B. H. (1998). Memory dysfunction in fatiguing illness: Examining interference and distraction in short-term memory. *Cognitive Neuropsychiatry, 3*, 269–285.

Johnson, S. K., Lange, G., DeLuca, J., Korn, L. R., & Natelson, B. (1997). The effects of fatigue on neuropsychological performance in patients with chronic fatigue syndrome, multiple sclerosis, and depression. *Applied Neuropsychology, 4*, 145–153.

Kohl, A. D., Wylie, G. R., Genova, H. M., Hillary, F. G., & DeLuca, J. (2009). The neural correlates of cognitive fatigue in traumatic brain injury using functional MRI. *Brain Injury, 23*, 420–432.

Krupp, L. B., & Elkins, L. E. (2000). Fatigue and declines in cognitive functioning in multiple sclerosis. *Neurology, 55*, 934–939.

Kujala, P., Portin, R., Revonsuo, A., & Ruutiainen, J. (1995). Attention related performance in two cognitively different subgroups of patients with multiple sclerosis. *Journal of Neurology, Neurosurgery, & Psychiatry, 59*, 77–82.

LaChapelle, D. L., & Finlayson, M. A. (1998). An evaluation of subjective and objective measures of fatigue in patients with brain injury and healthy controls. *Brain Injury, 12*, 649–659.

LaManca, J. J., Sisto, S. A., DeLuca, J., Johnson, S. K., Lange, G., Pareja, J., et al. (1998). Influence of exhaustive treadmill exercise on cognitive functioning in chronic fatigue syndrome. *American Journal of Medicine, 105*, 59S–65S.

Leavitt, V. M., & DeLuca, J. (2010). Central fatigue: Issues related to cognition, mood and behavior, and psychiatric diagnoses. *Physical Medicine & Rehabilitation, 2*, 332–337.

Levine, J., & Greenwald, B. D. (2009). Fatigue in Parkinson disease, stroke, and traumatic brain injury. *Physical Medicine & Rehabilitation Clinics of North America, 20*, 347–361.

Lezak, M. D. (1995). *Neuropsychological assessment* (3rd ed.) New York: Oxford University Press.

Lorist, M. M., & Faber, L. G. (2011). Consideration of the influence of mental fatigue on controlled and automatic cognitive processes and related neuromodulatory effects. In P. L. Ackerman (Ed.), *Cognitive fatigue: Multidisciplinary perspectives on current research and future applications* (pp. 105–126). Washington, DC: American Psychological Association.

Martinez-Martin, P., Catalan, M. J., Benito-Leon, J., Moreno, A. O., Zamarbide, I., Cubo, E., et al. (2006). Impact of fatigue in Parkinson's disease: the Fatigue Impact Scale for Daily Use (D-FIS). *Quality of Life Research, 15*, 597–606.

Mathiowetz, V. (2003). Test-retest reliability and convergent validity of the Fatigue Impact Scale for persons with multiple sclerosis. *Americal Journal of Occupational Therapy, 57*, 389–395.

Mead, G. E., Graham, C., Dorman, P., Bruins, S. K., Lewis, S. C., Dennis, M. S., et al. (2011). Fatigue after stroke: Baseline predictors and influence on survival. Analysis of data from UK patients recruited in the International Stroke Trial. *PLoS One, 6*, e16988.

Mead, G., Lynch, J., Greig, C., Young, A., Lewis, S., & Sharpe, M. (2007). Evaluation of fatigue scales in stroke patients. *Stroke, 38*, 2090–2095.

Morgan, R. M., Parry, A. M., Arida, R. M., Matthews, P. M., Davies, B., & Castell, L. M. (2007). Effects of elevated plasma tryptophan on brain activation associated with the Stroop task. *Psychopharmacology (Berl), 190*, 383–389.

Morrow, S. A., Weinstock-Guttman, B., Munschauer, F. E., Hojnacki, D., & Benedict, R. H. (2009). Subjective fatigue is not associated with cognitive impairment in multiple sclerosis: Cross-sectional and longitudinal analysis. *Multiple Sclerosis, 15*, 998–1005.

Mosso, A. (1904). *Fatigue.* London: Swan Sonnenschein.

Multiple Sclerosis Council (1998). *Fatigue and multiple sclerosis—Clinical practice guidelines.* Washington, DC: Paralyzed Veterans of America.

Muscio, B. (1921). Is a fatigue test possible? *British Journal of Psychology, 12*, 31–46.

Naess, H., Lunde, L., Brogger, J., & Waje-Andreassen, U. (2012). Fatigue among stroke patients on long-term follow-up. The Bergen Stroke Study. *Journal of the Neurological Sciences, 312*, 138–141.

Niepel, G., Tench, C., Morgan, P. S., Evangelou, N., Auer, D. P., & Constantinescu, C. S. (2006). Deep gray matter and fatigue in MS: A T1 relaxation time study. *Journal of Neurology, 253*, 896–902.

Pan, J. C., & Bressler, D. N. (2009). Fatigue in rheumatologic diseases. *Physical Medicine & Rehabilitation Clinics of North America, 20*, 373–387.

Pardini, M., Bonzano, L., Mancardi, G. L., & Roccatagliata, L. (2010). Frontal networks play a role in fatigue perception in multiple sclerosis. *Behavioral Neuroscience, 124*, 329–336.

Pardini, M., Krueger, F., Raymont, V., & Grafman, J. (2010). Ventromedial prefrontal cortex modulates fatigue after penetrating traumatic brain injury. *Neurology, 74*, 749–754.

Parmenter, B. A., Denney, D. R., & Lynch, S. G. (2003). The cognitive performance of patients with multiple sclerosis during periods of high and low fatigue. *Multiple Sclerosis, 9*, 111–118.

Paul, R. H., Beatty, W. W., Schneider, R., Blanco, C. R., & Hames, K. A. (1998). Cognitive and physical fatigue in multiple sclerosis: Relations between self report and objective performance. *Applied Neuropsychology, 5*, 143–148.

Rao, S. M., Leo, G. J., Bernardin, L., & Unverzagt, F. (1991). Cognitive dysfunction in multiple sclerosis. I. Frequency, patterns, and prediction. *Neurology, 41*, 685–691.

Roelcke, U., Kappos, L., Lechner-Scott, J., Brunnschweiler, H., Huber, S., Ammann, W., et al. (1997). Reduced glucose metabolism in the frontal cortex and basal ganglia of multiple sclerosis patients with fatigue: An 18F-fluorodeoxyglucose positron emission tomography study. *Neurology, 48*, 1566–1571.

Schwartz, C. E., Coulthard-Morris, L., & Zeng, Q. (1996). Psychosocial correlates of fatigue in multiple sclerosis. *Archives of Physical Medicine & Rehabilitation, 77*, 165–170.

Schwid, S. R., Tyler, C. M., Scheid, E. A., Weinstein, A., Goodman, A. D., & McDermott, M. P. (2003). Cognitive fatigue during a test requiring sustained attention: A pilot study. *Multiple Sclerosis, 9*, 503–508.

Sepulcre, J., Masdeu, J. C., Goni, J., Arrondo, G., Velez de, M. N., Bejarano, B., et al. (2009). Fatigue in multiple sclerosis is associated with the disruption of frontal and parietal pathways. *Multiple Sclerosis, 15*, 337–344.

Shah, A. (2009). Fatigue in multiple sclerosis. *Physical Medicine & Rehabilitation Clinics of North America, 20*, 363–372.

Shorter, E. (2005). The diagnosis and treatment of fatigue in psychiatry: A historical overview. In J. DeLuca (Ed.), *Fatigue as a window to the brain* (pp. 127–136). Cambridge, MA: MIT Press.

Siegel, S., & Schneiderman, N. (2005). Heart disease, cardiovascular functioning, and fatigue. In J. DeLuca (Ed.), *Fatigue as a window to the brain* (pp. 229–242). Cambridge, MA: MIT Press.

Stulemeijer, M., Fasotti, L., & Bleijenberg, G. (2005). Fatigue after Stroke. In J. DeLuca (Ed.), *Fatigue as a window to the brain* (pp. 73–88). Cambridge, MA: MIT Press.

Tang, W. K., Lu, J. Y., Mok, V., Ungvari, G. S., & Wong, K. S. (2011). Is fatigue associated with suicidality in stroke? *Archives of Physical Medicine & Rehabilitation, 92,* 1336–1338.

Torres-Harding, S., & Jason, L. A. (2005). What is fatigue? History and epidemiology. In J. DeLuca (Ed.), *Fatigue as a window to the brain* (pp. 3–18). Cambridge, MA: Massachusetts Institute of Technology.

van der Linden, D., Frese, M., & Meijman, T. F. (2003). Mental fatigue and the control of cognitive processes: Effects on perseveration and planning. *Acta Psychologica (Amsterdam), 113,* 45–65.

van Zomeren, A. H., Brouwer, W. H., & Deelman, B. G. (1984). Attentional deficits: The riddles of selectivity, speed, and alertness. In D. Brooks (Ed.), *Closed head injury: Psychological, social, and family consequences.* Oxford, UK: Oxford University Press.

Walker, G. C., Cardenas, D. D., Guthrie, M. R., McLean, A., Jr., & Brooke, M. M. (1991). Fatigue and depression in brain-injured patients correlated with quadriceps strength and endurance. *Archives of Physical Medicine & Rehabilitation, 72,* 469–472.

Wessely, S., Hotopf, M., & Sharpe, M. (1998). *Chronic fatigue and its syndromes.* New York: Oxford University Press.

Whitehead, L. (2009). The measurement of fatigue in chronic illness: A systematic review of unidimensional and multidimensional fatigue measures. *Journal of Pain and Symptom Management, 37,* 107–128.

Ziino, C., & Ponsford, J. (2006a). Selective attention deficits and subjective fatigue following traumatic brain injury. *Neuropsychology, 20,* 383–390.

Ziino, C., & Ponsford, J. (2006b). Vigilance and fatigue following traumatic brain injury. *Journal of the International Neuropsychological Society, 12,* 100–110.

7

The Impact of Pain and Pain-Related Factors on Cognitive Functioning

JAKE EPKER AND MELISSA OGDEN

Pain is a prevalent problem in the United States. A current Institute of Medicine (2011) report indicates that 116 million Americans experience chronic pain (i.e., pain that persists for at least 6 months). This is a conservative estimate of the problem of pain in our society, as it does not include children or individuals suffering from acute pain conditions. The annual costs associated with chronic pain (CP),[1] including medical treatment and lost productivity, range from $560 to $635 billion annually. Many neurological conditions are accompanied by pain, and a large number of patients who present for neurological care complain of pain (Williams et al., 2003). As such, neuropsychologists are likely to have frequent encounters with CP patients. In order to understand and validly interpret neuropsychological results in an individual with pain, it is important to understand the roles pain and pain-related variables may be playing in an individual's cognitive status.

The impact of pain can be extensive. Beyond the obvious physical limitations that can occur with pain, large percentages of patients who experience pain also report cognitive problems. Studies indicate that between 42% and 60% of mixed CP patients report experiencing impairment in at least one cognitive domain (Jamison, Sbrocco, & Parris, 1989; McCracken & Iverson, 2001; Roth, Geisser, Theisen-Goodvich, & Dixon, 2005). Samples of patients with fibromyalgia (FM), migraine, and systemic lupus erythematosus also report high levels of cognitive impairment (Denburg, Stewart, Hart, & Denburg, 2003; Grace, Nielson, Hopkins, & Berg, 1999, Suhr, 2003). Complaints of impaired short-term memory, attention, and concentration are most common.

While perceived cognitive problems in patients with pain may be associated with true cognitive deficits, cognitive complaints are not always correlated with objective impairment, and some individuals with CP are prone to reporting levels of cognitive impairment that exceed objective neuropsychological findings

(Grace et al., 1999; Suhr, 2003). In CP patients who demonstrate objective cognitive impairment, the impairment may be a direct result of pain, stem from actual central nervous dysfunction (i.e., brain injury or neurological disease that is also causing pain), occur secondary to various non-neurological variables often associated with the experience of pain, or a combination of these factors. Neuroimaging studies have shown functional and structural neuroanatomical changes associated with CP, including reduced gray matter volume (particularly in the frontal cortex and thalamus) and involvement of the dorsolateral prefrontal cortex (Apkarian et al., 2004). It has also been demonstrated that successful treatment of chronic back pain can result in a reversal of functional and structural brain abnormalities (Seminowicz et al., 2011), providing support for a neuroanatomical basis of CP.

Investigating the influence of pain on cognitive functions is complicated by the fact that pain rarely occurs in isolation. Instead, individuals with pain often present with additional conditions that can independently affect cognitive performance, including concomitant mood disturbance, somatization, sleep dysregulation, fatigue, neurological injury or disease, and incentive for disability. It has also been suggested some prescribed treatments for pain, most notably opioid medication, can affect cognitive performance in some individuals. The etiology, intensity, and duration of the individual's pain condition may also mediate cognitive functions. Such complexities create a challenging situation when attempting to determine the extent to which pain impacts cognitive functioning in a patient who presents for neuropsychological evaluation.

Several thorough review articles have summarized the role of pain in cognitive functions, as well as the challenges faced by researchers in this area (Hart, Martelli, & Zasler, 2000; Kreitler & Niv, 2007; Moriarty, McGuire, & Finn, 2011). However, the literature investigating pain and cognition is plagued with inconsistencies and mixed findings. At the same time, studies that have shown a positive association between pain and cognitive difficulties have most consistently identified problematic cognitive functioning in the areas of attention, processing speed, psychomotor speed, mental flexibility, and recent memory. The domain of attention skills in patients with pain has received particular attention. It has been hypothesized that individuals are subject to "attention overload" when pain consumes large amounts of available attentional resources and leaves minimal attention to invest in other aspects of cognitive functioning. When viewed within the hypothesis of limited cognitive resources, attention to pain competes with a finite amount of cognitive resources relative to the attention necessary for a cognitive task (Norman & Bobrow, 1975; Eccleston & Crombez, 1999). This model predicts poor performance when attention is divided between two tasks. Put simply, the assumption is that when pain competes with other tasks for attentional resources, it usually wins.

Little has been reported regarding the effect size of chronic pain's impact on cognition. In samples of FM patients, CP patients, and healthy controls, Suhr (2003) reported very small effect sizes (.00 to .11) for measures of executive functions, memory, attention/working memory, and psychomotor speed. These results suggested no significant cognitive differences between the groups with pain and individuals without pain.

The CP and cognition literature varies greatly with regard to patient samples (i.e., acute versus chronic pain, type and location of pain), methodology, and selection of cognitive measures. There is also wide variability in these studies' methods to control for other variables that may mediate the role of pain in cognition, including etiology of pain, duration of the pain condition, pain intensity, treatment type, presence of emotional distress, fatigue, and patient effort level. Each of these variables can play an important role in a patient's presentation and is important to understand when assessing an individual with CP. There is significant variability in the research findings as they relate to the relationship between these pain-related factors and cognition. A sampling of research studies investigating these factors is presented below, followed by a summary of those findings.

PAIIN-RELATED FACTORS AND COGNITION

Pain Etiology

Numerous studies have attempted to determine whether the type or location of pain mediates cognitive performance. Amongst specific pain locations, it has been suggested that patients suffering from pain in cervical and head regions, including whiplash injuries, may be particularly vulnerable to disruption of cognitive functions (DiStefano & Radanov, 1995; Kessels, Aleman, Verhagen, & Van Luijtelaar, 2000; Radanov, Dvořák, & Valach, 1992). Several characteristics unique to populations with cervical and head pain have been posited as potential explanations for these findings, including more severe and widespread pain, poor effort associated with high incidences of litigation, impact of greater levels of emotional distress associated with these types of pain, and the influence of high levels of somatic focus (Antepohl, Kiviloog, Andersson, & Gerdle, 2003; Bosma & Kessels, 2002; Goldberg et al., 1996; Radanov & Dvořák, 1996; Radanov, Dvořák, & Valach, 1992; Schmand et al., 1998).

Other studies have not found a difference in cognitive performance between patients with headache and those with other types of pain. For example, Bell, Primeau, Sweet, and Lofland (1999) compared neuropsychological functioning in three patient groups: those with migraine headache pain, those with non-headache CP, and those suffering mild traumatic brain injury. The cognitive performances of the headache and non-headache pain groups did not differ and neither pain group displayed significant cognitive impairment. These findings do not support a link between migraine headache and cognitive impairment, which is consistent with earlier findings (Burker, Hannay, & Halsey, 1989; Leijdekkers, Passchier, Goudswaard, Menges, & Orlebeke, 1990).

Other studies have examined cognitive functions of different pain groups. Bee et al. (2007) compared cognitive functioning of patients with fibromyalgia (FM) and chronic back pain (CBP). They found no significant differences between these two pain groups on measures of attention/concentration, memory, or word finding. They also examined patient's responses to their pain condition and noted no differences between pain groups on measures of pain catastrophizing (i.e., an excessively negative orientation toward pain; characterizations of pain as awful, horrible, and unbearable) or pain-related anxiety, although the FM group demonstrated significantly higher levels of depression than the CBP group. To examine for differences in attention capabilities among types of CP patients, Dick, Eccleston, and Crombez (2002) administered the Test of Everyday Attention (Robertson, Ward, Ridgeway, & Nimmo-Smith, 1994) to groups of patients with FM, rheumatoid arthritis (RA), and musculoskeletal pain. All three groups were impaired relative to a healthy control group, but the level and pattern of performance on the task did not differ between the pain groups. Apkarian and colleagues (2004) investigated performance on the Iowa Gambling Task (IGT; Bechara, Damasio, Damasio, & Anderson, 1994) in patients with CBP, complex regional pain syndrome (CRPS) and in healthy controls. The authors hypothesized that the pain groups would show impairment on this emotional decision-making task given its relationship to integrity of orbitofrontal systems, as their research group previously demonstrated involvement of the prefrontal cortex in CP (Apkarian et al., 2001). Both pain groups performed poorly on the IGT when compared to controls and the CRPS group performed worse than the CBP group. IGT impairment was not associated with levels of anxiety or depression. No significant deficits or differences in cognitive performance occurred among the pain groups on tests of attention (i.e., Digit Span, Stroop), intellect (Wechsler Abbreviated Scales of Intelligence; Wechsler, 1999), or executive functioning (Wisconsin Card Sorting Test; Heaton, Chelune, Talley, Kay, & Curtiss, 1995).

Neuropathic pain is defined as pain arising as a direct consequence of a lesion or disease affecting the somatosensory system. Povedano, Gascón, Gálvez, Ruiz, and Rejas (2007) evaluated cognitive functioning in a sample of over 1500 patients with various types of neuropathic or mixed neuropathic and nociceptive pain (i.e., pain associated with tissue damage or irritation) and found significantly higher rates of cognitive impairment in those with neuropathic pain. However, the researchers' assessment of cognition was quite limited and consisted only of administration of the Mini Mental State Examination (Folstein, Folstein, & McHugh, 1975). Another study, reported only as an abstract, also showed higher levels of cognitive difficulty in patients with neuropathic pain than levels in patients with localized and generalized pain (Larsen et al., 2009). Overall, studies of cognitive functions in patients with neuropathic pain are limited, and more research in this area is needed.

Attempts have also been made to understand whether different pain types and syndromes lead to specific patterns of cognitive impairment. In other words, do patients with certain types of pain produce characteristic patterns of cognitive performance? Studies of patients with FM have indicated mild difficulties with memory, verbal fluency, and attention compared with these abilities in healthy control groups (Landrø, Stiles, & Sletvold, 1997; Sletvold, Stiles, & Landrø, 1995). More recently, Dick, Verrier, Harker, and Rashiq (2008) found that a group with FM displayed impairment on measures of everyday attention and working memory compared with such measures in healthy controls. They noted that these effects were independent of mood or sleep disturbances that are common in FM patients. However, when pain levels were statistically accounted for, there were no differences between groups on cognitive measures. In a well-controlled study of FM patients, Suhr (2003) found that FM and healthy control groups showed no differences on a comprehensive neuropsychological battery. This study also controlled for poor effort in the FM sample, a factor that is absent from many studies of cognitive functioning in CP, which will be discussed later in this chapter.

In summary, the majority of studies indicate that most groups of CP patients perform below expectation compared with controls on some cognitive tests. However, there is a lack of consistent data demonstrating pronounced differences in patterns of cognitive performance associated with different pain etiologies.

Pain Intensity

While there are inconsistencies among studies in this area, a review indicated that pain intensity has been correlated positively with subjective complaints of cognitive impairment and with objectively assessed impairment on tests of mental flexibility, memory, visual motor coordination, speed, and global cognitive functions (Kreitler & Niv, 2007). DiStefano and Radanov (1995) reported higher intensity of head pain associated with higher levels of impairment on the Paced Auditory Serial Addition Task (PASAT), and other studies found that neurocognitive performance decreased when pain intensity was high (Eccleston, 1995; Iezzi, Archibald, Barnett, Klinck, & Duckworth,, 1999). Pain intensity was correlated with neuropsychological impairment in other studies as well (Dick et al., 2008; Weiner, Rudy, Morrow, Slaboda, & Lieber, 2006). Lorenz, Beck, and Bromm (1997) showed improvements on a vigilance task following reductions in pain intensity associated with morphine treatment, but the power of this study's findings is limited by the small number of subjects examined ($n = 6$).

While such studies show clear evidence of cognitive impairment in patients with CP compared to those without pain, other studies evaluating between-group differences in patients with CP have demonstrated that deficits on tests of attention, memory, and emotional decision-making were not related primarily to pain intensity (Apkarian et al., 2004; Dick et al., 2002; Grisart & Van der Linden, 2001). Eccleston, Crombez, Aldrich, and Stannard (1997) evaluated patients with CP and found only those with high pain intensity and high somatic awareness demonstrated impairment on measures of attention, with this being a medium effect size. In this study, there was no significant main effect for medication use, pain intensity, or affective distress on attention in this subset of patients. Similarly, in a study of 736 CP patients evaluated at a pain management clinic in a medical center, Wade and Hart (2002) found that deficits in neuropsychological functioning were not related to pain intensity, and one study found that reduction in pain intensity was accompanied by improvements in subjective evaluation of cognitive functioning, but not an objective assessment of cognition (Sator-Katzenschlager et al., 2003).

Overall, a number of studies have demonstrated that cognitive dysfunction is present in patients with CP compared to those without pain, but many investigators have failed to find a strong relationship between pain intensity and cognitive dysfunction within samples of CP patients. In addition, the fact that pain intensity has been shown to have a less significant impact on cognitive dysfunction in CP than additional factors (e.g., somatic awareness) suggests the possibility that factors other than pain intensity mitigate the impact on cognitive function.

Pain Duration

Some researchers have proposed that longer durations of pain are associated with greater levels of cognitive impairment. Jongsma et al. (2011) evaluated patients with chronic pancreatic pain and found diminished psychomotor speed, memory, and executive functioning compared to that in normal controls. The authors examined the role of depression, sleep disturbance, use of opioids, and a history of alcohol abuse in their analyses, as such factors have all been associated with decreased cognitive abilities. While each of these factors offered an additional explanation for the observed cognitive decline in patients with severe pancreatic pain, the greatest effect size resulted from pain duration, with this being a large effect size. In contrast, Bell and colleagues (1999) found no correlation between duration of migraine and cognitive performance, and Apkarian et al. (2004) found that chronicity of pain did not account for differences between pain groups on a decision-making task (i.e., IGT).

Medication Effects

Opioid medications are frequently used to manage pain. Acute, time-limited opioid use has been associated with impairment in cognitive domains of attention, concentration, memory, visuospatial skills, and psychomotor speed in healthy samples without CP (Cherrier, Amory, Ersek, Risler, & Shen, 2009; Curran, Kleckham, Bearn, Strang, & Wanigaratne, 2001; Darke, Sims, McDonald, & Wickes, 2000; Davis, Liddiard, & McMillan, 2002; Gruber, Silveri, & Yurgelun-Todd, 2007).

It has been suggested that cognitive complaints and deficits in patients with CP may be related to the direct effects of narcotic and opioid use in medical treatment. A few studies have found support for an adverse effect of opioids on cognition in CP samples, with diminished performance on measures of attention and psychomotor speed associated with opioid use (Sjørgren, Christrup, Petersen, & Højsted, 2005; Sjøgren, Thomsen, & Olsen, 2000). These authors did not, however, find a dose-effect relationship between long-term oral opioid use and cognitive functioning. Other studies have failed to find a relationship between opioid use and cognitive impairment in patients with neuropathic pain (Raja et al., 2002; Rowbotham et al., 2003), and some even report beneficial effects of long-term opioid use on cognitive functions in mixed CP samples (Haythornthwaite, Menefee, Quatrano-Piacentini, & Pappagallo, 1998; Tassain et al., 2003). These authors posited that the observed improvements in cognition were a result of pain relief and associated improvements in mood.

Overall, the bulk of research in this area indicates that those who use opioids habitually are less likely to experience impaired cognitive processes secondary to opioid use. Cognitive deficits that may be present in the initial phase of opioid treatment often decrease in the face of long-term use (Ersek, Cherrier, Overman, & Irving, 2004; Zacny, 1995; Zenz, Strumpf, & Tryba, 1992). Impaired attention can follow a dose escalation or the addition of immediately released opioids to a regular sustained-release regimen (Bruera, Macmillan, Hanson, & MacDonald, 1989; Kamboj, Tookman, Jones, & Curran, 2005). These findings contradict clinical assumptions that opioid medications are associated with pronounced cognitive impairment. Instead, research indicates that any cognitive impairment associated with opioid use tends to be mild and, when present, is most likely to be an acute phenomenon that occurs after dose initiation or escalation.

Role of Emotional Distress

Cognitive impairment in patients with CP has been associated with mood changes, somatic preoccupation, sleep disturbance, and fatigue. Those who suffer from pain often experience limitations in daily activities, loss of sources of enjoyment and satisfaction, disruption of typical roles, and loss of self-esteem and identity. Many patients with CP report feelings of helplessness, hopelessness, fear, and perceived loss of control. Each of these factors can contribute to decreased quality of life and is a potential source of chronic stress. Such factors may in and of themselves contribute to worsening of pain and increased cognitive complaints.

Several studies have looked at the influence of anxiety on cognitive performance in CP populations. The majority of studies that used a measure of anxiety as a mood state found no significant relationship between anxiety and various aspects of cognition (Dick et al., 1988; Grisart & Plaghki, 1999; Apkarian et al., 2004). However, studies using a measurement of pain-related fear (as opposed to anxiety in general) typically demonstrate an association between pain-related fear, cognitive complaints, and objective cognitive difficulty (Grisart & Van der Linden, 2001; McCracken & Iverson, 2001).

Many patients with CP also report high levels of depression. In a sample of CP patients examined by Sjøgren et al. (2005), 50% had high levels of depression and 38% had significant levels of anxiety. This sample excluded individuals who met diagnostic criteria for a depressive disorder, suggesting that the incidence of depression is actually higher in the CP population.

As reviewed by Basso, Miller, Estevis, and Combs in Chapter 3 of this volume, the presence of depression has been associated with a high incidence of reported cognitive deficits, including problems with attention/concentration, memory, executive functioning, and visuospatial difficulties (see also Butters et al., 2000; Kuny & Stassen, 1995; Ravnkilde et al., 2002); Basso and colleagues provide a comprehensive review of the relationship between depression and cognitive dysfunction in Chapter 3. In addition, several studies have demonstrated that psychological distress and mood disturbance are more closely associated with the cognitive deficits seen in patients with CP than with the severity of pain (Di

Stefano & Radnov, 1995; Grace et al., 1999; Kewman, Vaishampayan, Zald, & Han, 1991; Landro et al., 1997; Radanov, Hirlinger, Di Stefano, & Valach, 1992).

Numerous studies have shown depression accounts for variance in subjective cognitive complaints and objective cognitive impairments demonstrated in CP samples. McCracken and Iverson (2001) found greater emotional distress associated with greater reports of cognitive dysfunction in CP patients. In fact, depression accounted for 29% of the variance in cognitive complaints, with this representing a medium effect size. Similarly, Roth et al. (2005) demonstrated that depressive symptoms, as assessed by the Beck Depression Inventory, made the greatest contribution to the prediction of cognitive complaints. Brown, Glass, and Park (2002) evaluated a sample of patients with rheumatoid arthritis. While high levels of pain and depression were associated with poor cognitive performance in all four areas assessed (information processing speed, working memory capacity, reasoning ability, and verbal memory), structural equation modeling indicated depression accounted for this relationship, with the effects of pain on cognition no longer being significant when controlling for depression. Along similar lines, Iezzi et al. (1999) noted those patients with the highest level of emotional distress also presented with the greatest cognitive impairment and analyses demonstrated these deficits were not related to pain intensity ratings, disability or legal status, or medication use. Studies that actively screened patients with CP for psychiatric illness or else had a narrow range of scores on measures of psychological distress did not find associations between CP and cognitive impairment (Eccleston, 1994, 1995).

Overall, most studies in this area indicate that depression contributes significantly to the experience of cognitive impairment in CP patients, with the effect sizes typically in the medium range.

Perception of Pain

It has long been understood that physiological factors alone cannot account for an individual's experience of pain (Beecher, 1956; Melzack & Wall, 1965), with psychological variables, including the perception of pain, playing an important role in determining the pain experience. *Pain catastrophizing* has been defined as a tendency to view pain in an overly negative and exaggerated manner. Individuals who view their pain in a catastrophic manner tend to ruminate about their pain, magnify their experience of pain, and feel helpless to effectively manage their pain (Sullivan, Bishop, & Pivik, 1995). Catastrophizing has been associated with increased disability, increased expression of pain behaviors, higher use of health care services, longer hospital stays, greater use of pain medications, and poor outcome from surgical procedures for treatment of back pain (Block et al., 2001; Sullivan, Rodgers, & Kirsch, 2001).

Chronic worry, hypervigilance to painful situations, and fear of engaging in actions that may be painful are also common manifestations of CP (Aldrich, Eccleston, & Crombez, 2000; Asmundson, Wright, & Hadjistavropoulos, 2005; Roelofs, Peters, McCracken, & Vlaeyen, 2003; Roelofs, Peters, & Vlaeyan, 2002). An association between hypervigilance, pain intensity, and catastrophizing has been shown (Crombez, Eccleston, Van den Broeck, Goubert, & Van Houdenhove, 2004), and individuals who view their pain in a catastrophic manner often fear re-injury. As a result, they tend to be less active, which leads to a deconditioned state in which pain is more easily exacerbated and opioid use is increased. In their discussion of the influence of worry on CP, Aldrich and colleagues (2000) note that patients typically worry not only about their chronic pain but also about a number of adverse threats that could possibly converge on them, with perseveration on misdirected attempts to achieve a lasting escape from pain.

An individual's perception of pain can influence cognitive functions. High levels of pain catastrophizing have been associated with increased attention problems (Crombez, Eccleston, Baeyens, & Eelen, 1998; Crombez, Eccleston, Van den Broeck, Van Houdenhove, & Goubert, 2002; VanCleef & Peters, 2006). Catastrophizing is correlated with difficulty suppressing pain-related thoughts (Crombez et al., 1998; Van Damme, Crombez, & Eccleston, 2004), which may lead to increased distractability and less availability of attention resources. This "attention overload," in which pain consumes large amounts of available attention resources and leaves minimal attention to invest in other aspects of cognitive functioning, is hypothesized to result in poor cognitive performance. The attention model of pain catastrophizing is supported by neuroimaging data in subjects with FM, showing a correlation between catastrophizing scores and activity in the dorsolateral prefrontal cortex, rostral anterior cingulate cortex, and medial prefrontal cortex (Gracely et al., 2004), which are cortical regions implicated in pain vigilance, attention, and awareness (Bornhövd et al., 2002; Büchel et al., 2002; Derbyshire & Jones, 1998; Valet et al., 2004).

Sleep Disturbance and Fatigue

Sleep is often disrupted as a result of pain. Rates of reported sleep disturbance among CP populations range from 55% to over 90% (Morin, Gibson, & Wade, 1998; O'Donoghue, Fox, Heneghan, & Hurley, 2009). In individuals without CP, sleep deprivation has been shown to contribute to detriments in various cognitive processes, including memory, attention, and visuomotor skills (Alhola & Polo-Kantola, 2007). Given the association between sleep disturbance and detriments in aspects of cognitive functioning, it is logical to assume that patients with pain who have disrupted sleep may also experience associated cognitive disruptions. When investigating this hypothesis, Roth et al. (2005) found fatigue to be highly correlated with cognitive complaints in a series of 222 CP patients. In a similar study of FM and generalized CP groups, FM patients reported significantly more fatigue than CP counterparts and healthy controls (Suhr, 2003). Self-reported fatigue was the variable most consistently related to subjective cognitive complaints in all three groups. Among objective cognitive findings, fatigue was significantly related to speed of processing. In particular, level of fatigue was associated with performance on the Trail Making Test B, Controlled Oral Word Association, and Digit Symbol tests.

There seems to be a general consensus in this area, with most studies finding a positive relationship between sleep dysregulation and objective cognitive deficits in CP patients, with typical effect sizes in the medium range. In addition, there tends to be a stronger association between fatigue and perceived cognitive problems, especially in the FM population, as compared to the link between fatigue and objective cognitive dysfunction.

Patient Effort Level

A review of inadequate effort as a potential confound to valid neuropsychological assessment can be found in Chapter 2 of this book and thus will not be repeated here. As with all neuropsychological evaluations, assessment of individuals with CP can be confounded by efforts to appear more cognitively impaired than is actually the case. Base rates of malingering in CP patients have ranged from 20% to 50%, depending on the classification system used to define malingering (Greve, Ord, Bianchini, & Curtis, 2009, Meyers, Millis, & Volkert, 2002). These rates are similar to the base rates of malingering that have been reported in individuals with mild traumatic brain injury (Mittenberg, Patton, Canyock, & Condit, 2002). Symptom validity tests (SVTs) are a late arrival on the scene of research investigating the impact of pain on cognition, and many studies in this area do not control for potentially poor effort. The importance of effective evaluation of effort in neuropsychological assessment of patients with pain cannot be overemphasized. As evidence, Gervais and colleagues (2001) examined effort in groups of FM and CP patients seeking disability benefits and found SVT failure rates of 35% and 40%, respectively. In contrast, only 4% of FM patients who were not seeking disability benefits failed validity testing. In another sample of FM patients, Suhr (2003) reported that significantly more individuals from FM and CP groups failed symptom validity tests relative to healthy controls.

Numerous studies have demonstrated the utility of traditional, stand-alone SVTs in detecting inadequate effort in CP patients (Gervais, Rohling, Green, & Ford, 2004), while others have examined embedded cognitive variables that measure for valid responding (Suhr, 2003). Larrabee (2003) used patient responses to a self-report measure of pain perception (Modified Somatic Pain Questionnaire; Main, 1983) to detect exaggerated pain symptoms. The importance of employing more than one SVT when assessing individuals with CP was demonstrated by Gervais and colleagues (2003), who showed that the sensitivity of SVTs varied substantially in a sample of disability claimants. Twice as many of their CP and FM subjects failed the Word Memory Test (Green, 2003b), compared with the Test of Memory Malingering (Tombaugh, 1996). Collectively, such research clearly indicates the benefit of assessing for effort, especially if there are current or future medicolegal ramifications for the individual presenting with CP and complaints of cognitive impairment.

Summary

Assessment of patients who present with CP poses a number of challenges. Pain is a subjective phenomenon, and thus accurate and objective measurement is challenging. The clinician must rely on a combination of patient self-report, behavioral observations, and effective interviewing to gain a fuller understanding of pain location, type, intensity, and duration. While these aspects of pain can contribute to cognitive complaints and impairment, there are numerous additional confounding factors typically associated with pain that additionally complicate assessment of the patient with CP (e.g., depression, pain catastrophizing, pain-related fear, possible medication effects, fatigue, and possibly poor motivation). While research that has attempted to elucidate the role of pain in cognitive functions has yielded inconsistent findings, the larger and well-controlled studies indicate a greater impact on cognition from non-pain-related factors than from actual pain. Since it is possible for any number of these domains to contribute to cognitive impairment, it is important for clinicians to gain an understanding of these factors in each individual patient. Table 7.1 provides a summary of levels of evidence supporting a link between cognition and the pain-related factors reviewed in this chapter.

CLINICAL ASSESSMENT

Cognitive complaints and impairment are common in the CP population. Self-reported cognitive difficulties are frequently inconsistent with objective findings on neuropsychological measures. As such, it is essential to use a multimodal assessment approach when asked to evaluate a patient with CP. It is recommended that such assessment include a clinical interview, behavioral observations, review of recent medical records, and psychometric testing, with emphasis on emotional functioning, coping skills, and cognitive abilities.

Clinical Interview

In addition to typical neuropsychological interview questions, it is recommended that interviews of patients with pain elicit information about the pain-related variables outlined above (i.e., etiology, intensity, and duration of pain). Asking the patient to rate current pain and highest and lowest levels of pain in the past week using an analog scale (most studies employ a 0–10 scale, with 10 representing "worst pain possible") provides useful clinical data concerning the individual's experience of pain intensity. It is also helpful to inquire about factors that tend to exacerbate the individual's pain, as well as factors that seem to make the pain more manageable. This helps the clinician gain an understanding of the extent to which patients feel they can control or manage pain and can be useful information when structuring treatment recommendations.

Interviews should also include inquiry about patients' current medications, including their perception of whether or not these provide the desired benefit. It is not unusual for CP patients who are taking high doses of opioids or other medications used for pain management (i.e., muscle relaxants) to report that the medications have no effect on their pain, calling into question the need for such medications. Current dosage and duration of pain medication use are also

Table 7.1 SECONDARY FACTORS ASSOCIATED WITH COGNITION
IN CHRONIC PAIN (CP)

Secondary Factors that Influence Cognition in CP	Level of Evidence[1]	Cognitive Domains[2]
Pain intensity	**	Mental flexibility, memory, visual motor coordination, speed, attention
Pain etiology		
Cervical/headache	**	Variable
Nociceptive pain	**	Variable
Fibromyalgia	**	Memory, verbal fluency, attention
Neuropathic pain	***	Problem solving
Pain duration	**	Psychomotor speed, executive functioning, memory
Opioid effects	*/**[3]	Attention, psychomotor speed (following dose escalation)
Sleep disturbance/fatigue	***	Psychomotor/processing speed
Emotional factors		
Depression	****	Processing speed, memory, executive functioning
Anxiety (general/mood state)	*	Minimal impairment
Anxiety (pain-related fear)[+]	***	Memory
Pain catastrophizing	****	Attention

[1] Studies showing significant associations with cognitive functioning.
  * Minimal evidence of positive association with cognitive dysfunction.
  ** Some evidence of positive association with cognitive dysfunction, but many contradictory findings.
  *** Majority find positive association with cognitive dysfunction.
  **** Scant limited or contradictory evidence.
[2] Cognitive domains in which impairment is most often found.
[3] There is minimal evidence for habitual use and moderate evidence when dose escalation or immediate-release narcotics are added to a sustained-release regimen.
[+] A limited number of studies have evaluated this relationship.

important variables, particularly since it has been shown that opioid-related cognitive changes can occur in opioid-naïve patients.

Patients should be asked about their mood, energy, and quality of sleep, as well as any significant psychosocial stressors they may be facing, including work-related issues, family problems, and financial difficulties. This helps to establish a sense of the overall level of distress and suffering the patient may be experiencing. Interview questions about subjective perceptions of cognitive abilities (particularly attention, memory, and processing speed) are also important. Some clinicians prefer to elicit information regarding subjective cognitive experience entirely through interview, while others use interview questions in conjunction with standardized questionnaires (i.e., Memory Complaints Inventory; Green, 2003a). In addition, observations of potential cognitive dysfunction by significant others can be helpful. However, regardless of the method of acquiring such subjective data, it is important for the clinician to remain mindful that self-reported cognitive complaints among patients with CP are often inconsistent with objective neuropsychological data. Thus, the need for objective assessment, particularly in the presence of self-reported cognitive problems, is crucial.

Inquiry should also be made as to whether the patient is involved in any type of compensation-seeking activities, as effort and motivation can explain large amounts of variance in cognitive functioning in populations who are applying for disability or involved in litigation. Poor effort in someone seeking compensation should alter a neuropsychologist's approach to test interpretation for that particular patient.

Medical Record Review

As is true in most neuropsychological evaluations, a review of medical records helps provide a more comprehensive understanding of the case and provides a framework for understanding cognitive test results. When available, it is helpful to review recent medical records for patients with pain conditions. Such reviews can provide useful information regarding current and past medications, aberrant medication behavior (i.e., frequently running out early, loss of controlled substances, etc.), medical diagnoses related to the pain condition, potential inconsistencies in patient behavior or presentation, evidence of significant emotional distress observed by medical providers, and other "yellow flags" identified during routine medical treatment for the pain condition. Such review can also help the neuropsychologist gain a better understanding of any other medical problems the patient may be experiencing, with particular attention to those potentially associated with cognitive impairment.

Behavioral Observations

Individuals with CP often demonstrate pain behavior that can be systematically observed and quantified. For example, Keefe and Block (1982) identified a number of pain behaviors that correlate well with pain ratings. These behaviors include bracing (using a limb to abnormally support weight), guarding (stiff or interrupted movement), grimacing (a facial expression of pain), rubbing (touching the affected area), and sighing (an exaggerated exhalation of air). It is important to note whether pain intensity and self-reported description of factors that contribute to exacerbation of pain (i.e., sitting for more than 15 minutes) correspond with observed pain behavior. It is often helpful to observe the patient for consistencies in pain behavior in various settings, including the waiting room or when walking down the hall, as well as during the evaluation. The presence of inconsistent or exaggerated pain behaviors suggests that psychosocial factors (i.e., high pain sensitivity and somatization, depression, motivation or secondary gain) are likely contributing to reported pain.

Testing

Neuropsychologists vary with regard to test selection, depending on test familiarity and comfort level, evaluation referral question, and theoretical orientation. The amount of cognitive testing administered in cases where pain is present will also vary depending on the referral question. For example, in CP patients referred for presurgical psychological screening evaluations, cognitive testing may be brief and focus on ruling out significant cognitive deficits that would interfere with one's ability to follow postsurgical recommendations. In patients with pain that stems from a neurological condition with the potential to interfere with cognitive skills, assessment of cognition would likely be more comprehensive. Regardless of a clinician's approach to neuropsychological assessment, it is important to obtain a comprehensive neuropsychological assessment of individuals with cognitive complaints and concomitant pain. Close attention should be paid to the domains of processing speed, attention, and memory. If performances in these areas are disproportionally diminished relative to expected patterns associated with the neurological condition being evaluated, pain-related variables may be playing a role. Unusual patterns of cognitive results would also suggest the role of various non-neurological, pain-related variables.

Given the relatively high base rates of malingering and symptom exaggeration in patients with CP, use of SVTs in the assessments of CP patients is highly recommended and considered essential when an evaluation occurs within a medicolegal or other compensation-seeking context.

Assessment of individuals with pain should include measures of psychological distress, particularly those which assess for symptoms of depression, anxiety, and somatic focus. A variety of questionnaires have been designed to assess an individual's perception of his or her pain and pain-related disability. Inclusion of measures which provide useful clinical information regarding somatization and pain-related coping styles (i.e., pain catastrophizing) are also quite useful in pain populations. A sample of well-validated measures that can be used to assess various domains of the biopsychosocial impact of pain can be found in Box 7.1.

CLINICAL IMPLICATIONS

Once the assessment is complete, relevant information from interview, behavioral observations, medical records, and testing should be integrated and treatment recommendations made on the basis of those findings. Providing direct, honest feedback about evaluation results that indicate maladaptive emotional or behavioral reactions to pain is an important first step in managing CP patients.

When pronounced symptoms of depression or anxiety are identified, cognitive behavioral therapy is often helpful. When symptoms are especially severe or significantly interfering with an individual's functional capabilities, facilitating a medication consult may be helpful. If pronounced somatization tendencies are identified, helping the patient develop more insight into the role psychosocial factors play in their physical symptoms and teaching strategies to enhance coping

---

Box 7.1 SUGGESTED PAIN-RELATED ASSESSMENT MEASURES

Pain

Visual Analog Scale (VAS)
Numerical Rating Scale (NRS)
McGill Pain Questionnaire (MPQ; Melzack, 1987)
Short Form McGill Pain Questionnaire (SF-MPQ; Dworkin et al., 2009)

Emotional Status-Affective

Minnesota Multiphasic Personality Inventory-2 (MMPI-2; Butcher, Dahlstrom, Graham, Tellegen, & Kaemmer, 1989)
Minnesota Multiphasic Personality Inventory-2-Restructured Form (MMPI-2-RF; Ben-Porath & Tellegen, 2008)
Battery for Health Improvement-2 (BHI-2; Bruns & Disorbio, 2003)
Brief Battery for Health Improvement-2 (BBHI-2; Disorbio & Bruns, 2002)
Beck Depression Inventory (BDI; Beck, Ward, Mendelson, Mock, & Erbaugh, 1961)

Somatization

Minnesota Multiphasic Personality Inventory-2 (MMPI-2)
Minnesota Multiphasic Personality Inventory-2-Restructured Form (MMPI-2-RF)
Battery for Health Improvement-2 (BHI-2)
Brief Battery for Health Improvement-2 (BBHI-2)
Modified Somatic Perceptions Questionnaire (MSPQ; Main, 1983)

Pain Perception

Sullivan Pain Catastrophizing Scale (PCS; Sullivan, Bishop, & Pivik, 1995)
Tampa Scale for Kinesiophobia (TSK; Kori, Miller, & Todd, 1990)
Fear-Avoidance Beliefs Questionnaire (FABQ; Waddell, Newton, Hinderson, Somerville, & Main, 1993)

Fatigue

Fatigue Scale (Chalder et al., 1993)
Fatigue Severity Scale (FSS; Krupp, LaRocca, Muir-Nash, & Steinberg, 1989)

---

skills would be warranted. Other approaches to managing somatization, including psychodynamic and interpersonal psychotherapies and affective cognitive behavioral therapy, are also available (Lamberty, 2008).

When there is evidence of pain catastrophizing, cognitive therapy should be included in treatment to help individuals learn techniques to modify their thinking. Education, graded exposure in vivo, graded activity, acceptance and commitment therapy (ACT), and cognitive behavioral therapy are most commonly described in the literature as treatment methods to help patients with pain reduce fear avoidance (de Jong et al., 2005, Woods & Asmundson, 2008). Graded in vivo exposure and ACT have been associated with the highest levels of effectiveness in reducing fear-avoidance behaviors (Bailey, Carleton, Valeyen, & Asmundson, 2010). For the patient with a high level of somatization, significant mood disturbance, and significant subjective complaints about cognitive ability who demonstrates few or no objective cognitive deficits, it will be relevant to focus primarily on addressing psychosocial issues such as mood, coping skills, and underlying personality factors that may be contributing to perceived cognitive inefficiencies.

When significant sleep disturbance is present, educating patients about sleep hygiene, teaching relaxation techniques, and facilitating a medication consultation can be helpful. Effectively reducing sleep disturbance helps decrease fatigue, improve quality of life, and may improve cognitive functions in some individuals.

Severity of impairment, level of concern by the individual about any impairment, and level of functional disability are important factors to consider when choosing an interventional strategy. As any of these increase, an approach of identifying potential contributors to impairment and then developing appropriate strategies to address those that are modifiable is likely to be useful. For example, if a recent increase in opioid medication seems to be correlated with cognitive impairment, consultation with the physician could be warranted.

CASE STUDY

Identifying Information and Reason for Evaluation: *P.T. is a 72-year-old, married, right-handed woman with 13 years of education who was referred for behavioral medicine evaluation by her pain management physician.*

History of Present Illness: *P.T. reported a 5-year history of pain in the lumbar region and right lower extremity. She reported that she had undergone seven spine surgeries within the past 5 years and that she was being considered for implantation of a spinal cord stimulator to more effectively manage her ongoing pain. Evaluation was requested to help identify potential psychosocial risk factors for poor surgical outcome and develop appropriate treatment recommendations. In addition, there were concerns about her cognitive status, her use of medication, and how these two factors interacted.*

Over the past several years, P.T. had reportedly experienced a decline in her memory, attention, and decision-making skills. Despite these problems, she reportedly functioned adequately in her daily life.

Medical History: *Apart from the aforementioned back problems, P.T. reported a prior diagnosis of fibromyalgia and thyroid disease. At the time of this evaluation, she was taking morphine sulfate (a long-acting narcotic) 15 mg bid, Lortab 7.5 mg bid prn for break-through pain, and Lyrica 75 mg bid for pain-related issues. She reported that these medications had been of questionable benefit and that her pain level rarely changed after taking them. She indicated that her pain typically ranged from a 3 to an 8 on a scale of 0 to 10, depending on her activity level.*

Psychiatric History: *The patient reported a history of depression since the onset of her pain condition. She was taking Cymbalta (30 mg qd) for treatment of her mood at the time of this evaluation. She reported that the medication had been beneficial.*

Chemical Dependency History: *Since the onset of her back pain, P.T. had been prescribed various opioid medications and her husband expressed concerns that she had been "overmedicated" at times. She had overused pain medications in the past and required inpatient detoxification for treatment of this problem in 2007. Despite her history, she was again prescribed these medications for pain control and reportedly took them as prescribed. Her husband reported that, even when using pain medications as prescribed, her use of opioids seemed to be associated with changes in cognitive status and emotional lability. She denied any history of alcohol or illicit drug use.*

Behavioral Observations and Test Results: *P.T. was pleasant and cooperative with the evaluation. Her speech was of normal, rate, volume, and tone. She had more difficulty than expected following test instructions, and frequently required repetition and simplification of directions to facilitate her comprehension. No pain-related behaviors were noted and she did not complain of pain during the evaluation. She did, however, complain of fatigue and appeared drowsy at times during the assessment.*

Her scores on a test of performance validity were adequate. Within this context, she demonstrated low-average global intellectual abilities, with somewhat stronger nonverbal (average) versus verbal (low average) intellectual performances. On a cognitive screening measure, she demonstrated significant impairment on indices of immediate memory (2nd percentile) and delayed memory (<1st percentile). Her score on an index of attention was also impaired (5th percentile). On a measure of emotional functioning (BHI-2), she demonstrated confusion in her responding, omitted numerous items, and produced an invalid profile.

Given her presentation, test results, and reported history of cognitive problems within the context of opioid use, it was concluded that the true nature of the patient's cognitive status was obscured by medication effects. Thus, it was recommended that her physician consider discontinuation of, or at least minimization of, opioid medication (especially since she reported limited pain relief from the medications). Repeat neuropsychological evaluation was recommended and took place 2 months later. In the meantime, the patient's pain-management physician worked with her to significantly reduce the level of opioids. At the time of re-evaluation, she was taking Percocet 5 mg bid.

During the second evaluation, P.T. was more alert and no fluctuations in her mental status were noted. She was cooperative and performed adequately on performance of validity testing. Whereas pronounced impairments on measures of attention and memory were noted during the initial evaluation, she now produced normal scores on tests of those abilities. She also produced average scores for someone of her age and educational background on tests of intellectual abilities, executive functions, visuospatial abilities, processing speed, and language skills. Emotionally, she denied significant depression, anxiety, or emotional distress. There was no evidence of pain catastrophizing or symptom magnification.

Overall, there was no evidence of a dementia or incipient neurodegenerative process, and no cognitive or emotional reasons to avoid implanting a stimulator in this individual were evident. It was recommended that she remain abstinent from opioid medications given her propensity to develop cognitive side effects and her history of medication abuse and dependence. She underwent surgery several months later following a successful stimulator trial. Her pain level decreased to approximately 50% and remained at that level 6 months after surgery.

Appendix

Pain-Related Acronyms

CP: chronic pain
CBP: chronic back pain
FM: fibromyalgia
RA: rheumatoid arthritis
CRPS: complex regional pain syndrome

Note

1. This and other pain-related acronyms can be found in the Appendix.

References

Aldrich, S., Eccleston, C., & Crombez, G. (2000). Worrying about chronic pain: Vigilance to threat and misdirected problem solving. *Behaviour Research and Therapy, 38*(5), 457–470.

Alhola, P., & Polo-Kantola, P. (2007). Sleep deprivation: Impact on cognitive performance. *Neuropsychiatric Disease and Treatment, 3*(5), 553–567.

Antepohl, W., Kiviloog, L., Andersson, J., & Gerdle, B. (2003). Cognitive impairment in patients with chronic whiplash-associated disorder—a matched control study. *NeuroRehabilitation, 18*(4), 307–315.

Apkarian, A. V., Sosa, Y., Krauss, B. R., Thomas, P. S., Fredrickson, B. E., Levy, R. E., et al. (2004). Chronic pain patients are impaired on an emotional decision-making task. *Pain, 108*(1–2), 129–136.

Apkarian, A. V., Thomas, P. S., Krauss, B. R., & Szeverenyi, N. M. (2001). Prefrontal cortical hyperactivity in patients with sympathetically mediated chronic pain. *Neuroscience Letters, 311*(3), 193–197.

Asmundson, G. J., Wright, K. D., & Hadjistavropoulos, H. D. (2005). Hypervigilance and attentional fixedness in chronic musculoskeletal pain: Consistency of findings across modified Stroop and Dot Probe tasks. *J Pain, 6*(8), 497–506.

Bailey, K. M., Carleton, R. N., Vlaeyen, J. W., & Asmundson, G. J. (2010). Treatments addressing pain-related fear and anxiety in patients with chronic musculoskeletal pain: A preliminary review. *Cognitive Behavior Therapy, 39*(1), 46–63.

Bechara, A., Damasio, A. R., Damasio, H., & Anderson, S. W. (1994). Insensitivity to future consequences following damage to human prefrontal cortex. *Cognition, 50*(1–3), 7–15.

Beck, A. T., Ward, C. H., Mendelson, M., Mock, J., & Erbaugh, J. (1961). An inventory for measuring depression. *Archives of General Psychiatry, 4*, 561–571.

Bee, S., Townsend, C., Bruce, B., Hayes, S., Utesch, S., Dokken, P., et al. (2007). Cognitive functioning of patients with fibromyalgia: A comparison to patients with chronic back pain. *The Journal of Pain, 8*(4, Supplement), S61.

Beecher, H. K. (1956). Relationship of significance of wound to pain experienced *Journal of the American Medical Association, 161*, 1609–1613.

Bell, B. D., Primeau, M., Sweet, J. J., & Lofland, K. R. (1999). Neuropsychological functioning in migraine headache, nonheadache chronic pain, and mild traumatic brain injury patients. *Archives of Clinical Neuropsychology, 14*(4), 389–399.

Ben-Porath, Y. S., & Tellegen, A. (2008). Minnesota Multiphasic Personality Inventory-2 Restructured Form. *Pearson Assessments.*

Block, A. R., Ohnmeiss, D. D., Guyer, R. D., Rashbaum, R. F., & Hochschuler, S. H. (2001). The use of presurgical psychological screening to predict the outcome of spine surgery. *The Spine Journal, 1*(4), 274–282.

Bornhövd, K., Quante, M., Glauche, V., Bromm, B., Weiller, C., & Büchel, C. (2002). Painful stimuli evoke different stimulus-response functions in the amygdala, prefrontal, insula and somatosensory cortex: A single-trial fMRI study. *Brain, 125*(6), 1326–1336.

Bosma, F. K., & Kessels, R. P. (2002). Cognitive impairments, psychological dysfunction, and coping styles in patients with chronic whiplash syndrome. *Neuropsychiatry, Neuropsychology, and Behavioral Neurology, 15*(1), 56–65.

Brown, S. C., Glass, J. M., & Park, D. C. (2002). The relationship of pain and depression to cognitive function in rheumatoid arthritis patients. *Pain, 96*(3), 279–284.

Bruera, E., Macmillan, K., Hanson, J., & MacDonald, R. N. (1989). The cognitive effects of the administration of narcotic analgesics in patients with cancer pain. *Pain, 39*(1), 13–16.

Bruns, D., & Disorbio, J. M. (2003). *Battery for Health Improvement 2 manual.* Minneapolis: Pearson.

Büchel, C., Bornhovd, K., Quante, M., Glauche, V., Bromm, B., & Weiller, C. (2002). Dissociable neural responses related to pain intensity, stimulus intensity, and stimulus awareness within the anterior cingulate cortex: A parametric single-trial laser functional magnetic resonance imaging study. *Journal of Neuroscience, 22*(3), 970–976.

Burker, E., Hannay, H. J., & Halsey, J. H. (1989). Neuropsychological functioning and personality characteristics of migrainous and nonmigrainous female college students. *Neuropsychology, 3*(2), 61–73.

Butcher, J. N., Dahlstrom, W. G., Graham, J. R., Tellegen, A., & Kaemmer, B. (1989). *Minnesota Multiphasic Personality Inventory-2 (MMPI-2): Manual for administration and scoring.* Minneapolis: University of Minnesota Press.

Butters, M. A., Becker, J. T., Nebes, R. D., Zmuda, M. D., Mulsant, B. H., Pollock, B. G., & Reynolds, C. F., 3rd. (2000). Changes in cognitive functioning following treatment of late-life depression. *The American Journal of Psychiatry, 157*(12), 1949–1954.

Chalder, T., Berelowitz, G., Pawlikowska, T., Watts, L., Wessely, S., Wright, D., et al. (1993). Development of a fatigue scale. *Journal of Psychosomatic Research, 37*(2), 147–153.

Cherrier, M. M., Amory, J. K., Ersek, M., Risler, L., & Shen, D. D. (2009). Comparative cognitive and subjective side effects of immediate-release oxycodone in healthy middle-aged and older adults. *The Journal of Pain, 10*(10), 1038–1050.

Crombez, G., Eccleston, C., Baeyens, F., & Eelen, P. (1998). When somatic information threatens, catastrophic thinking enhances attentional interference. *Pain, 75*(2–3), 187–198.

Crombez, G., Eccleston, C., Van den Broeck, A., Goubert, L., & Van Houdenhove, B. (2004). Hypervigilance to pain in fibromyalgia: The mediating role of pain intensity and catastrophic thinking about pain. *The Clinical Journal of Pain, 20*(2), 98–102.

Crombez, G., Eccleston, C., Van den Broeck, A., Van Houdenhove, B., & Goubert, L. (2002). The effects of catastrophic thinking about pain on attentional interference by pain: No mediation of negative affectivity in healthy volunteers and in patients with low back pain. *Pain Research & Management, 7*(1), 31–39.

Curran, H. V., Kleckham, J., Bearn, J., Strang, J., & Wanigaratne, S. (2001). Effects of methadone on cognition, mood and craving in detoxifying opiate addicts: A dose-response study. *Psychopharmacology, 154*(2), 153–160.

Darke, S., Sims, J., McDonald, S., & Wickes, W. (2000). Cognitive impairment among methadone maintenance patients. *Addiction, 95*(5), 687–695.

Davis, P. E., Liddiard, H., & McMillan, T. M. (2002). Neuropsychological deficits and opiate abuse. *Drug and Alcohol Dependence, 67*(1), 105–108.

de Jong, J. R., Vlaeyen, J. W. S., Onghena, P., Cuypers, C., Hollander, M. d., & Ruijgrok, J. (2005). Reduction of pain-related fear in complex regional pain syndrome type I: The application of graded exposure in vivo. *Pain, 116*(3), 264–275.

Denburg, S. D., Stewart, K. E., Hart, L. E., & Denburg, J. A. (2003). How "soft" are soft neurological signs? the relationship of subjective neuropsychiatric complaints to cognitive function in systemic lupus erythematosus. *The Journal of Rheumatology, 30*(5), 1006–1010.

Derbyshire, S. W. G., & Jones, A. K. P. (1998). Cerebral responses to a continual tonic pain stimulus measured using positron emission tomography. *Pain, 76*(1–2), 127–135.

Dick, B., Eccleston, C., & Crombez, G. (2002). Attentional functioning in fibromyalgia, rheumatoid arthritis, and musculoskeletal pain patients. *Arthritis Care & Research, 47*(6), 639–644.

Dick, B. D., Verrier, M. J., Harker, K. T., & Rashiq, S. (2008). Disruption of cognitive function in fibromyalgia syndrome. *Pain, 139*(3), 610–616.

Disorbio, J. M., & Bruns, D. (2002). *Brief Battery for Health Improvement 2 manual.* Minneapolis: Pearson.

Di Stefano, G., & Radanov, B. P. (1995). Course of attention and memory after common whiplash: A two-years prospective study with age, education and gender pair-matched patients. *Acta Neurologica Scandinavica, 91*(5), 346–352.

Dworkin, R. H., Turk, D. C., Revicki, D. A., Harding, G., Coyne, K. S., Peirce-Sandner, S., et al., (2009). Development and initial validation of an expanded and revised version of the short-form McGill pain questionnaire (SF-MPQ-2). *Pain, 144*(1–2), 35–42.

Eccleston, C. (1994). Chronic pain and attention: A cognitive approach. *British Journal of Clinical Psychology, 33*(4), 535–547.

Eccleston, C. (1995). The attentional control of pain: Methodological and theoretical concerns. *Pain, 63*(1), 3–10.

Eccleston, C., & Crombez, G. (1999). Pain demands attention: A cognitive–affective model of the interruptive function of pain. *Psychological Bulletin, 125*(3), 356 366.

Eccleston, C., Crombez, G., Aldrich, S., & Stannard, C. (1997). Attention and somatic awareness in chronic pain. *Pain, 72*(1–2), 209–215.

Ersek, M., Cherrier, M. M., Overman, S. S., & Irving, G. A. (2004). The cognitive effects of opioids. *Pain Management Nursing, 5*(2), 75–93.

Folstein, M. F., Folstein, S. E., & McHugh, P. R. (1975). "Mini-mental state". A practical method for grading the cognitive state of patients for the clinician. *Journal of Psychiatric Research, 12*, 189–198.

Gervais, R. O., Rohling, M. L., Green, P., & Ford, W. (2004). A comparison of WMT, CARB, and TOMM failure rates in non-head injury disability claimants. *Archives of Clinical Neuropsychology, 19*(4), 475–487.

Gervais, R. O., Russell, A. S., Green, P., Allen, L. M., 3rd, Ferrari, R., & Pieschl, S. D. (2001). Effort testing in patients with fibromyalgia and disability incentives. *Journal of Rheumatology, 28*(8), 1892–1899.

Goldberg, M. B., Mock, D., Ichise, M., Proulx, G., Gordon, A., Shandling, M., et al. (1996). Neuropsychologic deficits and clinical features of posttraumatic temporomandibular disorders. *Journal of Orofacial Pain, 10*(2), 126–140.

Grace, G. M., Nielson, W. R., Hopkins, M., & Berg, M. A. (1999). Concentration and memory deficits in patients with fibromyalgia syndrome. *Journal of Clinical and Experimental Neuropsychology, 21*(4), 477–487.

Gracely, R. H., Geisser, M. E., Giesecke, T., Grant, M. A., Petzke, F., Williams, D. A., & Clauw, D. J. (2004). Pain catastrophizing and neural responses to pain among persons with fibromyalgia. *Brain, 127*(4), 835–843.

Green, P. (2003a). *Green's Memory Complaints Inventory*. Edmonton, Canada: Green's Publishing.

Green, P. (2003b). *Green's Word Memory Test: User's manual*. Edmonton, Canada: Green's Publishing.

Greve, K. W., Ord, J. S., Bianchini, K. J., & Curtis, K. L. (2009). Prevalence of malingering in patients with chronic pain referred for psychologic evaluation in a medico-legal context. *Archives of Physical Medicine and Rehabilitation, 90*(7), 1117–1126.

Grisart, J. M., & Plaghki, L. H. (1999). Impaired selective attention in chronic pain patients. *European Journal of Pain, 3*(4), 325–333.

Grisart, J. M., & Van der Linden, M. (2001). Conscious and automatic uses of memory in chronic pain patients. *Pain, 94*(3), 305–313.

Gruber, S. A., Silveri, M. M., & Yurgelun-Todd, D. A. (2007). Neuropsychological consequences of opiate use. *Neuropsychol Rev, 17*(3), 299–315.

Hart, R. P., Martelli, M. F., & Zasler, N. D. (2000). Chronic pain and neuropsychological functioning. *Neuropsychology Review, 10*(3):131–149.

Haythornthwaite, J. A., Menefee, L. A., Quatrano-Piacentini, A. L., & Pappagallo, M. (1998). Outcome of chronic opioid therapy for non-cancer pain. *Journal of Pain and Symptom Management, 15*(3), 185–194.

Heaton, R. K., Chelune, G. J., Talley, J. L., Kay, G. G., & Curtiss, G. (1995). *Wisconsin Card Sorting Test*. Odessa, FL: *Psychological Assessment Resources*.

Iezzi, T., Archibald, Y., Barnett, P., Klinck, A., & Duckworth, M. (1999). Neurocognitive performance and emotional status in chronic pain patients. *Journal of Behavioral Medicine, 22*(3), 205–216.

Institute of Medicine Report, Committee on Advancing Pain Research, Care, and Education. (2011). *Relieving pain in America: A blueprint for transforming prevention, care, education and research*. Washington, DC: National Academies Press.

Jamison, R. N., Sbrocco, T., & Parris, W. C. (1989). The influence of physical and psychosocial factors on accuracy of memory for pain in chronic pain patients. *Pain, 37*(3), 289–294.

Jongsma, M. L. A., Postma, S. A. E., Souren, P., Arns, M., Gordon, E., Vissers, K.,. et al. (2011). Neurodegenerative properties of chronic pain: Cognitive decline in patients with chronic pancreatitis. *PLoS ONE, 6*(8), e23363.

Kamboj, S. K., Tookman, A., Jones, L., & Curran, H. V. (2005). The effects of immediate-release morphine on cognitive functioning in patients receiving chronic opioid therapy in palliative care. *Pain, 117*(3), 388–395.

Keefe, F. J., & Block, A. R. (1982). Development of an observation method for assessing pain behavior in chronic low back pain patients. *Behavior Therapy, 13*(4), 363–375.

Kessels, R. P., Aleman, A., Verhagen, W. I., & Van Luijtelaar, E. L. (2000). Cognitive functioning after whiplash injury: A meta-analysis. *Journal of the International Neuropsychology Society, 6*(3), 271–278.

Kewman, D. G., Vaishampayan, N., Zald, D., & Han, B. (1991). Cognitive impairment in musculoskeletal pain patients. *International Journal of Psychiatry in Medicine, 21*(3), 253–262.

Kori, S. H., Miller, R. P., & Todd, D. D. (1990). Kinesiophobia: A new view of chronic pain behavior. *Pain Management, Jan/Feb*, 35–43.

Kreitler, S., & Niv, D. (2007). Cognitive impairment in chronic pain. *Pain: Clinical Updates, 15*(4), 1–4.

Krupp, L. B., LaRocca, N. G., Muir-Nash, J., & Steinberg, A. D. (1989). The Fatigue Severity Scale: Application to patients with multiple sclerosis and systemic lupus erythematosus. *Archives of Neurology, 46*(10), 1121–1123.

Kuny, S., & Stassen, H. H. (1995). Cognitive performance in patients recovering from depression. *Psychopathology, 28*(4), 190–207.

Landrø, N. I., Stiles, T. C., & Sletvold, H. (1997). Memory functioning in patients with primary fibromyalgia and major depression and healthy controls. *Journal of Psychosomatic Research, 42*(3), 297–306.

Larrabee, G. J. (2003). Exaggerated pain report in litigants with malingered neurocognitive dysfunction. *Clinical Neuropsychology, 17*(3), 395–401.

Larsen, L. L., Øistensen Holthe, Ø., Landrø, N. I., Stiles, T. C., & Borchgrevink, P. C. (2009). Neuropsychological functioning in chronic pain: Complaints and objective test performance *European Journal of Pain, 13* (Suppl 1), S221.

Leijdekkers, M. L. A., Passchier, J., Goudswaard, P., Menges, L. J., & Orlebeke, J. F. (1990). Migraine patients cognitively impaired? *Headache: The Journal of Head and Face Pain, 30*(6), 352–358.

Lorenz, J., Beck, H., & Bromm, B. (1997). Cognitive performance, mood and experimental pain before and during morphine-induced analgesia in patients with chronic non-malignant pain. *Pain, 73*(3), 369–375.

Main, C. J. (1983). The modified somatic perception questionnaire (MSPQ). *Journal of Psychosomatic Research, 27*(6), 503–514.

McCracken, L. M., & Iverson, G. L. (2001). Predicting complaints of impaired cognitive functioning in patients with chronic pain. *Journal of Pain and Symptom Management, 21*(5), 392–396.

Melzack, R. (1975). The McGill pain questionnaire: Major properties and scoring methods. *Pain, 1*(3), 277–299.

Melzack, R., & Wall, P. D. (1965). Pain mechanisms: A new theory. *Science, 150*(3699), 971–979.

Meyers, J. E., Millis, S. R., & Volkert, K. (2002). A validity index for the MMPI-2. *Archives of Clinical Neuropsychology, 17*(2), 157–169.

Mittenberg, W., Patton, C., Canyock, E. M., & Condit, D. C. (2002). Base rates of malingering and symptom exaggeration. *Journal of Clinical and Experimental Neuropsychology, 24*(8), 1094–1102.

Moriarty, O., McGuire, B. E., & Finn, D. P. (2011). The effect of pain on cognitive function: A review of clinical and preclinical research. *Progress in Neurobiology, 93*(3), 385–404.

Morin, C. M., Gibson, D., & Wade, J. (1998). Self-reported sleep and mood disturbance in chronic pain patients. *The Clinical Journal of Pain, 14*(4), 311–314.

Norman, D. A., & Bobrow, D. G. (1975). On data-limited and resource-limited processes. *Cognitive Psychology, 7*(1), 44–64.

O'Donoghue, G. M., Fox, N., Heneghan, C., & Hurley, D. A. (2009). Objective and subjective assessment of sleep in chronic low back pain patients compared with healthy age and gender matched controls: A pilot study. *BMC Musculoskeletal Disorders, 10,* 122.

Povedano, M., Gascón, J., Gálvez, R., Ruiz, M., & Rejas, J. (2007). Cognitive function impairment in patients with neuropathic pain under standard conditions of care. *Journal of Pain and Symptom Management, 33*(1), 78–89. doi:10.1016/j.jpainsymman.2006.07.012

Radanov, B. P., & Dvorak, J. (1996). Spine update. impaired cognitive functioning after whiplash injury of the cervical spine. *Spine, 21*(3), 392–397.

Radanov, B. P., Dvorák, J., & Valach, L. (1992). Cognitive deficits in patients after soft tissue injury of the cervical spine. *Spine, 17*(2), 127–131.

Radanov, B. P., Hirlinger, I., Di Stefano, G., & Valach, L. (1992). Attentional processing in cervical spine syndromes. *Acta Neurologica Scandinavica, 85*(5), 358–362.

Raja, S. N., Haythornthwaite, J. A., Pappagallo, M., Clark, M. R., Travison, T. G., Sabeen, S., et al. (2002). Opioids versus antidepressants in postherpetic neuralgia: A randomized, placebo-controlled trial. *Neurology, 59*(7), 1015–1021.

Ravnkilde, B., Videbech, P., Clemmensen, K., Egander, A., Rasmussen, N. A., & Rosenberg, R. (2002). Cognitive deficits in major depression. *Scandinavian Journal of Psychology, 43*(3), 239–251.

Robertson, I. H., Ward, A., Ridgeway, V., & Nimmo-Smith, I. (1994). *Test of everyday attention.* Bury St. Edmunds, UK: Thames Valley Test Company.

Roelofs, J., Peters, M. L., McCracken, L., & Vlaeyen, J. W. S. (2003). The pain vigilance and awareness questionnaire (PVAQ): Further psychometric evaluation in fibromyalgia and other chronic pain syndromes. *Pain, 101*(3), 299–306.

Roelofs, J., Peters, M. L., & Vlaeyen, J. W. S. (2002). Selective attention for pain-related information in healthy individuals: The role of pain and fear. *European Journal of Pain, 6*(5), 331–339.

Roth, R. S., Geisser, M. E., Theisen-Goodvich, M., & Dixon, P. J. (2005). Cognitive complaints are associated with depression, fatigue, female sex, and pain catastrophizing in patients with chronic pain. *Archives of Physical Medicine and Rehabilitation, 86*(6), 1147–1154.

Rowbotham, M. C., Twilling, L., Davies, P. S., Reisner, L., Taylor, K., & Mohr, D. (2003). Oral opioid therapy for chronic peripheral and central neuropathic pain. *New England Journal of Medicine, 348*(13), 1223–1232.

Sator-Katzenschlager, S. M., Schiesser, A. W., Kozek-Langenecker, S. A., Benetka, G., Langer, G., & Kress, H. G. (2003). Does pain relief improve pain behavior and mood in chronic pain patients? *Anesthesia and Analgesia, 97*(3), 791–797.

Schmand, B., Lindeboom, J., Schagen, S., Heijt, R., Koene, T., & Hamburger, H. L. (1998). Cognitive complaints in patients after whiplash injury: The impact of malingering. *Journal of Neurology, Neurosurgery, and Psychiatry, 64*(3), 339–343.

Seminowicz, D. A., Wideman, T. H., Naso, L., Hatami-Khoroushahi, Z., Fallatah, S., Ware, M. A., et al. (2011). Effective treatment of chronic low back pain in humans reverses abnormal brain anatomy and function. *Journal of Neuroscience, 31*(20), 7540–7550.

Sjøgren, P., Christrup, L. L., Petersen, M. A., & Højsted, J. (2005). Neuropsychological assessment of chronic non-malignant pain patients treated in a multidisciplinary pain centre. *European Journal of Pain, 9*(4), 453–462.

Sjøgren, P., Thomsen, A. B., & Olsen, A. K. (2000). Impaired neuropsychological performance in chronic nonmalignant pain patients receiving long-term oral opioid therapy. *Journal of Pain and Symptom Management, 19*(2), 100–108.

Sletvold, H., Stiles, T. C., & Landrø, N. I. (1995). Information processing in primary fibromyalgia, major depression and healthy controls. *Journal of Rheumatology, 22*(1), 137–142.

Suhr, J. A. (2003). Neuropsychological impairment in fibromyalgia: Relation to depression, fatigue, and pain. *Journal of Psychosomatic Research, 55*(4), 321–329.

Sullivan, M. J. L., Bishop, S. R., & Pivik, J. (1995). The pain catastrophizing scale: Development and validation. *Psychological Assessment, 7*(4), 524–532.

Sullivan, M. J. L., Rodgers, W. M., & Kirsch, I. (2001). Catastrophizing, depression and expectancies for pain and emotional distress. *Pain, 91*(1–2), 147–154.

Tassain, V., Attal, N., Fletcher, D., Brasseur, L., Dégieux, P., Chauvin, M., & Bouhassira, D. (2003). Long term effects of oral sustained release morphine on neuropsychological performance in patients with chronic non-cancer pain. *Pain, 104*(1–2), 389–400.

Tombaugh, T,N,. (1996). *TOMM. Test of Memory Malingering.* Tonawanda, NY: Mulit-Health Systems.

Valet, M., Sprenger, T., Boecker, H., Willoch, F., Rummeny, E., Conrad, B., et al. (2004). Distraction modulates connectivity of the cingulo-frontal cortex and the midbrain during pain—an fMRI analysis. *Pain, 109*(3), 399–408.

Vancleef, L. M. G., & Peters, M. L. (2006). Pain catastrophizing, but not injury/illness sensitivity or anxiety sensitivity, enhances attentional interference by pain. *The Journal of Pain, 7*(1), 23–30.

Van Damme, S., Crombez, G., & Eccleston, C. (2004). Disengagement from pain: The role of catastrophic thinking about pain. *Pain, 107*(1–2), 70–76.

Waddell, G., Newton, M., Henderson, I., Somerville, D., & Main, C. J., (1993). A fear-avoidance beliefs questionnaire (FABQ) and the role of fear-avoidance beliefs in chronic low back pain and disability. *Pain, 52*(2), 157–168.

Wade, J. B., & Hart, R. P. (2002). Attention and the stages of pain processing. *Pain Medicine, 3*(1), 30–38.

Wechsler, D. (1999). *Wechsler Abbreviated Scale of Intelligence.* San Antonio, TX: The Psychological Corporation.

Weiner, D. K., Rudy, T. E., Morrow, L., Slaboda, J., & Lieber, S. (2006). The relationship between pain, neuropsychological performance, and physical function in community-dwelling older adults with chronic low back pain. *Pain Medicine, 7*(1), 60–70.

Williams, L. S., Jones, W. J., Shen, J., Robinson, R. L., Weinberger, M., & Kroenke, K. (2003). Prevalence and impact of depression and pain in neurology outpatients. *Journal of Neurology, Neurosurgery, & Psychiatry, 74*(11), 1587–1589.

Woods, M. P., & Asmundson, G. J. G. (2008). Evaluating the efficacy of graded in vivo exposure for the treatment of fear in patients with chronic back pain: A randomized controlled clinical trial. *Pain, 136*(3), 271–280.

Zacny, J. P. (1995). A review of the effects of opioids on psychomotor and cognitive functioning in humans. *Experimental and Clinical Psychopharmacology, 3*(4), 432–466.

Zenz, M., Strumpf, M., & Tryba, M. (1992). Long-term oral opioid therapy in patients with chronic nonmalignant pain. *Journal of Pain and Symptom Management, 7*(2), 69–77.

8

The Influence of Oral Motor Impairments
on Cognitive Functioning

PETER A. ARNETT, GRAY A. VARGAS, DEDE UKUEBERUWA,
AND AMANDA R. RABINOWITZ

Performance on neuropsychological tests requires both input and output. Examinees must take in information either auditorily or visually (input) and then produce some written, manual or oral response (output). Neuropsychologists are mostly interested in interpreting the meaning of the output in terms of higher-level cognitive functioning. However, in many neurological patients, the interpretation of such output is complicated by input and output problems, issues that have received some discussion in the neuropsychological literature for many years (Weintraub & Mesulam, 1985).

Regarding input, certain patients may have difficulty seeing or hearing the test stimuli, and thus the output they produce is not a clear reflection of the higher-order function that the test is designed to measure. For example, a patient who has primary problems with audition who cannot adequately hear a verbally presented story may perform poorly when asked to recall it; such poor performance may have nothing to do with the patient's verbal memory ability and may simply reflect the fact that the patient did not adequately hear the story. Regarding output, some patients have difficulty with fine-motor speed and coordination such that the output they produce on a neuropsychological task does not purely reflect the higher-order cognitive function that the task is designed to measure. To illustrate, a patient who has impaired fine-motor writing speed who is asked to perform an executive test such as a trail-making test may perform poorly; the impaired performance will very likely not exclusively reflect a deficit of higher-order cognitive functioning that the test is designed to measure but may also reflect the patient's fine-motor writing speed deficit.

Neuropsychologists are trained to be aware of the many confounding input and output factors in their interpretation of cognitive test results as a reflection of higher level cognitive functioning. An example of a common approach to addressing an input problem (hearing) is simply to ensure that patients with such difficulties wear their hearing aids to the testing. It is also useful to include some very basic auditory processing procedures in the test battery to ensure that patients can actually hear adequately during the testing. In cases where rudimentary auditory processing problems are suspected, Lezak, Howieson, and Loring (2004) recommend asking examinees to tell whether two spoken words are the same or different, such as "cat" and "cap" or "vie" and "thy," and then use identical word pairs. As an example of a method for addressing an output problem associated with impaired rudimentary fine-motor speed, neuropsychologists often include measures in their test batteries (e.g., Symbol Copy Test from the Wechsler Adult Intelligence Scale–III [WAIS-III], Grooved Pegboard Test) to assess it directly so that they can gauge the impact of such deficits on higher-order tasks that require fine-motor speed. Alternatively, when a patient or patient group is known to have problems with rudimentary fine-motor speed, a test battery can be constructed to limit the number of tasks that depend on this skill. The most commonly used test battery in multiple sclerosis (MS), for example, the Minimal Assessment of Cognitive Functioning in Multiple Sclerosis (MACFIMS) (Benedict et al., 2002), includes tasks that mostly require only a spoken response as the output (e.g., Verbal Fluency, Judgment of Line Orientation, Paced Auditory Serial Addition Task [PASAT]).

Although many of these approaches involve creative ways of circumventing the potentially confounding influence of input and output problems on neuropsychological test performance, there is one deficit in output that has received relatively little attention: rudimentary oral motor speed. As with the MACFIMS battery, when patients have difficulty with manual motor skill, neuropsychologists have typically circumvented the problem by relying more on tasks that only require a spoken response. However, such an approach is not without its own problems, because many patients seen by neuropsychologists have problems with slow, dysarthric speech. When a task requires examinees to produce a rapid spoken response, they may perform poorly not because of a deficit in higher level cognitive functioning but because of more fundamental problems in making a rapid oral motor response.

With these considerations in mind, the focus of this chapter is on research examining the contribution of rudimentary oral motor speed to neuropsychological test performance. Research in this area is decidedly limited; however, it addresses a topic that is critical for clinical neuropsychologists to understand. We will first discuss the construct of dysarthria generally, then consider it more specifically in neurological populations. Following that we will discuss research that has examined the impact of slowed speech on neuropsychological tests requiring a rapid spoken response in neurological patients. Using the limited research available, we will present some evidence-based guidelines for assessing dysarthria formally in neuropsychological evaluations and then discuss how results of such an assessment can be interpreted. Some consideration of how to circumvent this difficulty will also be discussed and evidence-based guidelines for practice provided. Finally, we will suggest some future research directions and provide a case study to illustrate some of the principles discussed in the chapter.

DYSARTHRIA

Dysarthria encompasses a range of motor speech disorders that involve defective articulation from weakness, slowness, or incoordination of the speech musculature (Beeson & Rapcsak, 2006; Lezak et al., 2004). Dysarthria can occur with aphasia, but it is thought to reflect a defect in speech rather than language. There is a high range of variability in the severity of dysarthric speech, from slightly distorted articulation to nearly unintelligible speech.

Dysarthria in Neurological Populations

Dysarthria is extremely common in patients with neurological disorders, including Huntington's disease (Hartelius, Carlstedt, Ytterberg, Lillvik, & Laakso, 2003), stroke (Kent & Kent, 2000), Parkinson's disease (Sapir et al., 2001), traumatic brain injury (TBI) (Guo & Togher, 2008; Murdoch, Kuruvilla, & Goozee, 2012), HIV (McCabe, Sheard, & Code, 2002), and MS (Darley, Brown, & Goldstein, 1972; Hartelius, Runmarker, & Andersen, 2000; Mackenzie & Green, 2009; Tröster & Arnett, 2006), among others. Duffy (2005) reported on a study from the Department of Neurology at the Mayo Clinic from 1987–1990 and 1993–2001 where 54% of 10,444 individuals with acquired neurological disorders had dysarthria.

Psychomotor slowing, including slowing of speech, also occurs with normal aging and may impact performance on higher-level cognitive tasks (e.g., verbal fluency) that require rapid articulatory speed (Rodriguez-Aranda, 2003). Given the pervasiveness of dysarthria in neurological patients as well as in normal aging, it is surprising that relatively little research has been devoted to the possible influence of slowed, dysarthric speech on performance on neuropsychological tasks requiring a rapid oral motor response.

Dysarthria in MS

The French neurologist Charcot may have been the first to formally describe dysarthria in MS. He considered dysarthria (or "scanning speech") to be one of the three characteristic neurological symptoms of MS, the others being intention tremor and nystagmus (Charcot, 1877; Darley et al., 1972). He reported observing dysarthria in 22 of 23 cases he examined. As he described it, "the words are as if measured or scanned; there is a pause after every syllable, and the syllables themselves are pronounced slowly" (p. 192). More recent descriptions of dysarthria in MS characterize it as difficulty with articulation and slowed speech rate (Darley et al., 1972; Hartelius, Runmarker, & Andersen, 2000; Hartelius, Runmarker, Andersen, & Nord, 2000). Work with more representative MS patient samples than those available to Charcot indicates that dysarthria is not quite as pervasive as his case reports suggested; still, it has been found to be quite common. Consistent with findings for neurological patients more generally (Duffy, 2005), Hartelius, Runmarker, and Andersen (2000) reported dysarthria prevalence rates in MS ranging from 40% to 55%.

Dysarthria in MS has been shown to be associated with neurological disability (Darley et al., 1972; Hartelius, Runmarker, & Andersen, 2000) and MS course type (Hartelius, Runmarker, & Andersen, 2000), with primary and secondary progressive patients displaying greater levels of dysarthria than relapsing–remitting patients. In MS, dysarthria does not appear to be associated with age or duration of illness.

Dysarthria and Neuropsychological Test Performance in MS

MS is one disorder in which at least some research has been conducted investigating dysarthria and performance on higher-level cognitive tasks. Smith and Arnett (2007) examined these associations in a sample of MS patients with mixed course types. Given that dysarthria is extremely common in MS and that many neuropsychological tests recommended for use with these patients require rapid speech (e.g., PASAT, oral version of the Symbol Digit Modalities Test [SDMT], Controlled Oral Word Association Test [COWAT]), the goal of this study was to evaluate whether dysarthria was associated with performance on such tests. The authors reasoned that MS patients might have particular difficulty with such tasks, in part because of slow speech. In this study, dysarthria was measured via an examiner rating scale. With these considerations in mind, it was predicted that (a) observer ratings of dysarthria would be higher for MS patients than for controls; (b) MS patients would perform worse than controls on neuropsychological tests requiring a rapid spoken response; and (c) dysarthria ratings would be correlated with performance on neuropsychological tests requiring a rapid spoken response.

The study compared 97 MS patients and 27 demographically matched controls. Overall, patients were characterized as having a moderate level of disability, with their score on the Extended Disability Status Scale (EDSS) being 4.57 (1.56). A psychosocial interview was conducted before administration of the cognitive tests, and the following 4-point rating scale was used to make dysarthria ratings for both MS patients and controls: 1 = normal, nothing unusual about the participant's speech; 2 = mildly dysarthric, participant's speech generally normal, but some words slurred or difficult to understand, or speech notably slow; 3 = mildly or moderately dysarthric, with more than a few words difficult to understand or slurred, with occasional requests for repetition, or speech very slow; and 4 = moderately dysarthric, frequent requests for repetition necessary because of difficulty understanding participant's speech, or speech extremely slow. Very few participants were rated at 3 or higher, so ratings were dichotomized into "normal speech" (score of 1) and "dysarthria" (scores of 2–4).

With this scale, even most of these moderately disabled MS patients ($n = 65$, 67%) were rated as having normal speech, with the other 32 (33%) patients showing some level of dysarthria but none showing severe dysarthria (rating of 4). All but one control participant was rated as having normal speech; this one individual was rated as mildly dysarthric (rating of 1). Consistent with the first prediction, it is not surprising that chi-squared analysis showed that significantly more MS participants than control participants were dysarthric: χ^2 (1, $N = 124$) = 9.28, $p < .005$.

In addition to measuring overall intellectual functioning, measures requiring a rapid speech response were employed, including the COWAT, Oral Symbol Digit Test, and the Visual Elevator subtest from the Test of Everyday Attention. Consistent with the second prediction and most prior work in MS, patients performed significantly worse than controls on all of these tasks. Additionally, regression analyses that controlled for variables on which MS patients and controls differed were conducted to examine the association between dysarthria ratings and rapid speech tasks, and significant associations ($p < .05$) were found for all tasks. Finally, performance on the tasks was compared between MS patients with normal speech ($n = 65$) and those with some dysarthria ($n = 32$). In each case the dysarthria group performed worse, with effect sizes ranging from small (COWAT = .44), to medium (Visual Elevator = .72), to large (Oral Symbol Digit = .84).

The Smith and Arnett (2007) study demonstrated that, at least on the basis of examiner dysarthria ratings, MS patients displayed greater dysarthria than controls, and dysarthria was significantly correlated with performance on all neuropsychological tasks requiring rapid speech. Also, even within the MS sample, dysarthric patients performed significantly worse on these tasks than patients with normal speech, with effect sizes ranging from small to large. With this said, the study nonetheless had some significant limitations, including the use of subjective dysarthria ratings, the possibility that the examiners' perception of patients' overall disability may have affected dysarthria ratings, and the fact that no tasks without rapid speech demands were used. This last factor is important because the association between dysarthria and task performance found in the study may have been due to dysarthria simply being a marker for disability and overall cognitive decline such that it would be associated with any cognitively demanding task, regardless of oral motor demands.

In a follow-up study (Arnett, Smith, Barwick, Benedict, & Ahlstrom, 2008), some of the limitations of Smith and Arnett's (2007) study were addressed by using an objective performance-based measure of dysarthria, adding tasks that did not have rapid speech demands, and including a larger control group. The predictions for the study were analogous to those in Smith and Arnett's study, with the additional prediction that the measure of dysarthria would be unrelated to neuropsychological tasks without rapid speech demands.

Fifty definite MS patients were included in the study, most of whom had either a relapsing–remitting ($n = 29$) or secondary progressive ($n = 14$) course. The measure of dysarthria used was a task known as the Maximum Repetition Rate of Syllables and Multisyllabic Combinations (MRR; Kent, Kent, & Rosenbek, 1987). This task is commonly used in the speech and language literature and in clinical settings to measure rapid speech. The MRR had also been previously recommended for inclusion in a consensus neuropsychological battery known as the MACFIMS that was designed for use with MS patients (Benedict et al., 2002), but prior to Arnett et al.'s (2008) study the MRR had never been examined empirically in MS. In reviewing tests of speech production, Kent and colleagues (1987) noted that "the monosyllabic triad [pa], [ta], [ka] has become a clinical standard" (p. 379) for which the greatest amount of normative data is available. The MRR involves having examinees repeat syllables as quickly as they can in one good breath lasting at least 6 seconds. Examinees repeat the syllables "pa," "ta," and "ka" in separate trials, then have a final trial in which they repeat "pa-ta-ka" in sequence. Syllables per second is the central measurement of this task.

In Arnett et al.'s (2008) study, the neuropsychological tasks requiring rapid speech included the COWAT (Benton & Hamsher, 1989), Animal Naming (Strauss, Sherman, & Spreen, 2006), the oral version of the Symbol Digit (Smith, 1982), and the PASAT (Rao et al., 1990). Tasks that did not require rapid speech were the California Verbal Learning Test, 2nd edition (CVLT-II; Delis, Kramer, Kaplan, & Ober, 2000) and the Brief Visual Memory Test–Revised (BVMT-R; Benedict, 1997). Depression and fatigue were also measured, respectively, by the Beck Depression Inventory, 2nd edition (BDI-II; Beck, Steer, & Brown, 1996) and the Fatigue Severity Scale (Krupp, LaRocca, Muir-Nash, & Steinberg, 1989), to measure the potential impact of these secondary factors on the test results.

Consistent with predictions, the MS group performed significantly more slowly across the MRR tasks (mean = 4.57 syllables/sec) compared with controls (5.06 syllables/sec). Thus, the MS participants produced, on average, about half a syllable less per second then controls. Although this may not seem clinically relevant, it is worth considering these findings in a broader temporal context. Such a difference would add up to 30 fewer syllables produced per minute in MS patients, 1800 fewer syllables per hour, and 43,200 fewer syllables per day. Thus a difference of half a syllable per second could have profound implications on the amount of speech a typical patient is able to produce in a given day. Also consistent with predictions and with prior MS research, the MS group performed worse on all neuropsychological tasks, including the tasks not requiring a rapid speech response, compared with controls. With the exception of the COWAT ($p < .07$), all group comparisons met traditional levels of statistical significance ($p < .05$).

Regarding the relationship between the MRR task and the neuropsychological tests requiring a rapid speech response, regression analyses (controlling for relevant demographic variables) revealed a significant relationship (semipartial correlations) with all tasks, including the Symbol Digit ($sr = .32$), combined PASAT ($sr = .25$), COWAT ($sr = .35$), and Animal Naming ($sr = .26$). Thus the effect sizes, using Cohen's (1992) guidelines, were small (PASAT, Animal Naming) to medium (Symbol Digit, COWAT). The correlation between the MRR and the tasks without rapid speech demands were lower in the case of the CVLT-II ($sr = .00$) but comparable for the BVMT-R ($sr = .22$). To determine whether group effects on the neuropsychological tasks would be reduced when controlling for differences in oral motor speed, regressions were conducted in which the MRR was entered in before the group effect. In the case of the neuropsychological tasks requiring rapid speech, group effects were reduced as follows: Symbol Digit ($sr = .32$ to.24), PASAT ($sr = .20$ to.14), COWAT ($sr = .22$ to.14), and Animal Naming ($sr = .33$ to .26). With the PASAT and COWAT, initially significant group effects were reduced to being statistically not significant. For the neuropsychological tasks not requiring rapid speech, group effects were reduced as follows: CVLT-II (sr = .25 to .20) and BVMT-R (sr = .28 to .24). Group effects remained significant regardless of the control of MRR performance for these latter tasks.

A final set of analyses was conducted to evaluate factors that might underlie group differences in rapid speech. As noted, the multivariate group effect for the MRR in the initial analyses was highly significant, F (1, 98) = 7.95, p < .01. When ANCOVAs were conducted, this effect was reduced to being nonsignificant (ns) when the fatigue measure, F (1, 97) = 1.33, ns, and the depression measure, F (1, 97) = 1.92, ns, were used as covariates.

The results of this study showed that (a) MS patients display objectively slower speech than controls; (b) slow speech is correlated with neuropsychological tasks requiring a rapid spoken response; (c) some of the MS patients' deficits on neuropsychological tasks requiring a rapid spoken response are due to their slower speech; and (d) the greater depression and fatigue in MS compared with controls fully accounts for their slower speech. The findings raised a number of intriguing interpretive possibilities. First, it may be that the greater depression and fatigue characterizing MS patients leads to slow speech, which in turn contributes to their poor performance on neuropsychological tasks requiring rapid speech. This suggests the possibility that treatment of depression in MS patients could lead to improved speech rate and ultimately contribute to better performance on such tasks. A second explanation for these findings is that slowed speech may be a marker for the extent of neuropathology present. Neuropsychological test performance in MS patients has been shown to be highly correlated with measures of neuropathology, including lesion load and atrophy (Feinstein et al., 2010). As such, slow speech and performance on neuropsychological tasks requiring rapid speech, as well as depression and fatigue, could be correlated given the underlying effects of neuropathology.

A final implication from this study is that eliminating manual or written motor responses from a neuropsychological test battery will not entirely remove the impact of primary motor deficits on test performance. Since MS patients and many other neurological patient groups commonly have dysarthria, clinicians who do not control for such basic speech impairments may erroneously conclude that patients have more severe cognitive deficits than they actually do and consequently make recommendations that are misleading and inaccurate. Ideally, neuropsychologists would develop tasks that allow for a more systematic control of oral motor slowing, making it possible for a clearer picture of the nature of the cognitive difficulties characterizing MS patients to emerge. Until that time, however, systematically measuring oral motor speed in clinical evaluations will be critical.

In another study, Mackenzie and Green (2009) examined the association between dysarthria and performance on higher-level cognitive tasks in MS patients. The study included 24 patients with "chronic progressive MS" and 24 matched controls. Participants were administered a "cognitive-linguistic" battery of tests in the form of the Arizona Battery for Communication Disorders of Dementia (ABCD). The adaptation of this battery used by these investigators included 15 subtests measuring the domains of mental status, episodic memory, linguistic expression, and linguistic comprehension. Dysarthria was measured with the Assessment of Intelligibility of Dysarthric Speech (AIDS) test. This test involves 22 sentences, varying in length from 5 to 15 words. Sentences are presented in written form and read aloud by the examiner, and then examinees read the sentence. Participants receive a point for every correctly articulated word, with scores ranging from 0 to 220. Within the MS group, the overall ABCD score was highly correlated with the AIDS score ($r = .64$). Because most of the subtests on the ABCD do not require rapid speech, and dysarthric patients performed poorly even on tasks requiring very little productive speech, these authors suggested that the association between the ABCD and AIDS score was most likely not mediated by motor speech deficits. On the one task that did require rapid speech, a generative naming task, the authors noted anecdotally that most of the participants finished generating words well before the 1-minute completion time. Still, they did not report on the quantitative association between performance on the generative naming task and overall AIDS score, so it is unclear whether objectively measured dysarthria was associated with this rapid speech task in their study. The authors acknowledged that in cases where dysarthria affects the rate of speech, the number of words generated on such a test would likely be reduced.

Slowed Speech and Neuropsychological Test Performance in Aging

In a study on aging, Rodriguez-Aranda (2003) examined the contribution of psychomotor factors to verbal fluency performance. This investigator suggested that, instead of higher-order cognitive processes, such as memory/executive skill, bringing about diminished verbal fluency, the well-documented psychomotor slowing with age may in fact be responsible for poor verbal fluency performance in the elderly. She noted the absence of any neuropsychological studies examining basic psychomotor mechanisms involved in verbal tasks requiring word production, such as verbal fluency tasks. Thus Rodriguez-Aranda designed a study to explore the extent to which rudimentary tasks of writing and reading were associated with written and oral verbal fluency task performance, respectively.

This study included 101 adults ranging in age from 20 to 88 years, divided into five age groups (20–39, 40–59, 60–69, 70–79, and 80 years and older). To measure simple oral motor speed, the Word-Reading Stroop test, involving the reading of 100 words in black ink, was used. Simple writing speed was measured by presenting examinees with an 18-word list and asking them to copy it as quickly as possible. Oral verbal fluency was measured with the COWAT and a category fluency test (animals, fruits, and professions). Written verbal fluency was measured using the Thurstone Word Fluency Test. This test involved having participants write as many words as possible that begin with the letters *S* and *K*, with a 4-minute time limit for each. The written semantic task required participants to write as many words as quickly as they could in 1 minute from a particular category (vegetables, sports, and farm animals).

Results showed that older age groups performed significantly worse on the oral semantic fluency task and both of the written fluency tests (phonemic and semantic). Significant age-related differences were also observed on the tasks of reading and writing speed, with declines most evident after age 60. When the author examined the oral semantic verbal fluency results, controlling for their measure of simple oral motor speed (word reading trial from the Stroop), the age effect remained significant, although the magnitude of the overall age group effect was reduced by approximately half ($F = 8.93$, $p < .0001$ without the covariate, and $F = 4.83$ with reading speed as the covariate). For both written fluency tasks, highly significant age group effects were reduced to being statistically non-significant when the author controlled for writing speed. Finally, and of greatest relevance to this chapter, the author found highly significant correlations between the measure of basic oral motor speed (word reading trial from the Stroop) and performance on both the COWAT ($r = .40$) and the category fluency ($r = .44$) test. Handwriting speed was even more highly associated with both the written phonemic fluency ($r = -.60$) and written semantic fluency ($r = -.64$) test.

Rodriguez-Aranda's (2003) study is provocative. It suggests the possibility that a significant proportion of the age-related decline in verbal fluency tasks may be due to age-related reductions in the more rudimentary skill of psychomotor speed. The study findings further underscore the importance of measuring rudimentary psychomotor speed in neuropsychological evaluations of patients presenting with age-related cognitive problems. One limitation to the study is that, although the psychomotor tasks chosen are designed to be relatively automatic, they may be more cognitively demanding than they first appear. For instance, while the Stroop Reading task measures articulatory speed, it also has significant visual scanning and sustained attention demands. Also, verbal-fluency tasks have significant sustained attention demands over a time period similar to that required to read a Stroop page (45 seconds) in the Golden version of the Stroop used in the study. With these limitations in mind, athough Rodriguez-Aranda's data are intriguing, they cannot be unambiguously interpreted as reflecting a clear contribution of rudimentary oral motor speed to verbal-fluency performance.

FUTURE RESEARCH DIRECTIONS

As noted earlier, dysarthria and slowed speech have been demonstrated in many neurological patient groups and they increase with age. However, there is little empirical research examining the relationship between basic rapid speech tasks and neuropsychological tests that require a rapid spoken response. Consensus guidelines in MS suggest the use of a rudimentary oral motor speech task (the MRR, as described above) in evaluations where patients present with evidence of dysarthria or slowed speech. However, there do not appear to be clear recommendations for addressing this issue in other neurological disorders.

Given the pervasiveness of dysarthria and slowed speech across neurological patient groups and aging, research is needed that uses rudimentary speech tasks in a variety of patient groups and examines the extent to which they are associated with commonly used neuropsychological tasks that require rapid speech (e.g., PASAT, Verbal Fluency Tasks, Oral Symbol Digit Test). Clinical neuropsychologists are well-versed in recognizing the importance of manual motor difficulties and the likely contribution they have on performance of neuropsychological tasks requiring manual manipulation or writing. However, less attention is paid to the possibility that slow and dysarthric speech can confound the interpretation of neuropsychological tasks that require rapid speech. Although research at this stage of our understanding is too limited to make unequivocal recommendations for future study, employing rudimentary oral motor tasks such as the MRR is preferable to relying on tasks (such as the Stroop Reading trial) that have cognitive demands other than the simple rate of speech.

EVIDENCE-BASED RECOMMENDATIONS

Research on the relationship between neuropsychological tasks requiring rapid speech and rudimentary oral motor speech tasks is extremely limited. The bulk of relevant published studies appear to be in the MS literature, with one additional study on aging. It is premature to make firm recommendations for practice. However, a few tentative recommendations and guidelines can be offered.

As noted earlier, the MRR task described above has been widely used in the speech and language literature and in clinical settings to measure rapid speech and is considered the clinical standard for which the greatest amount of normative data is available (Kent et al., 1987). Given that it has also been found to be significantly associated with neuropsychological tasks requiring rapid speech in at least one study with a neurological patient group (Arnett et al., 2008), it could be useful in clinical evaluations of other disorders. A reasonable guideline would be for clinicians to include the task in evaluations in which patients are observed to have slow and dysarthric speech. If patients perform poorly on the MRR task relative to normative data, then the extent to which such difficulties may have contributed to their performance on those neuropsychological tasks requiring rapid speech can be considered.

Regarding the use of a normative reference group that could be relevant for some disorders, Arnett and colleagues (2008) presented data for the MRR task on 50 healthy Caucasian controls with a mean age of 51.9 (9.3) years and educational level of 14.7 (2.1) years. On the basis of these reference data, standard MRR scores could be calculated for patients with comparable demographic characteristics. For younger, as well as geriatric patients, Kent and colleagues (1987) included normative data on the MRR from several published studies that could be used to calculate standard scores.

The Appendix at the end of this chapter provides instructions and a record form for the MRR that we developed for our MS study described earlier in the chapter (Arnett et al., 2008). The task requiring examinees to repeat the "pa-ta-ka" sequence can usually be recorded manually without difficulty on the record form. However, in our experience, it can be difficult to accurately record the number of specific phonemes (e.g., "pa" spoken repeatedly). Thus we recommend that, for the specific phoneme trials, examiners also record the examinee's spoken response with a recorder that makes it possible to slow down the response so that an accurate record can be made later. Alternatively, if this technology is not readily available or there are time constraints, recording only the "pa-ta-ka" trial would be reasonable, as performance on this trial is highly correlated with individual phoneme trials.

CASE STUDY

The following case study highlights themes presented in this chapter. In particular, this case study describes a patient who performed normally on a rudimentary oral motor speech task (the MRR, as described above) but scored in the impaired range on complex neuropsychological measures that require rapid speech. These latter tasks can be less ambiguously interpreted as reflecting deficits in higher-level cognitive functions and instead as reflecting problems with slowed speech.

Background and Presenting Concerns

Ms. P, a 56-year-old divorced, Caucasian, right-handed woman, was referred by Dr. J for an evaluation of increased cognitive difficulties that had developed over the past year or so. These manifested as memory problems, being forgetful, mixing up numbers, having difficulty focusing and concentrating, losing her train of thought, and forgetting names of people. She had always had a difficult time remembering names, but this problem had become more acute in the past year. A close friend of Ms. P's had also reportedly noticed an increase in her cognitive difficulties over the past year. Ms. P expressed concern about developing cognitive difficulties, in part because her mother was diagnosed with dementia at a relatively early age, 65. Ms. P attributed part of her cognitive difficulties over the past year to the increased scrutiny she experienced on her job. She was acutely aware of this increased scrutiny and that it had been distracting to her. She had been recently terminated from her job. Since then, she had noticed an improvement in her cognitive problems, now that she was not under such constant, intense scrutiny. Ms. P noted that, in addition to affecting her performance on the job, her cognitive difficulties had been affecting her social relationships, as well as her ability to maintain her household and do chores around the house.

Ms. P has a history of depression for which she is currently taking Zoloft, ongoing problems with chronic pain from a prior injury to her left leg, and intermittent migraine headaches. Her social and developmental history is unremarkable. She was a somewhat above-average student in high school and completed 4 years of college with a 2.5 GPA. Ms. P is a remitted alcoholic, having been sober for almost 20 years. She denied any other significant history of substance abuse and denied any regular current caffeine or tobacco intake.

Behavioral Observations

Ms. P was seen on one occasion for the interview and neuropsychological testing. She was appropriately and casually dressed and was oriented, alert, and cooperative throughout. Ms. P spoke fluently with normal prosody, rate, volume, and clarity and was able to comprehend all testing procedures. She recounted her history in a detailed manner. Her affect was generally euthymic, though she did become appropriately tearful momentarily when recounting the work-related difficulties she had encountered over the past several months.

On testing Ms. P clearly appeared to be putting forth good effort. This was corroborated by an objective test of effort administered. She responded to task difficulty in good humor, often laughing when she did not know the answers to things or when she had difficulty. Overall, the test results were thought to be an accurate reflection of Ms. P's current level of cognitive functioning.

Results, Interpretation, and Recommendations

In relation to her likely high-average premorbid level of cognitive functioning based on her high-average performance on measures of crystallized verbal intellectual functioning (WAIS-III Verbal Comprehension Index), Ms. P displayed a few select cognitive difficulties. In particular, she scored in the impaired range on measures of auditory and visual processing speed and verbal fluency (COWAT, PASAT, Symbol Digit), as well as on the first two learning trials of a measure of visual memory (BVMT-R). She further displayed impaired performance on a measure of right-sided fine-motor coordination (Grooved Pegboard). Ms. P also scored significantly below expectations (low average), but not in the impaired range, on a measure of visual processing speed (Digit Symbol—Coding), on the first two trials of a verbal learning task (CVLT-II), on measures of visual processing speed and sustained attention (Comprehensive Trail-Making Tests 2 and 4), and with her nondominant hand on a measure of fine-motor coordination (Grooved Pegboard).

What might account for these cognitive difficulties that Ms. P displayed? At the time of the evaluation, Ms. P reported mild levels of depression, so this is one possible contributor to her difficulties. High levels of fatigue are likely to play a greater role, however, as Ms. P reported fatigue levels at the 99th percentile on the Fatigue Severity Scale. Fatigue can affect sustained attention and processing speed, and most of the tasks on which she displayed difficulties had significant processing speed and sustained attentional demands. Many of the tests on which Ms. P scored in the impaired range (COWAT, PASAT, Oral Symbol Digit) also had rapid speech demands. However, Ms. P did not display any evidence of slow or dysarthric speech in conversation, and she performed in the average range on a test of rudimentary oral motor speed (MRR task). As such, her difficulty on the task, which required a rapid oral motor response, cannot be attributed to a more basic problem with slow speech.

Ms. P's history of alcoholism must also be considered. Although she has been sober for nearly 20 years, she did engage in heavy drinking for a number of years. Given that chronic alcohol use is associated with some of the difficulties she displayed on testing, it is possible that Ms. P's history of alcoholism is a contributor to her difficulties. However, this explanation for her problems seems less likely than her current fatigue.

As noted earlier, a significant concern that Ms. P expressed at the time of the evaluation was that her development of cognitive difficulties might reflect the early manifestations of dementia. At present, however, Ms. P does not show cognitive problems suggestive of Alzheimer's dementia. The latter is more typically characterized by difficulty learning new information as well as rapid forgetting. Furthermore, naming problems are often very salient in the early stages of Alzheimer's. In contrast to this, Ms. P's naming skills were excellent; she also displayed good learning of information with repetition and showed excellent retention of information on all measures of memory and learning administered. Thus there is nothing about her current pattern of difficulties to suggest that they are a precursor to more serious cognitive impairments that would more typically characterize a dementia such as Alzheimer's.

Poor effort on testing also cannot be invoked to explain Ms. P's difficulties, as she appeared to be putting forth excellent effort throughout testing; an objective measure of effort administered corroborated this impression. The impairments seen on objective neuropsychological testing are consistent with Ms. P's report of a high-average level of cognitive difficulties in her daily life. Her friend's perception of a high level of cognitive difficulties in Ms. P's daily life is also consistent with the objective neuropsychological findings.

Although Ms. P displayed difficulty primarily on measures of processing speed and sustained attention, she showed significant strengths on several tasks. She scored in the high-average range or above on measures of immediate and delayed recall of meaningful verbal information (Logical Memory I & II), learning with repetition and consistency of recall when learning nonmeaningful verbal information (CVLT-II), and learning with repetition on a visual memory task. These strengths should help Ms. P circumvent some of the cognitive difficulties she displays.

Recommendations for Ms. P included (1) pharmacological and nonpharmacological treatment of fatigue, (2) psychotherapy for depression, (3) use of an electronic planner and organizer, (4) work on developing compensatory strategies using cognitive strengths (e.g., repetition), and (5) medical workup to explore possible treatment for her lack of appetite.

ACKNOWLEDGMENTS

This chapter was supported in part by a grant to Peter Arnett from the National Multiple Sclerosis Society (PP0978). Also, special thanks go to our friend and colleague, the late Adele Miccio, Professor of Communication Sciences and Disorders at Penn State University, for her consultation on issues relating to the objective measurement of rudimentary oral motor speed.

Appendix

Maximum Repetition Rate Tests—Instructions and Record Form

Test Materials: Record Form, Recording Device, Stopwatch

Administration: "FOR THIS NEXT TEST WHAT I'D LIKE YOU TO DO IS TO SAY THE SYLLABLE 'Pa' AS MANY TIMES AS YOU CAN AND AS QUICKLY AS YOU CAN IN ONE BREATH. WHEN I SAY 'GO', *TAKE A DEEP BREATH,* AND YOU CAN BEGIN SAYING THE SYLLABLE. SO YOU WOULD GO LIKE THIS." (Demonstrate by taking a breath, then saying 9 syllables quickly and clearly

["Pa-Pa-Pa-Pa-Pa-Pa-Pa-Pa-Pa"]. When you're finished, say the following:) "TRY TO DO THE VERY BEST YOU CAN FOR AT LEAST 6 SECONDS IN ONE BREATH. BE SURE TO TAKE A GOOD BREATH, AND SPEAK AS CLEARLY AS YOU CAN. ARE YOU READY? OK, REMEMBER, SAY 'Pa-Pa-Pa' AS FAST AS YOU CAN. *TAKE A DEEP BREATH*, READY?" (Start recording.) "GO!!" (Start stopwatch and mark each "Pa" syllable on the record form as it is performed by the subject. When the subject stops, stop the stopwatch immediately and record the number of "pa's" and the time on the record form. Also, be sure to stop recording). REPEAT FOR "TA" AND "KA."

"FOR THIS NEXT TEST WHAT I'D LIKE YOU TO DO IS TO SAY THE SEQUENCE 'pa-ta-ka' AS MANY TIMES AS YOU CAN AND AS QUICKLY AS YOU CAN IN ONE BREATH. AGAIN, WHEN I SAY 'GO', *TAKE A DEEP BREATH,* AND YOU CAN BEGIN SAYING THE SEQUENCE. SO YOU WOULD GO LIKE THIS." (Demonstrate by taking a breath, then saying 9 syllables quickly and clearly ["Pa-ta-ka-Pa-ta-ka-Pa-ta-ka"]. When you're finished, say the following:) "TRY TO DO THE VERY BEST YOU CAN FOR AT LEAST 6 SECONDS IN ONE BREATH. BE SURE TO TAKE A GOOD BREATH, AND SPEAK AS CLEARLY AS YOU CAN. ARE YOU READY? OK, REMEMBER, SAY 'Pa-ta-ka-Pa-ta-ka-Pa-ta-ka' AS FAST AS YOU CAN. *TAKE A DEEP BREATH*, READY?" (Start recording.) "GO!!" (Start stopwatch and mark each "Pa-ta-ka" syllable on the record form as it is performed by the subject. When the subject stops, stop the stopwatch immediately and record the number of "pa-ta-ka's" and the time on the record form. Also, be sure to stop recording.)

MAXIMUM REPETITION RATE TEST SCORING

Syllable(s)	No. of Syllables	Time	Syllables per Second
PA			
TA			
KA			
	No. of Triads	Time	Triads per Second
PA-TA-KA			

References

Arnett, P. A., Smith, M. M., Barwick, F. H., Benedict, R. H. B., & Ahlstrom, B. (2008). Oral motor slowing in multiple sclerosis: Relationship to complex neuropsychological tasks requiring an oral response. *Journal of the International Neuropsychological Society, 14,* 454–462.

Beck, A. T., Steer, R. A., & Brown, G. K. (1996). *Beck Depression Inventory—second edition, manual.* San Antonio, TX: The Psychological Corporation.

Beeson, P. M., & Rapcsak, S. Z. (2006). The aphasias. In P. J. Snyder, P. D. Nussbaum, & D. L. Robins (Eds.), *Clinical neuropsychology: A pocket handbook for assessment* (2nd ed., pp. 436–459). Washington, DC: American Psychological Association.

Benedict, R. H. B. (1997). *Brief Visuospatial Memory Test—revised: Professional manual.* Odessa, FL: Psychological Assessment Resources.

Benedict, R. H. B., Fischer, J. S., Archibald, C. J., Arnett, P. A., Beatty, W. W., Bobholz, J., et al. (2002). Minimal neuropsychological assessment of MS patients: A consensus approach. *The Clinical Neuropsychologist, 16,* 381–397.

Benton, A. L., & Hamsher, K. d. (1989). *Multilingual Aphasia Examination.* Iowa City, IA: AJA Associates.

Charcot, J. M. (1877). *Lectures on the diseases of the nervous system* (G. Sigerson, Trans., Vol. 1): London: New Sydenham Society.

Cohen, J. (1992). A power primer. *Psychological Bulletin, 112,* 155–159.

Darley, F. L., Brown, J. R., & Goldstein, N. P. (1972). Dysarthria in multiple sclerosis. *Journal of Speech and Hearing Research, 15,* 229–245.

Delis, D. C., Kramer, J. H., Kaplan, E., & Ober, B. A. (2000). *California Verbal Learning Test manual: Second edition, Adult version.* San Antonio, TX: The Psychological Corporation.

Duffy, J. R. (2005). *Motor speech disorders: Substrates, differential diagnosis and management* (2nd ed.). St. Louis, MO: Elsevier Mosby.

Feinstein, A., O'Connor, P., Akbar, N., Moradzadeh, L., Scott, C. J. M., & Lobaugh, N. J. (2010). Diffusion tensor imaging abnormalities in depressed multiple sclerosis patients. *Multiple Sclerosis, 16,* 189–196.

Guo, Y. L., & Togher, L. (2008). The impact of dysarthria on everyday communication after traumatic brain injury: A pilot study. *Brain Injury, 22,* 83–97.

Hartelius, L., Carlstedt, A., Ytterberg, M., Lillvik, M., & Laakso, K. (2003). Speech disorders in mild and moderate Huntington disease: Results of dysarthria assessments of 19 individuals. *Journal of Medical Speech-Language Pathology, 11,* 1–14.

Hartelius, L., Runmarker, B., & Andersen, O. (2000). Prevalence and characteristics of dysarthria in a multiple-sclerosis incidence cohort: Relation to neurological data. *Folia Phoniatrica et Logopedica, 52,* 160–177.

Hartelius, L., Runmarker, B., Andersen, O., & Nord, L. (2000). Temporal speech characteristics of individuals with multiple sclerosis and ataxia dysarthria: "Scanning speech" revisited. *Folia Phoniatrica et Logopedica, 52,* 228–238.

Kent, R. D., & Kent, J. F. (2000). Task-based profiles of the dysarthrias. *Folia Phoniatrica et Logopedica, 52,* 48–53.

Kent, R. D., Kent, J. F., & Rosenbek, J. C. (1987). Maximum performance tests of speech production. *Journal of Speech and Hearing Disorders, 52,* 367–387.

Krupp, L. B., LaRocca, N. G., Muir-Nash, J., & Steinberg, A. D. (1989). The Fatigue Severity Scale: Application to patients with multiple sclerosis and systemic lupus erythematosus. *Archives of Neurology, 46,* 1121–1123.

Lezak, M. D., Howieson, D. B., & Loring, D. W. (2004). *Neuropsychological assessment* (4th ed.). New York: Oxford University Press.

Mackenzie, C., & Green, J. (2009). Cognitive-linguistic deficit and speech intelligibility in chronic progressive multiple sclerosis. *International Journal of Language and Communication Disorders, 44,* 401–420.

McCabe, P., Sheard, C., & Code, C. (2002). Acquired communication impairment in people with HIV. *Journal of Medical Speech-Language Pathology, 10,* 183–199.

Murdoch, B. E., Kuruvilla, M. S., & Goozee, J. V. (2012). Effect of speech rate manipulations on articulatory dynamics in severe traumatic brain injury: An EMA and EPG study. *Brain Injury, 26,* 241–260.

Rao, S. M., and the Cognitive Function Study Group of the National Multiple Sclerosis Society. (1990). *Manual for the brief repeatable battery of neuropsychological tests in multiple sclerosis.* New York: National Multiple Sclerosis Society.

Rodriguez-Aranda, C. (2003). Reduced writing and reading speed and age-related changes in verbal fluency tasks. *The Clinical Neuropsychologist, 17,* 203–215.

Sapir, S., Pawlas, A. A., Ramig, L. O., Countryman, S., O'Brien, C., & Hoehn, M. M. (2001). Voice and speech abnormalities in Parkinson disease: Relation to severity of motor impairment, duration of disease, medication, depression, gender, and age. *Journal of Medical Speech-Language Pathology, 9,* 213–226.

Smith, A. (1982). *Symbol Digit Modalities Test (SDMT) manual (revised).* Los Angeles: Western Psychological Services.

Smith, M. M., & Arnett, P. A. (2007). Dysarthria predicts poorer performance on cognitive tasks requiring a speeded oral response in an MS population. *Journal of Clinical & Experimental Neuropsychology, 29,* 804–812.

Strauss, E., Sherman, E. M. S., & Spreen, O. (2006). *A compendium of neuropsychological tests: Administration, norms, and commentary* (3rd ed.). New York: Oxford University Press.

Tröster, A. I., & Arnett, P. A. (2006). Assessment of movement and demyelinating disorders. In P. J. Snyder, P. D. Nussbaum, & D. L. Robins (Eds.), *Clinical neuropsychology: A pocket handbook for assessment* (2nd ed., pp. 243–293). Washington, DC: American Psychological Association.

Weintraub, S., & Mesulam, M.-M. (1985). Mental state assessment of young and elderly adults in behavioral neurology In M.-M. Mesulam (Ed.), *Principles of behavioral neurology.* F.A. Davis.

9

Response Expectancies and Their Potential Influence in Neuropsychological Evaluation

JULIE A. SUHR AND CHRISTINA WEI

Ohio University

CASE REPORT

Ms. L. was a 54-year-old female referred by her neurologist because of her concerns about memory loss and confusion. She reported experiencing a sudden and dramatic change to her cognitive abilities while at a mid-summer social event. The temperatures were extremely hot, and she felt dizzy and confused and disoriented. She managed to drive herself home and did not seek immediate medical attention, but over the year since the incident, she had experienced a decline in her cognitive abilities. She also indicated that 4 years prior to the evaluation, she experienced a "dangerously high" fever, leading to delirium and hospitalization for several days "near death." She indicated she had "never been right since," although the more recent event had led to further decline in functioning. Of note, she mentioned that she knew a lot about "heat stroke" and expressed great concern that she had a particular "brain vulnerability" to heat, given these two incidents.

Her current complaints included worsening memory, occasional disorientation and confusion, and daily headaches and other physical complaints that had also increased over the past year. She indicated that she would find herself wandering at night unaware of what she was doing and starting tasks but then not finishing them (for example, washing her hair only half way so that soap remained in her hair; talking on the phone but forgetting to hang the phone up after the call was finished). She stated that she was incapable of working as a secretary anymore, because she couldn't remember how to file, how to answer office phones, or procedures for routing mail within the departments she was in charge of.

The neurological examination, including EEG and MRI and a full metabolic panel, was normal. Mental status exam was notable for poor performance on attention, working memory, and figure copy tasks. The neurologist diagnosed her with an anxiety disorder but referred her for further assessment at her insistence. Her presentation during the neuropsychological evaluation was notable for her extremely fashionable and overdressed appearance for the setting. She reported a significant amount of concern about her own cognitive abilities and became easily flustered and anxious about questions, often hyperventilating and appearing flushed. During many tasks, she reported that she forgot the purpose of the task and needed repetition of directions. She repeatedly asked whether testing could be done with the door or windows opened, as she felt the room was hot and stuffy and she worried about the effect of this on her ability to complete the tasks. During a list-learning task, she discontinued after three trials, sobbing, "How can anyone in my condition be expected to perform such a difficult task?"

INTRODUCTION

Response expectancies, expectations for automatic emotional, physical, or behavioral responses as reactions to specific situational cues (Kirsch, 1999), contribute to the outcomes of a variety of diagnostic and evaluative situations, including neuropsychological assessment. Response expectancies influence one's personal response to events and situations, often without conscious awareness (Kirsch, 2004), and are likely associated with recall of the past (Hirt, Lynn, Payne, Krackow, & McCrea, 1999). Response expectancies are acquired and shaped by past experiences, suggestions by others, or even through observational learning (Benedetti, 2009; Kirsch, 1999; Stewart-Williams & Podd, 2004). Even well-intentioned provision of information (for example, public health announcements regarding medications and their side effects, or symptoms of a disease or disorder that "you may have") can lead to unintended and quite specific negative consequences due to response expectancies. In general, response expectancies are one way in which human beings try to provide meaning to their world, allowing for immediate, automatic responses in new situations similar to those previously encountered, and are encoded into expectancy "templates." These templates influence our attention to and perception of our present, our explanations and understanding of our past, and our prediction of our own future behavior, directly affecting our behavioral output and affective experience (Benedetti, 2009; Goldman, Darkes, & Del Boca, 1999; Maddux, 1999).

The purpose of this chapter is to review evidence that response expectancies, particularly expectancies regarding neuropsychological dysfunction, can influence patients' behavioral responses, as well as their report of current and past symptoms and history. Such findings have direct implications for interpretation of neuropsychological evaluation results as reflective of brain damage and dysfunction.

PLACEBO AND NOCEBO EFFECTS

The study of response expectancies has been best documented in placebo and nocebo effect research. In such studies, the application of some external agent (medication, a medical procedure) leads to expected and stereotyped responses (positive for placebo, negative for nocebo), even when the external agent is in fact neutral and should not lead to the expected outcomes. Some of the most robust placebo effects have been shown in pain (Benedetti, 2006; Turner, Deyo, Loeser, Von Korff, & Fordyce, 1994; Vase, Riley, & Price, 2002), but placebo effects have also been demonstrated in the experience of asthma symptoms and attacks, motor symptoms, and sleep (Benedetti, 2009; Joyce, Jackevicius, Chapman, McIvor, & Kesten, 2000; Kemeny et al., 2007; Ross, Nelson, & Finegold, 2000; Sodergren & Hyland, 1999). Nocebo effects are less often the subject of experimental manipulation, for obvious ethical reasons, but are also well documented in research on pain, medication side effects, asthma and allergy symptoms, seizures, and motor symptoms (Beneditti, 2009; Colloca, Sigaudo, & Benedetti, 2008; Hahn, 1999; Liccardi et al., 2004; Rief et al., 2009). Reviews in specific placebo and nocebo domains suggest effect sizes that are generally large (for example, .95 for placebo analgesia, 1.16 for placebo antidepressant medication) (Kirsch & Sapirstein, 1998; Vase et al., 2002).

The literature on medication side effects demonstrates the amazing specificity of nocebo effects. For example, Pogge (1963) found that, while 17% of patients given placebo estrogen experienced nausea and vomiting, an expected side effect, only 6% of those given placebo analgesia and only 2% of those given placebo antiobesity drugs reported this particular side effect. Similarly, a meta-analysis examining the reported side effects for placebo groups in clinical trials for antidepressant medications (Rief et al., 2009) showed that individuals prescribed placebo medication but told they were taking tricyclic antidepressants reported more negative side effects compared to individuals prescribed placebo medication but told they were taking selective serotonin reuptake inhibitors, a pattern consistent with known side effect history for both medications.

For the most part, the effects of placebo and nocebo are measured by report of increased or decreased current symptoms (pain, allergy symptoms, mood changes, etc.). The more ambiguous and common the symptoms, the more vulnerable they seem to be to the effect (Benedetti, 2009). We have previously suggested that misattribution bias in postconcussive syndrome symptom report is an example of the nocebo effect working in a retrospective fashion (Gunstad & Suhr, 2001; 2002). That is, when people know they have suffered a head injury (the "nocebo"), not only might they report increased current symptoms consistent with expected consequences of a head injury (from widely available and sometimes inaccurate information about head injury), but they may also recall having fewer symptoms prior to having sustained the injury than base rates in the general population would suggest. Mittenberg, DiGiulio, Perrin, and Bass (1992) were the first to document misattribution bias in postconcussive symptom report, demonstrating that individuals with a history of mild head injury not only over-reported current symptoms (i.e., had higher rates than non-head-injured participants at baseline) but also underreported having those symptoms in the past (relative to non-head-injured controls at baseline). Their findings were replicated by Ferguson, Mittenberg, Barone, and Schneider (1999) and expanded beyond head injury into other illness domains, such as depression and headache, by Suhr and Gunstad (2002).

Although most placebo and nocebo effects documented in the literature are based on self-reported symptom changes, one interesting study examined the effects of nocebo on neuropsychological performance (Smith & Sullivan, 2003). These authors evaluated patients diagnosed with chronic fatigue syndrome who also had complaints of multiple chemical sensitivity symptoms, including cognitive dysfunction. Patients participated in a double-blind exposure paradigm in which they were exposed to either allergens they had reported reactions to in prior testing or to placebo (random administration on two separate occasions). They were given neuropsychological assessment prior to and 1 hour post-exposure. Patients were asked to predict what they had been exposed to at each administration. Although there was a general trend toward worse performance regardless of agent of exposure, it was patients' predictions of what they had been exposed to (i.e., their response expectancy templates) that were related to neuropsychological performance, with small effect size for attention measures and medium effect sizes for sustained attention, psychomotor processing speed, and memory measures.

STEREOTYPE THREAT

In placebo and nocebo research, the response expectancy template follows the pattern "if X is done to me, than Y will occur." However, response expectancy templates can also be based on beliefs about oneself, following the pattern "because I am X, than Y will occur." A line of research that examines the effect of this type of expectancy template is stereotype threat (Steele, 1997). Stereotype-threat research has focused primarily on stigmatized groups about whom well-known stereotypes exist with regard to academic and ability performance (African Americans and academic achievement and intelligence, females and math ability and achievement). Such stereotypes permeate our society, and members of stereotyped groups are well aware of the stereotypes from early in life, whether or not they personally believe them. A recent meta-analysis of evidence for stereotype-threat effects in race and ethnicity studies and gender studies (Nguyen & Ryan, 2008) showed, on average, a small effect size of .26, with stronger effects for ethnicity- and race-based stereotype threat ($d = .32$) than for gender-based stereotype threat ($d = .21$). Thus, being exposed to stereotypic negative information about a group in which one is a member (i.e., the response expectancy template of "because I am X, I will likely perform this way on test Y") has a small effect size for performance on ability and achievement tests. However, stereotype-threat research also suggests that the size of the effect is moderated by several variables.

One variable that moderates the effects of stereotype threat is task difficulty, with more difficult tasks showing average effect sizes of .36 (ethnicity/race research) and .42 (gender research), and easier tasks showing a smaller effect size of .18, regardless of sample. Stronger effects on more difficult tasks may be related to the increased cognitive demands associated with such tasks, which may more easily convince a test taker that a stereotype is true, or may be more threatening to someone who is already feeling threatened by their response expectancy template. Within the female and math stereotype-threat research, the size of the stereotype-threat effect was also moderated by how strongly one identified with the math domain (having a high math identity resulted in a small effect size of .20, while a low math identity showed a medium effect size of .52). Interestingly, an earlier meta-analysis of stereotype-threat research (Walton & Cohen, 2003) found that those with lower math identification showed *less* stereotype threat, which may be related to differences in what the measure of "math identity" used in these studies was actually measuring. On the one hand, a measure of strong domain identification could actually reflect having high personal value for being successful in that domain, which might lead to feeling more threatened by any challenge to that value. On the other hand, those who identify as "good" in math may have enough personal experience that their response expectancy template of "I am good at math" is more resistant to exposure to the larger cultural stereotype "women are bad at math," resulting in a smaller stereotype-threat effect. Finally, within ethnicity and race studies, the size of the effect was moderated by whether the stereotype threat was subtle or was explicitly induced (effect size for subtle threats $d = .22$, for moderately explicit threats $d = .64$, and for blatant threats $d = .41$). However, the opposite pattern was seen in the gender-based research, with more explicit threats producing smaller effect sizes than more subtle threats.

An important consideration in stereotype-threat research is not only whether individuals in stereotyped groups perform differently when exposed to the threat as compared to non-threat conditions but whether their performance differs from individuals *not* in the stereotyped groups, under either conditions of threat or non-threat. Within the race and ethnicity research, the majority versus minority effect size was .56 in non-threat conditions and .67 in threat conditions. Within the gender research, the male versus female effect size was .26 in non-threat conditions and .39 in threat conditions. Thus, stereotype threat as manipulated in these studies did not account entirely for the group differences, although group differences were larger under stereotype threat.

Stereotype-threat effects have also been documented in another group of individuals who often seek neuropsychological evaluation: older adults. Table 9.1 summarizes the results of studies examining stereotype threat effects in aging, with effect sizes where available. In general, older adults exposed to stereotype threat are more likely to perform worse than older adults not exposed to stereotype threat, with on average a medium to large effect ($d = .71$). As in the literature on race/ethnicity- and gender-based stereotype threat, larger effect sizes were seen when the task was more difficult (free recall, relative to basic attention or recognition tasks). At least one study directly comparing subtle with explicit threat induction (Hess, Hinson, Statham, 2004) showed that explicit stereotype-threat induction was not as strong an effect as implicit induction, but overall the aging literature is not clear on the effects of implicit versus explicit induction of threat. Although there is some suggestion that age may moderate the effect, evidence is mixed on whether younger-old adults or older-old adults are more vulnerable

Table 9.1 Effect Sizes in Studies of Aging-Stereotype Threat
(Effect Is Comparing Older Adults Exposed to Threat to
Older Adults in Neutral Conditions)

Study	Threat Manipulation	Measures	Effect Sizes
Levy (1996)	Implicit activation	Visuospatial recall, photo recall, auditory recall of word list	Could not be calculated
Levy et al. (2000)	Implicit activation	Mathematical challenge	.86
Stein et al. (2002)	Implicit activation	Dot location task and photo recall task	.04 (opposite direction), .11
Rahhal et al. (2001)	Explicit activation	Recall of sentence feedback, recognition of exposure to sentence	.23, .34, .04, .32, .20, .06, .15, .33, .19 .46 (opposite direction)
Hess et al. (2003)	Explicit activation	Free recall of word list	.70
Hess et al. (2004)	Implicit and explicit activation	Free recall of word-list task	Implicit: .84, .96 Explicit: .22, .03 (opposite direction)
Chasteen et al. (2005)	Explicit activation	Sentence memory task and recognition task	.82, .83, .63
Desrichard & Kopetz (2005)	Explicit activation	"Running an errand task" (efficiency of planning route for errands), story memory task, shape memory task, visuospatial attention span task	5.57, 2.49, 1.97, 1.1
Hess, Emery, & Queen (2009)	Explicit activation	Free recall of word list	Could not be calculated
Hess, Hinson, & Hodges (2009)	Explicit activation	Free recall of word list	Could not be calculated
Levy & Leifheit-Limson (2009)	Implicit activation of either cognitive threat or physical threat	Photo recall task	Difference in scores on memory performance when threat cognitive versus physical 2.16

to the effects of threat. We would argue that the age effect is probably related to how strongly one's personal response-expectancy template is focused on negative and pathological aspects of aging based on one's own personal experience (thus perhaps more of a perceived threat of a diagnosis such as Alzheimer's rather than aging per se; Suhr & Kinkela, 2007). At least one study showed that achievement motivation moderated the size of the effect, with those who value the threatened skill more being more strongly affected by the threat (Hess, Auman, Colcombe, & Rahhal, 2003).

It is also important to consider not only whether older adults exposed to ste-reotype threat perform differently than older adults not exposed to stereotype threat but also whether older and younger adults perform differently in either threat or non-threat conditions. Of the studies in Table 9.1 providing such data, the average age effect was 1.16 in non-stereotype-threat conditions and 1.55 in threat conditions. Thus, there is a large effect of age on neuropsychological test results even without exposure to threat, which would be expected; it is unlikely that stereotype threat can completely explain cognitive differences in older and younger adults. However, the addition of stereotype threat clearly increases the differences in neuropsychological performance between older and younger adults.

Although stereotype-threat studies typically focus on behavioral performance as outcome variables, aging stereotype research suggests that older adults are more likely to attribute minor memory glitches to permanent, internal causes (related to aging stereotype templates) than younger adults who make the same memory errors (Lachman, Weaver, Bandura, Elliott, & Lewkowicz, 1992). We have previously argued that self-reported memory decline in older adults may be related to perceived threat of Alzheimer's disease (Suhr & Kinkela, 2007). In a review of the predictive accuracy of self-reported memory complaints in older adults, Jonker, Jackevicius, Chapman, McIvor, and Kesten (2000) observed that self-reported memory complaints were not accurate predictors of concur-rent or future memory test performance in self-referred clinical samples, but self-reported memory complaints were more accurate predictors of concurrent and future memory test performance in community-based samples recruited and paid for their participation. Suhr and Kinkela (2007) argued that such a pattern makes sense if one considers the response expectancy template of individuals who present with concerns that they have dementia. People with personal history of a loved one showing abnormal cognitive decline with age (family members, caregivers of dementia patients) hold more negative stereo-types about aging and cognition than the general aging population. These indi-viduals may repeatedly check themselves for "signs" of dementia and interpret their own cognitive glitches in a more pathological manner (Caprio-Prevette & Fry, 1996; Hodgson, Cutler, & Livingston, 1999; Lachman et al., 1992), which can influence both current report of memory impairment (i.e., overreport-ing memory symptoms in an inaccurate fashion) and report of the degree of memory decline from the past (underreporting the frequency of such common memory errors in past years).

DIAGNOSIS THREAT

Thus far, our review has focused on stereotypes that are well-known in the general population and that are about large groups of individuals in the general population. However, stereotypes also exist about specific diseases and illnesses, an effect we have termed "diagnosis threat" (Suhr & Gunstad, 2002; 2005). Hahn (1999) considered how culture and society are sources of information about disease and illness, including typical symptoms, causes, prognoses, and treatments, and effects of an illness on social roles and responsibilities. As in other response expectancies, disease-specific beliefs may be learned through not only personal experience but also the suggestions of others (news media, public health announcements, physician suggestion) and can even be learned through observation (e.g., epidemic hysteria; Hahn, 1999). In other words, when one is given diagnosis X and then reads about diagnosis X, hears about it on television, attends support groups for diagnosis X, and meets others with diagnosis X, etc., this can create response expectancy templates that include how X might affect cognitive abilities and performance on tasks within a neuropsychological assessment. Within the domain of neuropsychological illness and injury, research shows that people do expect neurological injury and psychological illness to lead to cognitive impairments (Dilorio et al., 2004, Ferguson et al., 1999; Gunstad & Suhr, 2001; 2002; Mittenberg et al., 1992; Wong, Regennitter, & Barrios, 1994). As noted above, we have previously interpreted misattribution-bias findings as consistent with the nocebo effect ("the head injury harmed my brain"), but over time, with repeated experience relevant to the diagnosis and reinforcement of the response expectancy template, it is likely that a strong personal diagnosis or patient identity emerges that is consistent with diagnosis threat (i.e., "I am brain injured").

Table 9.2 summarizes existing studies of the diagnosis-threat effect on actual neuropsychological test performance. Three studies (two from our lab) have examined the effects of diagnosis threat on individuals with mild head injury. Effect sizes varied slightly by neuropsychological domain, with an average effect size of .31 in the domain of memory, an average effect size of .39 in the domain of attention, an average effect size of .32 in motor speed tasks, and an average effect size of .68 in intellectual and executive tasks. Overall, the effect is similar to that seen in existing studies on race and ethnicity and gender stereotype threat but smaller than that seen in aging-stereotype threat. An important consideration in interpreting the results of existing diagnosis-threat studies is the nature of the participant samples—these individuals were highly functioning and educated young adults who happened to have a head injury history but who were not seeking treatment or compensation for the injury. Response expectancies associated with stereotype threat involve two dimensions: internalized expectations about oneself (membership in the group and the stereotype about the group) and expectations about the situation one is in (this testing situation is relevant, evaluative, diagnostic; in other words, an external threat). Because the participants in these studies were not patients with a strong "patient identity," their personal expectancy beliefs are not likely as strong as those that would be seen in clinical samples. In support of this,

Table 9.2 EFFECT SIZES IN STUDIES OF DIAGNOSIS THREAT (EFFECT IS COMPARING
GROUPS UNDER THREAT TO GROUPS IN NEUTRAL CONDITION)

Study	Measures	Effect Sizes
Suhr & Gunstad (2002)	Auditory Verbal Learning Test, Complex Figure Recall, Information, Block Design, Digit Span, Letter Number Sequencing, Trail-Making Test, Controlled Oral Word Association	Memory .27, .53, .55 Intellect .72, .84 Attention .15, .18 Processing speed .24, .31, .03 (opposite direction)
Suhr & Gunstad (2005)	Complex Figure Recall, Word Memory Test memory subtests, Trail-Making Test, Digit Symbol, Digit Span, Letter Number Sequencing, Mental Arithmetic, Wisconsin Card Sorting Test	Memory .74, .50, .13, .18 Processing speed .26, .30, .63 Attention .74, .90, .65 Executive function .47
Cole et al. (2006)	Rivermead Behavioral Memory Test prose recall, Digit Span, Controlled Oral Word Association	.52 for memory; no effect size could be calculated for other tasks
Suhr & Spickard (2006)	Word Memory Test long-delay free recall, Digit Span, Trail-Making Test, Digit Symbol, Letter Number Sequencing, Mental Arithmetic	Memory .65 Attention .11 (opposite direction), .09, .16 Processing speed .27, .41
Suhr & Nemitz (2006)	Word list learning Delayed recall Semantic fluency	1.09 .32 1.09
Looby & Earleywine (2010)	California Verbal Learning Test-II Controlled Oral Word Association Digit Symbol	Men .05, women 1.01 (opposite direction) Men 1.17, women .68 (opposite direction) Men .47, women .93 (opposite direction)
Isgrigg & Suhr (2010)	Word-list learning Semantic fluency	.15 .05 (opposite direction)

Note. All studies used explicit activation.

Ozen and Fernandes (2011) found that the effect size for traumatic brain injury
(TBI) was −.10 across all cognitive domains in the no-stereotype threat condition,
a much smaller group effect than in other existing stereotype-threat work and
likely reflective of the nonclinical sample recruited for the study. Furthermore,
in the diagnosis-threat condition, the TBI group actually performed better than

controls ($d = .16$). In addition, participants in these three studies had extensive previous experience with difficult cognitive tasks, and the tasks administered may not have been as difficult for them, further weakening the diagnosis-threat effect. In that context, it is notable that the largest diagnosis-threat effect sizes were in the intelligence and executive-function domain.

Five other stereotype-threat studies have examined stereotype threat in samples that may have stronger patient identity response expectancy templates for cognitive-task performance. Two existing studies focused on substance abusers. Cole, Michailidou, Jerome, and Sumnall (2006) reported a medium effect of diagnosis threat on a memory test in ecstasy users who were exposed to stereotype threat. However, Looby and Earleywine (2010) found no memory diagnosis-threat effect for male marijuana users, although they did perform worse on speeded information-processing tasks (medium to large effect size). By contrast, in female marijuana users, there was evidence of stereotype lift (i.e., female marijuana users exposed to the stereotype performed better). In our laboratory, we have examined diagnosis threat in recurrent headache (Suhr & Spickard, 2006), with a memory effect size of .65, an attention/working memory effect size of .05, and a processing-speed effect size of .34. We have also examined two separate samples of pregnant women exposed to a "pregnancy dementia" stereotype, with mixed findings. In the first study (Suhr & Nemitz, 2006), pregnant women told that the study was specifically examining cognitive changes in pregnancy performed worse on memory and speed of processing tasks (large effect sizes) than women told that the study was about anticipation of pain experiences in pregnancy and during delivery. However, in the second study (Isgrigg & Suhr, 2010), the effect size for cognitive tasks was negligible. Of note, with regard to self-report measures, pregnant women who thought the study was specifically assessing cognitive changes in pregnancy self-reported more current memory problems (effect size .50) and a higher degree of change from prior to pregnancy (effect size .35) compared to pregnant women who thought the study was about pain. One possible reason for the differences in the cognitive-test findings across the two pregnancy threat studies may have been related to changes in pre-study awareness of the diagnosis threat. Debriefing at the end of the second pregnancy study showed that all participants reported not only knowledge of the pregnancy dementia stereotype but also a belief that the study's purpose was to examine pregnancy and memory, despite attempts to hide the purpose of the study in the non-threat condition. When asked, the pregnant women indicated that their own physicians had told them to expect cognitive decline while pregnant, and that they had also read this information in highly popular books on preparing for pregnancy and delivery. These findings point to the widespread availability of negative stereotypes about cognitive performance, which may contribute to strong and difficult-to-manipulate preexisting response expectancy templates in certain populations or certain individuals during neuropsychological evaluation.

In general, studies of diagnosis threat are limited in number, and further work needs to be conducted in this area, particularly in clinical patients, in whom stronger and more established diagnosis-based response expectancy templates likely exist. However, it is important that such studies be conducted outside of a true clinical evaluation, in which the goal is to have the most valid and accurate data available for interpretation, given existing evidence of a meaningful, though small, effect of diagnosis threat on both self-report and test performance. Future studies should continue to examine the effects of diagnosis threat on retrospective recall, current symptom report, and actual test performance across multiple cognitive domains.

POTENTIAL PROCESSES UNDERLYING RESPONSE EXPECTANCIES

Several potential mediators of response expectancies have gained theoretical and research attention in existing placebo/nocebo and stereotype and diagnosis threat research, including emotional change such as increased or decreased anxiety, physiological change, behavioral change, and selective processing. In placebo and nocebo research, decreased (or increased) anxiety as a result of positive (or negative) expectancies is assumed to cause decrease (or increase) in nonspecific physical symptoms, which are then interpreted by the experiencer to be consistent with and specific to the expected effect (Osborne, 2007; Stewart-Williams & Podd, 2004). Anxiety has also been suggested as a mediator of the relationship of stereotype threat to cognitive outcomes, perhaps tied to physiological changes such as cortisol or blood pressure, which may influence cognitive performance (Kit, Tuokko, & Mateer, 2008; Osborne, 2007). Response expectancies may also lead individuals to alter their behavior in ways that then increase the likelihood that the expected outcome will occur. In the realm of gender-based stereotype threat, females exposed to stereotype threat have been shown to alter their behavior in ways that might affect task performance, such as choosing to complete verbal items over math items, or spending less time on math items (Davies, Spencer, Quinn, & Gerhardstein, 2002; Spencer, Steele, & Quinn, 1999). Selective processing may also explain the relationship of response expectancies to outcomes, particularly for self-reported symptoms. For example, expectations about the outcome of a treatment can guide an individual to attend to symptoms and experiences that are consistent with their expectations, interpret ambiguous information in a way that is consistent with their expectations, and dismiss inconsistent information (Brody & Brody, 2000; Hirt et al., 1999). Overall, however, mediators of response expectancy effects on self-report and cognitive performance have not been carefully examined in the literature to date.

Individuals do not appear to be equally vulnerable to response expectancies. Unfortunately, researchers have only begun to identify individual difference variables that may moderate placebo/nocebo and stereotype or diagnosis threat effects. Factors that may potentially make individuals more vulnerable to response expectancies include having stronger preexisting response expectations (Kit et al., 2008; Vase et al., 2002), having previous experiences consistent with the response expectations (such as previous side effects of a medication) (Liccardi et al., 2004; Price, Finniss, & Benedetti, 2008), scoring higher on neuroticism (Kit et al., 2008), and holding a social role that deemphasizes control (Hahn, 1999). Factors that have been proposed to make a person more vulnerable specifically to stereotype or diagnosis threat include a strong identification with the group that is being stereotyped, having less confidence in or self-efficacy for one's performance prior to being exposed to the threat, or having mild premorbid impairments in a cognitive area that is being assessed (Kit et al., 2008). As with potential mediators of response expectancy effects, moderators of response expectancy effects are understudied and should be examined in future research.

IMPLICATIONS FOR CLINICAL PRACTICE

Response expectancies appear to have small to medium-sized effects on both self-report and behavioral performance in the neuropsychological evaluation context. In effect, response expectancy templates are the "lenses" that a given patient wears when presenting for evaluation; their self-reported history, prior symptoms, current symptoms, and appraisal of the "threat" of the evaluative situation are all viewed through this lens. There are several important implications of this work for clinical practice, which we will illustrate by returning to our case, Ms. L.

With regard to interviewing patients about their history and their present and past symptoms and experiences, it is important to recognize the possible effects of response expectancies on patient presentation and communication. Kunda (1990) emphasized that there are two possible motivational goals at the time of information retrieval: (1) to be accurate, and (2) to arrive at a desired conclusion. If that desired conclusion is to help an evaluator understand the patient's past and present in the context of the active response expectancy template "I have X, that causes Y," the likelihood that the patient will engage in efforts to accurately recall the past decreases, as the literature on misattribution bias reviewed above suggests. The possibility of distorted recall of the past (and the present) emphasizes the need for neuropsychological evaluation to include not only self-reported current and past experiences and symptoms but also collateral reports and objective records to confirm what is reported. Recently, researchers have suggested that misattribution bias may play a role in the overdiagnosis of mild head injury in the military and provided suggestions for approaches to evaluation of such individuals (Howe, 2009; Iverson, Langlois, McCrea, & Kelly, 2009).

In the case of Ms. L., although she recalled a prior hospitalization in which she was reportedly "near death," hospital records showed that she had presented to the emergency room complaining of several days of vomiting and diarrhea and had been hospitalized for dehydration and given IV fluids. While she did develop a fever on the second day, it was not life threatening and responded quickly to medications. She was awake, alert, and oriented through her brief hospital stay, with the exception of a few hours around the fever. Her discharge diagnosis was urinary tract infection and dehydration. These records were a sharp contrast to her self-reported account of this incident and its importance to her presenting complaints.

Another key implication for clinical practice is the importance of knowing the broader history of the patient in terms of family history and experience with similar disorders. Response expectancy research in placebo/nocebo and stereotype and diagnosis threat has emphasized the role of personal experience in establishing the response expectancy. We have worked with many middle-aged adults who, because of their own experience with caring for someone or being related to someone with Alzheimer's disease, are convinced they "have the same thing," to the point of noticing only those cognitive symptoms that most remind them of the early stages of their loved one's decline. Such observations prompted our work on perceived Alzheimer's disease threat (Suhr & Kinkela, 2007). Thus, listening for and asking about a patient's personal history with similar symptoms and similar conditions, in family members and in others they are close to, may provide important clues for the source of the "lenses" they are wearing when interpreting their own everyday behavior.

In the case of Ms. L., when she was a child, one of her family members had collapsed and died from heat stroke (note, a history confirmed by spouse report). She mentioned this family member repeatedly when expressing her concerns about her own functioning.

Another important consideration is the context of the evaluation. Stereotype- and diagnosis-threat research has shown inconsistent effects of explicit versus subtle induction of threat. Researchers have argued that if an individual is unaware of the nature of the threat, the stereotype may not be activated, but other researchers have pointed out that even subtle manipulations of threat can be potent. Attempts to remove stereotype threat in ethnic and minority studies have actually resulted in greater group differences, although attempts to minimize gender-based stereotype threat tend to be effective (Nguyen & Ryan, 2008). As noted earlier, response expectancies associated with stereotype and diagnosis threat involve both internalized expectations about oneself (membership in the group and the stereotype about the group) and expectations about the situation one is in. Given that the context of neuropsychological evaluation is diagnostic and prognostic, the situation is always somewhat threatening. To some extent then, the context of clinical evaluation is always one of diagnosis threat, with the size of the effect dependent on the degree to which the individual patient has a particular patient identity (i.e., how distorted the "lens" of their response expectancy template is), as well as the degree to which any individual task within the testing session will be viewed as threatening. In this context, the effect of diagnosis threat on measures of noncredible responding (i.e., so-called malingering measures) is critical to understand, but as yet unknown. Given that such measures are actually psychometrically very easy but are difficult in appearance, it is important for future studies to determine whether inclusion of such measures would help detect the influence of diagnosis threat in a neuropsychological evaluation.

In the case of Ms. L., not only was she so distressed during a list-learning task that the task had to be discontinued, but she also failed two measures of noncredible responding on two separate testing occasions. In fact, right after completing one of the subtests on the first measure of noncredible responding, she said, "Part of me wants to do [the task] but part of me says I can't do it, it's paralyzing."

Finally, response expectancy research has implications for feedback in neuropsychological assessment and for treatment and rehabilitation of neuropsychological dysfunction. The use of therapeutic feedback is of growing importance in psychological and neuropsychological assessment (Finn, 2003; Gorske & Smith, 2009; Meyer et al., 2003). Such feedback should include accurate interpretation of neuropsychological test results, as well as consideration of both neurological and non-neurological contributions to the overall presentation of the patient during the evaluation. Mittenberg, Tremont, Zielinski, Fichera, and Rayls (1996) showed that providing more accurate response expectancy templates for head injury symptoms and recovery at the time of the injury (in the emergency room) resulted in better long-term outcomes than provision of standard head-injury feedback. These findings have since been replicated by several others (Paniak, Toller-Lobe, Durand, & Nagy, 1998; Paniak, Toller-Lobe, Reynolds, Melnyk, & Nagy, 2000; Ponsford et al., 2002). Interestingly, research on memory training for older adults has shown that provision of accurate information about age-associated changes leads to improved self-reported memory performance, even when actual test scores do not improve (Lachman et al., 1992; Schmidt, Zwart, Berg, & Deelman, 1999; Turner & Pinkston, 1993). However, response expectancy research and the social-cognitive theories it is based on clearly suggest that the continued, repeated, and reinforced encoding that is part of a well-established response expectancy template will be more difficult to change. Nevertheless, from a treatment standpoint, cognitive and cognitive-behavioral therapies are based on disconfirming existing maladaptive beliefs (i.e., response expectancy templates) through changing statements and real-world exposure and experience to experiences that contradict those beliefs (Goldman et al., 1999; Weinberger & Eig, 1999). More research needs to be conducted specifically on the power of such interventions to improve functioning in those with neuropsychological dysfunction and impairments that do not appear to be neurologically based.

With regard to Ms. L., all neuropsychological test results suggested severe impairment, but given the inconsistency of these scores with her general presentation and her performance on multiple measures of noncredible responding, these were believed to be invalid. Her MMPI-2 profile showed a 1–3 profile, with 3 higher than 1, consistent with a conversion presentation. We also diagnosed her with anxiety disorder NOS. As we prepared to provide her with feedback about her performance and our recommendation for psychological intervention, we considered that, over the year since her second heat-related incident, her place of employment had been very supportive of her performance decline, and in fact had hired an assistant for her to help her complete her daily work. In addition, her husband had taken over most home management responsibilities over the past year. Unfortunately, this likely led to reinforcement of her belief that she was impaired and needed assistance, helping to strengthen her response expectancy template. Therefore, we prepared for resistance to our interpretation of her presentation as non-neurological. However, immediately prior to feedback, her husband asked to talk with the first author privately. He indicated that he had been doing some reading on his own, and he was starting to wonder whether she was just "really anxious." He had come to recognize the inconsistencies in her belief that she was impaired and her actual ability to accomplish many tasks, and he had also witnessed several panic-type episodes, which we saw repeatedly throughout the evaluation. With his support during feedback, we were therefore able to offer her a therapeutic interpretation of her distress, her beliefs about her performance, her concerns about her brain, and her ability to function, and provide a recommendation for cognitive-behavioral therapy. Given that we received a request for records from a local mental health agency within a month of our evaluation, we were hopeful that our feedback was successful and that she was able to follow through with therapy and change her maladaptive response expectancies in a way that would allow her to return to normal, healthy functioning.

References

Benedetti, F. (2006). Placebo and endogenous mechanisms of analgesia. *Handbook of Experimental Pharmacology, 177,* 393–413.

Benedetti, F. (2009). *Placebo effects: Understanding the mechanisms in health and disease.* New York: Oxford.

Brody, H., & Brody, D. (2000). Three perspectives on the placebo response: expectancy, conditioning, and meaning. *Advances in Mind-Body Medicine, 16,* 211–232.

Caprio-Prevette, M. D., & Fry, P. S. (1996). Memory enhancement program for community-based older adults. *Experimental Aging Research, 22,* 281–303. doi:10.1080/03610739608254012

Chasteen, A. L., Bhattacharyya, S., Horhota, M., Tam, R., & Hasher, L. (2005). How feelings of stereotype threat influence older adults' memory performance. *Experimental Aging Research, 31,* 235–260. doi:10.1080/03610730590948177

Cole, J. C., Michailidou, K., Jerome, L., & Sumnall, H. R. (2006). The effects of stereotype threat on cognitive function in ecstasy users. *Journal of Psychopharmacology, 20,* 518–525. doi:10.1177/0269881105058572

Colloca, L., Sigaudo, M., & Benedetti, F. (2008). The role of learning in nocebo and placebo effects. *Pain, 136,* 211–218. doi:10.1016/j.pain.2008.02.006

Davies, P. G., Spencer, S. J., Quinn, D. M., & Gerhardstein, R. (2002). Consuming images: How television commercials that elicit stereotype threat can restrain women academically and professionally. *Personality and Social Psychology Bulletin, 28,* 1615–1628. doi:10.1177/014616702237644

Desrichard, O., & Kopetz, C. (2005). A threat in the elder: The impact of task instructions, self-efficacy and performance expectations on memory performance in the elderly. *European Journal of Social Psychology, 35*, 537–552. doi:10.1002/ejsp.249

Dilorio, C. A., Kobau, M., Holden, E. W., Berkowitz, J. M., Kamin, S. L., Antonak, R. F.,... Price, P. H. (2004). Developing a measure to assess attitudes toward epilepsy in the US population. *Epilepsy & Behavior, 5*, 965–975. doi:10.1016/j.yebeh.2004.08.020

Ferguson, R. J., Mittenberg, W., Barone, D. F., & Schneider, B. (1999). Postconcussion syndrome following sports-related head injury: Expectation as etiology. *Neuropsychology, 13*, 582–589. doi:10.1037/0894-4105.13.4.582

Finn, S. E. (2003). Therapeutic assessment of a man with "ADD." *Journal of Personality Assessment, 80*, 115–129. doi:10.1207/S15327752JPA8002_01

Goldman, M. S., Darkes, J., & Del Boca, F. K. (1999). Expectancy mediation of biopsychosocial risk for alcohol use and alcoholism. In I. Kirsch (Ed.), *How expectancies shape experience* (pp. 233–262). Washington, DC: American Psychological Association. doi:10.1037/10332-010

Gorske, T. T., & Smith, S. R. (2009). *Collaborative therapeutic neuropsychological assessment.* New York: Springer.

Gunstad, J., & Suhr, J.A. (2001). "Expectation as etiology" versus "the good old days": Postconcussion syndrome symptom reporting in athletes, headache sufferers, and depressed individuals. *Journal of the International Neuropsychological Society, 7*, 323–333. doi:10.1017/S1355617701733061

Gunstad, J., & Suhr, J. A. (2002). Perception of illness: nonspecificity of postconcussion syndrome symptom expectation. *Journal of the International Neuropsychological Society, 8*, 37–47. doi:10.1017/S1355617702811043

Hahn, R. A. (1999). Expectations of sickness: Concept and evidence of the nocebo phenomenon. In I. Kirsch (Ed.), *How expectancies shape experience* (pp. 333–356). Washington, DC: American Psychological Association. doi:10.1037/10332-014

Hess, T. M., Auman, C., Colcombe, S. J., & Rahhal, T. A. (2003). The impact of stereotype threat on age differences in memory performance. *The Journals of Gerontology: Series B: Psychological Sciences and Social Sciences, 58*, 3–11.

Hess, T. M., Emery, L., & Queen, T. L. (2009). Task demands moderate stereotype threat effects on memory performance. *The Journals of Gerontology: Series B: Psychological Sciences and Social Sciences, 64*, 482–486. doi:10.1093/geronb/gbp044

Hess, T. M., & Hinson, J. T. (2006). Age-related variation in the influences of aging stereotypes on memory in adulthood. *Psychology and Aging, 21*, 621–625. doi:10.1037/0882-7974.21.3.621

Hess, T. M., Hinson, T. J., & Hodges, E. A. (2009). Moderators of and mechanisms underlying stereotype threat effects on older adults' memory performance. *Experimental Aging Research, 35*,153–177. doi:10.1080/03610730802716413

Hess, T.M., Hinson, J.T., & Statham, J.A. (2004). Explicit and implicit stereotype activation effects on memory: Do age and awareness moderate the impact of priming? *Psychology and Aging, 19*(3), 495–505. doi:10.1037/0882-7974.19.3.495

Hirt, E. R., Lynn, S. J., Payne, D. G., Krackow, E., & McCrea, S. M. (1999). Expectancies and memory: Inferring the past from what must have been. In I. Kirsch (Ed.), *How expectancies shape experience* (pp. 93–124). Washington, DC: American Psychological Association. doi:10.1037/10332-004

Hodgson, L. G., Cutler, S. J., & Livingston, K. (1999). Alzheimer's disease and symptom seeking. *American Journal of Alzheimer's Disease, 14*, 264–274.

Howe, L. L. S. (2009). Giving context to post-deployment post-concussive-like symptoms: Blast-related potential mild traumatic brain injury and comorbidities. *The Clinical Neuropsychologist, 23*, 1315–1337. doi:10.1080/13854040903266928

Isgrigg, A., & Suhr, J. (2010, April). *Diagnosis threat and cognitive performance during pregnancy.* Annual meeting of the Society for Behavioral Medicine, Seattle, WA.

Iverson, G. L., Langlois, J. A., McCrea, M. A., & Kelly, J. P. (2009). Challenges associated with post-deployment screening for mild traumatic brain injury in military personnel. *The Clinical Neuropsychologist, 23*, 1299–1314. doi:10.1080/1385404090315902

Jonker, E., Geerlings, M. I., & Schmand, B. (2000). Are memory complaints predictive for dementia: A review of clinical and population-based studies. *International Journal of Geriatric Psychiatry, 15*, 983–991. doi:10.1002/1099-1166(200011)15:11<983::AID-GPS238>3.0.CO;2-5

Joyce, D. P., Jackevicius, C., Chapman, K. R., McIvor, A., & Kesten, S. (2000). The placebo effect in asthma drug therapy trials: A meta-analysis. *Journal of Asthma, 37*, 303–318.

Kemeny, M. E., Rosenwasser, L. J., Panettieri, R. A., Rose, R. M., Berg-Smith, S. M., & Kline, J. N. (2007). Placebo response in asthma: A robust and objective phenomenon. *Journal of Allergy and Clinical Immunology, 119*, 1375–1381. doi:10.1016/j.jaci.2007.03.016

Kirsch, I. (Ed.) (1999). *How expectancies shape experience.* Washington, DC: American Psychological Association.

Kirsch, I. (2004). Conditioning, expectancy, and the placebo effect: Comment on Stewart-Williams and Podd (2004). *Psychological Bulletin, 130*, 341–343. doi:10.1037/0033-2909.130.2.341

Kirsch, I., & Sapirstein, G. (1998). Listening to Prozac but hearing placebo: A meta-analysis of antidepressant medication. *Prevention & Treatment, 1*, 2–18. doi:10.1037/1522-3736.1.1.12a

Kit, K. A., Tuokko, H. A., & Mateer, C. A. (2008). A review of the stereotype threat literature and its application in a neurological population. *Neuropsychological Review, 18*, 132–148. doi:10.1007/s11065-008-9059-9

Kunda, Z. (1990). The case for motivated reasoning. *Psychological Bulletin, 108*, 480–498. doi:10.1037/0033-2909.108.3.480

Lachman, M. E., Weaver, S. L., Bandura, M., Elliott, E., & Lewkowicz, C. J. (1992) Improving memory and control beliefs through cognitive restructuring and self-generated strategies. *Journals of Gerontology Series B: Psychological Sciences and Social Sciences, 47*, 293–299. doi:10.1093/geronj/47.5.P293

Levy, B. (1996). Improving memory in old age through implicit self-stereotyping. *Journal of Personality and Social Psychology, 71*, 1092–1107. doi:10.1037/0022-3514.71.6.1092

Levy, B., Hausdorff, J., Hencke, R., & Wei, J. Y. (2000). Reducing cardiovascular stress with positive self-stereotypes of aging. *The Journals of Gerontology: Series B: Psychological Sciences and Social Sciences, 55*, 205–213.

Levy, B. R., & Leifheit-Limson, E. (2009). The stereotype-matching effect: Greater influence on functioning when age stereotypes correspond to outcomes. *Psychology and Aging, 24*, 230–233. doi:10.1037/a0014563

Liccardi, G., Senna, G., Russo, M., Bonadonna, P., Crivellaro, M., Dama, A., et al. (2004). Evaluation of the nocebo effect during oral challenge in patients with adverse drug reactions. *Journal of Investigational Allergology and Clinical Immunology, 14*, 104–107.

Looby, A., & Earleywine, M. (2010). Gender moderates the impact of stereotype threat on cognitive function in cannabis users. *Addictive Behaviors, 35*, 834–839. doi:10.1016/j.addbeh.2010.04.004

Maddux, J. E. (1999). Expectancies and the social-cognitive perspective: Basic principles, processes, and variables. In I. Kirsch (Ed.), *How expectancies shape experience* (pp. 17–40). Washington, DC: American Psychological Association. doi:10.1037/10332-001

Meyer, G. J., Finn, S. E., Eyde, L. D., Kay, G. G., Moreland, K. L., Dies, R. R., et al. (2003). Psychological testing and psychological assessment: A review of evidence and issues. In A. E. Kazdin (Ed.), *Methodological issues and strategies in clinical research* (3rd ed., pp. 265–345). Washington, DC: American Psychological Association.

Mittenberg, W., DiGiulio, D. V., Perrin, S., & Bass, A. E. (1992). Symptoms following mild head injury: Expectation as aetiology. *Journal of Neurology, Neurosurgery & Psychiatry, 55*, 200–204. doi:10.1136/jnnp.55.3.200

Mittenberg, W., Tremont, G., Zielinski, R. E., Fichera, S., & Rayls, K. R. (1996). Cognitive-behavioral prevention of postconcussion syndrome. *Archives of Clinical Neuropsychology, 11*, 139–145. doi:10.1016/0887-6177(95)00006-2

Nguyen, H-H. D., & Ryan, A. M. (2008). Does stereotype threat affect test performance of minorities and women? A meta-analysis of experimental evidence. *Journal of Applied Psychology, 93*, 1134–1334. doi:10.1037/a0012702

Osborne, J. W. (2007). Linking stereotype threat and anxiety. *Educational Psychology, 27*, 135–154. doi:10.1080/01443410601069929

Ozen, L. J. & Fernandes, M. A. (2011). Effects of "diagnosis threat" on cognitive and affective functioning long after mild head injury. *Journal of the International Neuropsychological Society, 17*, 219–229. doi:10.1017/S135561771000144X

Paniak, C., Toller-Lobe, G., Durand, A., & Nagy, J. (1998). A randomized trial of two treatments for mild traumatic brain injury. *Brain Injury, 12*, 1011–1023. doi:10.1080/026990598121927

Paniak, C., Toller-Lobe, G., Reynolds, S., Melnyk, A., & Nagy, J. (2000). A randomized trial of two treatments for mild traumatic brain injury: 1 year follow-up. *Brain Injury, 14*, 219–226. doi:10.1080/026990500120691

Pogge, R. C. (1963). The toxic placebo: Part I: Side and toxic effects reported during the administration of placebo medicine. *Medical Times, 91*, 773–778.

Ponsford, J., Willmott, C., Rothwell, A., Cameron, P., Kelly, A-M., Nelms, R., & Curran, C. (2002). Impact of early intervention on outcome following mild head injury in adults. *Journal of Neurology, Neurosurgery, and Psychiatry, 73*, 330–332. doi:10.1136/jnnp.73.3.330

Price, D. D., Finniss, D. G., & Benedetti, F. (2008). A comprehensive review of the placebo effect: Recent advances and current thought. *Annual Review of Psychology, 59*, 565–590. doi:10.1146/annurev.psych.59.113006.095941

Rahhal, T. A., Hasher, L., & Colcombe, S. J. (2001). Instructional manipulations and age differences in memory: Now you see them, now you don't. *Psychology and Aging, 16*, 697–706. doi:10.1037/0882-7974.16.4.697

Rief, W., Nestoriuc, Y., von Lilienfeld-Toal, A., Dogan, I., Schreiber, F., Hofmann, S.G., Barsky, A.J., & Avorn, J. (2009). Differences in adverse effect reporting in placebo groups in SSRI and tricyclic antidepressant trials. *Drug Safety, 32*, 1041–1056. doi:10.2165/11316580-000000000-00000

Ross, R. N., Nelson, H. S., & Finegold, I. (2000). Effectiveness of specific immunotherapy in the treatment of asthma: A meta-analysis of prospective, randomized, double-blind, placebo-controlled studies. *Clinical Therapeutics, 22*, 329–341. doi:10.1016/S0149-2918(00)80037-5

Schmidt, I. W., Zwart, J. F., Berg, I. J., & Deelman, B. D. (1999). Evaluation of an intervention directed at the modification of memory beliefs in older adults. *Educational Gerontology, 25*, 365–385. doi:10.1080/036012799267792

Smith, S., & Sullivan, K. (2003). Examining the influence of biological and psychological factors on cognitive performance in chronic fatigue syndrome: A randomized, double-blind, placebo-controlled, crossover study. *International Journal of Behavioral Medicine, 10,* 162. doi:10.1207/S15327558IJBM1002_05

Sodergren, S. C., & Hyland, M. E. (1999). Expectancy and asthma. In I. Kirsch (Ed.), *How expectancies shape experience* (pp. 197–212). Washington, DC: American Psychological Association. doi:10.1037/10332-008

Spencer, S. J., Steele, C. M., & Quinn, D. M. (1999). Stereotype threat and women's math performance. *Journal of Experimental Social Psychology, 35,* 4–28. doi:10.1006/jesp.1998.1373

Steele, C. M. (1997). A threat in the air: How stereotypes shape intellectual identity and performance. *American Psychologist, 52,* 613–629. doi:10.1037/0003-066X.52.6.613

Stein, R., Blanchard-Fields, F., & Hertzog, C. (2002). The effects of age-stereotype priming on the memory performance of older adults. *Experimental Aging Research, 28,* 169–181. doi:10.1080/03610730252800184

Stewart-Williams, S., & Podd, J. (2004). The placebo effect: Dissolving the expectancy versus conditioning debate. *Psychological Bulletin, 130,* 324–340. doi:10.1037/0033-2909.130.2.324

Suhr, J. A. & Gunstad, J. (2002). "Diagnosis threat": The effect of negative expectations on cognitive performance in head injury. *Journal of Clinical and Experimental Neuropsychology, 24,* 448–457. doi:10.1076/jcen.24.4.448.1039

Suhr, J. A. & Gunstad, J. (2005). Further exploration of the effect of "diagnosis threat" on cognitive performance in individuals with mild head injury. *Journal of the International Neuropsychological Society, 11,* 23–29. doi:10.1017/S1355617705050010

Suhr, J. A., & Kinkela, J. (2007). Perceived threat of Alzheimer's disease (AD): The role of personal experience with AD. *Alzheimer Disease and Associated Disorders, 21,* 225–231. doi:10.1097/WAD.0b013e31813e6683

Suhr, J., & Nemitz, J. (2006, February). *Diagnosis threat and neuropsychological performance in pregnancy.* Annual meeting of the International Neuropsychological Society, Boston, MA.

Suhr, J., & Spickard, B. (2006, February). *Exploration of the diagnosis treat effect in a chronic pain population.* Annual meeting of the International Neuropsychological Society, Boston, MA.

Turner, J. A., Deyo, R. A., Loeser, J. D., Von Korff, M., & Fordyce, W. E. (1994). The importance of placebo effects in pain treatment and research. *Journal of the American Medical Association, 271,* 1609–1614. doi:10.1001/jama.271.20.1609

Turner, M. L., & Pinkston, R. S. (1993). Effects of a memory and aging workshop on negative beliefs of memory loss in the elderly. *Educational Gerontology, 19,* 359–373. doi:10.1080/0360127930190501

Vase, L., Riley III, J. L., & Price, D. D. (2002). A comparison of placebo effects in clinical analgesic trials versus studies of placebo analgesia. *Pain, 99,* 443–452. doi:10.1016/S0304-3959(02)00205-1

Walton, G. M., & Cohen, G. L. (2003). Stereotype lift. *Journal of Experimental Social Psychology, 39,* 456–467. doi:10.1016/S0022-1031(03)00019-2

Weinberger, J., & Eig, A. (1999). Expectancies: The ignored common factor in psychotherapy. In I. Kirsch (Ed.), *How expectancies shape experience* (pp. 357–382). Washington, DC: American Psychological Association. doi:10.1037/10332-015

Wong, J., Regennitter, R., & Barrios, F. (1994). Base rate and simulated symptoms among normals. *Archives of Clinical Neuropsychology, 9,* 411–425. doi:10.1016/0887-6177(94)90004-3

Complexities in Assessing Secondary Influences in Specific Neurologic Conditions

10

Secondary Influences on Cognition in Multiple Sclerosis

JARED M. BRUCE, JOANIE M. THELEN, AND
HOLLY JAMES WESTERVELT

Multiple sclerosis (MS) is an autoimmune, demyelinating disease of the central nervous system (CNS), characterized by a wide spectrum of physical, cognitive, emotional, and behavioral symptoms. More frequently affecting females than males, it is the most common neurological disease among young adults, affecting approximately 1 in 1000 people in northern regions of Europe and North America (Alonso & Hernan, 2008). The neurological symptoms often reflect the location of lesions within the CNS, and patients with MS commonly experience a wide variety of symptoms, including ataxia, fatigue, spasticity, vision and speech disturbances, bladder dysfunction, mood changes, and cognitive impairment. Despite the highly variable and unpredictable nature of MS, the disease course can be classified into four subtypes (Lublin & Reingold, 1996). Approximately 85% of patients present with a relapsing-remitting form of MS (RRMS), typified by isolated "attacks" or relapses followed by recovery. Ten years post-onset, a significant majority of RRMS patients will experience a slowly progressive decline in function, labeled secondary progressive MS (SPMS). About 15% of patients have a progressive course from onset, either without superimposed attacks, termed primary progressive MS (PPMS), or more rarely, with a steady development of disability and superimposed relapses throughout the disease course, called progressive relapsing MS (PRMS).

COGNITIVE IMPAIRMENT IN MS

Cognitive impairment can be found in up to 65% of MS patients (Amato, Zipoli, & Portaccio, 2006). Impaired cognitive function can occur in any disease subtype at any point in the course of the disease. Deficits tend to progress over time and are modestly related to overall levels of physical disability (Lynch, Parmenter, &

Denney, 2005). Progressive forms of MS typically result in more severe cognitive impairment than RRMS (Huijbregts et al., 2004). Cognitive dysfunction can dramatically affect patients' quality of life, employment status, relationships, and adherence to treatment regimens (Benedict et al., 2005; Bruce, Hancock, Arnett, & Lynch, 2010; Rao, Leo, Ellington, et al., 1991). Researchers have suggested that these cognitive deficits may have a larger impact on daily functioning than the more visible physical symptoms frequently experienced by patients with MS (Amato et al., 2006). Although problems with visuospatial abilities, language, and basic attention are sometimes observed, the most common cognitive deficits in MS include problems with speeded information processing, memory, and executive functioning (Winkelmann, Engel, Apel, & Zettl, 2007).

Information Processing

Slowed processing speed has been described as the primary cognitive deficit in patients with MS (DeLuca, Chelune, Tulsky, Lengenfelder, & Chiaravalloti, 2004) and is related to coincident deficits in working memory, long-term memory, and executive functioning (Denney, Lynch, & Parmenter, 2008). Several studies have found that memory impairment is positively correlated with slowed processing speed (DeLuca et al., 2004). It has also been suggested that as working memory demand increases, processing speed and working memory deficiencies become more pronounced (Lengenfelder et al., 2006). Thus, patients with MS tend to be more impaired on complex, speeded tests of information processing. Two tests that are frequently used to assess processing speed and working memory in MS are the Symbol Digit Modalities Test (SDMT; Smith, 1982) and the Paced Auditory Serial Addition Test (PASAT; Gronwall, 1977).

Memory

Between 40% and 65% of patients with MS experience impaired long-term memory (Chiaravalloti & DeLuca, 2008). Early research suggested that poor retrieval from long-term storage was the main cause for these memory deficits (Rao, Leo, & St Aubin-Faubert, 1989). However, recent studies reveal that a decline in initial learning efficiency may contribute to memory difficulties in MS, as patients with MS have been shown to require more stimuli exposure than controls to encode information (DeLuca, Barbieri-Berger, & Johnson, 1994; Demaree, Gaudino, DeLuca, & Ricker, 2000). Measures commonly used to assess memory in MS include list-learning tasks (e.g., California Verbal Learning Test [CVLT], Delis, Kramer, Kaplan, & Ober, 2000; Selective Reminding Test [SRT], Buschke & Fuld, 1974) and nonverbal memory measures in which patients learn, recall, and reproduce visual information, such as a display of geometric shapes (e.g., Brief Visuospatial Memory Test—Revised [BVMT-R], Benedict, 1997) or the location of 10 tiles on a 6 × 6 grid (10/36 Spatial Recall Test [10/36], Barbizet & Cany, 1968).

Executive Functioning

Executive functions describe a set of behaviors that encompass planning, organization, decision making, and abstract reasoning. Between 17% and 25% of individuals with MS demonstrate impaired executive functions across a broad range of abilities, including shifting, response inhibition, problem solving, and verbal fluency (Drew, Tippett, Starkey, & Isler, 2008; Rao, Leo, Bernardin, & Unverzagt, 1991). Fluency tests involve the spontaneous generation of words starting with a specific letter or belonging to a certain semantic category and are sensitive to neurological impairment in MS (Henry & Beatty, 2006). Other methods frequently used to assess executive dysfunction include the Wisconsin Card Sorting Test (WCST; Heaton, Chelune, Talley, Kay, & Curtiss, 1993), the Sorting Test from the Delis-Kaplan Executive Function System (DKEFS; Delis, Kramer, Kaplan, & Holdnack, 2004), and tower tasks. Impaired executive performance is more frequent in patients with progressive forms of MS (Huijbregts et al., 2004) and may interfere with performing jobs and other cognitively demanding daily activities. As such, the social and occupational impact of executive dysfunction may be particularly salient to patients and clinicians.

Batteries Used for Assessment of Cognitive Functioning

Two commonly used neuropsychological batteries have been specifically developed and validated for the assessment of cognitive dysfunction in MS. Using a consensus approach, a panel of MS experts developed the Minimal Assessment of Cognitive Function in MS (MACFIMS), a 90-minute battery made up of seven tests measuring executive function, processing speed, working memory, word fluency, visuospatial ability, visuospatial memory, and verbal memory (Benedict et al., 2002). The MACFIMS is a valid and reliable method of quantifying cognitive dysfunction in MS (Benedict & Zivadinov, 2007). Patients with MS perform significantly worse on the MACFIMS than healthy controls. Moreover, patients with secondary progressive MS perform worse than relapsing-remitting patients in each cognitive domain. The MACFIMS also predicts real-world functioning, with several measures accounting for unique variance in employment status above and beyond depression, demographic variables, and disease course (Benedict, Cookfair, et al., 2006).

Taking approximately 25 minutes to administer, the Rao Brief Repeatable Neuropsychological Battery (BRNB; Rao, 1991) is also commonly used to assess cognitive functioning in MS. In comparing the MACFIMS and the BRNB, Strober and colleagues (2009) determined that the sensitivity of the batteries' verbal/auditory memory tests is comparable, but the Brief Visuospatial Memory Test—Revised used in the MACFIMS may be more sensitive to impairment than the 10/36 Spatial Recall Test used in the BRNB. Overall, the MACFIMS and BRNB were comparable in their discriminative validity and were both endorsed for the neuropsychological assessment of patients with MS.

PRIMARY FACTORS THAT IMPAIR COGNITION IN MS

The neurodegeneration characteristic of MS produces generalized brain atrophy, lesions, and inflammation, all of which directly contribute to impaired cognition. Specifically, increased cortical and subcortical lesion load, decreased white matter volume, and decreased gray matter volume are correlated with cognitive dysfunction in MS (Benedict, Bruce, et al., 2006; Sanfilipo, Benedict, Weinstock-Guttman, & Bakshi, 2006). Lesion location may also be associated with the nature of the cognitive deficit. For example, Arnett and colleagues (1994) found that MS patients with frontal white matter lesions perform worse than patients with minimal frontal lesions on the WCST. Measures of generalized brain atrophy are also strong predictors of cognitive impairment in MS and can distinguish secondary progressive from relapsing-remitting courses of the disease (Benedict, Bruce, et al., 2006). It should be noted, however, that many of the correlations between magnetic resonance imaging (MRI) findings and cognition are surprisingly modest, and some studies have found no significant relationship between global lesion load and cognitive impairment (Heesen et al., 2010; Rovaris et al., 2002). As a result, several researchers have investigated additional, secondary factors that contribute to cognitive dysfunction in MS.

SECONDARY FACTORS ASSOCIATED WITH IMPAIRED COGNITION IN MS

Because the impact of primary factors on cognitive functioning is often salient in neurologic disorders, the potential influences of secondary factors are often overlooked. Fatigue and emotional disturbances, particularly depression, commonly emerge as correlates of cognitive impairment in MS, although personality, various aspects of physical disability, medication side effects, and cognitive reserve have also been explored as significant contributors to neuropsychological performance.

Fatigue

Fatigue has been reported in approximately 90% of patients with MS, and many patients characterize it as the most troubling symptom of their disease (Krupp, Alvarez, LaRocca, & Scheinberg, 1988). Fatigue in MS includes both physical and cognitive components, including overwhelming weariness and desire to rest, along with limited mental endurance and motivation (Krupp, 2003). Fatigue can be brought on by primary MS pathology, as well as by mental or physical activity, sleep disorders, acute infection, medications, deconditioning, and heat or humidity (Kos, Kerckhofs, Nagels, D'Hooghe M, & Ilsbroukx, 2008). The underlying pathophysiology of fatigue, however, is still debated.

Fatigue is an inherently challenging phenomenon to study, as it is subjective. Measurement relies on self-report, with instruments such as the Fatigue Impact Scale (FIS; Fisk et al., 1994; modified version, MFIS: Kos et al., 2005) or the

Fatigue Severity Scale (FSS; Krupp, LaRocca, Muir-Nash, & Steinberg, 1989). The construct validity of these (and similar) measures is difficult to establish given the subjective nature of fatigue, though they have been shown to distinguish patient groups who complain of fatigue from those who do not. Perhaps as a function of the measurement challenges, cognitive fatigue has proven difficult to study empirically, despite the high frequency of the complaint.

Studies examining the cognitive impact of fatigue fall into two broad categories: correlational observations and induction studies. Among the correlational studies, results have been mixed, with several showing no relationship between self-reported fatigue and objective cognitive performance (Bol, Duits, Hupperts, Verlinden, & Verhey, 2010; Morrow, Weinstock-Guttman, Munschauer, Hojnacki, & Benedict, 2009), and others showing the anticipated relationship, particularly between measures of fatigue and processing speed or attentional control (Andreasen, Spliid, Andersen, & Jakobsen, 2010; Bruce, Bruce, & Arnett, 2010; Holtzer & Foley, 2009). The discrepancies in these studies do not appear to be simply a measurement issue, as divergent findings have been noted with the same cognitive tasks and fatigue measure.

In induction studies, participants are typically administered a cognitive battery twice, with or without some intervening, fatigue-inducing task or event. Most of these studies have failed to demonstrate any adverse effect of fatigue on cognition, despite diverse study designs ranging from variations on basic battery-followed-by-battery designs (Jennekens-Schinkel, Sanders, Lanser, & Van der Velde, 1988; Paul, Beatty, Schneider, Blanco, & Hames, 1998) to more naturalistic designs including examination of cognition before and after the participant's work day (Beatty et al., 2003) and during the patient's reported times of highest and lowest fatigue (Parmenter, Denney, & Lynch, 2003). When subjective ratings of fatigue have been examined in these studies, participants report the expected increase in fatigue following the fatiguing task or event, which suggests that the fatigue was successfully induced. However, the expected objective decline in performance has not been observed in these studies, with MS patients and controls showing the same degree of improvement across administrations due to practice. A smaller number of studies have demonstrated an objective negative impact of fatigue (Claros-Salinas et al., 2010; Kujala, Portin, Revonsuo, & Ruutiainen, 1995; Schwid et al., 2003). Schwid et al. (2003) reported a statistically significant decline in performance within trials of the PASAT in patients with MS relative to controls, although the raw score differences were of doubtful clinical significance. In the study by Krupp and Elkins (2000), administrations of a cognitive battery were separated by a lengthy continuous performance task, with the overall assessment period lasting approximately 4 hours. Following the continuous task, the patients with MS showed a decline in performance on several measures, whereas the healthy control participants showed the expected practice effect. The authors suggest that the prolonged period of sustained focus was necessary to induce fatigue. Criticism of this study surrounds the continuous performance task, suggesting that it is artificially long and arduous. However, the other two studies that successfully induced fatigue on vigilance measures used much briefer tasks, ranging from 3 minutes (Claros-Salinas et al., 2010) to 15 minutes (Kujala et al., 1995).

There are several possible explanations for the relatively limited success in demonstrating a relationship between fatigue and cognitive performance in MS. Given the subjective nature of fatigue, measurement concerns have frequently arisen, including questions about the construct validity of the self-report measures, uncertainty of an individual's ability to accurately rate his or her own fatigue, and the potential of "trait" (i.e., more chronic tolerance for mental effort) versus "state" (i.e., in the moment) fatigue varying as a function of the scale, how individuals may interpret the scales, or how individuals may interpret their own experiences. Recent neuroimaging studies suggest an alternative explanation. Studies using functional MRI (fMRI) to measure region of activation during fatiguing and nonfatiguing tasks indicate that relative to controls, fatigued patients tend to marshal more brain activation and recruit additional brain regions to complete the study tasks, although performance on the measures may not differ between the fatigued patients and controls (Tartaglia, Narayanan, & Arnold, 2008). As with findings from structural imaging studies examining the relationship between regional atrophy and fatigue (Andreasen, Jakobsen, et al., 2010; Sepulcre et al., 2009), consistent relationships appear between fatigue and the basal ganglia, frontal lobes, and parietal lobes. These brain regions are thought to be critical in speeded processing and attentional control. Although there are exceptions, overwhelmingly, when significant relationships between fatigue and cognition have been observed or when fatigue has been induced on objective performance, the affected cognitive areas include attention and processing speed. Thus, this literature suggests that the brain of a fatigued patient is essentially working harder on these tasks, regardless of whether the end performance is affected. This provides a possible explanation for mismatch between patient perception (as rated on self-report measures) and cognitive performance (as observed on objective measures), as patients often perceive that they are "failing" at tasks that now require more effort than in the past or than would be anticipated by the patient, based on the nature of the task.

Emotional Disturbances

Patients with MS are more likely to experience psychiatric symptoms than people with other chronic health conditions (Minden & Schiffer, 1990). In a sample of 86 patients with MS, Figved and colleagues (2005) found that 80% presented with at least one neuropsychiatric condition, the most common being depression, sleep disturbance, irritability/emotional lability, and apathy. Other common psychiatric disturbances in MS include excessive anxiety (Korostil & Feinstein, 2007), personality change (Benedict, Priore, Miller, Munschauer, & Jacobs, 2001), bipolar affective disorder (Iacovides & Andreoulakis, 2011), and pseudo-bulbar affect (Feinstein, O'Connor, Gray, & Feinstein, 1999). Affective disturbances may reduce the accuracy of self-reported cognition (Bruce, Bruce, Hancock, & Lynch, 2010), are related to poorer performance of objective neuropsychological measures

(Arnett, Barwick, & Beeney, 2008), and may be predictive of a more rapid cognitive decline (Christodoulou et al., 2009).

DEPRESSION

Major depression in MS has been estimated to have a lifetime prevalence as high as 50% (Sadovnick et al., 1996) and a 1-year prevalence of 15.7%, compared to 9% in patients with other chronic diseases and 4% in people without chronic disease (Patten, Beck, Williams, Barbui, & Metz, 2003). Major depression significantly contributes to reduced quality of life (Benedict et al., 2005), poor treatment adherence (Bruce, Hancock, et al., 2010), greater social dysfunction (Gilchrist & Creed, 1994), and increased suicidal ideation (Turner, Williams, Bowen, Kivlahan, & Haselkorn, 2006), consequently increasing the overall distress and disability of MS patients (Feinstein, 2004).

Although non-neurological depressed patients may experience deficits in executive functioning and effortful cognitive processes (Hartlage, Alloy, Vazquez, & Dykman, 1993), in MS the relationship has been less consistently demonstrated, with both positive (Arnett, Higginson, & Randolph, 2001; Arnett et al., 1999; Filippi et al., 1994) and null findings (DeLuca et al., 1994; Minden & Schiffer, 1990; Rao, Leo, Bernardin, & Unverzagt, 1991). Differences in subject recruitment may partially account for these discrepant findings; for example, one study found that the significant correlation between depression and cognitive impairment may only hold true for paid research volunteers, who tend to be younger and less cognitively impaired than clinically referred patients (Duquin, Parmenter, & Benedict, 2008). In a review of the literature, Arnett and colleagues confirmed a positive relationship between depression and cognitive functioning in studies that are sufficiently powered and involve a representative sample of patients with MS. Furthermore, the relationship between depression and cognitive functioning may be moderated by stress, social support, coping, and conceptions of the self and illness (Arnett, Barwick, & Beeney, 2008). Depressed MS patients are most likely to be impaired during effortful (rather than automatic) information processing, such that performance worsens on tasks that place higher demands on attentional resources (Arnett et al., 1999). Specifically, depressive symptoms are associated with impaired performance on tasks calling for complex speeded attention, working memory, and planning (Arnett, 2005). Depression is also associated with perceived memory problems. A theoretical model proposed by Bruce and colleagues suggests that this relationship is mediated by normative dissociation experiences (Bruce, Bruce, Hancock, & Lynch, 2010). According to this model, depressed MS patients are more likely to experience normative dissociative experiences (such as daydreaming and absent-mindedness); these normative dissociative experiences are, in turn, associated with more self-reported memory problems.

It should be noted that all of these studies are correlational, so it is unknown whether cognitive dysfunction causes depression, whether depression causes cognitive dysfunction, or whether a third variable such as disease progression causes both. Only one study has longitudinally examined changes in cognition following treatment of depression in MS. This study found improvements in accuracy of perceived cognition following treatment but no concomitant improvements in objective neuropsychological performance (Kinsinger, Lattie, & Mohr, 2010). This result weakens the claim that depression directly contributes to objective cognitive deficits in MS. Replications of this finding and additional modeling and longitudinal studies are needed to further determine the causal nature of this relationship. Regardless of disputed levels of causation, in general, when studies are appropriately powered with large sample sizes, a positive association emerges between depression and cognitive impairment, with mostly moderate effect sizes.

Depression may frequently be misdiagnosed in MS because of an overlap between common symptoms of depression and neurological symptoms often encountered in MS. Sleep disturbances, psychomotor retardation, concentration difficulties, sexual dysfunction, and insomnia can be caused by both major depression and primary neurological dysfunction. For example, approximately 25% of individuals with MS experience sleep disturbances. Clark et al. (1992) have suggested that neurological symptoms of MS, such as bladder dysfunction and spasticity, can disrupt sleep cycles, which in turn leads to increased fatigue and depression. Fatigue is another symptom common to both depression and MS proper. Depression and fatigue in MS are significantly correlated, and the successful treatment of depression reduces (but does not eliminate) patient reports of fatigue (Mohr, Hart, & Goldberg, 2003). In short, although neurovegetative symptoms may be a sign of depression in patients with MS, vegetative symptoms of depression might be disproportionately endorsed because of the presence of MS-related symptoms (Beeney & Arnett, 2008). Thus, it is important to use questionnaires that minimize the vegetative component of mood disorders to avoid inflated estimates of depression. Instead, more weight should be given to mood and evaluative depression symptoms, as these symptoms are more specific indicators of depression in MS (Rabinowitz, Fisher, & Arnett, 2011). Several depression scales eliminate or separate items that are associated with both depression and general neurological illness, such as the Beck Depression Inventory—Fast Screen (BDI-Fast Screen; Beck, Steer, & Brown, 2000) and the Chicago Multiscale Depression Inventory (CMDI; Nyenhuis et al., 1998). The proper assessment and diagnosis of depression in MS has significant implications, as depression can be effectively treated in patients with MS with either antidepressant medication or cognitive-behavioral psychotherapy (Mohr & Goodkin, 1999).

ANXIETY

The lifetime prevalence of any anxiety disorder in individuals with MS is reported to be 35.7%, with generalized anxiety disorder (GAD; 18.6%), panic disorder (10%), and obsessive-compulsive disorder (OCD; 8.6%) being the most frequent diagnoses (Korostil & Feinstein, 2007). Lifetime prevalence rates in the general population for these anxiety disorders are notably lower (GAD, 5%; panic disorder, 1–2%; OCD, 2.5%) (American Psychiatric Association, 2000). Patients with MS also report significantly more chronic worry, a defining component of GAD, than do normal controls; this elevated worry is correlated with problem-solving deficits, sleep disturbance, and fatigue (Bruce & Arnett, 2009). It has been suggested that anxiety in MS may be a reactive response to the chronic and unpredictable nature of the disease and psychosocial challenges experienced by the patient (Janssens et al., 2003). The lack of association between anxiety and MRI abnormalities supports the assertion that anxiety is more likely reactive than a neuropsychiatric consequence of the disease (Zorzon et al., 2001). The demonstrated relationship between life stressors and subsequent exacerbations among relapsing-remitting patients, however, hints at a possibly more complex biological interplay (Brown, Tennant, Dunn, & Pollard, 2005). Some studies have described a significant relationship between anxiety and cognitive impairment in MS (Gold, Schulz, Monch, Schulz, & Heesen, 2003; Julian & Arnett, 2009). Consistent with findings among neurologically intact psychiatric patients (Eysenck, Derakshan, Santos, & Calvo, 2007), these studies generally yield small to moderate effects and find that patients with increased anxiety experience concomitant deficits in executive functioning and attentional control. As with depression, a causal relationship, however, cannot be inferred. Moreover, other studies have not found a relationship between anxiety and cognition in MS (DeLuca, Johnson, Beldowicz, & Natelson, 1995).

Despite significant overlap between symptoms of generalized anxiety and MS-related neurological dysfunction (e.g., sleeplessness, muscle tension, fatigue, and difficulty concentrating), how best to assess anxiety disorders in MS has been relatively neglected in the literature. Nevertheless, screening for anxiety disorders in MS is crucial, as they are often overlooked and left untreated (Korostil & Feinstein, 2007). The State-Trait Anxiety Inventory (STAI; Spielberger, Gorsuch, Lushene, Vagg, & Jacobs, 1983) and the Hospital Anxiety and Depression Scale (HADS; Zigmond & Snaith, 1983) are both used to measure anxiety in MS.

PERSONALITY

Patients with MS may experience personality changes during the course of their illness, with emotional lability, disinhibition, apathy, social inappropriateness, and impulsivity most frequently noted (Benedict et al., 2001). Mood and anxiety disorders are also associated with personality disturbances in MS, specifically increased neuroticism and decreased agreeableness, conscientiousness, and extroversion (Bruce & Lynch, 2011). Benedict and colleagues examined the relationship between personality disorder and cognitive impairment, using both self and informant reports on the NEO Personality Inventory (NEO-PI; Costa & McCrae, 1992) and the Hogan Empathy Scale (HES; Hogan, 1969). Worse performance on tests of executive functioning was associated with increased euphoria and decreased altruism and empathy, possibly suggestive of a neurogenic, frontal lobe syndrome (Benedict et al., 2001). This is consistent with findings that personality disturbance in MS is associated with reduced cortical volume (Benedict, Hussein, et al., 2008). However, a larger study that included more relapsing-remitting patients with less cognitive impairment found no significant relationship between personality and cognition in MS (Benedict, Hussein, et al., 2008). Regardless, accurate identification of personality dysfunction in MS may have important implications for treatment. For instance, one study found that counseling can improve social functioning among MS patients with personality or behavior problems (Benedict et al., 2000).

Physical Symptoms

Overall, cognitive impairment is only modestly correlated with physical disability measured by a commonly administered measure of symptom severity, the Expanded Disability Status Scale (EDSS; Kurtzke, 1983) (Achiron & Barak, 2003; Lynch et al., 2005; Rao, Leo, Bernardin, & Unverzagt, 1991). However, neuropsychological tasks requiring rapid written or oral responses may be affected by primary sensory or motor deficits, such as visual or oculomotor problems or reduced motor and vocal control. Consequently, when possible, neuropsychologists employ batteries that minimize the impact of their patients' specific physical disability. For instance, the MACFIMS requires mostly vocal responses, which may be optimal for a patient with physical deficits but may not be ideal for a dysarthric patient.

DYSARTHRIA

Dysarthria, or slowed speech due to oral motor articulation problems, is present in 23% to 51% of patients with MS (Beukelman, Kraft, & Freal, 1985; Hartelius, Runmarker, & Andersen, 2000). In one study, Arnett and colleagues found that oral motor slowing interferes with performance on neuropsychological assessments demanding a rapid oral response, including the PASAT and SDMT (Arnett, Smith, Barwick, Benedict, & Ahlstrom, 2008). In another study, Smith and Arnett (2007) found a small to moderate association between dysarthria and performance on the SDMT and a test of speeded verbal switching. In contrast, Bodling, Denney, and Lynch (2008) concluded that verbal motor deficits had a minimal impact on the performance of a speeded Picture Naming Test in MS. While Bodling and colleagues agreed that moderate to severe dysarthria would negatively impact neuropsychological test performance, they argued that most patients with MS have relatively mild or no dysarthria. More research is needed to better understand how differing levels of dysarthria negatively affect performance on oral neuropsychological tests.

VISUAL IMPAIRMENT

Visual disturbance is a common and disabling symptom of MS, with up to 80% of patients developing vision impairment during the course of their disease (Jacobs & Galetta, 2004). MS patients with poor corrected near visual acuity may show impaired functioning on visually oriented neuropsychological tests, particularly conventional measures of information processing such as the SDMT (Bruce, Bruce, & Arnett, 2007). However, upon exploration, Feaster and Bruce (2011) found that poorer high-contrast, near, and low-contrast visual acuity were significantly related to worse performance on visual, nonvisual, and motor-based neuropsychological tests, suggesting that general disease progression might partially explain the relationships. Overall, relatively little work has been done examining the association between visual abnormalities and cognition in MS. For instance, future studies may wish to examine the potential impact of oculomotor dysfunction, scotoma, and visual-field cuts on cognitive-test performance in MS.

Medication Effects and Polypharmacy

Many of the drugs typically used by patients with MS can cause side effects that influence neuropsychological test performance (Stein & Strickland, 1998), particularly medications aimed at managing MS symptoms (rather than disease-modifying agents), such as spasticity, pain, mood disorders, and bladder dysfunction (Brichetto, Messmer Uccelli, Mancardi, & Solaro, 2003). Many of these drugs affect CNS activity, including benzodiazepines, antiepileptics, antimuscarinics, selective serotonin reuptake inhibitors (SSRIs), corticosteroids, and tricyclic antidepressants and other anticholinergics. In an analysis of medication use among patients with MS, Oken and colleagues (2006) found that 74% used at least one CNS-active medication. With a range from one to five medications, these patients were taking two CNS-active drugs on average, the most frequent being SSRIs, antiepileptics, and baclofen. Compared to MS patients taking no CNS-active medications, patients using at least one CNS-active medication performed significantly worse on cognitive tests of processing speed and sustained attention and reported more fatigue. Though it could not be determined that the drugs directly caused these symptoms, results suggested that more research is needed to improve our understanding of the association between polypharmacy and cognition in MS.

FACTORS THAT IMPROVE OR PROTECT COGNITIVE FUNCTIONING

Medication

The U.S. Food and Drug Administration has not approved any medications for the treatment of cognitive dysfunction in MS. However, several studies have examined the efficacy of medications to improve cognition in individuals with MS, with mixed outcomes (Lyros, Messinis, Papageorgiou, & Papathanasopoulos, 2010). Donepezil has been associated with improved memory, semantic word fluency, and executive function in some smaller studies (Krupp et al., 2004) but not in a large multisite trial (Krupp et al., 2011). Treatment with interferon beta (IFN-β-1a) has been proposed to reduce fatigue and improve information processing and learning and memory in RRMS patients (Melanson et al., 2010), although effect sizes were small and others have found no such cognitive benefit among SPMS patients (Cohen et al., 2002). Other studies have examined the benefit of l-amphetamine on reduced processing speed in MS, finding small to medium effect sizes on PASAT and SDMT performance (Benedict, Munschauer, et al., 2008). Recently, in a larger multisite trial, Morrow and colleagues failed to replicate these findings on their primary outcome measures, though performance on measures of visual and verbal delayed recall was significantly improved (Morrow, Kaushik, et al., 2009). Reanalyzing data from the same trial, Sumowski et al. (2011) found that l-amphetamine yielded large memory gains, but only in patients with objective memory impairments at baseline. While some mixed success has been observed, more research needs to be done to further evaluate the efficacy of potential pharmacological cognitive interventions in MS.

Cognitive Reserve

The theory of cognitive reserve proposes that innate premorbid intelligence and lifetime intellectual enrichment (including educational or professional accomplishment) may provide "reserve," allowing some people to better cope with neurological pathology (Scarmeas & Stern, 2003). Cognitive reserve is typically estimated with proxies such as vocabulary knowledge and years of education and may predict the ability to endure a higher burden of neuropathology before developing cognitive impairment or dementia (Stern, 2002). There is considerable evidence supporting this concept in the Alzheimer's disease (AD) literature (Stern, 2006). While the course of cognitive impairment in MS differs significantly from that in AD, the cognitive-reserve hypothesis may be equally relevant in MS. Benedict et al. (2010) concluded that more cognitive reserve, as operationalized by years of education or higher premorbid intelligence, protects against the development of cognitive impairment in MS. Additionally, premorbid cognitive leisure activity (e.g., doing puzzles, playing card games) is associated with current cognitive status in patients with MS, even after controlling for vocabulary and education levels (Sumowski, Wylie, Gonnella, Chiaravalloti, & Deluca, 2010). Furthermore, lifetime intellectual enrichment is suggested to moderate the adverse impact of brain atrophy on memory and learning in individuals with MS (Sumowski, Chiaravalloti, Wylie, & Deluca, 2009). Hypothetically, one's "reserve" can be modified by providing cognitively enriching experiences, though there are no current prospective intervention studies in MS that have examined if cognitive decline can be prevented or minimized with this type of cognitive stimulation.

Cognitive Training

Cognitive training is increasingly becoming a treatment option among patients with cognitive dysfunction. Evidence for the efficacy of rehabilitative cognitive training in MS is inconsistent, as research in this area is nascent. Several studies have found benefits associated with cognitive training (Brenk, Laun, & Haase, 2008; Hildebrandt et al., 2007), while others have found no significant impact (Lincoln et al., 2002; Solari et al., 2004). In a review of the current literature, O'Brien and colleagues highlighted the methodological differences that may account for the discrepancy in findings. Some studies focused on attention as the target cognitive domain, while others aimed to improve memory, and several training programs were nonspecific or targeted multiple skills. These studies also varied widely in terms of the sample size, MS subtypes included, frequency and duration of training, and intervention technique. Many of these studies did not employ the appropriate level of evidence classification; problematic issues included lack of appropriate control groups, lack of appropriate blinding, and use

of identical training and outcome measures. Furthermore, insufficient information regarding the methodology (including training and assessment paradigms)
prevents replication by future researchers (O'Brien, Chiaravalloti, Goverover, &
Deluca, 2008). More methodologically rigorous studies will be required to determine the value of cognitive rehabilitation interventions.

CONCLUSIONS

Cognitive impairment is frequently experienced in patients with MS and has serious
implications for daily functioning, occupational status, interpersonal relationships,
treatment adherence, and overall quality of life (Benedict et al., 2005; Bruce, Hancock,
et al., 2010; Morrow et al., 2010; Patti, 2010; Rao, Leo, Ellington, et al., 1991). While
it is recognized that neurological damage caused by MS can impact cognition, many
factors secondary to MS-related pathology can also account for significant variance
in cognitive functioning. Conditions such as fatigue, depression, peripheral motor
deficits, cognitive reserve, and polypharmacy may be particularly salient when evaluating neuropsychological performance in patients with MS. Consideration of these
secondary factors can provide a more complete and nuanced understanding of the
contributors to cognitive impairment. Tables 10.1 and 10.2 summarizes the evidence
for these various secondary factors in relation to cognitive functioning in MS.

Table 10.1 SECONDARY FACTORS ASSOCIATED WITH COGNITION IN MS

Secondary Factors that Influence Cognition in MS	Level of Evidence[1]	Range of Effect Sizes (Pearson's *r*)
Fatigue		
Self-reported fatigue	***	.33–.58
Induced fatigue	*	.10–.33
Emotional factors		
Depression	***	.20–.62
Anxiety	***	.05–.37
Personality	**	.28–.63
Physical Factors		
Visual impairment	*	.10–.21
Dysarthria	*	.20–.40
Medication effects	*	.19–.36
Protective factors		
Cognitive training	**	.04–.52
Nootropic medications	**	.11 –.44
Cognitive reserve	**	.21–.39

[1] Studies showing significant associations with cognitive functioning.
* 1–5 studies.
** 6–10 studies.
*** ≥11 studies.

Table 10.2. Suggested Measures for the Assessment of Secondary Factors in MS.

Secondary Factors	Measures
Fatigue *****	Fatigue Severity Scale
	Modified Fatigue Impact Scale
Depression *****	Beck Depression Inventory – FastScreen
	Chicago Multi-Scale Depression Inventory
	Hamilton Rating Scale for Depression
	Structured Psychiatric Clinical Interview
Anxiety****	Hospital Anxiety and Depression Scale
	State Trait Anxiety Inventory
	Structured Psychiatric Clinical Interview
Personality/Behavior***	Frontal Systems Behavior Scale
	NEO Personality Inventory
	Structured Psychiatric Clinical Interview
Visual Impairment**	Low Contrast Visual Acuity Chart
	High Contrast Visual Acuity Chart
	Near Visual Acuity Chart
	Visual Field Exam
	(Full Ophthalmologic Exam)
Dysarthria*	Dysarthria Rating Scale
	(Speech pathology evaluation)

Note: More stars indicate increased importance of routine assessment, as determined by prevalence, impact on overall quality of life, and impact on neuropsychological evaluation.

CASE STUDY

Patricia (pseudonym) was a 48-year-old, married, right-handed, Caucasian high school graduate with a history of relapsing-remitting multiple sclerosis (MS) who was referred by her neurologist because of concerns of cognitive change. She stated that she had experienced a gradual loss of short-term memory, cognitive slowing, decreased concentration, and word-finding difficulties. She also noted that she lost her train of thought in conversation. These symptoms had began several months prior to her evaluation and had progressively worsened; she was frustrated and overwhelmed by her cognitive difficulties and worried about her cognitive future. An administrative assistant in a physician's office, Pat stated that it took her much longer to do her work. She also reported fatigue that worsened in the afternoon.

Medical and Psychiatric History: *Pat was diagnosed with clinically definite relapsing-remitting MS at age 42. She had been treated for 5 years with Avonex but discontinued the disease-modifying medication because of repeated rejection-site reactions. Her most recent MRI of the brain showed moderate periventricular and subcortical white matter T2 hyperintensities; there were no enhancing lesions. Her most recent neurological examination revealed mild bilateral dysmetria and reduction in vibration sense, although her elemental neurological examination was otherwise normal. Pat noted difficulties falling asleep and that she sometimes awakened during the night because of pain from a remote back injury. Thus she had been taking Xanax nightly as a sleep aid. Pat also had a diagnosis of depression that was being treated by her primary care physician. She reported no history of substance abuse. At the time of the evaluation, she was taking Celexa, Wellbutrin, Trazadone, Xanax, hydrochlorothiazide, and oxycodone.*

Behavioral Observations and Test Results: *Pat was pleasant and cooperative during the evaluation. She was tearful at times during the interview and during tests that she found challenging. She occasionally paused in the middle of a sentence and asked the examiner to restate a question because she had forgotten it. When asked about her current mood, Pat replied that she felt anxious and depressed. She declined offers to take breaks. Her scores on a test of symptom credibility were well within normal limits.*

Estimated Premorbid Intelligence: *Based on testing of reading ability and several demographic variables, Pat's premorbid intellectual abilities were estimated to be at least within the average range.*

Attentional Functions: *Basic attention, working memory, psychomotor speed, and processing speed were average. Sustained attention was impaired, with Pat's performance declining over the course of the task.*

Executive Functions: *Planning and organizational skills were high average. Abstract reasoning and letter fluency were average. Multitasking and cognitive flexibility on a problem-solving task were mildly impaired. Category fluency was severely impaired.*

Motor Functions: *Speed of finger tapping and fine motor coordination were mildly impaired bilaterally.*

Language and Related Functions: *Language skills were intact, including reading, writing, repetition, comprehension, naming, mathematical computations, and praxis.*

Visuospatial Functions: *Constructional ability ranged from average to superior.*

Learning and Memory: *Story learning was below expectation, although recall following a 10-minute delay was average. List learning was mildly impaired, as were recall trials following brief and longer delay. Recognition discriminability was average, suggesting that Pat had encoded more information than she could freely recall. Learning and recall of visual information were average.*

Assessment of Secondary Factors: *A self-report measure of depression revealed severe depression. A measure of self-reported state and trait anxiety revealed extremely high elevations for both. A measure of fatigue symptoms revealed clinically significant fatigue.*

Impressions and Recommendations: *Consistent with what can be seen in MS, Pat's performance on this exam revealed deficits in sustained attention, aspects of executive functioning (e.g., multitasking and cognitive flexibility), fine-motor speed and coordination, and verbal learning and memory. Other areas of cognition were intact, including several performances within the high-average to superior range. Although they likely cannot solely account for her deficits, factors such as fatigue (FIS), severe depressive symptoms (BDI-FS), high levels of both situational and chronic anxiety (STAI), and potential adverse medication effects likely contributed to her cognitive difficulties. Some improvement in her cognition may occur following a reduction in these symptoms and changes in her medication regimen. The following evidence-based recommendations were suggested:*

1. Pat may benefit from more aggressive treatment of her depression and anxiety. At the time of the exam, she was provided with contact information for a psychologist and psychiatrist. Successful treatment of her depression and anxiety may partially ameliorate her perceived and objective cognitive deficits.

2. Given the number of medications she is currently taking, a medication review may be warranted. Polypharmacy has been associated with cognitive complaints, fatigue, and cognitive difficulties among various patient populations, including patients with MS.

3. Given her current cognitive complaints and cognitive difficulties, physician-supervised discontinuation of Xanax is also recommended. Regular use of benzodiazepines is associated with cognitive deficits that can persist at least 6 months beyond discontinuation in chronic users. Prior to discontinuation, Pat may benefit from behavioral health counseling to improve her sleep hygiene.

4. Pat was encouraged to engage in regular moderate physical exercise, within her physician's guidelines. Ideally, this would include activities with both aerobic and strength-building components at least 3 times per week for more than a half an hour at a time. Mindfulness-based exercises such as yoga have been shown to be particularly helpful. Regular exercise may help to improve and maintain brain functioning, reduce stress and fatigue, and serve as a buffer against negative mood states (Dalgas, Stenager, & Ingemann-Hansen, 2008).

5. We encouraged Pat to talk with her physician about reinstating a disease-modifying therapy. Disease-modifying therapies can slow the progression of MS and reduce future exacerbations and brain lesions. Along these lines, Pat may benefit from counseling that includes motivational interviewing. Research suggests that a combination of motivational interviewing and patient education can help patients with MS overcome barriers to treatment and improve medication adherence (Berger, Liang, & Hudmon, 2005). Similarly, successful treatment of her depression and anxiety may improve her treatment adherence (Mohr et al., 1997).

6. In general, Pat may benefit from maximizing use of organizational strategies. For example, a checklist may be useful to keep track of daily tasks and work-related goals, and it may be helpful to request that her boss provide her with written instructions and task lists. An electronic organizer or smart phone may be especially useful, as she could receive

auditory alerts for time-sensitive tasks. Given Pat's difficulties with sustained attention, she may also benefit from frequent breaks when performing monotonous tasks, either with rest or by switching tasks. Similarly, she may benefit from rechecking any important work after she has had a break from that task.

References

Achiron, A., & Barak, Y. (2003). Cognitive impairment in probable multiple sclerosis. *Journal of Neurology, Neurosurgery, and Psychiatry, 74*(4), 443–446.

Alonso, A., & Hernan, M. A. (2008). Temporal trends in the incidence of multiple sclerosis: A systematic review. *Neurology, 71*(2), 129–135. doi:10.1212/01.wnl.0000316802.35974.34

Amato, M. P., Zipoli, V., & Portaccio, E. (2006). Multiple sclerosis-related cognitive changes: A review of cross-sectional and longitudinal studies. *Journal of the Neurological Sciences, 245*(1–2), 41–46. doi:10.1016/j.jns.2005.08.019

American Psychiatric Association. (2000). *Diagnostic and statistical manual of mental disorders* (4th ed., text rev.). Washington, DC: Author.

Andreasen, A. K., Jakobsen, J., Soerensen, L., Andersen, H., Petersen, T., Bjarkam, C. R., & Ahdidan, J. (2010). Regional brain atrophy in primary fatigued patients with multiple sclerosis. *NeuroImage, 50*(2), 608–615. doi:10.1016/j.neuroimage.2009.12.118

Andreasen, A. K., Spliid, P. E., Andersen, H., & Jakobsen, J. (2010). Fatigue and processing speed are related in multiple sclerosis. *European Journal of Neurology, 17*(2), 212–218. doi:10.1111/j.1468-1331.2009.02776.x

Arnett, P. A. (2005). Longitudinal consistency of the relationship between depression symptoms and cognitive functioning in multiple sclerosis. *CNS Spectrums, 10*(5), 372–382.

Arnett, P. A., Barwick, F. H., & Beeney, J. E. (2008). Depression in multiple sclerosis: Review and theoretical proposal. *Journal of the International Neuropsychological Society, 14*(5), 691–724. doi:10.1017/S1355617708081174

Arnett, P. A., Higginson, C. I., & Randolph, J. J. (2001). Depression in multiple sclerosis: relationship to planning ability. *Journal of the International Neuropsychological Society, 7*(6), 665–674.

Arnett, P. A., Higginson, C. I., Voss, W. D., Bender, W. I., Wurst, J. M., & Tippin, J. M. (1999). Depression in multiple sclerosis: Relationship to working memory capacity. *Neuropsychology, 13*(4), 546–556.

Arnett, P. A., Rao, S. M., Bernardin, L., Grafman, J., Yetkin, F. Z., & Lobeck, L. (1994). Relationship between frontal lobe lesions and Wisconsin Card Sorting Test performance in patients with multiple sclerosis. *Neurology, 44*(3 Pt 1), 420–425.

Arnett, P. A., Smith, M. M., Barwick, F. H., Benedict, R. H., & Ahlstrom, B. P. (2008). Oralmotor slowing in multiple sclerosis: relationship to neuropsychological tasks requiring an oral response. *Journal of the International Neuropsychological Society, 14*(3), 454–462. doi:10.1017/S1355617708080508

Barbizet, J., & Cany, E. (1968). Clinical and psychometrical study of a patient with memory disturbances. *International Journal of Neurology, 7*(1), 44–54.

Beatty, W. W., Goretti, B., Siracusa, G., Zipoli, V., Portaccio, E., & Amato, M. P. (2003). Changes in neuropsychological test performance over the workday in multiple sclerosis. *The Clinical Neuropsychologist, 17*(4), 551–560. doi:10.1076/clin.17.4.551.27942

Beck, A. T., Steer, R. A., & Brown, G. K. (2000). BDI—Fast screen for medical patients manual. San Antonio, TX: The Psychological Corporation.

Beeney, J. E., & Arnett, P. A. (2008). Endorsement of self-report neurovegetative items of depression is associated with multiple sclerosis disease symptoms. *Journal of the International Neuropsychological Society, 14*(6), 1057–1062. doi:10.1017/S1355617708081265

Benedict, R. H., Bruce, J. M., Dwyer, M. G., Abdelrahman, N., Hussein, S., Weinstock-Guttman, B.,... Zivadinov, R. (2006). Neocortical atrophy, third ventricular width, and cognitive dysfunction in multiple sclerosis. *Archives of Neurology, 63*(9), 1301–1306. doi:10.1001/archneur.63.9.1301

Benedict, R. H., Cookfair, D., Gavett, R., Gunther, M., Munschauer, F., Garg, N., & Weinstock-Guttman, B. (2006). Validity of the minimal assessment of cognitive function in multiple sclerosis (MACFIMS). *Journal of the International Neuropsychological Society, 12*(4), 549–558.

Benedict, R. H., Fischer, J. S., Archibald, C. J., Arnett, P. A., Beatty, W. W., Bobholz, J.,...Munschauer, F. (2002). Minimal neuropsychological assessment of MS patients: A consensus approach. *The Clinical Neuropsychologist, 16*(3), 381–397. doi:10.1076/clin.16.3.381.13859

Benedict, R. H., Hussein, S., Englert, J., Dwyer, M. G., Abdelrahman, N., Cox, J. L.,... Zivadinov, R. (2008). Cortical atrophy and personality in multiple sclerosis. *Neuropsychology, 22*(4), 432–441. doi:10.1037/0894-4105.22.4.432

Benedict, R. H., Morrow, S. A., Weinstock Guttman, B., Cookfair, D., & Schretlen, D. J. (2010). Cognitive reserve moderates decline in information processing speed in multiple sclerosis patients. *Journal of the International Neuropsychological Society, 16*(5), 829–835. doi:10.1017/S1355617710000688

Benedict, R. H., Munschauer, F., Zarevics, P., Erlanger, D., Rowe, V., Feaster, T., & Carpenter, R. L. (2008). Effects of *l*-amphetamine sulfate on cognitive function in multiple sclerosis patients. *Journal of Neurology, 255*(6), 848–852. doi:10.1007/s00415-008-0760-7

Benedict, R. H., Priore, R. L., Miller, C., Munschauer, F., & Jacobs, L. (2001). Personality disorder in multiple sclerosis correlates with cognitive impairment. *Journal of Neuropsychiatry and Clinical Neurosciences, 13*(1), 70–76.

Benedict, R. H., Shapiro, A., Priore, R., Miller, C., Munschauer, F., & Jacobs, L. (2000). Neuropsychological counseling improves social behavior in cognitively-impaired multiple sclerosis patients. *Multiple Sclerosis, 6*(6), 391–396.

Benedict, R. H., Wahlig, E., Bakshi, R., Fishman, I., Munschauer, F., Zivadinov, R., & Weinstock-Guttman, B. (2005). Predicting quality of life in multiple sclerosis: Accounting for physical disability, fatigue, cognition, mood disorder, personality, and behavior change. *Journal of the Neurological Sciences, 231*(1–2), 29–34. doi:10.1016/j.jns.2004.12.009

Benedict, R. H., & Zivadinov, R. (2007). Reliability and validity of neuropsychological screening and assessment strategies in MS. *Journal of Neurology, 254*(Suppl 2), II22–II25. doi:10.1007/s00415-007-2007-4

Benedict, R. H. B. (1997). Brief visuospatial memory test—revised: Professional manual. Odessa, FL: Psychological Assessment Resources.

Berger, B. A., Liang, H., & Hudmon, K. S. (2005). Evaluation of software-based telephone counseling to enhance medication persistency among patients with multiple sclerosis. *Journal of the American Pharmacists Association, 45*(4), 466–472.

Beukelman, D. R., Kraft, G. H., & Freal, J. (1985). Expressive communication disorders in persons with multiple sclerosis: A survey. *Archives of Physical Medicine and Rehabilitation, 66*(10), 675–677.

Bodling, A. M., Denney, D. R., & Lynch, S. G. (2008). Rapid serial processing in patients with multiple sclerosis: The role of peripheral deficits. *Journal
of the International Neuropsychological Society, 14*(4), 646–650. doi:10.1017/
S1355617708080739

Bol, Y., Duits, A. A., Hupperts, R. M., Verlinden, I., & Verhey, F. R. (2010). The impact
of fatigue on cognitive functioning in patients with multiple sclerosis. *Clinical
Rehabilitation, 24*(9), 854–862. doi:10.1177/0269215510367540

Brenk, A., Laun, K., & Haase, C. G. (2008). Short-term cognitive training improves
mental efficiency and mood in patients with multiple sclerosis. *European Neurology,
60*(6), 304–309. doi:10.1159/000157885

Brichetto, G., Messmer Uccelli, M., Mancardi, G. L., & Solaro, C. (2003). Symptomatic
medication use in multiple sclerosis. *Multiple Sclerosis, 9*(5), 458–460.

Brown, R. F., Tennant, C. C., Dunn, S. M., & Pollard, J. D. (2005). A review of stress-
relapse interactions in multiple sclerosis: Important features and stress-mediating
and -moderating variables. *Multiple Sclerosis, 11*(4), 477–484.

Bruce, J. M., & Arnett, P. (2009). Clinical correlates of generalized worry in multiple
sclerosis. *Journal of Clinical and Experimental Neuropsychology, 31*(6), 698–705.
doi:10.1080/13803390802484789

Bruce, J. M., Bruce, A. S., & Arnett, P. A. (2007). Mild visual acuity disturbances are
associated with performance on tests of complex visual attention in MS. *Journal
of the International Neuropsychological Society, 13*(3), 544–548. doi:10.1017/
S1355617707070658

Bruce, J. M., Bruce, A. S., & Arnett, P. A. (2010). Response variability is associated with
self-reported cognitive fatigue in multiple sclerosis. *Neuropsychology, 24*(1), 77–83.
doi:10.1037/a0015046

Bruce, J. M., Bruce, A. S., Hancock, L., & Lynch, S. (2010). Self-reported memory problems in multiple sclerosis: Influence of psychiatric status and normative dissociative
experiences. *Archives of Clinical Neuropsychology, 25*(1), 39–48. doi:10.1093/arclin/
acp092

Bruce, J. M., Hancock, L. M., Arnett, P., & Lynch, S. (2010). Treatment adherence in multiple sclerosis: Association with emotional status, personality, and cognition. *Journal
of Behavioral Medicine, 33*(3), 219–227. doi:10.1007/s10865-010-9247-y

Bruce, J. M., & Lynch, S. G. (2011). Personality traits in multiple sclerosis: Association
with mood and anxiety disorders. *Journal of Psychosomatic Research, 70*(5), 479–485.
doi:10.1016/j.jpsychores.2010.12.010

Buschke, H., & Fuld, P. A. (1974). Evaluating storage, retention, and retrieval in disor-
dered memory and learning. *Neurology, 24*(11), 1019–1025.

Chiaravalloti, N. D., & DeLuca, J. (2008). Cognitive impairment in multiple sclerosis.
Lancet Neurology, 7(12), 1139–1151. doi:10.1016/S1474-4422(08)70259-X

Christodoulou, C., Melville, P., Scherl, W. F., Macallister, W. S., Abensur, R. L.,
Troxell, R. M., & Krupp, L. B. (2009). Negative affect predicts subsequent cognitive
change in multiple sclerosis. *Journal of the International Neuropsychological Society,
15*(1), 53–61. doi:10.1017/S135561770809005X

Clark, C. M., Fleming, J. A., Li, D., Oger, J., Klonoff, H., & Paty, D. (1992). Sleep disturbance, depression, and lesion site in patients with multiple sclerosis. *Archives of
Neurology, 49*(6), 641–643.

Claros-Salinas, D., Bratzke, D., Greitemann, G., Nickisch, N., Ochs, L., & Schroter, H.
(2010). Fatigue-related diurnal variations of cognitive performance in multiple
sclerosis and stroke patients. *Journal of the Neurological Sciences, 295*(1–2), 75–81.
doi:10.1016/j.jns.2010.04.018

Cohen, J. A., Cutter, G. R., Fischer, J. S., Goodman, A. D., Heidenreich, F. R., Kooijmans, M. F.,...Whitaker, J. N. (2002). Benefit of interferon beta-1a on MSFC progression in secondary progressive MS. *Neurology, 59*(5), 679–687.

Costa, P. T., Jr., & McCrae, R. R. (1992). *Revised NEO Personality Inventory (NEO PI-R) and NEO Five-Factor Inventory (NEO-FFI) professional manual*. Odessa, FL: Psychological Assessment Resources.

Dalgas, U., Stenager, E., & Ingemann-Hansen, T. (2008). Multiple sclerosis and physical exercise: recommendations for the application of resistance-, endurance- and combined training. *Multiple Sclerosis, 14*(1), 35–53. doi:10.1177/1352458507079445

Delis, D. C., Kramer, J. H., Kaplan, E., & Holdnack, J. (2004). Reliability and validity of the Delis-Kaplan Executive Function System: An update. *Journal of the International Neuropsychological Society, 10*(2), 301–303. doi:10.1017/S1355617704102191

Delis, D. C., Kramer, J. H., Kaplan, E., & Ober, B. A. (2000). *California Verbal Learning Test: Second edition*. San Antonio, TX: Psychological Corporation.

DeLuca, J., Barbieri-Berger, S., & Johnson, S. K. (1994). The nature of memory impairments in multiple sclerosis: acquisition versus retrieval. *Journal of Clinical and Experimental Neuropsychology, 16*(2), 183–189. doi:10.1080/01688639408402629

DeLuca, J., Chelune, G. J., Tulsky, D. S., Lengenfelder, J., & Chiaravalloti, N. D. (2004). Is speed of processing or working memory the primary information processing deficit in multiple sclerosis? *Journal of Clinical and Experimental Neuropsychology, 26*(4), 550–562. doi:10.1080/13803390490496641

DeLuca, J., Johnson, S. K., Beldowicz, D., & Natelson, B. H. (1995). Neuropsychological impairments in chronic fatigue syndrome, multiple sclerosis, and depression. *Journal of Neurology, Neurosurgery, and Psychiatry, 58*(1), 38–43.

Demaree, H. A., Gaudino, E. A., DeLuca, J., & Ricker, J. H. (2000). Learning impairment is associated with recall ability in multiple sclerosis. *Journal of Clinical and Experimental Neuropsychology, 22*(6), 865–873. doi:10.1076/jcen.22.6.865.961

Denney, D. R., Lynch, S. G., & Parmenter, B. A. (2008). A 3-year longitudinal study of cognitive impairment in patients with primary progressive multiple sclerosis: Speed matters. *Journal of the Neurological Sciences, 267*(1–2), 129–136. doi:10.1016/j.jns.2007.10.007

Drew, M., Tippett, L. J., Starkey, N. J., & Isler, R. B. (2008). Executive dysfunction and cognitive impairment in a large community-based sample with multiple sclerosis from New Zealand: A descriptive study. *Archives of Clinical Neuropsychology, 23*(1), 1–19. doi:10.1016/j.acn.2007.09.005

Duquin, J. A., Parmenter, B. A., & Benedict, R. H. (2008). Influence of recruitment and participation bias in neuropsychologic research among MS patients. *Journal of the International Neuropsychological Society, 14*(3), 494–498.

Eysenck, M. W., Derakshan, N., Santos, R., & Calvo, M. G. (2007). Anxiety and cognitive performance: Attentional control theory. *Emotion, 7*(2), 336–353. doi:10.1037/1528-3542.7.2.336

Feaster, H. T., & Bruce, J. M. (2011). Visual acuity is associated with performance on visual and non-visual neuropsychological tests in multiple sclerosis. *The Clinical Neuropsychologist, 25*(4), 640–651. doi:10.1080/13854046.2011.565075

Feinstein, A. (2004). The neuropsychiatry of multiple sclerosis. *Canadian Journal of Psychiatry, 49*(3), 157–163.

Feinstein, A., O'Connor, P., Gray, T., & Feinstein, K. (1999). Pathological laughing and crying in multiple sclerosis: A preliminary report suggesting a role for the prefrontal cortex. *Multiple Sclerosis, 5*(2), 69–73.

Figved, N., Klevan, G., Myhr, K. M., Glad, S., Nyland, H., Larsen, J. P., . . . Aarsland, D. (2005). Neuropsychiatric symptoms in patients with multiple sclerosis. *Acta Psychiatrica Scandinavica, 112*(6), 463–468. doi:10.1111/j.1600-0447.2005.00624.x

Filippi, M., Alberoni, M., Martinelli, V., Sirabian, G., Bressi, S., Canal, N., & Comi, G. (1994). Influence of clinical variables on neuropsychological performance in multiple sclerosis. *European Neurology, 34*(6), 324–328.

Fisk, J. D., Ritvo, P. G., Ross, L., Haase, D. A., Marrie, T. J., & Schlech, W. F. (1994). Measuring the functional impact of fatigue: Initial validation of the fatigue impact scale. *Clinical Infectious Diseases, 18*(Suppl 1), S79–83.

Gilchrist, A. C., & Creed, F. H. (1994). Depression, cognitive impairment, and social stress in multiple sclerosis. *Journal of Psychosomatic Research, 38*(3), 193–201.

Gold, S. M., Schulz, H., Monch, A., Schulz, K. H., & Heesen, C. (2003). Cognitive impairment in multiple sclerosis does not affect reliability and validity of self-report health measures. *Multiple Sclerosis, 9*(4), 404–410.

Gronwall, D. M. (1977). Paced auditory serial-addition task: A measure of recovery from concussion. *Perceptual and Motor Skills, 44*(2), 367–373.

Hartelius, L., Runmarker, B., & Andersen, O. (2000). Prevalence and characteristics of dysarthria in a multiple-sclerosis incidence cohort: Relation to neurological data. *Folia Phoniatrica et Logopaedica, 52*(4), 160–177.

Hartlage, S., Alloy, L. B., Vazquez, C., & Dykman, B. (1993). Automatic and effortful processing in depression. *Psychological Bulletin, 113*(2), 247–278.

Heaton, R. K., Chelune, G. J., Talley, J. L., Kay, G. G., Curtiss, G. (1993). *Wisconsin Card Sorting Test manual: Revised and expanded*. Odessa, FL: Psychological Assessment Resources.

Heesen, C., Schulz, K. H., Fiehler, J., Von der Mark, U., Otte, C., Jung, R., . . . Gold, S. M. (2010). Correlates of cognitive dysfunction in multiple sclerosis. *Brain, Behavior, and Immunity, 24*(7), 1148–1155. doi:10.1016/j.bbi.2010.05.006

Henry, J. D., & Beatty, W. W. (2006). Verbal fluency deficits in multiple sclerosis. *Neuropsychologia, 44*(7), 1166–1174. doi:10.1016/j.neuropsychologia.2005.10.006

Hildebrandt, H., Lanz, M., Hahn, H. K., Hoffmann, E., Schwarze, B., Schwendemann, G., & Kraus, J. A. (2007). Cognitive training in MS: Effects and relation to brain atrophy. *Restorative Neurology and Neuroscience, 25*(1), 33–43.

Hogan, R. (1969). Development of an empathy scale. *Journal of Consulting and Clinical Psychology, 33*(3), 307–316.

Holtzer, R., & Foley, F. (2009). The relationship between subjective reports of fatigue and executive control in multiple sclerosis. *Journal of the Neurological Sciences, 281*(1–2), 46–50. doi:10.1016/j.jns.2009.02.360

Huijbregts, S. C., Kalkers, N. F., de Sonneville, L. M., de Groot, V., Reuling, I. E., & Polman, C. H. (2004). Differences in cognitive impairment of relapsing remitting, secondary, and primary progressive MS. *Neurology, 63*(2), 335–339.

Iacovides, A., & Andreoulakis, E. (2011). Bipolar disorder and resembling special psychopathological manifestations in multiple sclerosis: A review. *Current Opinion in Psychiatry, 24*(4), 336–340. doi:10.1097/YCO.0b013e328347341d

Jacobs, D. A., & Galetta, S. L. (2004). Multiple sclerosis and the visual system. *Ophthalmology Clinics of North America, 17*(3), 265–273, v. doi:10.1016/j.ohc.2004.05.011

Janssens, A. C., van Doorn, P. A., de Boer, J. B., van der Meche, F. G., Passchier, J., & Hintzen, R. Q. (2003). Impact of recently diagnosed multiple sclerosis on quality of life, anxiety, depression and distress of patients and partners. *Acta Neurologica Scandinavica, 108*(6), 389–395.

Jennekens-Schinkel, A., Sanders, E. A., Lanser, J. B., & Van der Velde, E. A. (1988). Reaction time in ambulant multiple sclerosis patients. Part I. Influence of prolonged cognitive effort. *Journal of the Neurological Sciences, 85*(2), 173–186.

Julian, L. J., & Arnett, P. A. (2009). Relationships among anxiety, depression, and executive functioning in multiple sclerosis. *The Clinical Neuropsychologist, 23*(5), 794–804. doi:10.1080/13854040802665808

Kinsinger, S. W., Lattie, E., & Mohr, D. C. (2010). Relationship between depression, fatigue, subjective cognitive impairment, and objective neuropsychological functioning in patients with multiple sclerosis. *Neuropsychology, 24*(5), 573–580. doi:10.1037/a0019222

Korostil, M., & Feinstein, A. (2007). Anxiety disorders and their clinical correlates in multiple sclerosis patients. *Multiple Sclerosis, 13*(1), 67–72.

Kos, D., Kerckhofs, E., Carrea, I., Verza, R., Ramos, M., & Jansa, J. (2005). Evaluation of the Modified Fatigue Impact Scale in four different European countries. *Multiple Sclerosis, 11*(1), 76–80.

Kos, D., Kerckhofs, E., Nagels, G., D'Hooghe M, B., & Ilsbroukx, S. (2008). Origin of fatigue in multiple sclerosis: Review of the literature. *Neurorehabilitation and Neural Repair, 22*(1), 91–100. doi:10.1177/1545968306298934

Krupp, L. B. (2003). Fatigue in multiple sclerosis: definition, pathophysiology and treatment. *CNS Drugs, 17*(4), 225–234.

Krupp, L. B., Alvarez, L. A., LaRocca, N. G., & Scheinberg, L. C. (1988). Fatigue in multiple sclerosis. *Archives of Neurology, 45*(4), 435–437.

Krupp, L. B., Christodoulou, C., Melville, P., Scherl, W. F., MacAllister, W. S., & Elkins, L. E. (2004). Donepezil improved memory in multiple sclerosis in a randomized clinical trial. *Neurology, 63*(9), 1579–1585.

Krupp, L. B., Christodoulou, C., Melville, P., Scherl, W. F., Pai, L. Y., Muenz, L. R.,... Wishart, H. (2011). Multicenter randomized clinical trial of donepezil for memory impairment in multiple sclerosis. *Neurology, 76*(17), 1500–1507. doi:10.1212/WNL.0b013e318218107a

Krupp, L. B., LaRocca, N. G., Muir-Nash, J., & Steinberg, A. D. (1989). The Fatigue Severity Scale. Application to patients with multiple sclerosis and systemic lupus erythematosus. *Archives of Neurology, 46*(10), 1121–1123.

Kujala, P., Portin, R., Revonsuo, A., & Ruutiainen, J. (1995). Attention related performance in two cognitively different subgroups of patients with multiple sclerosis. *Journal of Neurology, Neurosurgery, and Psychiatry, 59*(1), 77–82.

Kurtzke, J. F. (1983). Rating neurologic impairment in multiple sclerosis: An expanded disability status scale (EDSS). *Neurology, 33*(11), 1444–1452.

Lengenfelder, J., Bryant, D., Diamond, B. J., Kalmar, J. H., Moore, N. B., & DeLuca, J. (2006). Processing speed interacts with working memory efficiency in multiple sclerosis. *Archives of Clinical Neuropsychology, 21*(3), 229–238. doi:10.1016/j.acn.2005.12.001

Lincoln, N. B., Dent, A., Harding, J., Weyman, N., Nicholl, C., Blumhardt, L. D., & Playford, E. D. (2002). Evaluation of cognitive assessment and cognitive intervention for people with multiple sclerosis. *Journal of Neurology, Neurosurgery, and Psychiatry, 72*(1), 93–98.

Lublin, F. D., & Reingold, S. C. (1996). Defining the clinical course of multiple sclerosis: results of an international survey. National Multiple Sclerosis Society (USA) Advisory Committee on Clinical Trials of New Agents in Multiple Sclerosis. *Neurology, 46*(4), 907–911.

Lynch, S. G., Parmenter, B. A., & Denney, D. R. (2005). The association between cognitive impairment and physical disability in multiple sclerosis. *Multiple Sclerosis, 11*(4), 469–476.

Lyros, E., Messinis, L., Papageorgiou, S. G., & Papathanasopoulos, P. (2010). Cognitive dysfunction in multiple sclerosis: The effect of pharmacological interventions. *International Review of Psychiatry, 22*(1), 35–42. doi:10.3109/09540261003589455

Melanson, M., Grossberndt, A., Klowak, M., Leong, C., Frost, E. E., Prout, M.,... Namaka, M. (2010). Fatigue and cognition in patients with relapsing multiple sclerosis treated with interferon beta. *The International Journal of Neuroscience, 120*(10), 631–640. doi:10.3109/00207454.2010.511732

Minden, S. L., & Schiffer, R. B. (1990). Affective disorders in multiple sclerosis. Review and recommendations for clinical research. *Archives of Neurology, 47*(1), 98–104.

Mohr, D. C., & Goodkin, D. E. (1999). Treatment of depression in multiple sclerosis: Review and meta-analysis. *Clinical Psychology: Science and Practice, 6*(1), 1–9.

Mohr, D. C., Goodkin, D. E., Likosky, W., Gatto, N., Baumann, K. A., & Rudick, R. A. (1997). Treatment of depression improves adherence to interferon beta-1b therapy for multiple sclerosis. *Archives of Neurology, 54*(5), 531–533.

Mohr, D. C., Hart, S. L., & Goldberg, A. (2003). Effects of treatment for depression on fatigue in multiple sclerosis. *Psychosomatic Medicine, 65*(4), 542–547.

Morrow, S. A., Drake, A., Zivadinov, R., Munschauer, F., Weinstock-Guttman, B., & Benedict, R. H. (2010). Predicting loss of employment over three years in multiple sclerosis: Clinically meaningful cognitive decline. *The Clinical Neuropsychologist, 24*(7), 1131–1145. doi:10.1080/13854046.2010.511272

Morrow, S. A., Kaushik, T., Zarevics, P., Erlanger, D., Bear, M. F., Munschauer, F. E., & Benedict, R. H. (2009). The effects of L-amphetamine sulfate on cognition in MS patients: Results of a randomized controlled trial. *Journal of Neurology, 256*(7), 1095–1102. doi:10.1007/s00415-009-5074-x

Morrow, S. A., Weinstock-Guttman, B., Munschauer, F. E., Hojnacki, D., & Benedict, R. H. (2009). Subjective fatigue is not associated with cognitive impairment in multiple sclerosis: Cross-sectional and longitudinal analysis. *Multiple Sclerosis, 15*(8), 998–1005. doi:10.1177/1352458509106213

Nyenhuis, D. L., Luchetta, T., Yamamoto, C., Terrien, A., Bernardin, L., Rao, S. M., & Garron, D. C. (1998). The development, standardization, and initial validation of the Chicago Multiscale Depression Inventory. *Journal of Personality Assessment, 70*(2), 386–401. doi:10.1207/s15327752jpa7002_14

O'Brien, A. R., Chiaravalloti, N., Goverover, Y., & Deluca, J. (2008). Evidenced-based cognitive rehabilitation for persons with multiple sclerosis: A review of the literature. *Archives of Physical Medicine and Rehabilitation, 89*(4), 761–769. doi:10.1016/j.apmr.2007.10.019

Oken, B. S., Flegal, K., Zajdel, D., Kishiyama, S. S., Lovera, J., Bagert, B., & Bourdette, D. N. (2006). Cognition and fatigue in multiple sclerosis: Potential effects of medications with central nervous system activity. *Journal of Rehabilitation Research and Development, 43*(1), 83–90.

Parmenter, B. A., Denney, D. R., & Lynch, S. G. (2003). The cognitive performance of patients with multiple sclerosis during periods of high and low fatigue. *Multiple Sclerosis, 9*(2), 111–118.

Patten, S. B., Beck, C. A., Williams, J. V., Barbui, C., & Metz, L. M. (2003). Major depression in multiple sclerosis: A population-based perspective. *Neurology, 61*(11), 1524–1527.

Patti, F. (2010). Optimizing the benefit of multiple sclerosis therapy: The importance of treatment adherence. *Patient Preference and Adherence, 4*, 1–9.

Paul, R. H., Beatty, W. W., Schneider, R., Blanco, C. R., & Hames, K. A. (1998). Cognitive and physical fatigue in multiple sclerosis: Relations between self-report and objective performance. *Applied Neuropsychology, 5*(3), 143–148. doi:10.1207/s15324826an0503_5

Rabinowitz, A. R., Fisher, A. J., & Arnett, P. A. (2011). Neurovegetative symptoms in patients with multiple sclerosis: fatigue, not depression. *Journal of the International Neuropsychological Society, 17*(1), 46–55. doi:10.1017/S1355617710001141

Rao, S. M. (1991). *A manual for the brief, repeatable battery of neuropsychological tests in multiple sclerosis.*

Rao, S. M., Leo, G. J., Bernardin, L., & Unverzagt, F. (1991). Cognitive dysfunction in multiple sclerosis. I. Frequency, patterns, and prediction. *Neurology, 41*(5), 685–691.

Rao, S. M., Leo, G. J., Ellington, L., Nauertz, T., Bernardin, L., & Unverzagt, F. (1991). Cognitive dysfunction in multiple sclerosis. II. Impact on employment and social functioning. *Neurology, 41*(5), 692–696.

Rao, S. M., Leo, G. J., & St Aubin-Faubert, P. (1989). On the nature of memory disturbance in multiple sclerosis. *Journal of Clinical and Experimental Neuropsychology, 11*(5), 699–712. doi:10.1080/01688638908400926

Rovaris, M., Iannucci, G., Falautano, M., Possa, F., Martinelli, V., Comi, G., & Filippi, M. (2002). Cognitive dysfunction in patients with mildly disabling relapsing-remitting multiple sclerosis: An exploratory study with diffusion tensor MR imaging. *Journal of the Neurological Sciences, 195*(2), 103–109.

Sadovnick, A. D., Remick, R. A., Allen, J., Swartz, E., Yee, I. M., Eisen, K.,... Paty, D. W. (1996). Depression and multiple sclerosis. *Neurology, 46*(3), 628–632.

Sanfilipo, M. P., Benedict, R. H., Weinstock-Guttman, B., & Bakshi, R. (2006). Gray and white matter brain atrophy and neuropsychological impairment in multiple sclerosis. *Neurology, 66*(5), 685–692. doi:10.1212/01.wnl.0000201238.93586.d9

Scarmeas, N., & Stern, Y. (2003). Cognitive reserve and lifestyle. *Journal of Clinical and Experimental Neuropsychology, 25*(5), 625–633. doi:10.1076/jcen.25.5.625.14576

Schwid, S. R., Tyler, C. M., Scheid, E. A., Weinstein, A., Goodman, A. D., & McDermott, M. P. (2003). Cognitive fatigue during a test requiring sustained attention: A pilot study. *Multiple Sclerosis, 9*(5), 503–508.

Sepulcre, J., Masdeu, J. C., Goni, J., Arrondo, G., Velez de Mendizabal, N., Bejarano, B., & Villoslada, P. (2009). Fatigue in multiple sclerosis is associated with the disruption of frontal and parietal pathways. *Multiple Sclerosis, 15*(3), 337–344. doi:10.1177/1352458508098373

Smith, A. (1982). *Symbol Digits Modalities Test.* Los Angeles: Western Psychological Services.

Smith, M. M., & Arnett, P. A. (2007). Dysarthria predicts poorer performance on cognitive tasks requiring a speeded oral response in an MS population. *Journal of Clinical and Experimental Neuropsychology, 29*(8), 804–812. doi:10.1080/13803390601064493

Solari, A., Motta, A., Mendozzi, L., Pucci, E., Forni, M., Mancardi, G., & Pozzilli, C. (2004). Computer-aided retraining of memory and attention in people with multiple sclerosis: A randomized, double-blind controlled trial. *Journal of the Neurological Sciences, 222*(1–2), 99–104. doi:10.1016/j.jns.2004.04.027

Spielberger, C. D., Gorsuch, R. L., Lushene, P. R., Vagg, P. R., & Jacobs, A. G. (1983). Manual for the State-Trait Anxiety Inventory (Form Y). Palo Alto, CA: Consulting Psychologists Press.

Stein, R. A., & Strickland, T. L. (1998). A review of the neuropsychological effects of commonly used prescription medications. *Archives of Clinical Neuropsychology, 13*(3), 259–284.

Stern, Y. (2002). What is cognitive reserve? Theory and research application of the reserve concept. *Journal of the International Neuropsychological Society, 8*(3), 448–460.

Stern, Y. (2006). Cognitive reserve and Alzheimer disease. *Alzheimer Disease and Associated Disorders, 20*(2), 112–117. doi:10.1097/01.wad.0000213815.20177.19

Strober, L., Englert, J., Munschauer, F., Weinstock-Guttman, B., Rao, S., & Benedict, R. H. (2009). Sensitivity of conventional memory tests in multiple sclerosis: comparing the Rao Brief Repeatable Neuropsychological Battery and the Minimal Assessment of Cognitive Function in MS. *Multiple Sclerosis, 15*(9), 1077–1084. doi:10.1177/-1352458509106615

Sumowski, J. F., Chiaravalloti, N., Erlanger, D., Kaushik, T., Benedict, R. H., & Deluca, J. (2011). L-amphetamine improves memory in MS patients with objective memory impairment. *Multiple Sclerosis, 17*(9), 1141–1145. doi:10.1177/1352458511404585

Sumowski, J. F., Chiaravalloti, N., Wylie, G., & Deluca, J. (2009). Cognitive reserve moderates the negative effect of brain atrophy on cognitive efficiency in multiple sclerosis. *Journal of the International Neuropsychological Society, 15*(4), 606–612. doi:10.1017/S1355617709090912

Sumowski, J. F., Wylie, G. R., Gonnella, A., Chiaravalloti, N., & Deluca, J. (2010). Premorbid cognitive leisure independently contributes to cognitive reserve in multiple sclerosis. *Neurology, 75*(16), 1428–1431. doi:10.1212/WNL.0b013e3181f881a6

Tartaglia, M. C., Narayanan, S., & Arnold, D. L. (2008). Mental fatigue alters the pattern and increases the volume of cerebral activation required for a motor task in multiple sclerosis patients with fatigue. *European Journal of Neurology, 15*(4), 413–419. doi:10.1111/j.1468-1331.2008.02090.x

Turner, A. P., Williams, R. M., Bowen, J. D., Kivlahan, D. R., & Haselkorn, J. K. (2006). Suicidal ideation in multiple sclerosis. *Archives of Physical Medicine and Rehabilitation, 87*(8), 1073–1078. doi:10.1016/j.apmr.2006.04.021

Winkelmann, A., Engel, C., Apel, A., & Zettl, U. K. (2007). Cognitive impairment in multiple sclerosis. *Journal of Neurology, 254*(Suppl 2), II35–42. doi:10.1007/s00415-007-2010-9

Zigmond, A. S., & Snaith, R. P. (1983). The hospital anxiety and depression scale. *Acta Psychiatrica Scandinavica, 67*(6), 361–370.

Zorzon, M., de Masi, R., Nasuelli, D., Ukmar, M., Mucelli, R. P., Cazzato, G., . . . Zivadinov, R. (2001). Depression and anxiety in multiple sclerosis. A clinical and MRI study in 95 subjects. *Journal of Neurology, 248*(5), 416–421.

11

The Role of Secondary Factors in HIV-Associated Neurocognitive Disorders

KAITLIN BLACKSTONE, DAVID J. MOORE, AND STEVEN PAUL WOODS

HIV AND THE BRAIN

Human immunodeficiency virus–1 (HIV) is a retrovirus that is associated with a wide range of neuropsychological problems among approximately half of infected individuals (Heaton et al., 2010). The introduction of improved antiretroviral treatment, while translating into improved longevity and quality of life among HIV-infected persons, has not significantly altered the prevalence of HIV-associated neurocognitive disorders (Heaton et al., 2011). The Centers for Disease Control and Prevention (CDC) delineates severity of HIV disease based on the lowest documented CD4 cell count and presence or previously diagnosed of HIV-related conditions. For example, the stages range from "medically asymptomatic" (CDC stage A1), in which CD4 count is $\geq$500 cells/μL and no diagnosed HIV-related conditions exist, to an AIDS classification (CDC stages A3, B3, C1–3), in which CD4 count <200 cells/μL and/or a specific HIV-related condition exists. Increased rates of neuropsychological impairment have been found at each of these successive stages of HIV infection (Heaton et al., 1995); importantly, however, the deleterious effect of disease severity on subsequent neuropsychological functioning may have dampened in the highly active antiretroviral therapy (HAART) era (Heaton et al., 2010). Although the exact neurobiological underpinnings of neurocognitive impairments associated with HIV infection have yet to be fully elucidated, the current working hypothesis is that HIV crosses the blood–brain barrier but does not directly infect neurons. Instead, central nervous system (CNS) viral replication mostly occurs via monocyte-derived macrophages (MDM)[1] and microglia. The host immune response to the presence of the virus activates a neurotoxic cascade of events, such as the release of chemokines and cytokines, which ultimately lead to neuronal damage and observed neurobehavioral complications (reviewed in Hult, Chana, Masliah, & Everall, 2008). While HIV-associated neuropathologies are observed throughout brain parenchyma, the effects are arguably most commonly observed in the white matter, frontal cortex, and basal ganglia (Jernigan et al., 2011). Frontostriatal systems may be particularly affected, and these systems are strongly tied to neurocognitive functioning (e.g., Mohamed et al., 2010). In the current era of efficacious antiretroviral therapy, there have been relatively few identified concrete biological susceptibility factors associated with neurocognitive impairment in HIV infection. One concept with some traction as a susceptibility factor for neurocognitive impairment is that individuals with lower nadir CD4 cell count, an indicator of lifetime disease severity rather than current HIV disease severity, may be more susceptible to neurocognitive impairment (Heaton et al., 2010; Muñoz-Moreno et al., 2008). Other co-occurring medical conditions (e.g., hepatitis C virus), substance use disorders (e.g., methamphetamine), and psychiatric conditions (e.g., bipolar disorder) exert a primary effect on the neurocognitive complications observed in HIV and can result in additive neurocognitive impairment among dually afflicted HIV-infected individuals (e.g., Cherner et al., 2005; Moore et al., 2008; Rippeth et al., 2004). In short, there is a great deal of work that remains in determining the neurobiological susceptibility factors, protective factors, and mechanisms that ultimately translate into HIV-associated neurocognitive impairment.

Given that the exact mechanisms of HIV-related neurocognitive impairment have yet to be fully identified, there is a particular need to examine the possible influence of secondary factors in the expression of HIV-associated neurocognitive disorders (HAND). These secondary factors, some of which have a substantially higher prevalence among HIV-infected persons than among the general population, include (1) affective disorders, (2) apathy, (3) suboptimal effort, (4) pain, (5) HIV-induced constitutional symptoms, and (6) primary perception and sensory deficits. The particular challenge for clinicians and researchers alike is to determine whether observed neurocognitive impairments in an HIV-infected person are the result of (1) primary HIV-related cognitive impairments, (2) secondary factors associated with HIV infection that may influence neurocognition (e.g., fatigue, neuropathic pain), or (3) a co-occurring confounding factor (e.g., substance abuse, hepatitis C virus [HCV] infection, serious mental illness). It is not the intent of this chapter to cover the primary CNS and neurocognitive complications associated with HIV infection (see Woods et al., 2009, for a review), nor is it to review specific comorbidities common among HIV infection with known cognitive effects. Our primary goal is to review the literature relating to the above secondary factors and provide a brief description of assessment instruments that may be useful to the reader in assessing for the potential influence of these factors. Additionally, we provide an example of an HIV-infected person with secondary factors and present future directions for properly accounting for these influences on neurocognitive performance among HIV-infected persons.

AFFECTIVE DISORDERS

Depression

Major depressive disorder (MDD) is one of the most common comorbidities in HIV infection; meta-analyses report that up to 50% of individuals with HIV experience co-occurring MDD (Ciesla & Roberts, 2001; Rabkin, 2008). Previous studies have established that, on its own, depression affects neurocognitive performance. Specifically, individuals with depression have been shown to have difficulties in attention, learning, memory, psychomotor speed, and executive functions (Austin et al., 1992; Cassens, Wolfe, & Zola, 1990). Importantly, MDD has also been shown to involve the same frontostriatal systems that are preferentially affected by HIV (Tekin & Cummings, 2002).

Despite this, studies have consistently shown that neuropsychological performance of individuals with HIV is not affected by comorbid depression. For example, Grant et al. (1993) examined HIV seropositive (HIV+) and HIV seronegative (HIV−) gay men and found that although depressive symptoms were more common in the HIV+ group, no relationship existed between neuropsychological performance and depression for these individuals. Similarly, a recent longitudinal study followed HIV+ men who did not meet criteria for a current major depressive episode at baseline for 2 years and found that neuropsychological performance did not differ between HIV+ individuals without depression and those with either a lifetime or incident major depressive episode (Cysique et al., 2007). Additionally, HIV+ individuals with depression do not evidence greater cognitive worsening over time than those HIV+ individuals without depression (Cysique et al., 2007; Goggin et al., 1997). As such, depressed mood and neurocognitive disturbances appear to retain unique relationships to HIV illness status and should be considered as independent processes. Cysique et al. (2007) proposed dissociable neuropathogenic mechanisms behind depression and HIV infection; however, future studies are still necessary to fully delineate the differential biological pathways affected by these conditions.

Nevertheless for both clinical and research settings it is important to note that depressed mood has been shown to significantly influence self-reported measures of cognitive complaints, as well as daily functioning in individuals with HIV. Not only is depression associated with more frequent and severe cognitive complaints in HIV+ individuals (Cysique et al., 2007; Mapou et al., 1993; Thames et al., 2010), but in a regression analysis, depressive symptoms were shown to account for most of the variance in cognitive complaints, which were not strongly related to objective neuropsychological performance (Rourke, Halman, & Bassel, 1999). Therefore, when using self-report measures of neurocognitive problems in individuals with HIV, it is essential to first consider whether such complaints may be secondary to a mood disturbance. Relatedly, depression is a reliable and salient predictor of a range of everyday functioning outcomes in persons living with HIV. For example, depression is independently associated with medication nonadherence (Tucker, Burnam, Sherbourne, Kung, & Gifford, 2003), unemployment (e.g., Heaton et al., 2004), and mortality (Ellis et al., 1997) in HIV+ individuals. Thus, while it is unlikely that depression would be an independent source of neuropsychological impairment in HIV infection, it warrants careful consideration when determining the etiology of everyday functioning declines when rendering diagnoses of symptomatic HAND. The recent Frascati criteria for HAND have outlined a helpful diagnostic algorithm for weighing depressive symptoms in the presence of cognitive complaints and/or declines in everyday functioning (Antinori et al., 2007; see flow chart in Appendix 11.2).

Anxiety

Estimated rates of co-occurring anxiety disorders among individuals with HIV vary widely, from less than 1% up to 43% (Beyer, Taylor, Gersing, & Krishnan, 2007; Elliot, 1998; O'Cleirigh, Hart, & James, 2008). As a subset of anxiety disorders independently evidence neuropsychological impairments (i.e., obsessive-compulsive disorder, posttraumatic stress disorder, and generalized anxiety disorder; Airaksinen, Larsson, & Forsell, 2005), it is important to ascertain how these conditions could influence cognitive functioning in HIV.

Although comorbid anxiety disorders in persons living with HIV are independently associated with poorer medication adherence and poorer heath-related quality of life (Tucker et al., 2003), they have not been related to the stage of HIV infection (Percides, Dunbar, Grunseit, Hall, & Cooper, 1992) and their role in the expression of HAND is not well understood. For instance, Mapou et al. (1993) reported that HIV+ individuals who complained of cognitive difficulties also reported anxiety symptoms more frequently, with those who complained more likely to reach the clinical anxiety cutoff than those HIV+ individuals who did not complain. More recently, Woods et al. (2007) showed that those HIV+ individuals who complain of prospective memory difficulties reported more symptoms of anxiety. However, these cognitive complaints in both studies related most strongly to current mood (i.e., reported anxiety and depressive symptoms) and were not associated with objective neuropsychological performance (Mapou et al., 1993; Woods et al., 2007). Similarly, generalized anxiety disorder diagnoses were not associated with neuropsychological impairment in a large sample of 500 HIV-infected adults (Heaton et al., 1995). The strongest association to anxiety symptoms in HIV+ individuals was the presence of psychological and psychosocial symptoms; constitutional symptoms as a result of HIV infection may also be a potential mediator to the development of anxiety symptoms (Percides et al., 1992). The literature on HIV and anxiety would benefit from future studies focusing at the neural level (e.g., neuroimaging and biomarkers) of these diseases to delineate the neuropathological systems underlying their etiologies in order to determine any shared versus distinct processes.

Bipolar Disorder

Rates of HIV infection are particularly elevated in individuals with bipolar disorder (BD) as compared to rates for the general population, with a recent study reporting a comorbidity rate of 2.8% (versus approximately 1% in the general population; Beyer, Kuchibhatla, Gersing, & Krishnan, 2005). On its own, BD has been associated with dysregulation of the limbic system (e.g., amygdala, anterior cingulated, hippocampus), as well as alterations along white matter tracts that connect prefrontal, subcortical, and medial–temporal structures (Bearden, Hoffman, & Cannon, 2001; Mahon, Burdick, & Szeszko, 2010; Phillips, Ladouceur, & Drevets, 2008; Strakowski, Adler, Holland, Mills, & DelBello,, 2005). These neural pathways are similar to those pathogenic neural systems associated with HIV infection (e.g., frontostriatal loops). Among individuals with both HIV infection and BD, frontostrial systems may experience a "double hit," possibly increasing the risk of neurocognitive and functional impairment.

A growing number of studies illustrate that individuals with bipolar I and II disorders show impairments on objective neurocognitive measures, especially in the domains of executive functions and verbal learning (Bearden et al., 2001; Quraishi & Frangou, 2002; Robinson et al., 2006). Neurocognitive dysfunction appears to be most pronounced during acute manic and depressive episodes (Malhi et al., 2007; Martinez-Aran, Vieta, Reinares, et al., 2004; Murphy & Sahakian, 2001; Quraishi & Frangou, 2002); however, an increasing amount of research has demonstrated that cognitive deficits persist during periods of euthymia and in clinical remission as well (Clark & Goodwin, 2004; Kurtz & Gerraty, 2009; Martinez-Aran, Vieta, Colom, et al., 2004).

Although there is evidence of neuropsychological deficits independently in persons with either HIV infection or BD, few studies have examined neuropsychological performance in individuals who are dually affected. Data from our laboratory suggested that HIV-infected individuals with BD (HIV+/BD+) demonstrate greater global cognitive impairment, and specifically, greater impairment in the domains of attention, processing speed, motor, and episodic memory than individuals with only one condition or healthy comparison subjects (Moore et al., 2006). A subsequent study more closely examined the effects of BD on attentional deficits in HIV infection using a well-validated measure of sustained attention (i.e., Conner's Continuous Performance Test-II). Results showed that HIV+/BD+ individuals ($n = 39$) performed significantly worse on accuracy (omission errors; $\delta = .7$) and variability of the response time (reaction time standard error, $\delta = .6$ and variability of the standard error, $\delta = .7$) compared to HIV+/BD– individuals (Posada et al., 2012).

These emerging data suggest an additive effect of BD on the neuropsychological performance of individuals with HIV. However, research is still needed to fully delineate the degree and scope to which BD may influence neuropsychological performance beyond the effect of HIV, by comparing findings among dually affected persons to HIV-uninfected persons with BD as well. As it remains, however, it is important for researchers and clinicians to be aware of this potentially additive detrimental cognitive effect that can be expected in individuals with HIV+/BD+. These findings are in contrast to the lack of influence that the other affective disorders appear to have on neuropsychological performance in HIV. Our results suggest that a distinct neuropathogenic system exists in BD, particularly compared to MDD, in the context of HIV infection, that is important for clinicians and researchers to recognize.

Other areas that warrant future research in HIV+ individuals with co-occurring BD is the impact that neuropsychological impairment has on emotional cognition and everyday functioning. Emotional cognition is widely recognized as the cognitive processing of emotionally laden stimuli. Such processes are particularly salient in neurological and psychiatric disorders given that impairment is often observed in both domains. Emotional dysregulation is commonly reported in HIV+ patients, including increased rates of depression as well as secondary mania and psychosis, especially among those with advanced immunosuppression (Cruess et al., 2003; Ellen, Judd, Mijch, & Cockram, 1999; Sewell et al., 1994). Additionally, deficits in emotional regulation are the core characteristics of BD (American Psychiatric Association, 2000). Therefore, HIV+ individuals with BD are likely highly susceptible to dysfunctional emotional cognition, the impact of which could have important implications on how these individuals interpret and react to emotional stimuli in their environment. Similarly, as a linear relationship has been shown to exist between neurocognitive impairment and functional declines in individuals with HIV (Heaton et al., 2004) and those with BD (Green, 2006) independently, individuals with HIV and BD are likely also at risk for such deficits. For example, medication adherence is consistently related to cognitive abilities independently among individuals with HIV infection (Hinkin et al., 2002, 2004; Selnes, 2002) and those with BD (Berk, Berk, & Castle, 2004; Colom, Vieta, Tacchi, Sanchez-Moreno, & Scott, 2005; Danion, Neunrither, & Kreger-Finance, 1987). Those domains which have been shown to be important for successful medication adherence (i.e., executive functions, attention, and memory) are also at particular risk for decline in persons with HIV and BD (Moore et al., 2008). These multiple risk factors may make individuals with HIV and BD susceptible to nonadherence and other declines in everyday functioning.

APATHY

Although apathy has long been recognized as a clinical feature of HAND (Navia, Jordan, & Price, 1986), our scientific understanding of the prevalence, neural underpinnings, and clinical correlates of this neuropsychiatric phenomenon has only begun to take shape in the past 10 years. *Apathy* broadly refers to a state of diminished interest and motivation that may be expressed in the realm of affect, neurocognition, and/or behavior (van Reekum et al., 2005), particularly as it concerns self-initiated actions (Stuss et al., 2000). At the group level, persons living with HIV infection consistently show higher levels of apathy than in demographically similar seronegative individuals (e.g., Castellon, Hinkin, & Myers, 1998). In fact, while prevalence estimates vary across the literature (e.g., Rabkin et al., 2000), as many as 50% of HIV-infected individuals might evidence clinically elevated levels of apathy (e.g., Castellon et al., 1998). However, the association between HIV infection and apathy appears to be largely unrelated to disease severity (e.g., Castellon et al., 1998; Rabkin et al., 2000; Paul,

Flanigan, et al., 2005), perhaps with the exception of longer duration of infection (Paul, Flanigan, et al., 2005).

Whether apathy in HIV infection is separable from depression, however, has been the subject of some debate. Clinical symptoms of apathy and depression ostensibly overlap and, as one might expect, these two neuropsychiatric features commonly co-occur (e.g., Castellon et al., 1998). Moreover, apathy and depression are reliably and strongly associated with one another in HIV-infected samples (e.g., Castellon et al., 1998; Rabkin et al., 2000; cf. Paul, Flanigan, et al., 2005). Castellon and colleagues (1998), for example, showed that HIV-infected persons with clinically elevated scores on the Beck Depression Inventory (BDI) evidenced significantly greater signs of apathy on the Neuropsychiatric Interview. HIV-associated apathy may be particularly related to cognitive symptoms of depression (Castellon et al., 1998) and alexithymia (Bogdanova, Dìaz-Santos, & Cronin-Golomb, 2010). Nevertheless, the effect sizes of these associations do not indicate a one-to-one correspondence between apathy and depression; in fact, one recent study found elevated clinical ratings of apathy in a sample of nondepressed HIV-infected persons as compared to seronegatives, suggesting that these two neuropsychiatric syndromes may be more separable than previously thought (Hoare et al., 2010).

At the level of neural systems, one might expect that HIV-associated neural injury to frontostriatal pathways (e.g., anterior cingulate, ventral striatum) would underlie the expression of apathy in this population (van Reekum et al., 2005). To this end, Paul, Brickman, and colleagues (2005) reported a specific association between apathy and nucleus accumbens volume, independent of HIV disease severity. In a more recent study using diffusion tensor imaging, Hoare et al. (2010) observed that apathy was associated with lower fractional anisotropy (i.e., an index of microstructural integrity) in white matter pathways of the medial frontal cortex (e.g., corona radiata). Despite these reliable and direct relationships with neural systems, there is some controversy regarding the extent to which apathy is associated with the cognitive expression of frontostriatal neural injury in HIV, which would include deficits in working memory, executive functions, episodic memory, and psychomotor efficiency (e.g., Woods et al., 2009). Two prior studies have reported small and nonsignificant correlations between a range of neurocognitive functions and apathy in persons infected with HIV (Rabkin et al., 2000; Robinson-Papp et al., 2008). In contrast, a handful of other studies suggest at least modest associations between apathy and working memory ($r = -.36$ to $-.46$, Castellon et al., 1998; $r = -.43$, Bogdanova et al., 2010), learning (visual: $r = -.30$, verbal: $r = -.43$; Paul, Flanigan, et al., 2005), aspects of executive functions, including dual task performance (Castellon, Hinkin, & Myers, 2000), set shifting ($r = .31$; Paul, Flanigan, et al., 2005), and response inhibition (Castellon et al., 2000). Further study is clearly warranted, perhaps to include a broader range of cognitive functions that may assess other ability areas that directly correspond to the neural circuitry of apathy (e.g., decision making, prospective memory).

Of greater clinical interest, elevated apathy may be associated with worse overall everyday functioning outcomes for persons infected with HIV. For example, two prior studies suggest that higher levels of apathy are associated with lower health-related quality of life (Rabkin et al., 2000; Tate et al., 2003) and that this association is independent of the severity of depressive symptomatology (Tate et al., 2003). With regard to antiretroviral medication management, apathy has been linked to medication nonadherence in younger HIV-infected persons (Barclay et al., 2007), as well as to determinants of medication adherence, such as intention to adhere (Rabkin et al., 2000). However, in both of these studies of adherence, the strength and independence of the apathy effect was tempered by consideration of other predictors (e.g., depression). Nevertheless, apathy's potentially unique role in other important functional outcomes such as vocational functioning (e.g., unemployment), engagement in HIV risk behaviors (e.g., unprotected sex), and various instrumental (e.g., financial management, household chores) and basic (e.g., grooming) activities of daily living remains to be determined.

SUBOPTIMAL EFFORT

Suboptimal effort is another potentially important secondary factor that can influence data interpretation in the neuropsychological evaluation of HIV infection. Suboptimal test-taking effort may be observed for a variety of reasons among persons living with HIV infection, ranging from constitutional symptoms to acute substance intoxication to secondary gain. Regarding the latter, declines in the independent performance of basic and instrumental activities of daily living are prevalent and may be secondary to myriad physical, cognitive, and psychiatric complications of HIV disease. In fact, HIV is recognized under the Americans with Disabilities Act, and thousands of persons living with HIV infection receive benefits. Thus, it is possible that a small subset of HIV-infected individuals might feign or exaggerate neurocognitive deficits in an effort to secure monetary compensation and service benefits (Slick, Hinkin, van Gorp, & Satz, 2001).

Assessment of possible suboptimal effort in HIV infection is thus essential to both clinical and research evaluations of persons living with HIV infection. Ideally, such an evaluation would involve multiple indicators of suboptimal effort, including careful behavioral observations, effort indices that can be derived from standard clinical tests (e.g., reliable digits), and formal symptom validity tests (SVTs; Woods et al., 2003). SVTs commonly use a forced-choice format and are designed to be highly specific, meaning that they are passable for all individuals in the absence of severe neurocognitive impairment (Bianchini, Mathias, & Greve, 2001). Interpreting effort tests, such as SVTs, in clinical populations is greatly enhanced by the availability of base rate data on test failures (i.e., possible false positives) in the population of interest. Unfortunately, only two studies have been published on the topic of effort testing in persons living with HIV infection. In the first study, Slick et al. (2001) reported a tolerable 7% false-positive error rate among 55 HIV-infected persons on the "embedded" effort index from the Wechsler Memory Scale-Revised (WMS-R; Psychological Corporation, 1987), which was calculated by subtracting the WMS-R Attention/Concentration Index (ACI) score from the General Memory Index (GMI; Mittenberg, Azrin, Millsaps,

& Heilbronner, 1993). However, the false-positive error rate rose to 18.2% when the analysis was restricted to individuals with above-average GMI scores, possibly tempering the usefulness of this approach in this subpopulation. Although the WMS-R does not provide a base rate for false-positive errors on the GMI-ACI effort index in a normative sample, prior studies have found an 8% false-positive error rate among inpatient substance users (Iverson, Slick, & Franzen, 2000) and a 10% false-positive error rate among healthy individuals who were instructed to malinger head trauma symptoms on the WMS-R (Mittenberg et al., 1993). These findings suggest that the 7% false-positive error rate found in the general HIV-infected Slick et al. (2001) sample may be acceptable; whereas the reported 18.2% false-positive error rate among the Slick et al. cohort with above-average GMI scores indicates that the embedded WMS-R effort index may not be appropriate for these individuals.

In 2003, Woods and colleagues reported a 2% false-positive rate on the Hiscock Digit Memory Test (HDMT; Hiscock & Hiscock, 1989) in 82 non-compensation-seeking research subjects with HAND. Ninety-five percent of the sample achieved perfect scores on the HDMT, and no participants evidenced HDMT scores that fell near or below the level of chance. With regard to the two false-positive HDMT scores, both individuals were at least moderately impaired on the broader neu-rocognitive test battery, most prominently on measures of visual memory. Given that episodic memory impairments are highly prevalent in HAND (Heaton et al., 2009), caution should be exercised in interpreting SVT scores below cutoff in persons with viable evidence of impairment in this domain. Corroborating evidence for the viability of observed memory deficits in persons who fail the HDMT might be sought in the clinical interview, behavioral observations, patterns of test performance, and other SVTs. Future research is needed to examine the base rates of failures (i.e., specificity) on other, more commonly used SVTs and embedded indices in persons living with HIV infection, as well as the sensitivity of such measures to known malingerers and persons with substantial motivation to feign cognitive impairment (e.g., persons in litigation, applying for disability).

PAIN

Previous studies have reported that 30–90% of HIV patients experience clinically significant pain (Aouizerat et al., 2010; Breitbart et al., 1996; Marcus, Kerns, Rosenfeld, & Breitbart, 2000). Severity of HIV-associated pain has been shown to be related to disease severity (e.g., lower CD4 counts), ethnicity, sleep disturbances, and care setting (Aouizerat et al., 2010; Marcus et al., 2000) but has not been examined in the context of HAND. Previous research in other populations report models in which the effect of pain on cognition is mediated by affective state (e.g., depression and anxiety; Brown, Glass, & Park, 2002; Moroni & Laurent, 2006). Additionally, some studies examining the communication between the immune and central nervous systems suggest that the alteration in cytokine release, which is modulated by immune function, may in turn affect those cytokines in the brain, which play an important role in cognitive function (e.g., cytokines in the hippocampus may interfere with memory consolidation), as well as cytokines within the spinal cord that exaggerate pain (Maier, 2003; Maier & Watkin, 2003). As HIV infection is a disease primarily targeting CNS function and the immune system, these studies may have important implications for a potential pathogenic etiology by which cognition and pain may be associated in HIV.

Since no studies were found examining the role of pain on cognition in HIV, we examined 155 HIV+ participants (mean age = 40.3 ± 8.7 years; 90% male; 67% Caucasian, mean education = 12.7 ± 2.7 years) recruited at the HIV Neurobehavioral Research Center who completed the Brief Pain Inventory (BPI) and a neurocognitive battery covering seven major ability domains (see Heaton et al., 2009). The BPI assesses presence and severity of pain in the previous 24 hours as well as the degree to which pain has interfered with aspects of daily functioning. Presence and severity of pain were not associated with impairment in any of the cognitive domains or globally ($p > .05$), nor was the degree to which pain reportedly interfered with aspects of daily functioning ($p > .05$; see Fig. 11.1). However, presence and severity of pain in the past 24 hours was associated with lower nadir CD4 count ($\rho = -.21$, $p = .009$) and lower current CD4 count ($\rho = -.20$, $p = .02$), while pain that interfered with daily functioning was associated with HIV disease stage ($\chi^2 = 33.1$, $p < .001$) and lower nadir CD4 count ($\rho = -.22$, $p = .006$). Of clinical importance, both the presence and severity of pain as well as the degree to which pain interfered with daily functioning were predictive of self-reported functional declines in daily life ($\rho = .20$, $p = .01$; $\rho = .32$, $p < .001$, respectively). Lastly, both presence of pain and pain associated with daily functioning significantly

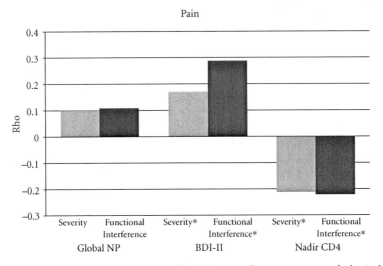

Figure 11.1 Depressive symptoms and nadir CD4 count, but not neuropsychological performance, are correlated to both severity of pain and the degree to which pain interferes with aspects of daily functioning in HIV-infected individuals. *p < 0.05.
Abbreviations: BDI-II, Beck Depression Inventory–II; Global NP, Global Deficit Score (neuropsychological performance).

correlated to depressive symptoms (i.e., BDI-II; $\rho = .17$, $p = .03$; $\rho = .29$, $p < .001$, respectively).

Our results suggest that pain, regardless of severity and interference with functional abilities, is not associated with neurocognitive functioning in HIV+ persons. Nonetheless, pain is a significant predictor of HIV disease severity (e.g., immunosuppression) as well as depressive symptoms and plays an important role in the functional abilities of individuals with HIV. These results are consistent with previous studies that have established that HIV-associated pain is significantly associated with decreased quality of life, functional dependence, and increased depression, including increased suicidal ideation (Breitbart et al., 1996; Holzemer, Henry, Reilly, 1998; Kowal et al., 2008; Marcus et al., 2000). Therefore, although there is likely no direct relationship between pain and cognitive function, assessment and treatment of HIV-associated pain has important implications in the daily lives of these patients.

CONSTITUTIONAL SYMPTOMS

Somatic complaints are common in HIV infection, particularly among individuals with advanced disease. Typical symptoms can include fevers, night sweats, fatigue, diarrhea, anorexia (including nausea and vomiting), or weight loss. The impact that such physical symptoms may have on neurocognitive performance in persons living with HIV infection is a practical and important issue, but there is little empirical data to guide clinical decision-making. For the few studies that have examined the effect of constitutional symptoms on neuropsychological performance in HIV, this question was not the primary focus of the analyses, and generally null findings have been reported. For example, in the pre-HAART era, Heaton et al. (1995) reported that there was relatively little relationship between symptoms and neuropsychological impairment in a large HIV+ cohort. In another study attempting to disentangle the relationship among cognitive complaints, constitutional symptoms, and mood state to neuropsychological functioning, Carter, Rourke, Murji, Shore, and Rourke (2003) found that mood and symptoms were significantly correlated to each other but not to neuropsychological performance.

Given the paucity of literature on this topic, we examined 131 HIV-infected individuals from our laboratory (mean age = 46.1 ± 8.4 years; 90% male; mean education = 13.6 ± 2.9 years; 67% Caucasian) who had completed a comprehensive neurocognitive test battery (see Woods et al., 2007, for a listing of specific tests), psychiatric assessment (Profile of Mood States; POMS), self-reported instrumental activities of daily living (i.e., Physical Activities of Daily Living and Instrumental Activities of Daily Living; Lawton & Brody, 1969), and a self-report measure of constitutional symptoms. Specifically, we extracted the 10 constitutional symptom items from the AIDS Clinical Trials Group Medication Adherence Questionnaire (i.e., fever, balance, pain, nausea, fatigue, diarrhea, sleep, skin problems, cough, and headache) that were coded on a frequency scale of 1 (never) to 4 (everyday).

Results showed no significant correlations between performance in any of the neuropsychological domains and number or severity of symptoms (p's > .05; see Fig. 11.2). However, all subscales on the POMS (i.e., tension/anxiety, depression/ dejection, anger/hostility, vigor/activation, fatigue/inertia, confusion/bewilderment) as well as total POMS mood disturbance were significantly associated with reports of constitutional symptoms (correlation range: $\rho = .47$ [number of total mood disturbance] to $\rho = -.37$ [number and severity of vigor/activation]; p's < .001). Additionally, both the number and severity of constitutional symptoms were significantly associated with the number of self-reported everyday functioning declines and severity of the decline in both basic and complex daily tasks (p's < .002). Lastly, both the number and severity of symptom complaint was associated with lower current CD4 count ($\rho = -.20$, $p = .02$; $\rho = -.27$, $p = .002$, respectively) but no other HIV-disease variables (i.e., nadir CD4 count, HIV disease stage, plasma or cerebrospinal fluid RNA viral load; p's > .05). These findings highlight the lack of influence of constitutional symptoms on neuropsychological performance; yet our findings show the importance of those symptoms to self-reported mood state and daily functioning reports. Additionally, physical symptoms may be a good indicator of current immunosuppression. Therefore, although neuropsychological performance can likely be reliably interpreted despite the presence of physical symptoms, it is important to consider how physical complaints may be affecting other areas of a patient's life. As some of these symptoms can be alleviated by changes in medication regimens, it is important

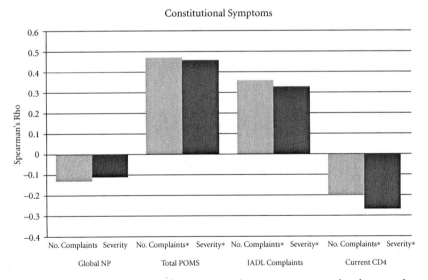

Figure 11.2 Number and severity of constitutional symptoms are correlated to mood, daily functioning, and current CD4, but not neuropsychological performance in HIV-infected individuals. *p < 0.05.

Abbreviations: Global NP, global clinical rating (neuropsychological performance); IADL complaints, number of instrumental activities of daily living complaints; total POMS, total score on the Profile of Mood States.

for patients to be aware of and report complaints to their physicians in order to achieve optimal functionality and quality of life with their illness.

Fatigue

Fatigue is the most common constitutional symptom reported in HIV infection; in a large HIV+ cohort, fatigue was reported to affect up to 26.8% of patients (Heaton et al., 1995). Similar to the other physical symptoms, however, fatigue has not been consistently shown to influence neuropsychological functioning (Heaton et al., 1995; Millikin, Rourke, Halman & Power, 2003). For example, in a large HIV cohort in the pre-HAART era, Heaton et al. (1995) found that fatigue severity was not associated with neuropsychological functioning; additionally, when fatigue was examined as a dichotomous variable (i.e., present versus absent), it still only reached a trend level. Nonetheless, studies have shown that complaints of fatigue are associated with self-reported cognitive complaints (e.g., prospective memory; Woods et al., 2007), affective distress (Ferrando et al., 1998; Millikin et al., 2002; Perkins et al., 1995; Woods et al., 2007), and limitations in daily functioning and disability (Darko, 1991; Ferrando et al., 1998). Mixed results have been reported regarding the relationship between fatigue and HIV-related disease variables. For example, some studies report that fatigue is not associated with AIDS and medication status (Millikin et al., 2002) or CD4 count and HIV viral load (Ferrando et al., 1998; Perkins et al., 1995). However, Darko (1991) reported that those HIV-infected individuals for whom fatigue interfered with their daily activities had significantly lower CD4 counts, higher total globulin, and lower hematocrit levels than those participants who did not report fatigue interfering in their daily lives. Therefore, although fatigue can manifest as a lack of motivation on neuropsychological testing, it does not appear to independently influence performance. However, determining fatigue severity may be a good indicator of affective distress, level of daily functioning, and potentially HIV disease severity in some patients.

PRIMARY PERCEPTION AND SENSORY DEFICITS

Disruption of basic perception and sensory functions often occurs in HIV infection and can consequently complicate interpretation of higher-order cognitive abilities. Heaton et al. (1995) reported that up to 28% of individuals with HIV-associated neurocognitive impairment also showed sensory-perceptual deficits. As such, it is important to determine what role, if any, these deficits play in neuropsychological performance.

Retinopathy is common in advanced stages in HIV infection and can manifest as infectious (e.g., cytomegalovirus) or noninfectious (e.g., cotton wool spots [CWS]) pathologies. Declines in color vision and contrast sensitivity (Quiceno, Capparelli, & Sadun, 1992; Geier et al., 1994) as well as decreased myelination of axons in the optic nerve (Tenhula et al., 1992) have been reported as a result of such retinopathies. Specifically, CWS, which are typically the result of the destruction of retinal ganglion cells by multiple infarcts, have been examined in relation to neuropsychological functioning in HIV infection. Geier et al. (1992) found significant correlations between the number of CWS in both eyes and neuropsychological performance on an auditory list learning task (i.e., Auditory-Verbal Learning Test; $r = -.56$), a perceptual test of line orientation (i.e., Judgment of Line Orientation Test; $r = -.51$), and a task that taps processing speed and executive functions (i.e., Stroop Color and Word; $r = -.50$). However, no association was found for a different task that assesses processing speed and executive function (i.e., Trail Making Test, Part B), or a Vocabulary for Measuring Premorbid Intelligence task (Geier et al., 1992). In a more recent study, Freeman et al. (2004) did not find any relationship between retinovascular disease (i.e., CWS) and any of the five major neurocognitive domains or global neuropsychological performance, but it was related to lower current CD4 counts. Therefore, it is clear that presence of CWS is associated with severity of HIV disease progression and is most likely to occur in later stages of infection. Future studies are warranted to determine what role retinovascular disease may or may not play in neuropsychological performance.

Impaired odor identification and recognition also exist in the context of HIV infection (Brody, Serby, Etienne, & Kalkstein, 1991; Hornung et al., 1998; Razani, Murphy, Davidson, Grant, & McCutchan, 1996; Westervelt, McCaffrey, Cousins, Wagle, & Haase, 1997). Studies have established that odor-identification deficits are present in individuals with HIV-associated dementia (Brody et al., 1991; Hornung et al., 1991) and, in particular, that individuals with HIV-associated neurocognitive impairment have worse odor sensitivity thresholds than either seronegative individuals or HIV+ individuals without neurocognitive impairment (Razani et al., 1996). In a longitudinal study, Westervelt et al. (1997) found that individuals with cognitively symptomatic HIV infection showed significant declines in odor detection across time, while individuals with asymptomatic HIV infection and seronegative controls remained stable. At the 2-year follow-up, up to 71% of the symptomatic participants obtained an abnormal odor-detection score, with no participants with an abnormal odor score showing improvement at subsequent testing (Westervelt et al., 1997). Therefore, odor-detection deficits may be a good marker of CNS involvement and advanced disease status, including symptomatic or progressed cognitive impairment. Importantly, however, odor-detection studies in other neurologically impaired populations (e.g., patients with Alzheimer's disease or Huntington's disease) have shown that deficits in odor identification and recognition can exist despite normal performance in other cognitive domains and after controlling for the lexical components (i.e., cognitively demanding aspects) of odor detection (Moberg et al., 1987; Morgan, Nordin, Murphy, 1995). Therefore, although those HIV+ individuals who show cognitive impairment are also more likely to show deficits in odor detection, cognitive impairment may not necessitate odor-detection impairment. In particular, it is unclear how, or if any, interaction exists between odor-detection impairment and cognitive performance. Given the similar neuropathogenic systems underlying deficits in both odor detection and cognition in HIV+ individuals (i.e., frontostriatal regions), it is likely that odor detection deficits and cognitive impairment are indicators of disease severity along parallel pathways but do not necessarily directly influence one another.

Audiological disorders have been shown to affect up to a third of HIV-infected patients, including deficits in middle-ear function and high-frequency sensorineural hearing loss (Chandrasekhar et al., 2000; Kohan, Rothstein, & Cohen, 1988). Severity of senorineural hearing loss is associated with severity of HIV disease progression as well as older age (Chandrasekhar et al., 2000). Additionally, studies have shown that HIV+ patients who complain of hearing loss demonstrate discernibly worse otopathology than those without complaints and should thus be taken seriously (Chandrasekhar et al., 2000; Kohan et al., 1988). However no studies have been found that examine to what extent, if any, ear disease influences neuropsychological performance.

Sensory neuropathy is the most prevalent neuropathy associated with HIV/AIDS. Specifically, distal sensory polyneuropathy (DSPN), a neuropathy in which the distal degeneration of long axons occurs, has been reported to affect from 19% to 66% of HIV+ patients (Letendre et al., 2009). Clinical manifestation of DSPN varies depending on HIV disease stage, type of antiretroviral therapy, current CD4 count, age, and height but can include painful dysesthesias, paresthesias, and numbness (Letendre et al., 2009; Schifitto et al., 2002; Watters et al., 2004). Such symptoms may compromise aspects of daily functioning and particularly quality of life. Previous studies have hypothesized that, pathologically, HIV-associated dementia and sensory neuropathy have similar pathways not only in the spinal cord but also in the brain and peripheral nerves (Tan & Guiloff, 1998; Tyor et al., 1995). In fact, Watters et al. (2004) found that 36% of older HIV-infected adults (≥50 years old) had both sensory DSPN and HIV-associated dementia. However, directionality was not examined in this study, so it is unclear if this relationship reflects independent indicators of disease severity rather than the impact of DSPN on cognitive functioning. Future studies are needed to directly examine the potential influence of sensory neuropathy on neuropsychological performance.

ASSESSMENTS

Establishing the measures that will be most sensitive and specific in detecting neuropsychological impairment, functional status, as well as psychiatric and symptom assessment in individuals with HIV infection is critical for determining the course and implications of the disease. Determining accurate diagnoses in the context of HIV infection is also essential, to facilitate communication of research findings and in tailoring patient intervention and treatment (American Association of Neurology, 1991). Identification of the presentation and etiology of cognitive and psychiatric symptoms is critical to establishing effective treatment strategies. Additionally, misdiagnosis of neurodegenerative and psychiatric disorders has important social and health care consequences (e.g., a misdiagnosed patient may engage in activities that are inappropriate for his or her current symptoms and may inadvertently misuse health care dollars). A better understanding of HIV-associated cognitive and functional declines as well as co-occurring conditions can enhance the ability to diagnose and successfully treat these impairments.

In response to such needs, the guidelines for classifying HAND were updated to include additional operationalization of the diagnostic criteria for determining neurocognitive and daily functioning decline (Antinori et al., 2007). More specifically, the current nomenclature for diagnosing "asymptomatic" HAND (i.e., asymptomatic neurocognitive impairment; ANI) requires neurocognitive deficits in at least two ability domains that are attributable to HIV infection but that do not meaningfully influence daily functioning (Antinori et al., 2007). In contrast, "symptomatic" HAND diagnoses require significant HIV-associated neurocognitive deficits that interfere with functional capabilities at either a mild (i.e., mild neurocognitive disorder, MND) or moderate-to-severe (HIV-associated dementia, HAD) level. Such guidelines provide clear and concrete assessments and cutoffs that must be met in order to classify HAND, thereby enhancing the standardization and reliability of such diagnoses (see Antinori et al., 2007, for in-depth discussion of recommended measures and criteria listings).

In terms of assessing for co-occurring conditions in HIV, several general types of measures exist, including self-report of complaints, performance-based ability measures, and clinician-rated assessments. For a full listing of the gold-standard measures used to assess comorbid conditions in HIV+ individuals, see Table 11.1.

Table 11.1 Gold Standard Assessments of Secondary Influences on Neuropsychological Performance in HIV

	Levels of Evidence[†]	Importance[‡]
Depression		*****
Beck Depression Inventory–II	*****	
Hamilton Rating Scale for Depression	****	
POMS—Depression/Dejection subscale	***	
Structured psychiatric clinical interview (e.g., SCID, CIDI)	*****	
Anxiety		****
Beck Anxiety Inventory	*****	
Hamilton Rating Scale for Anxiety	****	
POMS—Tension/Anxiety subscale	**	
Spielberger State-Trait Anxiety Inventory	***	
Structured psychiatric clinical interview (e.g., SCID, CIDI)	*****	
Bipolar		****
Young Mania Rating Scale	**	
Beck Depression Inventory–II	****	
Structured psychiatric clinical interview (e.g., SCID, CIDI)	*****	

(Continued)

Table 11.1 (Continued)

	Levels of Evidence	Importance
Constitutional Symptoms		***
ACTG Medication Adherence Questionnaire	***	
Chalder Fatigue Scale	*	
Fatigue Severity Scale	**	
Brief Symptom Inventory	*****	
Clinical interview (e.g., clinician-developed symptom checklist)	*****	
Apathy		***
POMS—Apathy/Fatigue subscale	**	
Neuropsychiatric interview (NPI)	***	
Suboptimal Effort		****
Hiscock Digit Memory Test	****	
Portland Digit Recognition Test	*	
WMS-R (embedded effort index)	*****	
Recognition Memory Test	**	
Test of Memory Malingering	***	
Pain		**
Brief Pain Inventory (Cleeland, 1989)	****	
Memorial Symptom Assessment Scale	****	
MOS-HIV Health Survey (pain subscale)	*****	
Sensory & Perceptual Deficits		****
Reitan-Kløve Sensory–Perceptual Exam	*	
University of Pennsylvania Smell Identification Test	****	
Ophthalmological examination	*****	
Audiological examination	*****	
Neurological examination (e.g., neuropathy)	*****	

Support ranges from *poor to *****strong support.

[†]Levels of Evidence: indicates the frequency with which measure has been used in peer-reviewed studies examining people with HIV infection (i.e., number of studies that were found in a literature search using the measure name and "HIV" in the search field).

[‡]Levels of Importance: indicates the importance of evaluating the secondary factor in HIV as rated by a combination of how common the secondary condition occurs in HIV as well as the impact the condition has on neurocognition, everyday functioning, and general quality of life in people with HIV.

Abbreviations: ACTG, AIDS Clinical Trial Group; CIDI, Composite International Diagnostic Interview; MOS-HIV Health Survey, Medical Outcomes Study HIV Health Survey; POMS, Profile of Mood States; SCID, Structured Clinical Interview for *DSM-IV-R*; WMS-R, Wechsler Memory Scale–Revised.

Self-report measures remain the most common assessments used in psychiatric and somatic symptom evaluations. Self-report measures have several advantages, including low cost, minimal participant burden, and high face validity. However, self-report can be a susceptible to social desirability and recall inaccuracies or biases, which may over- or underestimate the severity of such conditions. In particular, depressed mood has been shown to inflate self-reported cognitive complaints among HIV+ individuals (Rourke et al., 1999; Thames et al., 2010). Although for some conditions, such as evaluation of pain, self-report assessment is the gold standard, complaints on such measures should be taken within the context of the patient, including psychosocial factors (e.g., vocational functioning, homelessness), which could influence outcomes.

Performance-based measures evaluate patients' ability to complete tasks relevant to the construct in question (Moore et al., 2007). Of the conditions discussed, performance-based measures would be most appropriate when evaluating suboptimal effort (e.g., SVTs). During such tasks, important information can be gathered from both the performance score on the task as well as behavioral observation of strategies used by the patient, which cannot be assessed via self-report measures. However, performance-based assessments can be time-intensive and require additional training and tools to administer. Yet they have been shown to be highly valid and reliable in predicting outcomes and may be less influenced by affective state than self-report measures (Blackstone et al., 2012).

Clinician-rated assessments incorporate the trained judgment of the task administrator, allowing the administrator the final verdict in determining presence and severity of the symptoms assessed. A disadvantage of clinician-rated evaluations is that they can only be administered by a clinician or by personnel who are highly trained on the measure; these measures require more time and potential costs. On the other hand, the advantage of these measures is the additional training and, therefore, judgment that is incorporated into such evaluations. For example, if a patient is clearly depressed when reporting somatic complaints, the test administrator can take that into account in his or her ratings.

CASE STUDY

In order to illustrate the points raised in this chapter regarding the role of secondary factors in the expression of neurocognitive deficits among HIV-infected persons, we present a case study here. This case is an example of a person who has significant secondary influences that do not result in neurocognitive impairment. Some individuals with these influences may indeed show neurocognitive impairments; yet the prototypical error that we have routinely observed among clinicians is that the presence of these secondary factors necessitates neurocognitive impairment. While the data below are generated from an actual participant evaluated at our research center, we have altered some information not critical to the neuropsychological outcomes to maintain confidentiality.

Background

Mr. Webb (a pseudonym) is a 42-year-old, English-speaking, Caucasian man with 11 years of formal education. He has no history of learning disabilities or special education, but did leave school early because of behavioral problems. He has been unemployed for the past 8 years and his highest level of employment attained was as an apartment manager. He has been unable to hold a job because of his substance use difficulties. He has been married for the past 10 years. The patient was first diagnosed with HIV infection when he was 24 years of age. He meets criteria for AIDS as a result of having a CD4 T-cell count <200 at some point in his life. Currently, Mr. Webb's plasma HIV RNA viral levels are undetectable and his most recent CD4 count is 260. He is currently taking a common protease inhibitor–based regimen to manage his HIV disease. In terms of other medical comorbidities, he is hepatitis C antibody negative and is considered to be in excellent overall health.

Mr. Webb has a significant psychiatric and substance abuse history. He was first diagnosed with major depressive disorder at the age of 28. He currently meets DSM-IV criteria for major depressive disorder, and his self-reported depressive symptoms according to the Beck Depression Inventory–II are in the mild range (i.e., 19). Mr. Webb also has lifetime diagnoses of alcohol and cocaine abuse and methamphetamine dependence. His substance abuse and dependence problems began when he was 18, and he used a significant amount of alcohol (approximately 12 drinks per day for 24 years), cocaine (approximately 0.1 g/day for approximately 12 years), and methamphetamine (approximately 0.5 g/day for 24 years). He stopped using methamphetamine 4 months prior to the present evaluation. He has not used cocaine for 5 years. He reported 1.25 g marijuana use 2 days before testing. Mr. Webb is currently taking a selective serotonin reuptake inhibitor for depression and a protease inhibitor–based anti-HIV medication for HIV. He reported taking both medications this morning. Other than over-the-counter pain medications, he is taking no other medications.

In addition, Mr. Webb reports some secondary factors that may influence his neurocognitive testing. Specifically, he complained of constitutional symptoms consistent with HIV infection, including fatigue and diarrhea (likely a side effect of his antiretroviral medications). He has been experiencing these symptoms for the last 4 years. He also reports mild-to-moderate neuropathic pain that occurs primarily in the fingers of both hands.

Behavioral Observations

Mr. Webb was well groomed and on time for his appointment. He reported having a restful night of sleep the night before the assessment. He was alert and oriented to time, date, and place. The examiner reported a friendly demeanor, adequate effort and cooperation, a good ability to understand and follow directions, and no noticeable sensory or perceptual deficits. Certain neuropsychological tests requiring intact color vision were not administered, since the participant is colorblind.

The examiner also noted that the participant was often tangential and needed a great deal of redirection during the evaluation.

Neuropsychological Test Results

Mr. Webb's effort was good as evidenced by his perfect score on the Hiscock Digit Memory Test. Mr. Webb performed well on a test of basic word identification, indicating an estimated verbal IQ of 117 based on the Wide Range Achievement Test–3. On a comprehensive battery of neurocognitive tests covering seven domains of functioning, Mr. Webb also performed well. Utilizing T-scores corrected for age, education, sex, and ethnicity, Mr. Webb performed in the normal range in the domains of verbal fluency, motor skills, working memory, executive functioning, speed of information processing, and learning. He evidenced isolated mild impairment in the domain of delayed verbal recall, as he was only able to retain 4 of 12 words after a 20-minute delay on a standardized list-learning test. With regard to visual recall, his delayed recall was within normal limits and his percent retained was 100%. Overall, his neuropsychological performance was considered to be normal (see Table 11.2). Mr. Webb only reported one instrumental activity of daily living (IADL) complaint (current unemployment), which represents a significant downward change from his previous positions in the hospitality and retail business. Mr. Webb did not report any cognitive complaints in his everyday functioning and is considered to be functionally independent.

RELEVANCE OF CASE STUDY TO LITERATURE REVIEW

Mr. Webb represents an HIV-infected individual presenting with several secondary factors (e.g., neuropathic pain, fatigue) and comorbidities (e.g., depression, history of significant substance use) that are common within the HIV population. Consistent with our literature review above, however, despite these additional risk factors, Mr. Webb presents with intact neurocognitive functioning and reported independence in his everyday functioning. Certainly, not all persons with Mr. Webb's risk factors are cognitively normal, but it is important to note that the presence of secondary factors (and other comorbidities) does not necessitate neurocognitive impairment in individuals with HIV infection.

CONCLUSIONS AND FUTURE DIRECTIONS

In summary, from the literature and data available, there do not appear to be many significant secondary influences on neuropsychological performance in the context of HIV infection. Those contributing factors that impact cognition the most appear to be co-occurring bipolar disorder, apathy, and, to a lesser extent, suboptimal effort. Specifically, if comorbid bipolar disorder is hypothesized,

Table 11.2 SUMMARY OF MR. WEBB'S NEUROPSYCHOLOGICAL PERFORMANCE BY ABILITY DOMAIN (RAW AND T-SCORES)

Test	Raw Score	T-Score
Suboptimal Effort		
Hiscock Digit Memory Test	100%	
WRAT-3 Reading	57	61
Speed of Information Processing		
WAIS-III Digit Symbol	60	42
WAIS-III Symbol Search	41	62
WAIS-III SIP Index	99	52
Trail-Making: Part A	20	59
Verbal Fluency		
COWAT—correct words	31	42
Animals—correct words	22	52
Actions—correct words	23	64
Learning		
HVLT-R total recall	26	48
BVMT-R total recall	26	53
Memory		
HVLT-R percent retained	40	24
BVMT-R percent retained	92	40
Executive Functions		
Trail Making: Part B	58	54
Working Memory		
PASAT 50	35	47
WMS-III Spatial Span	19	59
Motor		
Pegboard: dominant	61	56
Pegboard: nondominant	74	46

Abbreviations: BVMT-R, Brief Visuospatial Memory Test–Revised; COWAT, Controlled Oral Word Association Test; HVLT-R, Hopkins Verbal Learning Test–Revised; PASAT, Paced Auditory Serial Addition Test; WAIS-III, Wechsler Adult Intelligence Scale–III; WMS-III, Wechsler Memory Scale–III; WRAT-3, Wide Range Achievement Test–3.

performance on verbal memory and executive functions should be interpreted with caution, as these domains have been shown to be disparately affected by both conditions. Additionally, tasks of working memory, episodic memory, and executive functions may be associated with elevated levels of apathy and should thus be closely examined if apathy is reported. Lastly, although the reported prevalence of suboptimal effort is low in individuals with HIV (2–7%), individual effort is a critical aspect in obtaining valid neuropsychological data in any population and should be evaluated and taken into account accordingly. Although the somatic and medical factors examined (i.e., constitutional symptoms, pain, sensory and perceptual deficits) do not appear to influence neuropsychological performance, further research is clearly necessary in this area to rule them out. Instead, these physical symptoms may be best conceptualized as clinical indicators of disease progression and status of everyday functioning, two clinically relevant aspects to patient care. Similarly, depressed and anxious mood states have not been shown to be significantly associated with cognitive performance in HIV+ individuals but have important implications for patients' everyday functioning, including vocational status and antiretroviral medication adherence. Therefore, although there are several factors that do not appear to directly influence cognitive performance, they do play a significant role in important "real-life" aspects of individuals with HIV, including both quality of life and daily functional abilities, and should be taken into account accordingly.

Importantly, the general absence of overt cognitive manifestation with several of these secondary conditions does not preclude any changes or disruptions at the neural level. Neuroimaging will play an important role in future studies examining the interplay among co-occurring conditions in HIV. Disentangling the etiology of each factor at the neuropathic level will help elucidate any potential differential influences that each symptomatic condition contributes to neurocognitive functioning in the context of HIV infection and is an integral area of study that clearly warrants more research.

ACKNOWLEDGMENTS

The HIV Neurobehavioral Research Center (HNRC) is supported by Center award MH62512, T32DA031098, and R01MH073419. We also thank Matthew Dawson for his help in preparing this book chapter.

The San Diego HIV Neurobehavioral Research Center [HNRC] group is affiliated with the University of California, San Diego, the Naval Hospital, San Diego, and the Veterans Affairs San Diego Healthcare System, and includes Director: Igor Grant, M.D.; Co-Directors: J. Hampton Atkinson, M.D., Ronald J. Ellis, M.D., Ph.D., and J. Allen McCutchan, M.D.; Center Manager: Thomas D. Marcotte, Ph.D.; Jennifer Marquie-Beck, M.P.H.; Melanie Sherman; Neuromedical Component: Ronald J. Ellis, M.D., Ph.D. (P.I.), J. Allen McCutchan, M.D., Scott Letendre, M.D., Edmund Capparelli, Pharm.D., Rachel Schrier, Ph.D., Terry Alexander, R.N., Debra Rosario, M.P.H., Shannon LeBlanc; Neurobehavioral Component: Robert K. Heaton, Ph.D. (P.I.), Steven Paul Woods, Psy.D., Mariana Cherner, Ph.D., David J. Moore, Ph.D., Matthew Dawson; Neuroimaging Component: Terry Jernigan, Ph.D. (P.I.), Christine Fennema-Notestine, Ph.D., Sarah L. Archibald, M.A., John Hesselink, M.D., Jacopo Annese, Ph.D., Michael J. Taylor, Ph.D.; Neurobiology Component: Eliezer Masliah, M.D. (P.I.), Cristian Achim, M.D., Ph.D., Ian Everall, FRCPsych., FRCPath., Ph.D. (Consultant); Neurovirology Component: Douglas Richman, M.D. (P.I.), David M. Smith, M.D.; International Component: J. Allen McCutchan, M.D. (P.I.); Developmental Component: Cristian Achim, M.D.,

Ph.D. (P.I.), Stuart Lipton, M.D., Ph.D.; Participant Accrual and Retention Unit: J. Hampton Atkinson, M.D. (P.I.), Jenifer Marquie Beck, M.P.H.; Data Management Unit: Anthony C. Gamst, Ph.D. (P.I.), Clint Cushman (Data Systems Manager); Statistics Unit: Ian Abramson, Ph.D. (P.I.), Florin Vaida, Ph.D., Reena Deutsch, Ph.D., Anya Umlauf, M.S.

The views expressed in this chapter are those of the authors and do not reflect the official policy or position of the Department of the Navy, Department of Defense, or the United States Government.

APPENDIX 11.1

Abbreviations

ACI:	Attention/Concentration Index (of the Wechsler Memory Scale–Revised)
ACTG:	AIDS Clinical Trial Group
AIDS:	acquired immune deficiency syndrome
ANI:	asymptomatic neurocognitive impairment
BD:	bipolar disorder
BPI:	Brief Pain Inventory
BVMT-R:	Brief Visuospatial Memory Test–Revised
CD4:	cluster of differentiation 4
CDC:	Centers for Disease Control and Prevention
CIDI:	Composite International Diagnostic Interview
CNS:	central nervous system
COWAT:	Controlled Oral Word Association Test
CSF:	cerebrospinal fluid
CWS:	cotton wool spots
DSM-IV:	*Diagnostic and Statistical Manual of Mental Disorders*—fourth edition
DSPN:	distal sensory polyneuropathy
GMI:	General Memory Index (of the Wechsler Memory Scale–Revised)
HAART:	highly active antiretroviral therapy
HAD:	HIV-associated dementia
HAND:	HIV-associated neurocognitive disorder
HCV:	hepatitis C virus
HDMT:	Hiscock Digit Memory Test
HIV:	human immunodeficiency virus–1
HVLT-R:	Hopkins Verbal Learning Test-Revised
IADL:	instrumental activities of daily living
MDD:	major depressive disorder
MDM:	monocyte derived macrophages
MND:	mild neurocognitive disorder
MOS-HIV Health Survey:	Medical Outcomes Study HIV Health Survey

Nadir CD4:	lowest ever CD4 count
NP:	neuropsychological
PASAT:	Paced Auditory Serial Addition Test
POMS:	Profile of Mood States
RNA:	ribonucleic acid
SCID:	Structured Clinical Interview for DSM-IV-R
SVT:	symptom validity test
WAIS-III:	Wechsler Adult Intelligence Scale-III
WMS-III:	Wechsler Memory Scale-III
WMS-R:	Wechsler Memory Scale-Revised
WRAT-3:	Wide Range Achievement Test-3

Appendix 11.2

Decision-tree for diagnosing HIV-associated neurocognitive disorders (HAND) according to the "Frascati criteria."

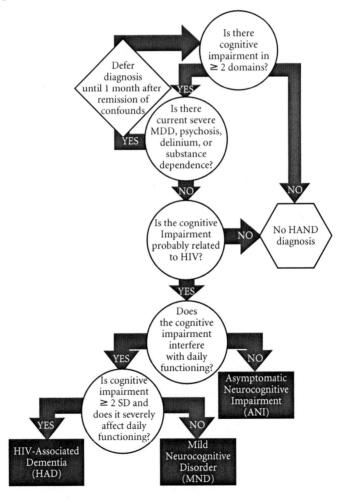

Notes

1. Acronyms frequently used in this chapter are spelled out in Appendix 11.1.

References

American Psychiatric Association. (2000). *Diagnostic and statistical manual of mental disorders* (4th ed., text rev.). Washington, DC: Author.

Angelino, A. F., & Treisman, G. J. (2008). Issues in co-morbid severe mental illnesses in HIV infected individuals. *International Review of Psychiatry, 20*(1), 95–101.

Aouizerat, B. E., Miaskowski, C. A., Gay, C., Portillo, C. J., Coggins, T., Davids, H., et al. (2010). Risk factors and symptoms associated with pain in HIV-infected adults. *Journal of the Association of Nurses in AIDS Care, 21*(2), 125–133.

Austin, M. P., Ross, M., Murray, C., O'Cairoll, R. E., Ebmeier, K. P., & Goodwin, G. M. (1992). Cognitive function in major depression. *Journal of Affective Disorders, 25*(1), 21–29.

Bearden, C. E., Glahn, D. C., Monkul, E. S., Barrett, J., Najt, P., Kaur, S., et al. (2006). Sources of declarative memory impairment in bipolar disorder: mnemonic processes and clinical features. *Journal of Psychiatric Research, 40*(1), 47–58.

Berk., M., Berk., L., & Castle, D. (2004). A collaborative approach to the treatment alliance in bipolar disoder. *Bipolar Disorder, 6*, 504–518.

Beyer, J., Kuchibhatla, M., Gersing, K., & Krishnan, K. R. R. (2005). Medical comorbidity in a bipolar outpatient clinical population. *Neuropsychopharmacology, 30*, 401–404.

Beyer, J., Taylor, L., Gersing, K. R., & Krishnan, R. R. (2007). Prevalence of HIV infection in a general psychiatric outpatient population. *Psychosomatics, 48*, 31–37.

Bianchini, K. J., Mathias, C. W., & Greve, K. W. (2001). Symptom validity testing: A critical review. *The Clinical Neuropsychologist, 15*, 19–45.

Blackstone, K., Moore, D. J., Heaton, R. K., Franklin, D. R., Woods, S. P., Clifford, D. B., et al., for the CHARTER Group (2012). Diagnosing symptomatic HIV-associated neurocognitive disorders: Self-report versus performance-based assessment of everyday functioning. *Journal of the International Neuropsychological Society, 18*(1), 79–88.

Bogdanova, Y., Díaz-Santos, M., & Cronin-Golomb, A. (2010). Neurocognitive correlates of alexithymia in asymptomatic individuals with HIV. *Neuropsychologia, 48*(5), 1295–1304.

Breitbart, W., McDonald, M. V., Rosenfeld., B., Passik, S. D., Hewitt, D., Thaler, H., & Portenoy, R. K. (1996). Pain in ambulatory AIDS patients: I. Pain characteristics and medical correlates. *Pain, 68*, 315–321.

Brody, D., Serby, M., Etienne, N., & Kalkstein, D. S. (1991). Olfactory identification deficits in HIV infection. *American Journal of Psychiatry, 148*, 248–250.

Brown, S. C., Glass, J. M., & Park, D. C. (2002). The relationship of pain and depression to cognitive function in rheumatoid arthritis patients. *Pain, 96*(3), 279–284.

Carey, C. L., Woods, S. P., Gonzalez, R., Conocer, E., Marcotte, T. D., Grant, I., Heaton, R. K., & the HNRC Group (2004). Predictive validity of global deficit scores in detecting neuropsychological impairment in HIV infection. *Journal of Clinical and Experimental Neuropsychology, 26*(3), 307–319.

Carter, S. L., Rourke, S. B., Murji, S., Shore, D., & Rourke, B. P. (2003). Cognitive complaints, depression, medical symptoms, and their association with neuropsychological functioning in HIV infection: A structural equation model analysis. *Neuropsychology, 17*(3), 410–419.

Cassens, G., Wolfe, L., & Zola, M. (1990). The neuropsychology of depression. *Journal of Neuropsychiatry in Clinical Neuroscience, 2*(2), 202–213.

Castellon, S. A., Hinkin, C. H., & Myers, H. F. (1998). Apathy, depression, and cognitive performance in HIV-1 infection. *The Journal of Neuropsychiatry and Clinical Neurosciences, 10*, 320–329.

Castellon, S. A., Hinkin, C. H., & Myers, H. F. (2000). Neuropsychiatric disturbance is associated with executive dysfunction in HIV-1 infection. *Journal of the International Neuropsychological Society, 6*(3), 336–347.

Chandrasekhar, S. S., Connelly, P. E., Brahmbhatt, S. S., Shah, C. S., Kloser, P. C., & Baredes, S. (2000). Otologic and audiologic evaluation of human immunodeficiency virus-infected patients. *American Journal of Otolaryngology, 21*(1), 1–9.

Cherner, M., Letendre, S., Heaton, R. K., Durelle, J., Marquie-Beck, J., Gragg, B., Grant, I., & the HIV Neurobehavioral Research Center Group (2005). Hepatitis C augments cognitive deficits associated with HIV infection and methamphetamine. *Neurology, 64*(8), 1343–1347.

Ciesla, J. A., & Roberts, J. E. (2001). Meta-analysis of the relationship between HIV infection and risk for depressive disorders. *American Journal of Psychiatry, 158*, 725–730.

Clark, L., & Goodwin, G. M. (2004). State- and trait-related deficits in sustained attention in bipolar disorder. *European Archives of Psychiatry and Clinical Neuroscience, 254*(2), 61–68.

Cole, M. A., Castellon, S. A., Perkins, A. C., Ureno, O. S., Robinet, M. B., Reinhard, M. J., et al. (2007). Relationship between psychiatric status and frontal-subcortical systems in HIV-infected individuals. *Journal of the International Neuropsychological Society, 13*(3), 549–554.

Colom, F., Vieta, E., Tacchi, M. J., Sanchez-Moreno, J., & Scott, J. (2005). Identifying and improving non-adherence in bipolar disorders. *Bipolar Disorder, 7*(Suppl 5), S24–S31.

Cruess, D. G., Evans, D. L., Repetto, M. J., Gettes, D., Douglas, S. D., & Petitto, J. M. (2003). Prevalence, diagnosis, and pharmacological treatment of mood disorders in HIV disease. *Biological Psychiatry, 54*(3), 307–316.

Cysique, L. A., Deutsch, R., Atkinson, J. H., Young, C., Marcotte, T. D., Dawson, L., et al., & the HNRC Group (2007). Incident depression does not affect neuropsychological functioning in HIV-infected men. *Journal of the International Neuropsychological Society, 13*, 1–11.

Danion, J., Neunrither, C., & Kreger-Finance, F. (1987). Compliance with long-term lithium treatment in major affective disorders. *Pharmacopsychiatry, 20*, 230–231.

Darko, D. F., Miller, J. C., Gallen C., White, J., Koziol, J., Brown, S. J., et al. (1995). Sleep electroencephalogram delta-frequency amplitude, night plasma levels of tumor necrosis factor alpha, and human immunodeficiency virus infection. *Proceedings of the National Academy of Science of the U.S.A., 92*, 12080–12084.

Ellen, S. R., Judd, F. K., Mijch, A. M., & Cockram, A. (1999). Secondary mania in patients with HIV infection. *Australian and New Zealand Journal of Psychiatry, 33*(3), 353–360.

Elliot, A. (1998). Anxiety and HIV. *STEP Perspective, 98*, 11–14.

Ellis, R. J., Deutsch, R., Heaton, R. K., Marcotte, T. D., McCutchan, J. A., Nelson, J. A., et al. (1997). Neurocognitive impairment is an independent risk factor for death in HIV infection. *Archives of Neurology, 54*(4), 416–424.

Ferrando, S., Evans, S., Goggin, K., Sewell, M., Fishman, B., & Rabkin, J. (1998). Fatigue in HIV illness: Relationship to depression, physical limitations, and disability. *Psychosomatic Medicine, 60*, 759–764.

Freeman, W. R., McCutchan, J. A., Arevalo, J. F., Wolfson, T., Marcotte, T. D., Heaton, R. K., Grant, I., & the HNRC Group (2004). The relationship between AIDS retinal cotton wool spots and neuropsychological impairment in HIV-positive individuals in the pre-highly active antiretroviral therapy era. *Ocular Immunology and Inflammation, 12*, 25–33.

Geier, S. A., Hammel, G., Bogner, J. R., Kronawitter, U., Berninger, T., & Goebel, F. D. (1994). HIV-related ocular microangiopathic syndrome and color contrast sensitivity. *Investigative Ophthalmology & Visual Science, 35*, 3011–3021.

Geier, S. A., Perro, C., Klaub, V., Naber, D., Kronawitter, U., Bogner, J. R., et al. (1992). HIV-related ocular microanguipathic syndrome and cognitive functioning. *Journal of Acquired Immune Deficiency Syndromes, 6*, 252–258.

Goggin, K. J., Zisook, S., Heaton, R. K., Atkinson, J. H., Marshall, S., McCutchan, J. A., et al., & The HNRC Group (1997). Neuropsychological performance of HIV-1 infected men with major depression. *Journal of the International Neuropsychological Society, 3*, 457–464.

Grant, I., Oishen, R. A., Atkinson, J. H., Heaton, R. K., Nelson, J., McCutchan, J. A., et al. (1993). Depressed mood does not explain neuropsychological deficits in HIV-infected persons. *Neuropsychology, 7*, 53–61.

Green, M. F. (2006). Cognitive impairment and functional outcomes in schizophrenia and bipolar disorder. *Journal of Clinical Psychiatry, 67*(e12).

Green, M. J., Cahill, C. M., & Malhi, G. S. (2007). The cognitive and neurophysiological basis of emotion dysregulation in bipolar disorder. *Journal of Affective Disorders, 103*(1–3), 29–42.

Heaton, R. K., Grant, I., Butters, N., White, D. A., Kirson, D., Atkinson, J. H., et al., & the HNRC Group (1995). The HNRC 500—neuropsychology of HIV infection at different disease stages. HIV Neurobehavioral Research Center. *Journal of the International Neuropsychological Society, 1*(3), 231–251.

Heaton, R. K., Marcotte, T. D., Mindt, M. R., Sadek, J., Moore, D. J., Bentley, H., et al., & the HNRC Group (2004). The impact of HIV-associated neuropsychological impairment on everyday functioning. *Journal of the International Neuropsychological Society, 10*(3), 317–331.

Hinkin, C. H., Castellon, S. A., Durvasula, R. S., Hardy, D. J., Lam, M. N., Mason, K. I., et al. (2002). Medication adherence among HIV+ adults: Effects of cognitive dysfunction and regimen complexity. *Neurology, 59*, 1944–1950.

Hinkin, C. H., Hardy, D. J., Mason, K. I., Castellon, S. A., Durvasula, R. A., Lam, M. N., & Stefaniak, M. (2004). Medication adherence in HIV-infected adults: Effects of patient age, cognitive status, and substance abuse. *AIDS, 18*(Suppl 1), S19–S25.

Hiscock, M., & Hiscock, C. K. (1989). Refining the forced-choice method for the detection of malingering. *Journal of Clinical and Experimental Neuropsychology, 11*, 967–974.

Hoare, J., Fouche, J. P., Spottiswoode, B., Joska, J. A., Schoeman, R., Stein, D. J., & Carey, P. D. J. (2010). White matter correlates of apathy in HIV-positive subjects: A diffusion tensor imaging study. *Neuropsychiatry Clinical Neuroscience, 22*(3), 313–20.

Holzemer, W. L., Henry, S. B., & Reilly, C. A. (1998). Assessing and managing pain in AIDS care: The patient perspective. *Journal of the Association of Nurses in AIDS Care, 9*(1), 22–30.

Hornung, D. E., Kurtz, D. B., Bradshaw, C. B., Seipel, D. M., Kent, P. F., Blair, D. C., & Emko, P. (1998). The olfactory loss that accompanies an HIV infection. *Physiology & Behavior, 64*(4), 549–556.

Hult, B., Chana, G., Masliah, E., & Everall, I. (2008). Neurobiology of HIV. *International Review of Psychiatry, 20*(1), 3–13.

Iverson, G. L., Slick, D. J., & Franzen, M. D. (2000). Evaluation of a WMS-R malingering index in a non-litigating clinical sample. *Journal of Clinical and Experiment Neuropsychology, 22*(2), 191–197.

Jernigan, T. L., Archibald, S. L., Fennema-Notestine, C., Taylor, M. J., Theilmann, R. J., Julaton, M. D., et al., for the CHARTER Group (2011). Clinical factors related to brain structure in HIV: The CHARTER study. *Journal of Neurovirology, 17*(3), 248–257.

Kohan, D., Rothstein, S. G., & Cohen, N. L. (1988). Otologic disease in paitents with acquired immunodeficiny syndrome. *Annals of Otology, Rhinology, and Laryngology, 97,* 636–640.

Kowal, J., Overduin, L. Y., Balfour, L., Tasca, G. A., Corace, K., & Cameron, W. (2008). The role of the psychological and behavioral variables in quality of life and the experience of bodily pain among persons living with HIV. *Journal of Pain and Symptom Management, 36*(3), 247–258.

Kurtz, M. M., & Gerraty, R. T. (2009). A meta-analytic investigation of neurocognitive deficits in bipolar illness: Profile and effects of clinical state. *Neuropsychology, 23*(5), 551–562.

Lawton, M. P., & Brody, E. M. (1969). Assessment of older people: Self-maintaining and instrucmental activities of daily living. *Gerontologist, 9,* 179–186.

Letendre, S. L., Ellis, R. J., Everall, I., Ances, B., Bharti, A., & McCutchan, J. A. (2009). Neurologic complications of HIV disease and their treatment. *Topics in HIV Medicine, 17*(2), 46–56.

Mahon, K., Burdick, K. E., & Szeszko, P. R. (2010). A role for white matter abnormalities in the pathophysiology of bipolar disorder. *Neuroscience & Biobehavioral Reviews, 34*(4), 533–554.

Maier, S. F. (2003). Bidirectional immune-brain communication: Implications for understanding stress, pain, and cognition *Brain, Behavior, and Immunity, 17*(2), 69–85.

Maier, S. F., & Watkin, L. R. (2003). Immune-to-central nervous system communication and its role in modulating pain and cognition: Implications for cancer and cancer treatment. *Brain, Behavior, and Immunity, 17*(S1), 125–131.

Malhi, G. S., Ivanovski, B., Hadzi-Pavlovic, D., Mitchell, P. B., Vieta, E., & Sachdev, P. (2007). Neuropsychological deficits and functional impairment in bipolar depression, hypomania and euthymia. *Bipolar Disorder, 9*(1–2), 114–125.

Mapou, R. L., Law, W. A., Martin, A., Kampen, D., Salzar, A. M., & Rundell, J. R. (1993). Neuropsychological performance, mood, and complaints of cognitive and motor difficulties in individuals infected with the human immunodeficiency virus. *The Journal of Neuropsychiatry and Clinical Neurosciences, 5,* 86–93.

Marcus, K. S., Kerns, R. D., Rosenfeld, B., & Breitbart, W. (2000). HIV/AIDS-related pain as a chronic pain condition: Implications of a biopsychosocial model for comprehensive assessment and effective management. *Pain Medicine, 1*(3), 260–273.

Martinez-Aran, A., Vieta, E., Colom, F., Torrent, C., Sanchez-Moreno, J., Reinares, M., et al. (2004). Cognitive impairment in euthymic bipolar patients: Implications for clinical and functional outcome. *Bipolar Disorder, 6*(3), 224–232.

Martinez-Aran, A., Vieta, E., Reinares, M., Colom, F., Torrent, C., Sanchez-Moreno, J., et al. (2004). Cognitive function across manic or hypomanic, depressed, and euthymic states in bipolar disorder. *American Journal of Psychiatry, 161*(2), 262–270.

McKinnon, K., Cournos, F., Sugden, R., Guido, J. R., Herman, R. (1996). The relative contributions of psychiatric symptoms and AIDS knowledge to HIV risk behaviors among people with severe mental illness. *Journal of Clinical Psychiatry, 57,* 506–513.

Millikin, C. P., Rourke, S. B., Halman, M. H., & Power, C. (2003). Fatigue in HIV/AIDS is associated with depression and subjective neurocognitive complaints but not neuropsychological functioning. *Journal of Clinical and Experimental Neuropsychology, 25*(2), 201–215.

Mittenberg, W., Azrin, R., Millsaps, C., & Heilbronner, R. (1993). Identification of malingered head injury on the Wechsler Memory Scale—Revised. *Psychological Assessment, 5*, 34–40.

Moberg, P. J., Pearlson, G. D., Speedie, L. J., Lipsey, J. R., Strauss, M. E., & Folstein, S. E. (1987). Olfactory recognition: Differential impairments in early and late Huntington's and Alzheimer's diseases. *Journal of Clinical and Experimental Neuropsychology, 9*, 650–664.

Mohamed, M. A., Barker, P. B., Skolasky, R. L., Selnes, O. A., Moxley, R. T., Pomper, M. G., & Sacktor, N. C. (2010). Brain metabolism and cognitive impairment in HIV: A 3-T magnetic resonance spectroscopy study. *Magnetic Resonance Imaging, 28*(9), 1251–1257.

Moore, D. J., Depp, C. A., Posada, C., Parikh, M., Bhatt, A., Moseley, S., et al., & the HNRC Group (2008). Risk for cognitive impairment among HIV-infected persons with bipolar disorder. *Dialogues in Clinical Neuroscience, 10*, 2, 256–260.

Moore, D. J., Woods, S. P., Lazzaretto, D. L., Depp, C. A., Atkinson, J. H., Heaton, R. K., et al. (2006). Cognitive impairment among individuals with bipolar disorder and HIV infection. *Journal of the International Neuropsychological Society, 11*(S1), 175.

Morgan, C. D., Nordin, S., & Murphy, C. (1995). Odor identification as an early marker for Alzheimer's disease: Impact of lexical functioning and detection sensitivity. *Journal of Clinical and Experimental Neuropsychology, 17*, 793–803.

Moroni, C., & Laurent, B. (2006). Pain and cognition. *Psychologie & Neuropsychiatrie du Vieillissement, 4*(1), 21–30.

Muñoz-Moreno, J. A., Fumaz, C. R., Ferrer, M. J., Prats, A., Negredo, E., Garolera, M., et al. (2008). Nadir CD4 cell count predicts neurocognitive impairment in HIV-infected patients. *AIDS Research in Human Retroviruses, 24*(10), 1301–1307.

Murphy, F. C., & Sahakian, B. J. (2001). Neuropsychology of bipolar disorder. *British Journal of Psychiatry Supplement, 41*, s120–127.

Navia, B. A., Jordan, B. D., & Price, R. W. (1986). The AIDS dementia complex: I. Clinical features. *Annals of Neurology, 19*(6), 517–524.

O'Cleirigh, C., Hart, T. A., & James C. A. (2008). HIV and Anxiety. M. J. Zvolensky & J. A. Smits (eds.), Anxiety in Health Behaviors and Physical Illness.

Paul, R. H., Brickman, A. M., Navia, B., Hinkin, C., Malloy, P. F., Jefferson, A. L., et al. (2005). Apathy is associated with volume of the nucleus accumbens in patients infected with HIV. *Journal of Neuropsychiatry & Clinical Neuroscience, 17*(2), 167–171.

Paul, R. H., Flanigan, T. P., Tashima, K., Cohen, R., Lawrence, J., Alt, E., et al. (2005). Apathy correlates with cognitive function but not CD4 status in patients with human immunodeficiency virus. *Journal of Neuropsychiatry & Clinical Neuroscience, 17*(1), 114–118.

Percides, M., Dunbar, N., Grunseit, A., Hall, W., & Cooper D. A. (1992). Anxiety, depression, and HIV related symptomatology across the spectrum of HIV disease. *Australian and New Zealand Journal of Psychiatry, 26*(4), 560–566.

Perkins, D. O., Laserman, J. Stern, R. A., Baum, S. F., Liao, D., Golden, R. N., & Evans, D. L. (1995). Somatic symptoms of HIV infection: Relationship to depressive symptoms and indicators of HIV disease. *American Journal of Psychiatry, 152*, 1776–1781.

Phillips, M. L., Drevets, W. C., Rauch, S. L., & Lane, R. (2003). Neurobiology of emotion perception II: Implications for major psychiatric disorders. *Biological Psychiatry, 54*(5), 515–528.

Posada, C., Moore, D. J., Letendre, S. L, Parikh, M., Gouaux, B., Umlauf, A., et al., & the HIV Neurobehavioral Research Center (HNRC) Group. (2012). Sustained attention deficits among HIV-infected individuals with bipolar disorder. *Journal of Neuropsychiatry & Clinical Neuroscience, 24*(1), 61–70.

Psychological Corporation. (1987). *Wechsler Memory Scale—Revised.* San Antonio, TX: Author.

Quiceno, J. I., Capparelli, E., & Sadun, A. A. (1992). Visual dysfunction without retinitis in patients with the acquired immunodeficiency syndrome. *American Journal of Ophthalmology, 113*, 8–13.

Quraishi, S., & Frangou, S. (2002). Neuropsychology of bipolar disorder: A review. *Journal of Affective Disorders, 72*(3), 209–226.

Rabkin, J. G. (2008). HIV and depression: 2008 review and update. *Current HIV/AIDS Reports, 5*, 163–171.

Razani, J., Murphy, C., Davidson, T. M., Grant, I., & McCutchan, A. (1996). Odor sensitivity is impaired in HIV-positive cognitively impaired patients. *Physiology & Behavior, 59*(4/5), 877–881.

Rippeth, J. D., Heaton, R. K., Carey, C. L., Marcotte, T. D., Moore, D. J., Gonzalez, R., et al., & the HNRC Group (2004). Methamphetamine dependence increases risk of neuropsychological impairment in HIV infected persons. *Journal of the International Neuropsychological Society, 10*(1), 1–14.

Robinson, L. J., Thompson, J. M., Gallagher, P., Goswami, U., Young, A. H., Ferrier, I. N., et al. (2006). A meta-analysis of cognitive deficits in euthymic patients with bipolar disorder. *Journal of Affective Disorders, 93*(1–3), 105–115.

Rourke, S. B., Halman, M. H., & Bassel, C. (1999). Neurocognitive complaints in HIV-infection and their relationship to depressive symptoms and neuropsychological functioning. *Journal of Clinical and Experimental Neuropsychology, 21*(6), 737–756.

Schifitto, G., McDermott, M. P., McArthur, J. C., Marder, K., Sacktor, N., Epstein, L., Kieburtz, K., & the Dana Consortium on the Therapy of HIV Dementia and Related Cognitive Disorders. (2002). Incidence of and risk factors for HIV-associated distal sensory polyneuropathy. *Neurology, 58*(12), 1764–1768.

Selnes, O. A. (2002). Neurocognitive aspects of medication adherence in HIV infection. *Journal of Acquired Immune Deficiency Syndrome, 31*(Suppl 3), S132–S135.

Sewell, D. D., Jeste, D. V., Atkinson, J. H., Heaton, R. K., Hesselink, J. R., Wiley, C., et al. (1994). HIV-associated psychosis: a study of 20 cases. San Diego HIV Neurobehavioral Research Center Group. *American Journal of Psychiatry, 151*(2), 237–242.

Slick, D. J., Hinkin, C. H., van Gorp, W., & Satz, P. (2001). Base rate of a WMS-R malingering index in a sample of non-compensation-seeking men infected with HIV-1. *Applied Neuropsychology, 8*, 185–189.

Strakowski, S. M., Adler, C. M., Holland, S. K., Mills, N., & DelBello, M. P. (2004). A preliminary FMRI study of sustained attention in euthymic, unmedicated bipolar disorder. *Neuropsychopharmacology, 29*(9), 1734–1740.

Tan, S. V., & Guiloff, R. J. (1998). Hypothesis on the pathogenesis of vacuolar myelopathy, dementia and peripheral neuropathy in AIDS. *Journal of Neurology Neurosurgery Psychiatry, 65*, 23–28.

Tate, D., Paul, R. H., Flanigan, T. P., Tashima, K., Nash, J., Adair, C., et al. (2003). The impact of apathy and depression on quality of life in patients infected with HIV. *AIDS Patient Care STDS, 17*(3), 115–120.

Tekin, S., & Cummings, L. J. (2002). Frontal-subcortical neuronal circuits and clinical neuropsychiatry: An update. *Journal of Psychosomatic Research, 53*, 647–654.

Tenhula, W. N., Szhizao, X., Madigan, M. C., et al. (1992). Morphometric comparisons of optic nerve axon loss in AIDS: Morphometric comparisons. *American Journal of Ophthalmology, 113*, 14–20.

Thames, A. D., Becker, B. W., Marcotte, T. D., Hines, L. J., Foley, J. M., Ramezani, A., et al. (2010). Depression, cognition, and self-appraisal of functional abilities in HIV: An examination of subjective appraisal versus objective performance. *The Clinical Neuropsychologist*, 1–20.

Tucker, J. S., Burnam, M. A., Sherbourne, C. D., Kung, F. K., & Gifford, A. L. (2003). Substance use and mental health correlates of nonadherence to antiretroviral medications in a sample of patients with human immunodeficiency virus infection. *The American Journal of Medicine, 114*(7), 573–580.

Tyor, W. R., Wesselingh, S. L. Griffin, J. W., McArthur, J. C., & Griffin, D. E. (1995). Unifying hypothesis for the pathogenesis of HIV-associated dementia complex, vacuolar myelopathy, and sensory neuropathy. *Journal of Acquired Immune Deficiency Syndromes & Human Retrovirology, 9*(4), 379–388.

Watters, M. R., Poff, P. W., Shiramizu, B. T., Holck, P. S., Fast, K. M. S., Shikuma, C. M., & Valcour, V. G. (2004). Symptomatic distal sensory polyneuropathy in HIV after age 50. *Neurology, 62*, 1378–1383.

Westervelt, J. H., McCaffrey, R. J., Cousins, J. P., Wagle, W. A., & Haase, R. F. (1997). Longitudinal analysis of olfactory deficits in HIV infection. *Archives of Clinical Neuropsychology, 12*(6), 557–565.

Woods, S. P., Carey, C. L., Moran, L. M., Dawson, M. S., Letendre, S. L., Grant, I., & the HIV Neurobehavioral Research Center (HNRC) Group. (2007). Frequency and predictors of self-reported prospective memory complaints in individuals infected with HIV. *Archives of Clinical Neuropsychology, 22*(2), 187–195.

Woods, S. P., Conover, E., Weinborn, M., Rippeth, J. D., Brill, R. M., Heaton, R. K., Grant, I., & the HNRC Group. (2003). Base rate of Hiscock Digit Memory Test failure in HIV-associated neurocognitive disorders. *The Clinical Neuropsychologist, 17*, 383–389.

12

Parkinson's Disease: Secondary Influences on Cognition

ALEXANDER I. TRÖSTER, LINDSAY P. PRIZER, AND
AMBER BAXLEY

Parkinson's disease (PD) is a movement disorder characterized by tremor, rigidity, bradykinesia, postural instability, or a combination of these symptoms. Contrary to James Parkinson's original description of the disease, it is widely recognized that cognition is mildly or severely compromised in many of those afflicted with PD. Numerous neuropsychiatric conditions such as depression, apathy, anxiety, psychosis, and sleep disorders can accompany PD, and, indeed, several of these conditions occur with greater frequency in PD than in the general population. In addition, antiparkinsonian (dopaminergic) medications such as levodopa and dopamine agonists are associated with hallucinations as well as excessive daytime sleepiness and paroxysmal sleep in patients with PD. This co-occurrence of PD and several neuropsychiatric conditions raises the question of whether conditions such as depression are a reaction to the disease, related to PD, independent pathophysiologic mechanisms, or a result of treatments such as medication or deep brain stimulation. Clinical neuropsychologists need to be aware of not only how PD affects cognition but also how some of these neuropsychiatric conditions might exert a secondary influence on neuropsychological test performance. Regardless of whether secondary influences represent an additive or interactive effect on cognition in PD, knowledge of such conditions' effects on cognition can facilitate etiological determination of cognitive compromise, treatment recommendations, and prognosis.

In this chapter, after reviewing the cognitive profile of PD, we identify several potential secondary influences on cognition, including depression, apathy, anxiety, hallucinations, and disorders of sleep and wakefulness. The impact of these conditions on performance on various neuropsychological instruments as well as on cognitive functioning (including attention, executive functions, language, visuo-perceptual functions, and memory) is described. Where possible, the magnitude of secondary influences on test performance is estimated by effect sizes of differences between PD patients with and without these comorbid conditions. We then offer recommendations for the quantitative assessment of various secondary conditions, typically by referring to expert consensus or evidence-based recommendations made by Movement Disorder Society (MDS) task forces. Where available, modifications in instrument diagnostic or screening cutoff scores for use in PD are identified.

COGNITIVE IMPAIRMENT IN PARKINSON'S DISEASE

A substantial proportion of persons with PD develop cognitive impairment. Traditionally it was believed that about 25% of persons with PD have mild forms of cognitive impairment and that up to half develop dementia late in the disease course. Research over the past decade has challenged some of these notions. First, it has been observed that 25–30% of persons with PD have impairments detectable on neuropsychological testing already at or near the time of PD diagnosis (Elgh et al., 2009; Foltynie, Brayne, Robbins, & Barker, 2004; Muslimovic, Post, Speelman, & Schmand, 2005). Second, although a frontosubcortical pattern of cognitive deficits may represent the "average" profile in PD, recent attempts to define a syndrome of mild cognitive impairment (MCI) in PD has highlighted considerable heterogeneity in the cognitive domains impaired in PD. Previous studies of PD-MCI used various definitions, and PD-MCI criteria have only recently been proposed (Litvan et al., 2012; Tröster, 2011). The variety of definitions used notwithstanding, reviews of PD-MCI studies show that impairments are more common in single than in multiple cognitive domains (Litvan et al., 2011; Tröster, 2011) and that, although nonamnestic MCI is the most common form of single-domain MCI in PD, amnestic forms are observed with considerable frequency (Aarsland et al., 2010).

Unfortunately, research has yet to show how secondary influences such as depression impact different types of MCI. For this reason, we will review here the typical cognitive profile and neuropsychological test performances in persons with PD without dementia. It is this more typical profile that has been contrasted in PD with and without secondary conditions such as depression.

Attention and Working Memory

Simple attention task performance, such as on forward digit span, is typically intact in PD (Sullivan, Sagar, Gabrieli, Corkin, & Growdon, 1989). Patients with PD have limited attention resources and difficulty shifting attentional set (Dujardin, Degreef, Rogelet, Defebvre, & Destee, 1999; Woodward, Bub, & Hunter, 2002) and consequently perform poorly on tasks demanding sustained, selective, and divided attention (e.g., Stroop task, visual search, Trail Making). Deficits in PD on tests requiring efficient manipulation of information within working memory (Gabrieli, Singh, Stebbins, & Goetz, 1996) might be related to difficulty manipulating information within working memory (Lewis et al., 2003), to difficulty inhibiting responses (Kensinger, Shearer, Locascio, & Growdon, 2003; Rieger, Gauggel, & Burmeister, 2003), or to diminished storage capacity (Lee et al., 2010).

Executive Function

Executive dysfunction, including problems with planning, conceptualization, cognitive flexibility, insight, judgment, self-monitoring, and regulation, are considered a hallmark of PD, and a variety of tests have been used to assess these functions (Kudlicka, Clare, & Hindle, 2011). Alterations in these functions can often be seen early in PD and, although some deficits may be linked to visuospatial demands of the tasks (McKinlay, Grace, Dalrymple-Alford, & Roger, 2010), they traditionally have been attributed to dopaminergic deficits (Kehagia, Barker, & Robbins, 2010). Cholinergic mechanisms may also be implicated in some of the executive deficits observed (Bohnen et al., 2006).

Impairments observed on tower tests (e.g., Tower of London or Hanoi) in PD may be related to slow processing (Morris et al., 1988) or impairments in planning accuracy (Owen et al., 1995; Saint-Cyr, Taylor, & Lang, 1988). Card sorting test deficits are associated with difficulty with set formation, set maintenance, and set shifting (Bondi, Kaszniak, Bayles, & Vance, 1993; Pillon, Dubois, Ploska, & Agid, 1991) or with set loss later in PD (Bowen, Kamienny, Burns, & Yahr, 1975; Taylor, Saint-Cyr, & Lang, 1986).

Motor Skills and Information-Processing Speed

Diminished information-processing speed in postencephalitic parkinsonism was recognized in the 1920s, when the term *bradyphrenia* was coined (Naville, 1922). Early in PD processing speed deficits may be ameliorated by dopaminomimetic medications (Cools, 2006). Motor symptoms such as bradykinesia, rigidity, and tremor are a hallmark of PD, but patients do not have an apraxia.

Language

Motor speech abnormalities (e.g., dysarthria) are common in advanced PD. Despite the absence of aphasia, subtle alterations in performance on language tasks are observed in patients with PD, perhaps secondary to diminished attention, working memory, or inefficient information-processing strategy development and deployment (Murray, 2000).

Visual confrontation naming is preserved in PD (Levin, Llabre, & Weiner, 1989; Lewis, Lapointe, & Murdoch, 1998) but becomes compromised in patients with obvious cognitive impairment (Beatty & Monson, 1989). Lexical and semantic verbal fluency is often intact in patients without dementia (Lewis et al., 1998), but alternating word fluency (requiring retrieval of consecutive words from alternate semantic or letter categories) (Zec et al., 1999) and verb fluency tasks requiring naming of actions are sensitive to PD (Piatt, Fields, Paolo, Koller, & Tröster, 1999). Verbal-fluency impairments may be related to general retrieval deficits (Randolph, Braun, Goldberg, & Chase, 1993) or to a deficit in switching (i.e., disengaging from one category of words to produce those from another category) (Tröster et al., 1998; Troyer, Moscovitch, Winocur, Leach, & Freedman, 1998) or in processing speed (McDowd et al., 2011).

Learning and Memory

Impairments in episodic memory may be evident in the earliest stages of PD (Foltynie et al., 2004; Muslimovic et al., 2005). Learning of new information is slowed in PD (Faglioni, Saetti, & Botti, 2000), as is deployment of semantic encoding (Buytenhuijs et al., 1994). While free recall is impaired recognition is relatively preserved (Beatty, Staton, Weir, Monson, & Whitaker, 1989) but not necessarily intact (Whittington, Podd, & Kan, 2000). Patients with PD have retrieval deficits, and they may also have encoding difficulties (Bronnick, Alves, Aarsland, Tysnes, & Larsen, 2011; Buytenhuijs et al., 1994; Weintraub, Moberg, Culbertson, Duda, & Stern, 2004). In contrast to semantic encoding, serial encoding appears to be preserved (Berger et al., 1999; Buytenhuijs et al., 1994). Retention of word lists is usually normal (Massman, Delis, Butters, Levin, & Salmon, 1990), and intrusion errors are typically semantically related to the words on the list and are qualitatively similar to those of normal elderly (Massman et al., 1990; Rouleau, Imbault, Laframboise, & Bedard, 2001).

Recollection of information from the past (remote memory) is usually preserved (Fama et al., 2000; Leplow et al., 1997), and only rarely are subtle abnormalities revealed (Sagar, Cohen, Sullivan, Corkin, & Growdon, 1988; Venneri et al., 1997). Patients may have poorer memory for recent than remote autobiographical events (Smith, Souchay, & Conway, 2010). Patients with PD also demonstrate deficits on some prospective memory tasks, that is, for intended, future actions (Kliegel, Altgassen, Hering, & Rose, 2011; Pagni et al., 2011; Raskin et al., 2011; Smith, Souchay, & Moulin, 2011).

Visuoperception

Visuospatial deficits independent of motor symptoms are quite common in PD (Lee, Harris, & Calvert, 1998; Levin et al., 1991). Facial-matching tasks reveal impairments in PD (Levin et al., 1989); the facial-recognition impairment in PD is related to configural processing difficulties (Cousins, Hanley, Davies, Turnbull, & Playfer, 2000). On a task requiring persons to match lines of similar spatial orientation, PD patients make more serious errors than controls, for example, confusing an oblique line with one from the same quadrant that was displaced by two or three 18° segments from the target line, and mismatching horizontal lines.

DEPRESSION

Depression is common in patients with PD. The topic has attracted more empirical attention than any other psychiatric comorbid conditions. Depression is one of the most important determinants of quality of life for individuals with PD (Schrag, Jahanshahi, & Quinn, 2000) and is associated with dementia (Marder, Tang, Cote,

Stern, & Mayeux, 1995), disability (Cole et al., 1996; Menza & Mark, 1994), and increased health care utilization (Chen et al., 2007). Indeed, depression may be a risk factor for PD (Hubble, Cao, Hassanein, Neuberger, & Koller, 1993) and speed up disease progression (Starkstein, Mayberg, Leiguarda, Preziosi, & Robinson, 1992). Furthermore, depression in patients with PD negatively affects caregivers' quality of life (Aarsland, Larsen, Karlsen, Lim, & Tandberg, 1999) and is associated with depression in caregivers (Fernandez, Tabamo, David, & Friedman, 2001). Despite the importance of the timely recognition and treatment of depression, in PD it may be underdiagnosed (Shulman, Taback, Rabinstein, & Weiner, 2002) and undertreated (Weintraub, Moberg, Duda, Katz, & Stern, 2003).

Prevalence and Incidence

Prevalence and incidence estimates of depression in PD differ depending on the diagnostic criteria used and the patient population studied. Authors of a review of prevalence studies found that the method of ascertaining DSM criteria is an important determinant of prevalence: Higher prevalence of depression was reported in studies using structured or semistructured interviews to establish DSM criteria fulfillment (19%) than in studies not using structured interviews (7%) (Reijnders, Ehrt, Weber, Aarsland, & Leentjens, 2008).

Studies of patients in hospital and specialty clinics have yielded much higher point prevalence estimates than those in community-based studies. Whereas the prevalence of major depression among patients with PD has been reported to be about 25–40% in tertiary-care samples (Davous, Auquier, Grignon, & Neukirch, 1995; Dooneief et al., 1992), community studies reported a prevalence of only about 3–8% (Hantz, Caradoc-Davies, Caradoc-Davies, Weatherall, & Dixon, 1994; Tandberg, Larsen, Aarsland, & Cummings, 1996).

Clinically relevant depressive symptoms occur in about 35% of PD patients (Reijnders et al., 2008). In that study, the average weighted point prevalence was found to be 17% for major depression, 22% for minor depression, and 13% for dysthymia.

Diagnosis

Several *Diagnostic and Statistical Manual of Mental Disorders* (4th ed., text revision; *DSM-IV-TR*; American Psychiatric Association, 2000) entities involving depressive features are relevant to PD. These include depressive disorders (major depressive disorder, dysthymic disorder), other mood disorders, and adjustment disorders. Depression in the context of PD is typically diagnosed under the rubric of mood disorders due to a general medical condition (Kremer & Starkstein, 2000), which permits specification of whether the mood disorder involves a major depressive episode, depressive features (when criteria for a major depressive episode are not met), or manic features. Adjustment disorders are thought to be rare in PD (Cummings & Masterman, 1999), and although levodopa can induce depression, presumably by affecting serotonin (Andersen, Aabro, Gulmann, Hjelmsted, & Pedersen, 1980), this is rare.

Three types of depression are thought to occur in PD, namely major depression, minor depression, and dysthymia. Major and minor depression differ largely in the number of symptoms present and the extent of accompanying functional impairment: Per *DSM-IV-TR*, a diagnosis of major depression requires the presence of at least five of nine symptoms and functional impairment, whereas minor depression (listed as a depressive disorder not otherwise specified) requires only two to four symptoms, one of which is depressed mood or loss of interest or pleasure. In both major and minor depression, symptoms are present for at least 2 weeks. Per *DSM-IV-TR* criteria, the core features of a depressive episode include a pervasive negative mood disturbance or anhedonia characterized by diminished interest and motivation. Associated symptoms involve feelings of helplessness, indecisiveness and impaired concentration, worry, insomnia or hypersomnia, appetite changes, slowed movements, or restlessness. Dysthymia, by contrast, does not follow an episodic pattern. Instead, depressed mood occurs for much of the day on more days than not for at least 2 years. At least two of six symptoms must be present during depressed mood: appetite disturbance, sleep disturbance, anergia or fatigue, diminished self-esteem, poor concentration, and hopelessness.

The practical application of *DSM-IV-TR* criteria in PD occasionally faces difficulties. Somatic features of depression overlap with PD symptoms (e.g., appetite and sleep changes, slowness of movement, restlessness), as do some cognitive features (e.g., poor concentration) and diminished energy and fatigue. Consequently, several modifications to the *DSM-IV-TR* criteria have been proposed to enhance the reliability and sensitivity (despite possibly diminished specificity) of diagnosis of depression in PD (Marsh, McDonald, Cummings, & Ravina, 2006). These suggested modifications include the following: (1) consideration of all depression symptoms regardless of etiology; (2) elimination of a general medical condition etiology from being exclusionary; (3) requirement of depressed mood or anhedonia as a core feature of minor depression; (4) consideration of the motor state of the patient during the diagnostic assessment, which is preferably to be conducted in the "on" state; and (5) use of informants when patients are cognitively impaired.

Impact of Depression on Cognition in PD

Empirical studies are in general agreement that depression exerts an adverse effect on cognition in PD. Studies differ in their findings as to the nature and extent of cognitive impairment produced by depression, and this may be related to methodological differences among studies. Some studies used correlational methods, meaning they explored the relationship between severity of cognitive impairments and severity of depression symptoms, usually measured by self-report scales (Youngjohn, Beck, Jogerst, & Caine, 1992). Other studies compared the neuropsychological test performance of groups of PD patients with and without depression (Boller, Marcie, Starkstein, & Traykov, 1998; Starkstein et al., 1989; Starkstein, Preziosi, Bolduc, & Robinson, 1990; Tröster, Stalp, Paolo, Fields, & Koller, 1995) and occasionally to patients with depression but without PD (Kuzis, Sabe, Tiberti, Leiguarda, & Starkstein, 1997; Norman, Tröster, Fields, & Brooks,

2002; Uekermann et al., 2003). These group comparison studies differ with regard to how depression was defined (e.g., by symptom inventories or formal criteria confirmed per interview).

One question that studies have addressed is the extent of depression required to exert effects on cognition. Starkstein and colleagues proposed that major but not minor depression was associated with cognitive impairment in PD (Starkstein & Robinson, 1991). However, depression-associated cognitive deficits may exist along a continuum of depression severity. One study of DSM-classified minor and major depression in PD found that only the group with major depression evidenced significantly worse performance than that of the nondepressed group on tests of verbal memory, reasoning, and executive function. Although the performance of the minor-depression group did not differ significantly from that of the nondepressed group, the scores on the same tests were in the intermediate range of those for the nondepressed and major-depression group and did not differ significantly from those of the major-depression group (Costa, Peppe, Carlesimo, Pasqualetti, & Caltagirone, 2006). Patients with minor depression also show less rapid cognitive decline than persons with PD and major depression (Starkstein, Mayberg, Leiguarda, et al., 1992). The only study of the effects of dysthymia on cognition in PD reported that cognitive function is similarly impaired in PD with and without dysthymia (Stefanova et al., 2006). It is noteworthy that a history of depression prior to PD may have a negative effect independent of current depression on executive functions such as set shifting and response inhibition (Klepac, Hajnsek, & Trkulja, 2010).

A second important question is whether depression produces a pattern of cognitive deficits that differs not only in quantity but also in quality from that observed in PD. One study suggested that major depression in PD produces a qualitatively distinct pattern of deficits from PD (Costa et al., 2006), but that study did not compare the performance of the patient groups to that of normal controls, a comparison necessary before one can conclude that PD and depression have qualitatively different impacts on cognition. Another study found that, in comparison to a healthy control group, a depressed (defined by depression inventory score) PD group, but not a nondepressed PD group, demonstrated impairment in visual confrontation naming. However, the overall pattern of deficits on memory, letter fluency, naming, and attention measures differed only in severity, not in quality (Tröster et al., 1995).

Of relevance to neuropsychologists are the effects of depression on various cognitive domains and performance on specific neuropsychological tests. One means of estimating the extent of the influence of depression on cognition on a given test is to examine the effect size of the difference in mean scores obtained by PD patients with and without depression. For purposes of this review, the thresholds for effect sizes (d) are 0.2 for small, 0.5 for medium, and 0.8 for large effects in studies reporting statistically significant findings. The range of these effect size values as reported in the studies discussed in this chapter is presented in Table 12.1.

In terms of attention, the most widely used test in PD depression studies has been the digit span task. Findings have been equivocal, with some studies reporting

Table 12.1. EFFECT SIZE (COHEN'S *D*) RANGE OF DIFFERENCES BETWEEN PARKINSON'S DISEASE (PD) GROUPS WITH AND WITHOUT THE SECONDARY INFLUENCE CONDITION ON VARIOUS DOMAINS OF COGNITION*

Secondary Influence	Cognitive Domain	Effect Size Range	Number of Studies
Depression			
	Attention	0.06–1.02	7
	Executive function	0.11–1.70	10
	Language[†]	0.32–1.20	5
	Visuospatial	0.46–0.79	2
	Memory	0.28–0.92	5
Apathy			
	Attention	0.17–1.69	2
	Executive function[‡]	0.34–1.12	3
	Language[†,‡]	0.81–1.54	2
	Visuospatial	–	0
	Memory	0.82–1.45	2
Psychosis (Hallucinations)			
	Attention	0.96–1.85	2
	Executive function	0.83–1.05	2
	Language	0.56–0.77	1
	Visuospatial	0.70–1.22	2
	Memory		
Sleep Disorders			
	Attention	0.28–1.10	2
	Executive function	0.12–0.65	2
	Language[†]	0.92–1.62	2
	Visuospatial	0.62–1.82	2
	Memory	0.17–1.04	3

* Cognitive screening measures mentioned in the text are excluded from cognitive domains; anxiety is not included because only one correlational study was available.
[†] Based largely on verbal-fluency test score differences.
[‡] One study compared PD + depression with PD + depression + apathy, and a second study compared PD within tertiles of apathy scores.

impairments in PD depression (Kuzis et al., 1997; Tröster et al., 1995; Uekermann et al., 2003) but others not (Boller et al., 1998; Costa et al., 2006; Klepac et al., 2010). Comparisons of PD with and without depression using the digit span task, when significant, have generally revealed differences of medium effect size. If backward digit span (which is demanding of working memory) performance is considered alone, the effect size is large (Starkstein et al., 1989; Uekermann et al., 2003). Testing with the Trail Making Test, Part A has also shown differences of medium to large effect sizes (Starkstein et al., 1989; Stefanova et al., 2006). In contrast, performance on the spatial span task has not been found to differ significantly between depressed and nondepressed individuals with PD (Boller et al.,

1998; Costa et al., 2006), and findings from Symbol Digit Modalities and screening tests (such as the Dementia Rating Scale [DRS] and Repeatable Battery for Neuropsychological Assessment [RBANS]) are equivocal.

It has been suggested that depression especially affects executive function in PD. The two most commonly used tests evaluating executive function in studies of PD and depression are the Wisconsin Card Sorting Test (WCST) and letter fluency test (Kudlicka, Clare, & Hindle, 2011). Several studies have reported medium to large differences between depressed and nondepressed PD patients' letter fluency (Kuzis et al., 1997; Stefanova et al., 2006; Uekermann et al., 2003), whereas a few have reported small effects (Santangelo et al., 2009; Tröster et al., 1995). It appears that higher levels of depression are associated with greater impairment in letter fluency and that patients with minor depression may be relatively unimpaired on this task (Costa et al., 2006). The WCST (trials, categories and perseverative errors) has generally not shown significant differences between depressed and nondepressed patients with PD (Butterfield, Cimino, Oelke, Hauser, & Sanchez-Ramos, 2010; Cooper, Sagar, Jordan, Harvey, & Sullivan, 1991; Starkstein, Mayberg, Leiguarda, et al., 1992; Tröster et al., 1995). However, medium-to-large differences may be observed in terms of categories attained and perseverations if patients with major depression are studied (Costa et al., 2006; Kuzis et al., 1997). The Stroop test, too, has not identified marked differences between depressed and nondepressed PD, nor has it shown a relationship with severity of depressive symptoms once education is accounted for (Klepac et al., 2010; Santangelo et al., 2009). The Trail Making test is rarely reported on but may reveal large differences between depressed and nondepressed PD (Starkstein et al., 1989).

Language function, with the exception of verbal fluency, is rarely affected by depression beyond the effect attributable to PD alone, although this domain of cognition has rarely been explored in PD and depression studies. No differences have been found on tests of comprehension such as the Token test (Cooper et al., 1991), on tests of sentence construction (Costa et al., 2006) or on global screening measures such as the RBANS Language score (Ryder et al., 2002). By contrast, several studies have reported greater (medium effect sizes) impairment in visual confrontation naming in depressed than in nondepressed PD patients (Dobkin et al., 2010; Tröster et al., 1995), and large effect sizes may be observed in those patients with major depression (Stefanova et al., 2006). Category fluency deficits in depressed relative to nondepressed patients (medium to large effect sizes) have been found in some studies (Dobkin et al., 2010; Stefanova et al., 2006; Tröster et al., 1995) but not in others (Santangelo et al., 2009; Uekermann et al., 2003).

Visuoperceptual and spatial task performance has been reported to be not significantly associated with depression or to be comparable in PD with and without depression, on a large number of tasks: face recognition and line orientation (Fernandez et al., 2009), complex figure copy (Costa et al., 2006; Klepac et al., 2010), and visuoperceptual gestalt formation (Hooper Visual Organization Test; HVOT; Stefanova et al., 2006). Occasional reports of impaired performance by depressed relative to nondepressed PD patients on tasks such as Picture Arrangement (requiring sequencing of cartoon-like pictures to tell a meaningful story) (Cooper et al., 1991) or figure copy tests (Santangelo et al., 2009) are difficult to interpret given the lack of replication.

Memory and learning differences have been observed between depressed and nondepressed PD patients on prose memory tasks (Dobkin et al., 2010), but some studies have found the impairment only in immediate but not delayed recall (Stefanova et al., 2006; Tröster et al., 1995). Recall of word lists such as the Auditory Verbal Learning Test (AVLT) and Hopkins Verbal Learning Test (HVLT) and paired associates is poorer in depressed than in nondepressed PD patients (Butterfield et al., 2010; Costa et al., 2006; Starkstein, Bolduc, Mayberg, Preziosi, & Robinson, 1990) and in one study correlated with severity of depression symptoms (Fernandez et al., 2009). These studies' differences were associated with medium-to-large effect sizes. A few studies, however, have failed to find differences between depressed and nondepressed groups using list-learning tasks (Kuzis et al., 1997; Stefanova et al., 2006; Uekermann et al., 2003).

Treatment with antidepressants has not been found to improve cognitive function, but baseline verbal memory and executive dysfunction and diminished processing speed are predictive of treatment nonresponse (Dobkin et al., 2010).

APATHY

Apathy often co-occurs with depression, but in PD it clearly also exists independent of depression (Kirsch-Darrow, Fernandez, Marsiske, Okun, & Bowers, 2006; Kirsch-Darrow, Marsiske, Okun, Bauer, & Bowers, 2011; Louis, Huey, Gerbin, & Viner, 2012; Richard, 2007; Starkstein et al., 1992). Apathy involves an absence or lack of feeling, concern, emotion, motivation, and interest (Marin, 1990). Apathy may be mistaken for depression in PD, with which it shares features of anhedonia, diminished motivation, and fatigue. An important feature distinguishing apathy and depression is the mood valence, which is neutral in apathy but negative in depression. Apathy also may be mistaken for PD itself, given overlapping signs and symptoms such as reduced facial animation, socialization, and interest in hobbies (Shulman, 2000).

Prevalence and Incidence

Estimates of prevalence of apathy in PD are based on small research samples and varying methods of ascertainment. Most often various versions of Marin's Apathy Evaluation Scale (Marin, Biedrzycki, & Firinciogullari, 1991) have been used. Pure apathy has been reported to occur in 5–28% of PD patients (Kirsch-Darrow et al., 2006; Levy et al., 1998; Starkstein, Mayberg, Preziosi, et al., 1992), and about another 30% have combined apathy and depression at any given time (Levy et al., 1998; Starkstein, Mayberg, Preziosi, et al., 1992).

Diagnosis

Diagnostic criteria for apathy in PD have been proposed but evaluated inadequately (Drijgers, Dujardin, Reijnders, Defebvre, & Leentjens, 2010; Robert et al.,

2009; Starkstein & Leentjens, 2008). Most studies have used scales rather than diagnostic criteria to identify apathy in PD.

Impact of Apathy on Cognition in PD

Although reliable morphometric correlates of apathy have not been identified in PD (Isella et al., 2002), a consistent finding is that, among cognitive impairments, executive dysfunction in particular is more pronounced in those with than without apathy, and in those with higher than lower levels of apathy (Isella et al., 2002; Pluck & Brown 2002; Starkstein, Mayberg, Leiguarda, et al., 1992). This strongly suggests that frontal systems are implicated in the apathy of PD. Apathy is not only more common in PD patients with than without dementia (Dujardin et al., 2007), but it may be a marker for incipient dementia (Dujardin, Sockeel, Delliaux, Destee, & Defebvre, 2009).

In terms of the impact of apathy on specific cognitive domains and test performance, most studies have found limited impact of apathy on tests of attention such as digit and spatial span, Trail Making Part A, Brief Test of Attention, Symbol Digit, and the Stroop task (Isella et al., 2002; Starkstein, Mayberg, Preziosi, et al., 1992; Varanese, Perfetti, Ghilardi, & Di Rocco, 2011; Zgaljardic et al., 2007). A very limited number of studies identified differences of large effect sizes between apathetic and nonapathetic PD patients on the Stroop, letter-number sequencing, Symbol Digit Modalities (Dujardin et al., 2009), and backward digit span tasks (Varanese et al., 2011).

Numerous executive-function tests are sensitive to apathy in PD, including letter and category verbal fluency (large effects) (Dujardin et al., 2009; Isella et al., 2002; Starkstein, Mayberg, Preziosi, et al., 1992; Zgaljardic et al., 2007), Trail Making Part B (large effect compared to normal controls) (Starkstein, Mayberg, Preziosi, et al., 1992), the WCST (Butterfield et al., 2010; Varanese et al., 2011), and the Executive Interview (EXIT) (Isella et al., 2002).

Language measures other than verbal fluency have not been evaluated in apathetic patients, and visuoperceptual tasks tend not to reveal significant differences between apathetic and nonapathetic patients (Isella et al., 2002; Zgaljardic et al., 2007). There appears to be a dichotomy between learning and memory measures affected by apathy in PD. Whereas performance on list learning (immediate and delayed recall) reveals large differences between apathetic and nonapathetic PD patients (Butterfield et al., 2010; Dujardin et al., 2009; Varanese et al., 2011), prose recall may not vary as a function of apathy (Isella et al., 2002).

ANXIETY

Anxiety disorders also contribute substantially to morbidity and caregiver burden (Marsh, 2000). A wide range of anxiety conditions have been identified in PD, including generalized anxiety, panic disorder and attacks, specific and social phobias, and obsessive-compulsive disorder.

Prevalence and Incidence

Anxiety disorders, including generalized anxiety, panic, social phobia, and obsessive-compulsive disorder, have a point prevalence of about 25–50% among patients with PD (Richard, 2005). Generalized anxiety is evident in about 11–20% of PD patients and is unrelated to motor disability or levodopa use (Nuti et al., 2004; Stein, Heuser, Juncos, & Uhde, 1990). Panic disorder may occur in as many as 30% of PD patients (Nuti et al., 2004), and 24% of levodopa-treated patients may have recurrent panic attacks (Vazquez, Jimenez-Jimenez, Garcia-Ruiz, & Garcia-Urra, 1993). Stein and colleagues (1990) found that nearly 20% of their subjects met diagnostic criteria for social phobia and an additional 20% experienced disabling social anxiety specifically related to their symptoms of PD. Social anxiety was also reported to be evident in 16% in another study (Bolluk, Ozel-Kizil, Akbostanci, & Atbasoglu, 2010). In another study, the prevalence of social phobia in a movement disorders clinic convenience sample was 50% (Kummer, Cardoso, & Teixeira, 2008). Only about 3% of patients with PD meet diagnostic criteria for obsessive-compulsive disorder (Nuti et al., 2004). Patients are more likely to experience obsessive-compulsive symptoms than the disorder, and the symptoms tend to appear late in the course of the disease (Stein et al., 1990) and be more severe in those with left-sided motor symptoms (Tomer, Levin, & Weiner, 1993).

Diagnosis

Typically, studies have applied DSM criteria to ascertain presence of anxiety disorders, but some studies have focused on clinician-rated or patient-reported symptoms. Recognition of anxiety disorder in patients with PD can be difficult because of frequent overlap between anxiety and depression (Menza, Robertson-Hoffman, & Bonapace, 1993) and overlap between anxiety and PD symptoms (e.g., tremulousness, faintness).

Impact of Anxiety on Cognition in PD

One study using a brief neuropsychological test battery (RBANS) found that the State-Trait Anxiety Inventory correlated negatively with cognitive performance in a sample of 27 PD patients. The trait anxiety score was negatively associated with each of the RBANS scales (language, attention, immediate and delayed memory, and visuospatial/construction) ($r = -.41$ to $-.62$). In contrast, the state anxiety score was negatively associated with only three of the five scales (immediate memory, attention, language), and to a lesser extent ($r = -.27$ to $-.46$). It is possible, however, that certain cognitive functions, such as working memory, are affected by anxiety in only those with left-sided motor symptoms (Foster et al., 2010). In a recent study of 513 patients with PD, 40% were categorized as having anxious and depressive symptoms: 22% were said to have anxiety symptoms only, 9% depression symptoms only, and 9% to have both (Brown et al., 2011). High levels of cognitive impairment, assessed with the Addenbrooke Cognitive Examination—revised (ACE-R; Mioshi, Dawson, Mitchell, Arnold, & Hodges,

2006), were found in the depressed (possibly also apathetic) group but not the anxious group.

OTHER SECONDARY INFLUENCES ON COGNITION IN PARKINSON'S DISEASE

Sleep Disorders and Fatigue

Disorders of sleep and wakefulness represent one of the most common non-motor features in PD. As many as 90% of patients complain of insomnia, hypersomnia, REM sleep behavior disorder (RBD), sleep fragmentation, periodic limb movements during sleep, and nightmares or sleep terrors (Chaudhuri et al., 2010; Stacy, 2002). Patients with PD, especially when treated with dopamine agonists, frequently experience excessive daytime sleepiness (EDS) and paroxysmal sleep (suddenly dozing off), and, per one estimate, 70% of patients with disease duration of 20 or more years have EDS (Hely, Reid, Adena, Halliday, & Morris, 2008).

Relatively few studies have examined the impact of disorders of sleep and wakefulness on cognition. The most widely examined sleep-disorder in PD is RBD, perhaps because this disorder has been identified as one often preceding PD and as a risk factor for dementia with Lewy bodies (DLB). Mild cognitive impairment was identified in 73% of PD patients with RBD but in only 11% of PD patients without RBD (Gagnon et al., 2009). In comparison to PD patients without RBD, those with RBD have most reliably been found to have greater visuoperceptual and constructional and spatial impairments, a feature also observed in DLB (Gagnon et al., 2009; Marques et al., 2010; Vendette et al., 2007). Whereas medium-sized differences have been observed on the Rey Complex Figure task, large effects have been shown using the block design test. A significant RBD effect on memory and learning is less reliably observed. Two studies found greater impairments in immediate and delayed recall of the AVLT word list (large effect) (Gagnon et al., 2009; Vendette et al., 2007). However, groups with and without RBD failed to differ significantly on prose recall (Sinforiani et al., 2006), and compared to controls, patients may show normal performance on the Selective Reminding Test (Marques et al., 2010).

Regrading executive function, a medium-sized difference was reported between PD patients with RBD and those without RBD on Trail Making Part B (Gagnon et al., 2009; Vendette et al., 2007) (but not Part A) and on the WCST (specific score unspecified) (Sinforiani et al., 2006). Verbal fluency has been shown to be significantly poorer in patients with RBD in two studies (Gagnon et al., 2009; Vendette et al., 2007) (large effect sizes), but some studies failed to find significant differences in letter fluency (Sinforiani et al., 2006; Vendette et al., 2007). The Stroop task, especially the error score, tends to highlight differences between those with RBD and those without RBD (large effect) (Gagnon et al. 2009; Sinforiani et al., 2006; Vendette et al., 2007).

Attention has only inconsistently been shown to be affected by RBD in PD. In one study, digit span performance differed between PD patients with RBD and those without RBD (Gagnon et al., 2009), but digit and spatial span results did not differ in another study (Sinforiani et al., 2006).

While fatigue was observed in 44% of a community sample (Karlsen, Larsen, Tandberg, & Jorgensen, 1999), fatigue's effects on cognition have not been adequately studied. The suggestion that fatigue might impact WCST performance (Abe, Takanashi, & Yanagihara, 2000) remains to be evaluated. A recent study found that poor sleep quality in patients with PD was associated with impairments in attention and executive function but not psychomotor or memory functions (Stavitsky, Neargarder, Bogdanova, McNamara, & Cronin-Golomb, 2012).

Hallucinations

Only about 10% of untreated PD patients have hallucinations. In PD as a whole, visual hallucinations occur in 25–35% of patients and auditory hallucinations in as many as 20% (Fenelon & Alves, 2010). Visual illusions and hallucinations of sense of presence and passage occurred in 45% of PD patients in one study (Fenelon, Soulas, Zenasni, & de Langavant, 2010). Only recently (in the past 5 years) has the relationship between hallucinations and cognitive impairment in PD begun to be explored. Cognitive impairment in PD with visual hallucinations is comparable to that observed in patients with multimodality hallucinations (Katzen et al., 2010). Hallucinations often co-exist with RBD. PD patients with RBD and hallucinations may have greater cognitive (memory and executive) impairment than those with RBD alone (Sinforiani et al., 2006) and show greater cognitive and motor decline and mortality after 2-year follow-up (Sinforiani et al., 2008).

Attention tests that are demanding of working memory tend to be sensitive to presence of hallucinations in PD patients with or without dementia, but simpler attention tests tend not to reveal differential impairments in those with and without hallucinations. Thus impairments (usually of large effect size) in patients with, relative to those without, hallucinations have been reported on tasks such as the Paced Auditory Serial Addition Test (PASAT) (Katzen et al., 2010), the Stroop task (Barnes & Boubert, 2008; Imamura, Wada-Isoe, Kitayama, & Nakashima, 2008), and in choice reaction time in patients with PD dementia (Bronnick, Emre, Tekin, Haugen, & Aarsland, 2011). In contrast, performance on the digit span, simple reaction time, and other less demanding attention tasks may not be significantly affected in those with hallucinations (Bronnick, Emre, et al., 2011; Imamura et al., 2008; Katzen et al., 2010).

Executive-function tests such as the WCST reveal large differences between PD patients with and without hallucinations (Katzen et al., 2010), but hallucinations may not exert a significant additional impact on executive function in PD patients who have dementia (Bronnick, Emre, et al., 2011) or RBD (Sinforiani et al., 2006). Whereas letter fluency has not been shown to differ in those with and those without hallucinations (Bronnick, Emre, et al., 2011; Ramirez-Ruiz, Junque, Marti, Valldeoriola, & Tolosa, 2006), category or semantic fluency is typically worse in patients with hallucinations (Barnes & Boubert, 2008; Imamura et al., 2008; Ramirez-Ruiz et al., 2006).

Consistent with the posterior cortical correlates of visual hallucinations, hallucinations have been found to negatively impact performance on several language tasks (small to medium effect sizes), such as visual confrontation naming, category fluency, comprehension (Token test), and commands (Barnes & Boubert, 2008; Bronnick, Emre, et al., 2011; Imamura et al., 2008; Ramirez-Ruiz et al., 2006). However, this has not been a uniform finding (Katzen et al., 2010). One study failed to find significant differences in visuoperceptual functioning between those with and those without hallucinations on facial recognition, visuoperceptual gestalt formation (HVOT), and Ghent Embedded figures tasks, but the authors did find a difference on the Judgment of Line Orientation task (medium effect size) (Katzen et al., 2010). In contrast, another study found significant differences (medium to large effect sizes) between PD patients with and those without visual hallucinations on facial recognition and visual-form discrimination tasks (Ramirez-Ruiz et al., 2006).

Learning and memory have only inconsistently been shown to differ between PD patients with and those without hallucinations. Two studies found differences in list learning and memory (medium to large) (Bronnick, Emre, et al., 2011; Ramirez-Ruiz et al., 2006) but another study did not (Katzen et al., 2010). Spatial memory deficits have been observed in those with hallucinations (Barnes & Boubert, 2011), but performance on simpler recognition tests may be relatively intact in PD patients with hallucinations as compared to those without hallucinations (Ramirez-Ruiz et al., 2006).

ASSESSMENT OF SECONDARY INFLUENCES

Initial determination of the existence of possible secondary influences on cognition in PD should be based on record review and thorough interview. Even if a patient does not meet strict criteria for a psychiatric disorder, a quantitative assessment should be undertaken to help determine whether symptoms are present to an extent that might impact test performance.

The quantitative assessment of secondary influences can be achieved by self-report or clinician-rated instruments. The Movement Disorder Society (MDS) has an ongoing task force to evaluate various rating scales for use in PD. MDS Task Forces have used three broad criteria to determine whether a scale is recommended, suggested, or listed. To be included under any of these categories, a scale must have been applied to a PD population. A suggested scale has also been used in clinical studies beyond the initial study reporting development or use of that scale in PD, or it has been subjected to clinimetric/psychometric study establishing adequate reliability, validity, and sensitivity. A recommended scale meets all of these criteria. The MDS has published papers relevant to the use of scales of depression (Schrag et al., 2007), anxiety (Leentjens et al., 2008a), apathy and anhedonia (Leentjens et al., 2008b), psychosis (Fernandez et al., 2008), disorders of sleep and wakefulness (Hogl et al., 2010), and fatigue (Friedman et al., 2010). Table 12.2 provides an overview of the rating scales (and cutoff scores, where available) recommended for various domains.

Table 12.2 MOVEMENT DISORDER SOCIETY (MDS) RECOMMENDED AND SUGGESTED RATING SCALES FOR ASSESSMENT OF NEUROPSYCHOLOGICAL AND PSYCHIATRIC FEATURES OF PARKINSON'S DISEASE

Feature	Recommended Scales (Stronger Evidence)	Suggested Scales (Weaker Evidence)
Depression (Schrag et al., 2007)	Screening (and recommended cutoff in PD): Hamilton Depression Rating Scale (HAM-D, 9/10); Beck Depression Inventory (BDI, 13/14); Hospital Anxiety and Depression Scale (HADS, 10/11); Montogomery-Asberg Depression Rating Scale (MADRS; 14/15); Geriatric Depression Scale (GDS-30: 9/10; GDS-15: 4/5)	For patients with dementia (though insufficient evidence): MADRS; GDS; Cornell Scale for Depression in Dementia (CSDD, 5/6)
Anxiety (Leentjens et al., 2008a)	None	Beck Anxiety Inventory (BAI), Hospital Anxiety and Depression Scale (HADS), Zung Self-Rated Anxiety Scale (Zung SAS), Zung Anxiety Status Inventory (Zung ASI), State-Trait Anxiety Inventory (STAI), Hamilton Anxiety Rating Scale (HARS), Neuropsychiatric Inventory (NPI) anxiety section
Apathy and anhedonia (Leentjens et al., 2008b)	Apathy Scale (Starkstein, Mayberg, Preziosi, et al., 1992; screening cutoff 13/14); Unified Parkinson's Disease Rating Scale (UPDRS) item 4 (motivation/initiative) (screening cutoff 2/3)	Apathy Evaluation Scale (AES; Marin, et al., 1991; screening cutoff 38/39); Lille Apathy Rating Scale (LARS; screening cutoff 16/17); Neuropsychiatric Inventory (NPI) item 7; Snaith-Hamilton Pleasure Scale (SHAPS; screening cutoff 2/3)
Psychosis (Fernandez et al., 2008)	Neuropsychiatric Inventory (NPI); Brief Psychiatric Rating Scale (BPRS); Positive and Negative Syndrome Scale (PANNS); Schedule for Assessment of Positive Symptoms (SAPS)	Parkinson Psychosis Rating Scale (PPRS); Parkinson Psychosis Questionnaire (PPQ); Behavioral Pathology in Alzheimer's Disease Rating Scale (Behave-AD); Clinical Global Impression Scale (CGIS)

(Continued)

Table 12.2. (Continued)

Feature	Recommended Scales (Stronger Evidence)	Suggested Scales (Weaker Evidence)
Sleep disturbances (Hogl et al., 2010)	*Daytime sleepiness:* Epworth Sleepiness Scale (ESS) *Overall sleep impairment:* Parkinson's Disease Sleep Scale (PDSS); Pittsburgh Sleep Quality Index (PSQI); Scales for Outcomes in Parkinson's Disease (SCOPA-Sleep)	*Daytime sleepiness:* Inappropriate Sleep Composite Score (ISCS); Stanford Sleepiness Scale (SSS)
Fatigue (Friedman et al., 2010)	Fatigue Severity Scale (for severity and screening); Multidimensional Fatigue Inventory (for severity); Parkinson's Fatigue Scale (for screening); Functional Assessment of Chronic Illness Therapy—Fatigue Scale (for screening)	Multidimensional Fatigue Inventory (for screening); Fatigue Assessment Inventory (for severity and screening); Functional Assessment of Chronic Illness Therapy—Fatigue Scale (for severity); Parkinson's Fatigue Scale (for severity); Fatigue Impact Scale for Daily Use (for severity)

Symptoms of PD overlap frequently with those of depression, anxiety, apathy, and fatigue (Higginson, Fields, Koller, & Tröster, 2001; Menza, Palermo, DiPaola, Sage, & Ricketts, 1999). Most attention regarding this overlap has been devoted to assessment of depression and anxiety, and several studies have provided revised cutoff scores for the screening or diagnosis of these conditions in PD. Table 12.3 provides revised cutoff scores (along with their sensitivity and specificity) for depression scales in PD.

Few studies have recommended revised cutoff scores for other conditions in PD. For detection of generalized anxiety, the Hamilton Anxiety Rating Scale (HARS) cutoff of 10/11 has been recommended (Kummer, Cardoso, & Teixeira, 2010). For social phobia, a cutoff of 41/42 on the Liebowitz Social Anxiety scale has been suggested (Kummer et al., 2008). To identify PD patients with sleep problems, cutoffs of 82/83 for the Parkinson's Disease Sleep Scale and 6/7 for the Scales for Outcomes in PD-Sleep Scale (SCOPA-S) (Martinez-Martin et al., 2008) have been proposed.

CASE EXAMPLE

Through the following case example we attempt to tease apart the effects of depression and apathy and consider their potential impact on cognition in the differential diagnosis.

A 59-year-old African-American man with a high school education presented at the request of his primary care physician (PCP) to facilitate determination of the extent and possible causes of his cognitive problems. The PCP was told that the

Table 12.3 Self-Report and Rating Scales with Empirically Modified Cutoff Scores to Detect Depression in Parkinson's Disease

Scale (Reference)	Number of Items; Maximum Score; Traditional Cutoff*	PD Cutoffs Recommended By:	Recommended Cutoff to Distinguish Depressed vs. NonDepressed PD (Sensitivity/Specificity)	Recommended Screening Cutoff for PD (Sensitivity/Specificity)	Recommended Diagnostic Cutoff for PD (Sensitivity/Specificity)
Beck Depression Inventory (Beck, Ward, Mendelson, Mock, & Erbaugh, 1961)	21 items; Maximum = 63; 10 = mild; 12 = moderate; 30 = severe	Leentjens, Verhey, Luijckx, & Troost (2000)	13/14 (0.67/0.88)	8/9 (0.92/0.59)	16/17 (0.42/0.98)
Hamilton Rating Scale for Depression (17-item) (Hamilton, 1960)	17 items; Maximum = 50; 8 = mild; 14 = moderate; 19 = severe; 23 = very severe; 24 items	Leentjens, Verhey, Lousberg, Spitsbergen, & Wilmink (2000); Naarding, Leentjens, Van Kooten, & Verhey (2002); Dissanayaka et al. (2007); Weintraub, Oehlberg, Katz, & Stern (2006)	13/14 (0.88/0.89); 12/13 (0.80/0.92); 12/13; 9/10 (0.89/0.93); (0.88/0.78)	11/12 (0.94/0.75); 9/10 (0.95/0.98); NA; NA	16/17 (0.75/0.98); 15/16 (0.99/0.93); 18/19 (1.00/0.99); NA
Hamilton Depression Inventory (17-item) (Reynolds & Kobak, 1995)	17 items; Maximum = 52	Dissanayaka et al. (2007)	13.5/14 (0.78/0.90)	NA	15.5/16 (0.89/0.93)

Measure	Description	Reference			
Geriatric Depression Scale (15-item) (Sheikh & Yesavage, 1986)	15 items; Maximum = 15	Weintraub et al. (2006); Dissanayaka et al. (2007)	4/5 (0.88/0.85) 6/7 (0.89/0.87)	NA NA	NA 8/9 (0.89/0.87)
Geriatric Depression Scale (30-item) (Yesavage et al., 1983)	30 items; Maximum = 30 10 = mild 20 = severe	Mondolo et al. (2006)	10/11 (1.00/0.76)	10/11 (1.00/0.76)	12/13 (0.80/0.85)
Montgomery-Åsberg Depression Rating Scale (Montgomery & Asberg, 1979)	10 items; Maximum = 60 15 = mild 25 = moderate 31 = severe 44 = very severe	Leentjens, Verhey, Lousberg et al. (2000)	14/15 (0.88/0.89)	14/15 (0.88/0.89)	17/18 (0.63/0.94)
Hospital Anxiety and Depression Scale (Zigmond & Snaith, 1983)	Depression subscale 7 items; Maximum = 21 8 = mild 11 = severe	Mondolo et al. (2006)	10/11 (1.00/0.95)	10/11 (1.00/0.95)	11/12 (0.80/0.98)

* Traditional cutoffs from test manuals or per Task Force for the Handbook of Psychiatric Measures (American Psychiatric Association, 2000).

patient had had a shuffling gait for 3–4 months and cognitive changes (forgetful-ness) for 3 months. On physical examination he was noted to have a masked face, stooped posture, bradykinesia, rigidity, and, per history, nocturia. At his PCP visit the patient was unable to draw a clock, and recall was 2/3 words.

At neuropsychological evaluation, the patient's wife revealed that her husband, previously a truck driver, had declined functionally after he had to stop work because of back pain about 4 years previously. She initially attributed his gradual decline in function to his back problems but acknowledged that he had had a masked face for at least 2 years and that he had had a progressively slow, shuffling gait for more than 2 years. In addition, in the past 6 months she had observed her husband having episodes of upper and lower extremity resting tremor once or twice per day and poorer handwriting.

The patient's cognitive changes became of particular concern to his wife about a year ago, although he had seemed less sharp (difficulty focusing attention and forgetting conversations) for 2–3 years. In the past year, the patient had developed difficulty handling finances. For example, despite specific instructions, he would deposit checks into an incorrect account and have trouble operating an automated teller machine. He had difficulty recalling his PIN, and when he did, occasionally typed it incorrectly into the machine (he thought this was due to cataracts, but the problem had not improved after cataract surgery). His wife perceived him to be more moody, irritable, and as trying to justify his errors. He seemed less active but still enjoyed his favorite hobbies and activities (although on the Beck depression Inventory [BDI] he expressed anhedonia). During his interview, the patient stated that his orthopedic surgeon had treated him with an antidepressant, but he per-ceived no change in mood or cognition. The patient felt a sense of loss and thought his depression was largely due to declining function and activities in daily living. He denied anxiety, impulse control disorder, and vivid dreams or hallucinations. Although he did not report features of RBD, he acknowledged disruption of sleep by pain, estimating 5 hours of sleep nightly on a long-standing basis.

The patient's scores on cognitive and neuropsychiatric measures are presented in Table 12.4. An IQ estimate was slightly below premorbid estimates, and the cognitive screening instrument (Dementia Rating Scale) disclosed impairment in overall level of cognitive functioning, with particular impairment of concep-tual abilities (also seen on matrix reasoning, a visual reasoning task). Executive function was also shown to be compromised by a card sorting test demanding of conceptualization and cognitive flexibility (WCST). He demonstrated impair-ments on most tests (except digit span) of attention, working memory, and psy-chomotor speed (Trail Making, Stroop, spatial span, letter-number sequencing). Language, including verbal fluency and visual confrontation naming, appeared well preserved (low average to average, consistent with premorbid expectations). The patient demonstrated markedly compromised visuoperceptual and spatial abilities (despite adequate acuity). He was unable to complete correctly even the sample items of the Judgment of Line Orientation test requiring matching of pairs of lines of similar spatial orientation. He had difficulty drawing or copying a clock, Greek cross, and three-dimensional cube.

Table 12.4 PATIENT WITH PARKINSON'S DISEASE, MILD DEMENTIA, AND
DEPRESSION: NEUROPSYCHOLOGICAL TEST SCORES

Test	Raw Score	Standard Score or Percentile
Wechsler Test of Adult Reading Estimated Verbal IQ	25	90
Wechsler Abbreviated Scale of Intelligence		
Vocabulary	43	38
Matrix Reasoning	5	28
Dementia Rating Scale–2		Age scaled
Attention (/37)	35	10
Initiation/Perseveration (/37)	36	10
Construction (/6)	6	10
Conceptualization (/39)	25	3
Memory	24	10
Total (/144)	126	5
Wechsler Memory Scale–III		Scaled
Letter–Number Sequencing	4	4
Spatial Span	5	5
Digit Span	15	8
Trail Making Test		T-score
A	108 sec, 1 error	23
B	300+ sec, 5 errors	25
Stroop (SNST)		Percentile
Color (/112)	94	<2
Color–Word (/112)	25 (29 errors)	
Wisconsin Card Sorting Test 64–Card Version		Percentile: 2–5 T-score: 25
Categories	0	Percentile: <1
Perseverative errors	34	
Trials to first category	65	
FAS words (180 sec)	25	T-score: 40
Animal naming words (60 sec)	18	T-score 52
Boston Naming Test (/60)	53	T-score 53
Judgment of Line Orientation (/30)	Unable to complete sample items	
BDAE Clock, Cube, Cross Drawings (/7)	Command: 3 Copy: 3	
Wechsler Memory Scale–III		Age scaled
Logical Memory I	28	7
Logical Memory II	15	8

(*Continued*)

Table 12.4 (CONTINUED)

Test	Raw Score	Standard Score or Percentile
Hopkins Verbal Learning Test–Revised		T-score
Trials 1–3 Total (/36)		<20
Delayed (/12)	15	30
Retention (%)	6	46
Recognition	86	
Hits	8	
False alarms	1	
Brief Visuospatial Memory Test–Revised		T-score
Trials 1–3 total (/36)		<20
Delayed (/12)	5	23
Retention (%)	3	Percentile: >16
Recognition	150	Percentile: <1
Hits (/6)	3	Percentile: >16
False alarms	0	
Beck Depression Inventory–II (/63)	24	Moderate

Abbreviations: BDAE, Boston Diagnostic Aphasia Examination; FAS, Fatigue Assessment Scale; SNST Stroop Neuropsychological Screening Test.

Memory was better (intact) for externally structured material (prose passages) but poor on tasks requiring self-initiated deployment of efficient learning strategies (word list and figure learning). While immediate recall of a word list was impaired, delayed recall was more mildly affected. Rate of forgetting was not accelerated and there were no significant numbers of perseverations or intrusions. The patient did not benefit from recognition relative to recall testing. When asked to learn the identity and location of six designs, recall was again poor, but delayed recall was no more impaired than immediate recall.

The patient endorsed moderate symptoms of depression on the BDI. Scrutiny of item endorsements revealed hopelessness, pessimism, guilt, anhedonia, loss of self-confidence, tearfulness, indecisiveness, poor concentration, increased sleep, irritability, fatigue, and loss of libido. These scores were above cutoff for moderate depressive symptomatology, and symptoms were unlikely simply related to PD or apathy given the items endorsed.

Given his impairment in activities of daily living; the range of cognitive impairments, especially pronounced in visuoperceptual function, attention, and executive function; as well as the problems encoding material (in the absence of rapid forgetting), a possible diagnosis of mild Parkinson's disease dementia or DLB was considered. The timeline of cognitive and motor symptom onset were difficult to pinpoint given family observations, but because the motor and cognitive symptoms had evolved almost in tandem, a provisional diagnosis of DLB was entertained. The absence of fluency and naming impairments made Alzheimer's disease (AD) less likely. Although an early, highly asymmetric (right hemisphere predominant pathology) AD could not be excluded by the neuropsychological test results, the unremarkable MRI, and especially the absence of asymmetric cortical atrophy, suggested this etiology as less likely. The patient had depression, which might exacerbate executive, working-memory, and episodic-memory impairments. However, the depressive symptoms were not severe enough to be the sole cause of cognitive deficits, and prior depression treatment did not result in any perceived symptomatic benefit.

References

Aarsland, D., Bronnick, K., Williams-Gray, C., Weintraub, D., Marder, K., Kulisevsky, J., ... Emre, M. (2010). Mild cognitive impairment in Parkinson disease: A multi-center pooled analysis. *Neurology, 75,* 1062–1069. doi:75/12/1062 [pii] 10.1212/WNL.0b013e3181f39d0e

Aarsland, D., Larsen, J. P., Karlsen, K., Lim, N. G., & Tandberg, E. (1999). Mental symptoms in Parkinson's disease are important contributors to caregiver distress. *International Journal of Geriatric Psychiatry, 14,* 866–874.

Abe, K., Takanashi, M., & Yanagihara, T. (2000). Fatigue in patients with Parkinson's disease. *Behavioural Neurology, 12,* 103–106.

Andersen, J., Aabro, E., Gulmann, N., Hjelmsted, A., & Pedersen, H. E. (1980). Antidepressive treatment in Parkinson's disease. A controlled trial of the effect of nortriptyline in patients with Parkinson's disease treated with L-DOPA. [Clinical Trial]. *Acta Neurologica Scandinavica, 62,* 210–219.

Barnes, J., & Boubert, L. (2008). Executive functions are impaired in patients with Parkinson's disease with visual hallucinations. [Research Support, Non-U.S. Gov't]. *Journal of Neurology, Neurosurgery, and Psychiatry, 79,* 190–192. doi:10.1136/jnnp.2007.116202

Barnes, J., & Boubert, L. (2011). Visual memory errors in Parkinson's disease patient with visual hallucinations. *The International journal of neuroscience, 121,* 159–164. doi:10.3109/00207454.2010.539308

Beatty, W. W., & Monson, N. (1989). Lexical processing in Parkinson's disease and multiple sclerosis. *Journal of Geriatric Psychiatry and Neurology, 2,* 145–152.

Beatty, W. W., Staton, R. D., Weir, W. S., Monson, N., & Whitaker, H. A. (1989). Cognitive disturbances in Parkinson's disease. *Journal of Geriatric Psychiatry and Neurology, 2,* 22–33.

Beck, A. T., Ward, C. H., Mendelson, M., Mock, J., & Erbaugh, J. (1961). An inventory for measuring depression. *Archives of General Psychiatry, 4,* 53–63.

Berger, H. J., van Es, N. J., van Spaendonck, K. P., Teunisse, J. P., Horstink, M. W., van 't Hof, M. A., & Cools, A. R. (1999). Relationship between memory strategies and motor symptoms in Parkinson's disease. *Journal of Clinical and Experimental Neuropsychology, 21,* 677–684.

Bohnen, N. I., Kaufer, D. I., Hendrickson, R., Ivanco, L. S., Lopresti, B. J., Constantine, G. M., et al. (2006). Cognitive correlates of cortical cholinergic denervation in Parkinson's disease and parkinsonian dementia. *Journal of Neurology, 253,* 242–247.

Boller, F., Marcie, P., Starkstein, S., & Traykov, L. (1998). Memory and depression in Parkinson's disease. *European Journal of Neurology, 5,* 291–295.

Bolluk, B., Ozel-Kizil, E. T., Akbostanci, M. C., & Atbasoglu, E. C. (2010). Social anxiety in patients with Parkinson's disease. *The Journal of Neuropsychiatry and Clinical Neurosciences, 22*, 390–394. doi:10.1176/appi.neuropsych.22.4.390

Bondi, M. W., Kaszniak, A. W., Bayles, K. A., & Vance, K. T. (1993). Contributions of frontal system dysfunction to memory and perceptual abilities in Parkinson's disease. *Neuropsychology, 7*, 89–102.

Bowen, F. P., Kamienny, R. S., Burns, M. M., & Yahr, M. (1975). Parkinsonism: Effects of levodopa treatment on concept formation. *Neurology, 25*, 701–704.

Bronnick, K., Alves, G., Aarsland, D., Tysnes, O. B., & Larsen, J. P. (2011). Verbal memory in drug-naive, newly diagnosed Parkinson's disease. The retrieval deficit hypothesis revisited. *Neuropsychology, 25*, 114–124. doi:10.1037/a0020857

Bronnick, K., Emre, M., Tekin, S., Haugen, S. B., & Aarsland, D. (2011). Cognitive correlates of visual hallucinations in dementia associated with Parkinson's disease. *Movement Disorders, 26*, 824–829. doi:10.1002/mds.23525

Brown, R. G., Landau, S., Hindle, J. V., Playfer, J., Samuel, M., Wilson, K. C., . . . Burn, D. J. (2011). Depression and anxiety related subtypes in Parkinson's disease. [Research Support, Non-U.S. Gov't]. *Journal of Neurology, Neurosurgery, and Psychiatry, 82*, 803–809. doi:10.1136/jnnp.2010.213652

Butterfield, L. C., Cimino, C. R., Oelke, L. E., Hauser, R. A., & Sanchez-Ramos, J. (2010). The independent influence of apathy and depression on cognitive functioning in Parkinson's disease. *Neuropsychology, 24*, 721–730. doi:10.1037/a0019650

Buytenhuijs, E. L., Berger, H. J., Van Spaendonck, K. P., Horstink, M. W., Borm, G. F., & Cools, A. R. (1994). Memory and learning strategies in patients with Parkinson's disease. *Neuropsychologia, 32*, 335–342.

Chaudhuri, K. R., Prieto-Jurcynska, C., Naidu, Y., Mitra, T., Frades-Payo, B., Tluk, S., . . . Martinez-Martin, P. (2010). The nondeclaration of nonmotor symptoms of Parkinson's disease to health care professionals: An international study using the nonmotor symptoms questionnaire. [Multicenter Study Research Support, Non-U.S. Gov't]. *Movement Disorders, 25*, 704–709. doi:10.1002/mds.22868

Chen, P., Kales, H. C., Weintraub, D., Blow, F. C., Jiang, L., Ignacio, R. V., & Mellow, A. M. (2007). Depression in veterans with Parkinson's disease: Frequency, co-morbidity, and healthcare utilization. *International Journal of Geriatric Psychiatry, 22*, 543–548. doi:10.1002/gps.1712

Cole, S. A., Woodard, J. L., Juncos, J. L., Kogos, J. L., Youngstrom, E. A., & Watts, R. L. (1996). Depression and disability in Parkinson's disease. *Journal of Neuropsychiatry and Clinical Neuroscience, 8*, 20–25.

Cools, R. (2006). Dopaminergic modulation of cognitive function-implications for L-DOPA treatment in Parkinson's disease. *Neuroscience and Biobehavioral Reviews, 30*, 1–23.

Cooper, J. A., Sagar, H. J., Jordan, N., Harvey, N. S., & Sullivan, E. V. (1991). Cognitive impairment in early, untreated Parkinson's disease and its relationship to motor disability. *Brain, 114*, 2095–2122.

Costa, A., Peppe, A., Carlesimo, G. A., Pasqualetti, P., & Caltagirone, C. (2006). Major and minor depression in Parkinson's disease: A neuropsychological investigation. *European Journal of Neurology, 13*, 972–980.

Cousins, R., Hanley, J. R., Davies, A. D., Turnbull, C. J., & Playfer, J. R. (2000). Understanding memory for faces in Parkinson's disease: The role of configural processing. *Neuropsychologia, 38*, 837–847.

Cummings, J. L., & Masterman, D. L. (1999). Depression in patients with Parkinson's disease. *International Journal of Geriatric Psychiatry, 14*, 711–718.

Davous, P., Auquier, P., Grignon, S., & Neukirch, H. C. (1995). A prospective study of depression in French patients with Parkinson's disease: The Depar Study. *European Journal of Neurology, 2,* 455–461.

Dissanayaka, N. N., Sellbach, A., Matheson, S., Marsh, R., Silburn, P. A., O' Sullivan, J. D., et al. (2007). Validity of Hamilton Depression Inventory in Parkinson's disease. *Movement Disorders, 22,* 399–403.

Dobkin, R. D., Menza, M., Bienfait, K. L., Gara, M., Marin, H., Mark, M. H., ... Troster, A. (2010). The impact of antidepressant treatment on cognitive functioning in depressed patients with Parkinson's disease. [Randomized Controlled Trial Research Support, N.I.H., Extramural Research Support, Non-U.S. Gov't]. *The Journal of Neuropsychiatry and Clinical Neurosciences, 22,* 188–195. doi:10.1176/appi.neuropsych.22.2.188

Dooneief, G., Mirabello, E., Bell, K., Marder, K., Stern, Y., & Mayeux, R. (1992). An estimate of the incidence of depression in idiopathic Parkinson's disease. *Archives of Neurology, 49,* 305–307.

Drijgers, R. L., Dujardin, K., Reijnders, J. S., Defebvre, L., & Leentjens, A. F. (2010). Validation of diagnostic criteria for apathy in Parkinson's disease. [Validation Studies]. *Parkinsonism & Related Disorders, 16,* 656–660. doi:10.1016/j.parkreldis.2010.08.015

Dujardin, K., Degreef, J. F., Rogelet, P., Defebvre, L., & Destee, A. (1999). Impairment of the supervisory attentional system in early untreated patients with Parkinson's disease. *Journal of Neurology, 246,* 783–788.

Dujardin, K., Sockeel, P., Delliaux, M., Destee, A., & Defebvre, L. (2009). Apathy may herald cognitive decline and dementia in Parkinson's disease. *Movement Disorders, 24,* 2391–2397. doi:10.1002/mds.22843

Dujardin, K., Sockeel, P., Devos, D., Delliaux, M., Krystkowiak, P., Destee, A., & Defebvre, L. (2007). Characteristics of apathy in Parkinson's disease. *Movement Disorders, 22,* 778–784. doi:10.1002/mds.21316

Elgh, E., Domellof, M., Linder, J., Edstrom, M., Stenlund, H., & Forsgren, L. (2009). Cognitive function in early Parkinson's disease: A population-based study. *European Journal of Neurology, 16,* 1278–1284. doi:ENE2707[pii]10.1111/j.1468-1331.2009.02707.x

Faglioni, P., Saetti, M. C., & Botti, C. (2000). Verbal learning strategies in Parkinson's disease. *Neuropsychology, 14,* 456–470.

Fama, R., Sullivan, E. V., Shear, P. K., Stein, M., Yesavage, J. A., Tinklenberg, J. R., & Pfefferbaum, A. (2000). Extent, pattern, and correlates of remote memory impairment in Alzheimer's disease and Parkinson's disease. *Neuropsychology, 14,* 265–276.

Fenelon, G., & Alves, G. (2010). Epidemiology of psychosis in Parkinson's disease. [Review]. *Journal of the Neurological Sciences, 289,* 12–17. doi:10.1016/j.jns.2009.08.014

Fenelon, G., Soulas, T., Zenasni, F., & de Langavant, L. C. (2010). The changing face of Parkinson's disease-associated psychosis: A cross-sectional study based on the new NINDS-NIMH criteria. *Movement Disorders, 25,* 763–766. doi:10.1002/mds.22839

Fernandez, H. H., Aarsland, D., Fenelon, G., Friedman, J. H., Marsh, L., Troster, A. I., ... Goetz, C. G. (2008). Scales to assess psychosis in Parkinson's disease: Critique and recommendations. [Validation Studies]. *Movement Disorders, 23,* 484–500. doi:10.1002/mds.21875

Fernandez, H. H., See, R. H., Gary, M. F., Bowers, D., Rodriguez, R. L., Jacobson, C. T., & Okun, M. S. (2009). Depressive symptoms in Parkinson disease correlate with impaired global and specific cognitive performance. *Journal of Geriatric Psychiatry and Neurology, 22,* 223–227. doi:10.1177/0891988709335792

Fernandez, H. H., Tabamo, R. E., David, R. R., & Friedman, J. H. (2001). Predictors of depressive symptoms among spouse caregivers in Parkinson's disease. *Movement Disorders, 16*, 1123–1125.

Foltynie, T., Brayne, C. E., Robbins, T. W., & Barker, R. A. (2004). The cognitive ability of an incident cohort of Parkinson's patients in the UK. The CamPaIGN study. *Brain, 127*, 550–560.

Foster, P. S., Drago, V., Yung, R. C., Skidmore, F. M., Skoblar, B., Shenal, B. V., … Heilman, K. M. (2010). Anxiety affects working memory only in left hemibody onset Parkinson disease patients. *Cognitive and Behavioral Neurology, 23*, 14–18. doi:10.1097/WNN. 0b013e3181cc8be9

Friedman, J. H., Alves, G., Hagell, P., Marinus, J., Marsh, L., Martinez-Martin, P., … Schrag, A. (2010). Fatigue rating scales critique and recommendations by the Movement Disorders Society task force on rating scales for Parkinson's disease. [Review]. *Movement Disorders, 25*, 805–822. doi:10.1002/mds.22989

Gabrieli, J. D. E., Singh, J., Stebbins, G., & Goetz, C. G. (1996). Reduced working memory span in Parkinson's disease: Evidence for the role of a frontostriatal system in working and strategic memory. *Neuropsychology, 10*, 322–332.

Gagnon, J. F., Vendette, M., Postuma, R. B., Desjardins, C., Massicotte-Marquez, J., Panisset, M., & Montplaisir, J. (2009). Mild cognitive impairment in rapid eye movement sleep behavior disorder and Parkinson's disease. [Research Support, Non-U.S. Gov't]. *Annals of Neurology, 66*, 39–47. doi:10.1002/ana.21680

Hamilton, M. (1960). A rating scale for depression. *Journal of Neurology, Neurosurgery, and Psychiatry, 23*, 56–62.

Hantz, P., Caradoc-Davies, G., Caradoc-Davies, T., Weatherall, M., & Dixon, G. (1994). Depression in Parkinson's disease. *American Journal of Psychiatry, 151*, 1010–1014.

Hely, M. A., Reid, W. G., Adena, M. A., Halliday, G. M., & Morris, J. G. (2008). The Sydney multicenter study of Parkinson's disease: The inevitability of dementia at 20 years. *Movement Disorders, 23*, 837–844. doi:10.1002/mds.21956

Higginson, C. I., Fields, J. A., Koller, W. C., & Tröster, A. I. (2001). Questionnaire assessment potentially overestimates anxiety in Parkinson's disease. *Journal of Clinical Psychology in Medical Settings, 8*, 95–99.

Hogl, B., Arnulf, I., Comella, C., Ferreira, J., Iranzo, A., Tilley, B., … Goetz, C. G. (2010). Scales to assess sleep impairment in Parkinson's disease: Critique and recommendations. [Research Support, N.I.H., Extramural Research Support, Non-U.S. Gov't]. *Movement Disorders: official journal of the Movement Disorder Society, 25*, 2704–2716. doi:10.1002/mds.23190

Hubble, J. P., Cao, T., Hassanein, R. E., Neuberger, J. S., & Koller, W. C. (1993). Risk factors for Parkinson's disease. *Neurology, 43*, 1693–1697.

Imamura, K., Wada-Isoe, K., Kitayama, M., & Nakashima, K. (2008). Executive dysfunction in non-demented Parkinson's disease patients with hallucinations. *Acta Neurologica Scandinavica, 117*, 255–259. doi:10.1111/j.1600-0404.2007.00933.x

Isella, V., Melzi, P., Grimaldi, M., Iurlaro, S., Piolti, R., Ferrarese, C., et al. (2002). Clinical, neuropsychological, and morphometric correlates of apathy in Parkinson's disease. *Movement Disorders, 17*, 366–371.

Karlsen, K., Larsen, J. P., Tandberg, E., & Jorgensen, K. (1999). Fatigue in patients with Parkinson's disease. [Research Support, Non-U.S. Gov't]. *Movement Disorders, 14*, 237–241.

Katzen, H., Myerson, C., Papapetropoulos, S., Nahab, F., Gallo, B., & Levin, B. (2010). Multi-modal hallucinations and cognitive function in Parkinson's disease. *Dementia and Geriatric Cognitive Disorders, 30*, 51–56. doi:10.1159/000314875

Kehagia, A. A., Barker, R. A., & Robbins, T. W. (2010). Neuropsychological and clinical heterogeneity of cognitive impairment and dementia in patients with Parkinson's disease. [Research Support, Non-U.S. Gov't Review]. *Lancet Neurology, 9*, 1200–1213. doi:10.1016/S1474-4422(10)70212-X

Kensinger, E. A., Shearer, D. K., Locascio, J. J., & Growdon, J. H. (2003). Working memory in mild Alzheimer's disease and early Parkinson's disease. *Neuropsychology, 17*, 230–239.

Kirsch-Darrow, L., Fernandez, H. H., Marsiske, M., Okun, M. S., & Bowers, D. (2006). Dissociating apathy and depression in Parkinson disease. *Neurology, 67*, 33–38. doi:67/1/33 [pii] 10.1212/01.wnl.0000230572.07791.22

Kirsch-Darrow, L., Marsiske, M., Okun, M. S., Bauer, R., & Bowers, D. (2011). Apathy and depression: separate factors in Parkinson's disease. [Research Support, N.I.H., Extramural Research Support, Non-U.S. Gov't]. *Journal of the International Neuropsychological Society, 17*, 1058–1066. doi:10.1017/S1355617711001068

Klepac, N., Hajnsek, S., & Trkulja, V. (2010). Cognitive performance in nondemented nonpsychotic Parkinson disease patients with or without a history of depression prior to the onset of motor symptoms. *Journal of Geriatric Psychiatry and Neurology, 23*, 15–26. doi:10.1177/0891988709351831

Kliegel, M., Altgassen, M., Hering, A., & Rose, N. S. (2011). A process-model based approach to prospective memory impairment in Parkinson's disease. *Neuropsychologia, 49*, 2166–2177. doi:10.1016/j.neuropsychologia.2011.01.024

Kremer, J., & Starkstein, S. E. (2000). Affective disorders in Parkinson's disease. *International Review of Psychiatry, 12*, 290–297.

Kudlicka, A., Clare, L., & Hindle, J. V. (2011). Executive functions in Parkinson's disease: Systematic review and meta-analysis. [Research Support, Non-U.S. Gov't]. *Movement Disorders, 26*, 2305–2315. doi:10.1002/mds.23868

Kummer, A., Cardoso, F., & Teixeira, A. L. (2008). Frequency of social phobia and psychometric properties of the Liebowitz social anxiety scale in Parkinson's disease. [Research Support, Non-U.S. Gov't]. *Movement Disorders, 23*, 1739–1743. doi:10.1002/mds.22221

Kummer, A., Cardoso, F., & Teixeira, A. L. (2010). Generalized anxiety disorder and the Hamilton Anxiety Rating Scale in Parkinson's disease. [Research Support, Non-U.S. Gov't]. *Arquivos de Neuro-Psiquiatria, 68*, 495–501.

Kuzis, G., Sabe, L., Tiberti, C., Leiguarda, R., & Starkstein, S. E. (1997). Cognitive functions in major depression and Parkinson disease. *Archives of Neurology, 54*, 982–986.

Lee, A. C., Harris, J. P., & Calvert, J. E. (1998). Impairments of mental rotation in Parkinson's disease. *Neuropsychologia, 36*, 109–114.

Lee, E. Y., Cowan, N., Vogel, E. K., Rolan, T., Valle-Inclan, F., & Hackley, S. A. (2010). Visual working memory deficits in patients with Parkinson's disease are due to both reduced storage capacity and impaired ability to filter out irrelevant information. [Research Support, N.I.H., Extramural Research Support, Non-U.S. Gov't]. *Brain, 133*, 2677–2689. doi:10.1093/brain/awq197

Leentjens, A. F., Dujardin, K., Marsh, L., Martinez-Martin, P., Richard, I. H., Starkstein, S. E., ... Goetz, C. G. (2008a). Anxiety rating scales in Parkinson's disease: Critique and recommendations. *Movement Disorders, 23*, 2015–2025. doi:10.1002/mds.22233

Leentjens, A. F., Dujardin, K., Marsh, L., Martinez-Martin, P., Richard, I. H., Starkstein, S. E., ... Goetz, C. G. (2008b). Apathy and anhedonia rating scales in Parkinson's disease: Critique and recommendations. *Movement Disorders, 23*, 2004–2014. doi:10.1002/mds.22229

Leentjens, A. F., Verhey, F. R., Lousberg, R., Spitsbergen, H., & Wilmink, F. W. (2000). The validity of the Hamilton and Montgomery-Asberg depression rating scales as screening and diagnostic tools for depression in Parkinson's disease. *International Journal of Geriatric Psychiatry, 15*, 644–649.

Leentjens, A. F., Verhey, F. R., Luijckx, G. J., & Troost, J. (2000). The validity of the Beck Depression Inventory as a screening and diagnostic instrument for depression in patients with Parkinson's disease. *Movement Disorders, 15*, 1221–1224.

Leplow, B., Dierks, C., Herrmann, P., Pieper, N., Annecke, R., & Ulm, G. (1997). Remote memory in Parkinson's disease and senile dementia. *Neuropsychologia, 35*, 547–557.

Levin, B. E., Llabre, M. M., Reisman, S., Weiner, W. J., Sanchez-Ramos, J., Singer, C., & Brown, M. C. (1991). Visuospatial impairment in Parkinson's disease. *Neurology, 41*, 365–369.

Levin, B. E., Llabre, M. M., & Weiner, W. J. (1989). Cognitive impairments associated with early Parkinson's disease. *Neurology, 39*, 557–561.

Levy, M. L., Cummings, J. L., Fairbanks, L. A., Masterman, D., Miller, B. L., Craig, A. H., et al. (1998). Apathy is not depression. *Journal of Neuropsychiatry and Clinical Neurosciences, 10*, 314–319.

Lewis, S. J., Cools, R., Robbins, T. W., Dove, A., Barker, R. A., & Owen, A. M. (2003). Using executive heterogeneity to explore the nature of working memory deficits in Parkinson's disease. *Neuropsychologia, 41*, 645–654.

Lewis, F. M., Lapointe, L. L., & Murdoch, B. E. (1998). Language impairment in Parkinson's disease. *Aphasiology, 12*, 193–206.

Litvan, I., Aarsland, D., Adler, C. H., Goldman, J. G., Kulisevsky, J., Mollenhauer, B.,... Weintraub, D. (2011). MDS Task Force on mild cognitive impairment in Parkinson's disease: Critical review of PD-MCI. *Movement Disorders, 26*, 1814–1824. doi:10.1002/mds.23823

Litvan, I., Goldman, J. G., Troster, A. I., Schmand, B. A., Weintraub, D., Petersen, R. C.,... Emre, M. (2012). Diagnostic criteria for mild cognitive impairment in Parkinson's disease: Movement Disorder Society Task Force guidelines. *Movement Disorders, 27*, 349–356. doi:10.1002/mds.24893

Louis, E. D., Huey, E. D., Gerbin, M., & Viner, A. S. (2012). Apathy in essential tremor, dystonia, and Parkinson's disease: A comparison with normal controls. *Movement Disorders, 27*, 432–434. doi: 10.1002/mds.24049

Marder, K., Tang, M. X., Cote, L., Stern, Y., & Mayeux, R. (1995). The frequency and associated risk factors for dementia in patients with Parkinson's disease. *Archives of Neurology, 52*, 695–701.

Marin, R. S. (1990). Differential diagnosis and classification of apathy. [Research Support, U.S. Gov't, P.H.S. Review]. *The American Journal of Psychiatry, 147*, 22–30.

Marin, R. S., Biedrzycki, R. C., & Firinciogullari, S. (1991). Reliability and validity of the Apathy Evaluation Scale. [Research Support, U.S. Gov't, P.H.S.]. *Psychiatry Research, 38*, 143–162.

Marques, A., Dujardin, K., Boucart, M., Pins, D., Delliaux, M., Defebvre, L.,... Monaca, C. (2010). REM sleep behaviour disorder and visuoperceptive dysfunction: A disorder of the ventral visual stream? *Journal of Neurology, 257*, 383–391. doi:10.1007/s00415-009-5328-7

Marsh, L. (2000). Anxiety disorders in Parkinson's disease. *International Review of Psychiatry, 12*, 307–318.

Marsh, L., McDonald, W. M., Cummings, J., & Ravina, B. (2006). Provisional diagnostic criteria for depression in Parkinson's disease: Report of an NINDS/NIMH Work Group. *Movement Disorders, 21*, 148–158. doi:10.1002/mds.20723

Martinez-Martin, P., Visser, M., Rodriguez-Blazquez, C., Marinus, J., Chaudhuri, K. R., & van Hilten, J. J. (2008). SCOPA-sleep and PDSS: Two scales for assessment of sleep disorder in Parkinson's disease. [Multicenter Study Research Support, Non-U.S. Gov't]. *Movement Disorders, 23*, 1681–1688. doi:10.1002/mds.22110

Massman, P. J., Delis, D. C., Butters, N., Levin, B. E., & Salmon, D. P. (1990). Are all subcortical dementias alike? Verbal learning and memory in Parkinson's and Huntington's disease patients. *Journal of Clinical and Experimental Neuropsychology, 12*, 729–744.

McDowd, J., Hoffman, L., Rozek, E., Lyons, K. E., Pahwa, R., Burns, J., & Kemper, S. (2011). Understanding verbal fluency in healthy aging, Alzheimer's disease, and Parkinson's disease. [Research Support, N.I.H., Extramural]. *Neuropsychology, 25*, 210–225. doi:10.1037/a0021531

McKinlay, A., Grace, R. C., Dalrymple-Alford, J. C., & Roger, D. (2010). Characteristics of executive function impairment in Parkinson's disease patients without dementia. [Research Support, Non-U.S. Gov't]. *Journal of the International Neuropsychological Society, 16*, 268–277. doi:10.1017/S1355617709991299

Menza, M. A., & Mark, M. H. (1994). Parkinson's disease and depression: The relationship to disability and personality. *Journal of Neuropsychiatry and Clinical Neurosciences, 6*, 165–169.

Menza, M. A., Palermo, B., DiPaola, R., Sage, J. I., & Ricketts, M. H. (1999). Depression and anxiety in Parkinson's disease: Possible effect of genetic variation in the serotonin transporter. *Journal of Geriatric Psychiatry and Neurology, 12*, 49–52.

Menza, M. A., Robertson-Hoffman, D. E., & Bonapace, A. S. (1993). Parkinson's disease and anxiety: Comorbidity with depression. *Biological Psychiatry, 34*, 465–470.

Mioshi, E., Dawson, K., Mitchell, J., Arnold, R., & Hodges, J. R. (2006). The Addenbrooke's Cognitive Examination Revised (ACE-R): A brief cognitive test battery for dementia screening. [Evaluation Studies Research Support, Non-U.S. Gov't Validation Studies]. *International Journal of Geriatric Psychiatry, 21*, 1078–1085. doi:10.1002/gps.1610

Mondolo, F., Jahanshahi, M., Grana, A., Biasutti, E., Cacciatori, E., & Di Benedetto, P. (2006). The validity of the hospital anxiety and depression scale and the geriatric depression scale in Parkinson's disease. [Research Support, Non-U.S. Gov't Validation Studies]. *Behavioural Neurology, 17*, 109–115.

Montgomery, S. A., & Asberg, M. (1979). A new depression scale designed to be sensitive to change. *British Journal of Psychiatry, 134*, 382–389.

Morris, R. G., Downes, J. J., Sahakian, B. J., Evenden, J. L., Heald, A., & Robbins, T. W. (1988). Planning and spatial working memory in Parkinson's disease. *Journal of Neurology, Neurosurgery, and Psychiatry, 51*, 757–766.

Murray, L. L. (2000). Spoken language production in Huntington's and Parkinson's diseases. *Journal of Speech, Language, and Hearing Research, 43*, 1350–1366.

Muslimovic, D., Post, B., Speelman, J. D., & Schmand, B. (2005). Cognitive profile of patients with newly diagnosed Parkinson disease. *Neurology, 65*, 1239–1245.

Naarding, P., Leentjens, A. F., Van Kooten, F., & Verhey, F. R. (2002). Disease-specific properties of the Hamilton Rating Scale for depression in patients with stroke, Alzheimer's dementia, and Parkinson's disease. *Journal of Neuropsychiatry and Clinical Neurosciences, 14*, 329–334.

Naville, F. (1922). Les complications et let sequelles mentales de l'encephalite epidemique. *Encephale, 17*, 369–375 and 423–336.

Norman, S., Tröster, A. I., Fields, J. A., & Brooks, R. (2002). Effects of depression and Parkinson's disease on cognitive functioning. *Journal of Neuropsychiatry and Clinical Neuroscience, 14*, 31–36.

Nuti, A., Ceravolo, R., Piccinni, A., Dell'Agnello, G., Bellini, G., Gambaccini, G.,...
Bonuccelli, U. (2004). Psychiatric comorbidity in a population of Parkinson's disease patients. [Comparative Study]. *European Journal of Neurology, 11*, 315–320. doi:10.1111/j.1468-1331.2004.00781.x

Owen, A. M., Sahakian, B. J., Hodges, J. R., Summers, B. A., Polkey, C. E., & Robbins, T. W. (1995). Dopamine-dependent fronto-striatal planning deficits in early Parkinson's disease. *Neuropsychology, 9*, 126–140.

Pagni, C., Frosini, D., Ceravolo, R., Giunti, G., Unti, E., Poletti, M.,...Tognoni, G. (2011). Event-based prospective memory in newly diagnosed, drug-naive Parkinson's disease patients. *Journal of the International Neuropsychological Society, 17*, 1158–1162. doi:10.1017/S1355617711001214

Piatt, A. L., Fields, J. A., Paolo, A. M., Koller, W. C., & Tröster, A. I. (1999). Lexical, semantic, and action verbal fluency in Parkinson's disease with and without dementia. *Journal of Clinical and Experimental Neuropsychology, 21*, 435–443.

Pillon, B., Dubois, B., Ploska, A., & Agid, Y. (1991). Severity and specificity of cognitive impairment in Alzheimer's, Huntington's, and Parkinson's diseases and progressive supranuclear palsy. *Neurology, 41*, 634–643.

Ramirez-Ruiz, B., Junque, C., Marti, M. J., Valldeoriola, F., & Tolosa, E. (2006). Neuropsychological deficits in Parkinson's disease patients with visual hallucinations. [Research Support, Non-U.S. Gov't]. *Movement Disorders, 21*, 1483–1487. doi:10.1002/mds.20965

Randolph, C., Braun, A. R., Goldberg, T. E., & Chase, T. N. (1993). Semantic fluency in Alzheimer's, Parkinson's, and Huntington's disease: Dissociation of storage and retrieval failures. *Neuropsychology, 7*, 82–88.

Raskin, S. A., Woods, S. P., Poquette, A. J., McTaggart, A. B., Sethna, J., Williams, R. C., & Troster, A. I. (2011). A differential deficit in time- versus event-based prospective memory in Parkinson's disease. *Neuropsychology, 25*, 201–209. doi:10.1037/a0020999

Reijnders, J. S., Ehrt, U., Weber, W. E., Aarsland, D., & Leentjens, A. F. (2008). A systematic review of prevalence studies of depression in Parkinson's disease. *Movement Disorders, 23*, 183–189; quiz 313. doi:10.1002/mds.21803

Reynolds, W. M., & Kobak, K., A. (1995). *Hamilton Depression Inventory—a self-report version of the Hamilton Depression Rating Scale (HDRS)*. Odessa, FL: Psychological Assessment Resources.

Richard, I. H. (2005). Anxiety disorders in Parkinson's disease. [Research Support, N.I.H., Extramural Research Support, Non-U.S. Gov't Review]. *Advances in Neurology, 96*, 42–55.

Richard, I. H. (2007). Depression and apathy in Parkinson's disease. *Current Neurology and Neuroscience Reports, 7*, 295–301.

Rieger, M., Gauggel, S., & Burmeister, K. (2003). Inhibition of ongoing responses following frontal, nonfrontal, and basal ganglia lesions. *Neuropsychology, 17*, 272–282.

Robert, P., Onyike, C. U., Leentjens, A. F., Dujardin, K., Aalten, P., Starkstein, S.,... Byrne, J. (2009). Proposed diagnostic criteria for apathy in Alzheimer's disease and other neuropsychiatric disorders. *European Psychiatry, 24*, 98–104. doi:10.1016/j.eurpsy.2008.09.001

Rouleau, I., Imbault, H., Laframboise, M., & Bedard, M. A. (2001). Pattern of intrusions in verbal recall: Comparison of Alzheimer's disease, Parkinson's disease, and frontal lobe dementia. *Brain and Cognition, 46*, 244–249.

Ryder, K. A., Gontkovsky, S. T., McSwan, K. L., Scott, J. G., Bharucha, K. J., & Beatty, W. W. (2002). Cognitive function in Parkinson's disease: Association with anxiety but not depression. *Aging, Neuropsychology, and Cognition, 9*, 77–84.

Sagar, H. J., Cohen, N. J., Sullivan, E. V., Corkin, S., & Growdon, J. H. (1988). Remote memory function in Alzheimer's disease and Parkinson's disease. *Brain, 111,* 185–206.

Saint-Cyr, J. A., Taylor, A. E., & Lang, A. E. (1988). Procedural learning and neostriatal dysfunction in man. *Brain, 111,* 941–959.

Santangelo, G., Vitale, C., Trojano, L., Longo, K., Cozzolino, A., Grossi, D., & Barone, P. (2009). Relationship between depression and cognitive dysfunctions in Parkinson's disease without dementia. *Journal of Neurology, 256,* 632–638. doi:10.1007/s00415-009-0146-5

Schrag, A., Barone, P., Brown, R. G., Leentjens, A. F., McDonald, W. M., Starkstein, S., et al. (2007). Depression rating scales in Parkinson's disease: Critique and recommendations. *Movement Disorders, 22,* 1077–1092.

Schrag, A., Jahanshahi, M., & Quinn, N. (2000). What contributes to quality of life in patients with Parkinson's disease? *Journal of Neurology, Neurosurgery, and Psychiatry, 69,* 308–312.

Sheikh, J. I., & Yesavage, J. A. (1986). Geriatric Depression Scale (GDS): Recent evidence and development of a shorter version. *Clinical Gerontologist, 5,* 165–173

Shulman, L. M. (2000). Apathy in patients with Parkinson's disease. *International Review of Psychiatry, 12,* 298–306.

Shulman, L. M., Taback, R. L., Rabinstein, A. A., & Weiner, W. J. (2002). Non-recognition of depression and other non-motor symptoms in Parkinson's disease. *Parkinsonism and Related Disorders, 8,* 193–197.

Sinforiani, E., Pacchetti, C., Zangaglia, R., Pasotti, C., Manni, R., & Nappi, G. (2008). REM behavior disorder, hallucinations and cognitive impairment in Parkinson's disease: A two-year follow up. [Comparative Study]. *Movement disorders, 23,* 1441–1445. doi:10.1002/mds.22126

Sinforiani, E., Zangaglia, R., Manni, R., Cristina, S., Marchioni, E., Nappi, G.,… Pacchetti, C. (2006). REM sleep behavior disorder, hallucinations, and cognitive impairment in Parkinson's disease. [Comparative Study]. *Movement disorders, 21,* 462–466. doi:10.1002/mds.20719

Smith, S. J., Souchay, C., & Conway, M. A. (2010). Overgeneral autobiographical memory in Parkinson's disease. *Cortex, 46,* 787–793. doi:10.1016/j.cortex.2009.08.006

Smith, S. J., Souchay, C., & Moulin, C. J. (2011). Metamemory and prospective memory in Parkinson's disease. *Neuropsychology, 25,* 734–740. doi:10.1037/a0025475

Stacy, M. (2002). Sleep disorders in Parkinson's disease: Epidemiology and management. [Review]. *Drugs and Aging, 19,* 733–739.

Starkstein, S. E., Bolduc, P. L., Mayberg, H. S., Preziosi, T. J., & Robinson, R. G. (1990). Cognitive impairments and depression in Parkinson's disease: A follow up study. *Journal of Neurology, Neurosurgery, and Psychiatry, 53,* 597–602.

Starkstein, S. E., & Leentjens, A. F. (2008). The nosological position of apathy in clinical practice. [Research Support, Non-U.S. Gov't Review]. *Journal of Neurology, Neurosurgery, and Psychiatry, 79,* 1088–1092. doi:10.1136/jnnp.2007.136895

Starkstein, S. E., Mayberg, H. S., Leiguarda, R., Preziosi, T. J., & Robinson, R. G. (1992). A prospective longitudinal study of depression, cognitive decline, and physical impairments in patients with Parkinson's disease. *Journal of Neurology, Neurosurgery, and Psychiatry, 55,* 377–382.

Starkstein, S. E., Mayberg, H. S., Preziosi, T. J., Andrezejewski, P., Leiguarda, R., & Robinson, R. G. (1992). Reliability, validity, and clinical correlates of apathy in Parkinson's disease. *Journal of Neuropsychiatry and Clinical Neurosciences, 4,* 134–139.

Starkstein, S. E., Preziosi, T. J., Berthier, M. L., Bolduc, P. L., Mayberg, H. S., & Robinson, R. G. (1989). Depression and cognitive impairment in Parkinson's disease. *Brain, 112*, 1141–1153.

Starkstein, S. E., Preziosi, T. J., Bolduc, P. L., & Robinson, R. G. (1990). Depression in Parkinson's disease. *Journal of Nervous and Mental Disease, 178*, 27–31.

Starkstein, S. E., & Robinson, R. G. (1991). Dementia of depression in Parkinson's disease and stroke. *Journal of Nervous and Mental Disease, 179*, 593–601.

Stavitsky, K., Neargarder, S., Bogdanova, Y., McNamara, P., & Cronin-Golomb, A. (2012). The impact of sleep quality on cognitive functioning in Parkinson's disease. [Research Support, N.I.H., Extramural Research Support, Non-U.S. Gov't]. *Journal of the International Neuropsychological Society, 18*, 108–117. doi:10.1017/S1355617711001482

Stefanova, E., Potrebic, A., Ziropadja, L., Maric, J., Ribaric, I., & Kostic, V. S. (2006). Depression predicts the pattern of cognitive impairment in early Parkinson's disease. *Journal of the Neurological Sciences, 248*, 131–137. doi:S0022-510X(06)00227-9 [pii] 10.1016/j.jns.2006.05.031

Stein, M. B., Heuser, I. J., Juncos, J. L., & Uhde, T. W. (1990). Anxiety disorders in patients with Parkinson's disease. *American Journal of Psychiatry, 147*, 217–220.

Sullivan, E. V., Sagar, H. J., Gabrieli, J. D., Corkin, S., & Growdon, J. H. (1989). Different cognitive profiles on standard behavioral tests in Parkinson's disease and Alzheimer's disease. *Journal of Clinical and Experimental Neuropsychology, 11*, 799–820.

Tandberg, E., Larsen, J. P., Aarsland, D., & Cummings, J. L. (1996). The occurrence of depression in Parkinson's disease. A community-based study. *Archives of Neurology, 53*, 175–179.

Taylor, A. E., Saint-Cyr, J. A., & Lang, A. E. (1986). Frontal lobe dysfunction in Parkinson's disease. The cortical focus of neostriatal outflow. *Brain, 109*, 845–883.

Tomer, R., Levin, B. E., & Weiner, W. J. (1993). Side of onset of motor symptoms influences cognition in Parkinson's disease. *Annals of Neurology, 34*, 579–584.

Tröster, A. I. (2011). A précis of recent advances in the neuropsychology of mild cognitive impairment(s) in Parkinson's disease and a proposal of preliminary research criteria. *Journal of the International Neuropsychological Society, 8*, 1–14. doi:10.1017/S1355617711000257

Tröster, A. I., Fields, J. A., Testa, J. A., Paul, R. H., Blanco, C. R., Hames, K. A., . . . Beatty, W. W. (1998). Cortical and subcortical influences on clustering and switching in the performance of verbal fluency tasks. *Neuropsychologia, 36*, 295–304.

Tröster, A. I., Stalp, L. D., Paolo, A. M., Fields, J. A., & Koller, W. C. (1995). Neuropsychological impairment in Parkinson's disease with and without depression. *Archives of Neurology, 52*, 1164–1169.

Troyer, A. K., Moscovitch, M., Winocur, G., Leach, L., & Freedman, M. (1998). Clustering and switching on verbal fluency tests in Alzheimer's and Parkinson's disease. *Journal of the International Neuropsychological Society, 4*, 137–143.

Uekermann, J., Daum, I., Peters, S., Wiebel, B., Przuntek, H., & Muller, T. (2003). Depressed mood and executive dysfunction in early Parkinson's disease. [Comparative Study Research Support, Non-U.S. Gov't]. *Acta Neurologica Scandinavica, 107*, 341–348.

Varanese, S., Perfetti, B., Ghilardi, M. F., & Di Rocco, A. (2011). Apathy, but not depression, reflects inefficient cognitive strategies in Parkinson's disease. *PLoS one, 6*, e17846. doi:10.1371/journal.pone.0017846

Vazquez, A., Jimenez-Jimenez, F. J., Garcia-Ruiz, P., & Garcia-Urra, D. (1993). "Panic attacks" in Parkinson's disease. A long-term complication of levodopa therapy. *Acta Neurologica Scandanavica, 87*, 14–18.

Vendette, M., Gagnon, J. F., Decary, A., Massicotte-Marquez, J., Postuma, R. B., Doyon, J., . . . Montplaisir, J. (2007). REM sleep behavior disorder predicts cognitive impairment in Parkinson disease without dementia. [Comparative Study Research Support, Non-U.S. Gov't]. *Neurology, 69*, 1843–1849. doi:10.1212/01.wnl.0000278114.14096.74

Venneri, A., Nichelli, P., Modonesi, G., Molinari, M. A., Russo, R., & Sardini, C. (1997). Impairment in dating and retrieving remote events in patients with early Parkinson's disease. *Journal of Neurology, Neurosurgery, and Psychiatry, 62*, 410–413.

Weintraub, D., Moberg, P. J., Culbertson, W. C., Duda, J. E., & Stern, M. B. (2004). Evidence for impaired encoding and retrieval memory profiles in Parkinson disease. *Cognitive and Behavioral Neurology, 17*, 195–200.

Weintraub, D., Moberg, P. J., Duda, J. E., Katz, I. R., & Stern, M. B. (2003). Recognition and treatment of depression in Parkinson's disease. *Journal of Geriatric Psychiatry and Neurology, 16*, 178–183.

Weintraub, D., Oehlberg, K. A., Katz, I. R., & Stern, M. B. (2006). Test characteristics of the 15-Item Geriatric Depression Scale and Hamilton Depression Rating Scale in Parkinson disease. *American Journal of Geriatric Psychiatry, 14*, 169–175.

Whittington, C. J., Podd, J., & Kan, M. M. (2000). Recognition memory impairment in Parkinson's disease: Power and meta-analyses. *Neuropsychology, 14*, 233–246.

Woodward, T. S., Bub, D. N., & Hunter, M. A. (2002). Task switching deficits associated with Parkinson's disease reflect depleted attentional resources. *Neuropsychologia, 40*, 1948–1955.

Yesavage, J., Brink, T. L., Rose, T. L., Lum, O., Huang, V., Adey, M., & Leirer, V. O. (1983). Development and validation of a geriatric depression screening scale. *Journal of Psychiatric Research, 17*, 37–49.

Youngjohn, J. R., Beck, J., Jogerst, G., & Caine, C. (1992). Neuropsychological impairment, depression, and Parkinson's disease. *Neuropsychology, 6*, 149–158.

Zec, R. F., Landreth, E. S., Fritz, S., Grames, E., Hasara, A., Fraizer, W., et al. (1999). A comparison of phonemic, semantic, and alternating word fluency in Parkinson's disease. *Archives of Clinical Neuropsychology, 14*, 255–264.

Zgaljardic, D. J., Borod, J. C., Foldi, N. S., Rocco, M., Mattis, P. J., Gordon, M. F., . . . Eidelberg, D. (2007). Relationship between self-reported apathy and executive dysfunction in nondemented patients with Parkinson disease. [Research Support, N. I.H., Extramural Research Support, Non-U.S. Gov't]. *Cognitive and Behavioral Neurology, 20*, 184–192. doi:10.1097/WNN.0b013e318145a6f6

Zigmond, A. S., & Snaith, R. P. (1983). The hospital anxiety and depression scale. *Acta Psychiatrica Scandinavica, 67*, 361–370.

13

Traumatic Brain Injury and the Impact of Secondary Influences

CHAD SANDERS, ELIZABETH A. ZIEGLER, AND
MAUREEN SCHMITTER-EDGECOMBE

The definition used by the Centers for Disease Control and Prevention (CDC) and the National Center for Injury Prevention and Control (NCIPC) describes traumatic brain injury (TBI) as being caused by a bump, blow, or jolt to the head or a penetrating head injury that disrupts the normal function of the brain (Faul, Xu, Wald, & Coronado, 2010). Approximately 1.7 million individuals sustain a TBI each year in the United States (Faul et al., 2010); others estimate this number to be more than 2 million, as not all individuals that sustain TBIs are seen for care (Hoofien, Gilboa, Vakil, & Donovick, 2001; Kim et al., 2007). In addition, nearly 5.8 million individuals currently live with complications and lifelong difficulties associated with TBI, costing the United States $60 billion dollars in annual medical and other indirect costs (Cappa, Conger, & Conger, 2011; Kiraly & Kiraly, 2007; Roebuck-Spencer & Sherer, 2012). Within the military, where TBI is referred to as the "signature injury" of Operation Enduring Freedom (OEF) and Operation Iraqi Freedom (OIF), more than 30% of the 2 million troops have been estimated to have sustained a TBI (Belanger, Curtiss, Demery, Lebowitz, & Vanderploeg, 2009; Helmick, et al., 2006; McCrea et al., 2008; Polusny et al., 2011; see also Hoge, Goldberg, & Castro, 2009; Vasterling et al., 2006). Of note, this estimate has been considered by some a gross overestimation, especially for mild (MTBI) TBIs (Hoge et al., 2009; Howe, 2009; Nampiaparampil, 2008).

Given the large number of individuals who sustain TBIs, it is not surprising that neuropsychologists are called upon to assess the presence, severity, and potential impact that TBI may have on functioning, both immediately and long term. Neuropsychologists may also be charged with detecting and parsing out the effect that *secondary influences* may have on functioning, usually in conjunction with provision of appropriate recommendations for treatment aimed at ameliorating symptoms or remediating secondary factors. However, secondary influences on cognitive functioning following TBI have received limited consideration within the TBI literature. Thus, the purpose of this chapter is to review relevant findings and discuss the potential impact of secondary factors (e.g., depression, personality, acute stress reaction) on neuropsychological test data and recovery following TBI.

SEVERITY

In order to understand the potential influences of secondary factors, it is important to consider the severity of the TBI, which can range from mild to severe. MTBI presents quite differently than a severe TBI, so an accurate and comprehensive understanding of TBI severity is an essential factor to consider in the neuropsychological evaluation. The overwhelming majority of TBIs for both civilian and military populations, approximately 70–88%, can be classified as MTBIs (Bazarian et al., 2005; Faul et al., 2010; Howe, 2009; McCrea et al., 2009; Ruff & Jamora, 2009). An indication of severity *must* accompany a diagnosis of TBI, and the most reliable method for establishing TBI severity is to evaluate the acute injury characteristics, not the severity of residual symptoms post-injury (Management of Concussion/mTBI Working Group, 2009). Adjunctive medical records can be especially helpful in identifying day-of-injury characteristics as well as for cross-referencing self-report information obtained during a clinical interview (Larrabee, 2012; Management of Concussion/mTBI Working Group, 2009). Commonly used criteria include length of posttraumatic amnesia (PTA), duration of loss of consciousness (LOC), and Glasgow Coma Scale score ([GCS]; Teasdale & Jennett, 1974; see Table 13.1; McCrea et al., 2008; for additional details on assessment methods for severity of injury see Mittenberg & Roberts, 2008).

While several sets of diagnostic criteria have been offered for separating MTBI from more severe TBI (Hannay, Howieson, Loring, Fischer, & Lezak, 2004; Roebuck-Spencer and Sherer, 2012; Williams, Levin, & Eisenberg, 1990), the American Congress of Rehabilitation Medicine (ACRM; Kay et al., 1993) has provided the foremost reliable and accurate and commonly used clinical criteria to date (Management of Concussion/mTBI Working Group, 2009; McCrea et al., 2008; Nampiaparampil, 2008; Ruff, Iverson, Barth, Bush, Broshek, & the NAN Policy and Planning Committee, 2009; Ruff & Jamora, 2009). According to the ACRM, an individual with MTBI must have experienced a traumatically induced physiological disruption of brain function, manifested singly or as any combination of LOC, loss of memory for events immediately before or after the accident, alteration in mental state at the time of the accident, and focal neurological deficit(s) that may or may not be transient. The ACRM criteria also stipulate that for a TBI to be specified as mild, the individual must not experience LOC of 30 minutes or more, nor can they have experienced PTA greater than 24 hours. In addition, individuals with MTBI must have obtained a score of 13–15 on the GCS 30 minutes after sustaining the initial injury. Of note, these injury characteristics must result from biomechanical force to the brain and not be the result of other factors (e.g., psychological trauma, acute stress reaction), which can be difficult to ascertain, especially since many of these processes co-occur (McCrea et al., 2008). Furthermore, the Quality Standards Subcommittee of the American Academy of Neurology (AAN) has outlined the following grading scale for concussion, a term synonymous with MTBI: transient confusion without LOC occurring for <15 minutes (grade 1), >15 minutes (grade 2), or any LOC, either brief, resolving within seconds, or prolonged, lasting several minutes (grade 3) (Quality Standards Subcommittee of the American Academy of Neurology, 1997).

Injuries with more severe characteristics that exceed the thresholds outlined for MTBI reflect moderate or severe TBI. The Veterans Affairs/Department of Defense (VA/DoD) definitional criteria for TBI outline specific thresholds for classifying mild, moderate, and severe TBI and also highlight the important distinction between complicated and uncomplicated TBI, which is contingent upon normal or abnormal results of brain imaging, respectively (see Table 13.1).

CAUSES AND RISK FACTORS

Falls and motor vehicle accidents (MVAs) have been estimated to be responsible for 35.2% and 17.3% of all cases, respectively (Faul et al., 2010; see also Management of Concussion/mTBI Working Group, 2009; Roebuck-Spencer & Sherer, 2012). While falls accounted for approximately half of all head injuries sustained by children ages 0–4 years and adults over 64 years of age, MVAs were responsible for about half of all head injuries in other age groups. Other noteworthy causes of TBI were assault (10%) and "struck by or against" events (16.5%), while roughly 12% were precipitated by unknown causes (Faul et al., 2010; Hannay et al., 2004; Kiraly and Kiraly, 2007; Roebuck-Spencer & Sherer, 2012;). In the military, blast injuries

Table 13.1 CLASSIFICATION OF TBI SEVERITY

Criteria	Mild	Moderate	Severe
Structural imaging	Normal	Normal or abnormal	Normal or abnormal
Loss of consciousness (LOC)	0–30 min	>30 min and <24 hr	>24 hr
Alteration of consciousness/ mental state (AOC)	A moment up to 24 hr	>24 hr; severity based on other criteria	
Posttraumatic amnesia (PTA)	0–1 day	>1 and <7 days	>7 days
Glasgow Coma Scale (GCS): best available score in first 24 hr)	13–15	9–12	<9

Note: LOC: any period of loss of consciousness; AOC: any alteration of mental state at time of injury (e.g., disorientation, confusion, dizziness); PTA: period from time of injury involving inability to follow commands or encode new memories and lasting until continuous day-to-day memories return; GCS: state of consciousness as measured by visual, verbal, and motor responses/nonresponses to stimuli. Adopted from the VA/DoD Clinical Practice Guideline for Management of Concussion/MTBI, 2009; see also ACRM definitional criteria, 1993.

are the most common cause of TBI, estimated to account for 78–88% of injuries occurring in OEF and OIF. However, the cognitive sequelae of blast-related TBIs are relatively unknown. Also, given the problems currently affecting military over-estimations and misattribution of symptoms to TBI (e.g., flawed post-deployment screening processes based on assumptions that TBI causes long-term and persistent symptoms; poor risk communication; misuse of terminology; biased reports in the literature; misattribution of persistent post-deployment symptoms to TBI), accurate incidence estimations of blast-related TBI are not possible at this time (Belanger et al., 2009; Howe, 2009).

Children (ages 0 to 4), older adolescents (ages 15 to 19), and older adults (aged 75 and older) are more likely to sustain a TBI, with the highest rates of hospitalizations (339 per 100,000) and death (57 per 100,000) occurring among older adults (Faul et al., 2010; see also Hannay et al., 2004). With regard to gender differences, men are generally more likely to sustain TBI than women, with estimates placing men at about 1.4 to 2 times the risk of sustaining TBI compared to that for women (Faul et al., 2010; Hannay et al., 2004). Several studies have also found relationships between elevated risk of TBI and lowered socioeconomic status (SES), reduced years of education, and unstable work history or unemployment (Dikmen, Machamer, & Temkin, 2004; Hannay et al., 2004; Roebuck-Spencer & Sherer, 2008, 2012). In addition, alcohol use and higher blood alcohol content (BAC) have been implicated as factors associated with increased incidence of TBI (Hanks et al., 2003; Hannay et al., 2004). Having sustained a brain injury in the past has also been shown to increase risk of TBI in the future, estimated to be about 3 times higher than for those with no prior history of brain injury, and increasing further in magnitude following subsequent TBI (Roebuck-Spencer & Sherer, 2008).

MECHANISMS OF INJURY

In general, there are two types of TBI. The more common of the two, *closed head injury* (CHI), occurs when an object strikes the head with sufficient force to affect the brain. Alternately, individuals may sustain a *penetrating head injury* (PHI), when the skull has been breached (Belanger et al., 2009). While PHI occurs less frequently than CHI, PHIs tend to be more lethal, resulting in a higher incidence of brain damage and a mortality rate approximately 6 times higher than with CHI (Peek-Asa, McArthur, Hovda, & Kraus, 2001).

Primary and secondary injuries can occur with CHI. *Primary injury* refers to initial damage that results from the impact to the brain. One mechanism of primary injury, drubbing, occurs when the sharply edged ridges inside the skull directly damage the brain tissue, which is more likely to occur around the frontal and temporal lobes (Kiraly & Kiraly, 2007; Rao & Lyketsos, 2000). Contusion can occur at the site of contact, known as *coup injury*, or contralateral to the site of contact, known as *contre-coup injury*, and involve focal damage to brain tissue and vascular structure (Hannay et al., 2004; Kiraly & Kiraly, 2007; MacDonald et al., 2011; Rao & Lyketsos, 2000). Inertial force sustained via acceleration of the head is another mechanism of primary injury. Inertial force can be translational, when the brain moves in a straight line parallel to the head's center of gravity; rotational, involving rotation of the brain around its center of gravity; or angular, involving both translational and rotational forces (Hannay et al., 2004). In addition, damage to axons in cerebral and brainstem white matter, and even in the cerebellum, can be caused by rapid acceleration and deceleration of the brain, which involves wave-like expansion and contraction of brain matter (Gennarelli, Thibault, & Graham, 1998; Hannay et al., 2004). This rapid motion can cause *diffuse axonal injury* (DAI), which refers to damage from the shearing or tearing of axons (Adams, Graham, Murray, & Scott, 1982; Hannay et al., 2004; Palacios et al., 2011). More recently, the term *traumatic axonal injury* (TAI) has been suggested as a more fitting term encompassing both the primary shearing and tearing of axons resulting directly from impact as well as alterations of white matter that can result from several secondary forces, such as hypoxic or metabolic damage (Palacios et al., 2011).

Secondary injury involves either physiological processes that result directly from the primary injury within the brain or from events that lead to further brain damage following initial trauma. Typically, secondary brain insults are categorized as *systemic* (e.g., infection, hypotension, hypoxia, anemia, and hyper- or hypocapnia) or *intracranial* (severe intracranial hypertension, extra-axial lesions, seizures that cause focal brain hypermetabolism, and cerebral edema) (Hannay et al., 2004; Heegaard & Biros, 2007; Palmer et al., 1993; Vecht et al., 1995).

In 2009, Howe provided an extensive overview of blast-related mechanisms of injury that can potentially result in TBI. Typically, these injuries result from explosive mechanisms, such as improvised explosive devices (IEDs) and land-mines, which create a blast wave that spreads from the initial site of the explosion and consists of overpressurization (high-pressure shock wave) followed by a blast wind. As the shock wave begins to disperse, underpressurization occurs, caused by a reversal wind back toward the initial point of origin. Factors that can impact damage resulting from blast exposure include the type and location of the explosive device, peak and duration of overpressure, impulse (complex wave-forms), proximity and body orientation to the explosion, environmental hazards, and barriers. These comprise four potential mechanisms of injury, which are referred to as primary injuries resulting directly from the blast wave, secondary injuries from projectiles, tertiary injuries from impact after being thrown or moved by the blast wave, and quaternary injuries unaccounted for by the first three, such as burns, toxic exposure, etc. (Howe, 2009).

To date, most studies examining the differential effect of blast- versus non-blast-related TBI have been hampered by flawed methodological and sampling and diagnostic criteria, and there is significant controversy surrounding the issue of the primary blast wave's effects on the brain (Belanger et al., 2009; Howe, 2009; Larrabee, 2012; Luethcke, Bryan, Morrow, & Isler, 2010; MacDonald et al., 2011; Ropper, 2011). It is well established that air–fluid interfaces within the body, such as the pulmonary system, gastrointestinal tract, and middle ear, are most susceptible to damage from high-force blast waves. However, brain injuries may result more from the tertiary effects of a blast (e.g., being thrown back from the blast wave and subsequently striking the head on an object) than from the actual primary blast wave (DePalma, Burris, Champion, & Hodgson, 2005; Guy, Glover, & Cripps, 1998; Howe, 2009). Of the few studies with empirically sound methodology, there is very little support for any unique or atypical TBI outcomes attributable to blast-related versus non-blast mechanisms of injury based on neuropsychological test performance (Belanger et al., 2009; Larrabee, 2012; Luethcke et al., 2010).

COURSE OF RECOVERY AND PROGNOSIS

The severity of injury is likely to have a large, if not the largest, effect on post-injury recovery (Ghajar, 2000; Hoofien et al., 2001; see also Dikmen, Donovan, Loberg, Machamer, & Temkin, 2009; Teasdale, 1995). With regard to MTBI, self-reported symptoms most frequently include headache, blurred vision, dizziness, sleep problems, subjective memory problems, and other cognitive difficulties (Carroll et al., 2004). However, it is important to be aware of several key points. First, acute MTBI symptoms are usually only temporary, resolving within days to weeks post-injury (Belanger, Kretzmer, Yoash-Gantz, Pickett, & Tupler, 2005; Howe, 2009; McCrea et al., 2003, 2009). Symptoms that persist longer than several weeks post-injury, which some identify as postconcussive syndrome (PCS), are more likely attributable to factors unrelated to the MTBI itself (Belanger et al., 2005; Hoge et al., 2009; Howe, 2009; Iverson, 2005; Iverson, Lange, Brooks, & Rennison, 2010; Kay, Newman, Cavallo, Ezrachi, & Resnick, 1992; Kit, Mateer, & Graves, 2007; Larrabee, 2012; McCrea et al., 2003, 2008, 2009; Meares et al., 2011; Ruff et al., 2009; Suhr and Gunstad, 2002b). Symptoms of PCS commonly occurs in other populations, including non-clinical populations (Howe, 2009; Iverson & Lange, 2003; Meares et al., 2008), which is why PCS has received considerable scrutiny in the literature for not actually qualifying as a syndrome, given that the associated symptoms are not exclusive to TBI (Hoge et al., 2009; Howe, 2009; Iverson, 2005). Finally, the TBI literature has revealed several findings indicating that sustaining multiple MTBIs has no cumulative effect on recovery (Belanger, Spiegel, & Vanderploeg, 2010; Iverson, Brooks, Lovell, & Collins, 2005; Larrabee, 2012), while other studies have found that recurrent MTBIs can lead to increased self-reported memory problems and delayed symptom recovery (Guskiewicz et al., 2003, 2005). Drawing definitive conclusions in this area is made difficult by methodological issues. For example, it is important to separate out individuals who fully recover between MTBIs from those sustaining multiple concussions in close proximity to one another without adequate recovery between injuries, such as may be the case with boxers.

While the literature is less rich with efforts to explore outcomes directly attributable to moderate TBIs, there have been several important findings about expected recovery. Statistically, less than 10% of cases of moderate TBI result in death, usually attributable to complications. At 6 months following moderate TBI, estimates suggest that 0–14% of individuals are severely disabled, with up to 25% moderately disabled (Roebuck-Spencer & Sherer, 2012; Teasdale, 1995; Williams et al., 1990). Overall, recovery following moderate TBI tends to be positive, with individuals coming away largely intact across most cognitive and functional domains (Anderson, Brown, Newitt, & Hoile, 2011; Teasdale, 1995), though there is evidence of slightly slower processing speed and verbal-learning deficits (Kashluba, Hanks, Casey, & Millis, 2008; Williams et al., 1990; see Larrabee, 2012). Studies have shown that roughly 53–73% of individuals show good recovery by 6 months (Roebuck-Spencer & Sherer, 2012; Williams et al., 1990) and up to 18 months following moderate to severe TBI, with cognitive functions continuing to recover beyond this threshold (Dikmen et al., 2009; Millis et al., 2001; Roebuck-Spencer & Sherer, 2012).

Despite improved medical and rehabilitative techniques, individuals who sustain a severe TBI tend still to have relatively poor outcomes, both immediate and long term, with studies indicating that as many as 23–50% of hospitalized cases end in death (see Roebuck-Spencer & Sherer, 2012, for a review). These individuals typically experience greater residual cognitive and intellectual impairments, with deficits attributable to global or diffuse injury (e.g., TAI), focal impairments (e.g., right frontal contusion), or a combination of both. Common impairments following severe TBI typically include psychomotor slowness, decreased attention and cognitive information processing, memory impairment, and impaired executive function and complex language skills (Larrabee, 2012). These individuals may also experience problems related to disinhibition, hostility, reduced initiation, depression, anxiety, posttraumatic stress disorder (PTSD), and psychotic symptoms, and they are likely to have poor overall quality of life, higher unemployment rates, lowered work stability, and more long-term dependence on others (Anderson et al., 2011; Hoofien et al., 2001; Kreutzer, Gordon, & Wehman, 1989; Larrabee, 2012; Roebuck-Spencer, Banos, Sherer, & Novack, 2010; Teasdale, 1995).

SECONDARY INFLUENCES

The expected course of recovery and related outcome associated directly with TBI is relatively wide-ranging and complex and can be affected by secondary influences. Thus, the focus of the remainder of this chapter is to review the literature concerning secondary influences that can affect functioning and recovery from TBI. Of note, secondary factors should be considered when evaluating individuals with TBI, as most TBIs are mild, and acute symptoms should generally resolve within weeks following injury. In the vast majority of cases, persistent symptoms affecting functioning after MTBI are the result of secondary influences (Belanger et al., 2005; Carroll et al., 2004; Larrabee, 2012; McCrea et al., 2009). As evidenced by Iverson's meta-analysis in 2005, this is due to the significantly larger effect most secondary influences have on cognitive functioning than that of MTBI. By directly comparing the effect sizes of several secondary influences (e.g., litigation, ADHD, bipolar disorder, malingering), as well as moderate to severe TBI up to 24 months post-injury and MTBI up to 6 months post-injury, Iverson was able to illustrate that MTBI pales in comparison to the effect these other influences have on cognitive functioning (Iverson, 2005). Taken together, these points underscore the importance of secondary factors when working with individuals post-MTBI who are reporting high levels of impairment in broad areas of functioning.

Demographics

Unfortunately, it is not uncommon for studies in the TBI literature to overlook the sociodemographics of their samples as potential secondary influences (Cappa et al., 2011). The following section will delineate the secondary influence of several commonly documented demographic variables in the TBI literature.

AGE, GENDER, AND RACE

In addition to being related to increased risk of sustaining TBI (see Risk Factors section), age has been shown to serve as an important factor in determining the course of recovery post-injury. Findings have outlined a relationship between advancing age and increasingly poor outcomes following TBI, especially after age 65 (Roebuck-Spencer & Sherer, 2008; Senathi-Raja, Ponsford, & Schonberger, 2010; Teasdale, 1995). These findings include intensified cognitive decline following TBI (Raymont et al., 2008; Senathi-Raja et al., 2010), decreased motivation for major job and lifestyle changes, and reduced rates and delayed timing of returning to work (Dikmen et al., 2009; Kay et al., 1992). However, some studies have shown contrasting findings (Anderson, Brown, Newitt, & Hoile, 2009; Anderson et al., 2011, Kay et al., 1992; Senathi-Raja et al., 2010).

With regard to gender, females have been shown to be more likely than males to report persistent symptoms post-TBI (Bazarian, Blyth, Mooerjee, He, & McDermott, 2010; Halbauer et al., 2009; Meares et al., 2011; Ponsford et al., 2000.) Females have also been shown to be at greater risk than males to develop post-traumatic stress symptoms (Holbrook, Hoyt, Stein, & Seiber, 2002; Kim et al., 2007; Meares et al., 2008, 2011). In contrast, for individuals who worked pre-injury, one study found that females are more likely than males to be employed post-TBI, regardless of injury severity (Doctor et al., 2005).

After adjusting for other variables (e.g., age, marital status, education, cause and severity of injury, pre-injury employment, and other rehabilitation factors), several studies examining post-TBI employment have found that minority racial group members are approximately 1.27 to 3.5 times more likely than Caucasians to be unemployed or have unstable employment within the first 3 years post-TBI (Arango-Lasprilla et al., 2009; Kreutzer et al., 2003; Teasdale, 1995). However, other studies have found no significant racial differences in job stability post-TBI (Roebuck-Spencer & Sherer, 2008).

PRE- AND POST-INJURY EMPLOYMENT STATUS

Working in technical or managerial positions and having high job stability pre-TBI have been associated with returning to work earlier and more often following TBI (Brooks, McKinlay, Symington, Beattie, & Campsie, 1987; Dikmen et al., 2009; Nakase-Richardson, Yablon, & Sherer, 2007). Full-time employment post-TBI has been associated with increased job benefits and overall income pre-TBI, better functional outcomes at 1 month post-TBI (Arango-Lasprilla et al., 2009; Kreutzer et al., 2003; Machamer, Temkin, Fraser, Doctor, & Dikmen, 2005), and higher and more consistent pre- and post-TBI Wechsler Adult Intelligence Scale–Revised (WAIS-R) Full Scale IQ scores in comparison to part-time employment, sheltered or supported employment, and unemployment post-TBI (Fabiano & Crewe, 1995). Post-TBI employment has also been shown to be a primary indicator of community and social integration, financial capacity, and quality of life (Arango-Lasprilla et al., 2009). Full-time employment following severe TBI usually requires extremely high levels of support in the workplace, even when individuals perform within normal limits on tests of cognitive functioning (Hannay et al., 2004). Lastly, pre-TBI unemployment has been related to higher levels of persistent symptom reporting following MTBI (Kirsch et al., 2010; Larrabee, 2012).

SOCIAL NETWORK

Loss of social independence and autonomy has been identified as a significant barrier to successful recovery following TBI (Mukherjee, Heller, & Alper, 2001), and difficulties with day-to-day tasks (e.g., managing finances, writing letters, driving and using public transportation, weekly planning) have been shown to directly increase dependence on others (Mazaux et al., 1997). In addition, general levels of distress, adaptation, and resiliency in family members and caregivers can significantly affect an individual's short-term and long-term functional outcomes post-TBI (Bond, Draeger, Mandleco, & Donnelly, 2003).

FUTURE WORK

While the literature has provided some relatively consistent findings related to the influence that demographics can have on functioning and recovery post-TBI, there are several areas still lacking adequate methodology. First, researchers must consider the impact of demographic variables when interpreting data. For example, age effects on processing speed at different stages of the lifespan have been well documented, and researchers should ensure that these deleterious effects are taken into consideration when examining TBI across different age groups (see Bashore & Ridderinkhof, 2002). In addition, as suggested by Cappa et al. (2011), the TBI literature would benefit a great deal by adopting a more standardized and reliable system of organization and categorization of demographic variables. This would help avoid bias and increase the validity and generalizability of research findings, while also facilitating greater comparison of studies across the TBI literature. Lastly, it is pertinent to continue to conduct studies comparing TBI and non-TBI trauma groups, to potentially uncover patterns of outcome and neuropsychological test performance that may shed further light on the specific nature of TBI (see Larrabee, 2012).

Psychiatric Factors

Psychiatric symptoms following TBI are relatively common. These symptoms can negatively impact functional outcomes (Kilmer et al., 2006; Larson, Kaufman,

Kellison, Schmalfuss, & Perlstein, 2009; Ponsford et al., 2000) as well as caregivers and family members, sometimes to a greater extent than the physical repercussions of the TBI (Ponsford, Olver, Ponsford, & Nelms, 2003). The following section will discuss findings in the TBI literature related to the impact of secondary psychiatric factors on functioning post-TBI.

Pre-injury Psychiatric Influences

The presence of a premorbid psychiatric disorder has been shown to directly predict persistent symptom reporting at 3 months post-MTBI, as well as directly increase risk of post-TBI psychiatric issues regardless of injury severity (McCauley, Boake, Levin, Contant, & Sonx, 2001; Meares et al., 2011; Ponsford et al., 2000; Reekum, Cohen, & Wong, 2000). Pre-injury psychiatric problems have also been related to more severe symptom reporting (Kashluba, Paniak, & Casey, 2008).

Acute Stress Reaction and Posttraumatic Stress Disorder

There is considerable overlap between the symptoms of TBI, PTSD, and acute stress reaction (ASR), including noise sensitivity, fatigue, anxiety, insomnia, poor concentration, poor memory, irritability and anger, and depression (Helmick et al., 2006). This makes differential diagnosis difficult, especially with individuals who experience LOC or retrograde/anterograde amnesia surrounding the traumatic event itself (Belanger et al., 2009). Rates of PTSD are much higher for military populations than for civilians, especially for soldiers injured in combat (Howe, 2009), and PTSD tends to occur more frequently with MTBI than with moderate or severe injuries (Belanger et al., 2009; Glaesser, Neuner, Lütgehetmann, Schmidt, & Elbert, 2004; Helmick et al., 2006). PTSD can result in mild learning, memory, attention, and executive-functioning deficits (Brewin, Kleiner, Vasterling, & Field, 2007; Hannay et al., 2004), as well as more severe functional impairments (Prigerson, Maciejewski, & Rosenheck, 2001), dysregulation of psychophysiological arousal, frontal-systems and frontal-limbic dysfunction, stress-related hippocampal abnormalities, and long-term negative health consequences. PTSD often accompanies comorbid psychiatric illness. However, some have argued that these findings result from methodological issues in the PTSD literature, including pre-existing differences between individuals within sample groups, secondary factors and issues not controlled by researchers (e.g., incentives and external reinforcements), and failures to screen for malingering, and not PTSD per se (Armistead-Jehle, 2010; Howe, 2009; see also Arbisi, 2011; Vasterling, 2011). When PTSD and TBI co-occur, especially MTBI, PTSD may largely be responsible for many areas of functional impairment falsely attributed to the TBI (Hoge et al., 2008; Polusny et al., 2011), especially given that PTSD has been shown to magnify symptom perception and endorsement with general trauma (Geisser, Roth, Bachman, & Eckert, 1996; Nampiaparampil, 2008).

Depression and Anxiety

Some mood disorders, including mania and bipolar disorder, have received little to no support as being associated with TBI, regardless of severity (Hoge et al.,

2009; Larrabee, 2012; Rao and Lyketsos, 2000). In contrast, depression and anxiety disorders tend to be the most common psychiatric sequelae of TBI (Jorge et al., 2004; Larson et al., 2009; Rao and Lyketsos, 2000; Silver, Kramer, Greenwald, & Weissman, 2001), although these disorders are also highly comorbid in the general population (Larson et al., 2009). Negative affect, a term adopted by researchers to represent symptoms of both anxiety and depression (Hoofien et al., 2001; Larson et al., 2009, Malec, Brown, & Moessner, 2004; Silver et al., 2001), has been associated with difficulties in attention and memory, reduced motor functioning, and impaired executive functioning (Larson et al., 2009). When negative affect and TBI co-occur, findings have revealed disproportionately impaired performance monitoring and error processing, often referred to as a "double jeopardy" phenomenon (Botvinick, Carter, Braver, Barch, & Cohen, 2001; Dikmen, Machamer, & Temkin, 2004; Seel et al., 2003); executive functioning, processing speed, attention, and memory deficits (Jorge et al., 2004; Rapoport, McCullagh, Shammi, & Feinstein, 2005); decreased hippocampal volume (Jorge, Acion, Starkstein, & Magnotta, 2007); poorer functional outcomes and negatively biased perceptions of functioning (Malec et al., 2004); persistent emotional symptom reporting (Larson et al., 2009); impaired meta-memory with negative beliefs about memory functioning, self-efficacy, and strategy use (Kit et al., 2007); and increased drug use and abuse (Anson & Ponsford, 2006). Of note, Panayiotou, Jackson, and Crowe (2010) conducted a meta-analysis of studies focusing on emotional symptoms post-MTBI and concluded that the vast majority of persistent emotional symptoms following MTBI are more likely due to other factors, such as premorbid psychological issues, emotional reaction to trauma, poor motivation, and poor coping skills, not the actual MTBI.

Somatoform Disorders

Somatoform disorders are typically chronic conditions involving the experience of physical symptoms that can involve one or multiple parts of the body and are not fully explained by medical factors, the effects of substance use, or another psychological disorder (American Psychiatric Association, 2000). It is important to consider these disorders when individuals who have sustained MTBI are reporting persistent symptoms lasting well beyond the expected recovery timeline. In fact, theorists have argued that PCS, which is comprised of many persistent somatic complaints, should be classified as a type of cogniform disorder or condition, a diagnosis proposed for individuals exhibiting excessive or atypical symptom reporting without any evidence of neurological abnormality or malingering (Delis and Wetter, 2007; Larrabee, 2007, 2012). Furthermore, there has been limited evidence that certain somatic symptoms, including numbness, appetite disturbance, nausea, and smell or olfactory impairment, result from MTBI (Management of Concussion/mTBI Working Group, 2009). Several studies have also found that education and reassurance about expected outcomes following MTBI commonly leads to a reduction of somatic complaints, suggesting that somatic complaints following MTBI may be psychogenic (Management of Concussion/mTBI Working Group, 2009; Mittenberg, Tremont, Zielinski, Fichera, & Rayls, 1996;

Ponsford et al., 2002; Wang, Chan, Deng, 2006). Findings have also revealed that somatoform and chronic-pain conditions tend to impede effort during neuropsychological test performance post-TBI (Demakis et al., 2001), and increased somatic complaints pre-TBI have been associated with higher rates of health care utilization, litigation, and persistent symptom reporting post-TBI (Larrabee, 2012). Furthermore, concordance rates between somatoform disorders and PTSD are high (Bryant, Marosszeky, Crooks, Baguley, & Gurka, 1999), a finding suggesting that somatization may have similar effects on cognitive functioning to those evidenced with PTSD post-TBI.

PSYCHOTIC SYMPTOMS

The TBI literature has revealed that approximately 7%–15% of individuals develop symptoms of schizophrenia post-TBI, though faulty methodology and inclusion criteria have limited the validity of many of these findings (Rao and Lyketsos, 2000). In addition, schizophrenia is largely due to genetic influence, with heritability rates around 80% to 85% (Cardno & Gottésman, 2000; Harrison & Owen, 2003). Family history of schizophrenia is also more often associated with post-TBI psychotic symptoms than history of alcohol and drug use, post-TBI behavioral or personality changes, intelligence quotient (IQ), socioeconomic status, or age (Fujii and Ahmed, 2001; Sachdev, Smith, & Cathcart, 2001). Regardless of etiology, psychotic symptoms post-TBI have been associated with more widespread brain damage and cognitive impairment and commonly include paranoid delusions and auditory hallucinations, with negative symptoms, catatonic behaviors, and formal thought disorders occurring less often (Sachdev et al., 2001). Psychotic symptoms post-TBI have also been associated with significantly lowered IQ, semantic memory, verbal fluency, and executive abilities; however, the psychotic symptoms alone may also account for these deficits (Fujii, Ahmed, & Hishinuma, 2004).

FUTURE WORK

While psychiatric factors comprise a significant portion of the existing literature on secondary factors influencing functioning post-TBI, findings in this area have suffered from several methodological weaknesses. In their 2007 review of the TBI literature on psychiatric complications following TBI, Kim et al. (2007) provided excellent recommendations to strengthen research in this area. They call for the establishment of a clear, uniform, and standardized set of operational and definitional criteria for several of the psychiatric factors currently being studied, which would increase generalizability and between-study comparisons. The authors also emphasized the need for increased research identifying risk factors for post-TBI psychiatric symptoms and an overhaul of the excessive variability in diagnostic and selection criteria across many studies in this arena (Kim et al., 2007).

Personality

Because personality represents a very broad range of characteristics and behaviors, efforts to examine the impact of personality on functioning following TBI have required significant effort and resources. In addition, studies have revealed that changes to core personality traits following TBI are relatively rare (Rush, Malec, Brown, & Moessner, 2006; see also Kurtz et al., 1998;; Schretlen, 2000; Tate, 2003). Nevertheless, the following section will discuss several findings in the TBI literature on the influence of personality on functioning post-TBI.

TRAIT AND BEHAVIORAL CHANGE

Behavioral changes following TBI, potentially resulting from impaired brain systems or the adjustment process, are more commonly associated with emotional disturbances that can hinder functional outcomes than are personality traits, which have been shown to be relatively stable and unaffected by TBI (Malec et al., 2004; Rush et al., 2006; Rush, Malec, Moessner, & Brown, 2004). In fact, the overall distress experienced by caregivers and family members has been shown to be correlated with these behavioral changes post-TBI (Kilmer et al., 2006; Wade et al., 2002), with more disruptive behaviors limiting provision of care and, ultimately, increasing the likelihood of institutionalization (Kilmer et al., 2006). However, research has suggested that premorbid personality traits can affect how an individual interprets and responds to symptoms post-TBI, potentially magnifying or minimizing the impact of TBI (Kay et al., 1992; see also Rao & Lyketsos, 2000). Unfortunately, research identifying the role of personality secondary to TBI has been further hampered by measurement problems, namely that most personality tests are not normed with neurological populations, cannot be used to draw causal relationships between TBI and post-injury personality elevations, and potentially ignore acute-injury characteristics, all of which reduce the validity of potential interpretations of post-TBI functioning (Ruff & Jamora, 2009).

ANGER

Incidence rates for anger and aggression following TBI have been estimated to be as high as 33.7–49% (Max, Robertson, & Lansing, 2001; Tateno, Jorge, & Robinson, 2003). In addition, high levels of premorbid anger have been related to elevations in post-TBI aggression, though efforts to parse out the effect of anger and aggression on cognitive functioning post-TBI have been limited (Kim et al., 2007). This may be because most neuropsychological test batteries lack sufficient sensitivity to identify the subtle executive impairments that underscore many aspects of anger and aggression (Cicerone & Tanenbaum, 1997).

FUTURE WORK

Overall, the existing research examining personality traits and behavioral changes associated with TBI has revealed some interesting findings. However, as there have been several limitations to these efforts, some recommendations for future studies are warranted. First, researchers and clinicians should continue to make use of psychodiagnostic tests of personality, while working toward developing normative data that take neurological issues and premorbid personality traits into account. This would facilitate more accurate interpretations of findings and potentially yield useful information for clinicians interested in understanding the nature of personality and TBI. In addition, it is of the utmost importance that clinicians and researchers always take into consideration the severity of an individual's TBI when interpreting personality test results. This is essential because varying degrees of TBI can result in various elevations on personality tests that are neurological in nature but, when taken at face value, implicate personality and not the actual degree of impact to the brain (see Ruff and Jamora, 2009).

Medical Factors

In addition to psychiatric issues and personality, medical factors are another key category of potential secondary variables that can affect functioning post-TBI. The following section will explore findings in the literature regarding the secondary influence of several commonly reported medical and physiological symptoms attributed to TBI.

CHRONIC PAIN

Medically explained and unexplained chronic pain has been associated with recovery and outcomes following TBI throughout the past century of literature on head injury (Nampiaparampil, 2008; see also Myers, 1915). However, the relationship between chronic pain and TBI is not completely understood, as most studies have found higher prevalence rates of chronic pain following MTBI than after more severe injuries (Larrabee, 2012; Management of Concussion/mTBI Working Group, 2009; Nampiaparampil, 2008), likely due to a psychogenic process that partially, if not wholly, accounts for chronic-pain symptoms. In addition, research with improved methodology has revealed that TBI does not usually result in any persistent or significant chronic-pain problems after controlling for other comorbid disorders, with the exception of chronic headache (Hoge, McGurk, Thomas, Cox, Engel, & Castro, 2008; Nampiaparampil, 2008; Walker, Seel, Curtiss, & Warden, 2005). Chronic headache has been shown to persist in as many as 75.6% of cases, especially for those with pre-TBI headache conditions, and has been shown to interfere with completion of activities of daily living (ADLs), work-related activities, and other areas of functioning (Guidelines Development Team, 2011; Hoffman et al., 2007; Nampiaparampil, 2008).

Chronic pain has been shown to increase in severity in tandem with comorbid PTSD symptom severity post-TBI (Bryant et al., 1999; Geisser et al., 1996; Nampiaparampil, 2008), as well as depression and anxiety. Theoretically, this has been hypothesized to be driven by a "dysfunctional pain loop" in which pain impairs functioning, leading to depression and anxiety, which in turn maintains pain symptoms beyond actual brain injury (Kay et al., 1992). Chronic-pain symptoms may also occur as a product of increased attention to physical sensations, which intensifies somatic perception and reporting (Meares et al., 2011). Persistent pain symptoms have also been found to occur more often with females, non-Caucasians, and those who experience depression during post-TBI rehabilitation (Hoffman et al., 2007) and can affect reaction time (Meares et al., 2011) and effort during neuropsychological testing (Demakis et al., 2001). Severity of TBI has been shown to have an inverse relationship with incidence of chronic pain, with rates as high as 95% with MTBI, and as low as 22% with moderate to severe TBI (Guidelines Development Team, 2011; Larrabee, 2012; Nampiaparampil, 2008). Some have argued that this inverse relationship results from moderate to severe TBIs typically requiring bed rest and reduced activity following injury, thereby reducing potential strain to damaged muscles and other body parts. In addition, verbal communication, memory, and executive function are often impaired following moderate to severe TBI, further reducing the ability to accurately convey pain levels (Sherman, Goldberg, & Bell, 2006). Other hypotheses relate persistent post-MTBI complaints to premorbid psychiatric factors (e.g., depression, anxiety, somatization) and secondary gain.

Sleep Disturbance

Although sleep disturbance is commonly associated with TBI, specifically sleep onset and maintenance (Ouellet, Beaulieu-Bonneau, & Morin, 2006), it is also one of the least studied symptoms in the literature on the sequelae of TBI. Sleep disturbance is more common with MTBI than more severe head injuries and is more likely to result in impaired performance during neuropsychological testing when it occurs post-MTBI. However, subjective sleep complaints tend to be inconsistent with objective substantiation of sleep impairment, making it difficult to establish sleep disturbance as resulting directly from TBI or from other comorbid factors, such as mood or psychiatric issues (Guidelines Development Team, 2011; Orff, Avalon, & Drummond, 2009; Steele, Ponsford, Rajaratnam & Redman, 2006). The symptoms of sleep disturbance secondary to TBI typically include increased daytime fatigue and sleepiness, less time spent in REM, less overall time spent sleeping, increased tendency to fall asleep during the day, imbalanced circadian rhythms, and irregular sleep–wake patterns (Ayalon, Borodkin, Dishon, Kanety, & Dagan, 2007; Guidelines Development Team, 2011; Orff et al., 2009). Sleep disturbance post-TBI has also been shown to influence mood, mental capacity, social functioning, and work and employment (Ouellet et al., 2006). However, it is always important to consider non-TBI etiological factors when considering sleep disturbance (e.g., anxiety).

Fatigue

Fatigue has been shown to be one of the most commonly reported symptoms post-TBI (Kim et al., 2007; Management of Concussion/mTBI Working Group, 2009). In addition, research examining the magnitude of subjective reports of fatigue with mood disorders has revealed that comorbid TBI results in greater reported levels of fatigue than with mood disorders alone, regardless of severity (Management of Concussion/mTBI Working Group, 2009; Zinio & Ponsford, 2005). Similar to sleep disturbance, fatigue as a secondary influence following TBI can be one of the more prevalent symptoms, and evidence has suggested that general fatigue is not necessarily related to physical activity, potentially present with or without physical exertion. Post-TBI fatigue has been shown to affect a wide range of areas, including physical and cognitive functioning as well as subjective aspects of daily living, such as quality of life and general fulfillment and well-being (Cantor et al., 2008; Dijkers & Bushnik, 2008).

ALCOHOL USE

Individuals who have sustained a TBI with a premorbid history of alcohol abuse typically experience a poorer course of recovery (Dikmen, Bombardier, Machamer, Fann,, & Temkin, 1993), with higher levels of persistent symptom reporting (Kirsch et al., 2010; Larrabee, 2012) and delays in return to productivity (Turner et al., 2006), though these findings may be influenced by other premorbid factors, such as poor education and increased risk for TBI (Dikmen et al., 1993; Hannay et al., 2004). In addition, alcohol and other substances have been shown to be commonly used for self-medication and management of symptoms post-TBI (Hannay et al., 2004; Nampiaparampil, 2008).

FUTURE WORK

While the literature has outlined associations between several medical symptoms and TBI, it is important to note that the relationship between these variables is highly complex. Therefore, future research would likely benefit from efforts to separate symptoms occurring pre- and post-TBI in order to better understand the nature of these relationships (see Turner, Kivlahan, & Rimmele, 2006). In addition, researchers should continue to make efforts to properly select and document cases of TBI, so as to discriminate between true instances of head injury and those involving symptoms stemming from other medical conditions being attributed to TBI. Lastly, researchers and clinicians should strive to avoid the pitfall of ignoring acute-injury characteristics and relying on self-report, which can lead to faulty conclusions that potentially perpetuate misinformation and, ultimately, impede recovery following TBI.

Other Factors for Consideration

The following section covers factors that fall outside the scope of the previous categories. While not exhaustive, this section attempts to document some of the most strongly evidenced secondary factors and their relatively distinct impact on functioning post-TBI.

SECONDARY GAIN AND EFFORT

Secondary gain and the direct effects of effort on functioning with TBI are among some of the most pressing issues in the current neuropsychological literature. Several studies have illustrated the direct effect that effort can have on cognitive functioning, accounting for more variance than a severe TBI or other neurological or psychological conditions (Binder & Rohling, 1996; Green, Lees-Haley, & Allen, 2002; Howe, 2009; Iverson, 2005). Compensation seeking and litigation have been shown to be associated with poorer outcomes following MTBI (Binder & Rohling, 1996; Kashluba et al., 2008; Larrabee, 2012; Management of Concussion/mTBI Working Group, 2009), including greater levels of reported symptom severity and disability, prolonged unemployment (Carroll et al., 2004; Gotshall et al., 2007; Paniak et al., 2002; Reynolds, Paniak, Toller-Lobe, & Nagy, 2003), impaired neuropsychological functioning (Belanger et al., 2005), and greater impairment of neuropsychological test performance (Binder and Rohling, 1996). In fact, as many as 40% of MTBI cases involving litigation will demonstrate noncredible or malingered neurocognitive dysfunction (Armistead-Jehle, 2010; Larrabee, 2003; Mittenberg, Patton, Canyock, & Condit, 2002), and the magnitude of malingered symptom reporting directly increases in proportion to higher financial incentives (Bianchini, Curtis, & Greve, 2006).

With veterans, attending to potential secondary gain from service-connected injuries and disability status is especially important. Malingering base rates in veteran populations are highly variable and appear to vary depending on the evaluation context such as research, clinical, and forensic (Armistead-Jehle, 2010; Nelson et al., 2010; Whitney, Shepard, Williams, David, & Adams, 2009). For example, clinical samples with OEF/OIF veterans demonstrated SVT failure rates between 17% and 58% (Belanger et al., 2009; Armistead-Jehle, 2010; Whitney et al., 2009). In a research sample, Nelson et al. (2010) noted failed symptom validity test (SVT) performance in 8% of MTBI research subjects, whereas 67% of veteran disability claimants failed SVTs in the context of disability or forensic examinations. In addition, veterans with service connection status at the time of the assessment, regardless of amount, failed the Medical Symptom Validity Test (MSVT) at a higher rate than veterans without any service-connected injuries (Armistead-Jehle, 2010; Whitney et al., 2009). Various financial incentives available throughout the Veteran's Health Administration (VHA) system (Armistead-Jehle, 2010), as well as the pressure to earn and maintain these benefits during Compensation and Pension (C&P) examinations, may be contributing to the increased SVT failure rates and are an ever-present secondary influence with TBI for veterans.

EXPECTATIONS

It has been shown that negative expectations and overestimations of expected post-TBI symptoms can all negatively impact cognitive functioning following TBI (Kit et al., 2007). Several studies have shown that a large number of individuals who have sustained a TBI expect negative consequences to result from the injury, predominantly memory problems, and also underestimate the premorbid incidence rates of these symptoms, which typically have high base rates in the normal population (Ferguson, Mittenberg, Barone, & Schneider, 1999; Gunstad and Suhr, 2001; Iverson & Lange, 2003; Wang et al., 2006;). Thus, individuals should be educated as soon as possible following injury to avoid these negative effects on recovery (Howe, 2009; Kay et al., 1992; McCrea et al., 2009). In fact, several studies have shown that early intervention providing education about expected outcomes following TBI can directly reduce long-term symptom reporting (Kit et al., 2007; Management of Concussion/mTBI Working Group, 2009; Mittenberg et al., 1996; Nolan, 2005). In addition, researchers have recommended using selective terminology, such as replacing the term *MTBI* with *concussion*, and appropriate differential diagnosis and assessment to avoid potentially iatrogenic effects following TBI (Hoge et al., 2009; Howe, 2009).

Negative expectations following TBI can lead to selective attention focused on symptomatic impairment, which can exacerbate other symptoms, as well as performance-monitoring and error-focused attention, all of which can ultimately worsen cognitive functioning and potentially maintain persistent symptom reporting (Kit et al., 2007; Larson et al., 2009). Impaired performance and functioning can also occur when attention is drawn to the diagnosis of TBI, a phenomenon referred to as "diagnosis threat," which has been shown to influence expectations and negatively impact neuropsychological test performance (Howe, 2009; Suhr & Gunstad, 2002a, 2005). The "good old days" bias, a type of negative expectation documented across several studies in the literature, involves a skewed bias toward overreporting and amplification of currently experienced symptoms while at the same time perceiving premorbid functioning as consisting of high levels of health and reduced symptom presence and impairment. These types of expectations have been associated with increased symptom severity, misattribution of all symptoms to the injury of attention and focus, increased length of recovery following injury, delayed return to work, increased effort-test failure, and litigation (Iverson et al., 2010).

Future Work

Many of the secondary factors that influence functioning post-TBI fall into one of the more mainstream categories (e.g., personality, mood, psychiatric symptoms). However, this section illustrates that there are numerous other variables that can significantly affect functioning following TBI. In fact, this section also identifies the importance of incorporating a broad spectrum of sampling, testing, and diagnostic tools in order to avoid spurious conclusions and ensure that findings are sufficiently comprehensive. Of particular importance is consideration of effort and malingering, typically perpetuated by litigation, as this has been shown to explain more variance in cognitive and neuropsychological functioning than TBI, regardless of severity (Iverson, 2005).

RECOMMENDATIONS FOR ASSESSMENT

For neuropsychologists working with individuals who have sustained a TBI, the following section will outline recommendations for a comprehensive neuropsychological assessment. These recommendations will cover key aspects of assessing broad domains of functioning while integrating several components to ensure that secondary factors are identified and integrated into the neuropsychological assessment report.

First, clinicians should *always* identify and assess the severity of the TBI, since MTBI presents much differently than a severe TBI. As discussed in the first sections of this chapter, there are several important components required for adequate diagnosis of TBI (e.g., documentation of acute injury characteristics), and these should not be neglected. In addition, clinicians should strive to obtain day-of-injury records when establishing TBI, as most follow-up information is inadequate. Instead, marshaling emergency department and paramedic reports and other sources of day-of-injury information (e.g., knowledgeable and objective informant report, medical records, brain imaging, provider chart notes) avoids having to establish TBI on the basis of remote memory and self-report, which is inherently flawed; most acute-injury characteristics directly affect memory and consciousness at the time of injury. Self-report of acute-injury characteristics may also be flawed or biased because of external incentives or psychiatric factors (e.g., personality). In addition, when day-of-injury records and medical notes are unavailable because the individual did not seek or require medical care, this typically suggests a more mild TBI. Finally, clinicians should be aware of the residual symptoms and impairments likely to occur from focal brain damage resulting from the TBI, based on brain imaging and substantiated evidence of injury.

Aside from specific attention to the documented information related to TBI (e.g., day-of-injury records), it is recommended that clinicians conduct a standard neuropsychological assessment that includes a clinical interview, measures of cognitive and psychological functioning, and symptom validity testing. One major component of any standard neuropsychological assessment is the clinical interview. This stage provides the clinician the opportunity to obtain important information regarding presenting complaints and concerns, behavioral observations, and symptom progression over time. Information about various secondary factors currently affecting the individual should also be discussed, including being in the process of litigation, having military status, or seeking Social Security disability, as these may be contributing to current symptoms and level of functioning. Clinical interviews should also be used to establish historical information from a variety of domains (e.g., sociodemographic, medical, cognitive, emotional, behavioral, psychiatric, substance use). These areas should not be overlooked or "trumped" by TBI as there is ample evidence that many TBI-like symptoms, especially those of MTBI, are expressed and perpetuated by secondary issues (e.g., somatization, secondary gain). Lastly, neuropsychologists should be prepared to inquire about the reported TBI and how it has affected an individual's ability to function in daily life. This is useful for identifying functional impairment, based on self-report, but also to identify an individual's expectations, outlook, and overall perspective on TBI, which can be very important for differential diagnosis.

The other key component of the TBI assessment process is the neuropsychological testing. While standardized batteries vary greatly between individuals and clinics, the core goal of most batteries is relatively similar. Overall, neuropsychologists should aim to conduct a neuropsychological test battery with sufficient breadth to assess a variety of cognitive abilities. Neuropsychologists should also incorporate psychodiagnostic testing with embedded validity indicators to establish potential personality and psychological factors that may be contributing to current symptoms. Finally, as discussed in several practice standards and position papers (see Boone, 2009; Bush et al., 2005; Heilbronner et al., 2009), test batteries should incorporate multiple and heterogenous SVTs peppered throughout the assessment. This will be critical in determining levels of credible effort and motivation during testing, especially in situations where secondary gain and other external incentives may be pressuring an individual to exhibit suboptimal effort. In addition, it is important for the clinician to be mindful that secondary gain factors are not always known at the time of the evaluation. Therefore, cognitive- and psychological-based SVTs should be included regardless of whether the evaluation is clinical or forensic in nature.

Overall, the TBI neuropsychological assessment largely parallels the standard assessment formula for most neurological issues, although MTBI often requires more emphasis on non-injury factors, including assessment for the presence of depression, anxiety, PTSD, sleep disorders, somatoform disorders, and secondary gain. TBI is complex and dynamic, as well as highly variable, based on severity of injury and referral questions (e.g., mild versus severe, clinical versus forensic contexts). However, clinicians should always strive for thorough and comprehensive evaluation practices, as focusing on TBI alone is simply insufficient for differential diagnosis and can lead to iatrogenic effects and impede recovery. Table 13.2

Table 13.2 SUGGESTED MEASURES FOR ASSESSMENT OF
SECONDARY FACTORS WITH TBI

Injury Severity	**Frequency of use in peer-reviewed journals**
Glasgow Coma Scale (GCS) (i.e., score ranging from 3 to 15)	***
Loss of consciousness (LOC)	***
Posttraumatic amnesia (PTA)	***
Intracranial findings	***
Medical/archival records (i.e., day-of-injury records in order to determine acute injury characteristics)	***
Galveston Orientation and Amnesia Test (GOAT) (to assess length of PTA)	***
Motivation/Effort–Cognitive	
Computerized Assessment of Response Bias (CARB)	*
Dot Counting Test (DCT)	*
Medical Symptom Validity Test (MSVT)	*
Minnesota Multiphasic Personality Inventory–2 (MMPI-2) (e.g., Fake Bad Scale)	***
Minnesota Multiphasic Personality Inventory–2–Restructured Form (MMPI-2-RF) (e.g., Response Bias Scale, Symptom Validity Scale)	*
Portland Digit Recognition Test (PDRT)	*
Rey 15-Item Plus Recognition	*
Rey Word Test	*
Test of Memory Malingering (TOMM)	**
The b Test	*
Various embedded measures of effort should also be derived from the standard neuropsychological battery (e.g., Reliable Digit Span, CVLT-II/RAVLT/RCFT indicators, Finger Tapping Test)	***
Victoria Symptom Validity Test (VSVT)	*

(Continued)

Table 13.2 (CONTINUED)

Warrington Recognition Memory Test–Words (WRMT) (see Kim et al., 2010)	*
Word Memory Test (WMT)	**

Depression

Beck Depression Inventory, Second Edition (BDI-II)	**
Center for Epidemiological Studies–Depression Scale (CES-D)	*
Chicago Multi-Scale Depression Inventory	*
Hamilton Rating Scale for Depression	*
Millon Clinical Multiaxial Inventory–III (MCMI-III)	*
Minnesota Multiphasic Personality Inventory–2 (MMPI-2)	***
Minnesota Multiphasic Personality Inventory–2–Restructured Form (MMPI-2-RF)	*
Personality Assessment Inventory (PAI)	**
Structured Clinical Interview for *DSM-IV* (SCID)	***
Symptoms Check List 90 Revised (SCL-90-R)	***
Visual Analogue Scale of Depression (VASD)	*

Anxiety

Beck Anxiety Inventory (BAI)	**
Minnesota Multiphasic Personality Inventory–2 (MMPI-2)	***
Minnesota Multiphasic Personality Inventory–2–Restructured Form (MMPI-2-RF)	*
Millon Clinical Multiaxial Inventory–III (MCMI-III)	*
Personality Assessment Inventory (PAI)	**
Structured Clinical Interview for *DSM-IV* (SCID)	***
Symptoms Check List 90 Revised (SCL-90-R)	***
State Trait Anxiety Inventory	***

Acute Stress Reaction/PTSD

Clinician-Administered PTSD Scale for *DSM-IV* (CAPS)	**
Detailed Assessment of Post-Traumatic Stress (DAPS)	*
Millon Clinical Multiaxial Inventory–III (MCMI-III)	*
Minnesota Multiphasic Personality Inventory–2 (MMPI-2)	***
Minnesota Multiphasic Personality Inventory–2–Restructured Form (MMPI-2-RF)	*
Personality Assessment Inventory (PAI)	**
Post-Traumatic Stress Disorder Checklist	*
Structured Clinical Interview for *DSM-IV* (SCID)	***
Trauma Symptom Inventory–2 (TSI-2)	*

Sleep Disturbance/Fatigue

Epworth Sleepiness Scale (ESS)	**
Fatigue Severity Scale (FSS)	**
Insomnia Severity Index (ISI)	*
Modified Fatigue Impact Scale (MFIS)	*
Multidimensional Fatigue Inventory (MFI)	*
Pittsburgh Sleep Quality Index (PSQI)	**

Somatoform Disorders

Millon Clinical Multiaxial Inventory–III (MCMI-III)   *

Minnesota Multiphasic Personality Inventory-2 (MMPI-2)   ***

Minnesota Multiphasic Personality Inventory–2–Restructured Form   *
(MMPI-2-RF)

Personality Assessment Inventory (PAI)   **

Structured Clinical Interview for *DSM-IV* (SCID)   ***

Note. Literature search involved only peer-reviewed journals using search fields *subject heading* and *abstract* for "traumatic brain injury OR head injury OR TBI" and name of measure/instrument. Some studies examined several secondary factors and/or used multiple measures, namely the personality inventories, and these were compiled together. Given the methodological limitations currently present in the TBI literature, these frequencies may include studies with less than optimal inclusion criteria, diagnostic standards, or other issues possibly limiting interpretation of findings. *15 studies, **16–30 studies, ***>30 studies.

includes a list of secondary factors that can affect functioning with TBI as well as measures commonly used for their assessment. The etiology and subsequent impact of TBI is largely influenced by a very complex pool of individual characteristics (e.g., psychological, personality, cognitive). As referenced by Larrabee (2012), Symonds (1937) conveyed a seemingly perfect summation of the differential diagnostic process, stating "it is not only the kind of injury that matters, but the kind of head."

CASE EXAMPLE

The following case example illustrates a variety of the concepts discussed in this chapter. It also provides a demonstration of a neuropsychological assessment for a severe TBI involving secondary factors.

Referral Question

Mr. James Doe (plaintiff) is a 29-year-old, right-handed, married, Caucasian male who underwent a forensic neuropsychological evaluation 19 months following an assault and subsequent severe TBI. The forensic neuropsychological evaluation was requested by civil defense counsel under a major insurance carrier given alleged cognitive problems associated with the incident.

Circumstances of the Injury

Per the police report, the plaintiff and his friends were intoxicated and caused a disturbance at a downtown city bar. They were asked to leave the establishment by the bar manager and when they refused, they were removed from the bar by security personnel. Once outside of the bar, the security guard punched the plaintiff in the left temple area, causing him to fall down and strike his head on the pavement. Mr. Doe lost consciousness for approximately 1 minute. He demonstrated impaired and confused mental status upon waking, which his friends and bystanders attributed to intoxication. Emergency personnel were dispatched, and American Medical Response (AMR) records stated he was combative at the scene and was subsequently restrained. He was transported to the emergency department (ED) for treatment. Upon arrival to the ED, his neurological status declined sharply (i.e., GCS = 3, unresponsive). He was transferred to a trauma hospital where he was found to have frontotemporal contusions and a left subdural hematoma with midline shift. He underwent an emergent left frontotemporal decompressive craniectomy and evacuation of subdural hematoma and intraparenchymal hemorrhage. Preoperative and postoperative diagnoses were (1) left acute subdural hematoma and left anterior temporal intraparenchymal hemorrhage as a result of direct trauma, and (2) frontal temporal contusions and contrecoup right temporal contusion. He was placed on Keppra for seizure prophylaxis and reportedly had no seizures. There were episodes of agitation noted during his hospitalization, which required scheduled Seroquel and prn Haldol.

Approximately 1 week post-injury, Mr. Doe was transferred to an inpatient rehabilitation medicine unit. He completed 2 weeks of comprehensive inpatient brain injury rehabilitation and was subsequently discharged to home with 24-hour supervision by family and friends. Per medical records, Mr. Doe demonstrated good engagement with his therapies during his inpatient rehabilitation course. Therapies included rehabilitation psychology, speech therapy, occupational therapy, and physical therapy. Notable difficulties included impulsivity (e.g., needed frequent redirection to stay on topic) and awareness of limitations. He was independent with stand-by assistance for ambulation and basic ADLs. Goals included higher level ADL independence in outpatient rehabilitation. His physiatrist recommended ongoing support in recognizing his personal limitations, clearance from a physician before returning to work and driving, and outpatient rehabilitation. By the time of his rehabilitation medicine discharge, he evidenced significantly improved mental status and was alert and oriented to person, place, time, and date; however, it was noted that he continued to experience significant impulsivity, required 1-point locked restraints because of high fall risk, and could not remember to wear his helmet.

Mr. Doe underwent outpatient rehabilitation for 4 weeks and was noted to have made an excellent recovery. By 10 weeks post-injury, he denied any significant cognitive compromises other than difficulties with processing speed and language fluency. Emotional complaints included irritability, anger-prone tendencies, and depression. Notably, review of pre-injury medical records indicated a preexisting history of depression and anger tendencies. Physical complaints included headaches, neck pain, and anosmia. Pre-injury physical complaints and medical history were unremarkable per medical record review. At a 10-week post-injury evaluation, functional status was described as independent with mobility and self-care. He underwent a cranioplasty with no surgical or postsurgical complications 11 weeks post-injury. He returned to work on a half-time basis by 12 weeks post-injury and was full-time the following week. Given his injury and employer's concerns, he did not return to his previous supervisory position but rather as a safety inspector with no supervisory responsibilities. In a neurosurgical follow-up appointment 20 weeks post-injury, it was noted that Mr. Doe made a "complete and full recovery." His head CT showed the "presence of a 5-mm left frontal hygroma, which is postoperative in nature." There was no evidence of midline shift, sulcal effacement, hemorrhage, or infection.

Mr. Doe underwent a clinical neuropsychological evaluation 6 months post-injury at a local rehabilitation hospital with his treating rehabilitation psychologist. Findings were notable for significant deficits in aspects of language functioning (e.g., expressive vocabulary skills, confrontation naming) and verbal memory encoding and retrieval efficiency. It was noted that he benefited from repeated learning trials and retained what he encoded. Attention and executive functioning were considered intact. The results of the neuropsychological evaluation were reported as being consistent with impairment in left frontotemporal functioning. The neuropsychological evaluation was also notable for depression, anxiety, and chronic head and neck pain.

Mr. Doe underwent a forensic neuropsychological evaluation 19 months post-injury given legal claims that "he is suffering, and will continue to suffer from serious and permanent injuries as a result of the assault." He filed a personal injury lawsuit against the bar.

Presenting Complaints

- Cognitive:
  - *Attention/learning/memory difficulties: Learning and encoding new tasks at work, remembering to complete various tasks at work and home, paying attention during work seminars or online educational modules*
  - *Language: Word finding, spelling, verbal expression and fluency*
- Emotional:
  - *Variable symptoms of depression and anxiety—takes an SSRI and anxiolytic*
  - *Low frustration tolerance, irritability, anger prone*
- Physical:
  - *Sleep disturbance (onset and maintenance)*
  - *Chronic pain (headaches, neck pain)—takes Vicodin and trazadone daily*
  - *Anosmia*

Other Pertinent History

- Education/Occupational History:
  - *12 years of education*
  - *High school GPA = 2.4*
  - *History of special education (reading, spelling) in elementary school; does not know if he was diagnosed with a learning disorder. Academic records did not indicate a history of a learning disorder.*

- *Current job = full-time employment as a safety inspector for a technology company. Prior to the injury, he held a supervisory role. He returned to full-time employment 13 weeks post-injury.*
- *Prior to his injury, he was written up for excessive tardiness and not following through on tasks.*
- Medical History:
  - *Unremarkable*
  - *Family medical history: Unremarkable*
- Psychiatric History:
  - *Preexisting history of depression and anger-prone tendencies, exacerbated post-assault*
- Substance Abuse History:
  - *Denied a history of substance abuse during the interview, although endorsed a period of heavy drinking in late adolescence and early adulthood. He endorsed two DUIs (driving under the influence of alcohol) and one court-mandated substance abuse treatment program.*
  - *Experimental drug use in high school, primarily cocaine and marijuana*
  - *Currently uses marijuana 3–5 times per week and uses alcohol on weekends*
- Social History:
  - *Married, three children. Denied any marital or family stressors*
  - *No history of abuse, trauma, or neglect*
  - *Two prior DUIs, no other legal history, including lawsuits*

Evaluation

The forensic neuropsychological evaluation included assessment of intellectual function, attention, processing speed, working memory, language, visuospatial/construction ability, memory and learning, motor, and executive functioning. He was also administered the Multiphasic Minnesota Personality Inventory, 2nd Edition, Restructured Form, as well as 10 embedded and freestanding symptom validity tests that were scattered throughout the evaluation.

Mr. Doe performed credibly on the neuropsychological evaluation. He passed all measures of symptom validity and effort well above cutoffs. Symptom reporting style was credible (e.g., not consistent with somatoform tendencies) and not indicative of overreporting based on psychodiagnostic testing validity scales. Intellectual functioning was considered average, although there was a significant discrepancy between the Verbal Comprehension Index (VCI) and Perceptual Reasoning Index (PRI). The VCI was low average (89) and the Perceptual Reasoning Index was high average (113). The Working Memory Index was average (109), and the Processing Speed Index was low average (84). Attention was generally intact (50th–84th percentile), although there was some mild variability with sustained attention and vigilance on a continuous performance task. Processing speed ranged from borderline to average (5th–50th percentile). He was slow to complete tasks to ensure he did not make any errors (sacrificed speed for accuracy) but also appeared disengaged on some tasks early in the assessment. Language measures were variable.

A task of confrontational naming was significantly below expectation and notable for word-finding difficulty and paraphasic errors. Other language measures were low average to average (12th–63rd percentile). Conversational speech was intact and there was no evidence of receptive or expressive difficulties. However, on tasks that placed higher demands on verbal abilities (e.g., vocabulary task, verbal abstract reasoning), he demonstrated difficulty expressing fluent and logical answers. Visual spatial/constructional measures were average to superior (50th–95th percentile). Learning and memory measures were average to high average. On one task of verbal learning and memory that is particularly sensitive to brain injury, he was somewhat slow to initially encode the information, but with repeated learning trials, performance was average (42nd percentile). Visual learning and memory tasks were a notable strength with performance being consistently high average (76th–86th percentile). On measures of executive functioning, performance was average to very superior (42nd–99th percentile), and he performed better on nonverbal executive tasks without a time component. Motor tasks were variable, ranging from impaired to average (2nd–62nd percentile). There was a lateralizing pattern noted on two of three motor tasks, favoring the nondominant/left hand. Psychodiagnostic testing was remarkable for emotional distress (depression, anxiety) and anger proneness. There were no indications of somatization. On the first half of the assessment, behavioral observations were notable for being quick to give up on tasks even with repeated encouragement and appearing disengaged with the testing (likely due to the examiner being the opposing expert—he was slow to warm up and was very pleasant and polite during the latter half of testing). There was also notable fatigue throughout the evaluation (e.g., excessive yawning). He took several breaks and stated that he was "always tired" so he did not want to reschedule the examination for a day when he felt more alert. Behavioral observations were otherwise unremarkable.

Testing revealed relative strengths in visual-spatial reasoning, visual learning and memory, and executive functioning. Areas of relative weakness included range of vocabulary, remote historical knowledge, confrontational naming, processing speed, sustained attention/vigilance, and dominant/right-hand fine-motor speed and strength.

After a comprehensive review of the findings (clinical interview, neuropsychological test data, psychodiagnostic testing, medical, legal, and academic records, and behavioral observations), it was concluded that the verbal versus visual discrepancies noted were most likely related to his brain injury, although premorbid factors were also contributory given his history of special education in English-based classes and possible learning disability. Sustained attention/vigilance and processing speed were mildly variable but not indicative of impairment. Although the variability in his performance was likely related to his brain injury, other factors were also considered contributory:

- *Test-taking style (e.g., quick to give up, disengaged on some tasks early in the testing process; test-taking style improved on the latter half of testing and he was thoughtful and deliberate in his approach)*

- *Psychiatric factors (e.g., irritability, depression, variable anxiety)*
- *Sleep disturbance, daytime somnolence*
- *Stressors associated with his current job*
- *Litigation status*
- *Chronic pain*
- *Medication side effects*
- *Chronic marijuana use (denied use on the day of the examination)*

Had this been a clinical evaluation, rather than a forensic evaluation, Mr. Doe would have been referred for individual mental health therapy to address symptoms of depression, anger, irritability, and sleep disturbance. He has already completed comprehensive inpatient and outpatient brain injury rehabilitation treatment and uses a number of compensatory strategies to assist with cognitive complaints. Follow-up speech therapy or cognitive remediation treatment may be beneficial with any future job responsibility or job changes.

The case went to trial and Mr. Doe was awarded financial compensation to cover pain and suffering, medical expenses, and lost wages.

References

Adams, J. H., Graham, D. I., Murray, L. S., & Scott, G. (1982). Diffuse axonal injury due to non-missile head injury in humans: An analysis of 45 cases. *Annals of Neurology, 12*, 557–563.

American Psychiatric Association. (2000). *Diagnostic and statistical manual of mental disorders* (4th ed., text rev.). Washington, DC: Author.

Anderson, V., Brown, S., Newitt, H., & Hoile, H. (2009). Educational, vocational, psychosocial, and quality of life outcomes for adult survivors of childhood traumatic brain injury. *Journal of Head Trauma Rehabilitation, 24*, 303–312.

Anderson, V., Brown, S., Newitt, H., & Hoile, H. (2011). Long-term outcome from childhood traumatic brain injury: Intellectual ability, personality, and quality of life. *Neuropsychology, 25*(2), 176–184.

Anson, K. & Ponsford, J. (2006). Coping and emotional adjustment following traumatic brain injury. *Journal of Head Trauma Rehabilitation, 21*, 248–259.

Arango-Lasprilla, J. C., Ketchum, J. M., Gary, K. W., Kreutzer, J. S., O'Neil-Pirozzi, T. M., Wehman, P., et al. (2009). The influence of minority status on job stability after traumatic brain injury. *The American Academy of Physical Medicine and Rehabilitation, 1*, 41–49.

Arbisi, P. A. (May, 2011). *The neuropsychology of post-traumatic stress disorder*. Presented at the American Academy of Clinical Neuropsychology Conference, Washington, DC.

Armistead-Jehle, P. (2010). Symptom Validity Test performance in U.S. veterans referred for evaluation of mild TBI. *Applied Neuropsychology, 17*, 52–59.

Ayalon, L., Borodkin, K., Dishon, L., Kanety, H., & Dagan, Y. (2007). Circadian rhythm sleep disorders following mild traumatic brain injury. *Neurology, 68*, 1136–1140.

Bashore, T. R., & Ridderinkhof, K. R. (2002). Older age, traumatic brain injury, and cognitive slowing: Some convergent and divergent findings. *Psychological Bulletin, 128*(1), 151–198.

Bazarian, J. J., Blyth, B., Mookerjee, S., He, H., & McDermott, M. P. (2010). Sex differences in outcome after mild traumatic brain injury. *Journal of Neurotrauma, 27*, 527–539.

Bazarian, J. J., McClung, J., Shah, M. N., Cheng, Y. T., Flesher, W., & Kraus, J. (2005). Mild traumatic brain injury in the United States. *Brain Injury, 19*(2), 85–91.

Belanger, H. G., Curtiss, G., Demery, J. A., Lebowitz, B. K., & Vanderploeg, R. D. (2009). Cognitive sequelae of blast-related versus other mechanisms of brain trauma. *Journal of the International Neuropsychological Society, 15*, 1–8.

Belanger, H. G., Kretzmer, T., Yoash-Gantz, R., Pickett, T., & Tupler, L. A. (2005). Factors moderating neuropsychological outcomes following mild traumatic brain injury: A meta-analysis. *Journal of the International Neuropsychological Society, 11*(3), 215–227.

Belanger, H. G., Spiegel, E., & Vanderploeg, R. D. (2010). Neuropsychological performance following a history of multiple self-reported concussions: A meta-analysis. *Journal of the International Neuropsychological Society, 16*, 262–267.

Bianchini, K. J., Curtis, K. L. & Greve, K. W. (2006). Compensation and malingering in traumatic brain injury: A dose-response relationship? *The Clinical Neuropsychologist, 20*(4), 831–847.

Binder, L. M. & Rohling, M. L. (1996). Money matters: A meta-analytic review of the effects of financial incentives on recovery after closed-head injury. *The American Journal of Psychiatry, 153*(1), 7–10.

Bombardier, C. H., & Rimmele, C. T. (1999). Motivational interviewing to prevent alcohol abuse after traumatic brain injury. *Rehabilitation Psychology, 44*(1), 52–67.

Bond, A. E., Draeger, C. R., Mandleco, B., & Donnelly, M. (2003). Needs of family members of patients with severe traumatic brain injury. *Critical Care Nurse, 23*(4), 63–72.

Boone, K.B. (2009). The need for continuous and comprehensive sampling of effort/response bias during neuropsychological examinations. *The Clinical Neuropsychologist, 23*, 729–741.

Botvinick, M., Carter, C. S., Braver, T. S., Barch, D. M., & Cohen, J. D. (2001). Conflict monitoring and cognitive control. *Psychological Review, 108*, 624–652.

Brewin, C. R., Kleiner, J. S., Vasterling, J. J., & Field, A. P. (2007). Memory for emotionally neutral information in posttraumatic stress disorder: A meta-analytic investigation. *Journal of Abnormal Psychology, 116*(3), 448–463.

Brooks, N., McKinlay, W., Symington, C., Beattie, A., & Campsie, L. (1987). Return to work within the first seven years of severe head injury. *Brain Injury, 1*, 5–19.

Bryant, R. A., Marosszeky, J. E., Crooks, J., Baguley, I. J., & Gurka, J. A. (1999). Interaction of posttraumatic stress disorder and chronic pain following TBI. *Journal of Head Trauma Rehabilitation, 14*(6), 588–594.

Bush, S. S., Ruff, R. M., Tröster, A. I., Barth, J. T., Koffler, S. P., Pliskin, N. H., et al. (2005). Symptom validity assessment: Practice issues and medical necessity. *Archives of Clinical Neuropsychology, 20*, 419–426.

Cantor, J. B., Ashman, T., Gordon, W., Ginsberg, A., Engmann, C., Eqan, M., et al. (2008). Fatigue after traumatic brain injury and its impact on participation and quality of life. *Journal of Head Trauma Rehabilitation, 23*(1), 41–51.

Cappa, K. A., Conger, J. C., & Conger, A. J. (2011). Injury severity and outcome: A meta-analysis of prospective studies on TBI outcome. *Health Psychology, 30*(5), 542–560.

Cardno, A. G., & Gottesman, I. I. (2000). Twin studies of schizophrenia: From Bow-and-Arrow Concordances to Star Wars Mx and functional genomics. *American Journal of Medical Genetics, 97*, 12–17.

Carroll, L. J., Cassidy, D., Peloso, P. M., Borg, J., von Holst, H., Holm, L., et al. (2004). Prognosis for mild traumatic brain injury: Results of the WHO Collaborating Centre Task Force on Mild Traumatic Brain Injury. *Journal of Rehabilitation Medicine, 43*, 84–105.

Cicerone, K. D., & Tanenbaum, L. N. (1997). Disturbance of social cognition after traumatic orbitofrontal brain injury. *Archives of Clinical Neuropsychology, 12*, 173–188.

Delis, D. C., & Wetter, S. R. (2007). Cogniform disorder and cogniform condition: Proposed diagnoses for excessive cognitive symptoms. *Archives of Clinical Neuropsychology, 22*, 683–687.

Demakis, G. J., College, E., Sweet, J. J., Sawyer, T. P., Moulthrop, M., Illinois, E., et al. (2001). Discrepancy between predicted and obtained WAIS-R IQ scores discriminates between traumatic brain injury and insufficient effort. *Psychological Assessment, 13*(2), 240–248.

DePalma, R. G., Burris, D. G., Champion, H. R., & Hodgson, M. J. (2005). Blast injuries. *New England Journal of Medicine, 352*, 1335–1342.

Dijkers, M. P. J. M., & Bushnik, T. (2008). Fatigue after traumatic brain injury: An evaluation of the Barroso Fatigue Scale. *Journal of Head Trauma Rehabilitation, 23*, 3–16.

Dikmen, S. S., Bombardier, C. H., Machamer, J. E., Fann, J. R., & Temkin, N. R. (1993). Alcohol use and its effects on neuropsychological outcome in head injury. *Neuropsychology, 7*(3), 296–305.

Dikmen, S. S., Donovan, D. M., Loberg, T., Machamer, J. E., & Temkin, N. R. (2009). Neurobehavioral consequences of traumatic brain injury. In I. Grant & K. Adams (Eds.), *Neuropsychological assessment of neuropsychiatric and neuromedical disorders* (pp. 597–617). New York: Oxford University Press.

Dikmen, S., Machamer, J., & Temkin, N. (2004). Natural history of depression in traumatic brain injury. *Archives of Physical Medicine and Rehabilitation, 85*, 1457–1464.

Doctor, J. N., Castro, J., Temkin, N. R., Fraser, R. T., Machamer, J. E., & Dikmen, S. S. (2005). Workers' risk of unemployment after traumatic brain injury: A normed comparison. *Journal of the International Neuropsychological Society, 11*(6), 747–752.

Fabiano, R. J., & Crewe, N. (1995). Variables associated with employment following severe traumatic brain injury. *Rehabilitation Psychology, 40*(3).

Faul, M., Xu, L., Wald, M. M., & Coronado, V. G. (2010). *Traumatic brain injury in the United States: Emergency department visits, hospitalizations, and deaths 2002–2006.* Atlanta, GA: Centers for Disease Control and Prevention, National Center for Injury Prevention and Control.

Ferguson, R. J., Mittenberg, W., Barone, D. F., & Schneider, B. (1999). Postconcussion syndrome following sports-related head injury, expectation as etiology. *Neuropsychology, 13*, 582–589.

Fujii, D. E., & Ahmed, I. (2001). Risk factors in psychosis secondary to traumatic brain injury. *The Journal of Neuropsychiatry and Clinical Neurosciences, 13*, 61–69.

Fujii, D., Ahmed, I., & Hishinuma, E. (2004). A neuropsychological comparison of psychotic disorder following traumatic brain injury, traumatic brain injury without psychotic disorder, and schizophrenia. *The Journal of Neuropsychiatry and Clinical Neurosciences, 16*, 306–314.

Geisser, M. E., Roth, R. S., Bachman, J. E., & Eckert, T. A. (1996). The relationship between symptoms of post-traumatic stress disorder and pain, affective disturbance, and disability among patients with accident and non-accident related pain. *Pain, 66*(2–3), 207–214.

Gennarelli, T., Thibault, L. E., & Graham, D. I. (1998). Diffuse axonal injury: An important form of traumatic brain damage. *Neuroscientist, 4*, 202–215.

Ghajar, J. (2000). Traumatic brain injury. *The Lancet, 356*, 923–929.

Glaesser, J. N., Neuner, F., Lütgehetmann, R., Schmidt, R., & Elbert, T. (2004). Posttraumatic stress disorder in patients with traumatic brain injury. *BMC Psychiatry, 4*, 5.

Gotshall, K. R., Gray, N. L., Drake, A. I., Tejidor, R., Hoffer, M. E., & McDonald, E. C. (2007). To investigate the influence of acute vestibular impairment following mild traumatic brain injury on subsequent ability to remain on active duty 12 months later. *Military Medicine, 172*, 852–857.

Green, P., Lees-Haley, P. R., & Allen, L. M. (2002). The Word Memory Test and the validity of neuropsychological test scores. *Journal of Forensic Neuropsychology, 2*, 97–124.

Guidelines Development Team. (2011). *Guidelines for mild traumatic brain injury and persistent symptoms*. Toronto, Ontario: Ontario Neurotrauma Foundation (ONF).

Gunstad, J., & Suhr, J. A. (2001). "Expectation as etiology" versus the "good old days": Postconcussion syndrome symptom reporting in athletes, headache sufferers, and depressed individuals. *Journal of the International Neuropsychological Society, 7*, 323–333.

Guskiewicz, K. M., Marshall, S. W., Bailes, J., McCrea, M., Cantu, R. C., Randolph, C., et al. (2003). Cumulative effects associated with recurrent concussion in collegiate football players. The NCAA Concussion Study. *Journal of the American Medical Association, 290*, 2549–2555.

Guskiewicz, K. M., McCrea, M., Marshall, S. W., Cantu, R. C., Randolph, C., Barr, W. et al. (2005). Association between recurrent concussion and late-life cognitive impairment in retired professional football players. *Neurosurgery, 57*, 719–726.

Guy, R. J., Glover, M. A., & Cripps, N. P. (1998). The pathophysiology of primary blast injury and its implications for treatment. Part I: The thorax. *Journal of the Royal Naval Medical Service, 84*, 79–86.

Halbauer, J. D., Ashford, W., Zeitzer, J. M., Adamson, M., Lew, H. L., & Yesavage, J. A. (2009). Neuropsychiatric diagnosis and management of chronic sequelae of war-related mild to moderate traumatic brain injury. *Journal of Rehabilitation Research & Development, 46*, 757–796.

Hanks, R. A., Wood, D. L., Millis, S., Harrison-Felix, C., Pierce, C. A., Rosenthal, M., et al. (2003). Violent traumatic brain injury: Occurence, patient characteristics, and risk factors from the Traumatic Brain Injury Model Systems Project. *Archives of Physical Medicine and Rehabilitation, 84*(2), 249–254.

Hannay, H. J., Howieson, D. B., Loring, D. W., Fischer, J. S., & Lezak, M. D. (2004). Neuropathology for neuropsychologists. In M. D. Lezak (Ed.), *Neuropsychological assessment* (pp. 157–210). New York: Oxford University Press.

Harrison, P. J., & Owen, M. (2003). Genes for schizophrenia? Recent findings and their pathophysiological implications. *The Lancet, 361*, 417–419.

Heegaard, W., & Biros, M. (2007). Traumatic brain injury. *Emergency Medicine Clinics of North America, 25*, 655–678.

Heilbronner, R. L., Sweet, J. J., Morgan, J. E., Larrabee, G. J., Millis, S. R., & Conference Participants (2009). American Academy of Clinical Neuropsychology Consensus Conference Statement on the neuropsychological assessment of effort, response bias, and malingering. *The Clinical Neuropsychologist, 23*, 1093–1129.

Helmick, K., Guskiewicz, K., Barth, J., Cantu, R., Kelly, J. P., McDonald, E., et al. (2006). *Defense and Veterans Brain Injury Center Working Group on the acute management of mild traumatic brain injury in military operational settings*. Washington DC: Defense and Veterans Brain Injury Center (DVBIC).

Hoffman, J. M., Paqulayan, K. F., Zawaideh, N., Dikmen, S., Temkin, N., & Bell, K. R. (2007). Understanding pain after traumatic brain injury: Impact on community participation. *The American Journal of Physical Medicine & Rehabilitation, 86*(12), 962–969.

Hoge, C. W., Goldberg, H. M., Castro, C. A. (2009). Care of war veterans with mild traumatic brain injury—flawed perspectives. *New England Journal of Medicine, 360*(16), 1588–1591.

Holbrook, T. L., Hoyt, D. B., Stein, M. B., & Seiber, W. J. (2002). Gender differences in long-term posttraumatic stress disorder outcomes after major trauma: Women are at higher risk of adverse outcomes than men. *Journal of Trauma-Injury Infection & Critical Care, 53*(5), 882–888.

Hoofien, D., Gilboa, A. S., Vakil, E., & Donovick, P. J. (2001). Traumatic brain injury (TBI) 10–20 years later: A comprehensive outcome study of psychiatric symptomatology, cogntiive abilities, and psychosocial functioning. *Brain Injury, 15*(3), 189–209.

Howe, L. L. S. (2009). Giving context to post-deployment post-concussive-like symptoms: Blast-related potential mild traumatic brain injury and comorbidities. *The Clinical Neuropsychologist, 23*, 1315–1337.

Iverson, G. L. (2005). Outcome from mild traumatic brain injury. *Current Opinion in Psychiatry, 18*, 301–317.

Iverson, G. L., Brooks, B. L., Lovell, M. R., & Collins, M. W. (2005). No cumulative effects for one or two previous concussions. *British Journal of Sports Medicine, 40*, 72–75.

Iverson, G. L., & Lange, R. T. (2003). Examination of "postconcussion-like" symptoms in a healthy sample. *Applied Neuropsychology, 10*(3), 137–144.

Iverson, G. L., Lange, R. T., Brooks, B. L., & Rennison, V. L. (2010). "Good old days" bias following mild traumatic brain injury. *The Clinical Neuropsychologist, 24*, 17–37.

Jorge, R. E., Acion, L., Starkstein, S. E., & Magnotta, V. (2007). Hippocampal volume and mood disorders after traumatic brain injury. *Biological Psychiatry, 62*, 332–338.

Jorge, R. E., Robinson, R. G., Moser, D., Tateno, A., Crespo-Facorro, B., & Arndt, S. (2004). Major depression following traumatic brain injury. *General Psychiatry, 61*, 42–50.

Kashluba, S., Hanks, R. A., Casey, J. E., & Millis, S. R. (2008). Neuropsychologic functional outcome after complicated mild traumatic brain injury. *Archives of Physical Medicine and Rehabilitation, 24*, 24–31.

Kashluba, S., Paniak, C., & Casey, J. E. (2008). Persistent symptoms associated with factors identified by the WHO Task Force on Mild Traumatic Brain Injury. *The Clinical Neuropsychologist, 22*, 195–208.

Kay, T., Newman, B., Cavallo, M., Ezrachi, O., & Resnick, M. (1992). Toward a neuropsychological model of functional disability after mild traumatic brain injury. *Neuropsychology, 6*(4), 371–384.

Kilmer, R. P., Demakis, G. J., Hammond, F. M., Grattan, K. E., Cook, J. R., & Kornev, A. A. (2006). Use of the Neuropsychiatric Inventory in traumatic brain injury: A pilot investigation. *Rehabilitation Psychology, 51*(3), 232–238.

Kim, E., Lauterbach, E. C., Reeve, A., Arciniegas, D. B., Coburn, K. L., Mendez, M. F., et al. (2007). Neuropsychiatric complications of traumatic brain injury: A critical review of the literature (a report by the ANPA Committee on Research). *Journal of Neuropsychiatry and Clinical Neurosciences, 19*, 106–127.

Kiraly, M. A., & Kiraly, S. J. (2007). Traumatic brain injury and delayed sequelae: A review—traumatic brain injury and mild traumatic brain injury (concussion) are precursors to later-onset brain disorders, including early-onset dementia. *The Scientific World Journal, 7*, 1768–1776.

Kirsch, N. L., de Leon, M. B., Maio, R. F., Millis, S. R., Tan-Scrhiner, C. U., & Frederiksen, S. (2010). Characteristics of a mild head injury subgroup with extreme, persisting distress on the Rivermead Postconcussion Symptoms Questionnaire. *Archives of Physical Medicine and Rehabilitation, 91*, 35–42.

Kit, K. A., Mateer, C. A., & Graves, R. E. (2007). The influence of memory beliefs in individuals with traumatic brain injury. *Rehabilitation Psychology, 52*(1), 25–32.

Kreutzer, J. S., Gordon, W. A., & Wehman, P. (1989). Cognitive remediation following traumatic brain injury. *Rehabilitation Psychology, 34*(2).

Larrabee, G. J. (2003). Detection of malingering using atypical performance patterns on standard neuropsychological tests. *The Clinical Neuropsychologist, 17*, 410–425.

Larrabee, G. J. (2007). Commentary on Delis and Wetter, "Cogniform disorder and cogniform condition: Proposed diagnosis for excessive cognitive symptoms".*Archives of Clinical Neuropsychology, 22*, 683–687.

Larrabee, G. J. (2012). Mild traumatic brain injury. In G. Larrabee, *Forensic neuropsychology* (pp. 231–259). New York: Oxford University Press.

Larson, M. J., Kaufman, D. A. S., Kellison, I. L., Schmalfuss, I. M., & Perlstein, W. M. (2009). Double jeopardy! The additive consequences of negative affect on performance-monitoring decrements following brain injury. *Neuropsychology, 23*(4), 433–444.

MacDonald, C. L., Johnson, A. M., Cooper, D., Nelson, E. C., Werner, N. J., Shimony, J. S., et al. (2011). Detection of blast-related traumatic brain injury in U.S. military personnel. *New England Journal of Medicine, 364*(22), 2091–2100.

Machamer, J., Temkin, N., Fraser, R., Doctor, J., & Dikmen, S. (2005). Stability of employment after traumatic brain injury. *Journal of the International Neuropsychological Society, 11*(7), 807–816.

Malec, J. F., Brown, A. W., & Moessner, A. M. (2004). Personality factors and injury severity in the prediction of early and late traumatic brain injury outcomes. *Rehabilitation Psychology, 49*(1), 55–61.

Management of Concussion/mTBI Working Group. (2009). *VA/DoD clinical practice guideline for management of concussion/mild traumatic brain injury (mTBI)*. Washington, DC: Office of Quality and Performance, Veterans Affairs.

Max, J. E., Robertson, B. A., & Lansing, A. E. (2001). The phenomenology of personality change due to traumatic brain injury in children and adolescents. *The Journal of Neuropsychiatry and Clinical Neurosciences, 13*, 161–170.

Mazaux, J., Masson, F., Levin, H. S., Alaoui, P., Maurette, P., & Barat, M. (1997). Long-term neuropsychological outcome and loss of social autonomy after brain injury. *Archives of Physical Medicine and Rehabilitation, 78*, 1316–1320.

McCauley, S. R., Boake, C., Levin, H. S., Contant, C. F., & Sonx, J. X. (2001). Postconcussional disorder following mild to moderate traumatic brain injury: Anxiety, depression, and social support as risk factors and comorbidities. *Journal of Clinical and Experimental Neuropsychology, 23*(6), 792–808.

McCrea, M., Guskiewicz, K. M., Marshall, S. W., Barr, W. B., Randolph, C., Cantu, R. C., et al. (2003). Acute effects and recovery time following concussion in collegiate football players. *Journal of the American Medical Association, 290*, 2556–2563.

McCrea, M., Iverson, G. L., McAllister, T. W., Hammeke, T. A., Powell, M. R., Barr, W. B., & Kelly, J. P. (2009). An Integrated review of recovery after mild traumatic brain injury (MTBI): Implications for clinical management. *The Clinical Neuropsychologist, 23*, 8, 1368–1390.

McCrea, M., Pliskin, N., Barth, J., Cox, D., Fink, J., French, L., et al. (2008). Official position of the Military TBI Task Force on the role of neuropsychology and rehabilitation psychology in the evaluation, management, and research of military veterans with traumatic brain injury. *The Clinical Neuropsychologist, 22,* 10–26.

Meares, S., Shores, E. A., Taylor, A. J., Batchelor, J., Bryant, R. A., Baguley, I. J., et al. (2008). Mild traumatic brain injury does not predict acute postconcussion syndrome. *Journal of Neurology, Neurosurgery, & Psychiatry, 79,* 300–306.

Meares, S., Shores, E. A., Taylor, A. J., Batchelor, J., Bryant, R. A., Baguley, I. J., et al. (2011). The prospective course of postconcussion syndrome: The role of mild traumatic brain injury. *Neuropsychology, 25*(4), 454–465.

Mild Traumatic Brain Injury Committee of the Head Injury Interdisciplinary Special Interest Group of the American Congress of Rehabilitation Medicine. (1993). Definition of mild traumatic brain injury. *Journal of Head Trauma Rehabilitation, 8*(3), 86–87.

Millis, S. R., Rosenthal, M., Novack, T. A., Sherer, M., Nick, T. G., Kreutzer, J. S., et al. (2001). Long-term neuropsychological outcome after traumatic brain injury. *Journal of Head Trauma Rehabilitation, 16*(4), 343–355.

Mittenberg, W., Patton, C., Canyock, E. M., & Condit, D. C. (2002). Base rates of malingering and symptom exaggeration. *Journal of Experimental Neuropsychology, 24,* 1094–1102.

Mittenberg, W., &, Roberts, D. M. (2008). Mild traumatic brain injury and postconcussion syndrome. In J. E. Morgan & J. H. Ricker (Eds.), *Textbook of clinical neuropsychology* (pp. 430–436). New York: Taylor & Francis Group.

Mittenberg, W., Tremont, G., Zielinski, R. E., Fichera, S., & Rayls, K. R. (1996). Cognitive-behavioral prevention of postconcussion syndrome. *Archives of Clinical Neuropsychology, 11*(2), 139–145.

Mukherjee, D., Heller, W., & Alper, J. S. (2001). Social and institutional factors in adjustment to traumatic brain injury. *Rehabilitation Psychology, 46*(1), 82–99.

Myers, C. S. (1915). A contribution to the study of shellshock: Being an account of the cases of loss of memory, vision, smell, and taste admitted to the Duchess of Westminster's War Hospital, Le Touquet. *The Lancet, 1,* 316–320.

Nakase-Richardson, R., Yablon, S. A., & Sherer, M. (2007). Prospective comparison of acute confusion severity with duration of post-traumatic amnesia in predicting employment outcome after traumatic brain injury. *Journal of Neurology, Neurosurgery, and Psychiatry, 78*(8), 872–876.

Nampiaparampil, D. E. (2008). Prevalence of chronic pain after traumatic brain injury. *The Journal of the American Medical Association, 300*(6), 711–719.

Nelson, N. W., Hoelzle, J. B., McGuire, K. A., Ferrier-Auerbach, A. G., Charlesworth, M. J., & Sponheim, S. R. (2010). Evaluation context impacts neuropsychological performance of OEF/OIF veterans with reported combat-related concussion. *Archives of Clinical Neuropsychology, 25*(8), 713–723.

Nolan, S. (2005). Traumatic brain injury, a review. *Critical Care Nursing Quarterly, 28* (2), 188–194.

Orff, H. J., Ayalon, L., & Drummond, S. P. A. (2009). Traumatic brain injury and sleep disturbance: A review of the current research. *Journal of Head Trauma Rehabilitation, 24,* 155–165.

Ouellet, M. C., Beaulieu-Bonneau, S., & Morin, C. M. (2006). Insomnia in patients with traumatic brain injury: Frequency, characteristics, and risk factors. *Journal of Head Trauma Rehabilitation, 21,* 199–212.

Palacios, E. M., Fernandez-Espejo, D., Junque, C., Sanchez-Carrion, R., Roig, T., Tormos, J. M., et al. (2011). Diffusion tensor imaging differences relate to memory deficits in diffuse traumatic brain injury. *Neurology, 11*(24), 1–11.

Panayiotou, A., Jackson, M., & Crowe, S. F. (2010). A meta-analytic review of the emotional symptoms associated with mild traumatic brain injury. *Journal of Clinical and Experimental Neuropsychology, 32*, 463–473.

Paniak, C., Reynolds, S., Toller-Lobe, G., Melnyk, A., Nagy, J., & Schmidt, D. (2002). A longitudinal study of the relationship between financial compensation and symptoms after treated mild traumatic brain injury. *Journal of Clinical and Experimental Neuropsychology, 24*(2), 187–193.

Peek-Asa, C., McArthur, D., Hovda, D., & Kraus, J. (2001). Early predictors of mortality in penetrating compared with closed brain injury. *Brain Injury, 15*(9), 801–810.

Polusny, M. A., Kehle, S. M., Nelson, N. W., Erbes, C. R., Arbisi, P. A., & Thuras, P. (2011). Longitudinal effects of mild traumatic brain injury and posttraumatic stress disorder comorbidity on postdeployment outcomes in National Guard soldiers deployed to Iraq. *General Psychiatry, 68*(1), 79–89.

Ponsford, J., Olver, J., Ponsford, M., & Nelms, R. (2003). Long-term adjustment of families following traumatic brain injury where comprehensive rehabilitation has been provided. *Brain Injury, 17*, 453–468.

Ponsford, J., Willmott, C., Rothwell, A., Cameron, P., Kelly, A., Nelms, R., et al. (2000). Factors influencing outcome following mild traumatic brain injury in adults. *Journal of the International Neuropsychological Society, 6*, 568–579.

Ponsford, J., Willmott, C., Rothwell, A., Cameron, P., Kelly, A.-M., Nelms, R., et al. (2002). Impact of early intervention on outcome following mild head injury in adults. *Journal of Neurology, Neurosurgery, and Psychiatry, 73*, 330–332.

Prigatano, G. P. (1992). Personality disturbances associated with traumatic brain injury. *Journal of Consulting and Clinical Psychology, 60*(3), 360–368.

Prigerson, H. G., Maciejewski, P. K., & Rosenheck, R. A. (2001). Combat trauma: Trauma with highest risk of delayed onset and unresolved post-traumatic stress disorder symptoms, unemployment, and abuse among men. *Journal of Nervous and Mental Diseases, 189*(2), 99–108.

Quality Standards Subcommittee of the American Academy of Neurology. (1997). Practice parameter: The management of concussion in sports. *Neurology, 48*, 581–585.

Rao, V., & Lyketsos, C. (2000). Neuropsychiatric sequelae of traumatic brain injury. *Psychosomatics, 41*(2), 95–103.

Rapoport, M. J., McCullagh, S., Shammi, P., & Feinstein, A. (2005). Cognitive impairment associated with major depression following mild and moderate traumatic brain injury. *Journal of Neuropsychiatry and Clinical Neurosciences, 17*, 61–65.

Raymont, V., Greathouse, A., Reding, K., Lipsky, R., Salazar, A., & Grafman, J. (2008). Demographic, structural and genetic predictors of late cognitive decline after penetrating head injury. *Brain, 131*(2), 543–558.

Reekum, R. V., Cohen, T., & Wong, J. (2000). Can traumatic brain injury cause psychiatric disorders? *Journal of Neuropsychiatry and Clinical Neurosciences, 12*, 316–327.

Reynolds, S., Paniak, C., Toller-Lobe, G., & Nagy, J. (2003). A longitudinal study of compensation-seeking and return to work in a treated mild traumatic brain injury sample. *Journal of Head Trauma Rehabilitation, 18*(2), 139–147.

Roebuck-Spencer, T., & Sherer, M. (2008). Moderate and severe traumatic brain injury. In J. E. Morgan & J. H. Ricker (Eds.), *Textbook of clinical neuropsychology* (pp. 411–429). New York: Taylor & Francis Group.

Roebuck-Spencer, T., & Sherer, M. (2012). Moderate and severe traumatic brain injury. In G. Larrabee (Ed.), *Forensic neuropsychology* (pp. 260–280). New York: Oxford University Press.

Roebuck-Spencer, T. M., Banos, J., Sherer, M., & Novack, T. (2010). Neurobehavioral aspects of traumatic brain injury sustained in adulthood. In J. Donders & S. J. Hunter (Eds.), *Principles and practice of lifespan developmental neuropsychology* (pp. 329–344). Cambridge, UK: Cambridge University Press.

Ropper, A. (2011). Brain injuries from blasts. *New England Journal of Medicine, 364*, 22.

Ruff, R. M., Iverson, G. L., Barth, J. T., Bush, S. S., Broshek, D. K., & the NAN Policy and Planning Committee (2009). Recommendations for diagnosing a mild traumatic brain injury: A National Academy of Neuropsychology education paper. *Clinical Neuropsychology, 24*, 3–10.

Ruff, R. M., & Jamora, C. W. (2009). Myths and mild traumatic brain injury. *Psychological Injury and Law, 2*, 34–42.

Rush, B. K., Malec, J. F., Brown, A. W., & Moessner, A. M. (2006). Personality and functional outcome following traumatic brain injury. *Rehabilitation Psychology, 51*(3), 257–264.

Rush, B. K., Malec, J. F., Moessner, A. M., & Brown, A. W. (2004). Pre-injury personality traits and the prediction of early neurobehavioral symptoms following mild traumatic brain injury. *Rehabilitation Psychology, 4*, 275–281.

Sachdev, P., Smith, J. S., & Cathcart, S. (2001). Schizophrenia-like psychosis following traumatic brain injury: A chart-based descriptive and case-control study. *Psychological Medicine, 31*, 231–239.

Seel, R. T., Kreutzer, J. S., Rosenthal, M., Hammond, F. M., Corrigan, J. D., & Black, K. (2003). Depression after traumatic brain injury: A National Institute on Disability and Rehabilitation research model systems multicenter investigation. *Archives of Physical Medicine and Rehabilitation, 84*, 177–184.

Senathi-Raja, D., Ponsford, J., & Schonberger, M. (2010). Impact of age on long-term cognitive function after traumatic brain injury. *Neuropsychology, 24*(3), 336–344.

Sherman, K. B., Goldberg, M., & Bell, K. R. (2006). TBI and pain. *Physical Medicine & Rehabilitation Clinics of North America, 17*(2), 473–490.

Silver, J. M., Kramer, R., Greenwald, S., & Weissman, M. (2001). The association between head injuries and psychiatric disorders: Findings from the New Haven NIMH Epidemiologic Catchment Area Study. *Brain Injury, 15*, 935–945.

Stambrook, M., Moore, A. D., Peters, L. C., Deviaene, C., & Hawryluk, G. A. (1990). Effects of mild, moderate, and severe closed head injury on long-term vocational status. *Brain Injury, 4*, 183–190.

Steele, D., Ponsford, J., Rajaratnam, S., & Redman, J. (2006). Self-reported changes to night-time sleep following traumatic brain injury. *Archives of Physical Medicine and Rehabilitation, 87*, 278–285.

Suhr, J. A., & Gunstad, J. (2002a). "Diagnosis threat": The effect of negative expectations on cognitive performance in head injury. *Journal of Clinical and Experimental Neuropsychology, 24*(4), 448–457.

Suhr, J. A., & Gunstad, J. (2002b). Postconcussive symptom report: The relative influence of head injury and depression. *Journal of Clinical and Experimental Neuropsychology, 24*, 981–992.

Suhr, J. A., & Gunstad, J. (2005). Further exploration of the effect of "diagnosis threat" on cognitive performance in individuals with mild head injury. *Journal of the International Neuropsychological Society, 11*(1), 23–29.

Summers, C. R., Ivins, B., & Schwab, K. A. (2009). Traumatic brain injury in the United States: An epidemiologic overview. *Mount Sinai Journal of Medicine, 76*, 105–110.

Symonds, C. P. (1937). Mental disorder following head injury. *Proceedings of the Royal Society of Medicine, 30*, 1081–1094.

Tateno, A., Jorge, R. E., & Robinson, R. G. (2003). Clinical correlates of aggressive behavior after traumatic brain injury. *Journal of Neuropsychiatry and Clinical Neurosciences, 15*, 155–160.

Teasdale, G. M. (1995). Head injury. *Journal of Neurology, Neurosurgery, and Psychiatry, 58*, 526–539.

Turner, A. P., Kivlahan, D. R., & Rimmele, C. T. (2006). Does preinjury alcohol use or blood alcohol level influence cognitive functioning after traumatic brain injury? *Rehabilitation Psychology, 51*(1), 78–86.

Vasterling, J. J. (November, 2011). *Neuropsychology of PTSD.* Presented at the Pacific Northwest Neuropsychological Society Conference, Seattle, WA.

Vasterling, J. J., Proctor, S. P., Amoroso, P., Kane, R., Heeren, T., & White, R. F. (2006). neuropsychological outcomes of army personnel following deployment to the Iraq war. *Journal of the American Medical Association, 296*(5), 519–529.

Wade, S. L., Taylor, H. G., Drotar, D., Stancin, T., Yeates, K. O., & Minich, N. M. (2002). A Prospective study of long-term care-giver and family adaptation following brain injury in children. *Journal of Head Trauma Rehabilitation, 17*, 96–111.

Walker, W. C., Seel, R. T., Curtiss, G., & Warden, D. L. (2005). Headache after moderate and severe traumatic brain injury: A longitudinal analysis. *Archives of Physical Medicine and Rehabilitation, 86*(9), 1793–1800.

Wang, Y., Chan, R. C., & Deng, Y. (2006). Examination of postconcussion-like symptoms in healthy university students: Relationships to subjective and objective neuropsychological function performance. *Archives of Clinical Neuropsychology, 21*(4), 339–347.

Whitney, A. W., Shepard, P. H., Williams, A. L., Davis, J. J., & Adams, K. M. (2009). The Medical Symptom Validity Test in the evaluation of Operation Iraqi Freedom/Operation Enduring Freedom soldiers: A preliminary study. *Archives of Clinical Neuropsychology, 24*, 145–152.

Williams, D. H., Levin, H. S., & Eisenberg, H. M. (1990). Mild head injury classification. *Journal of Neurosurgery, 27*(3), 422–428.

Zinio, C., & Ponsford, J. (2005). Measurement and prediction of subjective fatigue following traumatic brain injury. *Journal of the International Neuropsychological Society, 11*(4), 416–425.

14

Secondary Factors in Alzheimer's Disease, Mild Cognitive Impairment, and Stroke

ANTONIO N. PUENTE AND L. STEPHEN MILLER

Appropriate neuropsychological assessment of Alzheimer's disease (AD), mild cognitive impairment (MCI), and stroke is vital for accurate diagnosis, effective intervention, and treatment, as well as for making everyday life adjustments and adaptations in living with these debilitating diseases. As the number of adults affected by these conditions continues to dramatically increase (Alzheimer's Disease International, 2008), precision of neuropsychological assessment has become of utmost importance. Several factors can compromise the reliability and validity of an assessment, including those related to the examiner, the examinee, and the environment. In this chapter we review the intra-examinee secondary factors of apathy, anxiety, and depression on cognitive performance in AD, MCI, and stroke. In our discussion of stroke we also attend to language disturbances, as these are uniquely associated with stroke presentation.

The goals of this chapter are to provide the reader with an understanding of the effects of these secondary factors on cognitive functioning in AD, MCI, and stroke, as well as to make recommendations toward mitigating these factors and increasing accurate interpretation and synthesis of clinical data. The empirical review is organized by neurological syndrome, and the influence of the different secondary factors on cognitive performance in each syndrome is discussed by cognitive domain. Following this review, empirically driven recommendations are provided, with the goal of assisting clinicians in assessing patients with AD, MCI, or stroke and co-occurring clinical conditions and psychiatric symptoms. We also discuss the specific limitations in research and how it could benefit from further investigation. Finally, a short case example is presented in which we attempt to investigate and integrate potential psychiatric symptoms.

ALZHEIMER'S DISEASE

The most common neurodegenerative disease and type of dementia, affecting 5.3 million Americans, is Alzheimer's disease (Alzheimer's Association, 2011). The prevalence of AD is growing and expected to increase by 300% in the United States by 2050 (Prigerson, 2003). AD is characterized by memory deficits and progressive cognitive decline (Hutchinson & Mathias, 2007). Despite the trajectory of AD, the onset is insidious, and symptoms only gradually become apparent. Typically, AD involves impairment in learning and recall of information, accompanied by another cognitive dysfunction. However, there are also other presentations of AD (i.e., nonamnestic) in which the most significant deficit is in a domain other than memory, such as language or executive functioning (McKhann et al., 2011). Cognitive disturbances are the diagnostic and traditional symptoms associated with AD; however, psychiatric symptoms are very common and are experienced by almost all individuals with AD at some point in the course of the disease (Lyketsos & Olin, 2002). These symptoms are associated with a more rapid decline and increased caregiver distress and may negatively impact cognition in AD (Malloy & Boyle, 2005). The effect of the most common psychiatric symptoms on cognitive performance in AD—depression, apathy, and anxiety—are reviewed here.

Depression

Depression is likely the most common psychiatric symptom and disorder accompanying AD (Prado-Jean et al., 2010; Starkstein, Mizrahi, & Power, 2008). Prevalence estimates range from 1% to 50% but most estimates fall between 20% and 50% (Holtzer et al., 2005; Lyketsos & Olin, 2002; Starkstein et al., 2008). This variability is attributed to differences in methodology, such as the sample, diagnostic criteria, and measures used (Starkstein et al., 2008).

The etiology of depression in AD is mixed. Some propose depression as a prodrome of AD (Bartolini, Coccia, Luzzi, Provinciali, & Ceravolo, 2005) whereas others indicate that it is a risk factor (Michelsen, Prickaerts, & Steinbusch, 2008; Ownby, Crocco, Acevedo, John & Loewenstein, 2006). Similarly, there is also debate over whether depression is an affective reaction to or results from AD (Lyketsos & Olin, 2002). Although the etiology is inconclusive, depression in AD has been associated with a decrease in noradrenergic and serotonergic nuclei in the locus ceruleus and dorsal raphe, supporting a neurobiological perspective (Lyketsos & Olin, 2002).

Depression in AD is reported to begin in the initial stages, before cognitive impairment is evident (Bartolini et al., 2005), and continues through the later stages (Fernandez-Martinez, Molano, Castro, & Zarranz, 2010). The relationship of depression with the course of AD (i.e., dementia severity) is an area of controversy; depression is typically quantified in relation to global measures of cognition. Depression and depressive symptoms have been reported to increase (Fernandez-Martinez et al., 2010), decline (Holtzer et al., 2005; Lopez et al., 2003), or not change as AD progresses (Wilson et al., 2010). As with prevalence rates, the variability is likely due to methodological differences, including diagnostic classification (e.g., cutoff scores versus diagnostic criteria) and assessment differences (e.g., self-report versus observer report versus collateral report). Despite these discrepancies, it is apparent that individuals are less able to describe their symptoms as the disease progresses and invades cortical areas, and psychiatric symptoms are more likely to manifest as abnormal behaviors (Lopez et al., 2003).

In addition to inconsistencies with the course of depressive symptoms and AD, the effect of depression on general and specific cognitive abilities is equivocal. Several investigations have found effects of depression in AD on measures of overall cognitive ability as well as various measures of specific cognitive abilities (Hudon, Voyer, Tremblay, Tardif & Carmichael, 2010; Nakaaki et al., 2007, 2008; Rubin, Kinscherf, Grant, & Storandt, 1991; Wefel, Hoyt, Massma, 1999). However, many other investigators have not found depression to have a deleterious impact on neuropsychological functioning (Backman, Hassing, Forsell, & Viitanen, 1996; Berger, Fahlander, Wahlin, & Backman, 2002; Fahlander, Berger, Backman, & Wahlin, 1999; Fernandez-Martinez et al., 2010; Garavello, Magaldi, Paschoal, & Filho, 2010; Lopez, Boller, Becker, Miller & Reynolds, 1990; Porta-Etessam, Tobaruela-Gonzalez, & Rabes-Berendes, 2011). Both conclusions warrant further discussion.

Depressed individuals with AD have been found to perform both worse on global measures of cognitive ability and no differently than AD participants without depression or depressive symptoms. Rubin et al. (1991) enrolled participants with mild AD (as defined by a Clinical Dementia Rating [CDR] = 1; Hughes et al., 1982) and either no depression or co-occurring major depressive disorder (MDD). AD participants with MDD received lower scores on the overall Blessed Dementia Scale, cognitive portion. This finding extended to individuals with AD and depressive symptoms (i.e., those persons displaying depressive symptoms but not diagnosed with MDD), as participants with AD and depressive symptoms had a greater level of cognitive impairment on the Hierarchic Dementia Scale (HDS) even though the groups were matched for dementia severity (Hudon et al., 2010).

To our knowledge, the finding by Hudon et al. (2010) has not been replicated, and in contrast, individuals with AD and depressive symptoms have been shown to perform the same on the Mini Mental Status Exam (MMSE), Delayed Recall of the Brief Cognitive Screening Battery, and Cognitive Section of the Cambridge Examination for Mental Disorders of the Elderly as AD participants without DS (Garavello et al., 2010). Correlation analyses between the MMSE and depressive symptoms in two additional investigations suggest little impact of depression on measures of global cognitive status (Fernandez-Martinez et al., 2010; Porta-Etessame et al., 2011). While the discrepancy of the effect of depression on measures of global cognitive status could be due to differences in classifying depression, results suggest performance on measures of global cognitive status will not likely be affected by depression unless the individual meets criteria for MDD.

There is some evidence to suggest a negative association specifically between depression and memory-functioning in older adults (McClintock et al., 2010). This negative association was found between collateral report of depressive symptoms and performance on the Benton Visual Retention Test 10 s delay ($r = -.16$) in AD

(Powlishta et al., 2004). However, others have not found this impaired memory–depression relationship and suggest that there is not a negative impact of depression on memory performance in AD.

On several measures of episodic memory (i.e., face recognition, word recall, and object recall) Backman et al. (1996) found no difference between AD participants with depression and those with AD alone. Fahlander et al. (1999) also found that depression in AD does not affect memory, as AD participants with dysthymic disorder or MDD did not perform any worse on a list-learning task than those without mood disorders. These results are also apparent when using a composite memory score from performance on Verbal Paired Associates, Face Name Paired Associates, Rey-Osterrieth Complex Figure Immediate Recall, and Logical Memory tests (Lopez et al., 1990). Although counterintuitive, depression in AD has been associated with better memory performance in individuals with AD (Wefel et al., 1999). Most of the evidence suggests that memory function in AD is not affected by depression and does not support generalizing the negative association of depression on memory in normal older adults to AD.

While the impact of depression on measures of exective function in AD has not been investigated extensively, there is some evidence from a few of studies. Depressed individuals with mild-to-moderate levels of AD (as defined by a CDR = 0.5–1) performed worse on Trail Making Test Part B (TMT-B) than individuals without depression (Nakaaki et al., 2007). However, there was no difference in performance between depressed and nondepressed AD patients on the Stroop Color and Word Test or letter fluency (Nakaaki et al., 2007). Berger et al. (2002) also found no difference between AD participants with depression and those without it on letter fluency. In a subsequent study by Nakaaki et al. (2008), depression had a negative impact on the performance of individuals with mild-to-moderate AD on a bedside battery of executive function, the Frontal Assessment Battery (FAB) total score, and specifically on two of the battery's subtests, conflicting instructions and go/no-go. The effect of depression on executive function in AD then is variable but does suggest a negative influence on various measures of executive function.

The amount of evidence examining the relationship between depression and working memory in AD is more limited than that for executive function. Powlishta et al. (2004) found a negative correlation between collateral report of depressive symptoms and performance on Digit Span–Backward ($r = -.18$) in AD. While this suggests that a greater number of depressive symptoms are associated with worse working memory, Fahlander et al. (1999) found that individuals with AD and depression did not perform worse than participants with AD and no depression on a working-memory task. Thus the limited evidence of the effect of depression in AD on working memory is variable, and much more research is required to determine this relationship.

Performance on attention and processing-speed measures has also been shown to be variably associated with depression in AD. Individuals with mild AD and co-occurring MDD performed worse than individuals with AD only on Digit Symbol and crossing-off tasks (Rubin et al., 1991). Wefel et al. (1999) reported that performance on the Digit Symbol task was negatively affected by depression in

AD. Depression in AD can also impact performance on the TMT-A and divided-attention tests (Nakaaki et al., 2007, 2008). However, not all results suggest that depression negatively affects attention and processing speed in AD. In one study, individuals with depression and AD performed on the Digit Symbol test as well as AD participants without depression (Nakaaki et al., 2007), and in another study there was no difference between depressed and nondepressed AD individuals on a composite score of attention (Lopez et al., 1990). Nevertheless, the bulk of the evidence indicates that depression in AD may result in worse performance on measures of attention and processing speed.

As with executive function, eveidence on the impact of depression on visuospatial functioning is inconsistent. Wefel et al. (1999) found that those with depression and AD performed worse on the Wechsler Block Design (BD) than individuals with AD but no depression, reporting an effect size of .43. Another investigation reported a negative association between self-reported depressive symptoms and BD performance. In contrast to these results, Berger et al. (2002) did not find depression to negatively affect performance on BD or clock drawing tests. No impact of depression on visuospatial tasks was found by Lopez et al. (1990) on a composite score of visuospatial functioning from the Visual Forms Discrimination task, the Rey-Osterrieth Complex Figure Copy, and BD.

There is very limited research on the effect of depression on language and motor functioning, and it shows mixed results Evidence indicates that depression does not have a negative impact on measures of language (Berger et al., 2002; Lopez et al., 1990). However, one investigation reported depression negatively affecting motor functioning, with an effect size of .42 (Wefel et al., 1999).

Overall, the impact of depression in AD on measures of global cognitive status will likely be limited to individuals with AD and a clinical diagnosis of depression. However, memory and language functioning in AD will likely not be negatively affected by depression, whereas executive function, attention/processing speed, and visuospatial ability may be decreased by depression in AD. Limited evidence also suggests that motor functioning may be worsened by depression.

Because depression does affect performance in several cognitive domains (Hudon et al., 2009; Nakaaki et al., 2007, 2008; Rubin et al., 1991; Wefel et al., 1999), a brief discussion about treatments for depression in AD and their impact on both depressive symptoms and cognition is provided here. In several studies, depressed individuals with AD treated with antidepressants exhibited decreased levels of depression and depressive symptoms compared to controls (Lyketsos et al., 2000, 2003; Mossello et al., 2008). However, others have suggested that there is no reduction in depressive symptoms in AD depressed patients compared to controls (Magai, Kennedy, Cohen, & Gomberg, 2000; Petracca, Chemerinski, & Starkstein, 2001; Rosenberg et al., 2010). Only one investigation has found improvement of cognition following treatment with antidepressants. This improvement in the treatment group on the MMSE (i.e., 1.6 points) was not statistically different from that of controls (Mossello et al., 2008), however. Thus, overall, the use of antidepressants for depressed individuals with AD is equivocal for significantly diminishing depressive symptoms, as some randomized clinical trials have found benefit (Lyketsos et al., 2000, 2003) while other investigations have not found pharmacological treatment to be effective for depressive symptoms (Magai et al., 2000; Petracca et al., 2001; Rosenberg et al., 2010). In contrast to the inconsistent effectiveness of antidepressants for treatment of depressive symptoms in AD, the influence of antidepressant treatment on cognitive ability appears clear. There is no substantive cognitive enhancement following treatment compared to that of controls (Lyketsos et al., 2000, 2003; Magai et al., 2000; Mossello et al., 2008; Petracca et al., 2001; Rosenberg et al., 2010).

In addition to pharmacological treatments for depression in AD there are alternative interventions for depressive symptom reduction, including group psychotherapy (e.g., Cheston, Jones, & Gilliard, 2003), music therapy (e.g., Guétin et al., 2009), and acetylcholinesterase inhibitors (used adjunctively; e.g., Holmes et al., 2004). Preliminary evidence suggests that these treatments decrease depressive symptoms but provide no improvement in cognition.

Apathy

Another neuropsychiatric syndrome to consider when assessing AD is apathy. *Apathy* is defined as a loss of motivation and is behaviorally evident as decreased initiation, persistence, interest, and social engagement as well as indifference, blunted emotional response, and lack of insight (Landes, Sperry, Strauss, & Geldmacher, 2001). Despite its symptom overlap and co-occurrence with depression, identifying apathy separately in AD is necessary because of its differential impact on cognitive functioning and differential treatment response.

Shared symptoms of apathy and depression include diminished interest, lack of insight, psychomotor slowing, and fatigue (Boyle & Malloy, 2003; Landes et al., 2001). Symptoms unique to apathy include blunted emotional response, indifference, decreased social engagement and initiation, and poor persistence, while symptoms specific to depression are dysphoria, hopelessness, guilt, suicidal ideation, sleep disturbances, and loss of appetite (Boyle & Malloy, 2003). Similar to depression, apathy manifests early in the disease process and fluctuates throughout the course of AD (Landes, Sperry & Strauss, 2005) but, in general, increases in prevalence and impact as the illness progresses (Boyle & Malloy, 2003). Prevalence estimates range from 24% (Starkstein, Jorge, Mizrahi & Robinson, 2005) to 72% (Mega, Cummings, Fiorello, & Gornbein, 1996) in mild-to-moderate stages and up 90% in more severe stages (Boyle & Malloy, 2003).

Several studies have failed to find an influence of apathy on measures of global cognition in AD (Drijgers, Verhey, Leentjens, Köhler, & Aalten, 2011; Kuzis, Sabe, Tiberti, Dorrego, & Starkstein, 1999; Landes et al., 2001). However, others have reported a negative association between apathy and global cognitive status (Chen, Sultzer, Hinkin, Mahler, & Cummings, 1998; Landes et al., 2001).

The effect of apathy on specific domains of cognition has not been well studied, with only a small number of studies reporting domain-level performance differences. In the case of memory, the few studies are variable in their findings. The presence of apathy in individuals with AD was not found to impact performance on broad measures of verbal and nonverbal memory (Drijgers et al., 2011; Kuzis et al., 1999; McPherson, Fairbanks, Tiken, Cummings, & Back-Madruga, 2002). However, Kuzis et al. (1999) found individuals with apathy to perform worse on a list-learning task. Although the bulk of evidence suggests that apathy in AD does not negatively affect memory performance, there is evidence indicating severe levels of apathy (i.e., 2 SD from mean) affecting learning and retrieval (Kuzis et al., 1999).

In contrast to memory, most of this limited research suggests that apathy in AD compromises executive function. Participants with apathy and AD performed worse on the Stroop task, TMT-B, Wisconsin Card Sorting Test (WCST), and Controlled Oral Word Association Test (COWAT) (Kuzis et al., 1999; McPherson et al., 2002). This negative relationship between apathy in AD and executive-function tasks has not been replicated in every investigation or across every measure of executive function, however, as Drijgers et al. (2011) did not find individuals with AD and apathy to perform any worse on the Stroop than AD participants without apathy. Additionally, McPherson et al. (2002) did not find that apathy negatively affected performance on a letter fluency task. In sum, despite somewhat inconsistent findings on the Stroop and letter fluency tasks and a relative paucity of empirical study, executive function in AD is likely decreased by apathy.

Apathy does not appear to be associated with decreased working-memory performance, as AD individuals with apathy performed the same as participants without apathy (Kuzis et al., 1999; McPherson et al., 2002). Nonetheless, there needs to be future investigation on the relationship between apathy in AD and working memory, given the limited amount of studies researching this relationship.

The association between apathy and attention/processing speed is also very limited and has only been investigated by McPherson et al. (2002). The authors found that individuals with apathy performed worse on the Digit Symbol task. They also examined the relationship between visuospatial ability and apathy in AD. Their findings suggest that apathy does not compromise performance on the BD or Rey–Osterrieth Figure Copy tests (Kuzis et al., 1999; McPherson et al., 2002).

Similar to visuospatial ability, apathy does not appear to impact performance on vocabulary, verbal reasoning, receptive language functions, or semantic fluency tasks (Drijgers et al., 2011; Kuzis et al., 1999; McPherson et al., 2002). There is however, evidence to suggest that naming may be negatively influenced by apathy (Kuzis et al., 1999). This result was not replicated by McPherson et al. (2002), and the discrepancy may be due to how apathy was operationalized. Similarly, there are inconsistent findings between apathy in AD and motor functioning. AD participants with apathy had poorer performance on the Purdue Pegboard (Kuzis et al., 1999) but demonstrated no differences on finger tapping (McPherson et al., 2002).

Collectively, apathy may have a modest impact on global cognitive status. Apathy could also decrease memory scores on measures of list learning but will not likely decrease performance on other memory measures. Despite some inconsistency in findings, apathy appears to be associated with compromised executive function. Additionally, it is possible that apathy also negatively affects attention/ processing speed, language, and motor functioning to some degree, but limited data are available. Apathy does not appear to be associated with visuospatial deficit or working-memory performance. More research is required to confirm and better understand the relationship of cognitive functioning and apathy in AD.

To attenuate any possible cognitive impact of apathy in AD, some treatments may be viable options. These include pharmacological and behavioral interventions. Both interventions may be mildly efficacious for decreasing apathy and have been associated with improved cognition (Malloy & Boyle, 2005). Cholinesterase inhibitors (ChE-Is), antidepressants, and stimulants are several different pharmacological agents suggested to be effective in decreasing apathy in AD (Malloy & Boyle, 2005).

ChE-Is are found to be somewhat efficacious in treating apathy even though they were originally developed and commonly prescribed for cognitive enhancement (Holmes et al., 2004; Malloy & Boyle, 2005). ChE-Is have received mixed reviews and have limitations as cognitive enhancers, although in some studies they have been found to improve cognitive functioning and delay deterioration in AD (Rockwood, 2004). Although decreasing apathy with ChE-Is is accompanied by improved cognitive functioning (Holmes et al., 2004), it is difficult to determine if decreasing apathy improves cognition or if improved cognition decreases apathy (Brousseau, Rourke, & Burke, 2007). To elucidate this relationship, Buettner, Fitzsimmons, Atav, and Sink (2011) reported on a nonpharmacological randomized, clinical trial investigating the efficacy of cognitive stimulation for depression and apathy. Cognitive stimulation included activities designed to stimulate and challenge individuals with novel tasks twice a week for 1 hour. The authors found that individuals who received cognitive stimulation had decreased levels of apathy and improved general cognitive ability. While more research is required to understand the direction of this relationship, evidence suggests that decreased apathy is associated with modestly improved cognition, even though it will likely not substantially alter neuropsychological performance of an individual with AD.

Anxiety

Another frequent and problematic neuropsychiatric symptom of AD is anxiety. Like depression, anxiety is sometimes conceptualized as a reaction to the diagnosis or cognitive decline and sometimes viewed as a result of the neurobiological aspects of AD (Chemerinski, Petracca, Manes, Leiguarda, & Starkstein, 1998). Prevalence estimates of anxiety symptoms and disorders in AD vary widely, ranging from 5% to 71% (Fernandez, Gobartt & Balana, 2010; Ferretti, McCurry, Logsdon, Gibbons, & Teri, 2001).

The relationship of anxiety symptoms to the course of AD is inconsistent. It has been found to be increased with lower MMSE scores (Lopez et al., 2003) as well as equally occur at any stage (Bierman, Comijs, Jonker & Beekman, 2007; Fernandez et al., 2010). There is a dearth of investigations examining the effect of anxiety on cognition. Bierman, Comijs, Jonker, Scheltens, and Beekman (2009) investigated the influence of anxiety on episodic memory in 44 older adults with probable AD at baseline and 1-year follow-up. No associations were found with anxiety symptoms and episodic memory performance at baseline or at follow-up.

However, contrary to expectations, a higher number of anxiety symptoms at baseline appeared to be protective. Individuals with a greater number of anxiety symptoms at baseline exhibited a smaller decline in memory over the 1-year period. Although the results are counterintuitive, the authors reported that the anxiety symptoms were subclinical and consistent with cross-sectional investigations of cognitive performance and anxiety in normal adults. Thus, subclinical levels of anxiety may act to preserve cognitive performance while more severe levels may impair performance. Further research is warranted to solidify the relationship between anxiety and cognition in AD.

Several investigations have explored the treatment of anxiety and its effect on cognition. Evidence suggests that individuals with anxiety and AD who are willing and able to discuss their everyday problems in psychotherapy experience a reduction in symptoms upon treatment completion (Cheston et al., 2003). Significant improvement in anxiety is also evident in individuals with AD after completion of music therapy (Guétin et al., 2009) as well as with ChE-I (Holmes et al., 2004). Despite the effectiveness of anxiety treatments in AD, what remains inconclusive and requires further investigation is if decreased anxiety actually improves cognition.

MILD COGNITIVE IMPAIRMENT

MCI has been theorized as a possible transitional stage between normal and pathological aging (Petersen, 2004). The MCI classification was developed to identify a pre-dementia phase of AD for possible intervention and slowing of any neurodegenerative process (Petersen et al., 2009). Theoretically, this syndrome is conceptualized as categorically distinct from normal aging and dementia but likely is on a continuum and has overlap with these two groups (Petersen, 2004). The original criteria for MCI (Petersen et al., 1999) required an individual to have (1) memory complaint, preferably corroborated by an informant; (2) memory impairment according to age and education expectations; (3) largely intact general cognitive function and performance in non-memory cognitive domains; (4) preserved activities of daily living; and (5) not demented. The diagnostic criteria and definition of MCI have evolved since their introduction (Albert et al., 2011; Petersen et al., 2009; Winblad et al., 2004), with the most recent adaptation completed by a National Institute of Aging and Alzheimer's Association workgroup (Albert et al., 2011). The clinical and cognitive criteria from this workgroup include the following: (1) cognitive concern reflecting a change in cognition reported by the patient or an informant or a clinician; (2) objective evidence of impairment in one or more cognitive domains, typically including memory; (3) preservation of independence in functional abilities; (4) not demented. It is important to recognize that these criteria (Albert et al., 2011) are not drastically different from the original ones (Petersen et al., 1999) or from subsequent adaptations (Petersen, 2004; Winblad et al., 2004), but they are not synonymous.

MCI is a beneficial construct and clinical syndrome given the rate at which individuals with MCI convert to AD (Gauthier et al., 2006). The conversion rate of normal older adults to probable AD is 1–2 % annually, while the rate of progression of those with MCI is 10–15% annually (Petersen et al., 2001). This conversion rate is influenced by several factors (e.g., type and age of sample), one of which is type of cognitive deficit. For example, a prospective investigation followed 141 individuals with MCI for 2½ years and found that 49% and 27% of amnestic and nonamnestic participants converted, respectively (Fischer et al., 2007).

In addition to the influence of type of cognitive deficit on conversion, neuropsychiatric symptoms also increase the progression rate, as individuals with MCI combined with a greater amount of neuropsychiatric symptoms have twice the risk of converting to AD as that of MCI patients without concomitant neuropsychiatric symptoms (Edwards, Spira, Barnes, & Yaffe, 2009). A higher number of neuropsychiatric symptoms in MCI are associated with increased comorbidity, cognitive impairment, and functional impairment (Edwards et al., 2009). Similar to AD, the prevalence of neuropsychiatric symptoms in MCI is variable. The Cardiovascular Health Study of Depression reported that 43% of MCI participants had neuropsychiatric symptoms in a 1-month period (Lyketsos et al., 2002). In contrast, a study of clinic-referred MCI patients reported the prevalence of neuropsychiatric symptoms to be 75% (Hwang, Masterman, Ortiz, Fairbanks, & Cummings, 2004). The range of prevalence estimates for neuropsychiatric symptoms in MCI, as identified in a comprehensive review of 21 studies, suggests the variability to be 35–75%, with reported depression, anxiety, and apathy being most common (Apostolova & Cummings, 2008).

Depression

Depressive features are consistently found to be the most prevalent neuropsychiatric symptoms in MCI (Apostolova and Cummings, 2008; Lyketsos et al., 2002; Fernandez-Martinez et al., 2010). Prevalence estimates range from 20% (Lyketsos et al., 2002) to approximately half (Feldman et al., 2004). Actual diagnoses of depression occur in MCI at somewhat lower rates, as minor depression was diagnosed in 17.2% of a community sample of 2551 older adults, and the occurrence of major depression was 3.4% (Kumar, Jorm, Parslow, & Sachdev, 2006). Several investigations comparing cognitive-test performance and rates of progression in individuals with and without depression in MCI have been conducted in an effort to determine the impact of depression and depressive symptoms on cognition in MCI.

Among 124 MCI outpatients, Chilovi et al. (2009) found that depressed patients did not perform worse on the MMSE. This also was found by Modrego and Ferrández (2004). Similarly, Fernandez-Martinez et al. (2010) and Teng, Lu, and Cummings (2007) failed to find a relationship between depressive symptoms and performance. In contrast to global measures of cognition, the impact of depression on memory function is less consistent.

Hudon, Belleville, and Gauthier (2008) investigated the influence of depressive symptoms in 44 participants with amnestic MCI (a-MCI) and 33 healthy older adults. Eighteen of the a-MCI individuals had depressive symptoms whereas 26 of 44 did not. The presence of these symptoms did not influence performance on the episodic memory measure. In contrast, Modrego and Ferrández (2004) found depression in a-MCI to negatively impact two of six memory measures (i.e., immediate visual recall and immediate Logical Memory).

List-learning memory tasks are not negatively affected in MCI by a mild number of depressive symptoms or a diagnosis of MDD or minor depression (Chilovi et al., 2009; Fernandez-Martinez et al., 2010; Hudon et al., 2008; Modrego & Ferrández, 2004). However, memory function on story tasks could be affected by depressive symptoms, as depressed participants with MCI performed worse than MCI participants without depressive symptoms on the immediate-recall portion of the Signoret Logical Memory Task. However, all other measures of various stories, such as Novelli's Short Story, New York Logical Memory Test, and delayed recall on the Signoret Logical Memory Task, were unaffected by the presence of depressive symptoms or a major depressive episode (MDE). Nonverbal memory performance also may be affected by depression, as participants with MCI and in an MDE performed worse on immediate recall of the Signoret Visual Figure Test but performed as well as MCI participants without depression on the delayed-recall portion (Modrego & Ferrández, 2004). Chilovi et al. (2009) found that MCI participants with depression performed as well as MCI individuals without depressive symptoms on the Rey-Osterrieth Complex Figure, delayed recall. Taken together, evidence indicates that retention and delayed recall will likely not be compromised by depression, but encoding and immediate recall may be affected.

Another cognitive domain that may be affected by depression in MCI is executive function. Hudon et al. (2008) found MCI participants with a score of ≥ 2 on the five-item Geriatric Depression Scale performed worse than MCI participants with only one or without depressive symptoms on the Stroop-Victoria. In contrast, depression does not decrease performance on the TMT-B or letter fluency (Chilovi et al., 2009). There is also no relationship between depressive symptoms and an executive-function composite score (Teng et al., 2007). Similarly, measures of working memory, attention/processing speed, visuospatial ability, or language functioning are not affected by (Chilovi et al., 2009; Modrego & Ferrández et al., 2004) or associated with depression (Fernandez-Martinez et al., 2010; Teng et al., 2007).

All told, the extant literature suggests that depression in MCI may modestly negatively impact inhibition and immediate recall (Hudon et al., 2008; Modrego & Ferrández, 2004). However, delayed recall and other measures of executive function, attention/processing speed, visuospatial abilities, language, and global cognitive ability are not significantly affected (Chilovi et al., 2009; Fernandez-Martinez et al., 2010). This interpretation is further supported by the finding that treating depression in MCI does not improve cognitive performance on measures of global cognitive status, orientation, long- and short-term memory, higher cortical and intellectual functions, visuospatial abilities, or language function (Adler, Chwalek, Jajcevic, 2004; Li, Meyer, & Thornby, 2001).

Although these results are informative, an examination of epidemiological studies will be helpful to better understand the association of depression in MCI with cognitive functioning. Gabryelewicz et al. (2007) enrolled 105 participants with

MCI and found that those with depressive symptoms were more likely to progress to dementia. Similarly, a clinic sample of MCI patients who progressed to AD had a greater number of depressive symptoms at baseline (Teng et al., 2007), and a community sample of Chinese older adults with MCI developed dementia at a greater rate if they were exhibiting depressive symptoms at baseline (Lam, Tam, Chiu, & Liu, 2007). Depressed individuals with MCI were more than twice as likely to convert to AD as MCI participants without depression (Modrego and Ferrández, 2004).

Still, other investigations have found contrasting results, with depression not being associated with an increased risk for converting. Rozzini, Chilovi, Trabucchi, and Padovani (2005) followed 46 individuals with MCI for 2 years. Approximately half of the participants were diagnosed with depression at baseline, and compared to individuals without a diagnosis, the depressed group did not develop dementia at a greater rate. These findings were replicated and extended by Palmer et al. (2010), as they found that participants with MCI and a diagnosis of depression or depressive symptoms did not have an increased risk for developing AD. Chilovi et al. (2009) and Ramakers, Visser, Aalten, Kester, Jolles, and Verhey (2009) also did not find a relationship between depression and depressive symptoms and increased risk for progressing into dementia from MCI and reported that depressive symptoms in MCI actually decreased the conversion rate to dementia.

Taken as a whole, epidemiological results are inconsistent and further research is warranted to elucidate this relationship. However, a preliminary conclusion from the reviewed studies suggests that a patient with MCI and comorbid depression will likely not be misclassified as more cognitively impaired (e.g., demented) but may progress in impairment more quickly. It is not yet clear if the depression or another unidentified variable may be the reason why individuals with MCI are more likely to convert to AD. This preliminary conclusion may be supported by the finding that donepezil slows the conversion rate of depressed individuals with MCI but does not decrease the amount of depressive symptoms (Lu et al., 2009).

Apathy

Apathy accompanies depression as one of the most frequent neuropsychiatric symptoms in MCI (Apostolova & Cummings, 2008). Prevalence estimates of apathy vary; however, they typically fall between 15% (Lyketsos et al., 2002) to 39% (Hwang et al., 2004). Apathy occurs more often in older adults with MCI than in those without it (Geda et al., 2008; Hwang et al., 2004; Lyketsos et al., 2002) and is associated with a higher risk of conversion to AD (Chilovi et al., 2009; Palmer et al., 2007; Robert et al., 2002, 2006; Teng et al., 2007). Apathy is nonetheless not always found to be a risk factor for AD conversion (Chen et al., 2012). Speculation from these data could lead to the conclusion that apathy in MCI negatively influences cognition; however, there could be several other factors (e.g., sample demographics and baseline cognitive functioning) accounting for this relationship. To accurately determine this relationship, it is necessary to examine investigations directly comparing the performance of individuals with and without apathy in MCI.

Individuals with MCI and apathy do not perform worse on measures of global cognitive status (Chilovi et al., 2009; Drijgers et al., 2011; Lam et al., 2007; Robert et al., 2006). Additionally, no relationship between symptoms of apathy and performance on the MMSE has been shown (Teng et al., 2007). The effect of apathy on memory functioning is less clear, as most individuals with apathy do not perform worse except on a few measures. In terms of memory performance, individuals with apathy recall less total information and have poorer performance on free recall (Robert et al., 2006). Nonetheless, individuals with MCI and apathy generally seem to perform as well as MCI participants without apathy when cued on immediate and delayed recall of a verbal learning test and a list-learning task, on Novelli's Short Story, and on the Rey-Osterrieth Complex Figure Recall (Chilovi et al., 2009; Drijgers et al., 2011; Robert et al., 2006). Additionally, Teng et al. (2007) reported no relationship between a composite score of memory and symptoms of apathy.

As in AD, executive function may be compromised by apathy in MCI. Participants with MCI and apathy performed worse than MCI individuals without apathy on the TMT-B (Drijgers et al., 2011) and Stroop (Robert et al., 2006) tests. This negative effect is not universal, as others have found no difference in performance between MCI participants with or without apathy on the TMT-B (Chilovi et al., 2009; Robert et al., 2006) or Stroop (Drijgers et al., 2011). Robert et al. (2006) and Chilovi et al. (2009) also did not find an impact of apathy on letter fluency.

There is a limited amount of evidence pertaining to apathy and its effect on working memory, but two separate observations suggest that apathy does not negatively impact working memory (Robert et al., 2006a, 2006b). Measures of attention/processing speed are also not affected by apathy in MCI, except for the TMT-A, which was compromised in one out of three observations (Drijgers et al., 2011).

Similar to working memory there is a limited amount of evidence specific on the affect of visuospatial ability on MCI; it suggests that apathy does not have a negative impact. As with attention/processing speed, every measure of language function was unaffected by apathy except for semantic fluency, which was decreased in one out of three observations (Drijgers et al., 2011). Collectively, results suggest little impact of apathy on cognitive functioning in MCI, but apathy may affect the recall of information without cues as well as total information learned and executive function. Therefore, apathy should not be neglected when interpreting findings.

Anxiety

In MCI, anxiety is frequently comorbid with depression, yet depression has been much more thoroughly investigated (Devier et al., 2009). Rozzini et al. (2009) has suggested that this may be due to problems with differentiating physical-disorder symptoms from anxiety, as well as inadequate diagnostic criteria. Like depression and apathy, the prevalence estimates of anxiety in MCI are variable, ranging from

9.9% (Lyketsos et al., 2002) to as high as 75% (Rozzini, Vicini Chilovi, et al., 2008). Anxiety symptoms and syndromes are reported by some to be more common in MCI (Forsell, Palmer, & Fratiglioni, 2003; Geda et al., 2008; Palmer et al., 2007); however, they have also been found to occur at the same rate as that for older adults without MCI (Kumar et al., 2006).

Anxiety in MCI does appear to be a risk factor for progression into AD. Gallagher et al. (2011) evaluated 161 memory clinic patients at baseline and approximately 27 months later. Of these individuals, 69 converted to AD and were more likely to have anticipatory anxiety at baseline than the non-converters. Controlling for age, gender, and education, individuals with anxiety were approximately twice as likely to develop AD earlier than those without anxiety. However, when global cognitive status at baseline was entered into the model the relationship did not remain. The authors interpreted their findings by suggesting that anxiety could be a marker of severity of cognitive impairment rather than being a predictor.

In a study of a sample of 232 Swedish older adults with and without MCI, in which age, gender, education, and global cognitive status were controlled for at baseline, Palmer et al. (2007) reported that MCI-diagnosed individuals who progressed to AD were more likely to have symptoms of anxiety. Compared to older adults without MCI, individuals with MCI and anxiety were 30 times more likely to develop AD, whereas persons with MCI without anxiety were 10 times more likely to develop AD than normal older adults. Analysis of reported anxiety separately indicated that each reported symptom increased the risk for progression to AD by almost two. These results underscore the importance of acknowledging individual anxiety symptoms, regardless of their immediate impact on cognitive task scores.

In contrast to Gallagher et al. (2011) and Palmer et al. (2007), Teng et al. (2007) did not find anxiety to be a predictor of progression to AD from MCI. The authors enrolled 51 patients from a memory disorders clinic and followed participants for an average of 2 years. Depression and apathy were predictive of those who progressed to AD compared to those who did not, and anxiety was not predictive of such progression. Devier et al. (2009) also found that current level of anxiety was unrelated, with an increased risk of converting to AD in 148 patients with MCI followed for 1 to 9 years. Taken together, anxiety in MCI has mixed evidence as a risk factor for progression to AD.

Regarding the direct impact of anxiety on cognition in MCI, several cross-sectional investigations using multiple neuropsychological measures have been conducted. Anxiety was not related to MMSE performance (Teng et al., 2007), nor did individuals with anxiety and MCI perform worse than MCI participants without anxiety on the MMSE (Rozzini et al., 2009). Memory performance in MCI also does not appear to be associated with or negatively affected by anxiety in MCI (Rozzini et al., 2009; Teng et al., 2007). However, there is some evidence to suggest that anxiety decreases performance on the TMT-B in MCI, as these patients required a substantially greater amount of time to complete the test (322.7 sec) than that required by those without anxiety (152.6 sec; Rozzini et al., 2009). Nonetheless, anxiety has not been found to be related to a composite score of executive-function measures

(Teng et al., 2007). The limited literature additionally suggests that MCI with anxiety is not related to nor affects performance on measures of attention/processing speed, language, or visuospatial ability. Thus, the small amount of literature suggests that performance across most cognitive domains is immune to anxiety, with the exception of executive function, which may be modestly negatively affected in MCI. Future research is needed to confirm current results and to provide a more comprehensive understanding of this relationship.

STROKE

Worldwide, cerebrovascular insult (CVI, or stroke) is a frequent cause of death and disability (Goljar et al., 2010). Generally speaking, there are two types of CVI, ischemic and hemorrhagic. The most common type, ischemic, occurs when there is a disruption of blood supply to the brain by a thrombosis or embolism. Hemorrhagic CVIs, or hemorrhages, are less likely but more dangerous, as they more frequently result in death or in damage to brain tissue. Given the variety in type, size, and location of CVIs, there is a large amount of variability in type and severity of cognitive changes. However, a comprehensive neuropsychological review suggests the most common cognitive impairments following CVI are those involving executive function, memory, language, and processing speed (Barker-Collo & Feigin, 2006). Cognitive changes are accompanied by emotional alterations, including depression (Hackett, Yapa, Parag, & Anderson, 2005), anxiety (Barker-Collo, 2007), and apathy (Carota, Staub, & Bogousslavsky, 2002). While depression, apathy, and anxiety are often comorbid with cognitive impairment, they are frequently assessed in isolation. Here we review how these conditions may impact cognitive test performance of post-CVI survivors. Language disturbances are a frequent concomitant to CVI, as language areas of the brain are commonly damaged from the mechanisms of cerebrovascular processes. Thus we also review the influence of language disturbance on other cognitive processes in CVI.

Depression

Depression is the most common post-CVI psychiatric syndrome (Burvill et al., 1995), with prevalence estimates ranging from 20% to 80% (Tharwani, Yerramsetty, Mannelli, Patkar, & Masand, 2007). A comprehensive review of 96 investigations estimated that 33% of post-CVI survivors experience depression at some point post-CVI (Hackett et al., 2005). Compared to older adults without a history of CVI, survivors were approximately six times more likely to experience a clinically significant level of depressive symptoms at follow-up 2 years later (Whyte, Mulsant, Vanderbilt, Dodge, & Ganguli, 2004). The course of post-CVI depression is thought to be dependent on the onset of the symptoms. Earlier symptom onset has a shorter course and greater probability of remission, without intervention (Santos et al., 2009). Onset of post-CVI depression is influenced by different factors, with later onset (i.e., >15 months) thought to be more associated with psychological instead of biological factors (Wilz & Barskova, 2007). The debate of psychological and biological hypotheses of post-CVI depression will not be thoroughly discussed here; for a comprehensive review, see Fang and Cheng (2009).

The occurrence of depression and association with lesion lateralization is another controversial topic with mixed evidence. Data suggest that post-CVI depression occurs more frequently following an infarct to the left hemisphere (Provinciali & Coccia, 2002; Provinciali et al., 2008; Spalletta, Guida, De Angelis & Caltagirone, 2002), while other investigations have found no difference (Carson et al., 2000), and a minority of studies have found the opposite (Yu et al., 2004). Despite these differences, lesion lateralization may be helpful in identifying which depressed individuals following CVI will experience cognitive impairment.

Spalletta et al. (2002) included 153 first-time post-CVI survivors and found that those with left-hemisphere lesions were more likely to experience greater levels of depression and increased cognitive impairment than those with right-hemisphere lesions. A similar finding was found by Robinson (2003). This relationship is notable; however, rather than dissect the relationship of lesion localization with post-CVI depression, this review will focus on the general effect of depression on cognition, highlighting specific lateralization effects as appropriate.

In a recent study, 94 CVI patients were evaluated at three separate time points: baseline, 6 months, and 12 months (Pirscoveanu et al., 2008). Those with depression performed worse on the MMSE and Montreal Cognitive Assessment (MoCA), and there was a negative relationship between depressive symptoms and global cognitive performance. A Brazilian cross-sectional study confirmed this finding with 300 post-CVI survivors, finding that depression was associated with decreased MMSE performance (Carod-Artal, Ferreira Coral, Trizotto, & Menezes Moreira, 2009). A significant negative impact of post-CVI depression on cognition is not limited to measures of global cognitive status but has also been shown to compromise test functioning in several cognitive domains, including language, temporal orientation, motor and executive functions (Bolla-Wilson, Robinson, Starkstein, Boston, & Price, 1989).

Post-CVI depression was also found to be associated with executive function in a group of 256 post-CVI survivors aged 55–85 with and without depressive symptoms. Measures of executive function included the WCST, TMT, Stroop, and semantic and letter verbal fluency tests (Pohjasvaara et al., 2002). The authors calculated a composite score from these measures and defined executive dysfunction as 1.5 standard deviations below the average composite score of a control. Compared to those without depression, individuals with post-CVI depression were more likely to have executive dysfunction.

Nys and colleagues (2005) found that depressive symptoms in post-CVI survivors were associated with language impairment but not with executive dysfunction in a sample of 126 first-time CVI patients. Investigators additionally found that individuals with a moderate to severe amount of depressive symptoms (i.e., Montgomery Asberg Depression Rating Scale >19) had worse cognitive performance on tasks of memory (i.e., Rey Auditory Verbal Learning Test and Rey–Osterrieth Complex Figure-Delay) and visual perception (i.e., Judgement of Line Orientation, Test of Facial Recognition, Rey–Osterrieth Complex Figure-Copy) than that of CVI survivors with mild (i.e., 8–19) or minimal depressive symptoms (i.e., <8).

Kauhanen et al. (1999) also found a negative effect of depression on memory in 106 post-CVI survivors with a depression diagnosis. As in Nys et al.'s (2005) study, depressed post-CVI survivors did not perform worse on a measure of executive function (verbal fluency). However, depression additionally impacted nonverbal problem solving (Wechsler, Picture Completion and Block Design) and attention (TMT-A).

Interestingly, the reviewed evidence suggests more consistently that post-CVI depression negatively affects cognition than does the literature on AD or MCI. While there are not many published studies on depression in post-CVI survivors, depression appears to affect global measures (Carod-Artal et al., 2009; Pirscoveanu et al., 2008; Spalletta et al., 2004), language (Bolla-Wilson et al., 1989; Nys et al., 2005), memory (Kauhanen et al., 1999; Nys et al., 2005), nonverbal problem solving (Kauhanen et al., 1999), attention (Kauhanen et al., 1999), orientation, and motor functions (Bolla-Wilson et al., 1989). More research is required to confirm the preliminary relationship between post-CVI depression and executive function.

Apathy

In CVI patients the occurrence of apathy ranges from 20% (Mayo, Fellows, Scott, Cameron, & Wood-Dauphinee, 2009) to 50% (Yamagata, Yamaguchi, & Kobayashi, 2004), and it is estimated to coexist in 17–9% of CVI survivors with depression (Mayo et al., 2009). Despite limited evidence, one study that examined 124 CVI patients at three time points post-CVI (i.e., 2, 6, and 12 months) suggests that the risk for developing apathy increases substantially with time. Patients were also three times more likely to develop apathy at 6 and 12 months post-CVI (Angelelli et al., 2004). There is limited evidence about the relationship between location of lesion and apathy, and it is inconsistent (Brodaty et al., 2005). Preliminary results suggest that apathy may be associated with insult to the frontostriatal network (Mayo et al., 2009).

While apathy in post-CVI survivors has not been extensively investigated there have been a few empirical studies examining the effect of post-CVI apathy on cognition. Apathy in post-CVI survivors has been associated with poorer global cognitive status. Study findings suggest poorer performance on the MMSE (Brodaty et al., 2005; Starkstein, Fedoroff, Price, Leiguarda, & Robinson, 1993), a brief measure of verbal intelligence (Hasegawa's Intelligence Scale; Okada, Kobayashi, Yamagata, Takahashi, & Yamaguchi, 1997), and an objective rater measure of global cognitive function (Hasegawa dementia rating scale; Yamagata et al., 2004).

Brodaty et al. (2005) examined 135 post-CVI patients with and without apathy and 92 controls with a neuropsychological assessment battery (NAB) consisting of eight cognitive domains: attention and concentration, memory, working memory, executive function, reasoning, language, visuoconstruction/praxis, and speed of information processing. Patients with apathy performed worse on measures of attention and concentration (Wechsler Adult Intelligence–Revised [WAIS-R] Digit Span Forward and Mental Control), working memory (WAIS-R Arithmetic and Digit Span Backward), and reasoning (WAIS-R Similarities and Picture Completion).

The negative effect of apathy in post-CVI survivors was also found in two Japanese investigations of 40 and 29 CVI patients, respectively (Okada et al., 1997; Yamagata et al., 2004). Okada et al. (1997) found that CVI patients with apathy performed worse than CVI patients without apathy on verbal fluency, and Yamagata et al. (2004) similarly found apathy to negatively influence semantic verbal fluency. Collectively, preliminary evidence suggests that there are effects of apathy on global cognition, attention, processing speed, and verbal fluency measures. These effects of apathy in CVI are similar to those of post-CVI depression, which may in part be due to the overlap between the constructs and frequent misdiagnosis and oversight of apathy as a separate syndrome (Withall, Brodaty, Altendorf, & Sachdev, 2010).

Anxiety

Up to 85% of individuals with post-CVI anxiety are additionally found to have post-CVI depression (Barker-Collo, 2007). Among first-time post-CVI survivors, 35% to 40% experience clinically elevated levels of anxiety within 1 month, 24 months post-CVI (Rasquin, Lodder, & Verhey, 2005). The percentage of individuals who experience generalized anxiety post-CVI is less frequent and reported to range from approximately 21% to 27% (Chemerinski & Levine, 2006). Anxiety is associated with left- and right-hemisphere CVIs; however, it is right-hemisphere CVIs that are typically more associated with anxiety disorders (Chemerinski & Levine, 2006). It has also been suggested that post-CVI anxiety is related to and may be maintained by cerebral atrophy (Chemerinski & Robinson, 2000).

Despite evidence of prevalence and etiology, post-CVI anxiety and its association with cognition has not been fully investigated. Post-CVI anxiety may be related to cognitive functioning, as Rasquin and colleagues (2005) found that individuals with post-CVI anxiety were more likely to experience cognitive decline within the first 6 months as measured by the Cognitive Section of the Cambridge Examination for Mental Disorders of the Elderly. However, individuals with generalized anxiety disorder do not decline more or perform worse on the MMSE than post-CVI survivors without anxiety (Shimoda & Robinson, 1998).

Consistent with these variable results, Barker-Collo (2007) reported that anxiety symptoms in post-CVI survivors were related to some but not all neuropsychological measures. Memory functioning, as measured by the California Verbal Learning Test (CVLT) short-delay free recall or Verbal Paired Associates immediate or delayed recall, was not related to anxiety symptoms on the Beck Anxiety Inventory (BAI). Anxiety was, nonetheless, related to performance on the CVLT long-delay free recall ($r = -.322$). Executive function was not related to anxiety symptoms, whereas attention/processing speed was inconsistently related to anxiety symptoms. No relationship between anxiety and attention/processing speed was found when quantified by the Integrated Visual Auditory Continuous Performance Test (IVA-CPT)—attention quotient. However, a relationship existed between attention/processing when measured by the IVA-CPT—prudence quotient and the baseline condition of the Victoria Stroop (dots). Anxiety symptoms 3 months post-CVI were predicted by a regression equation that included demographics, functional ability, and cognitive functioning. This model explained 50.7% of the variance and was driven by hemisphere of lesion and Stroop dots performance.

Evidence suggests that post-CVI anxiety is associated with and may be in part due to cognitive functioning, and specifically may affect and be related to performance on measures of global cognitive status, memory, and attention/processing speed. Despite these results, much more research is needed to confirm and clarify this relationship. To better understand this association, it would be best if future investigations administered comprehensive neuropsychological batteries over time to post-CVI survivors with and without anxiety. Additionally, the concomitant role of depression with anxiety effects remains poorly understood.

Language Disturbances

Aphasia is a disorder of language characterized by disruption or loss of language abilities due to brain damage (Berthier, 2005). It is evident in speech, writing, or reading and can be conceptualized as two different categories: disorders of comprehension and disorders of production (Kolb & Wishaw, 2009). Aphasia is often seen in CVI. Prevalence estimates range from 19% (Kyrozis et al., 2009) to 38% (Berthier, 2005), but large epidemiological investigations suggest that aphasia occurs in 26% (Croquelois & Bogousslavsky, 2011) to 5% (Dickey et al., 2010) of CVI survivors. The relation between type of aphasia and location of lesion is an investigative area of ongoing debate and requires further research; however, a recent neuroimaging investigation suggests that lesions in classic language centers (i.e., Broca's & Wernicke's; Yang, Zhao, Wang, Chen, & Zhang, 2008) still account for most exhibited language disturbances. Recovery of language is also variable, and investigators are still attempting to clarify prognosis on the basis of a variety of different variables. Nonetheless, current data suggest that lesion size and severity of aphasia at first assessment are typically the most consistent predictors of outcome, and aphasia in most CVI survivors improves in the first 3 months and almost always within the first year (Pedersen, Vinter, & Olsen, 2004).

Identifying aphasia can be challenging; however, neuropsychological techniques and language measures have improved and can now be used to to diagnose and label the type of aphasia accurately more often than not. The effect of aphasia on cognitive performance in "non-language" domains is less understood and, potentially, more complex. Nonetheless, within CVI survivors, some studies have shown a relationship between language disturbance and other cognitive processes.

Learning, retaining, and retrieving information is aided by language irrespective of type of material (i.e., verbal versus nonverbal). Several investigations have examined the relationship between language disturbances and memory functioning. Beeson, Bayles, Rubens, and Kazniak (1993) found that individuals with aphasia recalled fewer total words, on Trials 1 and 10, compared to controls with no history of neurological impairment. Location of lesion did not affect the number of words recalled on Trial 1, but on Trial 10 and delayed recall the anterior-injured group recalled fewer words.

Similarly, Ween, Verfaellie, and Alexander (1996) found aphasics performed worse on all five learning trials, free recall, short and long delay, and recognition than age-matched controls on the Rey Auditory Verbal Learning Test and a paired associate learning task. First-time CVI survivors with aphasia also had poorer nonverbal memory on the Benton Visual Retention Test compared to 28 demographically matched normal controls (Seniów, Litwin, & Lesniak, 2009). The provided samples of evidence indicate that aphasia is associated with negative performance on measures of memory.

However, given that the control groups of the reviewed studies are neurologically intact, it is not possible to conclude whether the behavioral aspects of aphasia negatively impact a CVI survivor's ability to encode, store, and retrieve information, or if this is due to the underlying neuroanatomical infarct. Results from Burgio and Basso (1997) help clarify this relationship. The authors included 78 left-hemisphere CVI patients (21 nonaphasic and 57 aphasic) and 135 normal controls. Participants completed five short- and long-term memory measures. All patients (aphasic and nonaphasic) were impaired on all memory tasks, except the story-learning task. Chi-square analyses revealed the presence of aphasia only exacerbated deficits on the paired-associated learning task. Thus, language disturbance may impact memory performance, but the majority of poor memory scores are probably due to underlying infarcts and not the behavioral language dysfunction.

Given that executive function is aided by language processes, this is another cognitive area that could be affected by language disturbances. Compared to healthy controls, CVI survivors with aphasia performed worse on the WCST. They completed fewer total categories (i.e., 2.7 versus 5.7), used a greater number of cards per category (i.e., 64.5 versus 18.1), and were slower to complete each category (i.e., 1973s versus 680s; Purdy, 2002). CVI survivors' performance on the WCST was related to several measures of language ability (aphasia quotient, $r = .33, p < .05$; naming, $r = .38, p < .05$; comprehension, $r = .43, p < .01$) but not all (fluency, $r = .20, p < .20$; repetition measures, $r = .24, p = .13$; Baldo et al., 2005). Although a CVI survivors' performance on the WCST was not related to all measures of language on the Western Aphasia Battery, it could be concluded that language ability likely impacts ability on the WCST.

CVI survivors with aphasia also perform worse on other executive tasks, such as the Porteus Maze Test. CVI survivors require more time and trials to complete the mazes than healthy older adults (Purdy, 2002). Similarly, on the Tower of London Test, aphasics required more time to complete items accurately (Purdy, 2002). Purdy (2002) additionally noted that only a very small percentage of CVI survivors with aphasia were able to complete the Tower of Hanoi Test, and they were less accurate than controls.

The ability to comprehend and express messages effectively was associated with both the Color Trails Test (CTT) and WCST-64 in 25 post-CVI survivors with aphasia (Fridriksson, Nettles, Davis, Morrow, & Montgomery, 2006). Errors and prompts given on the CTT and number of correct items and categories on the WCST were positively related to level of aphasia. Additionally, over half of the participants were unable to complete a category on the WCST and eight did not complete the WCST above chance levels.

As noted earlier with memory functioning, while individuals with CVI performed worse on a variety of EF measures, all comparison groups were neurologically intact healthy controls. Thus, negative associations may be attributed to either the underlying infarct or the behavioral impact of the language disturbances themselves. Evidence supporting the latter conclusion are the positive correlations reported by Baldo et al. (2005) between language functioning and the WCST, as well as the results from Fridriksson et al. (2006). Although it could be argued that language functioning after a CVI is a measure of the infarct's severity, language disturbances in CVI survivors could impact executive function.

Along this same line, compromised executive function in CVI survivors could be due to poor comprehension. This is supported by the qualitative differences reported by Baldo et al. (2005). Participants with nonfluent aphasias (e.g., anomic and Broca's) sorted more categories on the WCST than did individuals with fluent aphasias (i.e., Wernicke and Transcortical). However, there is evidence that this conclusion may be incorrect. For example, Purdy (2002) had participants complete practice items to ensure comprehension, and Baldo et al. (2005) and Fridriksson et al. (2006) noted that all participants responded to feedback in a manner suggesting that they understood the task (e.g., "Yes!" upon receiving correct feedback).

Baldo et al. (2005) provided behavioral evidence for an alternative conclusion. Fifty-one adults were separated into three groups and completed the WCST. Healthy adults were requested to either say "na" (i.e., verbal shadowing), tap the mouse after every beat (e.g., nonverbal shadowing), or only attend to the WCST (i.e., control). The verbal shadowing group performed worse than the control group, as they had more total, perseverative, and nonperseverative errors and had fewer correct consecutive responses. Articulatory suppression (i.e., verbal shadowing) disrupted performance, which supports the conclusion that intact language functioning aids executive functioning. Language may aid executive function through inner speech and covert language processes. Regardless, it can be concluded that language disruption, irrespective of etiology, could impact executive function.

Language disturbances in CVI survivors could also possibly impact working memory. Caspari, Parkinson, LaPointe, and Katz (1998) examined this association and found that CVI survivors' overall language ability and reading comprehension level was positively related to working-memory performance. Wright, Newhoff, Downey, and Austermann (2003) further explored the relationship between aphasia and working memory and found that CVI survivors with aphasia had more errors on a listening span task than those of demographically matched controls. Nonetheless, similar to memory and executive function, it is unclear if language dysfunction directly affects working-memory ability or if working memory–accompanied cognitive dysfunction is due to anatomical infarct.

Christensen and Wright (2010) attempted to clarify this relationship. Three separate n-back tasks, 0-, 1-, and 2-back, with varying linguistic load (i.e., low to high), were presented. Within-group analyses indicated a counterintuitive finding: the performance of aphasics improved as the language load on the task increased. Additionally, correlation analyses indicated no relationship between overall language ability (aphasia quotient on the WAB) and working-memory performance.

These data suggest that language dysfunction alone does not directly impact working memory, but the underlying insult likely accounts for decreased working memory in aphasics. This preliminary conclusion requires more support, and future research will be needed to confirm this perspective with CVI survivors with and without language disturbances.

Only a few investigations have examined visuospatial functioning in individuals with language disturbances. In one of these investigations Gorno-Tempini et al. (2004) conducted a cross-sectional study with 31 individuals with severe and isolated language impairment and 10 healthy, age-, gender-, and education-matched controls. Aphasics performed as well as controls on a modified Rey-Osterrieth Figure Copy and Cube Copy test. Correlation analyses also suggested that language dysfunction does not impact visuospatial ability, since no significant relationship was found between language ability and BD (Baldo et al., 2005). Nonetheless, the literature is limited, and more research is required to understand the association between language dysfunction and visuospatial ability.

The impact of language dysfunction on cognition is not completely understood. Investigations comparing CVI survivors with and without language disturbances are needed to determine if language dysfunction impairs cognition and, if so, how. The importance of further investigation is underscored by preliminary data suggesting that language dysfunction affects memory (Burgio & Basso, 1997; Seniów et al., 2009) and executive functioning (Baldo et al, 2005; Fridriksson et al., 2006; Purdy, 2002). The reason for this negative impact is unclear; it is likely due to various complex factors. One way in which language functioning may impact cognition is when self-talk and inner speech is prevented (Baldo et al., 2005). This process is probably affected in individuals with aphasia, but more research is required to ascertain this preliminary conclusion. Methods that could assist future investigations in understanding this intricate and multifaceted relationship are complex statistical analyses, such as structural equation modeling and path analysis.

RECOMMENDATIONS FOR ASSESSMENT

As should be obvious from the data presented here, the literature remains quite variable, and more research is needed for clarifying and confirming or disconfirming current findings. Nevertheless, a number of tentative conclusions are provided here to aid neuropsychologists in assessing these complex comorbid conditions. These guidelines should be viewed as preliminary and will likely be adjusted with future evidence.

AD

DEPRESSION
The current evidence (see Table 14.1) suggests that those with AD and MDD are rated as more impaired on dementia rating scales and perform worse on measures of global measures of cognition. However, individuals with depressive symptoms but without a formal diagnosis of depression are not rated as more demented and do not perform any worse on global measures of cognition. Therefore, if a client

Table 14.1 Impact of Psychiatric Conditions in Cognition in AD

Cognitive Domain	Effect	Measures	Study
Depression			
Global cognitive status	Depressed group more impaired	BDS; BDS-Cog P; HDS	Hudon et al. (2009); Rubin et al. (1991); Fernandez-Martinez et al. (2010); Garavello et al. (2010); Porta Etessam et al. (2011)
	No group differences	MMSE; DRBCSB; CAMCOG	
Memory	Depressed group more impaired	BVRT	Powlishta et al. (2004)
	No group differences	FRT; Word Recall; Object Recall	Backman et al. (1996); Fahlander et al. (1999)
Executive function	Depressed group less impaired	LM-II	Wefel et al. (1999)
	Depressed group more impaired	TMT-B; FAB	Nakaaki et al. (2007, 2008)
	No group differences	CS from VPA; FNPA; Rey-O IR; LM; Stroop; Letter Fluency	Berger et al. (2002); Lopez et al. (1990); Nakaaki et al. (2007)
Working memory	Depressed group more impaired	Digit Span B	Powlishta et al. (2004)
	No group differences	Digit Span F & B	Fahlander et al. (1999)
Attention & processing speed	Depressed group more impaired	Digit Symbol; Crossing Off; TMT-A; CS from LC; TMT-B	Lopez et al. (1990); Nakaaki et al. (2007); Rubin et al. (1991); Wefel et al. (1999)
	No group differences	Digit Symbol	Nakaaki et al. (2007)
Visuospatial ability	Depressed group more impaired	Divided Attention; BD	Nakaaki et al. (2007); Powlishta et al. (2004); Wefel et al. (1999)
	No group differences	BD; Clock Drawing; CS from VFD; Rey-O Copy	Berger et al. (2002); Lopez et al. (1990)

Domain	Finding	Tests	References
Language	No group differences	Semantic Fluency; CS from AC; RWAB; TT	Berger et al. (2002); Lopez et al. (1990)
Apathy			
Global cognitive status	Apathy symptoms were negatively associated	MMSE	Kuzis et al. (1999); Landes et al. (2001)
	No group differences or association	MMSE	Drijgers et al. (2011); Landes et al. (2001)
Memory	Apathy group more impaired	Buschke Selective Reminding Test	Kuzis et al. (1999)
	No group differences	BVRT; LM-II; Verbal Learning Test	Drijgers et al. (2011); Kuzis et al. (1999); McPherson et al. (2002)
Executive function	Apathy group more impaired	Stroop; TMT-B; WCST	McPherson et al. (2002)
	No group differences	Letter Fluency; Stroop	Drijgers et al. (2011); Kuzis et al. (1999); McPherson et al. (2002)
Working memory	No group differences	Digit Span F & B; Digit Span B	Kuzis et al. (1999); McPherson et al. (2002)
Attention & processing speed	Apathy group more impaired	Digit Symbol	McPherson et al. (2002)
Visuospatial ability	No group differences	BD; Rey-O Copy	Kuzis et al. (1999); McPherson et al. (2002)
Language	Apathy group more impaired	BNT	Kuzis et al. (1999)
	No group differences	BNT; Semantic Fluency; Token Test; WAIS-R Similarities & Vocabularly	Drijgers et al. (2011); Kuzis et al. (1999); McPherson et al. (2002)
Motor	Apathy group more impaired	Purdue Pegboard	Kuzis et al. (1999)

(Continued)

Table 14.1 (CONTINUED)

Cognitive Domain	Effect	Measures	Study
	No group differences	Finger Tapping	McPherson et al. (2002)
Anxiety			
Global cognitive status	Anxious group more impaired	MMSE	Lopez et al. (1993)
	No group differences	MMSE	Bierman et al. (2007); Fernandez et al. (2010); Shimoda & Robinson (1998)
Memory	No group differences, but anxious group declined more	Auditory Verbal Learning Test	Bierman et al. (2009)

Abbreviations: AC, auditory comprehension; B, backward; BD, Block Design; BDS, Blessed Dementia Scale; BDS-Cog P, Blessed Dementia Scale Cognitive Portion; BNT, Boston Naming Test; BVRT, Benton Visual Retention Test; CAMCOG, Cognitive Section of the Cambridge Examination for Mental Disorders of the Elderly; CS, composite score; DRBCSB, delayed recall of the Brief Cognitive Screening Battery; F, forward; FAB, Frontal Assessment Battery; FNPA, Face Name Paired Associates; FRT, Face Recognition Task; HDS, Hasegawa Dementia Rating Scale; LC, letter cancellation; LM-II, Logical Memory–II; MMSE, Mini-Mental Status Exam; Rey-O Copy, Rey–Osterrieth Complex Figure Copy; Rey-O IR, Rey–Osterrieth Complex Figure Immediate Recall; RWAB, reading portion of Western Aphasia Battery; TMT-A, Trail Making Test Part A; TMT-B, Trail Making Test Part B; VFD, Visual Forms Discrimination; VPA, Verbal Paired Associates; WAIS-R, Wechsler Adult Intelligence Scale, Revised; WCST, Wisconsin Card Sorting Test;

meets criteria for MDD as defined by the *DSM-III*, performance on measures of global cognition is likely to be affected; if a client has depressive symptoms without meeting a MDD diagnosis, his or her global cognition may not be significantly affected and depressive symptoms may not represent a potential explanation for cognitive findings, nor act as a confound.

Reviewed evidence suggests that depression does not affect performance on memory or language measures. In contrast, depression and depressive symptoms impact executive function, and one will need to consider depression and depressive symptoms as potential factors associated with an AD client's executive-function performance. Specifically, depression and depressive symptoms were found to affect executive functioning when operationalized by the provisional criteria for depression in AD (Nakaaki et al., 2007) and when patients had four or more depressive symptoms on the Neuropsychiatric Inventory (NPI) (Nakaaki et al., 2008).

Working memory may be negatively associated with depressive symptoms (e.g., Powlishta et al., 2004), but this relationship is modest, and in one study those with MDD or dysthymic disorder did not perform worse than those without a depression diagnosis (Fahlander et al., 1999). Thus, as with memory, one should not need to consider depression or depressive features when interpreting working-memory performance in AD.

In contrast, most measures of attention have been shown to be modestly affected by MDD, as measured by the *DSM-III* and provisional criteria for depression in AD (Nakaaki et al., 2007; Rubin et al., 1991), and depressive symptoms, as measured on the Geriatric Depression Scale (GDS) and NPI (Nakaaki et al., 2008; Wefel et al., 1999). Even though this association is not definitive, one should consider the negative effect of depression on attention in AD.

The relationship between visuospatial abilities and depression is also variable. However, depressive symptoms from a *DSM-IV*-defined MDE have shown a negative correlation with visualspatial performance (Powlishta et al., 2004). Additionally, individuals with AD who endorse 10 or more items on the GDS were found to perform worse on the Block Design task (Wefel et al., 1999). Thus, the GDS and symptoms from a *DSM-IV*-defined MDE may be particularly sensitive to impactful levels of depression on visuospatial measures, and clinicians must be cautious when interpreting visuospatial measures in depressed individuals with AD.

APATHY

Like depression, the impact of apathy on measures of global cognitive status is variable, and one must interpret carefully global cognitive status scores in individuals with AD and apathy. Despite the inconsistent effect of apathy found on global cognitive-status tests, particular measures sensitive to levels of apathy that can compromise performances on these measures include the NPI apathy scale (McPherson et al., 2002) and the Apathy Scale (Kuzis et al., 1999). While the relationship between memory performance and apathy in AD is also variable, most results indicate that apathy will probably not decrease performance unless severe levels are present, which seems to be restricted to list-learning tasks and when apathy is measured with the Apathy Scale (Kuzis et al., 1999).

Executive function is likely modestly compromised by apathy. It is recommended that clinicians consider the negative effect of apathy on executive function in patients with AD. Particular measures sensitive to impactful levels of apathy on executive function are the NPI (McPherson et al., 2002) and the Apathy Scale (Kuzis et al., 1999).

In contrast, working memory and visuospatial functioning are not affected by one's level of apathy. Although there is limited evidence on attention/processing speed and motor function measures in the context of AD, they may be negatively affected, and one should interpret performance on these measures with caution. Language measures will likely not be affected, but apathy may impact performance on naming; thus consideration of apathy is encouraged.

Overall, the effect of apathy on cognition in AD is variable, depending on the cognition domain being assessed. Measures found to be sensitive to impactful levels of apathy are the NPI and Apathy Scale. Specifically, a scores ≥1 and 2 standard deviations from the mean on the Apathy Scale are sensitive to cognition-compromising levels of apathy (McPherson et al., 2002).

Of note, the potential negative effect of apathy on cognitive functioning may be decreased by use of ChE-Is. Although most individuals may have already tried or are being prescribed ChE-Is, this may be a secondary treatment for cognitive change related (directly or indirectly) to apathy in persons with AD (Holmes et al., 2004; Malloy & Boyle, 2005). However, improvement will not be drastic.

ANXIETY

The relationship between anxiety and cognition in AD is inconsistent. Some evidence indicates poorer global cognition associated with anxiety (Lopez et al., 1993), but other data indicate no relationship between global cognitive status and anxiety (Bierman et al., 2007; Fernandez et al., 2010) in these patients. Additionally, anxiety does not impact memory and in one study was found to be a protective factor for memory decline (Bierman et al., 2009). This very limited evidence indicates that anxiety likely does not affect performance on measures of global cognitive status or memory. The inconsistent findings could be due to the measures used to assess anxiety. The one study to find anxiety negatively impacting cognition (Lopez et al., 1993) used the Consortium to Establish a Registry for Alzheimer's Disease Behavioral Rating Scale (CERAD), whereas the others measured anxiety with the Alzheimer's Disease Assessment Scale noncognitive subscale (ADAS-noncog) and the Hospital Anxiety and Depression Scale anxiety subscale (HADS-a). Thus, the CERAD may be more sensitive to capturing interfering levels of anxiety in AD.

MCI

DEPRESSION

Depressive symptoms do not appear to affect global cognitive status, working memory, attention/processing speed, language, or visuospatial ability (Chilovi et al., 2009; Fernandez-Martinez et al., 2010; Modrego & Ferrández, 2004) in persons diagnosed with MCI (see Table 14.2). However, the effect of depression on executive functioning and memory is inconclusive from the reviewed evidence. Despite the variable effect reported, cautious interpretation of measures of inhibition and memory in

Table 14.2 IMPACT OF PSYCHIATRIC CONDITIONS ON COGNITION IN MCI

Cognitive Domain	Effect	Measures	Study
Depression			
Global cognitive status	No group differences or association	MMSE	Chilovi et al. (2009); Fernandez-Martinez et al. (2010); Modrego & Ferrández (2004); Teng et al. (2007)
Memory	Depressed group more impaired	Signoret LM IR; Signoret Visual Figure Recall IR	Modrego & Ferrández (2004)
	No group differences or association	CERAD word list; CS from WAIS-R/III LM-II, VR-II, CVLT-I/II LDFR, Rey-O Figure Recall; Novelli's Short Story; NYULMT IR & DR; Rey's Word List IR & DR; RL/RI-16 memory test; Rey-O Figure Recall; Signoret List Learning Test IR & DR; Signoret LM DR; Signoret Visual Figure Recall DR	Chilovi et al. (2009); Fernandez-Martinez et al. (2010); Hudon et al. (2008); Modrego & Ferrández (2004); Teng et al. (2007)
Executive function	Depressed group more impaired	Stroop-Victoria	Hudon et al. (2008)
	No group differences or association	CS from COWAT, Stroop, TMT-B & WCST; Letter Fluency; TMT-B	Chilovi et al. (2009); Teng et al. (2007)
Working memory	No group differences	Signoret Digit Span Forward	Modrego & Ferrández (2004)
Attention & processing speed	No group differences or association	CS from WAIS-III Digit Span, Digit Symbol & TMT-A; TMT-A	Chilovi et al. (2009); Teng et al. (2007)
Visuospatial ability	No group differences or association	Clock Drawing Test; CS from WAIS-III PC, BD & Rey-O Figure Copy; Rey-O Figure Copy	Chilovi et al. (2009); Fernandez-Martinez et al. (2010); Teng et al. (2007)

(Continued)

Table 14.2 (Continued)

Cognitive Domain	Effect	Measures	Study
Language	No group differences or association	CS from BNT & Semantic Fluency; Semantic Fluency	Chilovi et al. (2009); Fernandez-Martinez et al. (2010); Teng et al. (2007)
Apathy			
Global cognitive status	No group differences or association	MMSE	Chilovi et al. (2009); Drijgers et al. (2011); Lam et al. (2007); Robert et al. (2006); Teng et al. (2007)
Memory	Apathy group more impaired	Free and cued selective reminding test TR & FR	Robert et al. (2006)
	No group differences or association	CS from WAIS-R/III LM II, VR II, CVLT I/II LDFR, Rey-O Figure Recall; Free and cued selective reminding test CR; Novelli's Short Story; Rey's word list IR & DR; Rey-O Figure Recall; Verbal Learning Test IR, DR, & Recognition	Chilovi et al. (2009); Drijgers et al. (2011); Robert et al. (2006); Teng et al. (2007)
Executive function	Apathy group more impaired	Stroop; TMT-B	Drijgers et al. (2011); Robert et al. (2006)
	No group differences	Letter Fluency; Stroop; TMT-B	Chilovi et al. (2009); Drijgers et al. (2011); Robert et al. (2006)
Working memory	No group differences	Digit Ordering; Dual Task	Robert et al. (2006)
Attention & processing speed	Apathy group more impaired	TMT-A	Drijgers et al. (2011)
	No group differences or association	CS from WAIS-III Digit Span, Digit Symbol, & TMT-A; Digit Symbol; Symbol Digit Modalities Test; TMT-A	Chilovi et al. (2009); Drijgers et al. (2011); Robert et al. (2006); Teng et al. (2007)

Domain	Finding	Measure	Citation
Visuospatial ability	No group differences or association	Clock Drawing Test; CS from WAIS-III PC; BD & Rey-O Figure Copy; Rey-O Figure Copy	Chilovi et al. (2009); Teng et al. (2007)
Language	Apathy group more impaired	Semantic Fluency	Drijgers et al. 2011
	No group differences or association	CS from BNT & Semantic Fluency; Naming; Semantic Fluency; Similarities	Chilovi et al. (2009); Robert et al. (2006); Teng et al. (2007)
Anxiety			
Global cognitive status	No group differences or association	MMSE	Rozzini et al. (2009); Teng et al. (2007)
Memory	No group differences or association	CS from WAIS-R/III LM II, VR II, CVLT I/II LDFR, Novelli Short Story; Rey-O Figure Recall	Rozzini et al. (2009); Teng et al. (2007)
Executive function	Anxious group more impaired	TMT-B	Rozzini et al. (2009)
	No group differences or association	CS from COWAT, Stroop, TMT-B, & WCST; Letter Fluency	Rozzini et al. (2009); Teng et al. (2007)
Attention & processing speed	No group differences or association	CS from WAIS-III Digit Span, Digit Symbol, & TMT-A; TMT-A	Rozzini et al. (2009); Teng et al. (2007)
Visuospatial ability	No group differences or association	CS from WAIS-III PC, BD, & Rey-O Figure Copy; Rey-O Figure Copy	Rozzini et al. (2009); Teng et al. (2007)
Language	No group differences or association	CS from BNT & Semantic Fluency; Semantic Fluency	Rozzini et al. (2009); Teng et al. (2007)

Abbreviations: BD, Block Design; BNT, Boston Naming Test; CERAD word list, Consortium to Establish a Registry for Alzheimer's Disease Behavioral Rating Scale word list; COWAT, Controlled Oral Word Association Test; CR, cued recall; CS, composite score; CVLT LDFR, California Verbal Learning Test long-delay free recall; DR, delayed recall; FR, free recall; IR, immediate recall; LM, Logical Memory; MMSE, Mini Mental Status Exam; NYULMT, New York University Logical Memory Test; PC, Picture Completion; Rey-O Figure Copy, Rey-Osterrieth Complex Figure Copy; Rey-O Figure Recall, Rey-Osterrieth Complex Figure Recall; TMT-A, Trail Making Test Part A; TMT-B, Trail Making Test Part B; TR, total recall; VR, Visual Reproduction; WAIS-R, Wechsler Adult Intelligence Scale, Revised; WCST, Wisconsin Card Sorting Test.

MCI is recommended, especially when an individual is experiencing an MDE as defined by the *DSM-IV* (Modrego & Ferrández, 2004) or they endorse ≥2 items on the GDS five-item scale (Hudon et al., 2008). Furthermore, despite depression's inconsistent effect on cognitive performance in MCI, it is important to remember that several studies have found older adults with MCI and depressive symptoms to be more likely to progress to dementia (Gabryelewicz et al., 2007; Lam et al., 2007; Modrego & Ferrández, 2004; Teng et al., 2007). Thus, the potential effect of depression on cognition in MCI should not be overlooked. Clinicians are encouraged to consider the relationship between future cognitive decline and current depressive symptoms. The GDS five-item scale and the *DSM-IV*'s criteria for depressive symptoms may be the most sensitive means of detecting levels of symptoms that interfere with cognitive function (Hudon et al., 2008; Modrego & Ferrández, 2004) and thus are recommended for assessing a client with MCI who has depressive symptoms.

APATHY

In MCI, apathy does not appear to affect global cognitive status, working memory, or visuospatial abilities (Drijgers et al., 2011; Lam et al., 2007; Robert et al., 2006a). The bulk of evidence reviewed indicates that apathy also typically does not impact performance on measures of executive function, attention/processing speed, language, and memory. Two measures of apathy associated with worse cognition performance in MCI were the NPI and the Apathy Inventory, Caregiver Version (Drijgers et al., 2011; Robert et al., 2006a). Specifically, a score >3 on the NPI was associated with worse performance on the TMT-B, TMT-A, and semantic fluency. A score of ≥1 was associated with poorer performance on the Stroop and on a memory test (i.e., Free and Cued Selective Reminding test). Thus, even though the relationship between apathy and cognitive performance in MCI is inconsistent, the NPI and the Apathy Inventory, Caregiver Version may be most helpful in identifying levels of apathy that could be interfering with cognition in MCI.

ANXIETY

There is extremely limited research on the relationship between anxiety and cognitive performance in MCI; more research is warranted. The current findings suggest that performance on at least the TMT-B may be negatively affected by anxiety (Rozzini et al., 2009). This investigation used the Geriatric Anxiety Inventory (GAI) to measure anxiety. Thus clinicians should be aware of the potential impact of anxiety on measures of executive function in MCI; the GAI may be the most sensitive means of detecting cognition-compromising anxiety in MCI (Rozzini et al., 2009). Additionally, clinicians need to be mindful that, like depression in MCI, anxiety may be a risk factor for future cognitive decline and conversion to AD (Gallagher et al., 2011; Palmer et al., 2007).

Stroke

DEPRESSION

In contrast to the other neurological conditions, there is a consistent negative relationship between post-CVI depression and performance on measures of global cognitive status (Bolla-Wilson et al., 1989; Carod-Artal et al. 2009; Pirscoveanu et al., 2008; see Table 14.3). This suggests that depressive presentations may account for a CVI patient's cognitive test performance and should be evaluated with this in mind. Depression measures and criteria that were associated with worse global cognitive status were the Hamilton Depression Rating Scale (HDRS), Hospital Anxiety and Depression Scale (HADS), GDS, and *DSM-III* crieteria for MDD (Bolla-Wilson et al., 1989; Carod-Artal et al., 2009; Pirscoveanu et al., 2008).

Memory functions are also affected by depression in individuals who have had a CVI. This effect, however, is variable, and interpretation of performance in an individual with a CVI and depression or depressive symptoms should be done with considerable caution. Psychiatric measures sensitive to compromising levels of depressive symptoms on memory functioning in CVI are the Montgomery Asberg Depression Rating Scale (MADS; Ny et a., 2004) and criteria for minor or major depression in the *DSM-III* (Kauhanen et al., 1999). Post-CVI depression as measured by the *DSM-III* (Bolla-Wilson et al., 1989) and Beck Depression Inventory (BDI; Pohjasvaara et al., 2002) also impacts an individual's performance on traditional measures of executive function (e.g., WCST, TMT-B, & Stroop). A tentative and preliminary recommendation is to use alternative measures of executive function (e.g., Visual Elevator & Brixton Spatial Anticipation Test) when assessing a post-CVI survivor with depression. There is very little evidence to suggest that depression does not impact attention/processing speed measures in CVI survivors; more research is needed in this area to allow for more informed recommendations.

The impact of depression in CVI on visuospatial instruments is inconsistent; much more empirical evidence is required in order to make sound recommendations for assessment. The evidence presented here indicates that the impact of depression on visuospatial measures may be mitigated by interpreting overall performance, as the majority of visuospatial composite scores were not decreased by depression in CVI survivors (Bolla-Wilson et al., 1989; Kauhanen et al., 1999; Nys et al., 2005).

Depression in CVI patients affects their receptive and expressive language functions but not their abilities to reason or to understand general principles and use social judgment (Bolla-Wilson et al., 1989; Kauhanen et al., 1999; Nys et al., 2005). This effect is specific to severe depression (Nys et al., 2005) and left-hemisphere lesions (Bolla-Wilson et al., 1989). Thus, with the measures reviewed, language functions can accurately be examined in depressed post-CVI survivors with right-hemisphere lesions and mild-to-moderate levels of depression. When examining a depressed client with a left-hemisphere lesion and/or severe symptomology, the clinician needs to be aware of the potential negative influence of language performance.

As in AD and MCI, the impact of depression on cognition in CVI is not universal. Its effect varies between and within cognitive domains. However, measures associated with compromising levels of depression in CVI include the HDRS, HADS, GDS, BDI, and MADS, as well as the depression criteria from the *DSM-*

Table 14.3 Impact of Secondary Factors on Cognition in Stroke

Cognitive Domain	Effect	Measures	Study
Depression			
Global cognitive status	Depressed group more impaired or negative association	CS from O & GI; MoCA; MMSE	Bolla-Wilson et al. (1989); Carod-Artal et al. (2009); Pirscoveanu et al. (2008)
Memory	Depressed group more impaired	CS from RAVLT & Rey-O FD; Serial Learning; LM DR; Visual Recognition and Reproduction	Kauhanen et al. (1999); Nys et al. (2005)
	No group differences or association	CS from GI & FFT; CS from LM IR & DR, RAVLT, RW, DS F & B; CS from Visual Reproduction IR & DR	Bolla-Wilson et al. (1989)
Executive function	Depressed group more impaired or negative association	CS from Verbal Fluency, AF & LMS; CS from WCST, Stroop, TMT-B, & VF	Bolla-Wilson et al. (1989); Pohjasvaara et al. (2002)
	No group differences	CS from BSAT, VE & LF	Nys et al. (2005)
Working memory	No group differences	CS from DS F & B, CBS & SC	Nys et al. (2005)
Attention & processing speed	No association	TMT-A	Kauhanen et al. (1999)
Visuospatial ability	Depressed group more impaired	BD; CS from JLO, TFR, & Rey-O FC; CS from Picture Completion	Kauhanen et al. (1999); Nys et al. (2005)
	No group differences or association	CS from BD, CDT, HVOT; CS from Copy Tasks & MCHT	Bolla-Wilson et al. (1989); Kauhanen et al. (1999)
Language	Depressed group more impaired	CS from RW&P, BNT, Reading, CTP, Comp., Letter & Semantic Fluency; CS from Token Test & BNT	Bolla-Wilson et al. (1989); Nys et al. (2005)

		No association	Kauhanen et al. (1999)
Apathy			
Global cognitive status	Apathy group more impaired	Comprehension; Similarities; Verbal Fluency	Brodaty et al. (2005); Okada et al. (1997); Starkstein et al. (1993); Yamagata et al. (2004)
		HDS-R; HIS; MMSE	
Memory	No group differences	CS from LM I & VR I; CS from LM II & VR II	Brodaty et al. (2005)
Executive function	No group differences	CS from CFST, TMT-B Verbal & Semantic Fluency; Letter Fluency	Brodaty et al. (2005); Okada et al. (1997)
Working memory	Apathy group more impaired	CS from DS B & Arithmetic	Brodaty et al. (2005)
Attention & processing speed	AP group more impaired	CS from DS F & Mental Control	Brodaty et al. (2005)
Visuospatial ability	No group differences	CS from TMT-A & Symbol Digit	Brodaty et al. (2005)
	No group differences	BD	Brodaty et al. (2005)
Language	AP group more impaired	Semantic Fluency	Okada et al. (1997); Yamagata et al. (2004)
	No group differences	BNT-15 item	Brodaty et al. (2005)
Anxiety			
Global cognitive status	Anxious group more impaired	CAMCOG	Rasquin et al. (2005)
	No group differences	MMSE	Shimoda & Robinson (1998)
Memory	Anxiety was negatively associated	CVLT Long Delay Free	Barker-Collo (2007)

(*Continued*)

Table 14.3 (CONTINUED)

Cognitive Domain	Effect	Measures	Study
	No group differences or association	CVLT Short Delay Free Recall; VPA Immediate; VPA Delayed	Barker-Collo (2007)
Executive function	No association	Interference ratio on Victoria Stroop	Barker-Collo (2007)
Attention & processing speed	Anxiety was negatively associated	IVA-CPT prudence; Victoria Stroop Dots	Barker-Collo (2007)
Language Dysfunction	No association	IVA-CPT attention	Barker-Collo (2007)
Memory	Aphasic group more impaired	BVRT; Corsi's Spatial Learning Test; CVLT; Paired Associate Learning; Paired Associates; RAVLT; Story Recall; Verbal Learning	Beeson et al. (1993); Burgio & Basso (1997); Gorno-Tempini et al. (2004); Seniów et al. (2009); Ween et al. (1996)
	No group differences	Levels of Processing; Recognition Memory; Rey-O FD; WMS-III Faces	Gorno-Tempini et al. (2004); Ween et al. (1996)
EF	APH group more impaired or negative association	CTT; Modified TMT; Porteus Maze Test; Tower of London; WCST	Baldo et al. (2005); Fridriksson et al. (2006); Gorno-Tempini et al. (2004); Purdy (2002)

Working memory	Aphasic group more impaired or negative association	1 & 2 n-back; Auditory DS; Consonant Trigrams; Corsi's spatial span; DS; DS F; Listening Span; Reading Span	Beeson et al. (1993); Burgio & Basso (1997); Caspari et al. (1998); Christensen & Wright (2010); Gorno-Tempini et al. (2004); Ween et al. (1996); Wright et al. (2003)
Visuospatial ability	No group differences	Tapping Forward	Beeson et al. (1993)
	No group differences or association	BD; Cube Copy; Rey-O FC	Baldo et al. (2005); Gorno-Tempini et al. (2004)

Abbreviations: AF, alternating fingers; B, backward; BD, Block Design; BNT, Boston Naming Test; BSAT, Brixton Spatial Anticipation Test; BVRT, Benton Visual Retention Test; CAMCOG, Cognitive Section of the Cambridge Examination for Mental Disorders of the Elderly; CBS, Corsi Block Span; CDT, Clock Drawing Test; CFST, Colour Form Sorting Test; Comp., comprehension; CS, composite score; CTP, Cookie Theft Picture; CTT, Color Trails Test; CVLT, California Verbal Learning Test; DR, delayed recall; DS, Digit Span; F, forward; FFT, Famous Faces Test; GI, general information; HDS-R, Hasegawa Dementia Rating Scale; HIS, Hasegawa's Intelligence Scale; HVOT, Hopper Visual Organization Test; IR, immediate recall; IVA-CPT, Integrated Visual Auditory Continuous Performance Test; JLO, Judgment of Line Orientation; LF, letter fluency; LM IR & DR, Logical Memory Immediate Recall & Delayed Recall; LMS, Luria Motor Sequences; MCHT, Modified Clock Hand Task; MMSE, Mini Mental Status Exam; MoCA, Montreal Cognitive Assessment; O, Orientation; RAVLT, Rey Auditory Verbal Learning Test; Rey-O FD, Rey–Osterrieth Complex Figure Delay; Rey-O FC, Rey–Osterrieth Complex Figure Copy; RW, recurrent words; RW&P, repetition of words and phrases; SC, Star Cancellation; TFR, Test of Facial Recognition; TMT-A, Trail Making Test Part A; TMT-B, Trail Making Test B; VE, Visual Elevator; VF, Verbal Fluency; VPA, Verbal Paired Associates; VR, Visual Recall; WCST, Wisconsin Card Sorting Test; WMS-III, Wechsler Memory Scale, Third Edition.

III. Thus, these measures should be used to identify potentially impactful levels of depression.

APATHY

Given apathy's influence on brief global cognitive measures, they are not recommended as stand-alone measures of cognition for CVI survivors with apathy. Further research is needed to determine if more comprehensive screeners would be immune to the impact of apathy in CVI. Apathy after CVI also may affect working memory, but existing studies are sparse and inconclusive. There are inconsistent relationships between apathy and performance on measures of attention/processing speed and language. Therefore, it is difficult to provide reliable recommendations to attenuate this effect. Given the lack of impact on the TMT-A and Symbol Digit, the use of measures requiring writing and physical engagement instead of verbal responses may be more resilient.

There is no impact of apathy on executive function, visuospatial ability, and memory in CVI survivors; the evaluation of executive function, visuospatial ability, and memory in CVI survivors appears warranted without adjustments, but future research is needed to confirm this recommendation. Measures sensitive to levels of apathy interfering with cognitive function are the Apathy Evaluation Scale (Brodaty et al., 2005) and the Apathy Scale (Okada et al., 1997; Starkstein et al., 1993; Yamagata et al., 2004).

ANXIETY

There is very limited evidence examining the influence of anxiety on cognitive functioning in CVI, but preliminary evidence suggests it may have a modest negative impact. Cross-sectional data indicate that global measures of cognition are not affected by anxiety (Shimoda & Robinson, 1998), but over time, individuals with anxiety following a CVI may have a faster rate of cognitive decline (Rasquin et al., 2005). Specific to memory, anxiety has only been found to be negatively related to long-delay free recall on a list-learning task. Anxiety does not have a negative association with immediate recall on list learning or with immediate or delayed recall on verbal paired associates (Barker-Collo, 2007). Thus, anxiety is not likely to confound interpretations of memory performance in these patients, although future investigations are needed to understand and clarify this relationship. Executive function was not related to anxiety following a CVI (Barker-Collo, 2007). Attention/processing speed is inconsistently related to anxiety. The impact of anxiety following CVI is only beginning to be understood; much more research is needed to further our minimal understanding.

LANGUAGE DISTURBANCE

Limited evidence suggests that language functioning is related to various other types of cognition, including executive function (Baldo et al., 2005; Fridriksson et al., 2006) and working memory (Caspari et al., 1998). There is also evidence that post-CVI survivors with language dysfunction (i.e., aphasia) perform worse on a variety of cognitive measures (Baldo et al., 2005; Beeson et al., 1993; Burgio

& Basso, 1997; Christensen & Wright, 2010; Gorno-Tempini et al., 2004; Ween et al., 1996; Wright et al., 2003). However, this evidence cannot distinguish what impacts cognitive performance—the behavioral manifestations of the language dysfunction or concomitant underlying neurological insult—given that the control groups for all investigations except one (Burgio & Basso, 1997) were individuals who had not had a CVI (i.e., neurologically intact). Results from this study suggest that the majority of compromised scores were probably due to underlying infarcts but may haveb been exacerbated by language dysfunction.

To attenuate the impact of language disturbances, clinicians should confirm with all clients with post-CVI language disturbances that they understand the task to be performed. If an individual with language disturbances comprehends administrative directions, the clinician should proceed cautiously with typical neuropsychological instruments and methods while being cognizant of the client's language difficulties. Furthermore, when considering measures to assess language dysfunction as it relates to cognitive functioning in CVI, it is recommended that the Western Aphasia Battery, Reading Comprehension Battery for Aphasia, and the Standard Language Examination for aphasia be completed.

CASE REPORT

GG, a 75-year-old retired accountant, is a bilingual Latina American woman referred by her neurologist for memory assessment following complaints of fairly acute memory decline. Testing was conducted over 2 days and included a detailed clinical interview with the client and her spouse; self- and informant-report memory questionnaires; the BDI, BAI, Wechsler Abbreviated Scale of Intelleigence (WASI), and NAB; Halstead-Reitan Neuropsychological Battery (HRNB) motor tasks;Medical Symptom Validity Test (MSVT) validity screen; and review of available medical records. GG reported moderate difficulties with recalling day-to-day information and that these negatively affected her mood and daily functioning. GG reported a great deal of distress related to her perceived memory difficulties, even though she reported overall adequate functioning through the use of calendars and lists. Her distress was further exacerbated by a family history (undocumented) of Alzheimer's disease. She reported considerable rumination on this and concern for herself. She reported difficulties remembering items, numbers, and taking her medications on her own, remarking that she would not remember certain items at the store or to take her medication without her list and calendar strategies. She also reported multiple instances of going to a cabinet or room in her home to retrieve a specific item and forgetting what she wanted or going to the incorrect place. Despite her reported difficulties, Ms. GG remained mostly in control of the family finances including a checking account, credit cards, home budgeting, and maintenance of savings and retirement accounts. She also maintained cooking responsibilities in the household and shared household cleaning responsibilities with her spouse. She no longer drove an automobile because of vision problems.

Overall results of intellectual and neuropsychological testing suggested a pattern of mild short-term memory difficulties consistent with the client's report. Intellectual functioning fell in the very superior range of functioning. She demonstrated memory and attentional impairments related to recalling and manipulating stimuli. Deficits were consistent across spatial and verbal domains, but difficulty was more pronounced with verbal information (e.g. words, stories). Spatial abilities were found to be as expected for her age and educational history. Executive functioning and language abilities appeared to serve as relative strengths for GG, who scored above expectations for her age and education-matched peers. Motor results from testing indicated a slightly below-average performance compared to that of age- and gender-matched peers. Thus, overall, it appeared that GG was experiencing primarily moderate short-term memory impairments across memory and attentional domains of functioning which were perceived as only mildly affecting daily living.

During detailed psychological interviewing and via self-report measures, GG denied any depressive symptoms. However, she reported during the interview, and was observed episodically throughout testing, symptoms consistent with acute anxiety, including loss of train of thought, heart palpitations, shortness of breath, and feelings of panic when she could not remember something. She became tearful on the second day of testing at two points—once during completion of the WASI regarding her father, and later, at the end of testing, when she expressed concerns about her neuropsychological status and what she felt was increased emotionality. She reported that her anxiety symptoms had begun approximately 6 months prior to the evaluation and had steadily increased in intensity and frequency over time. Given the empirical literature, we were concerned that her testing results may have been affected by her acute anxiety symptoms. As these symptoms were relatively new for her, a functional analysis focusing on potential antecedents was done in the context of follow-up interview. A review of her medication regimen identified Carvediol for heart regulation, Lipitor for cholesterol control, Detrol LA for occasional incontinence, and Omeprazole for gastroesophageal reflux (GERD).

It turned out that GG had been placed on the Carvediol approximately 5 months prior to our assessment. While rare, symptoms of anxiety, including palpitations, shortness of breath, and general feelings of nervousness, have been reported for this medication. Following consultation with her neurologist, Carvediol was discontinued. At 2-week follow-up with the client, she indicated a return to a pre-anxious state and increased attention and overall cognitive abilities. Because the client reported significantly decreased memory difficulties, no additional empirical testing was completed.

This case suggests that awareness of the types of potential influences that psychiatric features may have on neurocognitive testing can lead to additional hypothesis testing and investigation that may in turn be fruitful in understanding the presentation of our clients.

APPENDIX

a-MCI = amnestic MCI
AD = Alzheimer's disease

ADAS-noncog = Alzheimer's Disease Assessment Scale noncognitive subscale
BAI = Beck Anxiety Inventory
BD = Wechsler Block Design
BDI = Beck Depression Inventory
CDR = Clinical Dementia Rating Scale
CERAD = Consortium to Establish a Registry for Alzheimer's Disease Behavioral Rating Scale
ChE-Is = cholinesterase inhibitors
COWAT = Controlled Oral Word Association Test
CVI or Stroke = cerebrovascular insult
CVLT = California Verbal Learning Test
DSM-III = *Diagnostic and Statistical Manual of Mental Disorders, Third Edition*
DSM-IV = *Diagnostic and Statistical Manual of Mental Disorders, Fourth Edition*
GAI = Geriatric Anxiety Inventory
HADS =Hospital Anxiety and Depression Scale
HADS-a = Hospital Anxiety and Depression Scale–anxiety subscale
HDRS = Hamilton Depression Rating Scale
HDS = Hierarchic Dementia Scale
IVA-CPT = Integrated Visual Auditory Continuous Performance Test
MADS = Montgomery Asberg Depression Rating Scale
MCI = mild cognitive impairment
MDD = major depressive disorder
MDE = major depressive episode
MMSE = Mini-Mental Status Exam
NAB = neuropsycological assessment battery
NPI = Neuropsychiatric Inventory
TMT-A = Trail Making Test Part A
TMT-B = Trail Making Test Part B
WCST = Wisconsin Card Sorting Test

References

Adler, G., Chwalek, K., & Jajcevic, A. (2004). Six-month course of mild cognitive impairment and affective symptoms in late-life depression. *European Psychiatry, 19*(8), 502–505. doi:10.1016/j.eurpsy.2004.09.003

Albert, M. S., DeKosky, S. T., Dickson, D., Dubois, B., Feldman, H. H., Fox, N. C.,... Phelps, C. H. (2011). The diagnosis of mild cognitive impairment due to Alzheimer's disease: Recommendations from the National Institute on Aging-Alzheimer's Association workgroups on diagnostic guidelines for Alzheimer's disease. *Alzheimer's and Dementia, 7*(3), 270–279. doi:10.1016/j.jalz.2011.03.008

Alzheimer's Association (2011). Alzheimer's disease facts and figures. *Alzheimer's and Dementia, 7*(2), 208–244. doi:10.1016/j.jalz.2011.02.004

Alzheimer's Disease International. (2008, December). *The prevalence of dementia worldwide.* Retrieved from http://www.alz.co.uk/adi/pdf/prevalence.pdf.

Angelelli, P., Paolucci, S., Bivona, U., Piccardi, L., Ciurli, P., Cantagallo, A.,... Pizzamiglio, L. (2004). Development of neuropsychiatric symptoms in poststroke patients: A cross-sectional study. *Acta Psychiatrica Scandinavica, 110*(1), 55–63. doi:10.1111/j.1600-0 447.2004.00297.xACP297

Apostolova, L. G., & Cummings, J. L. (2008). Neuropsychiatric manifestations in mild cognitive impairment: A systematic review of the literature. *Dementia and Geriatric Cognitive Disorders, 25*(2), 115–126. doi:10.1159/000112509

Backman, L., Hassing, L., Forsell, Y., & Viitanen, M. (1996). Episodic remembering in a population-based sample of nonagenarians: Does major depression exacerbate the memory deficits seen in Alzheimer's disease? *Psychology and Aging, 11*(4), 649–657.

Baldo, J., Dronkers, N., Wilkins, D., Ludy, C., Raskin, P., & Kim, J. (2005). Is problem solving dependent on language? *Brain and Language, 92*(3), 240–250. doi:10.1016/j.bandl.2004.06.103

Barker-Collo, S. L. (2007). Depression and anxiety 3 months post stroke: Prevalence and correlates. *Archives of Clinical Neuropsychology, 22*(4), 519–531. doi:S0887-6177(07)00080-710.1016/j.acn.2007.03.002

Barker-Collo, S., & Feigin, V. (2006). The impact of neuropsychological deficits on functional stroke outcomes. *Neuropsychology Review, 16*(2), 53–64. doi:10.1007/s11065-006-9007-5

Barker-Collo, S., Feigin, V. L., Parag, V., Lawes, C. M., & Senior, H. (2010). Auckland Stroke Outcomes Study. Part 2: Cognition and functional outcomes 5 years poststroke. *Neurology, 75*(18), 1608–1616. doi:75/18/160810.1212/WNL.0b013e3181fb44c8

Bartolini, M., Coccia, M., Luzzi, S., Provinciali, L., & Ceravolo, M. G. (2005). Motivational symptoms of depression mask preclinical Alzheimer's disease in elderly subjects. *Dementia and Geriatric Cognitive Disorders, 19*(1), 31–36. doi:10.1159/00008096880968

Beeson, P. M., Bayles, K. A., Rubens, A. B., & Kaszniak, A. W. (1993). Memory impairment and executive control in individuals with stroke-induced aphasia. *Brain and Language, 45*(2), 253–275. doi:S0093-934X(83)71045-X10.1006/brln.1993.1045

Berger, A. K., Fahlander, K., Wahlin, A., & Backman, L. (2002). Negligible effects of depression on verbal and spatial performance in Alzheimer's disease. *Dementia and Geriatric Cognitive Disorders, 13*(1), 1–7. doi:dem13001

Berthier, M. L. (2005). Poststroke aphasia: epidemiology, pathophysiology and treatment. *Drugs & Aging, 22*(2), 163–182. doi:2226

Bhalla, R. K., Butters, M. A., Becker, J. T., Houck, P. R., Snitz, B. E., Lopez, O. L.,... Reynolds, C. F. (2009). Patterns of mild cognitive impairment after treatment of depression in the elderly. *American Journal of Geriatric Psychiatry, 17*(4), 308–316. doi:10.1097/JGP.0b013e318190b8d8

Bierman, E. J. M., Comijs, H. C., Jonker, C., & Beekman, A. T. F. (2007). Symptoms of anxiety and depression in the course of cognitive decline. *Dementia and Geriatric Cognitive Disorders, 24*(3), 213–219. doi:10.1159/000107083

Bierman, E. J. M., Comijs, H. C., Jonker, C., Scheltens, P., & Beekman, A. T. F. (2009). The effect of anxiety and depression on decline of memory function in Alzheimer's disease. *International Psychogeriatrics, 21*(06), 1142. doi:10.1017/s1041610209990512

Bolla-Wilson, K., Robinson, R. G., Starkstein, S. E., Boston, J., & Price, T. R. (1989). Lateralization of dementia of depression in stroke patients. *American Journal of Psychiatry, 146*(5), 627–634.

Boyle, P. A., & Malloy, P. F. (2003). Treating apathy in Alzheimer's disease. *Dementia and Geriatric Cognitive Disorders, 17*(1–2), 91–99. doi:10.1159/00007428074280

Brodaty, H., Sachdev, P. S., Withall, A., Altendorf, A., Valenzuela, M. J., & Lorentz, L. (2005). Frequency and clinical, neuropsychological and neuroimaging correlates of apathy following stroke—the Sydney Stroke Study. *Psychological Medicine, 35*(12), 1707. doi:10.1017/s0033291705006173

Brousseau, G., Rourke, B. P., & Burke, B. (2007). Acetylcholinesterase inhibitors, neuropsychiatric symptoms, and Alzheimer's disease subtypes: An alternate hypothesis to global cognitive enhancement. *Experimental and Clinical Psychopharmacology, 15*(6), 546–554. doi:10.1037/1064-1297.15.6.546

Bruce, J. M., Bhalla, R., Westervelt, H. J., Davis, J., Williams, V., & Tremont, G. (2008). Neuropsychological correlates of self-reported depression and self-reported cognition among patients with mild cognitive impairment. *Journal of Geriatric Psychiatry & Neurology, 21*(1), 34–40. doi: 089198870731103210.1177/08919887 07311032

Buettner, L. L., Fitzsimmons, S., Atav, S., & Sink, K. (2011). Cognitive stimulation for apathy in probable early-stage Alzheimer's. *Journal of Aging Research*, April 28, 480890. doi:10.4061/2011/480890

Burgio, F., & Basso, A. (1997). Memory and aphasia. *Neuropsychologia, 35*(6), 759–766. doi:S0028-3932(97)00014-6

Burvill, P. W., Johnson, G. A., Jamrozik, K. D., Anderson, C. S., Stewart-Wynne, E. G., & Chakera, T. M. (1995). Prevalence of depression after stroke: The Perth Community Stroke Study. *The British Journal of Psychiatry, 166*(3), 320–327. doi:10.1192/ bjp.166.3.320

Carod-Artal, F. J., Ferreira Coral, L., Trizotto, D. S., & Menezes Moreira, C. (2009). Poststroke depression: Prevalence and determinants in Brazilian stroke patients. *Cerebrovascular Diseases, 28*(2), 157–165. doi: 10.1159/000226114

Caroli, A., Lorenzi, M., Geroldi, C., Nobili, F., Paghera, B., Bonetti, M., ... Frisoni, G. B. (2010). Metabolic compensation and depression in Alzheimer's disease. *Dementia and Geriatric Cognitive Disorders, 29*(1), 37–45. doi:10.1159/000257761

Carota, A., Staub, F., & Bogousslavsky, J. (2002). Emotions, behaviours and mood changes in stroke. *Current Opinion in Neurology, 15*(1), 57–69.

Carson, A. J., MacHale, S., Allen, K., Lawrie, S. M., Dennis, M., House, A., & Sharpe, M. (2000). Depression after stroke and lesion location: A systematic review. *The Lancet, 356*(9224), 122–126. doi:10.1016/s0140-6736(00)02448-x

Caspari, I., Parkinson, S. R., LaPointe, L. L., & Katz, R. C. (1998). Working memory and aphasia. *Brain and Cognition, 37*(2), 205–223. doi:S0278-2626(97)90970-2 10.1006/ brcg.1997.0970

Chan, W. C., Lam, L. C. W., Tam, C. W. C., Lui, V. W. C., Leung, G. T. Y., Lee, A. T. C.,... Chan, W. M. (2010). Neuropsychiatric symptoms are associated with increased risks of progression to dementia: A 2-year prospective study of 321 Chinese older persons with mild cognitive impairment. *Age and Ageing, 40*(1), 30–35. doi:10.1093/ageing/ afq151

Chase, T. N. (2010). Apathy in neuropsychiatric disease: Diagnosis, pathophysiology, and Treatment. *Neurotoxicity Research, 19*(2), 266–278. doi:10.1007/ s12640-010-9196-9

Chemerinski, E., & Levine, S. R. (2006). Neuropsychiatric disorders following vascular brain injury. *Mount Sinai Journal of Medicine, 73*(7), 1006–1014.

Chemerinski, E., Petracca, G., Manes, F., Leiguarda, R., & Starkstein, S. E. (1998). Prevalence and correlates of anxiety in Alzheimer's disease. *Depression and Anxiety, 7*(4), 166–170. doi:10.1002/(SICI)1520-6394(1998)7:4<166::AID-DA4>3.0.CO;2-8

Chemerinski, E., & Robinson, R. G. (2000). The neuropsychiatry of stroke. *Psychosomatics, 41*(1), 5–14.

Chen, C. S., Ouyang, P., Yeh, Y. C., Lai, C. L., Liu, C. K., Yen, C. F., … Juo, S. H. (2012). Apolipoprotein E polymorphism and behavioral and psychological symptoms of dementia in patients with Alzheimer disease. *Alzheimer Disease & Associated Disorders, 26*(2), 135–139. doi:10.1097/WAD.0b013e31821f5787

Chen, S. T., Sultzer, D. L., Hinkin, C. H., Mahler, M. E., & Cummings, J. L. (1998). Executive dysfunction in Alzheimer's disease: Association with neuropsychiatric symptoms and functional impairment. *The Journal of Neuropsychiatry and Clinical Neurosciences, 10*(4), 426–432.

Cheston, R., Jones, K., & Gilliard, J. (2003). Group psychotherapy and people with dementia. *Aging & Mental Health, 7*(6), 452–461. doi:10.1080/136078603100015947

Chilovi, B. V., Conti, M., Zanetti, M., Mazzù, I.,… Padovani, A. (2009). Differential impact of apathy and depression in the development of dementia in mild cognitive impairment patients. *Dementia and Geriatric Cognitive Disorders, 27*(4), 390–398. doi:10.1159/000210045

Christensen, S. C., & Wright, H. H. (2010). Verbal and non-verbal working memory in aphasia: What three-back tasks reveal. *Aphasiology, 24*(6–8), 752–762. doi:10.1080/02687030903437690

Christy, E. M., & Friedman, R. B. (2005). Using non-verbal tests to measure cognitive ability in patients with aphasia: A comparison of the RCPM and the TONI. *Brain and Language, 95*(1), 195–196. doi:10.1016/j.bandl.2005.07.104

Coelho, C. (2005). Direct attention training as a treatment for reading impairment in mild aphasia. *Aphasiology, 19*(3–5), 275–283. doi:10.1080/02687030444000741

Croquelois, A., & Bogousslavsky, J. (2011). Stroke aphasia: 1,500 consecutive cases. *Cerebrovascular Diseases, 31*(4), 392–399. doi:00032321710.1159/000323217

Debruyne, H., Van Buggenhout, M., Le Bastard, N., Aries, M., Audenaert, K., De Deyn, P. P., & Engelborghs, S. (2009). Is the geriatric depression scale a reliable screening tool for depressive symptoms in elderly patients with cognitive impairment? *International Journal of Geriatric Psychiatry, 24*(6), 556–562. doi: 10.1002/gps.2154

Devier, D. J., Pelton, G. H., Tabert, M. H., Liu, X., Cuasay, K., Eisenstadt, R., … Devanand, D. P. (2009). The impact of anxiety on conversion from mild cognitive impairment to Alzheimer's disease. *International Journal of Geriatric Psychiatry, 24*(12), 1335–1342. doi:10.1002/gps.2263

Dickey, L., Kagan, A., Lindsay, M. P., Fang, J., Rowland, A., & Black, S. (2010). Incidence and profile of inpatient stroke-induced aphasia in Ontario, Canada. *Archives of Physical Medicine and Rehabilitation, 91*(2), 196–202. doi:10.1016/j.apmr.2009.09.020

Drijgers, R. L., Verhey, F. R. J., Leentjens, A. F. G., Köhler, S., & Aalten, P. (2011). Neuropsychological correlates of apathy in mild cognitive impairment and Alzheimer's disease: The role of executive functioning. *International Psychogeriatrics, 23*(08), 1327–1333. doi:10.1017/s1041610211001037

Edwards, E. R., Spira, A. P., Barnes, D. E., & Yaffe, K. (2009). Neuropsychiatric symptoms in mild cognitive impairment: Differences by subtype and progression to dementia. *International Journal of Geriatric Psychiatry, 24*(7), 716–722. doi:10.1002/gps.2187

Fahlander, K., Berger, A. K., Backman, L., & Wahlin, A. (1999). Depression does not aggravate the episodic memory deficits associated with Alzheimer's disease. *Neuropsychology, 13*(4), 532–538.

Fang, J., & Cheng, Q. (2009). Etiological mechanisms of post-stroke depression: A review. *Neurological Research, 31*(9), 904–909. doi:10.1179/174313209X385752

Feldman, H., Scheltens, P., Scarpini, E., Hermann, N., Mesenbrink, P., Mancione, L., … Ferris, S. (2004). Behavioral symptoms in mild cognitive impairment. *Neurology, 62*(7), 1199–1201.

Fernandez, M., Gobartt, A. L., & Balana, M. (2010). Behavioural symptoms in patients with Alzheimer's disease and their association with cognitive impairment. *BMC Neurology, 10*(1), 87. doi:10.1186/1471-2377-10-87

Fernandez-Martinez, M., Molano, A., Castro, J., & Zarranz, J. J. (2010). Prevalence of neuropsychiatric symptoms in mild cognitive impairment and Alzheimer's disease, and its relationship with cognitive impairment. *Current Alzheimer Research, 7*(6), 517–526. doi:CAR-79

Ferretti, L., McCurry, S. M., Logsdon, R., Gibbons, L., & Teri, L. (2001). Anxiety and Alzheimer's disease. *Journal of Geriatric Psychiatry and Neurology, 14*(1), 52–58. doi:10.1177/089198870101400111

Fischer, P., Jungwirth, S., Zehetmayer, S., Weissgram, S., Hoenigschnabl, S., Gelpi, E.,... Tragl, K. H. (2007). Conversion from subtypes of mild cognitive impairment to Alzheimer dementia. *Neurology, 68*(4), 288–291. doi:10.1212/01.wnl.0000252358.03285.9d

Forsell, Y., Palmer, K., & Fratiglioni, L. (2003). Psychiatric symptoms/syndromes in elderly persons with mild cognitive impairment. Data from a cross-sectional study. *Acta Neurologica Scandinavica, 107*(179), 25–28. doi:10.1034/j.1600-0404.107.s179.4.x

Fridriksson, J., Nettles, C., Davis, M., Morrow, L., & Montgomery, A. (2006). Functional communication and executive function in aphasia. *Clinical Linguistics & Phonetics, 20*(6), 401–410. doi:10.1080/02699200500075781

Friedmann, N., & Gvion, A. (2003). Sentence comprehension and working memory limitation in aphasia: A dissociation between semantic-syntactic and phonological reactivation. *Brain and Language, 86*(1), 23–39. doi:10.1016/s0093-934x(02)00530-8

Gabryelewicz, T., Styczynska, M., Luczywek, E., Barczak, A., Pfeffer, A., Androsiuk, W.,... Barcikowska, M. (2007). The rate of conversion of mild cognitive impairment to dementia: predictive role of depression. *International Journal of Geriatric Psychiatry, 22*(6), 563–567. doi:10.1002/gps.1716

Gallagher, D., Coen, R., Kilroy, D., Belinski, K., Bruce, I., Coakley, D., ... Lawlor, B. A. (2011). Anxiety and behavioural disturbance as markers of prodromal Alzheimer's disease in patients with mild cognitive impairment. *International Journal of Geriatric Psychiatry, 26*(2), 166–172. doi:10.1002/gps.2509

Garavello, A. P. E., Magaldi, R. M., Paschoal, S. M. P., & Filho, W. J. (2010). Impact of depressive symptoms on outcome of Alzheimer's disease. *Dementia & Neuropsychologia, 4*(4) 346-352.

Gauthier, S., Reisberg, B., Zaudig, M., Petersen, R. C., Ritchie, K., Broich, K., ... Winblad, B. (2006). Mild cognitive impairment. *The Lancet, 367*(9518), 1262–1270. doi:10.1016/s0140-6736(06)68542-5

Geda, Y. E., Roberts, R. O., Knopman, D. S., Petersen, R. C., Christianson, T. J. H., Pankratz, V. S., ... Rocca, W. A. (2008). Prevalence of neuropsychiatric symptoms in mild cognitive impairment and normal cognitive aging: Population-based study. *Archives of General Psychiatry, 65*(10), 1193–1198. doi:10.1001/archpsyc.65.10.1193

Goljar, N., Burger, H., Vidmar, G., Marincek, C., Krizaj, J., Chatterji, S., ... Bickenbach, J. E. (2010). Functioning and disability in stroke. *Disability & Rehabilitation, 32*(S1), S50-S58. doi:10.3109/09638288.2010.517598

Gorno-Tempini, M. L., Dronkers, N. F., Rankin, K. P., Ogar, J. M., Phengrasamy, L., Rosen, II. J., ... Miller, B. L. (2004). Cognition and anatomy in three variants of primary progressive aphasia. *Annals of Neurology, 55*(3), 335–346. doi:10.1002/ana.10825

Guétin, S., Portet, F., Picot, M. C., Pommié, C., Messaoudi, M., Djabelkir, L., ... Touchon, J. (2009). Effect of music therapy on anxiety and depression in patients with

Alzheimer's type dementia: Randomised, controlled study. *Dementia and Geriatric Cognitive Disorders, 28*(1), 36–46. doi:10.1159/000229024

Hackett, M. L., Yapa, C., Parag, V., & Anderson, C. S. (2005). Frequency of depression after stroke: A systematic review of observational studies. *Stroke, 36*(6), 1330–1340. doi:10.1161/01.str.0000165928.19135.35

Holmes, C., Wilkinson, D., Dean, C., Vethanayagam, S., Olivieri, S., Langley, A.,… Damms, J. (2004). The efficacy of donepezil in the treatment of neuropsychiatric symptoms in Alzheimer disease. *Neurology, 63*(2), 214–219. doi:63/2/214

Holtzer, R., Scarmeas, N., Wegesin, D. J., Albert, M., Brandt, J., Dubois, B., … Stern, Y. (2005). Depressive symptoms in Alzheimer's disease: Natural course and temporal relation to function and cognitive status. *Journal of the American Geriatrics Society, 53*(12), 2083–2089. doi:10.1111/j.1532-5415.2005.00535.x

Houde, M., Bergman, H., Whitehead, V., & Chertkow, H. (2008). A predictive depression pattern in mild cognitive impairment. *International Journal of Geriatric Psychiatry, 23*(10), 1028–1033. doi:10.1002/gps.2028

Hudon, C., Belleville, S., & Gauthier, S. (2008). The association between depressive and cognitive symptoms in amnestic mild cognitive impairment. *International Psychogeriatrics, 20*(4), 710–723. doi:10.1017/s1041610208007114

Hudon, C., Voyer, P., Tremblay, I., Tardif, S., & Carmichael, P.-H. (2010). Differentiation of the pattern of cognitive impairment between depressed and non-depressed patients with dementia living in long-term care facilities. *Aging & Mental Health, 14*(3), 293–302. doi:10.1080/13607860903191390

Hutchinson, A. D., & Mathias, J. L. (2007). Neuropsychological deficits in frontotemporal dementia and Alzheimer's disease: A meta-analytic review. *Journal of Neurology, Neurosurgery & Psychiatry, 78*(9), 917–928. doi:10.1136/jnnp.2006.100669

Hwang, T. J., Masterman, D. L., Ortiz, F., Fairbanks, L. A., & Cummings, J. L. (2004). Mild cognitive impairment is associated with characteristic neuropsychiatric symptoms. *Alzheimer Disease & Associated Disorders, 18*(1), 17–21.

Jefferies, E., Hoffman, P., Jones, R., & Lambon Ralph, M. A. (2008). The impact of semantic impairment on verbal short-term memory in stroke aphasia and semantic dementia: A comparative study. *Journal of Memory and Language, 58*(1), 66–87. doi:10.1016/j.jml.2007.06.004

Jehkonen, M., Laihosalo, M., & Kettunen, J. (2006). Anosognosia after stroke: Assessment, occurrence, subtypes and impact on functional outcome reviewed. *Acta Neurologica Scandinavica, 114*(5), 293–306. doi:10.1111/j.1600-0404.2006.00723.x

Kang, E. K., Sohn, H. M., Han, M.-K., Kim, W., Han, T. R., & Paik, N. -J. (2010). Severity of post-stroke aphasia according to aphasia type and lesion location in Koreans. *Journal of Korean Medical Science, 25*(1), 123. doi: 10.3346/jkms.2010.25.1.123

Kauhanen, M., Korpelainen, J. T., Hiltunen, P., Brusin, E., Mononen, H., Maatta, R.,… Myllyla, V. V. (1999). Poststroke depression correlates with cognitive impairment and neurological deficits. *Stroke, 30*(9), 1875–1880.

Kim, S. J., Moon, Y. S., Choi, N. K., Kim, Y. S., Son, K. B., Lee, S. K., & Kim D. (2004). Anatomical and clinical correlates of depression and anxiety after stroke. *Psychiatry Investigation, 1*(1), 44–49.

Kolb, B., & Wishaw, I. Q. (2009). *Fundamentals of human neuropsychology.* New York: Worth Publishers.

Kumar, R., Jorm, A. F., Parslow, R. A., & Sachdev, P. S. (2006). Depression in mild cognitive impairment in a community sample of individuals 60–64 years old. *International Psychogeriatrics, 18*(03), 471. doi:10.1017/s1041610205003005

Kuzis, G., Sabe, L., Tiberti, C., Dorrego, F., & Starkstein, S. E. (1999). Neuropsychological correlates of apathy and depression in patients with dementia. *Neurology, 52*(7), 1403–1407.

Kvaal, K., Ulstein, I., Nordhus, I. H., & Engedal, K. (2005). The Spielberger State-Trait Anxiety Inventory (STAI): The state scale in detecting mental disorders in geriatric patients. *International Journal of Geriatric Psychiatry, 20*(7), 629–634. doi:10.1002/gps.1330

Kyrozis, A., Potagas, C., Ghika, A., Tsimpouris, P. K., Virvidaki, E. S., & Vemmos, K. N. (2009). Incidence and predictors of post-stroke aphasia: The Arcadia Stroke Registry. *European Journal of Neurology, 16*(6), 733–739. doi:10.1111/j.1468-1331.2009.02580.x

Lam, L. C. W., Tam, C. W. C., Chiu, H. F. K., & Lui, V. W. C. (2007). Depression and apathy affect functioning in community active subjects with questionable dementia and mild Alzheimer's disease. *International Journal of Geriatric Psychiatry, 22*(5), 431–437. doi:10.1002/gps.1694

Landes, A. M., Sperry, S. D., & Strauss, M. E. (2005). Prevalence of apathy, dysphoria, and depression in relation to dementia severity in Alzheimer's disease. *The Journal of Neuropsychiatry and Clinical Neurosciences, 17*(3), 342–349. doi:17/3/34210.1176/appi.neuropsych.17.3.342

Landes, A. M., Sperry, S. D., Strauss, M. E., & Geldmacher, D. S. (2001). Apathy in Alzheimer's disease. *Journal of the American Geriatric Society, 49*(12), 1700–1707. doi:49282

Lazar, R. M., Speizer, A. E., Festa, J. R., Krakauer, J. W., & Marshall, R. S. (2008). Variability in language recovery after first-time stroke. *Journal of Neurology, Neurosurgery & Psychiatry, 79*(5), 530–534. doi: 10.1136/jnnp.2007.122457

Lee, A. C. K., Tang, S. W., Yu, G. K. K., & Cheung, R. T. F. (2007). Incidence and predictors of depression after stroke (DAS). *International Journal of Psychiatry in Clinical Practice, 11*(3), 200–206. doi:10.1080/13651500601091212

Lee, K. S., Cho, H. -S., Hong, C. H., Kim, D. G., & Oh, B. H. (2008). Differences in Neuropsychiatric Symptoms according to mild cognitive impairment Subtypes in the community. *Dementia and Geriatric Cognitive Disorders, 26*(3), 212–217. doi:10.1159/000153431

Lezak, M., Howieson, D. B., & Loring, D. W. (2004). *Neuropsychological assessment* (4th ed.). New York, NY: Oxford University Press.

Li, Y. S., Meyer, J. S., & Thornby, J. (2001). Longitudinal follow-up of depressive symptoms among normal versus cognitively impaired elderly. *International Journal of Geriatric Psychiatry, 16*(7), 718–727.

Lökk, J., & Delbari, A. (2010). Management of depression in elderly stroke patients. *Neuropsychiatric Disease and Treatment, 6*, 539–549. doi:10.2147/ndt.s7637

Lopez, O. L., Becker, J. T., Sweet, R. A., Klunk, W., Kaufer, D. I., Saxton, J., ... DeKosky, S. T. (2003). Psychiatric symptoms vary with the severity of dementia in probable Alzheimer's disease. *The Journal of Neuropsychiatry and Clinical Neurosciences, 15*(3), 346–353.

Lopez, O. L., Boller, F., Becker, J. T., Miller, M., & Reynolds, C. F., 3rd. (1990). Alzheimer's disease and depression: Neuropsychological impairment and progression of the illness. *American Journal of Psychiatry, 147*(7), 855–860.

Lu, P. H., Edland, S. D., Teng, E., Tingus, K., Petersen, R. C., & Cummings, J. L. (2009). Donepezil delays progression to AD in MCI subjects with depressive symptoms. *Neurology, 72*(24), 2115–2121. doi:72/24/2115 10.1212/WNL.0b013e3181aa52d3

Lyketsos, C. G., DelCampo, L., Steinberg, M., Miles, Q., Steele, C. D., Munro, C., ... Rabins, P. V. (2003). Treating depression in Alzheimer disease: Efficacy and safety of sertraline therapy, and the benefits of depression reduction: the DIADS. *Archives of General Psychiatry, 60*(7), 737–746. doi:10.1001/archpsyc.60.7.73760/7/737

Lyketsos, C. G., Lopez, O., Jones, B., Fitzpatrick, A. L., Breitner, J., & DeKosky, S. (2002). Prevalence of neuropsychiatric symptoms in dementia and mild cognitive impairment: Results from the cardiovascular health study. *Journal of the American Medical Association, 288*(12), 1475–1483. doi:joc20689

Lyketsos, C. G., & Olin, J. (2002). Depression in Alzheimer's disease: Overview and treatment. *Biological Psychiatry, 52*(3), 243–252. doi:S0006322302013483

Lyketsos, C. G., Sheppard, J. M., Steele, C. D., Kopunek, S., Steinberg, M., Baker, A. S., ... Rabins, P. V. (2000). Randomized, placebo-controlled, double-blind clinical trial of sertraline in the treatment of depression complicating Alzheimer's disease: Initial results from the depression in Alzheimer's disease study. *American Journal of Psychiatry, 157*(10), 1686–1689.

Lyketsos, C. G., Steele, C., Baker, L., Galik, E., Kopunek, S., Steinberg, M., & Warren, A. (1997). Major and minor depression in Alzheimer's disease: Prevalence and impact. *The Journal of Neuropsychiatry and Clinical Neurosciences, 9*(4), 556–561.

Magai, C., Kennedy, G., Cohen, C. I., & Gomberg, D. (2000). A controlled clinical trial of sertraline in the treatment of depression in nursing home patients with late-stage Alzheimer's disease. *American Journal Geriatric Psychiatry, 8*(1), 66–74.

Malloy, P. F., & Boyle, P. A. (2005, November 1). Apathy and its treatment in Alzheimer's disease and other dementias. *Psychiatric Times*, 29.

Mayer, L. S., Bay, R. C., Politis, A., Steinberg, M., Steele, C., Baker, A. S., ... Lyketsos, C. G. (2006). Comparison of three rating scales as outcome measures for treatment trials of depression in Alzheimer disease: Findings from DIADS. *International Journal of Geriatric Psychiatry, 21*(10), 930–936. doi:10.1002/gps.1583

Mayo, N. E., Fellows, L. K., Scott, S. C., Cameron, J., & Wood-Wood-Dauphinee, S. (2009). A longitudinal view of apathy and its impact after stroke. *Stroke, 40*(10), 3299–3307. doi:10.1161/strokeaha.109.554410

McKhann, G., Drachman, D., Folstein, M., Katzman, R., Price, D., & Stadlan, E. M. (1984). Clinical diagnosis of Alzheimer's disease. Report of the NINCDS—ADRDA work group under the auspices of the Department of Health and Human Services Task Force on Alzheimer's disease. *Neurology, 34*(7), 939–944.

McPherson, S., Fairbanks, L., Tiken, S., Cummings, J. L., & Back-Madruga, C. (2002). Apathy and executive function in Alzheimer's disease. *Journal of the International Neuropsychological Society, 8*(3), 373–381.

Mega, M. S., Cummings, J. L., Fiorello, T., & Gornbein, J. (1996). The spectrum of behavioral changes in Alzheimer's disease. *Neurology, 46*(1), 130–135.

Michelsen, K. A., Prickaerts, J., & Steinbusch, H. W. M. (2008). The dorsal raphe nucleus and serotonin: implications for neuroplasticity linked to major depression and Alzheimer's disease. *Progress in Brain Research, 172*, 233–264.

Modrego, P. J., & Ferr á ndez, J. (2004). Depression in patients with mild cognitive impairment increases the risk of developing dementia of Alzheimer type: A prospective cohort study. *Archives of Neurology, 61*(8), 1290–1293. doi:10.1001/archneur.61.8.129061/8/1290

Mossello, E., Boncinelli, M., Caleri, V., Cavallini, M. C., Palermo, E., Di Bari, M., et al. (2008). Is antidepressant treatment associated with reduced cognitive decline in Alzheimer's disease? *Dementia and Geriatric Cognitive Disorders, 25*(4), 372–379. doi:10.1159/000121334

Mulin, E., Leone, E., Dujardin, K., Delliaux, M., Leentjens, A., Nobili, F., ... Robert, P. H. (2011). Diagnostic criteria for apathy in clinical practice. *International Journal of Geriatric Psychiatry, 26*(2), 158–165. doi:10.1002/gps.2508

Mullerthomsen, T., Arlt, S., Mann, U., Mas, R., & Ganzer, S. (2005). Detecting depression in Alzheimer's disease: evaluation of four different scales. *Archives of Clinical Neuropsychology, 20*(2), 271–276. doi:10.1016/j.acn.2004.03.010

Murray, L. L. (1999). Review Attention and aphasia: theory, research and clinical implications. *Aphasiology, 13*(2), 91–111. doi:10.1080/026870399402226

Murray, L. L. (2011). Direct and indirect treatment approaches for addressing short-term or working memory deficits in aphasia. *Aphasiology,* 1–21. doi:10.1080/02687 038.2011.589894

Nakaaki, S., Murata, Y., Sato, J., Shinagawa, Y., Hongo, J., Tatsumi, H., ... Furukawa, T. A. (2008). Association between apathy/depression and executive function in patients with Alzheimer's disease. *International Psychogeriatrics, 20*(5), 964–975. doi:10.1017/ s1041610208007308

Nakaaki, S., Murata, Y., Sato, J., Shinagawa, Y., Tatsumi, H., Hirono, N., & Furukawa, T. A. (2007). Greater impairment of Ability in the Divided Attention Task Is Seen in Alzheimer's disease patients with depression than in Those without depression. *Dementia and Geriatric Cognitive Disorders, 23*(4), 231–240. doi:10.1159/000099633

Nakhutina, L., Borod, J., & Zgaljardic, D. (2006). Posed prosodic emotional expression in unilateral stroke patients: Recovery, lesion location, and emotional perception. *Archives of Clinical Neuropsychology, 21*(1), 1–13. doi:10.1016/j.acn.2005.06.013

Nys, G. M., van Zandvoort, M. J., van der Worp, H. B., de Haan, E. H., de Kort, P. L., & Kappelle, L. J. (2005). Early depressive symptoms after stroke: neuropsychological correlates and lesion characteristics. *Journal of Neurological Sciences, 228*(1), 27–33. doi:S0022–510X(04)00349–110.1016/j.jns.2004.09.031

Okada, K., Kobayashi, S., Yamagata, S., Takahashi, K., & Yamaguchi, S. (1997). Poststroke apathy and regional cerebral blood flow. *Stroke, 28*(12), 2437–2441.

Orfei, M. D., Caltagirone, C., & Spalletta, G. (2009). The evaluation of anosognosia in stroke patients. *Cerebrovascular Diseases, 27*(3), 280–289. doi:10.1159/000199466

Ownby, R. L., Crocco, E., Acevedo, A., John, V., & Loewenstein, D. (2006). Depression and risk for Alzheimer disease: Systematic review, meta-analysis, and metaregression analysis. *Archives of General Psychiatry, 63*(5), 530–538.

Pachana, N. A., Byrne, G. J., Siddle, H., Koloski, N., Harley, E., & Arnold, E. (2006). Development and validation of the Geriatric Anxiety Inventory. *International Psychogeriatrics, 19*(01), 103. doi:10.1017/s1041610206003504

Palmer, K., Berger, A. K., Monastero, R., Winblad, B., Backman, L., & Fratiglioni, L. (2007). Predictors of progression from mild cognitive impairment to Alzheimer disease. *Neurology, 68*(19), 1596–1602. doi: 68/19/1596 10.1212/01. wnl.0000260968.92345.3f

Panza, F., Frisardi, V., Capurso, C., D' Introno, A., Colacicco, A. M., Imbimbo, B. P., ... Solfrizzi, V. (2010). Late-Life depression, mild cognitive impairment, and dementia: Possible Continuum? *American Journal of Geriatric Psychiatry, 18*(2), 98–116. doi: 10.1097/JGP.0b013e3181b0fa13

Pedersen, P. M., Vinter, K., & Olsen, T. S. (2004). Aphasia after stroke: Type, severity and prognosis. The Copenhagen aphasia study. *Cerebrovascular Diseases, 17*(1), 35–43. doi:10.1159/000073896

Penn, C., Frankel, T., Watermeyer, J., & Russell, N. (2010). Executive function and conversational strategies in bilingual aphasia. *Aphasiology, 24*(2), 288–308. doi:10.1080/02687030902958399

Petersen, R. C. (2004). Mild cognitive impairment as a diagnostic entity. *Journal of Internal Medicine, 256*(3), 183–194. doi:10.1111/j.1365-2796.2004.01388.x

Petersen, R. C., Doody, R., Kurz, A., Mohs, R. C., Morris, J. C., Rabins, P. V., ... Winblad, B. (2001). Current concepts in mild cognitive impairment. *Archives of Neurology, 58*(12), 1985–1992. doi:10.1001/archneur.58.12.1985

Petersen, R. C., Roberts, R. O., Knopman, D. S., Boeve, B. F., Geda, Y. E., Ivnik, R. J.,... Jack, C. R. (2009). Mild cognitive impairment: Ten years later. *Archives of Neurology, 66*(12), 1447–1455. doi:10.1001/archneurol.2009.266

Petersen, R. C., Smith, G. E., Waring, S. C., Ivnik, R. J., Tangalos, E. G., & Kokmen, E. (1999). Mild cognitive impairment: Clinical characterization and outcome. *Archives of Neurology, 56*(3), 303–308. doi:10.1001/archneur.56.3.303

Petracca, G. M., Chemerinski, E., & Starkstein, S. E. (2001). A double-blind, placebo-controlled study of fluoxetine in depressed patients with Alzheimer's disease. *International Psychogeriatrics, 13*(2), 233–240.

Pirscoveanu, D., Zaharia, Tudorica, Matcau, Ene, & Ciobanu, (2008). Study on correlation between post stroke depression and cognitive impairment. *Romanian Journal of Neurology, 7*(3), 106.

Pohjasvaara, T., Leskela, M., Vataja, R., Kalska, H., Ylikoski, R., Hietanen, M.,... Erkinjuntti, T. (2002). Post-stroke depression, executive dysfunction and functional outcome. European Journal of Neurology, 9(3), 269–275. doi: 396

Porta-Etessam, J., Tobaruela-González, J. L., & Rabes-Berendes, C. (2011). Depression in patients with moderate Alzheimer disease: A prospective observational cohort study. *Alzheimer Disease & Associated Disorders, 25*(4), 317–325. doi:10.1097/WAD.0b013e31820e7c45

Powlishta, K. K., Storandt, M., Mandernach, T. A., Hogan, E., Grant, E. A., & Morris, J.C. (2004). Absence of effect of depression on cognitive performance in early-stage Alzheimer disease. Archives of Neurology, 61(8), 1265–1268. doi:10.1001/archneur.61.8.126561/8/1265

Prado-Jean, A., Couratier, P., Druet-Cabanac, M., Nubukpo, P., Bernard-Bourzeix, L., Thomas, P., ... Clément, J. P. (2010). Specific psychological and behavioral symptoms of depression in patients with dementia. *International Journal of Geriatric Psychiatry, 25*(10), 1065–1072. doi:10.1002/gps.2468

Prigerson, H. G. (2003). Costs to society of family caregiving for patients with end-stage Alzheimer's disease. *New England Journal of Medicine, 349*(20), 1891–1892. doi:10.1056/NEJMp038157

Provinciali, L., & Coccia, M. (2002). Post-stroke and vascular depression: A critical review. *Neurological Sciences, 22*(6), 417–428. doi:10.1007/s100720200000

Provinciali, L., Paolucci, S., Torta, R., Toso, V., Gobbi, B., & Gandolfo, C. (2008). Depression after first-ever ischemic stroke: The prognostic role of neuroanatomic subtypes in clinical practice. *Cerebrovascular Diseases, 26*(6), 592–599. doi:10.1159/000165112

Purdy, M. (2002). Executive function ability in persons with aphasia. *Aphasiology, 16*(4–6), 549–557. doi:10.1080/02687030244000176

Ramakers, I. H. G. B., Visser, P. J., Aalten, P., Kester, A., Jolles, J., & Verhey, F. R. J. (2009). Affective symptoms as predictors of Alzheimer's disease in subjects with mild cognitive impairment: A 10-year follow-up study. *Psychological Medicine, 40*(07), 1193–1201. doi:10.1017/s0033291709991577

Rasquin, S., Lodder, J., & Verhey, F. (2005). The association between psychiatric and cognitive symptoms after stroke: A prospective study. *Cerebrovascular Disorders, 19*(5), 309–316. doi:8449910.1159/000084499

Ready, R. E., Ott, B. R., Grace, J., & Cahn-Weiner, D. A. (2003). Apathy and executive dysfunction in mild cognitive impairment and Alzheimer disease. *American Journal of Geriatric Psychiatry, 11*(2), 222–228.

Robert, P., Berr, C., Volteau, M., Bertogliati, C., Benoit, M., Mahieux, F., ... Dubois, B. (2006a). Neuropsychological performance in mild cognitive impairment with and without apathy. *Dementia and Geriatric Cognitive Disorders, 21*(3), 192–197. doi:10.1159/000090766

Robert, P., Berr, C., Volteau, M., Bertogliati, C., Benoit, M., Sarazin, M., ... Dubois, B. (2006b). Apathy in patients with mild cognitive impairment and the risk of developing dementia of Alzheimer's disease: A one-year follow-up study. *Clinical Neurology and Neurosurgery, 108*(8), 733–736. doi:10.1016/j.clineuro.2006.02.003

Robert, P., Clairet, S., Benoit, M., Koutaich, J., Bertogliati, C., Tible, O., ... Bedoucha, P. (2002). The Apathy Inventory: Assessment of apathy and awareness in Alzheimer's disease, Parkinson's disease and mild cognitive impairment. *International Journal of Geriatric Psychiatry, 17*(12), 1099–1105. doi:10.1002/gps.755

Robinson, R. G. (2003). Poststroke depression: prevalence, diagnosis, treatment, and disease progression. *Biological Psychiatry, 54*(3), 376–387. doi:S0006322303004232

Rockwood, K. (2004). Size of the treatment effect on cognition of cholinesterase inhibition in Alzheimer's disease. *Journal of Neurology, Neurosurgery & Psychiatry, 75*(5), 677–685. doi:10.1136/jnnp.2003.029074

Rosenberg, P. B., Drye, L. T., Martin, B. K., Frangakis, C., Mintzer, J. E., Weintraub, D.,... Lyketsos, C. G. (2010). Sertraline for the treatment of depression in Alzheimer disease. *American Journal of Geriatric Psychiatry, 18*(2), 136–145. doi:10.1097/JGP.0b013e3181c796eb

Ross, E. D., & Monnot, M. (2008). Neurology of affective prosody and its functional–anatomic organization in right hemisphere. *Brain and Language, 104*(1), 51–74. doi:10.1016/j.bandl.2007.04.007

Rozzini, L., Chilovi, B. V., Peli, M., Conti, M., Rozzini, R., Trabucchi, M., & Padovani, A. (2009). Anxiety symptoms in mild cognitive impairment. *International Journal of Geriatric Psychiatry, 24*(3), 300–305. doi:10.1002/gps.2106

Rozzini, L., Chilovi, B. V., Trabucchi, M., & Padovani, A. (2005). Depression is unrelated to conversion to dementia in patients with mild cognitive impairment. *Archives of Neurology, 62*(3), 505; author reply 505–506. doi: 62/3/505 10.1001/archneur.62.3.505-a

Rozzini, L., Chilovi, B. V., Trabucchi, M., & Padovani, A. (2008). Re: Predictors of progression from mild cognitive impairment to Alzheimer disease. *Neurology, 70*(9), 735; author reply 735–736. doi:70/9/73510.1212/01.wnl.0000307674.94539.09

Rozzini, L., Vicini Chilovi, B., Conti, M., Delrio, I., Borroni, B., Trabucchi, M., & Padovani, A. (2008). Neuropsychiatric symptoms in amnestic and nonamnestic mild cognitive impairment. *Dementia and Geriatric Cognitive Disorders, 25*(1), 32–36. doi:10.1159/000111133

Rubin, E. H., Kinscherf, D. A., Grant, E. A., & Storandt, M. (1991). The influence of major depression on clinical and psychometric assessment of senile dementia of the Alzheimer type. *American Journal of Psychiatry, 148*(9), 1164–1171.

Santos, M., Kovari, E., Gold, G., Bozikas, V. P., Hof, P. R., Bouras, C., & Giannakopoulos, P. (2009). The neuroanatomical model of post-stroke depression: Towards a change of focus? *Journal of the Neurological Sciences, 283*(1–2), 158–162. doi:S0022-510X(09)00430–410.1016/j.jns.2009.02.334

Schepers, V. P., Visser-Meily, A. M., Ketelaar, M., & Lindeman, E. (2006). Poststroke fatigue: Course and its relation to personal and stroke-related factors. *Archives of Physical Medicine and Rehabilitation, 87*(2), 184–188. doi:10.1016/j.apmr.2005.10.005

Schuurmans, J., & Balkom, A. (2011). Late-life anxiety disorders: A review. *Current Psychiatry Reports, 13*(4), 267–273. doi:10.1007/s11920-011-0204-4

Seignourel, P. J., Kunik, M. E., Snow, L., Wilson, N., & Stanley, M. (2008). Anxiety in dementia: A critical review. *Clinical Psychology Review, 28*(7), 1071–1082. doi:10.1016/j.cpr.2008.02.008

Seniów, J., Litwin, M., & Leśniak, M. (2009). The relationship between non-linguistic cognitive deficits and language recovery in patients with aphasia. *Journal of the Neurological Sciences, 283*(1–2), 91–94. doi:10.1016/j.jns.2009.02.315

Shimoda, K., & Robinson, R. G. (1998). Effects of anxiety disorder on impairment and recovery from stroke. *The Journal of Neuropsychiatry and Clinical Neurosciences, 10*(1), 34–40.

Siegal, M., & Varley, R. (2006). Aphasia, language, and theory of mind. *Social Neuroscience, 1*(3–4), 167–174. doi:10.1080/17470910600985597

Spalletta, G., Baldinetti, F., Buccione, I., Fadda, L., Perri, R., Scalmana, S., . . . Caltagirone, C. (2004). Cognition and behaviour are independent and heterogeneous dimensions in Alzheimer's disease. *Journal of Neurology, 251*(6), 688–695. doi:10.1007/s00415-004-0403-6

Starkstein, S. E. (2006). A prospective longitudinal study of apathy in Alzheimer's disease. *Journal of Neurology, Neurosurgery & Psychiatry, 77*(1), 8–11. doi:10.1136/jnnp.2005.069575

Starkstein, S. E., Fedoroff, J. P., Price, T. R., Leiguarda, R., & Robinson, R. G. (1993). Apathy following cerebrovascular lesions. *Stroke, 24*(11), 1625–1630. doi:10.1161/01.str.24.11.1625

Starkstein, S. E., Mizrahi, R., & Power, B. D. (2008). Depression in Alzheimer's disease: Phenomenology, clinical correlates and treatment. *International Review of Psychiatry, 20*(4), 382–388. doi:10.1080/09540260802094480

Steinberg, M., Shao, H., Zandi, P., Lyketsos, C. G., Welsh-Bohmer, K. A., Norton, M. C., . . . Tschanz, J. T. (2008). Point and 5-year period prevalence of neuropsychiatric symptoms in dementia: The Cache County Study. *International Journal of Geriatric Psychiatry, 23*(2), 170–177. doi:10.1002/gps.1858

Stout, J. C., Ready, R. E., Grace, J., Malloy, P. F., & Paulsen, J. S. (2003). Factor analysis of the Frontal Systems Behavior Scale (FrSBe). *Assessment, 10*(1), 79–85. doi:10.1177/1073191102250339

Strober, L. B., & Arnett, P. A. (2009). Assessment of depression in three medically ill, elderly populations: Alzheimer's disease, Parkinson's disease, and stroke. *The Clinical Neuropsychologist, 23*(2), 205–230. doi:10.1080/13854040802003299

Teng, E., Lu, P. H., & Cummings, J. L. (2007). Neuropsychiatric symptoms are associated with progression from mild cognitive impairment to Alzheimer's disease. *Dementia and Geriatric Cognitive Disorders, 24*(4), 253–259. doi:10.1159/000107100

Tharwani, H. M., Yerramsetty, P., Mannelli, P., Patkar, A., & Masand, P. (2007). Recent advances in poststroke depression. *Current Psychiatry Reports, 9*(3), 225–231.

Thomas, S. A., & Lincoln, N. B. (2006). Factors relating to depression after stroke. *British Journal of Clinical Psychology, 45*(1), 49–61. doi:10.1348/014466505x34183

Trinh, N. H. (2003). Efficacy of cholinesterase inhibitors in the treatment of neuropsychiatric symptoms and functional impairment in Alzheimer disease: A meta-analysis.

Journal of the American Medical Association, 289(2), 210–216. doi:10.1001/jama.289.2.210

Vallat, C., Azouvi, P., Hardisson, H., Meffert, R., Tessier, C., & Pradat-Diehl, P. (2005). Rehabilitation of verbal working memory after left hemisphere stroke. *Brain Injury, 19*(13), 1157–1164. doi:10.1080/02699050500110595

Ween, J. E., Verfaellie, M., & Alexander, M. P. (1996). Verbal memory function in mild aphasia. *Neurology, 47*(3), 795–801.

Wefel, J. S., Hoyt, B. D., & Massma, P. J. (1999). Neuropsychological functioning in depressed versus nondepressed participants with Alzheimer's disease. *The Clinical Neuropsychologist, 13*(3), 249–257. doi:10.1076/clin.13.3.249.1746

Whyte, E. M., Mulsant, B. H., Vanderbilt, J., Dodge, H. H., & Ganguli, M. (2004). Depression after stroke: A prospective epidemiological study. *Journal of the American Geriatric Society, 52*(5), 774–778. doi:10.1111/j.1532-5415.2004.52217.xJGS52217

Wilson, R. S., Hoganson, G. M., Rajan, K. B., Barnes, L. L., Mendes de Leon, C. F., & Evans, D. A. (2010). Temporal course of depressive symptoms during the development of Alzheimer disease. *Neurology, 75*(1), 21–26. doi:75/1/2110.1212/WNL.0b013e3181e620c5

Wilz, G., & Barskova, T. (2007). Predictors of Psychological and somatic components of Poststroke depression: A longitudinal study. *Topics in Stroke Rehabilitation, 14*(3), 25–40. doi:10.1310/tsr1403-25

Winblad, B., Palmer, K., Kivipelto, M., Jelic, V., Fratiglioni, L., Wahlund, L., & ... Petersen, R. (2004). Mild cognitive impairment—beyond controversies, towards a consensus: Report of the International Working Group on Mild Cognitive Impairment. *Journal of Internal Medicine, 256*(3), 240–246.

Withall, A., Brodaty, H., Altendorf, A., & Sachdev, P. S. (2010). A longitudinal study examining the independence of apathy and depression after stroke: The Sydney Stroke Study. *International Psychogeriatrics, 23*(02), 264–273. doi:10.1017/s1041610209991116

Wright, H., Newhoff, M., Downey, R., & Austermann, S. (2003). Abstracts presented at the Thirty-First Annual International Neuropsychological Society Conference. *Journal of the International Neuropsychological Society, 9*, 135–330.

Yamagata, S., Yamaguchi, S., & Kobayashi, S. (2004). Impaired novelty processing in apathy after subcortical stroke. *Stroke, 35*(8), 1935–1940. doi:10.1161/01.STR.0000135017.51144.c9

Yang, Z. H., Zhao, X. Q., Wang, C. X., Chen, H. Y., & Zhang, Y. M. (2008). Neuroanatomic correlation of the post-stroke aphasias studied with imaging. *Neurological Research, 30*(4), 356–360. doi:10.1179/174313208X300332

Yu, L., Liu, C. K., Chen, J. W., Wang, S. Y., Wu, Y. H., & Yu, S. H. (2004). Relationship between post-stroke depression and lesion location: A meta-analysis. *Kaohsiung Journal of Medical Sciences, 20*(8), 372–380. doi:S1607-551X(09)70173-1

Secondary Influences on Neuropsychological Test Performance in Epilepsy

DALIN PULSIPHER, BRUCE HERMANN, DAVID LORING,
BRIAN BELL, AND MICHAEL SEIDENBERG

Epilepsy is a prevalent neurological disorder affecting an estimated 100 million people worldwide (World Health Organization, 2012). In addition to the important defining features of epilepsy, which include epilepsy syndrome, seizure frequency, and seizure severity, there is increasing awareness of the cognitive, behavioral, and medical comorbidities of the epilepsies. The term comorbidity is used here to refer to the occurrence of two clinical conditions with a greater frequency than that found in the general population (Gaitatzis, Trimble, & Sander, 2004; Tellez-Zenteno, Matijevic, & Wiebe, 2005). As reported by Boro and Haut (2003), "nearly every patient with epilepsy will experience a comorbid medical condition at some point during the course of treatment." These comorbidities not only affect health-related quality of life (HRQOL) but in many instances also exert secondary influences on neuropsychological test performance. In this chapter, we review several of the common neurobehavioral and medical comorbidities of epilepsy that may exert secondary influences on neuropsychological test performance.

NEUROPSYCHOLOGICAL COMORBIDITY

It has been appreciated for some time that epilepsy may adversely affect cognitive status. One of earliest formal studies examining cognitive impairment compared two epilepsy groups ("comparatively normal" and "marked dementia") to healthy controls (Smith, 1905). Epilepsy patients with "marked dementia" were found to be impaired on a number of measures, but of particular interest was the finding that this group showed an even greater impairment in "confusion between old and new" items during recognition memory testing, with a higher frequency of false-positive errors. "Everyone forgets many things from day to day, while errors of confusion occur relatively seldom and are much more noticeable when they do occur" (Smith, 1905). In a later report employing a more formal psychometric approach with standard testing with the Binet-Simon intelligence scale, institutionalized patients with epilepsy were found to have reduced scores, but they still had higher Binet-Simon mental ages than institutionalized patients who were classified as "feeble-minded" (Wallin, 1912). From these early beginnings, neuropsychological assessment has become an increasingly important component of patient care, and careful clinical work has identified a number of influences on task performance, several of which will be discussed here.

Antiepilepsy Medications

A potential secondary influence on neuropsychological performance among patients with epilepsy involves the very medications used to treat the disorder. Prior to the introduction of effective antiepilepsy drugs (AEDs) in the mid-nineteenth century, epilepsy was considered to be a progressive degenerative brain disease (Gross, 1992). Effective AEDs have permitted the separation of the effects of frequent uncontrolled seizures from those associated with underlying brain structure and epilepsy syndrome. Fortunately, the catastrophic epilepsy syndromes, such as Lennox-Gastaut, Sturge-Weber, or infantile spasms, occur relatively infrequently.

The introduction of AEDs for seizure control, however, adds a potentially new contributing factor to cognitive impairment in patients with epilepsy. Because AEDs decrease membrane excitability, increase postsynaptic inhibition, or alter synchronization of neural networks, AEDs are often associated with neuropsychological side effects (Meador, 2005). The importance of AED-induced cognitive comorbidity is that AED selection is under the control of the treating physician and family, and rational drug use considering AED-induced cognitive comorbidities can be used to guide treatment decisions. In one large phase III clinical trial establishing differential AED effectiveness in treating childhood absence epilepsy, ethosuximide was proposed as the initial recommended treatment over valproate because, despite comparable efficacy in treating seizures and normalizing the electroencephalogram (EEG), ethosuximide was associated with less attentional impairment (Glauser et al., 2010).

Of the older AEDs that were introduced prior to the 1990s, the greatest risk of cognitive impairment is associated with phenobarbital. In young children who were treated with phenobarbital following a febrile seizure for epilepsy prophylaxis, phenobarbital was associated with an IQ decline of slightly greater than ½ standard deviation (Fawell et al., 1990). Neuropsychological AED profiles are generally comparable for the other older-generation medications that include carbamazepine (CBZ), phenytoin (PHT), and valproate (VPA), as they display a similar pattern of a very mild encephalopathy such as would be expected in conditions like hyponatremia. Each AED is associated with modest psychomotor slowing accompanied by decreased attention and memory, and these cognitive side effects generally emerge according to a dose-dependent relationship (Loring, Marino, & Meador, 2007). Although the treating physician often is not concerned about AED side effects when anticonvulsant blood levels are within standard therapeutic ranges, quality of life and memory deficits may be seen with these medications even when serum concentrations are within standard therapeutic ranges (Gilliam, 2002; Meador et al., 1991).

With the exception of topiramate and possibly zonisamide, most newer-generation AEDs have more favorable tolerability and neuropsychological profiles than those of their predecessors. Like older-generation AEDs, the risk of cognitive impairment with topiramate is dose dependent (Loring, Williamson, Meador, Wiegand, & Hulihan, 2011) and does not habituate but affects different cognitive mechanisms, involving language output and "frontal lobe" functions (Kockelmann, Elger, & Helmstaedter, 2003; Martin et al., 1999). Although there is a tendency for drug-induced side effects to be greatest right after initiating treatment and then to habituate over time, individual patients who experience AED-related cognitive decline can often be identified within weeks of starting treatment so that different treatment approaches can be considered before prolonged complications occur.

AEDs are also a consideration for women with epilepsy of childbearing age, as recent research has characterized the in utero effects of AEDs on the fetus and subsequent cognitive development. The AED treatment of epilepsy in women of childbearing potential poses risks to the developing fetus and requires the balancing of risks that seizures pose to the mother and child with the risks of teratogenesis (i.e., congenital malformations and cognitive deficits). AEDs are one of the most common potentially teratogenic drugs taken by women of childbearing age and are associated with fetal risks including prematurity and low birth rate, congenital malformations, and even death (Perucca, 2005). In addition to anatomical abnormalities, AEDs can also contribute to neurobehavioral complications, including developmental delay, behavioral problems, and reduced school achievement (Palac & Meador, 2011). Of the various AEDs commonly used during pregnancy, VPA poses the most consistent, frequent, and severe risks for both anatomical and behavioral teratogenesis. In a recent prospective trial (Meador et al., 2009), children exposed to VPA had IQs 6–9 points lower than that of children exposed to other AEDs, a finding consistent with multiple retrospective analyses (Adab et al., 2004; Gaily et al., 2004). Children whose mothers took preconception folate exhibited higher IQ, which suggests its beneficial effect in the context of VPA. Across multiple studies, verbal abilities appear to be more affected by AEDs (and in particular, VPA) than nonverbal abilities. Fetal VPA exposure is associated with lower IQ and reduced cognitive abilities across a range of domains. Unfortunately, seizures in some women with generalized epilepsy can only be controlled by VPA, and it appears that fetal risks occur in a dose-dependent fashion. However, the evidence is certainly sufficiently strong that VPA should not be used as the initial treatment choice in women of childbearing age.

Developmental Comorbidities

Children with epilepsy have increased rates of learning disabilities as well as behavioral and attentional difficulties. In 1955, Ounsted was among the first to call attention to the syndrome of hyperkinetic disorder in children with epilepsy, including features of overactivity, distractibility, poor impulse control, and behavior problems (Ounsted, 1955). More contemporary studies now suggest that the general rate of attention deficit/hyperactivity disorder (ADHD) in pediatric epilepsy ranges from 10% to 40% (Dunn, 2011). The influence of AEDs is often cited as a potential cause for the observed co-occurrence, and several AED medications can produce the core symptoms of ADHD (e.g., high activity, aggressiveness, distractibility). However, ADHD has also been reported to predate the first seizure (and AED treatment) in a substantial number of children (Dunn et al., 2003; Hermann et al., 2007).

The association between epilepsy and ADHD (temporal contiguity) is consistent with the notion of a common underlying pathophysiological mechanism for the two disorders, whereby the order of their appearance is influenced by either or both genetic and environmental factors (e.g., perinatal insult and head injury). Common biological mechanisms suggested for the co-occurrence include disruption of lipid metabolism, the norepinepherine system or the dopamine transporter system (Hesdorffer et al., 2004). Hermann et al. (2007) reported that ADHD was significantly overrepresented in children with new- or recent-onset idiopathic epilepsies compared to controls, especially the inattentive variant. Also, compared to children with new- or recent-onset epilepsy without ADHD, children with epilepsy with comorbid ADHD had significantly more neuropsychological abnormalities, including executive dysfunction, educational complications requiring school assistance, and additional behavioral problems. In addition, children with ADHD and new-onset epilepsy showed significant volumetric abnormalities, especially in frontal lobe, compared with children with epilepsy alone (Hermann et al., 2007). Genetic mechanisms have also been suggested for this. Animal studies have demonstrated that rats bred to be seizure prone are more likely to display symptoms of ADHD than rats not bred to be seizure prone (McIntyre & Gilby, 2007).

Treatment of ADHD in children with epilepsy with psychostimulants is sometimes avoided by physicians because of concerns that this may result in lower seizure threshold and increase seizure frequency. Although anecdotal reports of increased seizures have been made, studies in children with epilepsy and ADHD have shown that stimulants (methylphenidate) are not only safe but also as effective as in the general population. A recent review of the prevalence, causes, and treatment approaches in children with epilepsy and ADHD has been provided by Dunn (2011).

Behavioral and Psychiatric Comorbidities

Mood disorders are the most common psychiatric comorbidity in epilepsy, but other psychiatric conditions are also represented. As with cognitive impairments, behavioral comorbidities may be associated with the underlying epilepsy syndrome as well the AED therapy.

Interictal depression is the most common psychiatric comorbidity in epilepsy and occurs more frequently in epilepsy than in other neurological conditions and other chronic non-neurological conditions (LaFrance, Kanner, & Hermann, 2008). Until recently, depression was viewed as a reaction to epilepsy (e.g., stigma and poor quality of life). Multiple risk factors, including seizure-related characteristics and social coping and adaptation skills, have been identified in the comorbidity of depression and epilepsy (Gaitatzis et al., 2004). A wide range of seizure-related factors have been implicated in the development of depression, including limbic-related seizures (e.g., temporal lobe epilepsy), left-temporal lobe seizure onset—particularly when involving concomitant frontal dysfunction (Hermann, Seidenber, Haltiner, & Wyler, 1991). Psychosocial variables are acknowledged to play an important role in the co-occurrence of epilepsy and depression. Perceived stigma associated with epilepsy also significantly contributes to poor self-esteem, rejection by peers, and avoidance of age-appropriate activities and social isolation in children (Austin & Caplan, 2007). Gilliam (2002) reported a robust "dose-related" or linear relationship between interictal depressive symptoms and reduced HRQOL, such that the more frequent and severe the symptoms of depression, the poorer the subjects' HRQOL. In addition to mood, adverse AED side effects also were a significant predictor of reduced HRQOL, whereas traditional clinical epilepsy variables such as seizure frequency were unrelated to patient-reported quality of life.

Rates of psychiatric disorders other than mood, such as anxiety disorders, are also increased in epilepsy and behave in much the same way on measures of quality of life. Johnson, Jones, Seidenberg, and Hermann (2004) examined anxiety symptoms in adults with epilepsy and their impact on HRQOL in epilepsy and found a strong relationship between increasing symptoms of anxiety and lower HRQOL in a "dose dependent" fashion as suggested by Gilliam (2002). Furthermore, psychiatric symptoms (depression or anxiety) were stronger predictors of HRQOL than were several clinical epilepsy variables combined.

What is the impact of psychiatric disorder on neuropsychological status in epilepsy? Paradiso, Hermann, Blumer, Davies, and Robinson (2001) examined a large group of patients with chronic temporal-lobe epilepsy who were seen and evaluated by a psychiatrist who conducted an independent assessment of mood status. Depressed mood was associated with significant adverse effects across a wide range of neuropsychological domains, including general intelligence, language, visuoperceptual abilities, memory, and executive functioning. There was no difference in the frequency of depression in left versus right temporal-lobe epilepsy groups, and the effects of depression on neuropsychological status seemed to be somewhat accentuated in patients with left temporal-lobe epilepsy. However, this has been a mixed literature, and there are investigations that have (Paradiso et al., 2001) or have not (Tracy et al., 2007) found robust effects of depression on neuropsychological status in patients with epilepsy, while others have found "nested effects," such as worse verbal memory, in left temporal-lobe epilepsy patients with depression compared to those without depression (Dulay, Schefft, Fargo, Privitera, & Yeh, 2004).

Possibly helping to understand the complex relationship between depressogenic effects of epilepsy on cognition is that recent evidence indicating that major depression represents a risk factor for developing epilepsy (Hesdorffer, Hauser, Annegers, & Cascino, 2000; Schmitz, 2005). The temporal sequence of the occurrence of depression and epilepsy appears bidirectional. Psychiatric symptoms have been found to predate the onset of epilepsy in up to 45% of patients (Ekinci, Titus, Rodopman, Berkem, & Trevathan, 2009; Jones et al., 2007; Kanner, 2003). These findings are consistent with the hypothesis that a shared underlying pathophysiological mechanism may form the basis for both conditions. Suggested biochemical factors include decreased serotonin (5HT), noradrenaline (NE), glutamate, and GABA, as well as reduced folate metabolism (Kanner, 2003; Rösche, Uhlmann, & Fröscher, 2003). Several other lines of research support the shared pathophysiology model of depression and epilepsy. Patients with new-onset epilepsy with symptoms of depression and anxiety at the time of diagnosis were significantly less likely to be seizure free following 1 year of treatment (Petrovski et al., 2010). Similarly, in a surgical series of patients undergoing temporal lobectomy, patients with a lifetime history of depression were 7 times less likely to be free of disabling seizures and 19 times less likely to be free of all seizures, including auras, than patients without a psychiatric history (Kanner, 2009). Thus, multiple data sources suggest a bidirectional relationship between depression and epilepsy, and this may make it more difficult to detect clear relationships between mood and cognition in epilepsy.

Many patients with epilepsy also exhibit "subsyndromal depression," which involves significantly depressed mood that falls short of meeting full *DSM-IV* diagnostic criteria for major depression. The same is true for anxiety disorders in which subsyndromal anxiety can be seen. Because ongoing depressed mood is distinct from postictal behavior change, it has previously been referred to as "interictal dysphoric disorder" (Blumer, Montouris, & Davies, 2004). Subsyndromal depression is commonly identified on the basis of depressed mood score on screening instruments such as the Beck Depression Inventory.

There is, however, a strong relationship between depression and decreased HRQOL. Surprisingly, however, epilepsy patients with diagnosed major depressive disorder or subsyndromal depression do not differ on HRQOL measures. That is, patients with subsyndromal depression do not report higher quality of life than that of similar patients meeting diagnostic criteria. However, comorbid depression and anxiety are associated with decreased HRQOL relative to either alone, as reviewed above.

AEDs also involve treatment-emergent risks for behavior complications (e.g., hyperactivity or mood change). These can be observed in children as well as in adults and are present for both older AEDs and newer-generation AEDs. Because of findings from 199 clinical trials of 11 AEDs for three different indications (including epilepsy), the U.S. Food and Drug Administration (FDA) issued a class-wide alert about an increased risk for suicidality associated with the use of antiepilepsy medications. This warning has been criticized (Hesdorffer & Kanner, 2009), in part on the grounds of different mechanisms being associated with different AEDs, as well as overreliance on self-report, which inflates estimates of occurrence but illustrates important risks of behavioral change associated with AED treatment. Many behavioral adverse effects are dose related, although individual response is variable; children with lower IQ levels often appear to be at greater risk.

EFFECTS OF EPILEPSY AND MOOD DISORDERS ON SUBJECTIVE COGNITIVE COMPLAINTS

Among the cognitive problems that may be associated with epilepsy, its cause, and its treatment, memory is among the most serious. Surveys of persons with epilepsy consistently reveal elevated rates of complaints and concerns regarding cognitive function in general, and memory in particular (Au et al., 2006; Corcoran & Thompson, 1993; Giovagnoli, Mascheroni, & Avanzini, 1997; Gleissner, Helmstaedter, Quiske, & Elger, 1998; Hendriks, Aldenkamp, van der Vlugt, Alpherts, & Vermeulen, 2002; Lineweaver, Naugle, Cafaro, Bingaman, & Lüders, 2004; Piazzini, Canevini, Maggiori, & Canger, 2001; Thompson & Corcoran, 1992; Vermeulen, Aldenkamp, & Alpherts, 1993).

Although some epilepsy studies have reported a veridical relationship between objective memory data and patient self-appraisal of memory functioning, usually it is weak and failure to find any significant association is relatively common (Hall, Isaac, & Harris, 2009). While some neurological illnesses are associated with underestimation of deficits (Giacino & Cicerone, 1998; Orfei, Robinson, Bria, Caltagirone, & Spalletta, 2008), patients with temporal-lobe epilepsy who are carefully investigated as part of a surgical workup most often overestimate their degree of memory impairment (Baxendale & Thompson, 2005; Hall et al., 2009).

There are methodological concerns in this area of research. Most studies have focused mainly on cases with intractable epilepsy, and so the veracity of self-report in those with controlled seizures is less well known. In addition, some subjective memory questionnaires are too brief, include non-memory items, or do not directly assess the type of memory that is measured by objective tests or pertinent to everyday functioning (Gleissner et al., 1998; Hall et al., 2009). One potential problem with standardized objective tests is that memory typically is not measured after a delay of more than 30 minutes (Blake, Wroe, Breen, & McCarthy, 2000; Butler et al., 2009); the relevance of this omission for the majority of temporal lobe epilepsy patients remains to be determined (Bell, 2006; Giovagnoli, Casazza, & Avanzini, 1995).

Overall, the discrepancy between objective and subjective memory findings is best explained not by methodological limitations but by the influence of affective variables on subjective measures. For example, in one study, anxiety and depression questionnaire scores explained 58% of the variance in subjective memory (Piazzini et al., 2001). The association between emotional distress and overestimation of memory impairment also has been discovered in other patient groups (Hermann, 1982; Kapur & Pearson, 1983; Lezak, 1995; Marino et al., 2009). This relationship and the susceptibility of patients with epilepsy to mood and anxiety disorders (Jones et al., 2005) highlights the need for assessment and treatment of psychological disorders toward maximization of quality of life in epilepsy (Au et al., 2006; Corcoran & Thompson, 1993; Hall et al., 2009).

MEDICAL COMORBIDITIES

Epidemiological findings are an important source of data concerning the issue of the medical comorbidities of epilepsy, and these investigations have demonstrated abnormalities associated with many organ systems (see Table 15.1). Six recent studies, surveying over 1.4 million subjects worldwide, reported that between 26.8% and 84% of patients with epilepsy had at least one comorbid medical condition (Forsgren, 1992; Gaitatzis, Carroll, Majeed, & Sander, 2004; Jalava & Sillanpää, 1996; Kobau et al., 2008; Strine et al., 2005; Tellez-Zenteno et al., 2005). Similarly, seven epidemiological or large-scale studies including approximately 300,000 people, reported rates of psychiatric comorbidity ranging from 5.9% to 64.1% in epilepsy patients, compared with 7–26.8% for nonepilepsy controls (Davies, Heyman, & Goodman, 2003; Forsgren, 1992; Gaitatzis et al., 2004; Jalava & Sillanpää, 1996; Kobau, Gilliam, & Thurman, 2006; Strine et al., 2005; Tellez-Zenteno, Patten, Jette, Williams, & Wiebe, 2007).

Table 15.1. COMORBID CONDITIONS WITH SIGNIFICANTLY HIGHER RATES IN EPILEPSY THAN IN THE GENERAL POPULATION

Medical
Musculoskeletal system disorders
Gastrointestinal and digestive disorders
Respiratory system disorders
Chronic pain disorders
Cerebrovascular accidents
Migraine
Neoplasia
Arthritis/rheumatism
Obesity
Diabetes
Infections
Fractures
Allergies

Psychiatric
Depression
Anxiety
Autism spectrum disorders
Interictal dysphoric disorder
Interictal behavior syndrome
Psychosis of epilepsy

Cognitive/Neuropsychological
Attention-deficit hyperactivity disorder
Learning disability
Developmental delay
Alzheimer's disease/dementia

Multiple causal models have been proposed to account for the co-occurrence of epilepsy with other medical, psychiatric, and cognitive conditions. The three most common models are (1) epilepsy (or its treatment) causes the comorbid condition(s); (2) the comorbid condition (or its treatment) leads to epilepsy; and (3) a shared underlying mechanism (biological or environmental factors) mediates the occurrence of both epilepsy and the comorbid condition(s). The first two possibilities are considered unidirectional models, whereby one condition leads to the occurrence of the other condition. The third possibility suggests that neither condition directly causes the other but instead, a third factor may underlie both the epilepsy and its comorbid condition. In these instances, the comorbid rate of occurrence is high in both directions (i.e., epilepsy shows higher incidence of comorbid condition and comorbid condition shows higher incidence of epilepsy), and data indicate that either condition may predate the occurrence of the other. Simple and direct cause–effect relationships, however, may not be sufficient to explain these comorbid associations. Instead, multiple causes that in some instances may include a shared underlying predisposition or pathogenesis may account for the co-occurrence.

Bone Health

Low bone mineral density and osteoporosis are common among people with epilepsy. Long-term AED use is considered etiologically relevant to bone health issues, particularly in women (Souverein, Webb, Weil, Van Staa, & Egberts, 2006). Cytochrome P450 enzyme–inducing AEDs (e.g., phenytoin, phenobarbital and carbamazepine) contribute to poor bone health because of their effect on vitamin D and resulting calcium deficiency. Other risk markers identified include older age, menopause in women, longer duration of AED use, and assisted ambulation. Poor bone health has been associated with risks for developing other comorbid conditions (e.g., obesity and depression) by reducing the opportunity for physical activity and reducing opportunities for social interaction (Vestergaard, 2005).

Bone fractures occur as much as 2 times more frequently in individuals with epilepsy than in the general population; however, the deficit in bone mineral density does not appear to fully account for the increased risk of fractures (Elliot, Lu, Moore, McAuley, & Long, 2005; Lado, Spiegel, Masur, Boro, & Haut, 2008). Fractures may also be due to the seizures themselves or to falls associated with adverse drug effects (e.g., dizziness and ataxia). For example, convulsions during the seizure may produce a fracture. People with tonic–clonic seizures are at higher risk for fractures than are people with other seizure types. Tonic and atonic seizures consist of a sudden onset of increased muscle tone, which is likely to include falls and increase the likelihood of bone fractures. Thus, the increased incidence of bone fractures in epilepsy appears to be associated with several risk factors.

Stroke

Stroke has long been established as a risk factor for epilepsy (also known as post-stroke epilepsy [PSE]), and in the elderly, it is the most common cause of new-onset epilepsy (Rowan, 2005). Several studies, which exclude acute seizures (first 2–4 weeks), indicate that 2–4% of stroke patients develop epilepsy over a period of several months, and people with stroke run a 23 times greater risk of developing seizures within the first year post-stroke than those who have not had a stroke (Bladin et al., 2000; So, Annegers, Hauser, O'Brien, & Whisnant, 1996). When the number of annual stroke cases in the United States is considered (approximately 600,000), this amounts to a relatively large number of cases of PSE . The temporal sequence of epilepsy emergence following stroke implicates the vascular event as the cause for the onset of epilepsy. Several stroke-related factors, such as severity, location of vascular abnormality, and type of vascular incident, have been shown to affect the occurrence of PSE (Kotila & Waltimo, 1992). In addition, residual hemosiderin is a form of iron, is epileptogenic, and is not absorbed during stroke recovery, giving rise to longstanding epilepsy risk. Among older patients who develop new-onset seizures, cardiovascular abnormalities were quite common (Rowan, 2005). The additional risk factors identified for developing PSE include preexisting dementia, possibly due to dysfunction in the excitatory amino acid pathways, and women appear to be more vulnerable than men (Cordonnier, Henon, Derambure, Pasquier, & Leys, 2005).

Less appreciated is the fact that multiple stroke risk factors are present in epilepsy before experiencing stroke, and it is not uncommon for people with epilepsy to have multiple stroke risk factors. Population-based surveys document higher rates of hypertension, ischemic heart disease, and diabetes in people with epilepsy. Disruption of folate metabolism and concomitant increase in homocysteine have been linked to enzyme-inducing AED medications. Abnormalities in cholesterol levels and lipoprotein homeostasis have also been reported. Compared with controls, young adults with epilepsy presented significantly increased carotid artery intima thickness (Chuang et al., 2012; Hamed, Hamed, Hamdy, & Nabeshima, 2007).

Migraine Headaches

Although the connection between epilepsy and migraine has long been recognized, questions remain regarding the temporal order of their occurrence and the basis for the association. The prevalence of migraine in epilepsy and epilepsy in migraine is increased compared with that in the general population, particularly in patients who experience a visual aura along with their migraine (Bazil, 2004; Ludvigsson, Hesdorffer, Olafsson, Kjartansson, & Hauser, 2006). Epilepsy and migraine co-occur with several of the same conditions, including stroke and depression. They also share a set of clinical features, including paroxysmal events, impaired consciousness, and focal neurological signs, as well as some common risk factors (Bigal, Lipton, Cohen, & Silberstein, 2003; Scher, Bigal, & Lipton, 2005). In addition, some AED medications are generally considered to be an effective treatment option for migraines, possibly by reducing neuronal instability and hyperexcitability (Calabresi, Galletti, Rossi, Sarchielli, & Cupini, 2007). Thus, one of the mainstay treatments for migraine headaches may themselves contribute to neuropsychological impairment. Patients with migraine headaches may also perform poorly on verbal, visuospatial memory, and selective attention tasks. Like epilepsy, the neuropsychological impairments may be present not only during the episode (ictus) but also after symptoms are no longer present. Migraine sufferers are also at increased risk for anxiety and depression (Ravishankar & Demakis, 2007).

Shared genetic and physiological mechanisms that have been identified include brain hyperexcitability originating from cortical depression (Gorji, 2001; Rogawski, 2008) and calcium-signal abnormalities (Gargus, 2009). Shared genetic susceptibility has also been identified. Specific subtypes of epilepsy (childhood epilepsy with occipital seizures and benign childhood epilepsy with centrotemporal spikes) and migraine (familial hemiplegic migraine) have been linked to genetic mutations in *CACNA1A*, *ATP1A2*, and *SCN1A* on chromosome 17 (Crompton & Berkovic, 2009; Gargus, 2009).

CASE STUDY

Ms. Smith is a 56-year-old woman with a history of cognitive disability, right temporal-lobe epilepsy, and depression with psychotic features.

Presenting Concern: *The concern for possible dementia is twofold. First, a close friend of the patient reported noticing changes in Ms. Smith's usual behavior, in approximately October 2011. This friend stated that Ms. Smith was becoming increasingly disinhibited socially, for instance, yelling at strangers in public. She also stated that the patient was becoming somewhat paranoid, accusing others of stealing items she misplaced. Second, Ms. Smith's limited outside records included a January 2012 neuroimaging study (CT), conducted at an outside hospital, that revealed atrophy accelerated for age (this study was not available for review). However, her social worker, Ms. Jones, reported that, considering Ms. Smith's baseline cognitive deficits, she had been functioning quite well before being hospitalized for depression with psychotic features in February. Before that time, Ms. Jones and staff at Ms. Smith's community-based living facility had discussed moving Ms. Smith to a more independent level of care because of her strong functioning. Ms. Jones stated with certainty that Ms. Smith has not returned to this prehospitalization baseline.*

Medical History: *Ms. Smith's lifelong right temporal-lobe epilepsy has been in remission since the patient entered menopause. She continues with her long-standing antiepileptic regimen of carbamazepine and phenobarbital. The small left temporal meningioma revealed on recent neuroimaging studies has remained stable, and her severe migraine headaches have largely resolved. Ms. Smith's records mention that she hit her head in a fall in March 2012; details regarding this are limited, but it seems that no significant neurological sequelae followed this fall. Ms. Smith's records also suggest that head trauma secondary to childhood abuse may have caused both her seizures and cognitive disability, but this cannot be definitively determined. Ms. Smith's general medical history is significant for hypertension, hypercholesterolemia, gastrointestinal problems, and sleeping problems. Any sleeping problems have been largely addressed, although Ms. Smith* complained that she did not sleep well the night before this evaluation because of wax in her ears. She admitted that she snores at times. There are no indications of illicit substance use or alcohol or tobacco abuse.

Psychiatric History: *Ms. Smith has a longstanding history of psychiatric distress. According to documentation from prior records, Ms. Smith has attempted suicide in the past and was once tazed during a confrontation with police, with no known neurological consequences. She has had at least two severe episodes of depression with psychotic features, one in 2007 or 2008 and the most recent one beginning in February 2012. Ms. Jones reported that Ms. Smith has had three total inpatient psychiatric admissions since February, most recently being discharged from the geropsychiatry unit at a local hospital the previous day. At the time of her most recent admission, her presentation was described as "almost catatonic with posturing behaviors at times," and she refused all oral intake, including food, water, and medications. With the cooperation of Ms. Smith's longtime neurologist, Dr. B, emergency detention paperwork and a court order to compel medications were obtained, after which Ms. Smith began to improve. At today's evaluation, Ms. Smith has stated that she feels better, but her mood continues to fluctuate during the day. She stated that her sleeping has improved (with the exception of last night), and she feels able to eat and take her medications. She is somewhat apprehensive about her new living situation, but she feels adequately supported at this time.*

Family History: *Ms. Smith's family neurological and psychiatric histories are largely unknown.*

Social History: *Although information about Ms. Smith's background is limited, it is known that she was born and raised in a small town in the upper Midwest, on a family farm with nine siblings. It is reported that her father was physically abusive, and Ms. Smith has stated that she was sexually abused at the age of 14 or 15 by a friend of her father. She entered foster care at age 16. Although Ms. Jones was unsure about how much formal education Ms. Smith had completed, the patient stated that she finished through at least the 10th grade. After leaving school, Ms. Smith resided in a group home that "helped prepare her for work." She has worked in cleaning and housekeeping jobs and at a local taco factory, where she met her late husband. She was widowed after over 30 years of marriage; Ms. Smith reported one instance of physical abuse in her marriage. Ms. Smith has one adult daughter who may also have cognitive delays. The patient has resided in community-based facilities since at least 2008, although she was discharged from her most recent placement because of her challenging behaviors (including striking out at staff) that preceded her February psychiatric admission. It is hoped that Ms. Smith will be able to return to either an adult group home or a community-based residential facility after her 30-day nursing home stay.*

Clinical Presentation: *Ms. Smith arrived on time for her outpatient evaluation accompanied by her social worker, Ms. Jones. Her overall presentation was quite flat, with restricted range of affect and monotonous intonation in her speech. The technician who conducted Ms. Smith's testing stated that the patient appeared markedly fatigued, appearing to doze off several times during the evaluation. Her gait was somewhat tentative, but she was able to walk without assistance for short distances. Significant fine-motor problems were not observed on subjective observation. No difficulties with expressive or receptive language were noted. Overall, Ms. Smith's attention and concentration were adequate for the completion of testing, and she appeared to place her best effort toward completing the evaluation tasks. Today's results are considered a valid representation of her current neuropsychological status.*

Results

Note: The following results are standard scores (mean = 100, standard deviation = 15) unless otherwise indicated.

Due to the patient's limited tolerance for testing, IQ estimates were not repeated today. *Outside records suggest that Ms. Smith's premorbid intellectual capacity is in the borderline intellectual functioning/mild mental retardation range (IQ 60–70).*

Performance on the Mini Mental Status Examination was impaired (MMSE = 21/30). *Ms. Smith received 6/10 points for orientation, misreporting the month, day of the week, state, and floor of the hospital. She was able to report the state correctly with querying. She learned 3 of 3 verbally presented words in one trial but recalled only 1 word spontaneously after a delay. She received 6/8 points available for language, losing points for repetition and writing, correctly completing items for confrontation naming, verbal comprehension, and reading comprehension. She spelled "world" backwards correctly but had difficulty copying the intersecting pentagons.*

Clock drawing was mildly impaired (CDT = 7/10). *The clock face was drawn without gross distortion, although it was quite large. Spacing errors were present in the placement of the numbers, although they were correctly sequenced. The requested time was not indicated correctly, with the hour hand of the clock pointing to 10 instead of 11.*

The Neurobehavioral Cognitive Status Examination (NCSE) was administered and the results are as follows:

Memory was within normal limits on this measure (Memory = 11/12). *Although Ms. Smith required 4 trials to encode 4 verbally presented words, she recalled 3 of these words spontaneously after a delay, recalling the other after a category clue.*

Moderate-to-severe impairment *was observed in attention (Attention = 2/8). Language comprehension and repetition (Comprehension = 3/6, Repetition = 7/12), visuospatial/constructional skills (Construction = 2/6), and basic social judgment (Judgment = 2/6) were* **moderately impaired.** *Orientation (Orientation = 8/12), confrontation naming (Naming = 6/8), elemental calculation (Calculation = 2/4), and verbal abstract reasoning (Similarities = 4/8) were* **mildly impaired.**

Learning and memory were severely impaired on a more challenging measure. *Learning of a 12-item word list was severely impaired over three learning trials (HVLT-R Trials 1–3 Total ≤55), learning a maximum of 3/12 words over the learning trials. Ms. Smith recalled only 1 word after a delay (33% information* *retention), and recognition clues did not facilitate additional, reliable recall (delayed recall and recognition memory both severely impaired).*

Executive functions were also significantly impaired. *Severe impairments were observed in basic attention (WAIS-III consistently correct Digit Span Forward = 2 digits), working memory (WAIS-III Digit Span Backwards = 0; WMS-III WMI = 57), and mental flexibility (TMT-B = Discontinued). Novel, abstract problem-solving was moderately impaired (WCST-64 = 0/6 categories completed), with a significantly perseverative response style (Perseverative Responses/Perseverative Errors = 69/68). Response inhibition was borderline impaired (Stroop interference = 70).*

Information processing speed was severely impaired. *Speeded word-reading and color-naming were in the severely impaired range (Stroop Word/Color = <55/58), as was performance on a task requiring visuomotor scanning and rapid number sequencing (TMT-A = 51).*

Summary: *This is a very abnormal cognitive status evaluation, with variable memory performances and marked impairment on the majority of measures administered today. The significance of these findings is unknown, however. It is uncertain if these results represent any change from Ms. Smith's cognitive baseline, especially as she has reportedly not yet returned to her prehospitalization baseline. Several other confounding factors are also possibly influencing Ms. Smith's performance today. First, her significant fatigue suggests that Ms. Smith is still adjusting to recent changes in her antipsychotic medication regimen and to her physical environment. The fatigue itself may have worsened her performance on formal testing today, in addition to any lingering depressive and/or psychotic symptoms. Given these findings, practical recommendations for intervention and follow-up are given below.*

Recommendations

1. **Medication Considerations:** *Ms. Smith's treatment team may wish to consider examining her medication list to reduce as much anticholinergic burden as possible, especially in her as-needed medications. Some of her prn drugs have high anticholinergic burdens that are even more potent in combination (such as cyclobenzaprine and phenergan). Ms. Smith may be increasingly vulnerable to these effects as she ages.*

2. **Sleep Apnea:** *Ms. Smith may be at increased risk for obstructive sleep apnea due to her body habitus. Her medical records indicate recommendations for sleep evaluation; we certainly concur with this recommendation. Obstructive sleep apnea has been associated with cognitive declines, particularly in memory, while appropriate treatment has been connected with cognitive improvements.*

3. **Psychiatric/Psychological Treatment:** *It is certainly recommended that Ms. Smith receive strong, ongoing psychiatric and psychological support. Her treatment team may wish to seek out Alan Bellack's Social Skills Training protocol, which is inexpensive and readily available through online retailers. This treatment protocol*

was initially designed for individuals with chronic schizophrenia, although it has been applied to other populations successfully, including people with depression, traumatic brain injury, and developmental delays.

4. **Follow-Up:** *No urgent follow-up with Neuropsychology is recommended at this time. However, repeated evaluation may be clinically indicated in Ms. Smith's care if cognitive declines are still noted after she becomes accustomed to her surroundings and daily routine.*

CONCLUSION

Epilepsy is comorbid with conditions that span the medical, psychiatric, and cognitive spheres of functions (summarized in Table 15.1) and provides a significant conundrum for diagnosis and treatment. Several conditions (e.g., depression, migraine, and ADHD) are proving to have a complex connection whereby a shared underlying pathogenic mechanism may be responsible for the co-occurrence of epilepsy with these conditions. The same can be said for several other comorbid conditions, including Alzheimer's disease, mental retardation, and autism spectrum disorder (Hermann et al., 2008; Levisohn, 2007). Understanding the basis for the association of epilepsy and comorbid conditions poses important challenges for the diagnosis and treatment of epilepsy.

References

Adab, N., Kini, U., Vinten, J., Ayres, J., Baker, G., Clayton-Smith, J., et al. (2004). The longer term outcome of children born to mothers with epilepsy. *Journal of Neurology, Neurosurgery, and Psychiatry, 75*(11), 1575–1583.

Au, A., Leung, P., Kwok, A., Li, P., Lui, C., & Chan, J. (2006). Subjective memory and mood of Hong Kong Chinese adults with epilepsy. *Epilepsy & Behavior, 9*(1), 68–72.

Austin, J. K., & Caplan, R. (2007). Behavioral and psychiatric comorbidities in pediatric epilepsy: Toward an integrative model. *Epilepsia, 48*, 1639–1651.

Baxendale, S., & Thompson, P. (2005). Defining meaningful postoperative change in epilepsy surgery patients: Measuring the unmeasurable? *Epilepsy Behavior, 6*(2), 207–211.

Bazil, C. W. (2004). Comprehensive care of the epilepsy patient—control, comorbidity, and cost. *Epilepsia, 45*, 3–12.

Bell, B. D. (2006). WMS-III Logical Memory Performance after a two-week delay in temporal lobe epilepsy and control groups. *Journal of Clinical and Experimental Neuropsychology, 28*(8), 1435–1443.

Bigal, M. E., Lipton, R. B., Cohen, J., & Silberstein, S. D. (2003). Epilepsy and migraine. *Epilepsy Behavior, 4*(Suppl 2), S13–S24.

Bladin, C. F., Alexandrov, A. V., Bellavance, A., et al. (2000). Seizures after stroke: A prospective multicenter study. *Archives of Neurology, 57*, 1617–1622.

Blake, R. V., Wroe, S. J., Breen, E. K., & McCarthy, R. A. (2000). Accelerated forgetting in patients with epilepsy. *Brain, 123*(3), 472–483.

Blumer, D., Montouris, G., & Davies, K. (2004). The interictal dysphoric disorder: Recognition, pathogenesis, and treatment of the major psychiatric disorder of epilepsy. *Epilepsy Behavior, 5*(6), 826–840.

Boro, A., & Haut, S. (2003). Medical comorbidities in the treatment of epilepsy. *Epilepsy Behavior, 4*, S2–S12.

Butler, C. R., & Zeman, A. Z. (2008). Recent insights into the impairment of memory in epilepsy: Transient epileptic amnesia, accelerated long-term forgetting and remote memory impairment. *Brain, 131*(9), 2243–2263.

Calabresi, P., Galletti, F., Rossi, C., Sarchielli, P., & Cupini, L. M. (2007). Antiepileptic drugs in migraine: From clinical aspects to cellular mechanisms. *Trends in Pharmacological Sciences, 28*, 188–195.

Chuang, Y. C., Chuang, H. Y., Lin, T. K., Chang, C. C., Lu, C. H., Chang, W. N., et al. (2012). Effects of long-term antiepileptic drug monotherapy on vascular risk factors and atherosclerosis. *Epilepsia, 53*(1), 120–128.

Corcoran, R., & Thompson, P. (1993). Epilepsy and poor memory: Who complains and what do they mean? *British Journal of Clinical Psychology, 32*(Pt 2), 199–208.

Cordonnier, C., Henon, H., Derambure, P., Pasquier, F., & Leys, D. (2005). Influence of pre-existing dementia on the risk of post-stroke epileptic seizures. *Journal of Neurology, Neurosurgery, and Psychiatry, 76*, 1649–1653.

Crompton, D. E., & Berkovic, S. F. (2009). The borderland of epilepsy: Clinical and molecular features of phenomena that mimic epileptic seizures. *Lancet Neurology, 8*, 370–381.

Davies, S., Heyman, I., & Goodman, R. (2003). A population survey of mental health problems in children with epilepsy. *Developmental Medicine and Child Neurology, 45*, 292–295.

Dulay, M. F., Schefft, B. K., Fargo, J. D., Privitera, M. D., & Yeh, H. S. (2004). Severity of depressive symptoms, hippocampal sclerosis, auditory memory, and side of seizure focus in temporal lobe epilepsy. *Epilepsy Behavior, 5*(4), 522–531.

Dunn, D. W., Austin, J. K., Harezlak, J., & Ambrosius, W. T. (2003). ADHD and epilepsy in childhood. *Developmental Medicine and Child Neurology, 45*, 50–54.

Ekinci, O., Titus, J. B., Rodopman, A. A., Berkem, M., & Trevathan, E. (2009). Depression and anxiety in children and adolescents with epilepsy: Prevalence, risk factors, and treatment. *Epilepsy Behavior, 14*, 8–18

Elliott, J. O., Lu, B., Moore, J. L., McAuley, J. W., & Long, L. (2008). Exercise, diet, health behaviors, and risk factors among persons with epilepsy based on the California Health Interview Survey, 2005. *Epilepsy Behavior, 13*, 307–315.

Eyrl, K. L. (2007). ADHD, neurological correlates and health-related quality of life in severe pediatric epilepsy. *Epilepsia, 48*, 1083–1091.

Fawell, J. R., Lee, Y. J., Hirtz, D. G., Sulzbacher, S. I., Ellenberg, J. H., & Nelson, K. B. (1990). Phenobarbital for febrile seizures—effects on intelligence and on seizure recurrence. *New England Journal of Medicine, 322*(6), 364–369.

Forsgren, L. (1992). Prevalence of epilepsy in adults in northern Sweden. *Epilepsia, 33*, 450–458.

Gaily, E., Kantola-Sorsa, E., Hiilesmaa, V., Isoaho, M., Matila, R., Kotila, M., et al. (2004). Normal intelligence in children with prenatal exposure to carbamazepine. *Neurology, 62*(1), 28–32.

Gaitatzis, A., Carroll, K., Majeed, A., & Sander, W. J. (2004). The epidemiology of the comorbidity of epilepsy in the general population. *Epilepsia, 45*, 1613–1622.

Gaitatzis, A., Trimble, M. R., & Sander, J.W. (2004). The psychiatric comorbidity of epilepsy. *Acta Neurologica Scandinavica, 110*, 207–220

Gargus, J. J. (2009). Genetic calcium signaling abnormalities in the central nervous system: Seizures, migraine, and autism. *Annals of the New York Academy of Science, 1151*, 133–156.

Giacino, J. T., & Cicerone, K. D. (1998). Varieties of deficit unawareness after brain injury. *Journal of Head Trauma Rehabilitation, 13*(5), 1–15.

Gilliam, F. (2002). Optimizing health outcomes in active epilepsy. *Neurology, 58*(8 Suppl 5), S9–20.

Giovagnoli, A. R., Casazza, M., & Avanzini, G. (1995). Visual learning on a selective reminding procedure and delayed recall in patients with temporal lobe epilepsy. *Epilepsia, 36*(7), 704–711.

Giovagnoli, A. R., Mascheroni, S., & Avanzini, G. (1997). Self-reporting of everyday memory in patients with epilepsy: Relation to neuropsychological, clinical, pathological and treatment factors. *Epilepsy Research, 28*(2), 119–128.

Glauser, T. A., Cnaan, A., Shinnar, S., Hirtz, D. G., Dlugos, D., Masur, D., et al.; Childhood Absence Epilepsy Study Group. (2010). Ethosuximide, valproic acid, and lamotrigine in childhood absence epilepsy. *New England Journal of Medicine, 362*(9), 790–799.

Gleissner, U., Helmstaedter, C., Quiske, A., & Elger, C. E. (1998). The performance-complaint relationship in patients with epilepsy: A matter of daily demands? *Epilepsy Research, 32*(3), 401–409.

Gorji, A. (2001). Spreading depression: A review of the clinical relevance. *Brain Research. Brain Research Reviews, 38*, 33–60.

Gross, R. A. (1992). A brief history of epilepsy and its therapy in the Western Hemisphere. *Epilepsy Research, 12*(2), 65–74.

Hall, K. E., Isaac, C. L., & Harris, P. (2009). Memory complaints in epilepsy: An accurate reflection of memory impairment or an indicator of poor adjustment? A review of the literature. *Clinical Psychology Review, 29*(4), 354–367.

Hamed, S. A., Hamed, E. A., Hamdy, R., & Nabeshima, T. (2007). Vascular risk factors and oxidative stress as independent predictors of asymptomatic atherosclerosis in adult patients with epilepsy. *Epilepsy Research, 74*, 183–192.

Hendriks, M. P. H., Aldenkamp, A. P., van der Vlugt, H., Alpherts, W. C. J., & Vermeulen, J. (2002). Memory complaints in medically refractory epilepsy: Relationship to epilepsy-related factors. *Epilepsy & Behavior, 3*(2), 165–172.

Hermann, B. P. (1982). Neuropsychological functioning and psychopathology in children with epilepsy. *Epilepsia, 23*(5), 545–554.

Hermann, B., Jones, J., Dabbs, K., et al. (2007). The frequency, complications and aetiology of ADHD in new onset paediatric epilepsy. *Brain, 130*, 3135–3148.

Hermann, B. P., Seidenberg, M., Haltiner, A., & Wyler, A. R. (1991). Mood state in unilateral temporal lobe epilepsy. *Biological Psychiatry, 30*, 1205–1218.

Hermann, B., Seidenberg, M., Sager, M., et al. (2008). Growing up with epilepsy: The neglected issue of cognitive and brain health in aging and elder persons with chronic epilepsy. *Epilepsia, 49*, 731–740.

Hesdorffer, D. C., Hauser, W. A., Annegers, J. F., & Cascino, G. (2000). Major depression is a risk factor for seizures in older adults. *Annals of Neurology, 47*, 246–249.

Hesdorffer, D. C., & Kanner, A. M. (2009). The FDA alert on suicidality and antiepileptic drugs: Fire or false alarm? *Epilepsia, 50*(5), 978–986.

Hesdorffer, D. C., Ludvigsson, P., Olafsson, E., Gudmundsson, G., Kjartansson, O., & Hauser, W. A. (2004). ADHD as a risk factor for incident unprovoked seizures and epilepsy in children. *Archives of General Psychiatry, 61*, 731–736.

Jalava, M., & Sillanpää, M. (1996). Concurrent illnesses in adults with childhood-onset epilepsy: A population-based 35-year follow-up study. *Epilepsia, 37*, 1155–1163.

Johnson, E. K., Jones, J. E., Seidenberg, M., & Hermann, B. P. (2004). The relative impact of anxiety, depression, and clinical seizure features on health-related quality of life in epilepsy. *Epilepsia, 45*(5), 544–550.

Jones, J. E., Hermann, B. P., Woodard, J. L., Barry, J. J., Gilliam, F., Kanner, A. M., et al. (2005). Screening for major depression in epilepsy with common self-report depression inventories. *Epilepsia, 46*(5), 731–735.

Jones, J. E., Watson, R., Sheth, R., et al. (2007). Psychiatric comorbidity in children with new onset epilepsy. *Developmental Medicine and Child Neurology, 49*, 493–497.

Kanner, A. M. (2003). Depression in epilepsy: Prevalence, clinical semiology, pathogenic mechanisms, and treatment. *Biological Psychiatry, 54*, 388–398.

Kanner, A. M. (2007). Epilepsy and mood disorders. *Epilepsia, 48*, 20–22.

Kanner, A. M. (2009). Depression and epilepsy: A review of multiple facets of their close relation. *Neurologic Clinics, 27*(4), 865–880.

Kapur, N., & Pearson, D. (1983). Memory symptoms and memory performance of neurological patients. *British Journal of Psychology, 74*(Pt 3), 409–415.

Kobau, R., Gilliam, F., & Thurman, D. J. (2006). Prevalence of self-reported epilepsy or seizure disorder and its associations with self-reported depression and anxiety: Results from the 2004 Healthstyles Survey. *Epilepsia, 47*, 1915–1921

Kobau, R., Zahran, H., Thurman, D. J., et al. (2008). Epilepsy surveillance among adults–19 states, behavioral risk factor surveillance system. *Morbidity and Mortality Weekly Report. Surveillance Summaries, 57*(6), 1–20.

Kockelmann, E., Elger, C. E., & Helmstaedter, C. (2003). Significant improvement in frontal lobe associated neuropsychological functions after withdrawal of topiramate in epilepsy patients. *Epilepsy Research, 54*(2–3), 171–178.

Kotila, M., & Waltimo, O. (1992). Epilepsy after stroke. *Epilepsia, 33*, 495–498.

Lado, F., Spiegel, R., Masur, J. H., Boro, A., & Haut, S. R. (2008). Value of routine screening for bone demineralization in an urban population of patients with epilepsy. *Epilepsy Research, 78*, 155–160.

LaFrance, W. C., Kanner, A. M., & Hermann, B. (2008). Psychiatric comorbidities in epilepsy. *International Review of Neurobiology, 83*, 347–383.

Levisohn, P. M. (2007). The autism–epilepsy connection. *Epilepsia, 48*(Suppl 9), 33–35.

Lezak, M. D., Howieson, D. B., & Loring, D. W. (2004). *Neuropsychological assessment* (4th ed.). New York: Oxford University Press.

Lineweaver, T. T., Naugle, R. I., Cafaro, A. M., Bingaman, W., & Lüders, H. O. (2004). Patients' perceptions of memory functioning before and after surgical intervention to treat medically refractory epilepsy. *Epilepsia, 45*(12), 1604–1612.

Loring, D. W., Marino, S., & Meador, K. J. (2007). Neuropsychological and behavioral effects of antiepilepsy drugs. *Neuropsychological Review, 17*(4), 413–425.

Loring, D. W., Williamson, D. J., Meador, K. J., Wiegand, F., & Hulihan, J. F. (2011). Topiramate cognitive dose effects: A randomized double-blind study with reliable change indices. *Neurology, 76*, 131–137.

Ludvigsson, P., Hesdorffer, D., Olafsson, E., Kjartansson, O., & Hauser, W. A. (2006). Migraine with aura is a risk factor for unprovoked seizures in children. *Annals of Neurology, 59*, 210–213.

Marino, S. E., Meador, K. J., Loring, D. W., Okun, M. S., Fernandez, H. H., Fessler, A. J., et al. (2009). Subjective perception of cognition is related to mood and not performance. *Epilepsy Behavior, 14*(3), 459–464.

Martin, R., Kuzniecky, R., Ho, S., Hetherington, H., Pan, J., Sinclair, K., & Faught, E. (1999). Cognitive effects of topiramate, gabapentin, and lamotrigine in healthy young adults. *Neurology, 52*(2), 321–327.

McIntyre, D. C., & Gilby, K. L. (2007). Genetically seizure-prone or seizure-resistant phenotypes and their associated behavioral comorbidities. *Epilepsia, 48*(Suppl 9), 30–32.

Meador, K. J. (2005). Cognitive effects of epilepsy and of antiepileptic medications. In E. Wyllie (Ed.), *The treatment of epilepsy* (4th ed., pp. 1215–1226). Baltimore, MD: Williams & Wilkins.

Meador, K. J., Baker, G. A., Browning, N., Clayton-Smith, J., Combs-Cantrell, D. T., Cohen, M., & Loring, D. W. (2009). Cognitive function at 3 years of age after fetal exposure to antiepileptic drugs. *New England Journal of Medicine, 360*(16), 1597–1605.

Meador, K. J., Loring, D. W., Allen, M. E., Zamrini, E. Y., Moore, E. E., Abney, O. L., & King, D. W. (1991). Comparative cognitive effects of carbamazepine and phenytoin in healthy adults. *Neurology, 41*(10), 1537–1540.

Orfei, M. D., Robinson, R. G., Bria, P., Caltagirone, C., & Spalletta, G. (2008). Unawareness of illness in neuropsychiatric disorders: Phenomenological certainty versus etiopathogenic vagueness. *Neuroscientist, 14*(2), 203–222.

Ounsted, C. (1955). The hyperkinetic syndrome in epileptic children. *Lancet, 269,* 303–311.

Palac, S., & Meador, K. J. (2011). Antiepileptic drugs and neurodevelopment: An update. *Current Neurology and Neuroscience Reports, 11*(4), 423–427.

Paradiso, S., Hermann, B. P., Blumer, D., Davies, K., & Robinson, R. G. (2001). Impact of depressed mood on neuropsychological status in temporal lobe epilepsy. *Journal of Neurology, Neurosurgery, and Psychiatry, 70*(2), 180–185.

Perucca, E. (2005). Birth defects after prenatal exposure to antiepileptic drugs. *Lancet Neurology, 4*(11), 781–786.

Petrovski, S., Szoeke, C. E., Jones, N. C., Salzberg, M. R., Sheffield, L. J., Huggins, R. M., & O'Brien, T. J. (2010). Neuropsychiatric symptomatology predicts seizure recurrence in newly treated patients. *Neurology, 75*(11), 1015–1021.

Piazzini, A., Canevini, M. P., Maggiori, G., & Canger, R. (2001). The perception of memory failures in patients with epilepsy. *European Journal of Neurology, 8*(6), 613–620.

Ravishankar, N., & Demakis, G. J. (2007). The neuropsychology of migraine. *Disease-a-Month, 53*(3), 156–161.

Rogawski, M. A. (2008). Common pathophysiologic mechanisms in migraine and epilepsy. *Archives of Neurology, 65,* 709–714.

Rösche, J., Uhlmann, C., & Fröscher W. (2003). Low serum folate levels as a risk factor for depressive mood in patients with chronic epilepsy. *Journal of Neuropsychiatry and Clinical Neuroscience, 15,* 64–66.

Rowan, A. J. (2005). Common morbidities influence development, treatment strategies, and expected outcomes. *Geriatrics, 60,* 30–34.

Scher, A. I., Bigal, M. E., & Lipton, R. B. (2005). Comorbidity of migraine. *Current Opinion in Neurology, 18,* 305–310.

Schmitz, B. (2005). Depression and mania in patients with epilepsy. *Epilepsia, 46,* 45–49.

Smith, W. G. (1905). A comparison of some mental and physical tests in their application to epileptic and to normal subjects. *British Journal of Psychology, 2,* 240–260.

So, E. L., Annegers, J. F., Hauser, W. A., O'Brien, P. C., & Whisnant, J. P. (1996). Population-based study of seizure disorders after cerebral infarction. *Neurology, 46,* 350–355.

Souverein, P. C., Webb, D. J., Weil, J. G., Van Staa, T. P., & Egberts, A. C. G. (2006). Use of antiepileptic drugs and risk of fractures: Case–control study among patients with epilepsy. *Neurology, 66,* 1318–1324.

Strine, T. W., Kobau, R., Chapman, D. P., et al. (2005). Psychological distress, comorbidities, and health behaviors among U.S. adults with seizures: Results from the 2002 National Health Interview Survey. *Epilepsia, 46,* 1133–1139.

Tellez-Zenteno, J. F., Matijevic, S., & Wiebe S. (2005). Somatic comorbidity of epilepsy in the general population in Canada. *Epilepsia, 46,* 1955–1962.

Tellez-Zenteno, J. F., Patten, S. B., Jette, N., Williams, J., & Wiebe, S. (2007). Psychiatric comorbidity in epilepsy: A population-based analysis. *Epilepsia, 48*, 2336–2344.

Thompson, P. J., & Corcoran, R. (1992). Everyday memory failures in people with epilepsy. *Epilepsia, 33*(Suppl 6), S18–20.

Tracy, J. I., Lippincott, C., Mahmood, T., Waldron, B., Kanauss, K., Glosser, D., & Sperling, M. R. (2007). Are depression and cognitive performance related in temporal lobe epilepsy? *Epilepsia, 48*(12), 2327–2335.

Vermeulen, J., Aldenkamp, A. P., & Alpherts, W. C. (1993). Memory complaints in epilepsy: Correlations with cognitive performance and neuroticism. *Epilepsy Research, 15*(2), 157–170.

Vestergaard, P. (2005). Epilepsy, osteoporosis and fracture risk—a meta-analysis. *Acta Neurologica Scandinavica, 112*, 277–286.

Wallin, J. E. W. (1912). Eight months of psycho-clinical research at the New Jersey State Village for Epileptics, with some results from the Binet-Simon testing. *Epilepsia, A3*, 366–380.

World Health Organization (2012). *Epilepsy*. Retrieved from http://www.who.int/topics/epilepsy/en.

Assessing Secondary Influences and Their Impact on Neuropsychological Test Performance: Summing Things up and Where We Need to Go from Here

PETER A. ARNETT

Thousands of evaluations are conducted by neuropsychologists each year on a wide range of neurological and neuropsychiatric patients. For most of these evaluations, neuropsychologists are keenly aware of primary influences on neuropsychological functioning relating to the extent and location of damage to the brain. Secondary influences on neuropsychological performance—those indirect factors associated with a brain injury—are often more likely to be overlooked. An important goal of this volume has been to bring greater attention to the prevalence of these secondary influences in neuropsychological assessments across a range of neurological disorders and conditions. It has also been a central goal of this book to make neuropsychologists aware of the literature on the more general influence of secondary factors that may cut across specific disorders. Thus, chapters focused on secondary influences involving symptom invalidity, depression, anxiety, fatigue, pain, response expectancies, and oral motor slowing have been included. Although most neuropsychologists are broadly familiar with the potential of these factors to influence cognitive test performance, prior to this book there has been no single source with evidence-based guidelines for evaluating the potential magnitude of these influences. By providing a comprehensive review of the range of key secondary influences that could impact neuropsychological test performance, this volume will be a resource that neuropsychologists can turn to for consideration when evaluating their patients. This book can also be a comprehensive source for research endeavors, as it provides an up-to-date review on these topics to guide the scholarship of investigators of secondary influences.

As a neuropsychologist who works in both research and clinical roles, I have always been most interested in pursuing research questions that have clinical significance and the potential for application. For the research program I have pursued in multiple sclerosis (MS), many of the studies we have conducted in my lab have involved pursuing issues related to the impact of secondary influences that I believe could have applied value. In fact, my initial foray into the MS literature, when I began studying MS during my postdoctoral fellowship with Steve Rao and Tom Hammeke at the Medical College of Wisconsin, was motivated by a clinical observation in the MS patients I saw for neuropsychological evaluation: Patients often presented with both depression and cognitive impairments. After seeing this repeatedly in my clinical work, I began perusing the MS literature to expand my knowledge of things. However, I was surprised to learn that the association between depression and cognitive impairment had been looked at repeatedly in MS, and the typical finding was that there was no relationship of this secondary factor (depression) with cognitive impairment. This led me to the following question: How could a relationship that seems so obviously present in a clinical evaluation be nonexistent in research studies? With that question, I embarked upon a research program that I have continued to this day that has attempted to understand secondary influences on cognitive test performance in MS.

The initial focus of my MS research involved the exploration of primary influences on cognitive functioning. In fact, my first publication on this topic with my mentor on my postdoctoral work, Steve Rao (Arnett et al., 1994), has been widely cited because it was the first clear demonstration that the location of white matter lesions in the brain of MS patients could have specific cognitive effects consistent with the area of damage to the brain. We followed up this study with a related publication demonstrating the association between white matter lesions in a specific brain region and a specific type of language impairment, conduction aphasia. Although I still regard the study of primary influences on cognitive functioning in MS as critical, I changed my emphasis to studying secondary factors for two reasons. First, it was apparent to me from my review of the MS literature that the possible influence of secondary factors on cognitive functioning in MS had only been minimally explored. Second, given the detrimental effects that cognitive impairments had been shown to have on the everyday functioning of MS patients, it occurred to me that some of these patients' cognitive impairments might be reversed, and their everyday functioning improved, if some of their cognitive problems were due to secondary factors. With these thoughts in mind, I began a research program designed to study secondary influences on cognitive functioning in MS.

As my students (especially Christopher Higginson, John Randolph, and Bill Voss) and I started exploring these issues when I began my first academic position at Washington State University, we made an interesting discovery in our MS sample: Cognitive dysfunction and the secondary influence of depression were in fact robustly correlated, but only when we removed neurovegetative symptoms of depression from the equation. In many lab discussions, we reasoned that depression and cognitive dysfunction might not be more consistently correlated in research because neurovegetative symptoms of depression may obscure that relationship. The problem with neurovegetative symptoms is that they are not clear indicators of depression but could also simply reflect MS symptomatology. Neurovegetative depression symptoms (e.g., fatigue, appetite disturbance, sleep dysfunction, concentration difficulties, and sexual dysfunction) are also common symptoms of MS. Because most MS studies had found that the severity of MS symptomatology was not associated with depression, it may have been that the inclusion of these overlapping symptoms when exploring the relationship of depression and cognitive dysfunction obscured a true relationship. With these thoughts in mind, we began restricting our operationalization of depression to include only mood and negative evaluative depression symptoms (thus excluding neurovegetative symptoms) and began finding robust relationships with cognitive dysfunction in MS.

Since our initial demonstration of a significant association between depression and cognitive functioning in MS (Arnett, Higginson, & Randolph, 2001; Arnett, Higginson, Voss, Bender, et al., 1999; Arnett, Higginson, Voss, Wright, et al., 1999), we have attempted to delve deeper into the complexities of these relationships. Although the relationships that we found in our data proved to be robust, they fell far short of accounting for all of the variance in cognitive functioning in MS. Consequently, we began to explore potential moderators, as well as alternative causal scenarios. In one study (Arnett, Higginson, Voss, & Randolph, 2002), we found that coping moderated the relationship between cognitive functioning and depression. Our data suggested that cognitive problems in MS were likely to predict depression if patients favored the use of maladaptive coping strategies involving high levels of avoidance or low levels of active coping. The data also suggested the possibility that even patients with significant levels of cognitive impairment might not suffer from depression if they used more adaptive approaches to coping. About 50% of the variance in depression in our MS patients could be explained by a combination of cognitive functioning, coping, and their interaction. I continued to follow this line of research, as well as other aspects of secondary influences, in the work I have pursued with my students at Penn State University (especially Jared Bruce, Lauren Strober, Laura Julian, Dawn Polen, Megan Smith, Amanda Schurle-Bruce, Fiona Barwick, Amanda Rabinowitz, Joe Beeney, Gray Vargas, and Dede Ukueberuwa). In a recent coping study (Rabinowitz & Arnett, 2009), we replicated our initial findings using a longitudinal framework. In a related study exploring longitudinal changes in depression in MS (Arnett & Randolph, 2006), we found that patients who displayed increased depressed mood over a 3-year period showed decreased used of adaptive (active) coping, whereas those patients who showed decreased depressed mood used more adaptive coping over time.

Beyond examining cognitive functioning and coping as predictors of depression in MS, we have explored more nuances of the influence of secondary factors in the form of cognitive-affective biases. In an initial study on this topic, we demonstrated that performance-based cognitive-affective biases predicted depression (Bruce & Arnett, 2005). Following this, we demonstrated that such biases interacted with both stress (Beeney & Arnett, 2008) and another secondary factor, pain (Bruce, Polen, & Arnett, 2007), to predict depression. Although both high levels of stress and pain are common in MS, our data showed that they did not necessarily lead to depression unless patients also exhibited negative cognitive biases. This finding suggested a possible avenue for treatment in patients experiencing high levels of stress or pain—specifically, reduction of negative cognitive biases might lead to reduced depression despite stress and pain. Our exploration of these various moderators and contributors to depression culminated in a theoretical review paper (Arnett, Barwick, & Beeney, 2008) that continues to guide our research program.

Another secondary influence on cognitive functioning that we have evaluated in MS is oral motor speed (i.e., the rate of speech). Much of this research is outlined in Chapter 8 (by Arnett, Vargas, Ukueberuwa, & Rabinowitz) of this book and touched on in Chapter 10 (by Bruce, Thelen, & Westervelt), where MS is discussed. As reviewed there, the basis of this research is that many neuropsychological tests used on individuals with MS require some type of motor response. Although many batteries recommended for use with MS now avoid tests that require significant motor writing or manual manipulation speed, many of the most sensitive commonly used cognitive tests still require some type of rapid *oral* motor response. Prior to our studies, the extent to which more primary problems with rapid speech in MS patients might influence neuropsychological test performance was unknown. If primary oral motor speed is slowed in MS patients, it may unduly contribute to patients' performance on these tests, inflating their deficit and inaccurately portraying patients' true level of cognitive impairment. In one study, we found evidence that a large proportion of the differences between MS patients and controls on neuropsychological tasks that required a rapid spoken response was due to the oral motor problems of patients with MS (Arnett, Smith, Barwick, Benedict, & Ahlstrom, 2008). We demonstrated this same phenomenon in another study using a different sample and a different method for measuring oral motor speed (Smith & Arnett, 2007). These data suggested the possibility that information-processing speed deficits in MS are influenced by the secondary effects of the slow oral motor speed that characterizes many MS patients.

Another potential secondary influence on cognitive functioning in MS that we have explored is visual acuity. We reasoned that if patients' difficulty with visually based neuropsychological tasks turns out to be related to more rudimentary visual acuity problems, it could have significant consequences for our understanding of the nature of cognitive dysfunction in MS and the way in which we measure cognitive deficits in MS patients neuropsychologically. In this study (Bruce, Bruce, & Arnett, 2007), we found that scores on a visual acuity test (Snellen chart) administered before testing accounted for significant variance in group (MS/Control) differences on one of the most sensitive clinical neuropsychological tests to cognitive dysfunction that is used in MS (Oral Symbol Digit Modalities Test).

In addition to exploring secondary factors in MS, we have investigated some secondary influences on neuropsychological test performance in sports-related concussion. My students and I (chiefly Chris Bailey, Jared Bruce, Aaron Rosenbaum, Amanda Rabinowitz, and Deepa Ramanathan) have tried to understand how motivational changes from baseline testing to postconcussion testing could influence test performance (Bailey, Echemendia, & Arnett, 2006). Based on the types of findings outlined in Christiansen and King's chapter in this volume (Chapter 4), we have tried to develop performance-based measures of depression that do not rely on self-report, to circumvent athletes' tendencies to underreport affective concerns (Ramanathan, Rabinowitz, Barwick, & Arnett, 2012). In this way, we are trying to develop ways in which to identify the potential impact of the secondary influence of depression when athletes minimize their reporting of depression because of their high motivation to return to play. Additionally, we have explored the secondary influence of fatigue by examining fatigue effects across multiple modalities (cognitive, self-report, EEG) over the course of a typical neuropsychological concussion battery (Barwick, Arnett, & Slobounov, 2012). I have devoted much of my career in neuropsychology to attempting to understand the influence of secondary factors on cognitive test performance and this has ultimately culminated in this edited book.

Although a great deal of research has been devoted to attempting to assess the impact of secondary influences on cognitive functioning, there is still much that we do not know. In the remainder of this chapter, I will highlight a few areas relating to secondary influences that warrant particular attention for future research.

AREAS FOR FUTURE RESEARCH

Clinically Normed Measures of Affective Bias

In this volume, Christiansen and King's chapter provides a scholarly, comprehensive review of affective bias in mood disorders. Despite the fact that a substantial body of research has accumulated over the past 30 years in which affective bias in depressed individuals was measured through the use of tasks involving memory, attention, and affective Stroop tasks, producing effect sizes typically in the medium range, no tasks have been developed for clinical use. As Christiansen and King note, "Currently, there are no commercially available or psychometrically tested instruments that directly assess the degree of affective bias among individual patients." Having such a tool available could be valuable for a variety of reasons. As we demonstrated in a recent study using an affective bias task in athletes at baseline (Ramanathan et al., 2012), because athletes are often motivated to underreport affective and other types of symptoms postconcussion, it would be valuable to have a clinical tool that depended on performance rather than self-report to assess possible depressed mood. In this study, we used a word-list learning test consisting of a mixture of affectively positive and negative words to be recalled, and divided up the sample into a group who displayed a recall bias toward negative versus positive words. We found that a substantially higher proportion of individuals in the negative-bias group reported depression compared to the positive-bias group. Now that we have validated this task in our athletes at baseline, we plan to use it to identify athletes postconcussion who may be at risk for mood disorders but who may be unwilling to self-report problems initially.

Our study provides one example of how the use of an affective bias task to identify those with mood disruption can be valuable. We have continued to use this task in our concussion program at Penn State to try and better understand these affective bias issues in the athletes. It would be useful to have such tasks available for more widespread use, because the underreporting of mood problems is likely to be present in other neurological populations as well. It would benefit clinical neuropsychologists to have such tools available to improve their clinical evaluations. However, the translation of robust research findings into tools for clinical use has been slow. At this stage in our knowledge of affective bias, enough replicated research has been conducted and effects have been robust enough for translation into clinical practice to be warranted. From Christiansen and King's review in this volume, the tasks that might be the best candidates, based on showing the best effect sizes combined with the most replication, include the Emotional Stroop Test, the Dot Probe Task, and the Autobiographical Memory Test. Effects for Affective List-Learning tests have been consistently replicated, but the effect sizes have tended to be smaller than those for the latter tasks.

Anxiety Bias and Traditional Neuropsychological Tests

In Chapter 5 in this book, Clarke and MacLeod provide a scholarly review of the literature on the impact of anxiety on cognitive test performance, which is extensive. They note, however, that there is limited research examining the ways in which anxiety-linked biases might be associated with traditional clinical neuropsychological tests. Listed in Table 5.1 are over 50 studies that have demonstrated a bias in anxious individuals on the Emotional Stroop Task; between 21 and 49 studies have demonstrated such biases using tasks involving the self-reported interpretation of scenarios, as well as the Attentional Probe task. These tasks might be good candidates for the examination of associations with traditional clinical neuropsychological tasks, as they have been thoroughly vetted in the literature as being sensitive to anxiety effects. Tasks identified as having the most robust and reliable associations with clinical neuropsychological test performance could then be developed for clinical use so that the influence of anxiety biases on neuropsychological test performance could more systematically be evaluated in clinical evaluations. Ultimately, the use of such tasks in clinical settings would be extremely helpful in identifying potential problems in anxiety in individuals who might be hesitant to report this, but also identify individuals who might show characteristic neuropsychological performance related to anxiety on more traditional clinical tasks.

Reasons Why Depression Affects Cognitive Functioning in Some Neurological Conditions and Not Others

As Basso and colleagues' chapter (Chapter 3) in this book demonstrates, there is a voluminous literature demonstrating that individuals with major depression show robust and chronic deficits in executive function, working memory, new learning, and speed of information processing. Additionally, it appears to be well established that depression affects cognitive functioning in a number of neurological disorders, such as MS, Parkinson's disease, and traumatic brain injury (TBI). However, it is surprising that in other disorders (e.g., HIV) there does not appear to be any association between depression and cognitive functioning. Why is this the case? More research is needed here to determine why these effects sometimes seem idiosyncratic to particular disorders. Additionally, even in disorders where reliable effects are typically found when comparing a clinical group to a matched control group, the effects are not pervasive across all patients. Why is depression associated with neurocognitive impairment in some patients but not in others? This inconsistency appears to be the case in patients with major depression who do not have any neurological condition, as Basso and colleagues' demonstrate. They identify several potential moderating variables. An exploration of other factors moderating the depression–cognitive dysfunction relationship in particular neurological patient groups would also be valuable, so that clinicians could be aware of factors to examine in clinical evaluations.

Development of Objective Clinical Tools to Measure Response Expectancies

As Suhr and Wei show in Chapter 9, response expectancies appear to impact cognitive functioning, but currently there are no standardized clinical tools available to assess such expectancies. It would be especially valuable for clinicians to have objective measures of response expectancies in relation to neuropsychological impairment, as such expectancy biases have been shown to be significantly associated with actual performance on neuropsychological tests. Additionally, response expectancies appear to affect patients' reports of their past symptoms and history. Response expectancy is typically studied using an experimental manipulation in which one group is under some expectancy or threat and the other is not, and performance on neuropsychological tasks between groups is then compared. Groups with a particular negative expectancy or who are under some threat typically show poorer performance, with small to medium effect sizes often reported. Although Suhr and Wei provide a number of excellent recommendations for addressing issues related to expectancy bias and threat in clinical evaluations, it would be useful if more work in this literature could be devoted to developing objective tasks to measure these constructs that could be normed and then translated for clinical practice.

Study of Potential Impact of Dysarthria on Cognitive Test Performance in a Greater Variety of Patient Groups

As Arnett and colleagues review in Chapter 8 on oral motor speed, dysarthria is typically found in over 50% of individuals with major neurological disorders, but few studies have empirically evaluated the relationship between slowed speech and neuropsychological test performance. A limited number of studies on oral motor speed in MS and aging have been conducted, and these studies have demonstrated that dysarthria manifested as slow speech is associated with poorer performance on neuropsychological tests. However, this issue does not appear to have been explored in any systematic way in other neurological disorders. Expanding this literature will be valuable to clinicians who can then rely on a greater evidence base to guide their care and treatment of patients and provide more accurate interpretation of the meaning of neuropsychological test results.

CONCLUSIONS

I hope you have enjoyed this book and will find it useful in clinical practice. The past 20–30 years have produced an impressive body of work addressing the impact of secondary influences on neuropsychological test performance. This book provides guidelines for using this evidence base and applying it in clinical practice. As this chapter highlights, although we have learned much about these often overlooked secondary influences, there is still much to be learned. Whole research programs could be devoted to exploring some of these issues further. My hope is that this book will not only be useful in guiding applied work but also inspire researchers to gain a better understanding of the complexities of these issues so that we can continue to improve the care and treatment of our patients and can fully understand the range of influences on neuropsychological test performance.

References

Arnett, P. A., Barwick, F. H., & Beeney, J. E. (2008). Depression in multiple sclerosis: Review and theoretical proposal *Journal of the International Neuropsychological Society, 14*, 691–724.

Arnett, P. A., Higginson, C. I., & Randolph, J. J. (2001). Depression in multiple sclerosis: Relationship to planning ability. *Journal of the International Neuropsychological Society, 7*, 665–674.

Arnett, P. A., Higginson, C. I., Voss, W. D., Bender, W. I., Wurst, J. M., & Tippin, J. (1999). Depression in multiple sclerosis: Relationship to working memory capacity. *Neuropsychology, 13*, 546–556.

Arnett, P. A., Higginson, C. I., Voss, W. D., & Randolph, J. J. (2002). Relationship between coping, depression, and cognitive dysfunction in multiple sclerosis. *The Clinical Neuropsychologist, 16*, 341–355.

Arnett, P. A., Higginson, C. I., Voss, W. D., Wright, B., Bender, W. I., Wurst, J. M., & Tippin, J. M. (1999). Depressed mood in multiple sclerosis: Relationship to capacity-demanding memory and attentional functioning. *Neuropsychology, 13*, 434–446.

Arnett, P. A., & Randolph, J. J. (2006). Longitudinal course of depression symptoms in multiple sclerosis. *Journal of Neurology, Neurosurgery, and Psychiatry, 77*, 606–610.

Arnett, P. A., Rao, S. M., Bernardin, L., Grafman, J., Yetkin, F. Z., & Lobeck, L. (1994). Relationship between frontal lobe lesions and Wisconsin Card Sorting Test performance in patients with multiple sclerosis. *Neurology, 44*, 420–425.

Arnett, P. A., Smith, M. M., Barwick, F. H., Benedict, R. H. B., & Ahlstrom, B. (2008). Oral motor slowing in multiple sclerosis: Relationship to complex neuropsychological tasks requiring an oral response. *Journal of the International Neuropsychological Society, 14*, 454–462.

Bailey, C. M., Echemendia, R. J., & Arnett, P. A. (2006). The impact of motivation on neuropsychological performance in sports-related mild traumatic brain injury. *Journal of the International Neuropsychological Society, 12*, 475–484.

Barwick, F., Arnett, P., & Slobounov, S. (2012). EEG correlates of fatigue during administration of a neuropsychological test battery. *Clinical Neurophysiology, 123,* 278–284.

Beeney, J. E., & Arnett, P. A. (2008). Stress and memory bias interact to predict depression
in multiple sclerosis *Neuropsychology, 22,* 118–126.

Bruce, J. M., & Arnett, P. A. (2005). Depressed MS patients exhibit affective memory
biases during and after a list learning task that suppresses higher-order encoding
strategies. *Journal of the International Neuropsychological Society, 11,* 514–521.

Bruce, J. M., Bruce, A. S., & Arnett, P. A. (2007). Mild visual acuity disturbances are associated with performance on tests of complex visual attention in MS. *Journal of the
International Neuropsychological Society, 13,* 544–548.

Bruce, J. M., Polen, D. M., & Arnett, P. A. (2007). Pain and affective memory biases interact
to predict depressive symptoms in multiple sclerosis. *Multiple Sclerosis, 13,* 58–66.

Rabinowitz, A. R., & Arnett, P. A. (2009). A longitudinal analysis of cognitive dysfunction, coping, and depression in multiple sclerosis. *Neuropsychology, 23,* 581–591.

Ramanathan, D. N., Rabinowitz, A. R., Barwick, F. H., & Arnett, P. A. (2012). Validity
of affect measurements in evaluating symptom reporting in athletes. *Journal of the
International Neuropsychological Society, 18,* 101–107.

Smith, M. M., & Arnett, P. A. (2007). Dysarthria predicts poorer performance on cognitive tasks requiring a speeded oral response in an MS population. *Journal of Clinical
& Experimental Neuropsychology, 29,* 804–812.

Index

Note: Page numbers followed by "*f*" and "*t*" denote figures and tables, respectively.

AD-related depression and, 331–32
anxiety and, 76, 94, 103–6
assessments, 108
BD and, 78
bias, 103–6
effect sizes for tests of, 84t
emotion and, 68–70
HIV and, 232
MDD and, 78–79
in mood disorders, 76–80
pain and, 143
pain perception and, 150
PD and, 260–61
PD-related depression and, 264–65
prioritizing, 68
selectivity, 105–6
self-reported fatigue and, 120
visual, 69
Attention/Concentration Index (ACI),
235–36
attention deficit/hyperactivity disorder
(ADHD)
cognitive SVTs and, 24
epilepsy and, 383
malingering and, 8, 22–26
audiological disorders, 242
Auditory Verbal Learning Test
(AVLT), 268
autonoetic consciousness, 81
AVLT. See Auditory Verbal Learning Test
Avonex, 216

BAC. See blood alcohol content
backward-masking techniques, 69
BAI. See Beck Anxiety Inventory
Bailey, Chris, 403
Barrow Neurological Institute (BNI)
Fatigue Scale, 133
BD. See bipolar disorder; Wechsler Block
Design
BDI. See Beck Depression Inventory
BDI-Fast Screen. See Beck Depression
Inventory-Fast Screen
BDI-II. See Beck Depression Inventory-
Second Edition
Beck Anxiety Inventory (BAI), 365
stroke-related anxiety and, 345
validity of, 11
Beck Depression Inventory (BDI), 365
CP and, 149
HIV-related apathy and, 234

Beck Depression Inventory-Fast Screen
(BDI-Fast Screen), 210
Beck Depression Inventory-Second
Edition (BDI-II), 11, 171
behavioral change
AEDs and, 385
comorbid disorders and, 383–86
fatigue and, 119
psychotic symptoms and, 303
response expectancies and, 192
of suboptimal effort, 235
TBI and, 304
behavioral observations, 9
of CP, 154
of oral motor speech tasks, 176–77
Benton Visual Retention Test, 330–31
benzodiazepines, 213, 218
BFI. See Brief Fatigue Inventory
bias. See also affective bias; cognitive bias;
response bias
anxiety, 96, 405
attention, 103–6
depression and, 2
"good old days," 13
interpretive, 102–3
judgment, 101–3
memory, 98–101
misattribution, 13, 193
mood-congruent, 76–77
Binet-Simon intelligence scale, 381
bipolar disorder (BD)
attention and, 78
depression and, 49–50
HIV and, 231–33
limbic system and, 232
memory and, 82
type II, 50
unipolar mood disorder versus,
49–50
Blessed Dementia Scale, 330
Block Design task, 353
blood alcohol content (BAC), 295
BNI Fatigue Scale. See Barrow
Neurological Institute Fatigue Scale
bone health, 388
BPI. See Brief Pain Inventory
bradyphrenia, 261
brain parenchyma, 229
Brief Cognitive Screening Battery, 330
Brief Fatigue Inventory (BFI), 130
Brief Pain Inventory (BPI), 237